T0178637

Lecture Notes in Computer Science   13948

Founding Editors

Gerhard Goos
Juris Hartmanis

Editorial Board Members

The series Lecture Notes in Computer Science (LNCS), including its subseries Lecture Notes in Artificial Intelligence (LNAI) and Lecture Notes in Bioinformatics (LNBI), has established itself as a medium for the publication of new developments in computer science and information technology research, teaching, and education.

LNCS enjoys close cooperation with the computer science R & D community, the series counts many renowned academics among its volume editors and paper authors, and collaborates with prestigious societies. Its mission is to serve this international community by providing an invaluable service, mainly focused on the publication of conference and workshop proceedings and postproceedings. LNCS commenced publication in 1973.

Abhinav Bhatele · Jeff Hammond ·
Marc Baboulin · Carola Kruse
Editors

High Performance Computing

38th International Conference, ISC High Performance 2023
Hamburg, Germany, May 21–25, 2023
Proceedings

 Springer

Editors
Abhinav Bhatele ⓘ
University of Maryland
College Park, MD, USA

Jeff Hammond ⓘ
NVIDIA
Helsinki, Finland

Marc Baboulin ⓘ
Université Paris-Saclay
Gif-sur-Yvette, France

Carola Kruse ⓘ
CERFACS
Toulouse, France

ISSN 0302-9743   ISSN 1611-3349 (electronic)
Lecture Notes in Computer Science
ISBN 978-3-031-32040-8   ISBN 978-3-031-32041-5 (eBook)
https://doi.org/10.1007/978-3-031-32041-5

Preface

ISC High Performance Computing—formerly known as the International Supercomputing Conference—was founded in 1986 as the Supercomputer Seminar. Originally organized by Hans Meuer, Professor of Computer Science at the University of Mannheim, and former director of its computer center, the seminar brought together a group of 81 scientists and industrial partners who shared an interest in high-performance computing (HPC). Since then, the annual conference has become a major international event within the HPC community. It has grown well beyond its humble beginnings, and moved out of Mannheim into other cities throughout the years: Frankfurt, Heidelberg, Dresden, Hamburg, and Leipzig. Over the years, the conference has witnessed a steady increase in the number of high-quality research papers submitted to the conference, and a corresponding growth in the number of conference attendees. ISC-HPC 2023 was held in person in Hamburg, Germany, from May 21–25.

The call for submissions to ISC-HPC 2023 was issued in Fall 2022, inviting the researcher and developer communities to submit their latest results for review by the Program Committee. In total, 78 papers were submitted by authors from all over the world. The Research Papers Program Committee consisted of 70 members from 16 countries. After at least three double-blind reviews were completed, a rebuttal process offered the authors an opportunity to respond to reviewers' questions and help clarify issues the reviewers might have had. To come to a final consensus on the papers, a virtual Program Committee meeting was held to discuss the papers. Finally, the committee selected 21 papers for publication.

For the past several years, the ISC-HPC conference has presented an ISC-sponsored award to encourage outstanding research in high-performance computing and to honor the overall best research paper accepted for publication at the conference. Some years ago, this annual award was renamed in memory of the late Dr. Hans Meuer, general chair of the ISC-HPC conference from 1986 through 2014, and a co-founder of the TOP500 project. This year, from the set of accepted research papers, the Research Papers Program Committee selected the best paper based on its technical merit, including its novelty and impact on the HPC community. During a live ceremony, the following paper was bestowed with the Hans Meuer Award: *Expression Isolation of Compiler-Induced Numerical Inconsistencies in Heterogeneous Code* by Dolores Miao from the University of California, Davis, USA, Ignacio Laguna from Lawrence Livermore National Laboratory, USA, and Cindy Rubio-González from the University of California, Davis, USA. The paper addresses the challenge of ensuring numerical accuracy in CPU- and GPU-based parallel applications using an automated approach that is both precise and efficient. Application programmers can spend weeks or months identifying numerical problems caused by compiler optimizations, and be forced to reduce the performance of their entire application just to solve a problem that might be caused by a single line of code. The winning paper implements a method that works with industry standard compilers for CPUs and GPUs, and is more than 99% accurate across a wide range of experiments. The tool developed by the authors provides hope for complex applications that cannot compromise on numerical accuracy or performance.

As chairs of the Research Papers Committee, we would like to express our gratitude to the HPC community for submitting papers to ISC-HPC. We also wish to extend our thanks to the track chairs, members of the Best Paper Committee, and members of the Research Papers Committee, who provided the reviews and helped us arrive at the final decisions for manuscript acceptance.

May 2023   Abhinav Bhatele
                                                              Jeff Hammond

Organization

Program Chair

John Shalf   Lawrence Berkeley National Laboratory, USA

Program Deputy Chair

Michela Taufer   University of Tennessee, USA

Research Papers Program Committee

Research Papers Chairs

Abhinav Bhatele (Chair)   University of Maryland, USA
Jeff Hammond (Deputy Chair)   NVIDIA, Finland

Architecture, Networks, and Storage

Venkatram Vishwanath (Chair)   Argonne National Laboratory, USA
James Dinan   NVIDIA, USA
Murali Emani   Argonne National Laboratory, USA
Maria Garzaran   Intel, USA
Sidharth Kumar   University of Alabama, USA
Julian Kunkel   Georg-August-Universität Göttingen, GWDG,
                                        Germany
Zhiling Lan   Illinois Institute of Technology, USA
Preeti Malakar   Indian Institute of Technology Kanpur, India
Hai Ah Nam   Lawrence Berkeley National Laboratory, USA
Sarp Oral   Oak Ridge National Laboratory, USA and
                                        OpenSFS, China
Swapna Raj   NVIDIA, USA
Aditya Tanikanti   Argonne National Laboratory, USA
François Tessier   Inria, France

HPC Algorithms and Applications

Cynthia Phillips (Chair)	Sandia National Laboratories, USA
Sameh Abdulah	KAUST, Saudi Arabia
Mehmet Belviranli	Colorado School of Mines, USA
Giselle Fernández-Godino	Lawrence Livermore National Laboratory, USA
Xing Cai	Simula Research Laboratory and University of Oslo, Norway
Lin Gan	Tsinghua University and National Supercomputing Center Wuxi, China
Christian Glusa	Sandia National Laboratories, USA
Clemens Grelck	University of Amsterdam, The Netherlands
Yang Ho	Sandia National Laboratories, USA
Israt Nisa	Lawrence Berkeley National Laboratory, USA
Gabriel Noaje	NVIDIA, Singapore
Lena Oden	Fernuniversität in Hagen, Germany
Swapna Raj	NVIDIA, USA
Johann Rudi	Virginia Tech, USA
George Slota	Rensselaer Polytechnic Institute, USA
Tuğba Torun	Koç University, Turkey
Miwako Tsuji	RIKEN, Japan
Ichitaro Yamazaki	Sandia National Laboratories, USA
Abdurrahman Yasar	NVIDIA, USA

Machine Learning, AI, and Quantum Computing

Bettina Heim (Chair)	NVIDIA, Switzerland
Michael Beverland	Microsoft, USA
Nikoli Dryden	ETH Zurich, Switzerland
Tobias Grosser	University of Edinburgh, UK
Thomas, Häner	AWS, Switzerland
Jiajia Li	North Carolina State University, USA
Bogdan Nicolae	Argonne National Laboratory, USA
Mostofa Patwary	NVIDIA, USA
Edgar Solomonik	University of Illinois at Urbana-Champaign, USA
Abhinav Vishnu	AMD, USA

Performance Modeling, Evaluation, and Analysis

Marc Casas (Chair)	Barcelona Supercomputing Center, Spain
Ivy B. Peng	Lawrence Livermore National Laboratory, USA
Jean-Baptiste Besnard	ParaTools, France
Wanling Gao	ICT, CAS, China
Diana Goehringer	Technische Universität Dresden, Germany
Bilel Hadri	KAUST Supercomputing Laboratory, Saudi Arabia
Andra Hugo	Apple, France
Tanzima Islam	Texas State University, USA
John Linford	NVIDIA, USA
Filippo Mantovani	Barcelona Supercomputing Center, Spain
Kengo Nakajima	University of Tokyo, Japan
Scott Pakin	Los Alamos National Laboratory, USA
Kento Sato	RIKEN, Japan
Nathan Tallent	Pacific Northwest National Laboratory, USA
Guangming Tan	Institute of Computing Technology, China
Michèle Weiland	University of Edinburgh, UK

Programming Environments and Systems Software

Ivona Brandić (Chair)	Vienna University of Technology, Austria
Bilel Hadri	KAUST Supercomputing Laboratory, Saudi Arabia
Guido Juckeland	HZDR, Germany
Michael Klemm	AMD and OpenMP ARB, Germany
Pouya Kousha	Ohio State University, USA
John Linford	NVIDIA, USA
István Z. Reguly	Péter Catholic University, Hungary
Martin Ruefenacht	Leibniz Supercomputing Centre, Germany
Roxana Rusitoru	Arm, UK
Thomas R.W. Scogland	Lawrence Livermore National Laboratory, USA
Hiroyuki Takizawa	Tohoku University, Japan
Christian Terboven	RWTH Aachen University, Germany

Proceedings Chairs

Marc Baboulin (Chair)	Université Paris-Saclay, France
Carola Kruse (Deputy Chair)	CERFACS, France

Contents

Machine Learning, AI, and Quantum Computing

Performance Modeling, Evaluation, and Analysis

Programming Environments and Systems Software

Architecture, Networks, and Storage

CPU Architecture Modelling and Co-design

Bine Brank[1] and Dirk Pleiter[2(✉)] [ID]

[1] Microsoft, Munich, Germany
[2] Division of Computational Science and Technology,
KTH Royal Institute of Technology, Stockholm, Sweden
`pleiter@kth.se`

Abstract. Co-design has become an established process for both developing high-performance computing (HPC) architectures (and, more specifically, CPU architectures) as well as HPC applications. The co-design process is frequently based on models. This paper discusses an approach to CPU architecture modelling and its relation to modelling theory. The approach is implemented using the gem5 simulator for Arm-based CPU architectures and applied for the purpose of generating co-design knowledge using two applications that are widely used on HPC systems.

Keywords: HPC architectures · computer architecture modelling · computer architecture simulation · HPC applications · gem5 · Arm · Graviton 2 · GROMACS · GPAW

1   Introduction

Co-design has become an established approach in the area of HPC (see, e.g., [20]). It is a process involving, on the one hand, computer architects and, on the other hand, experts that cover different aspects of the development and implementation of applications for HPC systems. The aim is to optimise HPC architectures, and more specifically CPU architectures, based on an understanding of the relevant workloads and conversely to optimise applications based on an understanding of the hardware architectures. One recent success story for this approach is the design of the Fugaku supercomputer and its Arm-based A64FX CPU [19] which involved HPC architects and application experts from Fujitsu and RIKEN. The co-design approach may become more relevant in the future as the ongoing need for reducing the energy consumption of a given workload may result in increased adoption of domain-specific accelerators, i.e. computer architectures optimised for applications from a particular domain [7].

Due to the high complexity of both modern computer architectures as well as HPC applications, implementing a co-design process can become extremely challenging. One strategy for reducing complexity and facilitating a faster and easier exploration of design spaces both for computer architectures as well as application and algorithms design is the use of models. Models can be created and implemented in different ways and with different levels of detail.

A. Bhatele et al. (Eds.): ISC High Performance 2023, LNCS 13948, pp. 3–21, 2023.
https://doi.org/10.1007/978-3-031-32041-5_1

In the context of the development of CPU architectures, the use of the gem5 simulator has become popular [5]. gem5 is an open-source simulator that continues to be actively developed (see, e.g., [15]), can model at cycle granularity, is fast enough to boot unmodified Linux-based operating systems and run full applications, and supports multiple instruction set architectures (ISA). This includes, in particular, recent versions of the Arm ISA.

The Arm ISA is increasingly used for CPU solutions suitable for HPC systems. The success of the aforementioned A64FX CPU was largely due to the recent extension of the ISA by the Scalable Vector Extension (SVE) [22]. SVE includes SIMD instructions with operands of different lengths (512 bit in the case of the A64FX). Various server-class CPU solutions that have been brought to market or are under development are based on Arm's new family of Neoverse cores [18] and do support SVE. Examples are CPUs from AWS (Graviton 2 and 3), NVIDIA (GRACE), Ampere, and SiPearl.

The focus of this paper is the development of gem5-based models for Arm-based CPU cores using Graviton 2 as a reference architecture. Particular attention is given to the use of the new SVE ISA. Our intention is to not only use gem5 for creating co-design input for future architectures but also for reviewing and analysing the performance of existing architectures. The resulting insights can be exploited by application developers.

This paper makes the following contributions:

1. We introduce an approach to CPU architecture modelling and discuss related relevant aspects of modelling theory.
2. Our approach is used for constructing a parametric model based on the gem5 simulator using the Graviton 2 CPU as a reference architecture. This Graviton 2 configuration for gem5 has been made publicly available for other researchers.
3. We use our parametric model to explore selected HPC applications and derive co-design insights for both CPU architects and application experts.

This paper is organised as follows: In the next section, we provide a discussion on the concept of modelling before introducing the technical details of our methodology in Sect. 3. In Sect. 4 we document our results for tuning the parameters of our model and model validation. Next, we describe the used workloads as well as the porting of these applications to the target architecture in Sect. 5. The results obtained from applying our parametric model for selected applications are presented in Sect. 6. In Sect. 7 we present related work before providing a summary and conclusions in Sect. 8.

2   Approach to Modelling

Models are crucial in research on the development of computer architectures (as well as their use for computational science research). For instance, performance models are used to predict the amount of work per time unit that can be performed by a given computer architecture. Models are also used for defining computer architectures or for design verification. However, connection to modelling theory is often lacking despite the merits of modelling theory being increasingly recognized including its value in education [10,11].

In this paper, we follow the definition of the term model as documented by Thalheim [24], who introduces models as material or virtual artefacts with nine abstract properties. Most importantly, a model should satisfy a *mapping property* that means that it relates to an origin, which can be a material world or an artificial artefact. The model and the latter typically share only relevant features, which is called the *truncation property*. Models may also deviate from the origin as they may feature extensions (*amplification property*), specific changes (*distortion property*), or be scoped to an ideal state of affairs (*idealisation property*). Furthermore, models are formulated in a particular language, e.g. for the purpose of using particular modelling tools (*carrier property*). Other important properties, which are often not explicitly specified, are the *pragmatic property* as well as the *purpose property* and *added value*. The former property takes into account that the use of models is only justified for particular model users within a particular scope. Both latter properties highlight that models are designed for a specific purpose and intended to generate specific values and benefits.

In the context of this work, the mainstream gem5 simulator framework is used to formulate a CPU architecture model. As the *origin*, a specific existing hardware implementation of an Arm-based CPU has been selected, namely the AWS Graviton 2 processor. The *purpose* of the model is the following:

1. Derive for selected applications, which are widely used on HPC systems, CPU architecture requirements, and
2. Derive implementation requirements for these applications based on insights into architectural constraints.

This defines also the *added value* we wanted to create as we generate knowledge relevant for CPU architects and/or implementers of applications as foreseen in a co-design process. Note that the purpose was not to create a model that is uniquely assigned to the chosen origin but to rather explore the design space taking ongoing evolutions of the market of Arm-based CPU implementations into account. For instance, the ISA of our model has been amplified by adding support for a recent SIMD ISA, namely SVE.

In the following, we distinguish between different model parameters: *configuration parameters*, *tuned parameters* and *variable parameters*. Configuration and tuned parameters are chosen to improve mapping between the origin and the model. The configuration parameters are chosen based on the technical specifications of the origin, e.g. size of caches. The tuned parameters are fixed such that observables like the execution time of a benchmark, which is run both on the origin and model, are similar. Such tuning is required due to the *truncation property* of the model, which does not implement all features of the origin. This was in parts due to simplifications of the architecture as our model includes, e.g., only one instead of 64 cores. Furthermore, not all architectural details of the origin are publicly known (e.g., the configuration of memory prefetchers).

Table 1. Key hardware characteristics of the Graviton 2 CPU.

Core model	Neoverse N1
Number of cores	64
Clock frequency	2.5 GHz
SIMD pipelines	2× Neon
L1-I&L1-D per core	64 kiByte
L2 per core	1 MiByte
L3 per core	512 kiByte
Nominal memory bandwidth	204.8 GByte/s
Number of memory channels	8

This tuning step also serves as a validation of the model. Variable parameters are used for systematic *distortion* of the model. This allows exploring the architectural design space, e.g. by changing the operand width of SIMD instructions or the number of SIMD pipelines.

3 Methodology

Model construction starts from a choice of origin. Here the Graviton 2 processor was chosen, which was the first widely accessible server-class CPU based on Arm's Neoverse family of cores, namely the Neoverse N1 core [18]. Selected hardware characteristics of the Graviton 2 processor are listed in Table 1.

Secondly, the model is defined within the gem5 framework. As a starting point, the available Arm_O3_v7 has been selected, which was adjusted to improve the mapping between the model and origin. The most significant changes were the configuration of instruction's execution latencies, the Execution Units (EU) in the core backend, and buffer sizes. Information about these is publicly available, yet the distorted mapping of instructions to functional units in the Gem5 model requires certain simplifications for branch and integer pipelines. Additionally, we modified the sizes of various buffers (most importantly, reorder buffer and load-store queue) for the out-of-order execution. Where these are not disclosed by Arm, we relied on unofficial sources and, to a small degree, other comparable processors.[1] A selection of the configuration parameters is documented in Table 2. Configuration parameters not listed there are set according to the hardware characteristics listed in Table 1. Compared to the origin, the model has been truncated in several ways. Only a single core is used, i.e. the on-chip network properties are not considered. For the memory, the simplest possible model, namely the gem5 simpleMemory model, was selected and only a single memory channel is used.

---

[1] The used simulator source including configuration are available at https://github.com/binebrank/gem5/tree/neoverse_model.

Table 2. Key gem5 configuration parameters.

Core model	O3CPU
Reorder buffer (ROB) size	128
Load (store) queue depth	68 (72)
Instruction queue depth	120
General-purpose registers	120
Vector registers	128
Number of cores	1
L3	8 MiByte
Memory model	Classic
Number of memory channels	1
Memory pre-fetcher	Tagged at L2 level (degree = 16)

Some hardware characteristics details are not publicly available, like for the memory pre-fetcher. Arm claims that their Neoverse N1 design includes a memory pre-fetcher that is able to detect different memory access patterns and coordinate the requests to multiple levels of cache [18]. We chose to use the tagged pre-fetcher available in gem5.

Next, the tuned parameters need to be identified. Here, the following tuned parameters have been chosen: Memory bandwidth and latency, L3 cache size, and the degree and queue size of the tagged pre-fetcher. To tune the mapping between the origin and model and validate the model, the following benchmarks are used:

- STREAM benchmarks with arrays of length 10^7 [16],
- Tinymembench[2] random dual read benchmark,
- C-version[3] of the NAS Parallel Benchmarks [4] using the small workloads (S).

Note that all benchmarks had been used to obtain a single setting for the given origin.

Fourthly, the variable parameters need to be selected that allow for systematic distortions of the model to reflect properties from CPU architectures different from the origin. The following variable parameters have been chosen:

- Number of SVE pipelines N_{SVE},
- Width of the SVE operands b_{SVE}.
- Configuration of execution latencies (either based on the N1 or A64FX backend).

---

[2] https://github.com/ssvb/tinymembench.
[3] https://github.com/benchmark-subsetting/NPB3.0-omp-C.

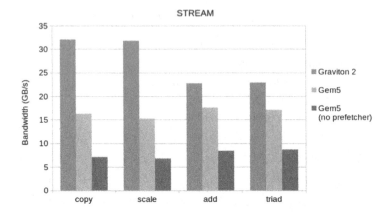

Fig. 1. Comparison of STREAM benchmarks results.

4   Model Tuning and Validation

This section shows the results of setting the tuned parameters of the model by comparing results obtained on the origin, i.e. a Graviton 2 CPU (using a single core), and the gem5-based model. We show that good results are obtained by setting the memory bandwidth to 25.6 GByte/s, the memory latency to 50 ns, the L3 cache size to 8 MiByte, and the degree and queue size of the tagged pre-fetcher to 16.

In Fig. 1 results are shown using a binary compiled for NEON. The bandwidth figures are as reported by the benchmark. There are several differences between the origin and the model that contribute to the observed differences. The origin features multiple memory channels. As the observed memory bandwidth exceeds the nominal bandwidth of a single channel, a Graviton 2 CPU core is able to saturate more than one channel. Furthermore, the model implements a write-allocate cache policy, while the origin features a write buffer that avoids reading cache lines that are fully overwritten. Finally, the memory pre-fetchers of origin and model can be expected to differ. Figure 1 shows gem5-based model results both with memory pre-fetcher disabled and enabled. The large difference between both results shows that the pre-fetcher has a strong impact on performance.

In Fig. 2 memory latency results are shown as a function of the size of the memory region used for random memory loads. The numbers are as reported by the Tinymembench dual random read benchmark. The results both for the origin and model reflect the cache structure with clearly visible changes in latency when L1, L2, and L3 capacity are exceeded. The different L3 sizes explain why for two data points larger differences are observed. For the Graviton 2 processor, an increase in the latency is observed for increasing memory region size that exceeds the L2 but fits in the L3 cache. This could be explained by the organisation of the L3 cache in 32 slices with a size of 1 MiByte each.

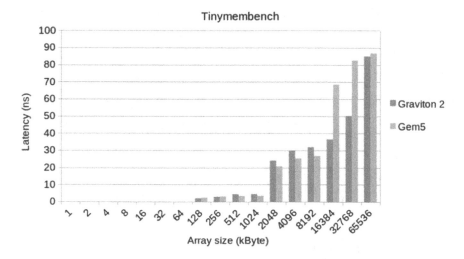

Fig. 2. Random read measurements using Tinymembench.

In Fig. 3 the performance results obtained for the NAS Parallel Benchmarks using origin and model are compared. The results are in units of million operations per second (MOp/s) as reported by the benchmark suite. The difference between the results does not exceed 15% for most benchmarks with the exceptions of the conjugate gradient (cg) and integer sort (is) benchmarks. The cg benchmark is memory bandwidth limited and the observed difference is in line with the observations for the STREAM benchmark. The integer sort benchmark is expected to be memory latency sensitive. However, the about 2.6 times lower performance observed for the model is not consistent with the results from Tinymembench. Further investigation of this difference has been deferred due to the focus on applications where floating-point instructions dominate.

In addition to the comparison of performance, also a comparison of the number of cache accesses has been performed as shown in Fig. 4. The counters have been measured using the perf tool for the Graviton 2 and gem5 statistics in the case of the model. The used counters are documented in Table 3. While a good agreement is observed for the L1 cache, the results for the L3 cache differ by up to an order of magnitude. This could be related to the different behaviour of the memory pre-fetchers. We note that we tried several configurations of different memory pre-fetcher parameters, and none yielded more satisfactory results.

Table 3. Measured cache-access statistics.

	Neoverse N1	gem5
L1	0x04 (L1 cache access)	dcache.overallAccesses::total
L2	0x16 (L2 data cache access)	l2cache.overallAccesses::total
L3	0x36 (last level cache access, read)	l3cache.overallAccesses::total

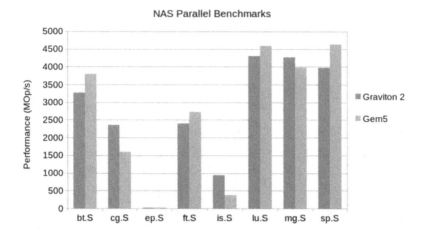

Fig. 3. NAS Parallel Benchmarks performance results.

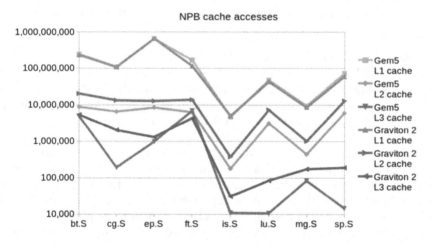

Fig. 4. Absolute cache access counters for the NAS Parallel Benchmarks.

5   Applications

In this section we introduce the co-design applications, document the relevant performance critical code regions (kernels), and describe efforts to add support for SVE instructions where needed.

5.1 GROMACS

GROMACS is a popular choice for molecular dynamics simulations in bio-chemistry, due to its high performance in high-performance computing (HPC) environments [1]. The software utilizes a modified Verlet algorithm and particle mesh Ewald algorithm to calculate forces and solve equations of motion. Its heterogeneous design, incorporating intrinsic functions, OpenMP, MPI, and GPU support, enables efficient simulation of both bonded and nonbonded interactions. In particular, the application has a dedicated SIMD back-end implemented with intrinsics with support for SVE.

The most computationally expensive part of simulations is the computation of the nonbonded interactions, on which we focus here. For performance evaluation, the nonbonded benchmark provided by GROMACS is used. GROMACS provides two different SIMD-optimised implementations of the kernel, called 4×M and 2×MM. Both feature a high fraction of SIMD floating-point instructions but differ in how data is distributed over SIMD registers. The 4×M kernel can be used for SIMD operands width of 128 and 256 bit, whereas the 2×MM kernel is used for 256 and 512 bit. The SVE version of these kernels leverages the Arm C Language Extensions (ACLE) with operand width fixed at compile time. The throughput of SIMD floating-point instructions is heavily affected by read-after-write dependencies between instructions.

5.2 GPAW

GPAW is a simulation software for calculating materials' electronic structures and atomic properties, applicable in various fields such as physics, chemistry, and materials sciences [8]. It is optimised for use on parallel architectures supporting MPI and OpenMP parallelization. The software utilizes functional density theory (DFT) based on the projector-augmented wave (PAW) method and the atomic simulation environment (ASE). It employs three main numerical methods: finite differences, linear combination of atomic orbitals, and plane-wave method. In this work, the carbon-nanotube use case from the Unified European Application Benchmark Suite (UEABS) [14] is used.

For this use case, a significant fraction of the execution time is spent in external numerical libraries, which are not considered here. Instead, we focus on the implementation of the discrete Laplace operator. This stencil-operator kernel is called bmgs_fd (see Listing 1.1). On the reference architecture about 15% of the execution time is spent there. While this is relatively small fraction of the overall execution time, the Laplace kernel is a good representation of a general class of stencil operators that are found in many HPC applications. The inner-most loop involves loading of 3 array elements and 3 arithmetic operations, i.e. the operational intensity is low. Note that the access to the array a is non-contiguous, and, therefore, requires gather-load instructions. The auto-vectorizer of GCC-11 is able to generate SVE instructions for the inner-most loop. The computation is performed using a normal fmul instruction in combination with the fadda instruction, which performs a sum-reduction to x.

For our analysis, we also study the outer-loop vectorisation. Due to the used compiler not being able to generate this type of vectorisation, we vectorised it manually using intrinsic functions. Compared to the inner-loop, vectorising the outer outer-loop kernel removes the latency-heavy `fadda` instruction, since different intermediate sums of x are computed concurrently in separate lanes of the SIMD register. Outer-loop vectorisation instead relies on normal `fadd` and `fmla` instructions. Also, the scalar stores of $b[j]$ is replaced by vector stores of subsequent elements of b.

To evaluate only this specific kernel, the `bmgs_fd` function has been extracted from the GPAW application into a standalone benchmark. Here we relied on the UEABS carbon-nanotube benchmark, to extract the relevant bmgsstencil data which uses a 19-point stencil (the inner-loop goes over 19 iterations).[4] All other used parameters are set to the same values to completely replicate the memory access of the real application.[5] The simulations are performed for 10 iterations of the kernel.

Listing 1.1. GPAW's `bmfs_fd` kernel.

```
void
Z(bmgs_fd)(const bmgsstencil* s, const T* a, T* b)
{
    /* Skip the leading halo area. */
    a += (s->j[0] + s->j[1] + s->j[2]) / 2;

    for (int i0 = 0; i0 < s->n[0]; i0++) {
        for (int i1 = 0; i1 < s->n[1]; i1++) {
#ifdef _OPENMP
#pragma omp simd
#endif
            for (int i2 = 0; i2 < s->n[2]; i2++) {
                int i = i2
                    + i1 * (s->j[2] + s->n[2])
                    + i0 * (s->j[1] + s->n[1] * (s->j[2] + s->n[2]));
                int j = i2 + i1 * s->n[2] + i0 * s->n[1] * s->n[2];
                T x = 0.0;

                for (int c = 0; c < s->ncoefs; c++)
                    x += a[i + s->offsets[c]] * s->coefs[c];
                b[j] = x;
            }
        }
    }
}
```

6   Results

In this section we document the results obtained for the application kernels introduced in the previous section using the earlier created model.

---

[4] In the carbon nanotube use case, 19-point stencil is used in combination with a 7-point stencil, which we have not evaluated.

[5] The used source code, together with manually vectorized functions, is available at https://gitlab.jsc.fz-juelich.de/brank1/gpaw-benchmarks.

6.1 GROMACS

In Fig. 5 nonbonded kernel performance results are shown for the Graviton 2 and A64FX processors using NEON and SVE instructions with operand widths of 128 and 512 bit, respectively. Furthermore, results obtained from the gem5-based model using SVE instructions of different widths are plotted. The simulations have been performed using different numbers of particles. Within the given range, the number of particles barely impacts the performance. Despite the use of slightly different SIMD ISA, the performance results obtained from the origin, i.e. the Graviton 2 processor, and the model agree well. More details obtained from the simulator are provided in Table 4 including the number of clock cycles (numCycles) and committed instructions (committedInsts) per kernel invocation. Also documented are the number of so-called fuBusy events. These events are triggered if a micro-instruction cannot be issued to the functional unit (FU) as soon as it is ready. This usually happens when the unit is stalled or if the CPU tries to issue several micro-instructions during the same clock cycle. The fuBusyRate denotes the number of fuBusy events per number of committed instructions. Furthermore, the number of times the re-order buffer (ROBFullEvents) and register file (fullRegistersEvents) become full are counted.

Table 4. GROMACS gem5 counters for 12,000 particles.

SVE configuration	2× SVE-128	2× SVE-256	2× SVE-256	2× SVE-512
Kernel implementation	4×M	4×M	2×MM	2×MM
numCycles	$56.4 \cdot 10^7$	$33.1 \cdot 10^7$	$35.7 \cdot 10^7$	$20.8 \cdot 10^7$
committedInsts	$141.6 \cdot 10^7$	$81.8 \cdot 10^7$	$70.2 \cdot 10^7$	$42.2 \cdot 10^7$
fuBusy	$83.2 \cdot 10^7$	$44.6 \cdot 10^7$	$21.2 \cdot 10^7$	$13.0 \cdot 10^7$
fuBusyRate	0.59	0.54	0.30	0.30
ROBFullEvents	$9.0 \cdot 10^6$	$9.4 \cdot 10^6$	$1.0 \cdot 10^6$	$1.5 \cdot 10^6$
fullRegistersEvents	$4.3 \cdot 10^7$	$2.5 \cdot 10^7$	$4.6 \cdot 10^7$	$2.7 \cdot 10^7$

For SVE operand width of 256 bit (SVE-256) both kernel implementations introduced in Sect. 5.1 can be used. It can be observed that for this configuration, the 4×M is 8% faster compared to the 2×MM kernel despite the 17% larger number of committed instructions. The larger fuBusyRate indicates a higher readiness of instructions to be executed, yet, the 4×M kernel executes 28% more instructions per cycle. The main reason for this is the reduced number of register file full events. We confirmed this by inspecting the rename stage of the model, where the 4×M kernel reported roughly 30% fewer cycles in which the rename component[6] of the model was blocked or idle. A large number of re-order buffer (ROB) and register file full events indicates that in the case of the SVE-256 configuration and the 4×M kernel implementation, the number of cycles could be reduced if the ROB or register file were enlarged.

---

[6] The rename component in gem5 stalls if there are no physical registers available or the ROB is full.

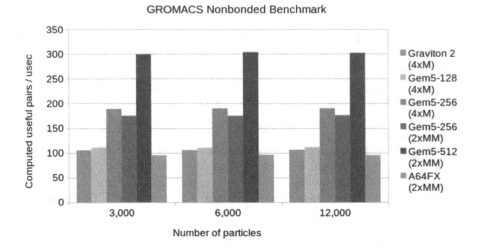

Fig. 5. GROMACS model and hardware results for different numbers of particles.

We now use the model to explore the performance of the GROMACS kernel for different configurations with different numbers of SVE pipelines N_{SVE} and SVE operand width b while keeping $N_{SVE} \cdot b = 512$ bit fixed. In other words, the throughput of floating-point instructions is the same for all three considered configurations. The results are documented in Table 5. The best performance is observed using a single SVE-512 pipeline. The performance noticeably drops using four SVE-128 pipelines. This is likely due to instruction dependencies that prevent the good filling of a larger number of pipelines, as indicated by the drop of the fuBusyRate. Better performance is expected from optimized kernel implementations.

Table 5. GROMACS model results for 3,000 particles using different core configurations with the same peak performance.

SVE configuration	4× SVE-128	2× SVE-256	2× SVE-256	1× SVE-512
Kernel implementation	4×M	4×M	2×MM	2×MM
Useful pairs/μsec	123	189	175	198
fuBusy	$24.7 \cdot 10^6$	$110.2 \cdot 10^6$	$52.4 \cdot 10^6$	$215.4 \cdot 10^6$
fuBusyRate	0.07	0.54	0.30	1.99
ROBFullEvents	$2.1 \cdot 10^6$	$2.2 \cdot 10^6$	$0.4 \cdot 10^6$	$0.8 \cdot 10^6$
fullRegistersEvents	$7.9 \cdot 10^6$	$6.3 \cdot 10^6$	$11.8 \cdot 10^6$	$12.7 \cdot 10^6$

From Fig. 5, a large deviation can be observed between the SVE-512 model and the A64FX hardware performance. A key difference between the Neoverse N1 core, used in the Graviton 2 processor that serves as the origin for our model, and the A64FX is the much larger latencies of the arithmetic pipelines. As the throughput of SIMD floating-point instructions, in the case of this kernel, is limited by read-after-write dependencies, this is a likely cause for reduced performance. To check this hypothesis, we changed the model configuration parameters defining the latency of the SVE instructions to match those of the A64FX CPU. For example, latencies for (fadd,fmul,fmla) instructions were changed from (2,3,4) to (9,9,9) cycles. The model statistics for both configurations are compared in Table 6. We observe a performance that is in much better agreement with what is observed on the A64FX processor hardware.

Table 6. GROMACS model results using different pipeline depths configured for the Neoverse N1 and A64FX architecture.

Model configuration	Neoverse N1	A64FX
Useful pairs/μsec	302	102
fuBusy	$129.6 \cdot 10^6$	$439.4 \cdot 10^6$
fuBusyRate	0.30	1.03
ROBFullEvents	$1.5 \cdot 10^6$	$2.2 \cdot 10^6$
fullRegistersEvents	$26.9 \cdot 10^6$	$40.5 \cdot 10^6$

6.2   GPAW

In Fig. 6, we compare execution times obtained for the bmgs_fd kernel. The implementation based on vectorisation of the inner-most loop (in the following labelled with Bf-1) is available for both NEON and SVE instructions. Therefore, a comparison between Graviton 2 and SVE-128 model results is possible. Again a good agreement between real hardware and the model is observed. Doubling the width of the SVE operands improves performance only by a factor of 1.61. Much less benefit is obtained when increasing the width to 512 bit.

The situation is much better in the case of outer-loop vectorisation (labelled Bf-2). When using 128 bit wide SIMD instructions, the outer-loop vectorisation improves performance compared to the inner-loop vectorisation case by 15%. Doubling and quadrupling the operand width results in a speed-up of 1.6 and 2.6, respectively.

To further explore the difference between both implementations, let us consider the gem5 statistics for the SVE-512 case shown in Table 7. The Bf-2 features both a smaller number of instructions as well as a higher throughput of instructions. In both cases, the number of executed micro-instructions is much larger than the number of instructions, which is a consequence of gather load instructions. (In the case of SVE-512, each gather load instruction is decoded into 8 micro-instructions.) Both kernels feature a rather high fuBusy rate indicating a high pressure on the execution pipelines. More specifically, the counter stat FUBusy::MemRead indicates a large number of load micro-instructions waiting to be executed. The behaviour of the caches in terms of the number of

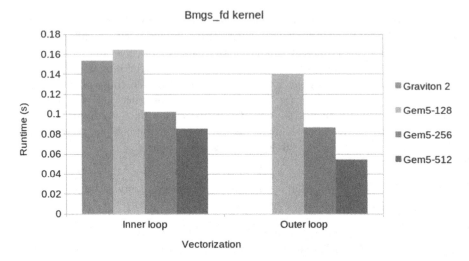

Fig. 6. GPAW results using inner-most (Bf-1) or outer-most loop vectorisation (Bf-2).

cache line replacements is almost the same in both cases. Since the application kernel features both low operational intensity as well as indirect memory accesses, performance is expected to be impacted both by memory bandwidth and latency. The gem5 simulator collects statistics on the time needed to complete requests in the load-store queue (LSQ). Table 7 shows the number of samples (lsq0.loadToUse::samples) as well as the average time for load micro-instructions to complete (lsq0.loadToUse::mean). The values are rather small, namely 4–6 cycles, indicating that most loads hit a cache line available in the L1 cache. Next, let us consider the bandwidth measured at the memory controller (mem_ctrls.bwTotal::total). From the difference in execution time and the observed similarity of cache line refill counters, the bandwidth for the Bf-2 implementation is expected to be about 60% larger compared to the Bf-1 implementation. This is indeed what is observed. However, both implementations utilize only a small fraction of the available memory bandwidth.

To explain this behaviour, we focus on the Bf-2 implementation. In our gem5 model, each gather load instruction is translated into multiple load micro-instructions, namely one per element of the SVE operand. As can be seen from the MemRead counters shown in Table 7, most of the committed instructions are load micro-instructions. Based on the assumption of perfect filling of the load-store pipelines (LSP) in the backend, a lower bound for the execution time $\Delta t_{\min}$ can be determined:

$$\Delta t_{\min} = \frac{\text{MemRead} + \text{MemWrite}}{N_{\text{LSP}}} = 100 \cdot 10^6 \text{ cycle}, \tag{1}$$

where $N_{\text{LSP}} = 2$ is the number of LSPs. Therefore, the model indicates that the Bf-2 implementation runs at 74% of the peak performance determined by the throughput of load/store micro-instructions.

In the case of Bf-1, a similar analysis shows that the model executes at 69% of peak performance. However, unlike Bf-2, Bf-1 is limited by SVE arithmetic instructions. Especially, the sum-reduction `fadda` instructions present a significant bottleneck. In our gem5 model, these are configured as non-pipelined, i.e. they block the SVE pipeline for 8 cycles. Such configuration was selected to mimic the Neoverse V1 and A64FX CPUs, where these instructions are decoded into b_{SVE} sequential micro-instructions. A way to reduce their high latency is to use `faddv` instructions, but this was not further investigated in the simulations.

Table 7. GPAW memory subsystem statistics for SVE-512.

Vectorization	Bf-1	Bf-2
numCycles	$213.0 \cdot 10^6$	$135.5 \cdot 10^6$
committedInsts	$325.9 \cdot 10^6$	$222.9 \cdot 10^6$
committedInsts/numCycles	1.53	1.64
MemRead	$232.3 \cdot 10^6$	$192.0 \cdot 10^6$
MemWrite	$7.7 \cdot 10^6$	$8.0 \cdot 10^6$
fuBusy	$155.7 \cdot 10^6$	$93.8 \cdot 10^6$
statFuBusy::MemRead	$90.6 \cdot 10^6$	$87.7 \cdot 10^6$
dcache.replacements	$8.1 \cdot 10^6$	$8.1 \cdot 10^6$
l2cache.replacements	$2.1 \cdot 10^6$	$2.1 \cdot 10^6$
l3cache.replacements	$2.1 \cdot 10^6$	$2.1 \cdot 10^6$
lsq0.loadToUse::samples	$232.3 \cdot 10^6$	$192.0 \cdot 10^6$
lsq0.loadToUse::mean	4.34	5.95
mem_ctrls.bwTotal::total (GByte/s)	2.3 GByte/s	3.7 GByte/s

7 Related Work

Computer architecture simulations in the context of HPC have a long history. One of the challenges is to obtain a good balance between the level of simulation granularity, the covered scope, and simulation performance. The simulation of full HPC systems requires the adoption of multi-level simulations. For the scope of a single processor, simulators like gem5 provide detailed granularity as well as good performance for evaluating full applications.

gem5 has, in particular, been used for exploring specific parts of the design space of modern CPU architectures like system-level cache designs [6], memory pre-fetchers [17], or on-chip network topologies [9]. More recently, extensions have been implemented to include the simulation of heterogeneous architectures with compute accelerators like gem5-Aladdin [21]. gem5 has been successfully used for full CPU architecture designs in the case of the A64FX processor [12]. A recent effort in the context of the EPI project resulted in a comparison of the gem5 simulator with two other simulators, namely MUSA and SESAM/VPSim

[26]. MUSA has the advantage of being a multi-level simulator, while SESAM supports coupling with detailed hardware simulators.

Some of the cited work does not involve detailed comparison with existing hardware. Work on Arm-based and x86-based architectures paid particular attention to a comparison between existing hardware and gem5-based models [2,25]. The approach taken in this work is to start from a model that reproduces the behaviour of existing hardware reasonably well and use this as a starting point for different model configurations.

Many of the papers presenting gem5-based result focus on hardware architectures. More recently, there is a growing interest in using gem5 for application development and preparing applications for upcoming architectures and ISA extensions. Examples are the work on preparing stencil applications [3] or the FFT library SPIRAL [23] for upcoming CPU architectures supporting SVE. This work extends this effort towards real-life HPC applications from the area of bio-physics and materials sciences.

With the improved support of gather/scatter instructions by modern CPU architectures and a large number of HPC applications with sparse memory access patterns, there is a growing interest in the performance of such instructions. Recently, a dedicated benchmarking framework has been developed, called Spatter [13]. The use of Spatter in conjunction with the model presented here would be an interesting next step.

8   Summary and Conclusions

A conceptional approach to the modelling of CPU architectures has been introduced and put into perspective with modelling theory. The approach has been used for creating a gem5-based model that uses AWS' Graviton 2 as the origin but includes amplifications and distortions suitable for exploring the design space and model more recent Arm-based server-class processors. One feature of the model is that thanks to the vector-length agnostic feature of the SVE ISA, different SIMD operand widths can easily be explored. The purpose of the model was to facilitate the generation of insights and knowledge for co-design processes, providing feedback to both CPU architects as well application developers.

In the case of the GROMACS kernel for computing non-bonded interactions, in certain configurations, frequent stalls due to full re-order buffer (ROB) and/or register file have been observed. Therefore, optimising their size should be considered for future CPU core architectures. Furthermore, the model results support the hypothesis that deep pipelines for floating-point SIMD instructions cause performance degradations as observed for the A64FX processor. The performance of the evaluated GPAW kernel was severely limited by the performance of SIMD gather load instructions. The resulting large number of load microinstructions caused the load pipeline to become a bottleneck. Optimised support of gather load instructions would improve the performance of this application.

In the case of GROMACS, the good exploitation of SIMD parallelism could be systematically explored by changing the operand width. Using the model a parallel efficiency of 68% has been found comparing operand widths of 128 and 512 bit. The current implementations of the kernel for computing non-bonded interactions are, however, lacking support for instruction-level parallelism (ILP), which is relevant for new CPU architectures like Graviton 3 and GRACE that feature a larger number of SIMD pipelines (here: 4) with more narrow operand width (here: 128 bit).

While also in case of GPAW wide SIMD instructions can be leveraged, the parallel efficiency breaks down due to the aforementioned serialisation of the SIMD gather load instructions. Assuming that it is difficult to avoid serialisation of SIMD gather load instructions, the feedback for application developers, therefore, is to consider improved data layouts that result in simpler memory access patterns.

An important outcome of this (and related work) is that gem5 has become a useful tool for application developers that could be more widely exploited. This requires, however, better availability of relevant models that can easily be used. Furthermore, an extension to multi-core simulations is desirable. In this work, due to the simplified memory model a simplified interconnect has been used, which cannot be expected to map well to the reference architecture. This shortcoming could be overcome by using the gem5's more detailed Ruby memory system with a network model based on Arm's AMBA 5 CHI architecture specification.

Acknowledgements. The authors would like to thank the Stony Brook Research Computing and Cyberinfrastructure, and the Furthermore, we want to thank the Open Edge and HPC Initiative for access to an Arm-based development Funding for parts of this work has been received from the European Commission H2020 program under Grant Agreement 779877 (Mont-Blanc 2020), and from the Swedish e-Science Research Centre (SeRC).

References

1. Abraham, M.J., et al.: GROMACS: high performance molecular simulations through multi-level parallelism from laptops to supercomputers. SoftwareX **1**, 19–25 (2015). https://doi.org/10.1016/j.softx.2015.06.001
2. Akram, A., Sawalha, L.: Validation of the gem5 simulator for x86 architectures. In: 2019 IEEE/ACM Performance Modeling, Benchmarking and Simulation of High Performance Computer Systems (PMBS), pp. 53–58 (2019). https://doi.org/10.1109/PMBS49563.2019.00012
3. Armejach, A., et al.: Stencil codes on a vector length agnostic architecture. In: Proceedings of the 27th International Conference on Parallel Architectures and Compilation Techniques (PACT 2018). Association for Computing Machinery, New York, NY, USA (2018). https://doi.org/10.1145/3243176.3243192
4. Bailey, D.H.: The NAS parallel benchmarks. Tech. rep., LBNL (2009). https://doi.org/10.2172/983318
5. Binkert, N., et al.: The gem5 simulator. SIGARCH Comput. Archit. News **39**(2), 1–7 (2011). https://doi.org/10.1145/2024716.2024718

6. Cataldo, R., et al.: Architectural exploration of last-level caches targeting homogeneous multicore systems. In: Proceedings of the 29th Symposium on Integrated Circuits and Systems Design: Chip on the Mountains (SBCCI 2016). IEEE Press (2017)

7. Dally, W.J., Turakhia, Y., Han, S.: Domain-specific hardware accelerators. Commun. ACM **63**(7), 48–57 (2020). https://doi.org/10.1145/3361682

8. Enkovaara, J., et al.: Electronic structure calculations with GPAW: a real-space implementation of the projector augmented-wave method. J. Phys.: Condens. Matter **22**(25), 253202 (2010). https://doi.org/10.1088/0953-8984/22/25/253202

9. Ghosh, A., Sinha, A., Chatterjee, A.: Exploring network on chip architectures using GEM5. In: 2017 International Conference on Information Technology (ICIT), pp. 50–55 (2017). https://doi.org/10.1109/ICIT.2017.16

10. Halloun, I.A.: Modeling Theory in Science Education, vol. 24. Springer, Dordrecht (2007). https://doi.org/10.1007/1-4020-2140-2

11. Hestenes, D.: Toward a modeling theory of physics instruction. Am. J. Phys. **55**(5), 440–454 (1987). https://doi.org/10.1119/1.15129

12. Kodama, Y., Odajima, T., Asato, A., Sato, M.: Evaluation of the RIKEN Post-K processor simulator. CoRR **abs/1904.06451** (2019). http://arxiv.org/abs/1904.06451

13. Lavin, P., et al.: Evaluating gather and scatter performance on CPUs and GPUs. In: The International Symposium on Memory Systems (MEMSYS 2020), pp. 209–222. Association for Computing Machinery, New York, NY, USA (2020). https://doi.org/10.1145/3422575.3422794

14. Lioen, W., et al.: D7.4: evaluation of benchmark performance (Final). Tech. rep., PRACE (2021). https://prace-ri.eu/wp-content/uploads/PRACE6IP-D7.4.pdf

15. Lowe-Power, J., et al.: The gem5 simulator: version 20.0+ (2020). https://doi.org/10.48550/ARXIV.2007.03152

16. McCalpin, J.D.: Memory bandwidth and machine balance in current high performance computers. IEEE Comput. Soc. Tech. Committee Comput. Archit. Newsl. **2**, 19–25 (1995)

17. Ortega, C., et al.: Data prefetching on in-order processors. In: 2018 International Conference on High Performance Computing and Simulation (HPCS), pp. 322–329 (2018). https://doi.org/10.1109/HPCS.2018.00061

18. Pellegrini, A., et al.: The Arm Neoverse N1 platform: building blocks for the next-gen cloud-to-edge infrastructure SoC. IEEE Micro **40**(2), 53–62 (2020). https://doi.org/10.1109/MM.2020.2972222

19. Sato, M., et al.: Co-design for A64FX manycore processor and "Fugaku". In: Proceedings of the International Conference for High Performance Computing, Networking, Storage and Analysis (SC 2020). IEEE Press (2020)

20. Shalf, J., Quinlan, D., Janssen, C.: Rethinking hardware-software codesign for exascale systems. Computer **44**(11), 22–30 (2011). https://doi.org/10.1109/MC.2011.300

21. Shao, Y.S., et al.: Co-designing accelerators and SoC interfaces using gem5-Aladdin. In: 2016 49th Annual IEEE/ACM International Symposium on Microarchitecture (MICRO), pp. 1–12 (2016). https://doi.org/10.1109/MICRO.2016.7783751

22. Stephens, N., et al.: The ARM scalable vector extension. IEEE Micro **37**(2), 26–39 (2017). https://doi.org/10.1109/MM.2017.35

23. Takahashi, D., Franchetti, F.: FFTE on SVE: SPIRAL-generated kernels. In: Proceedings of the International Conference on High Performance Computing in Asia-Pacific Region (HPCAsia2020), pp. 114–122. Association for Computing Machinery, New York, NY, USA (2020). https://doi.org/10.1145/3368474.3368488
24. Thalheim, B.: The conceptual model ≡ an adequate and faithful artifact enhanced by concepts. Front. Artif. Intell. Appl. **260**, 241–254 (2014). https://doi.org/10.3233/978-1-61499-361-2-241
25. Walker, M., et al.: Hardware-validated CPU performance and energy modelling. In: 2018 IEEE International Symposium on Performance Analysis of Systems and Software (ISPASS), pp. 44–53 (2018). https://doi.org/10.1109/ISPASS.2018.00013
26. Zaourar, L., et al.: Multilevel simulation-based co-design of next generation HPC microprocessors. In: 2021 International Workshop on Performance Modeling, Benchmarking and Simulation of High Performance Computer Systems (PMBS), pp. 18–29 (2021). https://doi.org/10.1109/PMBS54543.2021.00008

Illuminating the I/O Optimization Path of Scientific Applications

Hammad Ather[1,2], Jean Luca Bez[1]([✉]), Boyana Norris[2], and Suren Byna[1,3]

[1] Lawrence Berkeley National Laboratory, Berkeley, CA 94720, USA
{hather,jlbez,sbyna}@lbl.gov
[2] University of Oregon, Eugene, OR 97403, USA
hather@uoregon.edu, norris@cs.uoregon.edu
[3] The Ohio State University, Columbus, OH 43210, USA
byna.1@osu.edu

Abstract. The existing parallel I/O stack is complex and difficult to tune due to the interdependencies among multiple factors that impact the performance of data movement between storage and compute systems. When performance is slower than expected, end-users, developers, and system administrators rely on I/O profiling and tracing information to pinpoint the root causes of inefficiencies. Despite having numerous tools that collect I/O metrics on production systems, it is not obvious where the I/O bottlenecks are (unless one is an I/O expert), their root causes, and what to do to solve them. Hence, there is a gap between the currently available metrics, the issues they represent, and the application of optimizations that would mitigate performance slowdowns. An I/O specialist often checks for common problems before diving into the specifics of each application and workload. Streamlining such analysis, investigation, and recommendations could close this gap without requiring a specialist to intervene in every case. In this paper, we propose a novel interactive, user-oriented visualization, and analysis framework, called *Drishti*. This framework helps users to pinpoint various root causes of I/O performance problems and to provide a set of actionable recommendations for improving performance based on the observed characteristics of an application. We evaluate the applicability and correctness of *Drishti* using four use cases from distinct science domains and demonstrate its value to end-users, developers, and system administrators when seeking to improve an application's I/O performance.

Keywords: I/O · insights · visualization · I/O optimization

1 Introduction

The parallel I/O stack deployed on large-scale computing systems has a plethora of tuning parameters and optimization techniques that can improve application I/O performance [4,8]. Despite that, applications still face poor performance

A. Bhatele et al. (Eds.): ISC High Performance 2023, LNCS 13948, pp. 22–41, 2023.
https://doi.org/10.1007/978-3-031-32041-5_2

when accessing data. Harnessing I/O performance is a complex problem due to the multiple factors that can affect it and the inter-dependencies among the layers of the software and hardware stack.

When applications suffer from I/O performance slowdowns, pinpointing the root causes of inefficiencies requires detailed metrics and an understanding of the stack. There is a variety of I/O performance profiling and characterization tools, which are very helpful in diagnosing the I/O bottlenecks in an application. However, none of these tools provide a set of actionable items to guide users in solving the bottlenecks in the application. For instance, I/O profiling tools collect metrics to provide a coarse-grain view of the application's behavior when accessing data. Darshan [11] and Recorder [40] profilers can also trace I/O requests and provide a fine-grain view of the transformations the requests undergo as they traverse the parallel I/O software stack. Nonetheless, despite the availability of such fine-grained traces, there is a gap between the trace collection, analysis, and tuning steps.

A solution to close this gap requires analyzing the collected metrics and traces, automatically diagnosing the root causes of poor performance, and then providing user recommendations. Towards analyzing the collected metrics, Darshan [11,13] provides various utilities to summarize statistics. However, their interpretation is left to the user to identify root causes and find solutions. There have been many studies to understand the root causes of performance problems, including IOMiner [42] and Zoom-in I/O analysis [41]. However, these studies and tools are either application-specific or target general statistics of I/O logs. Existing technologies lack the provision of feedback and recommendation to improve the I/O performance or to increase utilization of I/O system capabilities [10].

To address these three components, i.e., analysis of profiles, diagnosis of root causes, and recommendation of actions, we envision a solution that meets the following criteria based on a visualization approach.

① Provide interactive visualization based on I/O trace files, allowing users to focus on a subset of MPI processes or zoom in to specific regions of the execution;
② Display contextual information about I/O calls (e.g., operation type, rank, size, duration, start and end times);
③ Understand how the application issues its I/O requests over time under different facets: operation, request sizes, and spatiality of accesses;
④ Observe transformations as the requests traverse the I/O software stack;
⑤ Detect and characterize the distinct I/O phases of an application;
⑥ Understand how the ranks access the file system in I/O operations;
⑦ Provide an extensible community-driven framework so new visualizations and analysis can be easily integrated;
⑧ Identify and highlight common root causes of I/O performance problems;
⑨ Provide a set of actionable items based on the detected I/O bottlenecks.

In this paper, we propose a novel interactive web-based analysis framework named *"Drishti"* to visualize I/O traces, highlight bottlenecks, and help understand the I/O behavior of scientific applications. Using *Drishti*, which is based on the nine requirements mentioned above, we aim to fill the gap between the trace collection, analysis, and tuning phases. However, designing this framework has several challenges in analyzing I/O metrics for extracting I/O behavior and illustrating it for users to explore, automatically detecting the I/O performance bottlenecks, and presenting actionable items to users. To tackle these challenges, we devised a solution that contains an interactive I/O trace analysis component for end-users to visually inspect their applications' I/O behavior, focusing on areas of interest and getting a clear picture of common root causes of I/O performance bottlenecks. Based on the automatic detection of I/O performance bottlenecks, our framework maps numerous common and well-known bottlenecks and their solution recommendations that can be implemented by users. This paper builds upon initial feedback on some of the components of *Drishti* [5,8]. Nonetheless, it describes a broader picture, encompassing novel work and features such as the I/O bottleneck detection from extended tracing logs, I/O phase analysis, and file system usage. Our proof-of-concept uses components and issues that are often investigated by I/O experts when end-users complain about I/O performance. Though some might be obvious to an I/O expert, end-users often face a barrier. *Drishti* seeks to streamline the process and empower the community to solve common I/O performance bottlenecks.

We designed *Drishti* to be scalable through different approaches, and not limited by the number of processes/cores. Our goal in using interactive visualizations is to overcome the limitations of static plots where information and bottlenecks cannot be displayed completely due to pixel limitations. In combination with the I/O analysis and recommendations of triggered issues, one can pinpoint the causes of those issues as they are highlighted in the visualization and zoom into areas of interest. A limiting issue might arise when an application issues millions of small requests using all the ranks for a longer period of time. To tackle this challenge, we provide options to generate multiple time-sliced plots. We also laid out the foundations for a community-based effort so that additional metrics could be added to *Drishti*, combined into more complex bottleneck detection, and integrated into the interactive visualization component. We demonstrate our framework with multiple case studies and visualize performance bottlenecks and their solutions.

The remainder of the paper is organized as follows. In Sect. 2, we discuss related work. Our approach to interactively explore I/O behaviors is detailed in Sect. 3, covering design choices, techniques to detect I/O phases and bottlenecks, and available features. We demonstrate its applicability with case studies in Sect. 4. We conclude the paper in Sect. 5 and discuss future efforts.

2   Related Work

We discuss a few tools that target I/O performance analysis, visualization, or bottleneck detection in HPC applications and highlight the novelty of our work.

NVIDIA Nsight [27] and TAU [29] are used for the performance analysis and visualization of HPC applications. They provide insights into issues from the perspective of CPU and GPU usage, parallelism and vectorization, and GPU synchronization, which can help optimize the overall performance of applications. In addition to these tools, Recorder [40] and IOMiner [42] are also used extensively to analyze the I/O performance of HPC applications. Some tools (e.g., TAU, Score-P [15], HPC Toolkit [1]) provide profiling/traces of I/O operations, with preliminary reports on observed performance. Furthermore, most of the performance visualization tools draw a line in displaying traces and metrics. The interpretation and translation of actions impose a steep learning curve for non-I/O experts. We push the state of the art by providing interactive visualizations with root cause analysis, bottleneck identification, and feedback to end-users.

The Total Knowledge of I/O (TOKIO) [21] framework provides a view of the performance of the I/O workloads deployed on HPC systems by connecting data and insights from various component-level monitoring tools available on HPC systems. It seeks to present a single coherent view of analysis tools and user interfaces. The Unified Monitoring and Metrics Interface (UMAMI) [22] introduces a holistic view of the I/O system of large-scale machines by integrating data from file systems, application-level profilers, and system components into a single interface. Both focus on the global view of the I/O system at a large scale rather than on the particular I/O issues of each application.

Tools like AI4IO [35] rely on artificial intelligence to predict and mitigate I/O contention in HPC systems. AI4IO includes two tools, PRIONN and CanarIO, which work together to predict I/O contention and take steps to prevent it. INAM [17] is a technique for profiling and analyzing communication across HPC middleware and applications, which can help identify bottlenecks and provide significant speedup by resolving those bottlenecks. H5tuner [4] is an auto-tuning solution for optimizing HPC applications for I/O usage.

All the aforementioned tools target I/O performance visualization and detecting I/O bottlenecks in HPC systems. Despite several efforts, none of the existing tools fill the translation gap which exists between determining the I/O bottlenecks and coming up with suggestions and recommendations to get rid of those bottlenecks. Our work fills this translation gap by providing interactive visualizations showing the I/O performance of the application and providing a set of actionable items or recommendations based on the detected I/O bottlenecks. Furthermore, auto-tuning approaches complement our work, as they could harness the provided insights and bottleneck detection to reduce their search space.

3 Visualization, Diagnosis, and Recommendations

We have designed and developed *Drishti* based on feedback gathered at two supercomputer facilities, the I/O-research community, and targeted end-users. In the following subsections, we discuss the design choices to support interactive visualizations, I/O behavior analysis, I/O phase detection, and how we efficiently map bottlenecks to a set of actionable items in a user-friendly way. In Fig. 1, we show the various components of *Drishti*.

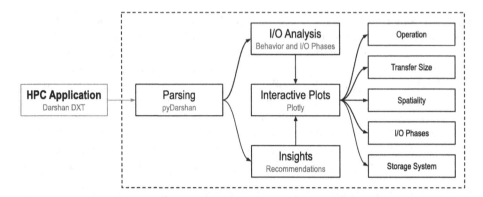

Fig. 1. *Drishti* generates meaningful interactive visualizations and a set of recommendations based on the detected I/O bottlenecks using Darshan DXT I/O traces.

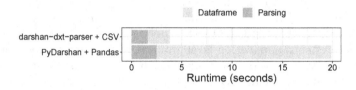

Fig. 2. Comparison of methods to extract and combine the I/O behavior metrics from Darshan DXT traces required to pinpoint I/O issues and generate visualizations.

3.1   Extracting I/O Behavior from Metrics

Darshan [11] is a tool deployed on several large-scale computing systems to collect I/O profiling metrics. Darshan collects aggregated statistics with minimal overhead providing a coarse-grain view of application I/O behavior. An extended tracing module of Darshan, DXT [44], can capture fine-grain POSIX and MPI-IO traces. Due to its widespread use, we use Darshan logs as input.

To characterize an application's I/O behavior, we require an efficient way to analyze possibly large traces collected by Darshan DXT logs that are in binary format. Darshan provides a command line solution named `darshan-dxt-parser` as part of the *darshan-util* library to parse DXT traces out of the binary Darshan log files. The parsed data is stored in a pre-defined textual format which could then be transformed into a CSV file to be analyzed. Figure 2 summarizes the time taken to obtain the required data in such approach. The trace file used in Fig. 2 is an OpenPMD use case with 1024 ranks over 64 nodes. The original trace file was of size 1.9 MB and after our transformations, the size was 23.6 MB.

Because of multiple conversions, these additional steps add to the user-perceived time. As an alternative, we have also explored PyDarshan [13], a novel Python package that provides interfaces to binary Darshan log files. With PyDarshan, we get direct access to the parsed DXT trace data in the form of a *pandas* [39] DataFrames. Figure 2 compares the performance of both approaches. However, PyDarshan also has shortcomings when the analysis requires an overall view of application behavior. It currently returns a dictionary of DataFrames containing all trace operations issued by each rank. This data structure is not optimal if the visualization requires an overall view of the application behavior, which is the case in *Drishti*. Therefore, an additional step has to be taken to iterate through the dictionary of DataFrames and merge them into a single DataFrame for both analysis and interactive visualization. For the trace in Fig. 2, this additional merging operation represents 87.3% of the time. If PyDarshan can provide direct access to all ranks in form of a single DataFrame, costly data transformations such as the one shown in Fig. 2 can be avoided.

3.2 Exploring I/O Behavior Interactively

I/O traces can be large for applications with longer runtimes or even for relatively short applications with a large number of small I/O requests, making analysis and visualization of the behavior difficult. Static plots have space constraints and pixel resolution issues. Thus they often hide the root causes of I/O bottlenecks in plain sight. For instance, when thousands of ranks issue I/O operations concurrently, but some of them suffer interference at the server level, those lines are not visible in a static plot at a regular scale.

Towards developing a modular and extensible framework (criterion ⑦ in §1), we consider two solutions. Our initial prototype to move from a static to interactive and dynamic visualization relied on plots generated in R using *ggplot2*. R is a programming language for statistical computing used in diverse fields such as data mining, bioinformatics, and data analysis. *ggplot2* is an open-source data visualization package for R to declaratively create graphics, based on The Grammar of Graphics [43] schema. A plot generated using this library could be converted into an interactive visualization by using the open-source *ggplotly* graphing library powered by *Plotly*. *Plotly* is a data visualization library capable of generating dynamic and interactive web-based charts.

However, integrating with the data extraction discussed in Sect. 3.1 would require the framework to combine features in different languages, compromising modularity, maintainability, and increasing software dependencies, possibly constraining its wide adoption in large-scale facilities. We have opted to rely on PyDarshan to extract the data. Using the open-source Plotly.py Python wrappers would simplify the code without compromising features or usability. Furthermore, it would easily allow I/O data experts to convert their custom visualizations into interactive ones and integrate them into *Drishti*. It also brought the advantage of reducing the total user-perceived time by 84.5% (from avg. of 69.45s to 10.74s), allowing such time to be better spent on detailed analysis of I/O behavior. Figure 3 summarizes this difference. This is the same OpenPMD use case, with write/read operations, of Fig. 2. Note that Fig. 3 only accounts for I/O phase analysis and plotting. The results on both Fig. 2 and Fig. 3 should be combined for the total runtime, i.e., they depict complementary information. Section 3.3 covers the I/O behavior analysis to pinpoint the root causes of bottlenecks.

As scientific applications often handle multiple files during their execution, which overlap in time (e.g., file-per-process or multiple processes to multiple

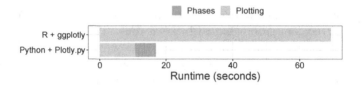

Fig. 3. Comparison of solutions to generate the interactive plots and detect I/O phases from Darshan DXT traces. Both approaches use the Plotly.js library under the hood to generate web-based interactive plots.

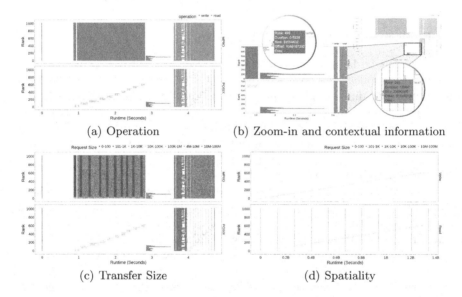

(a) Operation   (b) Zoom-in and contextual information

(c) Transfer Size   (d) Spatiality

Fig. 4. *Drishti* reports focusing on different facets of the I/O behavior: (a) operations; (b) contextual information regarding the operations; (c) transfer sizes; and (d) spatial locality of the requests into the file. Combined, they provide a clear picture of the I/O access pattern and help identify the root causes of performance problems.

files approaches), *Drishti* should provide a separate visualization for each. Furthermore, those visualizations should shine some light on the application's I/O behavior from multiple perspectives, i.e., criterion ③: operation, data transfer, and spatiality. Figure 4 shows the reports of particle and mesh-based data from a scientific simulation. Plotly also meets our criteria by allowing a user to dynamically narrow down the plot to cover a time interval of interest or zoom into a subset of ranks to understand the I/O behavior (criterion ①).

Because of the complexity of the parallel I/O stack, the requests issued by an application are transformed before reaching the file system. Those transformations originate from different mappings between the data model used by an application and its file representation or by the application of I/O optimization techniques such as collective buffering and data-sieving [37] or request scheduling [6,9,12]. To shed light on these transformations, *Drishti* depicts every plot using two synchronized facets: the first representing the MPI-IO level, and the second, its translation to POSIX level (criterion ④). For each request, by hovering over the depicted interval, it is possible to inspect additional details such as the operation type, execution time, rank, and transfer size, meeting criterion ②. Interactive examples are available in our companion repository jeanbez.gitlab.io/isc23.

When visualizing an application's I/O behavior, we are one step closer to understanding the root causes of any performance bottlenecks, demystifying data transformations, and guiding users to apply the most suitable set of optimization techniques to improve performance. We highlight that there is a lack of a straightforward translation of the I/O bottlenecks into potential tuning options. In this paper, we seek to close this gap by providing a framework to bring those issues to light, automatically detecting bottlenecks and meaningfully conveying actionable solutions to users.

3.3   Automatic Detection of I/O Bottlenecks

Several tools seek to analyze the performance of HPC applications, as discussed in Sect. 2. However, few of them focus on I/O and neither provide support for auto-detection of I/O bottlenecks in the application nor provide suggestions on how to fix those. We summarize common root causes of I/O performance bottlenecks in Table 1. Some issues require additional data or a combination of metrics collected from profilers, tracers, and system logs. For instance, Darshan's profiler only keeps track of the timestamp of the first and last operations to a given file. In contrast, its Extended Tracing module (DXT) tracks what happens in between, such as different behaviors or I/O phases.

Table 1. Root causes of I/O performance bottlenecks

Root Causes	Darshan	DXT	System	Drishti
Too many I/O phases [41]	✓	✓	✗	✓
Stragglers in each I/O phase [36]	✓	✓	✗	✓
Bandwidth limited by a single OST I/O bandwidth [23,41]	✗	✗	✓	✗
Limited by the small data size [41]	✓	✓	✗	✓
Rank 0 heavy-workload [46]	✓	✓	✗	✓
Unbalanced I/O workload among MPI ranks [41]	✓	✓	✗	✓
Large number of small I/O requests [41]	✓	✓	✗	✓
Unbalanced I/O workload on OSTs [41,46]	✓	✓	✓	✓
Bad file system weather [22,41]	✗	✗	✓	✗
Redundant/overlapping I/O accesses [12,30]	✓	✓	✗	✓
I/O resource contention at OSTs [32,45]	✗	✗	✓	✗
Heavy metadata load [23]	✓	✗	✗	✓

Drishti seeks to provide interactive web-based visualizations of the tracing data collected by Darshan, but it also provides a framework to detect I/O bottlenecks in the data (from both profiling and tracing metrics) and highlights criterion ⑧ those on the interactive visualizations along with providing a set of recommendations (criterion ⑨) to solve the issue. *Drishti* relies on counters available in Darshan profiling logs to detect common bottlenecks and classify the insights into four categories based on the impact of the triggered event and the certainty of the provided recommendation: HIGH (high probability of harming I/O performance), WARN (detected issues could negatively impact the I/O performance, but metrics might not be sufficient to detect application design, configuration, or execution choices), OK (the recommended best practices have been followed), and INFO (details relevant information regarding application configuration that could guide tuning solutions). The *insights* module is fully integrated with the parsing and visualization modules of the framework, so the identified issues and actionable items can enrich the reports.

Table 2. Triggers evaluated by *Drishti* for each Darshan log.

Level	Interface	Detected Behavior
HIGH	STDIO	High STDIO usage* ($> 10\%$ of total transfer size uses STDIO)
OK	POSIX	High number* of sequential read operations ($\geq 80\%$)
OK	POSIX	High number* of sequential write operations ($\geq 80\%$)
INFO	POSIX	Write operation count intensive* ($> 10\%$ more writes than reads)
INFO	POSIX	Read operation count intensive* ($> 10\%$ more reads than writes)
INFO	POSIX	Write size intensive* ($> 10\%$ more bytes written then read)
INFO	POSIX	Read size intensive* ($> 10\%$ more bytes read then written)
WARN	POSIX	Redundant reads
WARN	POSIX	Redundant writes
HIGH	POSIX	High number* of small† reads ($> 10\%$ of total reads)
HIGH	POSIX	High number* of small† writes ($> 10\%$ of total writes)
HIGH	POSIX	High number* of misaligned memory requests ($> 10\%$)
HIGH	POSIX	High number* of misaligned file requests ($> 10\%$)
HIGH	POSIX	High number* of random read requests ($> 20\%$)
HIGH	POSIX	High number* of random write requests ($> 20\%$)
HIGH	POSIX	High number* of small† reads to shared-files ($> 10\%$ of reads)
HIGH	POSIX	High number* of small† writes to shared-files ($> 10\%$ of writes)
HIGH	POSIX	High metadata time* (one or more ranks spend > 30 seconds)
HIGH	POSIX	Rank o heavy workload
HIGH	POSIX	Data transfer imbalance between ranks ($> 15\%$ difference)
HIGH	POSIX	Stragglers detected among the MPI ranks
HIGH	POSIX	Time imbalance* between ranks ($> 15\%$ difference)
WARN	MPI-IO	No MPI-IO calls detected from Darshan logs
HIGH	MPI-IO	Detected MPI-IO but no collective read operation
HIGH	MPI-IO	Detected MPI-IO but no collective write operation
WARN	MPI-IO	Detected MPI-IO but no non-blocking read operations
WARN	MPI-IO	Detected MPI-IO but no non-blocking write operations
OK	MPI-IO	Detected MPI-IO and collective read operations
OK	MPI-IO	Detected MPI-IO and collective write operations
HIGH	MPI-IO	Detected MPI-IO and inter-node aggregators
WARN	MPI-IO	Detected MPI-IO and intra-node aggregators
OK	MPI-IO	Detected MPI-IO and one aggregator per node

* Trigger has a threshold that could be further tunned. Default value in parameters.
† Small requests are consider to be < 1 MB.

The interactive visualizations are enhanced using multi-layered plots, with each layer activated according to the detected bottleneck keeping the original behavior in the background (criterion ⑧). The idea behind highlighting the bottlenecks on the interactive visualizations, apart from classifying the bottlenecks in different categories, is to allow the user to actually visualize where the bottlenecks are in the application. This will allow them to get more detailed information about the bottlenecks and give them more clarity about the application behavior which the textual information alone cannot provide. Furthermore, we complement the interactive visualization with a report based on 32 checks covering common I/O performance pitfalls and good practices, as summarized in Table 2. We provide the multi-layered plot functionality for the *operation* plot for now. Each layer of the plot shows a different variant of the base graph, for example, one layer can show one of the bottlenecks in the graph, and the other can show the base chart.

3.4   Exploring I/O Phases and Bottlenecks

HPC applications tend to present a fairly consistent I/O behavior over time, with a few access patterns repeated multiple times over their execution [20]. Request scheduling [6,9], auto-tuning [2–4] and reinforcement-learning [7,19] techniques to improve I/O performance also rely on this principle to use or find out the best configuration parameters for each workload, allowing the application to fully benefit from it in future iterations or executions. We can define an I/O phase as a continuous amount of time where an application is accessing its data following in a specific way or following one or a combination of access patterns. Nonetheless, factors outside the application's scope could cause an I/O phase to take longer, such as network interference, storage system congestion, or contention, significantly modifying its behavior. Seeking to detect I/O phases, *Drishti* adds an interactive visualization based on DXT trace data. This visualization gives a detailed picture of I/O phases and I/O patterns in the data and is very helpful in extracting information related to bottlenecks such as stragglers, meeting our criterion ⑤.

Finding the I/O phases from trace data is not trivial due to the sheer amount of data, often representing millions of operations in the order of milliseconds. We use PyRanges [31] to find similar and overlapping behavior between an application's MPI ranks and a threshold value to merge I/O phases closer to each other. PyRanges is a genomics library used for handling genomics intervals. It uses a 2D table to represent the data where each row is an interval (in our case, an operation), and columns represent chromosomes (i.e., interface and operation), the start and end of an interval (i.e., operation).

While identifying the I/O phases, we keep track of the duration between each I/O phase that represents computation or communication. Once we have the duration of all the intervals between the I/O phases, we calculate the mean and standard deviation of such intervals. A threshold is calculated by summing up the mean and the standard deviation, and it is used to merge I/O phases close to each other into a single I/O phase. We do that because due to the small

Algorithm 1. Merging I/O phases by a threshold

$end \leftarrow df[end][0]$
$prev\_end \leftarrow 0$
while $i < len(df)$ **do**
    if $df[start][i] - end <= threshold$ **then**
        $prev\_end \leftarrow df[end][i]$
    end if
    if $df[start][i] - end > threshold$ OR $i = len(df) - 1$ **then**
        $chunk\_end \leftarrow df[prev\_index : i].copy()$
        $end \leftarrow df[end][i]$
        $prev\_end \leftarrow i$
    end if
end while

---

time scale of the operations, we might end up with a lot of tiny I/O phases that, from the application's perspective, represent a single phase. As of now, the merging threshold cannot be changed dynamically from the visualization interface. Algorithm 1 describes the merging process. We take an I/O phase and check if the difference between the end of the last I/O phase and the start of this I/O phase is less than equal to the threshold value. We keep on merging the I/O phases till they satisfy this condition.

Figure 5 shows a sample I/O phases visualization, that is fully interactive supporting zoom-in/zoom-out. The phases are generated for MPIIO and POSIX separately. Hovering over an I/O phase displays the fastest and slowest rank in that phase and their durations.

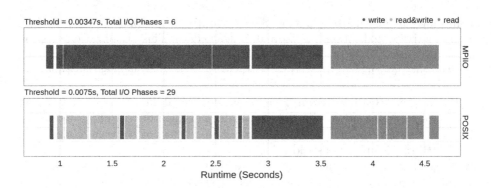

Fig. 5. Interactive I/O phases visualization in MPI-I/O and POSIX layers.

Understanding an application's I/O phases allow the detection of additional performance bottlenecks, as detailed by Table 1. To showcase how *Drishti* could be used in this context, we briefly cover synchronous and asynchronous requests, stragglers, and multiple I/O phases.

Blocking I/O Accesses. From a scientific application's perspective, I/O operations can be synchronous or asynchronous. Asynchronous I/O is becoming increasingly popular to hide the cost associated with I/O operation and improve overall performance by overlapping computation or communication with I/O operations [26,33]. Multiple interfaces (e.g., POSIX and MPI-IO) and high-level I/O libraries (e.g., HDF5) provide both blocking and non-blocking I/O calls. For HDF5, the Asynchronous I/O VOL Connector [34] can explore this feature.

If we consider only the profiling data available in Darshan, it only captures the number of non-blocking calls at the MPI-IO level and not when they happened. To provide a detailed and precise suggestion of when asynchronous could benefit the application, we rely on the I/O phases and the intervals between those to provide such recommendations. We demonstrate a use case with a block-structured adaptive mesh refinement application in Sect. 4.

I/O Stragglers. I/O stragglers in each phase define the critical path impairing performance. *Drishti* has an exclusive visualization to highlight the I/O phases and their stragglers (Fig. 6). We handle each interface separately due to the transformations that happen as requests go down the stack. The dotted lines represent the boundaries of an I/O phase. In each, the fastest and the slowest rank is shown. Combined with contextual information, it is possible to detect slow ranks across the entire execution or storage servers consistently delivering slow performance.

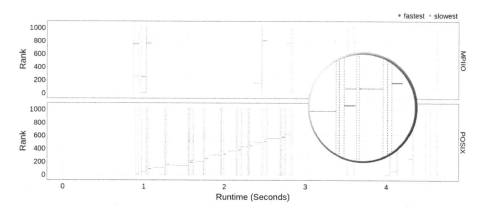

Fig. 6. Stragglers are identified in red for each I/O phase. (Color figure online)

3.5   Towards Exploring File System Usage

Additional logs are required to correctly detect bottlenecks related to unoptimized file system accesses, as detailed in Table 1. Nonetheless, Darshan DXT captures some information that could provide an initial overview of the storage servers' use if the underlying file system is Lustre and that integration is enabled. *Drishti* provides an exclusive visualization to explore the OST usage of the I/O requests, as depicted in Fig. 7. Furthermore, because of file stripping, a request at the MPI-I/O level might be broken down and require access to multiple storage devices to be completed, which explains why the information at both levels is not the same. *Drishti* can also depict the data transfer sizes (writes and reads) for each OST at both the MPI-I/O and POSIX levels.

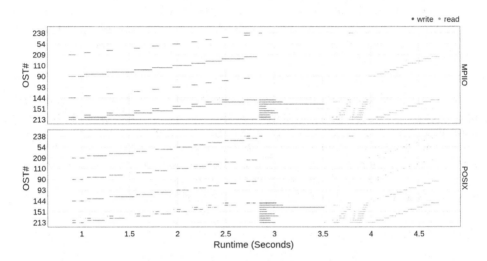

Fig. 7. Lustre data storage (OST) access over time.

4   Results

We selected the OpenPMD (Sect. 4.2) and AMReX (Sect. 4.3) use cases from distinct science domains to demonstrate *Drishti*'s value to end-users, developers, and system administrators. Both came from interactions with their core developers about concerns related to poor I/O performance. Existing solutions previously tried did not uncover all the root causes of performance inefficiencies. Experiments were conducted in two production supercomputing systems: Cori at the National Energy Research Scientific Computing Center (NERSC) and Summit at the Oak Ridge Leadership Computing Facility (OLCF). We have also probed the I/O research community and targeted end-users to gather feedback on the tool's features and helpfulness. For instance, highlighting bottlenecks uncovered by the heuristic analysis, indexing, and filtering the generated visualizations based on the file are some enhancements added from community-driven feedback. User-interface presentation of the contextual data was also shaped based on such evaluation.

4.1   I/O Systems in NERSC and OLCF

Cori is a Cray XC40 supercomputer at NERSC. It has $2,388$ Intel Xeon Haswell, and $9,688$ Intel Xeon Phi Knight's Landing (KNL) compute nodes. All compute nodes are connected to a ≈ 30 PB Lustre parallel file system with a peak I/O bandwidth of 744 GB/s. Cori's PFS is comprised of 244 Object Storage Servers.

Summit is a $4,608$ compute nodes IBM supercomputer at OLCF. Summit is connected to a center-wide 250 PB Spectrum Scale (GPFS) file system, with a peak bandwidth of 2.5 TB/s. It has 154 Network Shared Disk servers, each managing one GPFS Native RAID serving as data and metadata server.

4.2   I/O Bottlenecks in OpenPMD

Open Standard for Particle-Mesh Data Files (OpenPMD) [14] is an open metadata schema targeting particle and mesh data in scientific simulations and experiments. Its library [16] provides back-end support for multiple file formats such as HDF5 [38], ADIOS [25], and JSON [28]. In the context of this experiment, we focus on the HDF5 format to store the 3D mashes $[65536 \times 256 \times 256]$, represented as grids of $[64 \times 32 \times 32]$ composed by $[64 \times 32 \times 32]$ mini blocks. The kernel runs for 10 iteration steps writing after each one. Figure 8 depicts a baseline execution of OpenPMD in the Summit supercomputer, with 64 compute nodes, 6 ranks per node, and 384 processes, prior to applying any I/O optimizations alongside the triggered issues. For this scenario, OpenPMD takes on average 110.6 s (avg. of 5 runs).

Based on the initial visualization and the provided report (Fig. 8), it becomes evident that the application I/O calls are not using MPI-IO's collective buffering tuning option. Furthermore, the majority of the write and read requests are small (< 1MB), which is known to have a significant impact on I/O performance [41]. Moreover, *Drishti* has detected an imbalance when accessing the data. This is further highlighted when the user selects that issue in the interactive web-based visualization.

Nonetheless, after careful investigation, we confirmed that the application and the HDF5 library supposedly used collective I/O calls, though the visualization depicted something entirely different. *Drishti* aided in discovering an issue introduced in HDF5 1.10.5 that caused collective operations to be instead issued as independent by the library. Once that was fixed, we noticed that the application did not use collective metadata operations. Furthermore, *Drishti* reported misaligned accesses which pointed us toward tuning the MPI-I/O ROMIO collective buffering and data sieving sizes to match Alpine's 16MB striping configuration and the number of aggregators. Following the recommendations provided by *Drishti*, the runtime dropped to 16.1 seconds, a 6.8× speedup from the baseline execution. The complete interactive report for the optimized execution is available in our companion repository.

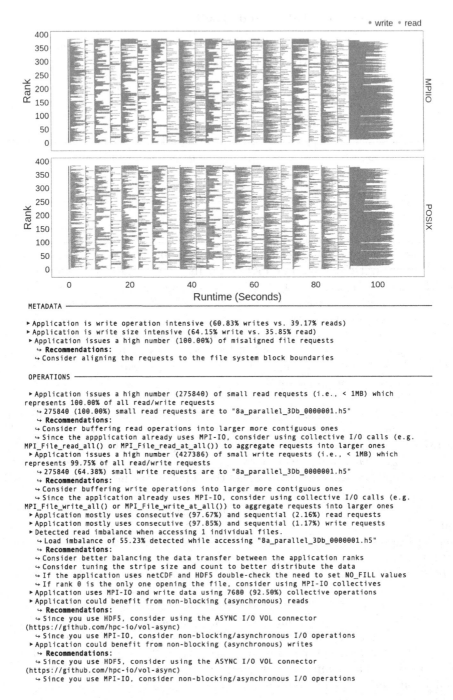

Fig. 8. Interactive visualization and recommendations report generated by *Drishti* for the OpenPMD baseline execution in Summit.

4.3   Improving AMReX with Asynchronous I/O

AMReX [47] is a C++ framework developed in the context of the DOE's Exascale Computing Project (ECP). It uses highly parallel adaptive mesh refinement (AMR) algorithms to solve partial differential equations on block-structured meshes. AMReX-based applications span different areas such as astrophysics, atmospheric modeling, combustion, cosmology, multi-phase flow, and particle accelerators. We ran AMReX with 512 ranks over 32 nodes in Cori supercomputer, with a 1024 domain size, a maximum allowable size of each subdomain used for parallel decomposal as 8, 1 level, 6 components, 2 particles per cell, 10 plot files, and a sleep time of 10 seconds between writes. Table 3 (left) shows the interactive baseline execution and the report generated by *Drishti*.

Table 3. *Drishti* report generated for the AMReX in Cori.

From the provided recommendations, since AMReX uses the high-level HDF5 library, we have added the asynchronous I/O VOL Connector [34] so operations are non-blocking and we could hide some of the time spent in I/O while the application continues its computation. Furthermore, as *Drishti* looks at the ratio of operations to trigger some insights, for this particular case, we can verify that the majority of write requests are small (< 1MB) for all 10 plot files. To increase those requests, we have set the stripe size to 16MB. Table 3 (right) shows the optimized version with a total speedup of 2.1× (from 211 to 100 s). The interactive report is available in our companion repository.

As demonstrated by design choices and these two use cases, *Drishti* meets all the initial criteria (defined in Sect. 1) we set to close the gap between analyzing the collected I/O metrics and traces, automatically diagnosing the root causes of poor performance, and then providing users with a set of actionable suggestions. The designed solution provides a framework that can further be extended and refined by the community to encompass additional triggers, interactive visualizations, and recommendations. We have also conducted a similar analysis for h5bench [18] and the end-to-end (E2E) [24] domain decomposition I/O kernel. These are available in our companion repository.

5   Conclusion

Pinpointing the root causes of I/O inefficiencies in scientific applications requires detailed metrics and an understanding of the HPC I/O stack. The existing tools lack detecting I/O performance bottlenecks and providing a set of actionable items to guide users to solve the bottlenecks considering each application's unique characteristics and workload. In this paper, we design a framework to face the challenges in analyzing I/O metrics: extracting I/O behavior and illustrating it for users to explore interactively, detecting I/O bottlenecks automatically, and presenting a set of recommendations to avoid them.

Drishti, an interactive web-based analysis framework, seeks to close this gap between trace collection, analysis, and tuning. Our framework relies on the automatic detection of common root causes of I/O performance inefficiencies by mapping raw metrics into common problems and recommendations that can be implemented by users. We have demonstrated its applicability and benefits with the OpenPMD and AMReX scientific applications to improve runtime.

Drishti is available on GitHub at github.com/hpc-io/drishti with an open-source license. Scientific community can expand the set of triggers and recommendations. Due to the interactive nature of our solution, we have also provided a companion repository jeanbez.gitlab.io/isc23 with all traces, visualizations, and recommendations in this work.

In our future work, we will integrate additional metrics and system logs to broaden the spectrum of I/O performance issues we can detect and visualize by providing a global API to consume metrics from distinct sources (e.g., Recorder's traces and parallel file system logs). We will also make the thresholds used for I/O phase visualization more generic so that they take into account different factors such as parallel file system performance degradation etc. Apart from this, we will work on approaches to map performance optimization recommendations to the exact source code line numbers through static code analysis and enhance the sample solutions in *Drishti* reports with modified code instead of generic snippets. Lastly, we plan to prepare guidelines on how the community can contribute to this tool as this will aid in keeping up with the latest advancements in I/O libraries and systems. As novel systems come online, we will also reach out to them to provide the necessary support.

Acknowledgment. This research was supported in part by the Exascale Computing Project (17-SC-20-SC), a collaborative effort of the U.S. Department of Energy
Office of Science and the National Nuclear Security Administration. This research was
also supported by The Ohio State University under a subcontract (GR130303), which
was supported by the U.S. Department of Energy (DOE), Office of Science, Office of
Advanced Scientific Computing Research (ASCR) under contract number DE-AC02-
05CH11231 with LBNL. This research used resources of the National Energy Research
Scientific Computing Center under Contract No. DE-AC02-05CH11231.

References

1. Adhianto, L., Banerjee, S., Fagan, M., Krentel, M., Marin, G., Mellor-Crummey, J.,
   Tallent, N.R.: HPCTOOLKIT: tools for performance analysis of optimized parallel
   programs. CCPE **22**(6), 685–701 (2010). https://doi.org/10.1002/cpe.1553
2. Agarwal, M., Singhvi, D., Malakar, P., Byna, S.: Active learning-based automatic
   tuning and prediction of parallel I/O performance. In: 2019 IEEE/ACM Fourth
   International Parallel Data Systems Workshop (PDSW), pp. 20–29 (2019). https://
   doi.org/10.1109/PDSW49588.2019.00007
3. Bağbaba, A.: Improving collective I/o performance with machine learning supported auto-tuning. In: IEEE International Parallel and Distributed Processing
   Symposium Workshops (IPDPSW), pp. 814–821 (2020). https://doi.org/10.1109/
   IPDPSW50202.2020.00138
4. Behzad, B., Byna, S., Prabhat, Snir, M.: Optimizing I/O performance of HPC
   applications with autotuning. ACM Trans. Parallel Comput. **5**(4) (2019). https://
   doi.org/10.1145/3309205
5. Bez, J.L., Ather, H., Byna, S.: Drishti: guiding end-users in the I/O optimization journey. In: 2022 IEEE/ACM International Parallel Data Systems Workshop
   (PDSW), pp. 1–6 (2022). https://doi.org/10.1109/PDSW56643.2022.00006
6. Bez, J.L., Boito, F.Z., Schnorr, L.M., Navaux, P.O.A., Méhaut, J.F.: TWINS:
   server access coordination in the I/O forwarding layer. In: 2017 25th Euromicro
   International Conference on Parallel, Distributed and Network-based Processing
   (PDP), pp. 116–123 (2017). https://doi.org/10.1109/PDP.2017.61
7. Bez, J.L., Zanon Boito, F., Nou, R., Miranda, A., Cortes, T., Navaux, P.O.: Adaptive request scheduling for the I/O forwarding layer using reinforcement learning.
   Futur. Gener. Comput. Syst. **112**, 1156–1169 (2020). https://doi.org/10.1016/j.
   future.2020.05.005
8. Bez, J.L., et al.: I/O bottleneck detection and tuning: connecting the dots using
   interactive log analysis. In: 2021 IEEE/ACM 6th International Parallel Data Systems Workshop (PDSW), pp. 15–22 (2021). https://doi.org/10.1109/PDSW54622.
   2021.00008
9. Boito, F.Z., Kassick, R.V., Navaux, P.O., Denneulin, Y.: AGIOS: application-
   guided I/O scheduling for parallel file systems. In: International Conference on Parallel and Distributed Systems, pp. 43–50 (2013). https://doi.org/10.1109/ICPADS.
   2013.19
10. Carns, P., Kunkel, J., Mohror, K., Schulz, M.: Understanding I/O behavior in
    scientific and data-intensive computing (Dagstuhl Seminar 21332). Dagstuhl Rep.
    11(7), 16–75 (2021). https://doi.org/10.4230/DagRep.11.7.16
11. Carns, P., et al.: Understanding and improving computational science storage
    access through continuous characterization. ACM Trans. Storage **7**(3) (2011).
    https://doi.org/10.1109/MSST.2011.5937212

12. Carretero, J., et al.: Mapping and scheduling hpc applications for optimizing I/O. In: Proceedings of the 34th ACM International Conference on Supercomputing. ICS'20 (2020). https://doi.org/10.1145/3392717.3392764
13. Darshan team: pyDarshan. https://github.com/darshan-hpc/darshan/tree/main/darshan-util/pydarshan
14. Huebl, A., et al.: openPMD: a meta data standard for particle and mesh based data (2015). https://doi.org/10.5281/zenodo.1167843
15. Knüpfer, A., et al.: Score-P: a joint performance measurement run-time infrastructure for periscope, scalasca, TAU, and vampir. In: Brunst, H., Müller, M.S., Nagel, W.E., Resch, M.M. (eds.) Tools High Perform. Comput., pp. 79–91. Springer, Berlin Heidelberg, Berlin, Heidelberg (2012). https://doi.org/10.1007/978-3-642-31476-6_7
16. Koller, F., et al.: openPMD-api: C++ & python API for scientific I/O with openPMD (2019). https://doi.org/10.14278/rodare.209
17. Kousha, P., et al.: INAM: cross-stack profiling and analysis of communication in MPI-based applications. In: Practice and Experience in Advanced Research Computing (2021). DOIurl10.1145/3437359.3465582
18. Li, T., Byna, S., Koziol, Q., Tang, H., Bez, J.L., Kang, Q.: h5bench: HDF5 I/O kernel suite for exercising HPC I/O patterns. In: CUG (2021)
19. Li, Y., Bel, O., Chang, K., Miller, E.L., Long, D.D.E.: CAPES: unsupervised storage performance tuning using neural network-based deep reinforcement learning. In: SC'17 (2017). DOIurl10.1145/3126908.3126951
20. Liu, Y., Gunasekaran, R., Ma, X., Vazhkudai, S.S.: Server-side log data analytics for I/O workload characterization and coordination on large shared storage systems. In: SC16: International Conference for High Performance Computing, Networking, Storage and Analysis, pp. 819–829. IEEE (2016). https://doi.org/10.1109/SC.2016.69
21. Lockwood, G.K., Wright, N.J., Snyder, S., Carns, P., Brown, G., Harms, K.: TOKIO on ClusterStor: connecting standard tools to enable holistic I/O performance analysis. CUG (2018). https://www.osti.gov/biblio/1632125
22. Lockwood, G.K., et al.: UMAMI: a recipe for generating meaningful metrics through holistic I/O performance analysis. In: PDSW-DISCS, p. 55–60 (2017). https://doi.org/10.1145/3149393.3149395
23. Lockwood, G.K., et al.: A year in the life of a parallel file system. In: SC'18 (2018). https://doi.org/10.1109/SC.2018.00077
24. Lofstead, J., et al.: Six degrees of scientific data: reading patterns for extreme scale science IO. In: HPDC'11, pp. 49–60. ACM, New York (2011). https://doi.org/10.1145/1996130.1996139
25. Lofstead, J.F., Klasky, S., Schwan, K., Podhorszki, N., Jin, C.: Flexible IO and integration for scientific codes through the adaptable IO system (ADIOS). In: CLADE, pp. 15–24. ACM, NY (2008). https://doi.org/10.1145/1383529.1383533
26. Nicolae, B., et al.: VeloC: towards high performance adaptive asynchronous checkpointing at large scale. In: IPDPS, pp. 911–920 (2019). https://doi.org/10.1109/IPDPS.2019.00099
27. NVIDIA: Nsight systems. https://developer.nvidia.com/nsight-systems
28. Pezoa, F., et al.: Foundations of JSON schema. In: Proceedings of the 25th International Conference on World Wide Web, pp. 263–273 (2016)
29. Shende, S., et al.: Characterizing I/O performance using the TAU performance system. In: ParCo 2011, Advances in Parallel Computing, vol. 22, pp. 647–655. IOS Press (2011). https://doi.org/10.3233/978-1-61499-041-3-647

30. Snyder, S., et al.: Modular HPC I/O characterization with darshan. In: ESPT '16, pp. 9–17. IEEE Press (2016). https://doi.org/10.1109/ESPT.2016.006
31. Stovner, E.B., Sætrom, P.: PyRanges: efficient comparison of genomic intervals in Python. Bioinformatics **36**(3), 918–919 (2019). https://doi.org/10.1093/bioinformatics/btz615
32. Sung, H., et al.: Understanding parallel I/o performance trends under various HPC configurations. In: Proceedings of the ACM Workshop on Systems and Network Telemetry and Analytics, pp. 29–36 (2019). https://doi.org/10.1145/3322798.3329258
33. Tang, H., Koziol, Q., Byna, S., Mainzer, J., Li, T.: Enabling transparent asynchronous I/O using background threads. In: 2019 IEEE/ACM 4th International Parallel Data Systems Workshop (PDSW), pp. 11–19 (2019). https://doi.org/10.1109/PDSW49588.2019.00006
34. Tang, H., Koziol, Q., Ravi, J., Byna, S.: Transparent asynchronous parallel I/O using background threads. IEEE TPDS **33**(4), 891–902 (2022). https://doi.org/10.1109/TPDS.2021.3090322
35. Taufer, M.: AI4IO: a suite of Ai-based tools for IO-aware HPC resource management. In: HiPC, pp. 1–1 (2021). https://doi.org/10.1109/HiPC53243.2021.00012
36. Tavakoli, N., Dai, D., Chen, Y.: Log-assisted straggler-aware I/O scheduler for high-end computing. In: 2016 45th International Conference on Parallel Processing Workshops (ICPPW), pp. 181–189 (2016). https://doi.org/10.1109/ICPPW.2016.38
37. Thakur, R., Gropp, W., Lusk, E.: Data sieving and collective I/O in ROMIO. In: Proceedings Frontiers '99 7th Symposium on the Frontiers of Massively Parallel Computation, pp. 182–189 (1999). https://doi.org/10.1109/FMPC.1999.750599
38. The HDF Group: Hierarchical data format, version 5 (1997). http://www.hdfgroup.org/HDF5
39. The pandas Development Team: pandas-dev/pandas: Pandas (2020). https://doi.org/10.5281/zenodo.3509134
40. Wang, C., et al.: Recorder 2.0: efficient parallel I/O tracing and analysis. In: 2020 IEEE International Parallel and Distributed Processing Symposium Workshops (IPDPSW), pp. 1–8 (2020). https://doi.org/10.1109/IPDPSW50202.2020.00176
41. Wang, T., et al.: A zoom-in analysis of I/O logs to detect root causes of I/O performance bottlenecks. In: CCGRID, pp. 102–111 (2019). https://doi.org/10.1109/CCGRID.2019.00021
42. Wang, T., et al.: IOMiner: large-scale analytics framework for gaining knowledge from I/O Logs. In: IEEE CLUSTER, pp. 466–476 (2018). https://doi.org/10.1109/CLUSTER.2018.00062
43. Wilkinson, L.: The Grammar of Graphics (Statistics and Computing). Springer-Verlag, Berlin (2005)
44. Xu, C., et al.: DXT: darshan eXtended tracing. CUG (2019)
45. Yildiz, O., et al.: On the root causes of cross-application I/O interference in HPC storage systems. In: IEEE IPDPS, pp. 750–759 (2016). https://doi.org/10.1109/IPDPS.2016.50
46. Yu, J., Liu, G., Dong, W., Li, X., Zhang, J., Sun, F.: On the load imbalance problem of I/O forwarding layer in HPC systems. In: International Conference on Computer and Communications (ICCC), pp. 2424–2428 (2017). https://doi.org/10.1109/CompComm.2017.8322970
47. Zhang, W., et al.: AMReX: block-structured adaptive mesh refinement for multiphysics applications. Int. J. High Perform. Comput. Appl. **35**(6), 508–526 (2021). https://doi.org/10.1177/10943420211022811

Efficient Large Scale DLRM Implementation on Heterogeneous Memory Systems

Mark Hildebrand$^{(\boxtimes)}$, Jason Lowe-Power , and Venkatesh Akella

University of California, Davis, USA
{mhildebrand,jlowepower,akella}@ucdavis.edu

Abstract. We propose a new data structure called *CachedEmbeddings* for training large scale deep learning recommendation models (DLRM) efficiently on heterogeneous (DRAM + non-volatile) memory platforms. *CachedEmbeddings* implements an implicit software-managed cache and data movement optimization that is integrated with the Julia programming framework to optimize the implementation of large scale DLRM implementations with multiple sparse embedded tables operations. In particular we show an implementation that is 1.4X to 2X better than the best known Intel CPU based implementations on state-of-the-art DLRM benchmarks on a real heterogeneous memory platform from Intel, and 1.32X to 1.45X improvement over Intel's 2LM implementation that treats the DRAM as a hardware managed cache.

1 Introduction

Deep Learning Recommendation Models (DLRM) are state of the art AI/ML workloads underlying large scale ML-based applications [16]. These models require hundreds of gigabytes of memory and thousands of sparse embedding table operations [16], which makes them challenging to implement on current computer systems. As shown in Fig. 1, DLRM model operates on a collection of dense features and sparse features. Dense features are processed by a standard Multi-Level Perceptron (MLP) network. The sparse features, on the other hand, are used to index into embedding tables to extract dense features. Sparse features can encode information such as a user id, product id, etc. The outputs of the individual embedding table lookups are concatenated together and combined with the output of the bottom MLP using various feature interaction techniques. Post interaction tensors are processed by a final top MLP before yielding a final result. The architectural implications of these networks has been investigated in depth in the literature [7]. Embedding table lookup and update operations are memory bandwidth intensive while the dense MLP layers, on the other hand, are compute intensive. This combination stresses many architecture subsystems. Further complicating matters is the size of these embedding tables, which can occupy tens to hundreds of gigabytes and are expected to grow [7,12].

A. Bhatele et al. (Eds.): ISC High Performance 2023, LNCS 13948, pp. 42–61, 2023.
https://doi.org/10.1007/978-3-031-32041-5_3

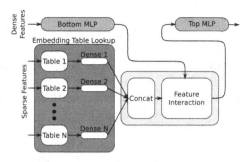

Fig. 1. *Generalized DLRM architecture*

Emerging heterogeneous memory based platforms that combine terabytes of non-volatile RAM such as 3DXpoint [11] and hundreds of gigabytes of DRAM are naturally attractive as they meet the memory demands of DLRM workloads at a reasonable power/cost [2,4]. When moving to these heterogeneous memory systems, we must manage the data movement and placement smartly to achieve the best performance. There are three classes of techniques to move data in these heterogeneous memory systems: hardware (usually at a 64-byte block granularity), operating system (usually at a page granularity), or directly by the application (at any granularity). Unfortunately, each of these techniques come with significant downsides. Hardware-based data movement wastes memory bandwidth by requiring up to four *extra* memory accesses on every demand request and can lead to poor performance [9]. OS-based data movement is not always timely and can be wasteful for applications with sparse memory access patterns [13,22]. Finally, requiring the application developer to manually move data is burdensome and requires modifying the algorithm and deep application changes [3,20].

Naive methods for heterogeneous memory embedding table management may fall short for several reasons. First, just placing the tables in non-volatile memory will not yield good performance due to the significantly lower performance of non-volatile memory technologies such as 3DXpoint when compared with DRAM. Next, the reuse pattern of entries within an embedding table can vary significantly from essentially random highly local and can change over time [5]. This suggests the need for a dynamic policy that is capable of meeting these different requirements. Further, while researchers have investigated using heterogeneous memory to store portions of these embedding tables [4], these works tend to focus on using NVMe SSDs for their tiered storage. The main issue with simple caching is that embedding table are sparsely accessed and lookups have little spatial locality and varying temporal locality.

In this paper, we focus on deep learning recommendation workloads with very large sparse embedding tables. We will show the data use/reuse patterns with sparse embedding tables is complex and there are complex interactions between due to the sparsity of the tables, batch size, features size, number of tables accessed, number of accesses, and parallelization techniques for lookup/update operation which cause poor performance for hardware caches. To decrease the burden on programmers but get the performance benefits of manually data movement, we introduce *CachedEmbeddings* which is a new runtime-optimized data structure for the embedding tables of the Deep Learning Recommendation Model (DLRM) workload. Specifically, we will target data movement during the embedding table lookup and gradient descent update operations. In this paper, we refer to a system with DRAM and non-volatile memory as a *heterogeneous memory* system and Intel's Optane Persistent Memory which is based on 3DXpoint non-volatile memory technology as **PM (Persistent Memory)**.

The novel contributions of this work are two fold. First, almost all the prior work in this area has focused on optimizing the embedding table operations on a homogeneous memory platform (CPU or GPU) taking advantage of the statistical distribution of the embedding table rows with clever partitioning and data layout techniques. In this work, we first perform benchmarking and analysis of a heterogeneous memory platform and show that it introduces a different set of tradeoffs (Sect. 3). Second, the core contribution of this work is a data tiering framework (or algorithm) that is centered around a new data structure (called *CachedEmbeddings*) and an API to implement different platform-specific data movement optimizations integrated with Julia programming framework. So, the proposed framework can be used for future workloads that may have different access patterns, model capacities, and statistical distributions, and more importantly different hardware platforms. The proposed data tiering framework goes beyond a traditional software-managed cache in terms of providing a comprehensive mechanism for memory allocation and deallocation, prefetching, and moving data at larger granularity that is closer to the semantics of the data. This makes it easier for the programmer to use the proposed API.

We evaluate our implementation of DLRM based on *CachedEmbeddings* and find it is 1.4X to 2X better than the best known Intel CPU based implementations on state-of-the-art DLRM benchmarks on a real heterogeneous memory platform from Intel [12], and 1.32X to 1.45X improvement over Intel's 2LM implementation that treats the DRAM as a hardware managed cache for the non-volatile memory.

2   Related Work

Bandana [5] aims to reduce the amount DRAM required for DLRM inference workloads on CPU clusters by using a combination of DRAM and SSDs, using heuristics to determine how to cache embedding vectors in DRAM. Like our work, Bandana also caches hot vectors in DRAM. However, Bandana needs to overcome the coarse read granularity of SSDs and must use hypergraph partitioning to group vectors with spatial locality to the same sector within the SSD. Persistent memory does not have this limitation, so this work investigates fine-grained vector caching while still maintaining high read and write bandwidth to PM. A performance model for DLRM training on GPUs is presented in [14] and using heterogeneous memory for DLRM inference to lower power consumption and cost is presented in [2] and DLRM inference on CPU cluster is presented in [8]. There are two state-of-the-art implementations of DLRM training in recent literature. Facebook's NEO [16] is software/hardware codesign of large scale DLRM models on a custom GPU-based hardware platform called ZionEX. It uses a customized 32-way set-associative software cache with LRU and LFU cache replacement policies and enables fine grain control of caching and replacement. Though NEO is focused on the GPU ecosystem, it provides motivation for the need of software managed caches to deal with large embedding tables. Intel's DLRM implementation [12] focuses on efficient parallelization across multiple CPU and a novel implementation of the SGD optimizer targeting mix-precision training. We extend this work by proposing a scale-up solution taking advantage of heterogeneous memory. Recently there has been work [1, 19, 21] in identifying and storing "hot" vectors in faster memory. Further, recent work [6] proposed a software caching idea similar to ours for GPU-based DLRM training, though with a different implementation mechanism.

To the best of our knowledge this is the first work on implementation and optimization of large scale DLRM *training* on a system with DRAM and non-volatile RAM (Intel's Optane Persistent Memory). In addition, this work introduces a generic data management API for optimizing embedded table implementations on heterogeneous memory systems that is useful beyond just DLRM workloads. This work goes beyond just *caching* frequently used vectors to providing a mechanism to the programmer to tailor the movement of data algorithmically to meet the unique constraints/features of the underlying hardware platform.

3 Implementing Embedding Tables in Heterogeneous Memory Systems

As noted in prior works [1, 16, 17, 19] embedding table operations have high bandwidth demands and low computation intensity, and moreover, one size doest not fit all. So, it is a challenge even on a homogeneous memory system like a CPU or GPU. Heterogeneous memory introduces new challenges. Performance of embedding tables depends on a variety of parameters such as number of threads, whether the feature size is fixed as a compiler-time parameter or dynamic, which means known at runtime, the feature size (we sweep from 16 to 256), the number of accesses, number of tables (we vary from 10 to 80), the location of the tables, whether they are in PM or DRAM, number of worker threads, direct vs indirect lookup (one memory access to retrieve the pointer to the vector and one more access to retrieve the vector) standard vs non-temporal stores for conducting the final write operation of an embedding table update. Non-temporal stores hint to the hardware that the associated data is not intended to be used in the near future, enabling CPU cache optimizations.

Methodology. Experiments were conducted on a single socket, with one thread per core on a 2-socket 56 core (112 thread) Intel Xeon Platinum 8276L running Ubuntu 21.10 with 192 GiB (6x32 GiB) DRAM and 1.5 TB (6x256 GiB) Optane DC NVRAM (3DXpoint-based PM) per socket. We used an embedding table library written in Julia[1] to decouple embedding table operations from data structure implement. For deep learning primitives, we wrote a Julia wrapper around Intel's oneDNN library[2].

The experiments consisted of running the kernel of interest multiple times until 20-s of wall-clock time had elapsed, the execution time for each invocation was logged. For each invocation of the kernel, new lookup/update indices where generated randomly from a uniform distribution. Execution time for the gradient descent update kernels includes the time for reindexing. In addition to execution time, hardware performance counters for DRAM and PM read and write traffic were also collected, sampled at the beginning and end of each kernel invocation. All experiments used a large batchsize of 16384. Embedding tables were sized to occupy a memory footprint between 1 GiB and 80 GiB to minimize the effect of the L3 cache.

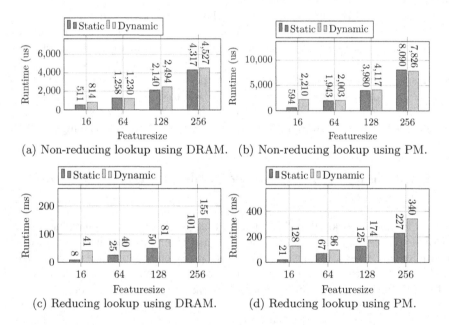

(a) Non-reducing lookup using DRAM.   (b) Non-reducing lookup using PM.

(c) Reducing lookup using DRAM.   (d) Reducing lookup using PM.

Fig. 2. *Comparing the execution time of static versus dynamic feature-sizes for a single embedding table lookup operation using a single thread. Figures cover the range of non-reducing and reducing (accesses = 40) operations with the embedding table in either DRAM or Optane PM. Within each regime, a range of feature sizes is explored. All runs used single-precision floating point with a batchsize of 16,384 and nvectors = 10,000,000*

---

[1] https://github.com/darchr/EmbeddingTables.jl.
[2] https://github.com/hildebrandmw/OneDNN.jl.

Systems equipped with Optane can run in two modes, an *app direct* mode where memory is explicitly allocated on PM with loads and stores going directly to the devices and a *2LM* cache mode where DRAM acts as a transparent direct-mapped cache for PM [11]. Unless otherwise specified, all of our experiments were conducted in *app direct* mode. Next, we present relevant and interesting results from the large number of experiments conducted.

Static and Dynamic Featuresize. First, we investigate the trade-off between dynamic and static feature size definitions for both reducing and non-reducing lookups. Figure 2 compares the execution time of static versus dynamic features sizes for a single embedding table lookup using a single thread across the combinations of reducing (*accesses* = 40) and non-reducing lookups with the embedding table in DRAM and Optane PM. In different situations, embedding table definitions may or may not know *a priori* the size of the embedding table entries, which leads to different code generation and different performance. With static feature sizes, the compiler can specialize the embedding table lookup code for a single feature size. In the dynamic case, the compiler cannot optimize the embedding table accesses. Additionally, when feeding the embedding table lookup results into the dense MLP in DLRM, sometimes a single embedding table entry is used (non-reducing) and other times many entries from the embedding table are *reduced* into a single value which is sent the MLP. We find that for non-reducing accesses there is little difference in performance, but when multiple lookups are required for each output, the static implementation outperforms the dynamic one in the reducing case. Finally, the performance of PM in these applications is on the order of 2× slower than DRAM showing that even for a single thread, memory location matters. This demonstrates that kernel implementation matters and knowledge of the underlying hardware is key to achieving high performance for these types of workloads.

To show that the lookup implementation is highly performant, we demonstrate that the implementation achieves close to the theoretical bandwidth of the platform. When the tables are located in DRAM, we achieve close to 100 GB/s of read bandwidth. This is close to the theoretical bandwidth of 110 GB/s. THe PM bandwidth achieved during ensemble lookup is between 10 GB/s (featuresize 16) and 25 GB/s (featuresize 256), which tracks well with the expected random-access read-only bandwidth for these devices [11].

SGD Update Performance - Worker Threads and Nontemporal Stores. Figure 3 shows an example ensemble gradient update performance broken down between DRAM and PM, number of worker threads, and usage of standard versus non-temporal stores. The performance of DRAM (Figs. 3a and 3b) increases with the number of threads with little performance difference between standard and non-temporal stores during the update phase. However, for DRAM, the indexing time to create the new CSR array for gradient updates dominates the total update time except for the largest embedding element sizes.

Persistent memory (Figs. 3c and 3d) exhibits more nuanced behavior. Because the write bandwidth to PM is much lower, reindexing time is less of a bottleneck than it is for DRAM. Furthermore, non-temporal stores tend to perform significantly better, especially for larger feature sizes. This is likely because non-temporal stores evict the corresponding cachelines from the cache. This causes the writes to appear at the memory controller as a group allowing for write-combining within the Optane memory controller (this generation of Optane DIMMs have a 256 B access granularity). Without non-temporal stores, the corresponding cache lines only arrive at the memory controller when evicted from the L3 cache, leading to lower spatial locality.

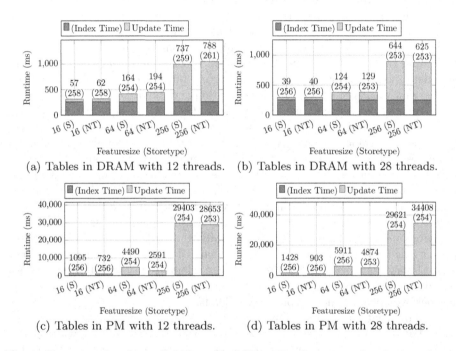

(a) Tables in DRAM with 12 threads.   (b) Tables in DRAM with 28 threads.

(c) Tables in PM with 12 threads.   (d) Tables in PM with 28 threads.

Fig. 3. *Execution time for embedding table SGD application comparing the use of non-temporal (NT) and standard (S) stores. 40 independent tables were used with 1 million vectors each, 40 tables accesses per output, batchsize 16384. Times to perform the update (no parentheses) and the indexing procedure (in parentheses) are given above each bar.*

For these experiments, the time taken by the reindexing procedure is mostly constant and takes a large fraction of the overall execution time when the embedding tables are in DRAM. This is largely because the reindexing procedure is largely targeted for situations where the number of unique indices accessed is relatively small compared to the number of vectors in the table. A choice of data structures and reindexing operation targeted more specifically at this "high density" situation may reduce the this time.

Note that in all cases exhibit a sharp increase in execution time when moving from a feature size of 64 (256 bytes) to 256 (1024 bytes). This is because the contiguous memory accesses of 1024 bytes are sufficient to trigger the streaming prefetcher, which fetches more than just the necessary cache lines causing bandwidth bloat. This phenomenon goes away when the streaming prefetcher is disabled in the system BIOS. In our experimental data is reported with the prefetcher enabled as we expect this to be a more common scenario.

Design Space Exploration Summary. Through our experiments, we make the following conclusions. First, placing the tables in PM results in lower performing lookup and update operations than DRAM. Further, this highlights the need to perform some kind of heterogeneous memory management to get the capacity advantage of PM without paying the full performance price. Second, higher performance implementations of embedding table operations requires cooperation with and understanding of the underlying hardware and the best implementation can change depending on the particular operation. For example, the use of non-temporal stores for update operations is beneficial for performance when embedding tables are in PM, but makes little difference when DRAM is used. Finally, in the context of multithreaded ensemble lookups and updates, an extra level of indirection can be tolerated limited performance penalty (about a 2× overhead for featuresize 16 down to about 10% for a feature size of 128). This is the main idea behind our idea of memory management for these tables which will be presented in the next section. Adding this indirection allows individual vectors to be stored in either PM or DRAM. With careful selection, we should be able to move frequently accessed vectors into DRAM while leaving infrequently accessed ones in PM, providing most of the performance of an all DRAM with the capacity of PM.

4   Cached Embeddings

In this section, we discuss how to apply the framework of heterogeneous memory management to embedding table lookups and updates into an approach called *CachedEmbeddings*.[3] Key aspects to keep in mind are that (1) access to each embedding table is performed on the granularity of feature vectors, (2) there is no reason to expect accesses to exhibit spatial locality, and (3) accesses *may* exhibit temporal locality. The key insight of *CachedEmbeddings* is to add an extra level of indirection to each feature vector access, allowing individual feature vectors to be cached in DRAM while stored in PM.

Figure 4 shows an overview of our approach. Base data for the embedding table is located in PM (beginning at address 0x1000 in the example). Each embedding table maintains a cache in DRAM that vectors can be migrated to. Internally, the embedding table maintains a vector of pointers, one for each row, pointing to where the primary region for that row is. Since embedding table rows are relatively large (>64 B), these pointers have unused lower order bits. We use the least significant bit (LSB) to encode whether the corresponding row is in the base data or in a cache page. The second LSB is used as a lock-bit. A thread

---

[3] https://github.com/darchr/CachedEmbeddings.jl.

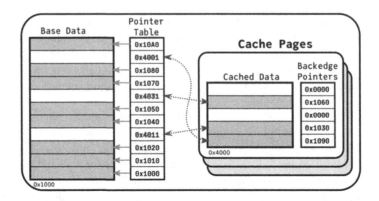

Fig. 4. Overview of *CachedEmbeddings*. *Base data lives in PM, (with a base address of 0x1000 as an example). In this example, each feature vector occupies 16 bytes. A pointer table tracks the actual location of each vector with the least significant bit indicating whether it's cached. Upon a lookup access, vectors are moved into cache pages. Each page contains backedges, which indicates whether the corresponding slot is filled and if so, the vectors original location.*

wanting to move a row uses an atomic compare-and-swap to gain ownership of the row. If ownership is acquired, the thread is free to move the row into the cache and unlock the row.

To support multithreaded access, the cache is composed of multiple cache pages with synchronization for allocation. If the most recent cache page is full, then the thread must acquire a lock for the table in order to allocate new cache page. The cache has a configurable maximum size, beyond which no more feature vectors can be migrated until the cache is flushed. Each cache page also maintains a vector of backedge pointers to each cached row's original location (or null if the slot is empty) to facilitate this flushing. The cache is flushed one page at a time. If the cache page is entirely clean (in the case that only lookups were performed with no update operations), flushing a cache page simply involves updating the *pointer table* back to each vector's original location and then deleting the cache page. If the vectors are dirty (e.g., the table was used during training) then the vectors within the cache page must also be written back to their original location.

The size of the cache is determined by two parameters. The parameter cachelower is a soft lower bound for the size of the cache. When the cache is flushed, pages will be sequentially flushed until the size of the cache is less than cachelower. The parameter cacheslack is flexible space to allow the cache to grow. New vectors can be cached until the total size of the cache exceeds cachelower + cacheslack. Thus, the size of the DRAM cache for each table can fluctuate between cachelower and cachelower + cacheslack.

Table 1 outline the API for a CachedEmbeddingTable. At a high level, the functions access_and_cache and access provides methods for retrieving feature vectors while optionally migrating vectors into the table's DRAM cache. Set-

Table 1. API for a CachedEmbeddingTable.

Operation	Description
access_and_cache	Get the pointer for the requested feature vector, caching it in DRAM if (1) the cache is not full, (2) the vector is not already cached, and (3) ownership of the row is acquired
access	Get the pointer for the requested feature vector without caching. This function is connected to the rowpointer function for all other access contexts besides Forward
set_cachelower	Set the cachelower variable
set_cacheslack	Set the cacheslack variable
isfull	Return true if the cache is full. Otherwise, return false
flush_clean	Purge the oldest cache pages until the size of the cache is less than cachelower. Do not write back data from cache pages to the base array
flush_dirty	Purge the oldest cache pages until the size of the cache is less than cachelower. Do write back data from cache pages to the base array

ters set_cachelower and set_cacheslack are used to modify their corresponding cache size parameter variables. Finally, flush_clean and flush_dirty provide methods for reducing the size of the cache to enable future vector accesses to be cached. With this API, we can simply extend *CachedEmbeddings* to new memory architectures (e.g., CXL) by modifying the backend implementations of these functions. On the user-facing side of the API, there will be no changes required to port the application to a new memory technology.

We evaluated the performance impact of a level of indirection and found it does not have a significant impact on the embedding table lookup time. An extra level of pointer chasing causes a slight slowdown when embedding tables are in DRAM, but it has roughly performance parity when the tables are in PM. In this bandwidth constrained environment with a large number of threads, the overhead introduced by an extra level of pointer chasing is negligible. Thus, we can add a level of indirection, allowing individual feature vectors to be located in either DRAM or PM, without a large sacrifice in performance.

4.1 *CachedEmbeddings* Performance

In this section, we perform experiments to determine the performance of the *CachedEmbeddings*.

Methodology. When comparing the performance of *CachedEmbeddings* to standard embedding tables, we focus on the lookup operation performance. This is because, in the context of DLRM training, feature vectors will be cached in DRAM during the lookup operation and simply accessed during the gradient descent operation. The performance of this update operation and subsequent cache flushing is harder to micro-benchmark for a couple of reasons. First, in the context of DLRM training, we would expect all embedding tables entries accessed during the update phase to already be cached. Second, the frequency of a flush operation is dependent on the input index distribution and thus doesn't necessarily occur on every training iteration. Consequently, we will examine update performance when we study then end-to-end performance of DLRM with *CachedEmbeddings* in Sect. 6.

For our benchmarks, we want to target conditions where a mix of DRAM and PM makes sense (i.e., the total memory footprint is high). To that end, we investigate ensemble lookups with 80 tables and 28 threads with featuresizes of 16 and 256 and accesses of 1 and 40. Furthermore, each table consisted of 1 million vectors and a batch size of 16384 was used. To investigate the effects of cache size, we set `cacheslack` to be 5% and `cachelower` to 10%, 25%, 50%, 75% and 100% of each table's total memory footprint.

To investigate the effects of temporal locality (e.g., users frequently returning to a web application), the lookup indices for each table are drawn from either a uniform distribution (which has low temporal locality) or a Zipf [18] distribution with $\alpha = 1$ (which has high temporal locality). In order to avoid spatial locality introduced by the Zipf distribution, the index sampling is followed by a maximum length linear feedback shift register (LFSR) using a different seed for each table.

For comparison points, the same experiments were run for standard embedding table with either all data stored in DRAM or PM and no indirection in the lookup accesses. As before, each lookup operation is invoked multiple time with different indices until the total benchmark runtime exceeds 20 s. For the experiments conducted using *CachedEmbeddings*, the `flush_clean` operation is run after each invocation.

Results. Figure 5 shows the results for a non-reducing embedding table ensemble lookup. The left-most and right-most bars in each figure show the performance of a standard embedding table with all DRAM and PM respectively. In between is shown the performance of a *CachedEmbeddings*, with the label giving the sum of `cachelower` and `cacheslack` as a percent of the ensemble's total memory footprint. For a featuresize of 16 (Fig. 5a and 5b), the overhead of cache management overheads dominates resulting in significant slowdown over the all PM simple table. Even with the larger featuresize of 256, *CachedEmbeddings* requires a fairly large cache size to outperform the all PM standard table.

There are a number of reasons for this. First, non-reducing lookups are essentially a memory copy from either DRAM to DRAM or PM to DRAM. This higher DRAM write traffic can, to some extent, help mitigate the lower read bandwidth of PM which we can see with the 2× lower performance of the PM based simple tables than the DRAM based ones for the uniform distribution. Second, because `flush_noclean` is called after every invocation and only at most 16384 are accessed on each lookup (around 1.6% of the embedding table) the table never reaches the state where the cache is full (recall that `cacheslack` was set to 5%

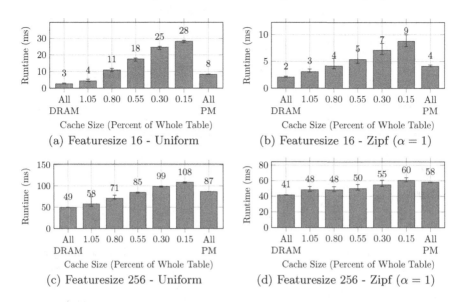

Fig. 5. *Comparison of CachedEmbeddings with standard embedding tables located in DRAM or PM for nonreducing lookups for uniform and zipf distributions. Runs were conducted with 80 embedding tables and 28 worker threads.*

of the overall table size). This means that the *CachedEmbeddings* table is always doing extra work and cannot necessarily take advantage of preexisting cached vectors.

Figure 6 shows the performance of *CachedEmbeddings* for reducing lookups (with *accesses* = 40). Again, the smaller feature sizes yield poorer performance advantages (or even performance regressions at smaller cache sizes) because the time spent moving data around is so low enough that the extra steps required by *CachedEmbeddings* can dominate. However, for larger feature sizes like 64 and 256, the performance of *CachedEmbeddings* nearly interpolates linearly between the performance of all DRAM and all PM. This is because with a batchsize of 16384 and 40 accesses per batch, a large portion of each embedding table is accessed on each lookup operation, resulting in the each embedding table's cache staying "full" for a large portion of the lookup operation. When full, the extra level of indirection for the embedding tables is amortized by the large number of worker threads, providing a performance benefit over all PM when an accessed vector is in DRAM with little overhead when it is not. This effect is magnified with the Zipf distribution which yields a very high DRAM hit rate with only a modest cache size.

Discussion. There are several regimes where this approach of fine-grained heterogeneous memory management can be effective. When the hit rate into the managed DRAM cache is sufficiently high (in the case of the Zipf index distribution) and the feature size is large enough to amortize the overhead of adding

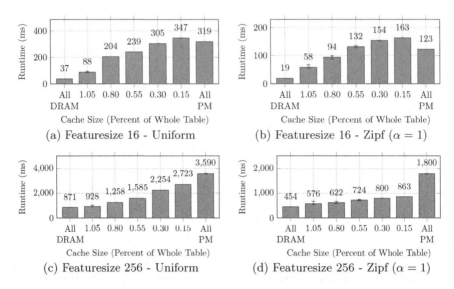

Fig. 6. *Comparison of CachedEmbeddings with standard embedding tables located in DRAM or PM for reducing lookups with 40 Runs were conducted with 80 embedding tables and 28 worker threads using the preallocation strategy.*

indirection to vector access, then *CachedEmbeddings* can outperform all PM with a relatively small amount of DRAM. Even in cases where the hit rate is not particularly high (the case of the uniform index distribution), *CachedEmbeddings* can still achieve a level of performance between all DRAM and all PM provided the cache becomes full and the amount extra work involved on each access decreases. At this operating point, each vector access just adds a level of indirection, sometimes hitting in DRAM and sometimes hitting in PM. Those accesses to DRAM are accelerated while those to PM have little penalty over the all PM case.

This suggests another use strategy for *CachedEmbeddings* called the *static* approach. If the input distribution is known to have little locality *or* if hot entries in the distribution are known *a priori*, then an appropriate subset of the table can be preemptively moved to DRAM (using `access_and_cache`) until the table's cache is full. At this point, further accesses will only fetch and not move feature vectors. This approach will not respond dynamically to changes in the input distribution, but as we pointed out, may be appropriate is some situations.

5   DLRM Implementation Methodology

We implemented the DLRM model in Julia[4], and to verify our model performance, we compared our DLRM implementation Intel's optimized PyTorch [12]

---

[4] https://github.com/darchr/DLRM.jl.

Table 2. Model hyperparameters used for DLRM PyTorch comparison.

	Small Mode	Large Model
Featuresize	16	128
Num Embeddings Tables	26	26
Embedding Table Sizes	min = 3, max = 8.9e6, $\mu \approx 1.2e6$, $\sigma = 2.6e6$	
Bottom MLP	512-256-64-16	512-256-128
Top MLP	512-256-1	1024-1024-512-256-1
Batchsize	8192	32768

submission to MLPerf [15]. This reference model using custom PyTorch extensions to enable BFloat16 for high performance dense network computations. We were able to acquire temporary access to an Intel Cooperlake server, a generation equipped with vector instructions for BFloat16 based dot products. Since our implementation is build on top of oneDNN (which supports the BFloat16 datatype), we incorporated the BFloat16 data type into our model as well.

We used two models for comparison, a small model used as Facebook's official DLRM sample model and the model used in MLPerf 2019 training [15]. The hyper parameters for these tables is shown in Table 2. The optimized PyTorch implementation used *split SGD* [12] for their BFloat16 weights. With this optimizer, MLP and embedding table weights are kept in BFloat16, and each weight array is associated with a similar sized array filled with 16-bit integers. During the weight update phase of training, these BFloat16 variables are concatenated with their respective 16-bit integer in their sibling array to create a full 32-bit float. The gradient update is applied to this 32-bit value, which is the decomposed back into a BFloat16 and 16-bit "mantissa". Using this strategy, the authors keep a full 32 bits of precision for training while using 16 bits of precision for inference. Importantly, this technique *does not* decrease the memory requirement of the embedding tables. Consequently, we implement the split SGD trick for the MLP layers of our implementation, but keep our embedding tables in full Float32.

Training data came from the Kaggle Display Advertising Challenge dataset. Both small and large models were run for a single epoch of training on the dataset, iterating over the data in the same order. Further, both our model and the PyTorch model began with the same initial weights.

Figure 7 shows the loss progression of our model and the optimized PyTorch model for the small and large networks. Figures 7a and 7c show loss as a function of iteration number while Figs. 7b and 7d show loss as a function of time.

We found that our model has slightly higher (worse) loss per iteration, implying our treatment of BFloat16 is not quite as precise as the PyTorch. However, our model has a significant less in loss over time because each iteration is processed much more quickly. When comparing end-to-end performance for training DLRM, our Julia model is slightly *faster* than the optimized PyTorch demonstrating that we have a high-performant implementation of DLRM to investigate the impacts of different embedding table lookup algorithms.

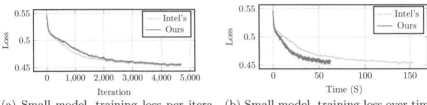

(a) Small model, training loss per itera- (b) Small model, training loss over time.
tion.

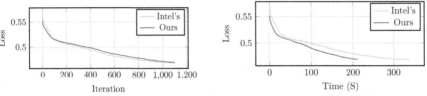

(c) Large model, training loss per itera- (d) Large model, training loss over time.
tion.

Fig. 7. Convergence comparison between the PyTorch optimized DLRM and ours. Our model has a slightly *higher* loss per iteration, but *lower* loss per wall clock time.

Figure 8 shows the time breakdown of each iteration for both implementations and models. Our performance benefit comes from three major areas. First, our MLP backward pass is much faster. This is because we are using an up to date version of oneDNN to compute our backward pass kernels while the PyTorch model at the time was using libxsmm. It should be noted that Intel's extensions for PyTorch have since switched to using oneDNN. Second, our implementation has a faster embedding table and weight update through our parallel embedding table update and parallel weight update strategies. Note that even though the wall-clock time for the large network embedding lookup is slightly larger than PyTorch, we're moving twice the amount of data because our tables were kept in Float32 while PyTorch used BFloat16. Finally, our implementation has less miscellaneous overhead, a factor especially apparent for the small network where PyTorch.

6   End-to-End DLRM Performance

In this section, we investigate the performance of *CachedEmbeddings* for full DLRM training. We investigate several different management schemes built on top of *CachedEmbeddings* and compare their performance with Intel's built-in 2LM hardware managed DRAM cache.

Policies. We implemented three simple policies on top of *CachedEmbeddings*. The *simple* policy leaves all embedding vectors in PM, using DRAM to store the results of an embedding table lookup and intermediate data for the dense computations. This policy uses a simple embedding table without the level of

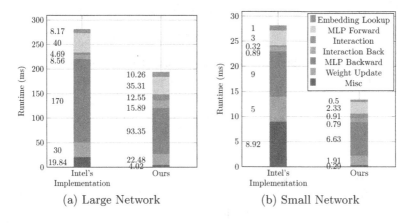

Fig. 8. *Timing breakdown of key layers in our DLRM comparison.*

indirection required for a CachedEmbedding table. The *static* policy allocates a specified amount of memory in DRAM as cache pages, fills these cache pages with random rows, then disables all dynamic row caching. At run time, a row access will either be serviced from DRAM (if one of the rows that was cached ahead of time) or from PM. The *dynamic* policy involves dynamically moves feature vectors into cache pages in DRAM. During lookup of a particular row, the current thread checks if the accessed row is cached and if so directly returns a pointer. If the row is not cached, the thread attempts to dynamically cache the row using the mechanism described above before returning the pointer. If the row fails to obtain ownership of the row, a pointer to the base data is used.

Over time, the *dynamic* policy will increase the footprint of the cache pages as more rows are moved into DRAM. In order to compare fairly with *memory mode* (which has access to all of DRAM), we need a per-table cache size small enough to fit in DRAM along side all memory used by the dense computations but large enough to achieve high utilization of the available DRAM. Thus, we set a cache size limit of 2 GiB for each table for a total memory footprint of 128 GiB across the ensemble. Cache pages are sized to be a fraction of this limit and when the limit is reached, the oldest cache page is cleaned up.

If the sparse input distributions are known, then policies can be updated on a per-table basis, (e.g., changing the amount of cache allowed for a table).

Methodology. To test *CachedEmbeddings*, we used a very large DLRM with the hyper parameters shown in Table 3. This model has large and deep MLPs and a memory footprint of around 393 GB for its embedding tables. For this large model, both embedding table operations and dense computations take a significant fraction of overall training iteration time. Models with smaller dense networks will be more bottlenecked on embedding table operations, and models with fewer tables or with fewer lookups per output will be more compute bound.

The input distributions for embedding tables used in industry are proprietary, though literature suggest that there is at least some temporal locality. In this

Table 3. Parameters for the large DLRM model used for benchmarking.

Parameter	Value	Parameter	Value
Number of Tables	64	Rows per Table	6000000
Featuresize	256	Lookups per Output	100
Bottom MLP Length	8	Bottom MLP Width	2048
Top MLP Length	16	Top MLP Width	4096
Batchsize	512		

work, we chose to select two extremes. First, we use a uniform random input distribution for all tables. This is nearly the worst case for caching as there is limited reuse. Second, we use a Zipf [18] distribution with $\alpha = 1$ for each table, scrambling the input for each table using a maximum length LFSR starting at a random phase. This distribution has significant temporal locality. Dense inputs were generated using a normal distribution.

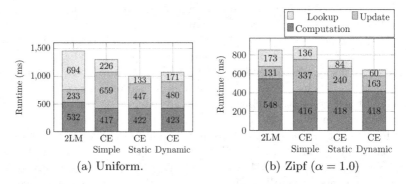

(a) Uniform.   (b) Zipf ($\alpha = 1.0$)

Fig. 9. *Performance with different sparse input distributions. Operations "Lookup" and "Update" refer to embedding table lookup and update respectively. All other operations are grouped into "Computation". Abbreviation "CE" stands for "CachedEmbeddings" and "2LM" stands for Intel's default hardware cache.*

Results. The results for our large DLRM model are shown in Fig. 9. Figure 9a shows performance when a uniform distribution is used to drive sparse accesses while Fig. 9b demonstrates the same model for the Zipf distribution. The *baseline* that we compare to is "2LM" or using the DRAM as a hardware-based cache for the PM. Since the embedding table size greatly exceeds the DRAM size, only a small part cache be cached in DRAM at any time, and during training all of these entries will be updated and must be written back to PM when new entires are moved into the DRAM (i.e., it is a writeback cache). These writebacks mostly occur during the lookup which is why that portion of the bar in Fig. 9a is dominate. In the case with more locality (Fig. 9b) the writebacks mostly occur during the MLP computation. By explicitly managing the memory movement in software, we avoid these hardware cache actions.

For the *CachedEmbeddings* runs, the performance of the dense layers is nearly the same. This is expected since now all dense computations are performed with memory in DRAM. The *simple* case is capable of achieving nearly the whole bandwidth of the PM devices. However, since embedding table updates must be done directly into PM, we see a performance degradation due to the low PM write bandwidth. The *static* policy performs the best. In this mode, embedding table lookup and update operations are serviced from both DRAM and PM. Thus, there is a performance benefit if for accessing rows in DRAM over the *simple* policy without a performance loss if the vector is in PM. The *dynamic* policy is able to perform a little better than the *simple* one because all embedding table updates go to DRAM. However, it is slower then *static* for embedding table lookups because the eager caching of embedding table vectors incurring more DRAM write bandwidth, competing with PM reads. Further more, *dynamic* incurs a slightly higher update penalty due to cache management (writing back dirty rows from old cache pages).

When switching from a uniform distribution (low reuse) to a Zipf distribution ($\alpha = 1$, high reuse), we observe speedups in embedding table and lookup performance across the board. Several factors are at play here. First, with this level of reuse, CPU caches become effective, reducing overall memory traffic. The embedding table update sees further performance increases due to our gradient aggregation strategy where the entire gradient for each embedding table vector is accumulated before applying the optimizer. With higher reuse, there are fewer indices per lookup and lower write traffic to PM.

Finally, we can see the effect of 2LM and *CachedEmbeddings* based caching mechanisms. The lookup performance of 2LM increases by 4× as the DRAM cache stops experiencing such a high miss rate. Further, the performance of *dynamic* improves by 2.85× compared to with the uniform distribution, surpassing the static strategy since it is able to correctly cache the hot vectors in DRAM. Indeed, we observe that there is a slight performance regression of *simple* when compared to 2LM as there is enough locality in the accessed vectors to overcome some of the issues associated with the hardware managed DRAM cache.

We again see the benefit of adding knowledge of program behavior to the memory management policy. When the sparse input distribution is uniform, our cache is too small to have a high enough hit rate to offset the overhead of moving vectors into the cache. In this case, a static partition of the data structures results in better utilization of the multiple levels of memory. However, when there *is* enough temporal locality in the input distribution for caching to be effective, fine grained memory management is exactly what we need. Tailoring of policy to the specifics of hardware and runtime situation is essential for performance.

7 Conclusions and Future Work

In this work, we presented the design space exploration of implementing multiple large and sparse embedding table operations on a heterogeneous memory platform using a new data structure called *CachedEmbeddings*. The main technique presented in this paper works best at larger feature sizes where the effort required to maintain the embedding table is out-weighed by the cost of the embedding table operation itself. Nevertheless, the existence of a caching mechanism for embedding table entries allows for custom policies to be implemented, tailored to the observed distribution in embedding table accesses.

Large and sparse embedding tables are not unique to DLRM workloads but also are useful in other ML workloads such as Transformers [10]. As a software-only technique, *CachedEmbeddings* can be adapted to future disaggregated memory systems, for instance CXL-based fabric-attached memory platforms.

References

1. Adnan, M., Maboud, Y.E., Mahajan, D., Nair, P.J.: Accelerating recommendation system training by leveraging popular choices. Proc. VLDB Endow. **15**(1), 127–140 (2021). https://doi.org/10.14778/3485450.3485462
2. Ardestani, E.K., et al.: Supporting massive DLRM inference through software defined memory. CoRR abs/2110.11489 (2021). https://arxiv.org/abs/2110.11489
3. Dhulipala, L., et al.: Sage: parallel semi-asymmetric graph algorithms for NVRAMs. Proc. VLDB Endow. **13**(9), 1598–1613 (2020). https://doi.org/10.14778/3397230.3397251
4. Eisenman, A., et al.: Reducing DRAM footprint with NVM in Facebook. In: Proceedings of the Thirteenth EuroSys Conference, EuroSys 2018, Porto, Portugal, 23–26 April 2018, pp. 42:1–42:13 (2018). https://doi.org/10.1145/3190508.3190524
5. Eisenman, A., et al.: Bandana: using non-volatile memory for storing deep learning models. CoRR abs/1811.05922 (2018). http://arxiv.org/abs/1811.05922
6. Fang, J., et al.: A frequency-aware software cache for large recommendation system embeddings (2022). https://arxiv.org/abs/2208.05321
7. Gupta, U., et al.: The architectural implications of Facebook's DNN-based personalized recommendation. CoRR abs/1906.03109 (2019). https://arxiv.org/abs/1906.03109
8. Gupta, U., et al.: Deeprecsys: a system for optimizing end-to-end at-scale neural recommendation inference. In: 2020 ACM/IEEE 47th Annual International Symposium on Computer Architecture (ISCA), pp. 982–995. IEEE (2020)
9. Hildebrand, M., Angeles, J.T., Lowe-Power, J., Akella, V.: A case against hardware managed dram caches for NVRAM based systems. In: 2021 IEEE International Symposium on Performance Analysis of Systems and Software (ISPASS), pp. 194–204 (2021)
10. Ivanov, A., Dryden, N., Ben-Nun, T., Li, S., Hoefler, T.: Data movement is all you need: a case study on optimizing transformers. Proc. Mach. Learn. Syst. **3**, 711–732 (2021)
11. Izraelevitz, J., et al.: Basic performance measurements of the Intel Optane DC persistent memory module. CoRR abs/1903.05714 (2019). http://arxiv.org/abs/1903.05714
12. Kalamkar, D., Georganas, E., Srinivasan, S., Chen, J., Shiryaev, M., Heinecke, A.: Optimizing deep learning recommender systems training on CPU cluster architectures. In: International Conference for High Performance Computing, Networking, Storage and Analysis, SC 2020, pp. 1–15. IEEE (2020)

13. Kim, J., Choe, W., Ahn, J.: Exploring the design space of page management for multi-tiered memory systems. In: 2021 USENIX Annual Technical Conference (USENIX ATC 2021), pp. 715–728 (2021)
14. Lin, Z., et al.: Building a performance model for deep learning recommendation model training on GPUs (2022). https://arxiv.org/abs/2201.07821
15. Mattson, P., et al.: MLPerf training benchmark (2019)
16. Mudigere, D., et al.: Software-hardware co-design for fast and scalable training of deep learning recommendation models. In: Proceedings of the 49th Annual International Symposium on Computer Architecture, ISCA 2022, pp. 993–1011. Association for Computing Machinery, New York (2022). https://doi.org/10.1145/3470496.3533727
17. Naumov, M., et al.: Deep learning recommendation model for personalization and recommendation systems. CoRR abs/1906.00091 (2019). http://arxiv.org/abs/1906.00091
18. Powers, D.M.W.: Applications and explanations of Zipf's law. In: New Methods in Language Processing and Computational Natural Language Learning (1998)
19. Sethi, G., Acun, B., Agarwal, N., Kozyrakis, C., Trippel, C., Wu, C.J.: RecShard: statistical feature-based memory optimization for industry-scale neural recommendation. In: Proceedings of the 27th ACM International Conference on Architectural Support for Programming Languages and Operating Systems, ASPLOS 2022, pp. 344–358. Association for Computing Machinery, New York (2022). https://doi.org/10.1145/3503222.3507777
20. Shanbhag, A., Tatbul, N., Cohen, D., Madden, S.: Large-scale in-memory analytics on intel® optane^{TM} DC persistent memory. In: Proceedings of the 16th International Workshop on Data Management on New Hardware, DaMoN 2020. Association for Computing Machinery, New York (2020). https://doi.org/10.1145/3399666.3399933
21. Xie, M., et al.: Fleche: an efficient GPU embedding cache for personalized recommendations. In: Proceedings of the Seventeenth European Conference on Computer Systems, EuroSys 2022, pp. 402–416. Association for Computing Machinery, New York (2022). https://doi.org/10.1145/3492321.3519554
22. Yan, Z., Lustig, D., Nellans, D., Bhattacharjee, A.: Nimble page management for tiered memory systems. In: Proceedings of the Twenty-Fourth International Conference on Architectural Support for Programming Languages and Operating Systems, ASPLOS 2019, Providence, RI, USA, 13–17 April 2019, pp. 331–345 (2019). https://doi.org/10.1145/3297858.3304024

HPC Algorithms and Applications

Efficient GPU Offloading with OpenMP for a Hyperbolic Finite Volume Solver on Dynamically Adaptive Meshes

Mario Wille[1]($\boxtimes$)(iD), Tobias Weinzierl[2](iD), Gonzalo Brito Gadeschi[3](iD), and Michael Bader[1]($\boxtimes$)(iD)

[1] TUM School of Computation, Information and Technology, Technical University of Munich, Garching, Germany
{mario.wille,michael.bader}@tum.de
[2] Department of Computer Science, Institute for Data Science—Large-scale Computing, Durham University, Durham, UK
tobias.weinzierl@durham.ac.uk
[3] NVIDIA, Munich, Germany
gonzalob@nvidia.com

Abstract. We identify and show how to overcome an OpenMP bottleneck in the administration of GPU memory. It arises for a wave equation solver on dynamically adaptive block-structured Cartesian meshes, which keeps all CPU threads busy and allows all of them to offload sets of patches to the GPU. Our studies show that multithreaded, concurrent, non-deterministic access to the GPU leads to performance breakdowns, since the GPU memory bookkeeping as offered through OpenMP's map clause, i.e., the allocation and freeing, becomes another runtime challenge besides expensive data transfer and actual computation. We, therefore, propose to retain the memory management responsibility on the host: A caching mechanism acquires memory on the accelerator for all CPU threads, keeps hold of this memory and hands it out to the offloading threads upon demand. We show that this user-managed, CPU-based memory administration helps us to overcome the GPU memory bookkeeping bottleneck and speeds up the time-to-solution of Finite Volume kernels by more than an order of magnitude.

Keywords: GPU offloading · Multithreading · OpenMP · Dynamically adaptive mesh refinement

This research has been supported by EPSRC's ExCALIBUR programme (projects EX20-9, PAX–HPC and MGHyPE), by the German Ministry of Education and Research (BMBF, project targetDART) and by Intel's Academic Centre of Excellence at Durham University. Supercomputing resources and support was provided by the ARCHER2 UK National Supercomputing Service, the Erlangen National High Performance Computing Center, Jülich Supercomputing Center and CINECA. See the Acknowledgements section for details.

© The Author(s) 2023
A. Bhatele et al. (Eds.): ISC High Performance 2023, LNCS 13948, pp. 65–85, 2023.
https://doi.org/10.1007/978-3-031-32041-5_4

1   Introduction

GPUs are the workhorses of exascale: In exascale machines, the biggest performance share is offered by multiple GPUs per node, being orchestrated by modestly powerful CPUs. However, exascale simulation software also needs to run efficiently on smaller machines, where more CPU-centric nodes are accompanied by few GPUs as accelerators for specific tasks. It is also not yet clear if future top-end systems will continue to be GPU-centric.

Various orthogonal concepts to operate GPUs exist: (i) GPUs can be the sole data owners [19], they can own parts of the data and be compute cores on equal footing with the host cores [13,14], or they can be treated as offloading devices providing services to the host for compute-heavy phases. (ii) GPUs can be interpreted as a few devices with large internal concurrency, or they can be read as compute units accepting many tasks concurrently. In this case, we either split up the GPU internally or toggle between tasks. (iii) Finally, GPUs can be associated statically to particular cores, or we can allow multiple cores to share them. Simulation software is expected to navigate flexibly within these dimensions, as it is not yet clear which paradigm will dominate the future. This challenges the software's design and parallelisation concept.

We study ExaHyPE [15], a wave equation solver that employs explicit time stepping and dynamically adaptive mesh refinement (AMR) with Peano [20]. It uses patches of cells constructed through octree-type AMR (cf. [6] and references therein), and implements a Finite Volume scheme over these patches[1].

ExaHyPE and Peano follow the MPI+X paradigm, i.e., we have many ranks, each hosting several threads. Each thread can take Finite Volume patches and offload them to the GPU. We work in a coupled multiscale and multiphysics environment. As the physics, control, and algorithmic logic reside on the CPU cores which in turn potentially needs access to all simulation data, the GPU is used in offloading mode for the "number crunching". This comes at the cost of additional data movement between GPU and CPU [19].

To construct GPU compute kernels with a high computational load, ExaHyPE provides the opportunity for the host to gather multiple of our patches into a batch of patch update tasks which are handled in one rush on the accelerator via one kernel call [22]. This way, one offload action potentially can occupy the whole GPU. Yet, as we work with dynamically adaptive meshes, we do not constrain at any point which core can access a GPU, and multiple cores potentially may hit the accelerator simultaneously.

ExaHyPE's reference implementation realises the offloading per thread via OpenMP's `target` constructs (cf. [10,18]). Our measurements suggest that the major OpenMP implementations avoid race conditions on the GPU by locking the GPU per data transfer: Whenever the runtime encounters a `target map` clause or implicit data offloading, the target GPU is halted. This is a reasonable design pattern to realise remote memory access in any system. Unfortunately, it

---

[1] Peano and ExaHyPE are available under a modified BSD license at https://gitlab.lrz.de/hpcsoftware/Peano.

introduces significant overhead and synchronisation. Developers face a triad of challenges: To design compute kernels of sufficient load, to overlap computation and data transfer, and to avoid that data is allocated or freed while computations run. Our work presents data for the NVIDIA ecosystem, but we have observed qualitatively the same challenging behaviour for core LLVM and AMD's offloading. Similar results have been reported for pure CUDA [14].

We study two approaches tackling the latter two challenges: The first approach reserves memory on the GPU upon demand, yet does not free it anymore. Instead, it hands out pre-reserved memory to threads whenever they decide to offload. As the memory ownership resides on the host, most synchronisation and coordination can be handled there. The GPU is only interrupted whenever we have to grow the pre-allocated memory. Approach number two relies on virtual shared memory between the GPU and the host. Pre-allocated shared memory regions are held on the host. Logical data transfers to the GPU become plain memory copies on the CPU into the pre-allocated shared memory regions, while the actual data transfer then is realised via the GPU's page fault mechanisms. The allocations on the host come along with overheads—offloading-ready data for example, has to be aligned properly and requires the operating system to physically allocate memory immediately—yet do not interrupt the accelerator.

Our studies suggest that it is reasonable to withdraw memory management from the accelerator where possible and to assign it to the host [14]. Through a host-centric realisation, we speed up some calculations by an order of magnitude, without imposing a static offloading pattern of patches, huge patches, fixed subtimestepping, or a distributed task/patch management [14,19]. Though motivated by a real-world science case, we deliberately work with a worst-case scenario—small kernels, a memory-bound numerical scheme, and an offloading-only approach—to spotlight the challenges. Yet, we think that our techniques are of relevance for a broad range of applications that require flexible GPU usage.

In Sects. 2, we sketch our software architecture and the science cases. Measurements for a straightforward realisation with OpenMP's `map` (Sect. 3) suggest that we have to avoid the allocation and deallocation on the GPU. We introduce a realisation of this approach in Sect. 4 before we provide experimental evidence of the payoff (Sect. 5). A longer discussion of our approach in the light of existing implementations vs. fundamental challenges as well as some generic lessons learned (Sect. 6) lead into an outlook closing the discussion (Sect. 7).

2   Science Case and Code Architecture

ExaHyPE's [15] finite volume solver, which is now in its second generation, accepts hyperbolic partial differential equations (PDEs) in first-order formulation

$$\frac{\partial Q}{\partial t} + \nabla \cdot F(Q) + \sum_{i=1}^{d} B_i(Q) \frac{\partial Q}{\partial x_i} = S(Q) \qquad \text{with } Q : \mathbb{R}^{3+1} \mapsto \mathbb{R}^N, \qquad (1)$$

describing time-dependent wave equations. ExaHyPE offers a suite of explicit time-stepping schemes for these equations: Finite Volumes (FVs), Runge-Kutta Discontinuous Galerkin (DG) and Arbitrary high order using Derivatives

(ADER)-DG (see [15,21]). Users are furthermore offered a set of solver ingredients from which they can pick to assemble their solver, while they can decide which terms of Eq. (1) to employ within the numerical scheme of choice.

Science Case. Our ambition is to study gravity and non-standard gravity models subject to strong solution gradients and solution localisation such as neutron stars or black holes. Two particular flavours of Eq. (1) demand our attention:

The Euler equations yield a system of $N = d + 2$ non-linear PDEs which describe the evolution of the scalar density, the scalar energy and the d-dimensional velocity on a cosmological scale. We employ the textbook Euler fluxes F in Eq. (1), while gravity enters the equations as source term $S(Q)$ with Q determined by the previous time step. $B_i = 0$, i.e., there are no non-conservative terms. Even though the governing PDE is non-linear, the arithmetic intensity of the arising functions is low.

With Euler, small inhomogeneities in the initial mass density distribution lead to a spherical accretion scenario: Gravity pulls more and more matter into a few overdensity centres, such that the Hubble expansion is locally compensated and we observe matter concentration instead of spreading out. Around the accretion centre, the density eventually exceeds a critical threshold and we obtain a shock which again pushes material outwards. It is an open question to which degree the temporal and spatial shape of the arising expansion and contraction horizons are preserved under non-standard gravity models [3,22].

Our second setup of interest results from a first-order formulation of the conformal and covariant Z4 (CCZ4) equations [1,8]. They are available for $d = 3$ only and model the evolution of the space-time curvature as a constrained wave equation. Different to the Euler equations, gravity is not modelled via a (quasi-)elliptic, Poisson-type term impacting some governing equations. Instead, we evolve it explicitly. CCZ4 models gravitational waves as they arise from rotating binary neutron stars, but also describes the environment around static and rotating black holes, i.e., singularities of the density concentration.

As we work with a first-order rewrite of CCZ4 to fit into the scheme of Eq. (1), we have to evolve $N = 59$ equations. Common to all codes working with variations of these equations (cf. [5,7,9,11], e.g.) is the observation that the arithmetic intensity within the PDE evaluations is very high; leading even to register spilling on GPUs [9]. In our first-order formulation (Eq. 1), this high arithmetic intensity materialises in complex B_i and S terms, while $F(Q) = 0$.

Problem Statement 1. *Both equations of interest require dynamic AMR as they study strongly localised effects. Both have high computational demands, but their compute characteristics are completely different.*

Software Architecture. For the spatial discretisation of the computational domain, ExaHyPE employs dynamically adaptive Cartesian meshes. It relies on the PDE framework Peano [20] to realise them through a generalisation of the popular octree approach: We embed the computational domain into a cube, and then subdivide this cube recursively and locally. This yields, on the finest subdivision level, an adaptive Cartesian mesh of cubes. The code thus falls into the class of octree AMR [6,14,19]. The grid structure can change at every time step.

While the code base supports various numerical discretisations, we focus in this paper on its straightforward Finite Volume solver with a generic Rusanov Riemann solver: The code embeds $p \times p$ (2D) or $p \times p \times p$ (3D) regular Cartesian meshes which we call patches into each and every cube, i.e., we work with a block-structured adaptive Cartesian mesh. This mixture of tree code and patches is popular to obtain a reasonable arithmetic load relative to the mesh management overhead (cf. [5,6,14,15,22], e.g.). The code base traverses through the mesh once per time step and progresses each patch in time. For this *compute kernel*, the actual update due to Eq. (1) is determined by the source term plus the flow through the volume faces. These terms are injected by the user via a callback mechanism. All other program logic including mesh traversal order, data storage and parallelisation is hidden. Other codes have propagated such an "inject your domain knowledge" before under the term *Hollywood principle* [20].

We employ three layers of parallelism: The domain spanned by the spacetree is first decomposed into non-overlapping chunks with one chunk per MPI rank. We cut the domain along a Peano space-filling curve (SFC) and hence end up with connected subdomains with a good surface-to-volume ratio, i.e., limited communication compared to compute load [2]. Next, we cut each MPI partition again into chunks along the SFC and deploy the resulting subdomains to the CPU's threads. We obtain hierarchical MPI+X parallelism where the threads own subdomains. Bulk-synchronous processing (BSP) is the programming model for the traversals, as the individual subdomain traversals are triggered at the same time per time step. Realisation via MPI and OpenMP is straightforward. In the context of quickly varying AMR, we however found this MPI+X parallelisation algorithmically insufficient (similar to observations by Dubey et al. [6]), as the domain decomposition on the threading side struggles to load balance.

Each thread, therefore, identifies within its subdomain patches to be deployed as separate tasks: All the patches which do feed into MPI—these patches are time-critical on supercomputers and they have to feed into MPI in-order—or have to realise adaptive mesh refinement are directly executed throughout the mesh traversals. The remaining patches are deployed as separate tasks. This *enclave tasking* concept [4] allows us to balance out imbalances between threads, i.e., within the BSP sections [16].

GPU Offloading. Furthermore, we can pool the tasks in a separate queue: We wait until this queue contains $\|\mathbb{P}_{GPU}\|$ enclave tasks ($\|\mathbb{P}_{GPU}\|$ being a user-defined threshold), and then deploy all patches within the queue in one rush to the GPU. The arising compute kernels over batches or sets of patches make up our fourth level of parallelism. Fifth, we note that our kernel implementations rely heavily on data parallelism yielding vector concurrency.

We note that the pooling or batching of tasks allows us to write GPU compute kernels that have very high concurrency [12]. The individual tasks within a batch are, by definition, all *ready* tasks, i.e., can be processed concurrently, and all of them expose additional internal concurrency on top. Our concept stands in the tradition of the enclave concept by Sundar et al. [17], who deployed subdomains to Intel Xeon Phi coprocessors. However, we do not identify the enclaves geometrically ahead of a mesh traversal—the "enclave" tasks enqueue on the fly—but can fuse segments of enclaves on the fly whenever a task that enqueues GPU tasks finds that the queue size exceeds the GPU threshold and hence deploys a whole batch to the accelerator. This added flexibility allows us to obtain large GPU offloading tasks even though the code might encounter geometrically small enclaves scattered among the threads' subregions.

Due to the processing in batches of size $\|\mathbb{P}_{\text{GPU}}\|$, a proper choice of $\|\mathbb{P}_{\text{GPU}}\|$ should allow users to exploit all parallel potential of a GPU. Contrary to that, a large $\|\mathbb{P}_{\text{GPU}}\|$ might imply that only a few batches become ready per time step and can, potentially, overlap each other [14]. We thus aim for a small $\|\mathbb{P}_{\text{GPU}}\|$ which is just about large enough to utilise the GPU efficiently. Let N_{threads} traverse their subdomain per node and produce tasks. Hence, up to N_{threads} might concurrently decide that they each would like to deploy a batch of $\|\mathbb{P}_{\text{GPU}}\|$ patches to the GPU. Many threads offload to the GPU simultaneously. A GPU serves multiple cores.

Problem Statement 2. *In ExaHyPE, multiple threads offload to the GPU simultaneously. Due to the dynamic AMR, the offloading pattern is not deterministic or known beforehand.*

3   A Realisation of GPU Offloads with target map

Let $\mathcal{K}_p^{\text{Euler,2D}}$, $\mathcal{K}_p^{\text{Euler,3D}}$ and $\mathcal{K}_p^{\text{CCZ4}}$ describe the compute kernels of interest. Each kernel takes the solution representation over a patch of $p \times p$ or $p \times p \times p$ finite volumes and returns the solution at the next timestep. When we benchmark the whole patch update cycle of such an update, we actually measure the cost including all data transfer, i.e., we measure

$$(\mathcal{R} \circ \mathcal{F} \circ \mathcal{K} \circ \mathcal{A} \circ \mathcal{P})Q(t)$$

where the operator $\mathcal{P}$ takes the solution $Q(t)$ and transports it to the GPU, while $\mathcal{R}$ retrieves the solution and brings it back into the user memory. $\mathcal{A}$ allocates on the device all temporary variables required by $\mathcal{K}$, while $\mathcal{F}$ frees these memory blocks. ExaHyPE works with sets of patches and therefore processes sets

$$\left\{ (\mathcal{R} \circ \mathcal{F} \circ \mathcal{K} \circ \mathcal{A} \circ \mathcal{P})Q_c(t) \right\}_{c \in [1, \|\mathbb{P}_{\text{GPU}}\|]}. \tag{2}$$

Realisation. Our plain realisation of the GPU offloading through OpenMP implements Eq. (2) as follows (also, cf. Algorithm 1):

1. The data per patch are stored en bloc in one large array of structures (AoS) on the host, but the individual patches are scattered over the main memory as we invoke the batched GPU kernel (cf. Eq. 2). We thus deep copy a list of

---

Algorithm 1: OffloadMap($\|\mathbb{P}_{\mathrm{GPU}}\|$):

Offloads $\|\mathbb{P}_{\mathrm{GPU}}\|$ to the GPU using OpenMP's map clause. First, patch and temporary data are allocated on the host and the respective device pointers are constructed. After offloading to the GPU, results are copied back to the host and the data is freed.

---

1 *Procedure* offload_map($\|\mathbb{P}_{\mathrm{GPU}}\|$, host_patch_data):
2   mapped_pointers ← allocate_host($\|\mathbb{P}_{\mathrm{GPU}}\|$)
3   **for** $i \leftarrow 0$ *to* $\|\mathbb{P}_{GPU}\|$ **do**
4 | patch_data ← host_patch_data[i]
5 | `#pragma omp target enter data map(to:patch_data)`
6 | mapped_pointers[i] ← `omp_get_mapped_ptr`(patch_data)
7   **end**
8   temporary_data ← allocate_host($\|\mathbb{P}_{\mathrm{GPU}}\|$)
9   `#pragma omp target teams distribute map(to:mapped_pointers)`
    `map(alloc:temporary_data)`
10 **for** $i \leftarrow 0$ *to* $\|\mathbb{P}_{GPU}\|$ **do**
11 | // Do computations on Finite Volumes
12 **end**
13 temporary_data ← free_host()
14 **for** $i \leftarrow 0$ *to* $\|\mathbb{P}_{GPU}\|$ **do**
15 | patch_data ← host_patch_data[i]
16 | `#pragma omp target exit data map(from:patch_data)`
17 **end**
18 mapped_pointers ← free_host()

---

    pointers to patch data to the device: A for loop maps each patch's data onto the device trough `omp target enter data map(to:...)`. Due to the loop, the kernel can handle arbitrary $\|\mathbb{P}_{\mathrm{GPU}}\|$. The copying per se is trivial, as the patch data is one large, continuous array of doubles. After that, we construct the list of pointers on the GPU and befill it with the device pointers. For this, OpenMP offers `declare mapper` constructs though we prefer to build up the list of device pointers via `omp_get_mapped_ptr`.

2. For all temporary data that the kernel requires to handle the $\|\mathbb{P}_{\mathrm{GPU}}\|$ patches, we allocate one large block. There is only one $\mathcal{A}_{\|\mathbb{P}_{\mathrm{GPU}}\|}$ allocation realised through a `map(alloc:...)`.

3. The actual kernel invocation is an `omp target` block supplemented with a `distribute` directive.

4. We free all temporary data in one rush.

5. With OpenMP's `map` clauses, copying the GPU outcomes back into the host memory is realised by a loop over the patches. We issue one `omp target exit data map(from:...)` call per patch and time step.

We conceptually end up with the following realisation of Eq. (2):

$$\left\{\mathcal{R}^{\mathrm{map}}\right\}_{c\in[1,\|\mathbb{P}_{\mathrm{GPU}}\|]} \circ \mathcal{F}_{\|\mathbb{P}_{\mathrm{GPU}}\|} \circ \left\{\mathcal{K}\right\}_{c\in[1,\|\mathbb{P}_{\mathrm{GPU}}\|]} \circ \mathcal{A}_{\|\mathbb{P}_{\mathrm{GPU}}\|} \circ \left\{\mathcal{P}^{\mathrm{map}}\right\}_{c\in[1,\|\mathbb{P}_{\mathrm{GPU}}\|]}. \tag{3}$$

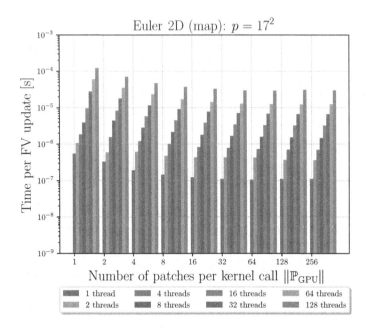

Fig. 1. Time per degree of freedom update for the 2D Euler equations with patch size 17×17. We benchmark the throughput for different numbers of patches $\|\mathbb{P}_{\mathrm{GPU}}\|$ handled by each kernel invocation (x-axis). We also let different thread counts N_{threads} access the GPU at the same time (different bars).

The scheme mirrors batched linear algebra, where a matrix is applied to multiple right-hand sides in one sweep. Each kernel $\mathcal{K}$ has some internal concurrency such as "loop over all faces" or "loop over all volumes". The batching pays off, as we obtain, on top of this, another outer loop over $[1, \|\mathbb{P}_{\mathrm{GPU}}\|]$ which we annotate with OpenMP's `distribute`. We leave it to OpenMP to distribute the patches over the streaming multiprocessors (SMs) or to deploy multiple patches onto one SM via multiple warps, while the SM threads are used to process all finite volumes within a patch.

Experimental Setup. To benchmark the offloading including all data transfers, we disable all calculations on the host, we artificially ensure that all work between the CPU threads is perfectly balanced, we make all cores use one GPU only, and we disable MPI. Next, we vary the number of threads N_{threads} which offload to the GPU simultaneously and let each thread deploy 100 patches, grouped into sets of $\|\mathbb{P}_{\mathrm{GPU}}\|$. In the big picture, it translates to a setup where each GPU of a compute node is governed by one MPI rank, in which multiple threads run in parallel, flooding the GPU with offloaded tasks. However, real simulations barely will encounter situations where all N_{threads} threads offload exactly at the same time. We focus on this worst-case constellation. It is a stress test.

All tests are run on the Alex cluster hosted by the Erlangen National High Performance Computing Center (NHR). Each node of our testbed is equipped with two AMD EPYC 7713 Milan processors (64 cores per chip) which accommodate eight NVIDIA A100 GPUs. Each GPU features 80 GB main memory. Our experiments use the NVIDIA HPC Software Development Kit (SDK) in the version 23.1 as well as the Compute Unified Device Architecture (CUDA) in the version 12.0 as the underlying software stack. NVIDIA SDK's collection of compilers, libraries, and software tools supports OpenMP GPU target offloading and OpenMP loop transformations as used by our compute kernels. However, some features have to be used with care[2].

Benchmark Results. For all different kernel variants as well as p choices, we get qualitatively similar results (Fig. 1):

Observation 1. *It is important to batch multiple patches into one GPU compute kernel to exploit the hardware concurrency of the accelerator.*

This is not a surprising observation once we take into account what hardware concurrency current GPUs offer. Our data however showcase that we quickly run into some saturation: Regardless of the number of threads used, the measured time per finite volume update decreases until it starts to saturate from around $\|\mathbb{P}_{GPU}\| = 16$ patches. It barely pays off to merge more than $\|\mathbb{P}_{GPU}\| = 16$ patches for the two-dimensional Euler. With a patch size of 17×17 and 128 threads, the GPU becomes saturated by keeping around $5.24 \cdot 10^5$ finite volume updates in flight at any point.

Observation 2. *If we launch multiple kernels from multiple threads, the performance of our straightforward implementation deteriorates.*

In theory, spawning kernels in parallel from multiple threads should pay off performance-wisely, as we can hide memory transfers of one kernel behind the computations of another kernel that has already started to work. Tutorials around the usage of streaming buffers or `nowait` (async) kernel launches exploit this. Even as the threads start to offload at the same time in a stress test, we should at least be able to scale up to the number of supported hardware streams. Our data however show that simultaneously firing kernels to the GPU reduces the throughput by at least two orders of magnitude. This is counterintuitive!

Observation 3. *The cheaper a compute kernel, the more severe the impact of concurrent data transfers.*

For the three-dimensional Euler, $\|\mathbb{P}_{GPU}\| = 8$ is reasonable, while CCZ4 has $\|\mathbb{P}_{GPU}\| = 4$ (not shown). As the saturation thresholds are lower, the penalties for concurrent kernel launches kick in stronger for lower thread counts.

Rationale. While modern GPUs can manage several compute kernels in flight, the maximum number of such kernels is relatively small, and each kernel launch

---

[2] See https://doi.org/10.5281/zenodo.7741217 for supplemental material.

introduces overhead. While this motivates why the code benefits from larger $\|\mathbb{P}_{\text{GPU}}\|$, it does not explain the penalties resulting from parallel kernel launches from multiple threads. It does not explain the performance degradation once we increase N_{threads}.

GPU offloading in OpenMP is realised through address mapping: The runtime manages a table per accelerator which stores which addresses from the CPU are mapped onto which GPU addresses including the corresponding memory sizes. From these data, the runtime can identify all reachable memory regions on the accelerator. An allocation of a new memory region on the GPU inserts a new entry into the device table. If an entry is removed, subsequent inserts will be able to use the "freed" memory regions again.

If any thread accesses the memory table, the runtime first has to avoid races with other threads. Secondly, the GPU itself might want to allocate GPU memory. Our kernels do not require dynamic memory, but it is not clear to what degree the compiler synthesises this knowledge from the source code. Thirdly, the GPU hardware can only read from page-locked host-pinned memory to copy data from the host to the device. In general, memory passed to `target map` is not page-locked. Therefore, additional `staging` is required. Our data suggest that this triad of challenges makes the memory manager suspend all running GPU kernels before it allocates or frees memory.

Observation 4. *Memory allocations on the GPU are expensive and potentially delay running kernels if multiple threads offload to the GPU concurrently.*

We consider this final Observation 4 to be a flaw in GPU offloading runtimes. To the best of our knowledge, it does not attract attention in current literature.

4   User-Managed Memory Management

To avoid memory allocations on the GPU, we propose to make the host the owner of the memory blocks on the GPU which are used for host-GPU data transfer. We propose to introduce a GPU memory manager [14], and we provide two realisations of such a manager.

Algorithmic Framework. Let each rank hold one instance of a GPU memory manager. Without loss of generality, we can assume that there is one manager per host CPU, i.e., for all N_{threads} threads sharing one GPU. If a code wants to deploy a memory chunk to the accelerator, it *allocates* memory through the GPU memory manager by passing the size of the memory chunk plus its address, as well as a device number if multiple GPUs are hosted on one node. The allocation routine returns a device pointer, i.e., an address that is valid on the respective device. The GPU memory manager guarantees that the resulting device pointer points to a valid device region that can be accessed consecutively from the calling code. The counterpart of the allocation is a *free* which releases the device memory. It is given another host address into which the GPU memory manager dumps the kernel results. Access to the GPU memory manager is made thread-safe through global semaphores—which is sufficient, as the map simply handles out pointers.

Internally, the GPU memory manager hosts a hash map of tuples of integers onto a sequence of tuples of device addresses plus a boolean marker:

$$M : \mathbb{N}^+ \times \mathbb{N}^+ \mapsto \left(\mathbb{A} \times \{\top, \bot\} \right)^+.$$

The key tuple represents the combination of the device number and memory block size (to be allocated). When the code requests (allocates) memory on a particular device of a particular size, we construct the key and study the image in M which is a sequence of addresses on the device. Each address either holds $\top$ which means that this address is currently in use. The manager may not hand out this address again. If it is labelled with $\bot$, then the address is not in use.

If the GPU memory manager can serve an allocation with an existing address with the label $\bot$, it toggles the flag to $\top$ and returns the corresponding address. If there is no address with $\bot$ available—and notably if a key tuple points to an empty list—it is the GPU memory manager's responsibility to acquire new GPU memory and then return the corresponding address. When memory is freed, the manager retrieves the result from the GPU into the user address space that is passed. After that, it sets the corresponding entry in M to $\bot$. As our compute kernels rely on the managed memory, they can use the manager's returned pointers within `target` compute kernels by labelling them as `is_device_ptr` and effectively avoiding the staging of host memory.

The algorithmic framework sketches a code utility that allocates memory and hands it out upon demand. As it does not free memory but re-uses memory blocks which are not in use anymore, we avoid repeated memory allocations. Notably, we share pre-allocated data between different threads. The exact allocation mechanism is subject to two different realisation flavours.

4.1   Data Pre-allocation on the GPU

A GPU-centric variant of the GPU memory manager acquires all memory requested via `omp_target_alloc` directly on the GPU: If no free memory blocks are held within M, we reserve GPU memory and store the GPU memory's address within the hash map. Whenever we identify a fitting pre-allocated memory region (or have literally just acquired memory), the manager transfers the user data to the allocated memory via an `omp_target_memcpy`. Bringing data back is another explicit `omp_target_memcpy` call (cf. Algorithm 2).

Employing the OpenMP API routines mirrors the behaviour behind the `map(alloc)` and `map(to)` pragma clauses. Internally, the compiler breaks down an `omp target enter data map(to: ...)` statement into $(\mathcal{P} \circ \mathcal{A})$, where the $\mathcal{A}$ operator denotes the explicit memory allocation on the GPU via `omp_target_alloc` which is followed by the actual data transfer.

Algorithm 2: OffloadManaged($\|\mathbb{P}_{\mathrm{GPU}}\|$):

Offloads $\|\mathbb{P}_{\mathrm{GPU}}\|$ to the GPU using the managed memory approach. We allocate patch and temporary data through the GPU memory manager. After offloading to the GPU, results are copied back to the host and the data handles are freed for re-use.

---

1 *Procedure* offload_managed($\|\mathbb{P}_{\mathrm{GPU}}\|$, host_patch_data):
2   patch_data ← GPUMemoryManager→allocate_device($\|\mathbb{P}_{\mathrm{GPU}}\|$)
3   patch_data ← omp_target_memcpy(host_patch_data, $\|\mathbb{P}_{\mathrm{GPU}}\|$)
4   temporary_data ← GPUMemoryManager→allocate_device($\|\mathbb{P}_{\mathrm{GPU}}\|$)
5   `#pragma omp target teams distribute is_device_ptr(patch_data, temporary_data)`
6   **for** $i \leftarrow 0$ *to* $\|\mathbb{P}_{GPU}\|$ **do**
7 | // Do computations on Finite Volumes
8   **end**
9   temporary_data ← GPUMemoryManager→free()
10   host_patch_data ← omp_target_memcpy(patch_data, $\|\mathbb{P}_{\mathrm{GPU}}\|$)
11   patch_data ← GPUMemoryManager→free()

Compared to Eq. (3), the present GPU memory manager variant eliminates, in most cases, the allocations, while we omit the frees. In all cases where our pre-allocated memory regions can serve the user code requests, we reduce the actual kernel invocation cost to

$$\left\{ \mathcal{R}^{\mathrm{copy}} \right\}_{c\in[0,|\mathbb{C}|-1]} \circ \left\{ \mathcal{K} \right\}_{c\in[0,|\mathbb{C}|-1]} \circ \left\{ \mathcal{P}^{\mathrm{copy}} \circ \hat{\mathcal{A}} \right\}_{c\in[0,|\mathbb{C}|-1]}, \qquad (4)$$

where $\hat{\mathcal{A}}$ is a no-operation. Only in the cases where we cannot serve a memory request with pre-allocated memory blocks, $\hat{\mathcal{A}}$ becomes an actual $\mathcal{A}$. As the $\mathcal{F}$ and $\mathcal{A}$ operations halt the GPU temporarily, we obtain a fast code stripped of these stops. Solely the orchestration overhead to launch the batched compute kernel for $\left\{ \mathcal{K} \right\}_{c\in[0,|\mathbb{C}|-1]}$ remains.

4.2 Pre-allocation on the CPU with Unified Memory

Our second approach works on GPUs which offer unified memory. In this case, we exploit that the GPU has full access to the host address space and that the hardware can migrate pages from the main memory via page faults to the CPU upon demand. GPU and CPU form one NUMA domain.

On such systems, it is possible to replace all memory allocations with a shared allocation, i.e., to enable the system to migrate any data automatically between host and accelerator. However, such allocations differ from "normal" allocations in that they induce particular memory layouts and arrangements. Even though the NVIDIA software stack allows developers to enable this *CUDA Unified Memory* globally at compile time through a flag, we refrain from using it globally, as it is not compatible with static memory regions employed for global constants, e.g. Instead, we distinguish the allocation on the GPUs $\mathcal{A}$ from an allocation $\mathcal{A}^{\text{shared}}$ on the CPU which allocates memory that can be transferred to the GPU. For the latter, we introduce the memory copy operators $\mathcal{C}^{\text{host}\mapsto\text{shared}}$ and $\mathcal{C}^{\text{shared}\mapsto\text{host}}$. While $\mathcal{P}$ transfers data directly to the GPU, both $\mathcal{C}$ operators copy data on the host from a "normal" memory region into a region that can be migrated to the GPU upon demand. They are plain CPU memory copies between two memory regions on the host.

Whenever the GPU kernel accesses a unified memory region that resides on the host the access might page fault and trigger a page migration to the GPU which we denote as $\mathcal{P}^{\text{pf}}$ with pf for page fault. Moving data back would be $\mathcal{R}^{\text{pf}}$. With this formalism, our kernel launch becomes

$$\left\{\mathcal{C}^{\text{shared}\mapsto\text{host}}\circ\mathcal{R}^{\text{pf}}\right\}_{c\in[0,|\mathbb{C}|-1]}\circ\left\{\mathcal{K}\circ\mathcal{P}^{\text{pf}}\right\}_{c\in[0,|\mathbb{C}|-1]}\circ\left\{\mathcal{C}^{\text{host}\mapsto\text{shared}}\right\}_{c\in[0,|\mathbb{C}|-1]}. \tag{5}$$

Initially, we simply copy our data on the host. This is cheap compared to the data transfer to the GPU. Notably, nothing stops multiple threads to copy their data in parallel, once the GPU memory manager has identified or created well-suited shared memory blocks. Immediately after that, we launch the kernel. In RAM, the algorithmic latency caused by memory transfers is significantly lower than in our previous managed approach, while the bandwidth is usually higher. While the kernel launches immediately, it has to retrieve data from the host via page fault $\mathcal{P}^{\text{pf}}$. The actual data transfer is prolonged yet has the potential to delay the kernel execution. However, it is realised in hardware, and the GPU is good at orchestrating such data transfer. Getting data back is again a relatively cheap host-internal memory transfer which might however trigger data transfers $\mathcal{R}^{\text{pf}}$ back from the GPU. There might be additional latency here, though the GPU hardware might also trigger the corresponding page faults ahead of time.

Technically, the second variant is close to trivial: We take the first managed approach and replace the OpenMP memory allocations with NVIDIA's CUDA allocations. The OpenMP data copies become plain C++ memory copies.

5   Results

We first benchmark the three-dimensional Euler equations and the CCZ4 setup where the offloading's data transfer is organised via a plain map. A fixed total number of patches is split into chunks (batches) of $\|\mathbb{P}_{\text{GPU}}\|$ and offloaded concurrently by the threads to the GPU. We vary the thread count N_{threads}. This is a classic strong scaling setup that again simplifies real-world simulation runs where the $N_{\text{threads}}\cdot\|\mathbb{P}_{\text{GPU}}\|$ patches never become available in one rush. The total number of patches used is empirically chosen such that the average runtime per patch becomes invariant, i.e., the experimental setup avoids burn-in effects.

Our data (Fig. 2) confirm that both bigger patch sizes p and higher number of patches per batch $\|\mathbb{P}_{\text{GPU}}\|$ pay off performance-wisely. However, the size of the individual patches is the more decisive performance lever: We can distribute a batch of patches over the GPU streaming multiprocessors but if the individual patch is very small, the batching is not able to close the performance gap to

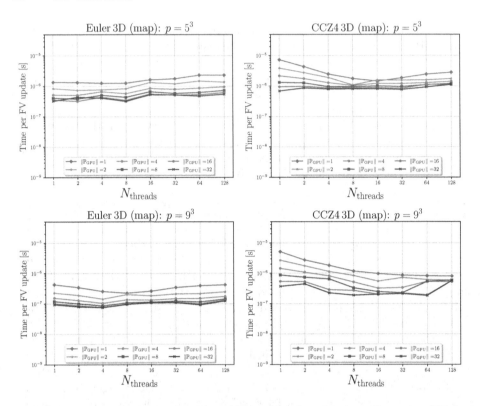

Fig. 2. Time per FV degree of freedom (volume) update for three-dimensional Euler (left) and CCZ4 (right). Lower is better. Each patch either hosts 5^3 (top) or 9^3 (bottom) Finite Volumes along each Cartesian coordinate axis. All data transfer is realised through OpenMP's `map` clauses (cf. Sect. 3).

a run employing big expensive patches right from the start. In any setup, the $N_{threads}$ hold $N_{threads} \cdot \|\mathbb{P}_{GPU}\| \cdot p^3$ finite volumes in flight on the GPU. While this corresponds to a reasonable memory footprint for CCZ4 with its 59 unknowns per volume—we also have to allocate temporary data for the non-conservative fluxes in all three directions plus the source term—the saturation for $\|\mathbb{P}_{GPU}\| \approx 8$ is reached early.

All measurements confirm that offloading to the GPU simultaneously from many threads comes along with a significant performance penalty. If we split up the total work equally among the threads and deploy the batches concurrently, the throughput relative to the threads plateaus quickly and eventually rises again. Indeed, we see a speedup if and only if the number of offloading threads is small, and if we offload only a few patches per batch.

When we rerun the experiments with our GPU memory manager, we dramatically improve the robustness of the concurrent offloading (Fig. 3). Batching, i.e., large $\|\mathbb{P}_{GPU}\|$, and reasonably large individual patches aka p remain key performance ingredients, but concurrent offloading can help robustly to improve

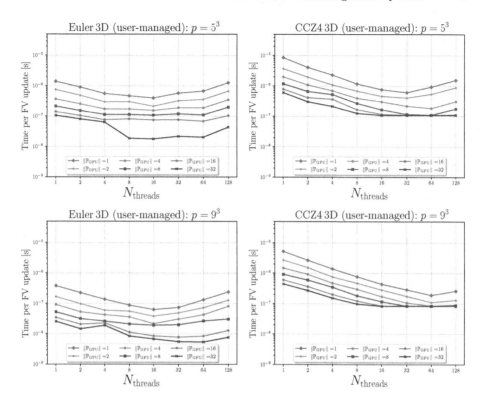

Fig. 3. Experiments from Fig. 2 with our user-managed memory (cf. Sect. 4.1).

performance. Robust here means that the gain through multi-threaded offloading might eventually plateau, yet, we do not pay a performance penalty. Given enough threads that access the GPU at the same time, setups employing smaller $\|\mathbb{P}_{\mathrm{GPU}}\|$ match the throughput of setups with large $\|\mathbb{P}_{\mathrm{GPU}}\|$. We also see that the best-case throughput becomes independent of the p-choice.

Once we replace our manual copies with pre-allocated GPU memory using CUDA unified memory, concurrent offloading to the GPU yields no performance improvement anymore and overall runtime suffers (Fig. 4). With CUDA unified memory, we postpone the data movement penalty to the point when the data is actually required. As the data access is spread out temporarily, bandwidth demands are spread out, too. This however does not manifest in better performance. Notably, it stops us from profiting from multiple threads which offload at the same time—we assume that the interconnect is kept busy by a single kernel already and multiple kernel launches interfere and compete with each other.

We provide full details on how to reproduce the results presented in this paper on https://doi.org/10.5281/zenodo.7741217.

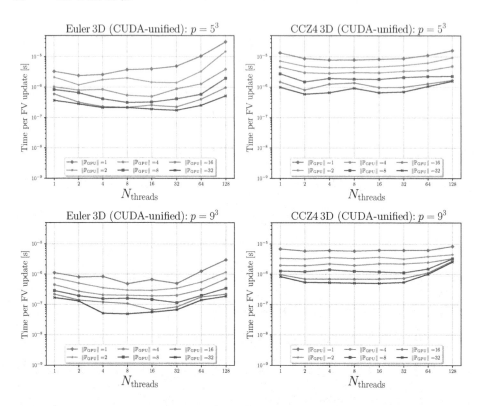

Fig. 4. Experiments from Fig. 2, using CUDA-unified memory (cf. Sect. 4.2): The GPU memory manager accepts data that has to be offloaded and packs it into unified memory on the host. It is then the responsibility of the CUDA runtime to bring the data from shared managed memory regions into the GPU.

6 Discussion and Conclusions

Our observations, proposed solutions, and runtime measurements allow us to draw conclusions for our algorithms as well as the used runtime:

Tasks of high computational load are important to exploit the concurrency on modern GPUs, and batching is one technique to construct such tasks while we stick to small patches (cf. Observation 1). With the concurrent offloading onto the GPU through multiple threads, we eventually manage to make the best-case throughput of this combination independent of p, and we are able to reduce the minimal batch size $\|\mathbb{P}_{\mathrm{GPU}}\|$. Yet, a reasonable value continues to depend on the algorithmic fingerprint of the underlying PDE. We assume that other discretisations such as DG have a major impact here, too.

The insight contradicts the rule of thumb knowledge which suggests that an efficient GPU utilisation becomes impossible in the presence of a totally adaptive AMR with tiny patches. If we employ tiny patches where the meshing has to track data flow and dependencies between small Cartesian meshes, the streaming compute properties per patch are not sufficient to keep a GPU busy [14]. However, small patches, i.e., small p-values in our case, are key to efficient AMR in an algorithmic sense: Large patches constrain the AMR, as we cannot represent rapid resolution changes accurately. They hence reduce the algorithmic efficiency, i.e., invested cost per numerical accuracy.

Conclusion 1. *The combination of parallel offloading, user-managed GPU memory, and batching yields a fast GPU code that works with relatively small patches.*

Indeed, our approach abandons the concept of a geometric "streamability" and instead translates this idea into the data space: Patches are batched into sets that can be processed in a streaming fashion, even though there might be no geometric correlation between those patches.

Our data suggest that OpenMP GPU offloading is vulnerable to concurrent access by multiple threads. Our GPU memory manager mitigates this shortcoming and renders Observations 2 and 3 invalid. It is not clear if the need for it (cf. Observation 4) is a shortcoming of the employed GPU runtime or an intrinsic property of any GPU runtime, as we obtained qualitatively comparable data for LLVM and AMD's runtime, too. We hypothesise that, as long as a GPU kernel is allowed to make dynamic allocations, any GPU allocation has to be thread-safe and hence introduces some synchronisation: To be thread-safe, any data transfer to the GPU has to stop all running kernels to prevent them to make allocations; unless the memory region for data exchange and the local heap is strictly separated, or a compiler derives a priori if a kernel does not require dynamic memory allocation and hence does not need to be stopped.

Conclusion 2. *Multithreaded access to GPU offloading in combination with dynamic memory allocation on the device requires special care on the programmer's side and eventually benefits from a deployment of the GPU's memory management onto the CPU.*

This argument gains importance for software which—in line with ExaHyPE—deploys algorithmically irregular and unstructured operations such as AMR administration to the CPU, yet keeps other data and work persistently on the GPU [19]. It might notably gain weight in the context of local time stepping, where patch interaction patterns quickly become challenging.

Conclusion 3. *Our data do not support the idea that managed memory is a competitive replacement for well-designed manual data migration of dynamically allocated memory regions.*

Our data yields "disappointing" results for managed memory, much in line with disappointing data of cache architectures compared to algorithms which explicitly exploit write-through or streaming capabilities. However, we have exclusively studied an offloading approach which requires dynamic allocations within the managed memory, and we have used a code base which is likely PCIe latency-bound. In this context, we assume that managed memory in combination with CUDA prefetching allows for significantly more elegant and faster code.

7   Summary and Outlook

With the advent of more and more cores on the host and with more GPUs being added to each node, in-depth analysis, and discussion around multi-threaded accelerator usage is imminent. Our work orbits around flaws that we document for the multithreaded usage of GPUs. Future versions of the employed OpenMP runtimes might fix those flaws and supersede our user-defined memory management. Even so, any future runtime development has to be contextualised in which way software operates GPUs:

Keeping data permanently on the accelerator [19] is beyond the scope of the present studies, as we let our ExaHyPE solver construct worst-case stress tests where each and every patch is offloaded to the GPU and eventually brought back. In contrast, many simulation codes try to hold data on the GPU as long as possible, i.e., let the GPU own the data, as the fastest data transfer is avoided data transfer. Therefore, it remains relevant to assess to which degree data transfer has to interrupt running GPU kernels. For our GPU memory manager, a fix could imply that parts of the memory administration are deployed to the GPU, i.e., that the GPU memory manager is distributed, too. We furthermore hypothesise that kernels could continue to run despite threads offloading to the GPU as long as the compiler is aware that no dynamic memory allocation is required for these kernels, and as long as the compiler can derive the maximum call stack size. No interaction with any dynamic memory management should be required.

Our work confirms that a GPU performs best if we deploy kernels with a huge concurrency level. We achieve this through batching. As the strict rule of lock-stepping comes to an end on the hardware side, we assume that smaller and smaller batch sizes become feasible. In this context, it remains to be seen if fewer restrictions on the lock-stepping side go hand in hand with the support of more active kernels and how this affects the concurrent offloading to the GPU from many threads.

Our GPU memory manager is basic and can be improved in many ways. A canonical extension is garbage collection, e.g., [14]. Fundamentally new challenges arise from switching to a multi-process view: Once multiple ranks are deployed per CPU—to accommodate multiple NUMA domains, e.g.,—our GPU memory manager becomes a distributed memory allocator which requires cross-process synchronisation and the coordination of multiple ranks requesting access to the GPU's pre-allocated memory at the same time. It remains open to which degree future OpenMP runtimes can and will accommodate the requirement to support multi-rank setups, and in which way they support a dynamic association of GPU compute resources to these ranks.

Acknowledgements. This research has been supported by EPSRC's ExCALIBUR programme through its cross-cutting project EX20-9 *Exposing Parallelism: Task Parallelism* (Grant ESA 10 CDEL). It uses the code base Peano as supported through ExCALIBUR's project *PAX–HPC—Particles At eXascale on High Performance Computers* (EP/W026775/1) and *MGHyPE—An ExCALIBUR Multigrid Solver Toolbox for ExaHyPE* (EP/X019497/1). We appreciate the support by the German Ministry of Education and Research (BMBF) via the project targetDART (16ME0634K), and by Intel's Academic Centre of Excellence at Durham University which allowed the team to investigate into OpenMP GPU offloading as facilitated through OpenMP. We also gratefully acknowledge support through the embedded CSE programme of the ARCHER2 UK National Supercomputing Service (http://www.archer2.ac.uk) under grant no ARCHER2-eCSE04-2, and the scientific support and HPC resources provided by the Erlangen National High Performance Computing Center (NHR@FAU) of the Friedrich-Alexander-Universität Erlangen-Nurnberg (FAU) under the NHR project PeanoMP. NHR funding is provided by federal and Bavarian state authorities. NHR@FAU hardware is partially funded by the German Research Foundation (DFG)—440719683. The authors acknowledge Jülich Supercomputing Center for providing access to the JURECA DC Evaluation Platform. This work was completed in part at the CINECA GPU Hackathon, part of the Open Hackathons program. Finally, the authors would like to acknowledge OpenACC-Standard.org for their support.

References

1. Alic, D., Bona-Casas, C., Bona, C., Rezzolla, L., Palenzuela, C.: Conformal and covariant formulation of the Z4 system with constraint-violation damping. Phys. Rev. D **85**(6), 064040 (2012)
2. Bader, M.: Space-Filling Curves–An Introduction with Applications in Scientific Computing. Texts in Computational Science and Engineering, vol. 9. Springer, Heidelberg (2013). https://doi.org/10.1007/978-3-642-31046-1
3. Bertschinger, E.: Self-similar secondary infall and accretion in an Einstein-de Sitter universe. Astrophys. J. Suppl. Ser. **58**, 39–65 (1985)
4. Charrier, D., Hazelwood, B., Weinzierl, T.: Enclave tasking for DG methods on dynamically adaptive meshes. SIAM J. Sci. Comput. **42**(3), C69–C96 (2020)
5. Daszuta, B., Zappa, F., Cook, W., Radice, D., Bernuzzi, S., Morozova, V.: GR-Athena++: puncture evolutions on vertex-centered oct-tree adaptive mesh refinement. Astrophys. J. Suppl. Ser. **257**(2), 25 (2021)
6. Dubey, A., Berzins, M., Burstedde, C., Norman, M.L., Unat, D., Wahib, M.: Structured adaptive mesh refinement adaptations to retain performance portability with increasing heterogeneity. Comput. Sci. Eng. **23**(05), 62–66 (2021)
7. Dumbser, M., Fambri, F., Tavelli, M., Bader, M., Weinzierl, T.: Efficient implementation of ADER discontinuous Galerkin schemes for a scalable hyperbolic PDE engine. Axioms **7**(3), 63 (2018)
8. Dumbser, M., Guercilena, F., Köppel, S., Rezzolla, L., Zanotti, O.: Conformal and covariant Z4 formulation of the Einstein equations: strongly hyperbolic first-order reduction and solution with discontinuous Galerkin schemes. Phys. Rev. D **97**, 084053 (2018)
9. Fernando, M., et al.: A GPU-accelerated AMR solver for gravitational wave propagation. In: 2022 SC22: International Conference for High Performance Computing, Networking, Storage and Analysis, pp. 1078–1092. IEEE Computer Society (2022)
10. Huber, J., et al.: Efficient execution of OpenMP on GPUs. In: 2022 IEEE/ACM International Symposium on Code Generation and Optimization (CGO), pp. 41–52 (2022)
11. Kidder, L., et al.: SpECTRE: a task-based discontinuous Galerkin code for relativistic astrophysics. J. Comput. Phys. **335**, 84–114 (2017)

12. Li, B., Schulz, H., Weinzierl, T., Zhang, H.: Dynamic task fusion for a block-structured finite volume solver over a dynamically adaptive mesh with local time stepping. In: Varbanescu, A.L., Bhatele, A., Luszczek, P., Marc, B. (eds.) ISC High Performance 2022. LNCS, vol. 13289, pp. 153–173. Springer, Cham (2022). https://doi.org/10.1007/978-3-031-07312-0_8

13. Peterson, B., et al.: Automatic halo management for the Uintah GPU-heterogeneous asynchronous many-task runtime. Int. J. Parallel Programm. **47**(5–6), 1086–1116 (2018). https://doi.org/10.1007/s10766-018-0619-1

14. Qin, X., LeVeque, R., Motley, M.: Accelerating an adaptive mesh refinement code for depth-averaged flows using GPUs. J. Adv. Model. Earth Syst. **11**(8), 2606–2628 (2019)

15. Reinarz, A., et al.: ExaHyPE: an engine for parallel dynamically adaptive simulations of wave problems. Comput. Phys. Commun. **254**, 107251 (2020)

16. Schulz, H., Gadeschi, G.B., Rudyy, O., Weinzierl, T.: Task inefficiency patterns for a wave equation solver. In: McIntosh-Smith, S., de Supinski, B.R., Klinkenberg, J. (eds.) IWOMP 2021. LNCS, vol. 12870, pp. 111–124. Springer, Cham (2021). https://doi.org/10.1007/978-3-030-85262-7_8

17. Sundar, H., Ghattas, O.: A nested partitioning algorithm for adaptive meshes on heterogeneous clusters. In: Proceedings of the 29th ACM on International Conference on Supercomputing, ICS 2015, pp. 319–328 (2015)

18. Tian, S., Chesterfield, J., Doerfert, J., Chapman, B.: Experience report: writing a portable GPU runtime with OPENMP 5.1. In: McIntosh-Smith, S., de Supinski, B.R., Klinkenberg, J. (eds.) IWOMP 2021. LNCS, vol. 12870, pp. 159–169. Springer, Cham (2021). https://doi.org/10.1007/978-3-030-85262-7_11

19. Wahib, M., Maruyama, N., Aoki, T.: Daino: a high-level framework for parallel and efficient AMR on GPUs. In: SC 2016: Proceedings of the International Conference for High Performance Computing, Networking, Storage and Analysis, pp. 621–632 (2016)

20. Weinzierl, T.: The Peano software–parallel, automaton-based, dynamically adaptive grid traversals. ACM Trans. Math. Softw. **45**(2), 14 (2019)

21. Zanotti, O., Fambri, F., Dumbser, M., Hidalgo, A.: Space-time adaptive ADER discontinuous Galerkin finite element schemes with a posteriori sub-cell finite volume limiting. Comput. Fluids **118**, 204–224 (2015)

22. Zhang, H., Weinzierl, T., Schulz, H., Li, B.: Spherical accretion of collisional gas in modified gravity I: self-similar solutions and a new cosmological hydrodynamical code. Mon. Not. Roy. Astron. Soc. **515**(2), 2464–2482 (2022)

Shallow Water DG Simulations on FPGAs: Design and Comparison of a Novel Code Generation Pipeline

Christoph Alt[1]([✉])[iD], Tobias Kenter[2][iD], Sara Faghih-Naini[1,3][iD], Jennifer Faj[2], Jan-Oliver Opdenhövel[2], Christian Plessl[2][iD], Vadym Aizinger[3][iD], Jan Hönig[1][iD], and Harald Köstler[1][iD]

[1] Friedrich Alexander Universität, Erlangen, Germany
{christoph.alt,jan.hoenig,harald.koestler}@fau.de
[2] Paderborn University, Paderborn, Germany
{kenter,jfaj,joo,plessl}@mail.uni-paderborn.de
[3] University of Bayreuth, Bayreuth, Germany
{sara.faghih-naini,vadym.aizinger}@uni-bayreuth.de

Abstract. FPGAs are receiving increased attention as a promising architecture for accelerators in HPC systems. Evolving and maturing development tools based on high-level synthesis promise productivity improvements for this technology. However, up to now, FPGA designs for complex simulation workloads, like shallow water simulations based on discontinuous Galerkin discretizations, rely to a large degree on manual application-specific optimizations. In this work, we present a new approach to port shallow water simulations to FPGAs, based on a code-generation framework for high-level abstractions in combination with a template-based stencil processing library that provides FPGA-specific optimizations for a streaming execution model. The new implementation uses a structured grid representation suitable for stencil computations and is compared to an adaptation from an existing hand-optimized FPGA dataflow design supporting unstructured meshes. While there are many differences, for example in the numerical details and problem scalability to be discussed, we demonstrate that overall both approaches can yield meaningful results at competitive performance for the same target FPGA, thus demonstrating a new level of maturity for FPGA-accelerated scientific simulations.

Keywords: FPGA · Reconfigurable Computing · Shallow Water Simulations · Code Generation · Dataflow · SYCL · OpenCL · Discontinuous Galerkin Method

1 Introduction

Porting applications to new hardware architectures often boils down to re-implementing major parts of the code, especially when some of the involved

A. Bhatele et al. (Eds.): ISC High Performance 2023, LNCS 13948, pp. 86–105, 2023.
https://doi.org/10.1007/978-3-031-32041-5_5

hardware is not based on a classical von Neumann architecture. Code generation is a promising way to overcome this difficulty as it allows to specify the application on an abstract, machine-independent level, whereas specialized backends take over the role of generating optimized code for various hardware architectures. FPGAs are a special target architecture that through its reconfigurability supports direct mapping of algorithmic behavior to the hardware. The recent generation of FPGAs provides ample resources, so FPGAs emerge as a relevant accelerator device for computationally intensive tasks in Scientific and High Performance Computing (HPC) – in this work represented by shallow water simulations.

Generation of Higher-Order Discretizations Deployed as ExaSlang Specifications (GHODDESS) [5] implements an abstract specification of a quadrature-free discontinuous Galerkin (DG) discretization of the *shallow water equations (SWE)* that uses a structured grid representation and so far has been used to generate code for CPUs and GPUs. In this work, we present a new Code Generation Pipeline (CGP) that uses *GHODDESS* specifications and a template-based FPGA-specific processing library for stencils called *StencilStream* to generate applications that fully run on FPGA hardware. This creates a beneficial separation of concerns, where the compiler and code generation chain performs optimization tasks like data layout transformations and symbolic expression simplification, whereas the FPGA-specific pipeline architecture with its customized streaming buffers is specified by the template library that can be separately improved over time and also be used directly from other application code. This is a difference to many other code generation approaches, where lots of target-specific knowledge is directly integrated into the code generation backend and cannot be improved without updating the compilation chain. The proposed methodology with its clear separation of application-, numerics-, algorithm-, and hardware-specific parts can be easily adapted to a very wide range of different numerical PDE solvers based on finite element or finite volume discretizations; the specific code generation and optimization techniques realized in our implementation may be directly transferred to many hyperbolic solvers (e.g. Euler equations of gas dynamics).

We compare the designs generated with this new approach to an existing hand-optimized FPGA dataflow design supporting unstructured grids, observing very similar performance for the piecewise constant problem formulation but also interesting differences and trade-offs. As further analysis, we present our adaption of the roofline model suitable for FPGA hardware and our CGP designs.

2 Background

2.1 Mathematical Model and Numerical Scheme

Using the methodology presented in [4,5,13] we consider the two-dimensional *SWE* model, which describes the time evolution of the free surface elevation and flow velocity in coastal ocean described by conservation of mass (1) and conservation of momentum (2) equations

$$\partial_t \xi + \nabla \cdot \boldsymbol{q} = 0, \tag{1}$$

$$\partial_t \boldsymbol{q} + \nabla \cdot \left(\boldsymbol{q} \boldsymbol{q}^T / H \right) + \tau_{\mathrm{bf}} \boldsymbol{q} + \begin{pmatrix} 0 & -f_c \\ f_c & 0 \end{pmatrix} \boldsymbol{q} + gH\nabla\xi = \boldsymbol{F}, \tag{2}$$

where ξ is the water elevation with respect to some datum (e.g., the mean sea level). We denote by $H = h_b + \xi$ the total water depth where h_b is the bathymetric depth (sea bed topography), and by $\boldsymbol{q} \equiv (U, V)^T$, the depth integrated horizontal velocity vector is denoted. f_c is the Coriolis coefficient, g the gravitational acceleration, and τ_{bf} the bottom friction coefficient. The body force $\boldsymbol{F} = (F_x, F_y)^T$ can contain gradients of atmospheric pressure and tidal potential. SWE are widely used for the simulation of tides, tsunamis, and storm surges or, augmented with additional equations, for ecological and environmental studies.

In our work, the numerical solution of the above nonlinear partial differential equation (PDE) system is carried out using the DG method [1,5]. Unlike classical finite elements, which only require evaluation of element integrals or finite volume methods relying on flux computations over edges, DG schemes contain both. However, due to the locality of DG stencils for all approximation orders, the element integrals can be computed on each element independently, whereas edge flux evaluations only involve two elements sharing the edge. Fluxes over exterior (land or sea) boundaries must be handled separately using physically relevant boundary conditions (e.g., prescribing known free surface elevation for open sea boundaries or enforcing no normal flow at the land boundaries). [5] introduced a new quadrature-free discretization which eliminated the innermost loop over the quadrature points, offering thereby a better code optimization and p-adaptivity potential. The accuracy and stability of this formulation were shown to be comparable to those of the quadrature-based method.

2.2   Simulation Scenario: Radial Dam Break

As a test problem, we have chosen a radial dam break scenario from [4]. Such problems serve as prototypes for flooding simulations and are often used as benchmarks since they pose high robustness requirements for the numerical scheme. Additionally, this test case is often used when developing and testing slope limiters, as in [9]. We set $\Omega = [0, 5] \times [0, 5]$, $g = 1$, and a constant bathymetry $h_b = 0$. The initial conditions are set as

$$\xi(x, y, t) = \begin{cases} 2, & (x - 2.5)^2 + (y - 2.5)^2 < 0.25, \\ 1, & \text{otherwise}, \end{cases} \qquad U(x, y, t) = 0, \; V(x, y, t) = 0.$$

The reference results for piecewise linear polynomials ($p = 1$) shown in Fig. 1 (left) were obtained using *GHODDESS* (c.f. Sect. 3.1) on a randomly perturbed uniform mesh with 512 triangles, whereas those displayed in Fig. 1 (middle: piecewise constants ($p = 0$), right: $p = 1$) used the same mesh refined twice in a uniform fashion, i.e., they contain 8,192 elements. Since all external boundaries use land boundary conditions, the wave is reflected as illustrated in Fig. 1 (bottom), which corresponds to $t = 3$ s. No limiting is used in the simulations.

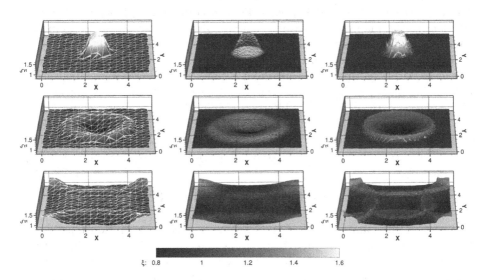

Fig. 1. Radial dam break: Elevation solution for $t = 0.1$ s (top), $t = 1$ s (middle), and $t = 3$ s (bottom). Linear approximation ($p = 1$) on a grid with 512 elements (left), constant ($p = 0$) (middle), and linear ($p = 1$) (right) approximations on a grid with 8,192 elements.

2.3   FPGAs

FPGAs are reconfigurable computing devices that are not defined by an instruction set but allow a direct mapping of algorithms to hardware similarly to the design of an application specific integrated circuit (ASIC). In contrast to ASICs, FPGAs can be (re-)configured repeatedly to fit different application needs. On a circuit level, FPGAs are built as an array of logic elements and RAM blocks that are connected with a configurable interconnect. The logic elements (denoted as ALMs for Intel FPGAs) contain Look Up Tables (LUT) and Flip-Flops (FFs), such that each LUT can represent every boolean function with a given number of inputs (typically 4–6) and the FFs allow to implement sequential circuits or to pipeline operations. The RAM blocks are used as an on-chip memory to store intermediate data that does not fit into FFs or requires a random access pattern. Since each RAM block provides a separate access port with single-cycle latency, enormous aggregate bandwidths can be achieved. In practice, multiple blocks are often combined to provide the required capacity and bit width required by a given data structure. In addition to logic blocks and RAM blocks, modern FPGAs typically contain Digital Signal Processing (DSP) blocks that provide more area-efficient and lower latency arithmetic operations compared to the logic resources. For a historic perspective on the evolution of FPGA architecture, also refer to Trimberger [21]. The DSP blocks of the Stratix 10 architecture targeted in this work can perform entire single precision floating-point operations without the use of additional logic resources. For applications like those shown in this work, the FPGA is configured to build a computation pipeline where the calculations are mapped (mostly) to DSPs and the data flow and the pipeline stages are realized with the help of logic elements and RAM blocks.

The process of creating a configuration from the developer's input is called synthesis. After multiple steps including a time-consuming resource placement and routing phase, a bitstream is generated that contains the configurations for all the blocks on the device. This bitstream can be generated from a specification in a hardware description language, like Verilog or VHDL, or via high-level synthesis also from a higher-level programming language, like *SyCL/oneAPI* or OpenCL respectively used in the two approaches in this work (see also [10]).

3   Proposed Code Generation Pipeline (CGP)

This section gives an overview of the implemented code generation pipeline by first briefly presenting the preexisting tools used (white boxes in Fig. 2) then describing the newly developed interface layers to integrate them (blue arrows in Fig. 2). Previously, *GHODDESS* (c.f. Sect. 3.1) and *pystencils* (c.f. Sect. 3.2) were only used to generate CPU and GPU code. To generate FPGA code, we now transform the abstract formulation of the *SWE* discretization scheme implemented in *GHODDESS* in such a way that it can be used as input for *pystencils* to generate code for *StencilStream* (c.f. Sect. 3.3) with a newly implemented *pystencils* backend. Finally we implemented a layer to automatically wrap this code into a full application, so that it can run completely on FPGA hardware.

3.1   GHODDESS

GHODDESS[1] is a *Python* package that implements a quadrature-free DG method for the *SWE* and generates *ExaSlang* Layer 4 specifications from it. *ExaSlang* is the layered Domain Specific Language (DSL) for *ExaStencils*, a code generation framework that transforms abstractions to an optimized *C++* or CUDA code, which can be compiled further to an executable [16].

GHODDESS [4] uses *SymPy* to implement the quadrature-free DG-scheme using piecewise constant (polynomial degree $p = 0$), linear ($p = 1$), quadratic ($p = 2$), and cubic ($p = 3$) DG discretizations. A major advantage of this technique is a representation of terms that is close to a mathematical expression and the use of basic abstractions for, e.g., basis functions just as classes representing triangles and data fields. To match the capabilities of the *ExaStencils* source-to-source compiler, the discretization uses a block-structured quadrilateral grid [23,24], which allows for predictable and regular memory access patterns. To apply our DG method that utilizes triangular meshes, we divide each

---

[1] https://i10git.cs.fau.de/ocean/ghoddess-release.

quadrilateral into a lower and an upper triangle and call it a *cell* in the following. For time integration, *GHODDESS* provides Runge-Kutta (RK) methods of orders 1, 2, and 3.

3.2 pystencils

pystencils[2] [2] is a *Python* package for generating stencil codes. It converts stencil operations formulated as assignments with the symbolic math library *SymPy* [17] to a target language such as C or CUDA. The output language is chosen along with a specific backend for each language with C and CUDA backends available as default options. It is possible to provide own, custom backends to add support for other languages or dialects, which we make use of in this work to generate the *StencilStream* kernel functions.

3.3 StencilStream

StencilStream[3] is a C++ template library that embeds an arbitrary stencil kernel function into an efficient FPGA design. This is done using Intel *oneAPI*, a toolchain that implements the *SyCL* standard and supports writing both host and FPGA device code in one source base.

StencilStream applications implement their stencil kernel function as an invocable class and use this class as a template parameter for the executor class. The executor encapsulates the FPGA-specific architecture, which streams the current state of the grid from memory, applies the kernel function to it, and writes the resulting stream back cell by cell. The stencil kernel function is inserted into this architecture, which results in a synthesizable, application-specific FPGA design. The part of the pipeline that applies the kernel function is called a stage and can be replicated, depending on resource availability. Every stage in the pipeline works independently from another, which exploits the temporal parallelism of stencil applications.

If applications need to alternate between different stencil kernel functions (denoted as kernels in Sect. 3.4), they can be expressed as different cases within a single kernel function. These cases are then implemented as separate, specialized stages. In the *StencilStream* repository, this is demonstrated for a finite-difference time-domain application with two alternating kernels but so far was not applied to an application as complex as targeted in this work.

3.4 Integration

Here we present the implemented interface layers, which are represented as the blue arrows in Fig. 2, and describe how they interact with the individual tools (white boxes in Fig. 2).

---

[2] https://i10git.cs.fau.de/pycodegen/pystencils.
[3] https://github.com/pc2/StencilStream.

Fig. 2. Structure of the code generation pipeline: the boxes represent the tools used, and the blue arrows represent the implemented interfaces. (Color figure online)

GHODDESS is the starting point of the pipeline, to which the designer provides the target grid size, the selected polynomial order p, the order of the RK method, and the desired number of temporal pipeline replications. From this specification, it generates an Abstract Syntax Tree (AST) that represents the discretization of the DG scheme to solve the *SWE*. During a regular run of *GHODDESS*, this AST is parsed and printed as *ExaSlang* specifications which are used as input for the *ExaStencils* compiler to generate *C++* source code. Here, instead of printing this AST to an *ExaSlang* file, it is converted to a new intermediate representation (IR) with an interface module that we call *ghoddess2pystencils*. In the *ghoddess2pystencils* phase, the data layout is transformed from multiple scalar-valued 2D fields to a single 2D field with a complex cell type. This is necessary because *StencilStream* can only modify a single grid, whereas *GHODDESS* defines numerous individual fields.

As mentioned in Sect. 3.2, *pystencils* builds its AST from a list of *SymPy* assignments. Therefore, in the *ghoddess2pystencils* layer, the *GHODDESS* discretizations are parsed, and the expressions are mapped to the corresponding *SymPy* expressions and assembled to *SymPy* assignments. In this step, the accesses to fields are replaced with accesses to the transformed field data structure. During this parsing process, these *SymPy* expressions are simplified with *SymPy*'s `simplify()` function. This is a crucial step to reduce the number of operations and thus save some resources on the FPGA later on.

The specification that is generated at this point consists of multiple loops over the domain arranged in functions. To map this to a single kernel function, as it is needed as input for *StencilStream*, the loops are transformed to kernels, and the function calls are flattened so that in the end the new AST is a list with 33 kernels for RK1 and 66 kernels for RK2 setups. These kernels are then mapped to *StencilStream* stages so that in the end it is possible to represent the whole *GHODDESS* application as a single kernel function. As *StencilStream* automatically decouples every stage from the previous one with row buffers to make sure the outputs of the previous stage are valid for every position within the stencil span, a dedicated stage for every original kernel may involve unnecessary resource usage for these buffers, if no direct dependency between two stages exists. These resource costs are particularly high for an application with many fields encoded in the cell status, like the one investigated in this work. To overcome that issue, the possibility to merge stages is implemented into the CGP. Since the kernels are gathered from loops, the same requirements need to be checked as it would be checked if these loops would be fused. Therefore, the assignments are analyzed for dependencies, and kernels are merged whenever there is no loop-carried dependency between them.

When the same function is invoked multiple times, as it happens with the higher order RK methods, the same kernels and, after transformations, the according stages are generated multiple times. In order to save resources, we implemented a mechanism that reorders these stages such that the logic can be reused without synthesizing them multiple times on the FPGA. Once all kernels are arranged, *pystencils* is used with a custom backend to transform every kernel into a *pystencils* AST. In this step, the assignments of every kernel are wrapped into guard nodes, which ensure that every assignment is only performed on cells that lay within the former loop bounds.

As *pystencils* itself is only intended as a code generation tool for stencils applications without further control flow, some extra effort is needed to generate a whole application. This is realized in the interface module we call *pystencils2program*. This module takes all the ASTs that were generated with *pystencils* and fuses them into a single AST. Thereby, AST nodes that represent control flow blocks like conditionals and loops are inserted, as *pystencils* user interface does not originally support such. Finally, this AST that now represents a complete *StencilStream* kernel function is printed with a modified *pystencils* code printer as *C++* code to a file. Further, *pystencils2program* generates a Makefile, header files, scripts for synthesis and execution, and other boilerplate code.

4   Existing Dataflow Design

The existing dataflow design used as reference here was implemented manually using OpenCL and first published in [13] in 2021. Its validation used a tidal wave simulation on an unstructured mesh for a bay in the Bahamas region. It uses traditional quadrature-based DG formulation in contrast to the novel quadrature-free approach based on *GHODDESS*. Apart from this, the support for unstructured meshes is a major difference to block-structured grids targeted by the new code generation approach that impacts the design in two regards.

Firstly, it is organized with lists of elements and edges, over which it iterates in two main kernels, correspondingly denoted as *element kernel* and *edge kernel*. When switching between the element and edge perspectives, it has to rely on indirect indexing, in particular, to access the two elements adjacent to an edge. Architecturally, this makes the access pattern behave as random access. Thus, in order to supply all inputs – including the indirectly indexed ones – with deterministic performance to the computation pipeline, the full mesh data is kept in on-chip RAM blocks for this design, thus limiting the design to smaller supported mesh sizes compared to the designs instantiated by *StencilStream*, which rely only on row buffers.

Secondly, given the quasi random access pattern during edge kernel, all updates from the previous step need to be completed before the calculations of edge integrals can begin. This enforces one synchronization point per step and prevents exploitation of temporal parallelism as used when *StencilStream* instantiates multiple execution units within the same pipeline. Only between two subsequent synchronization points, the dataflow design is able to overlap all kernel stages, such that asymptotically n elements are processed in $n + \lambda$ cycles, where λ denotes the aggregate latency of the pipeline. Figure 3 illustrates the execution schedule for 2,048 elements.

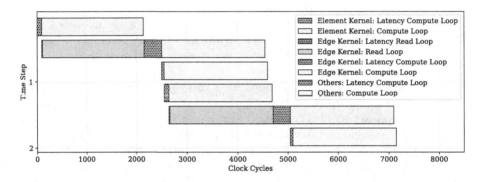

Fig. 3. Execution schedule of dataflow design for 2,048 elements.

In order to perform the simulations for the dam break scenario, a few adaptations were made for this work. Most importantly, an earlier optimization that exploited the property of the original mesh to contain only elements with at most one external (land or sea) edge had to be revised. This can either be done in a way that utilizes more on-chip memory resources but preserves the full throughput of the earlier design or by sharing local memory ports, such that the occupancy of the pipeline gets slightly reduced. By default, we use the former approach for the presented experiments, except for one design (denoted as *arbitration design*), where the latter approach is required to fit within the available resource budget. Further small changes include support for the required starting conditions and for time steps <1 s.

5   FPGA Designs, Experiments and Evaluation

Table 1 summarizes the key differences between the two presented FPGA design approaches along with a CPU reference that is generated via the *ExaStencils* optimization infrastructure from the same *GHODDESS* specification as the newly proposed FPGA CGP. The colors in the tables of this section and in Fig. 4 highlight combination of polynomial order and order of the RK-method where we had results to compare CGP, the exsiting dataflow designs and CPU. Thereby, encodes blue $p = 0$ with RK1, red $p = 1$ with RK1 and green $p = 1$ with RK2. Table 2 summarizes the synthesis results of different design points generated with both FPGA approaches. We see that, thanks to the underlying structured grid representation, the designs from the code-generation pipeline support much

Table 1. Overview of investigated designs.

	FPGA dataflow (Sect. 4)	FPGA CGP (Sect. 3)	CPU CGP
mesh	unstructured	structured quadrature-free	
DG formulation	normal quadrature		
tool flow	OpenCL Intel OpenCL SDK	GHODDESS pystencils StencilStream Intel oneAPI	GHODDESS exastencils GNU GCC 9.4
target platform	Stratix 10 GX2800	Stratix 10 GX2800	Xeon Gold 6148
base architecture	1 triangle per cycle	1 rectangle stencil = 2 triangles per cycle	vectorization with intrinsics
on-chip buffers	full mesh buffer	row buffers	cache blocking
replication	–	temporal replication	–
mesh size	upper limit fixed at compile time	fixed at compile time	
time step size	runtime parameter	fixed at compile time	

larger meshes, because they use on-chip RAM resources only for row buffers, in contrast the dataflow designs that keep the full mesh on-chip. When looking further at resources of comparable designs of both approaches, e.g. for $p = 0$ and $p = 1$, with RK1 and 2,048 elements and for the CGP with a single temporal replication, we need to first keep in mind that each step in the CGP processes two elements in contrast to one element in the dataflow approach. Considering this, we see that with regard to DSP usage, the CGP is more resource efficient, partially due to differences in the problem formulation (quadrature free), but mostly due to the combination of expression simplification in *SymPy* and automatic optimizations in the oneAPI phase, that lead to improved reuse of partial results. The logic (ALM) usage on the other hand is higher, partially because the complete cell data is moved through registers in every sub-stage of the stencil. The CGP allows for the automatic generation of temporally unrolled designs, which scales up to 8 temporal replications before being limited by logic resources. In contrast, the dataflow approach does not support this form of replication due to its synchronization point required by the unstructured mesh. Thus, lots of compute resources remain unused and only contribute in the $p = 1$ cases, where in turn the CGP is also limited to a single temporal replication and the efficiency gains of automatic optimizations seem to vanish.

Table 3 shows the performance measured with these generated designs. First looking at the time per RK-step, which is the metric that characterizes performance at the application level, for $p = 0$ with the CGP designs with the highest temporal parallelism, we see that both FPGA approaches reach a similar performance with around 7 μs per timestep for 2,048 elements and 22–26 μs for

Table 2. Resource usage and clock frequency for FPGA designs on *Intel Stratix 10 GX 2800*. Replicates is the number of temporal replications of the CGP designs (c.f. Sect. 3.3). Numbers in parenthesis relative to resources available for kernels on *Bittware 520N* cards with OpenCL BSP 20.4.0. For code generation based designs ALM: 705,500, RAM: 9,094 DSP: 4,713 using an area optimized *hpc* BSP; for dataflow designs ALM: 698,450, RAM: 8,953 DSP: 4,713 using the default *max* BSP; (*arbitration design variant).

p	integrator	elements	replicates	ALM		RAM		DSP		MHz
New FPGA CGP										
0	RK1	2,048	1	219,553	(31%)	1,097	(12%)	278	(6%)	423.33
			8	537,691	(76%)	4,304	(47%)	2,199	(47%)	262.50
		8,192	1	222,056	(31%)	1,097	(12%)	278	(6%)	423.33
			8	538,136	(76%)	4,304	(47%)	2,199	(47%)	235.42
		32,768	1	221,683	(31%)	1,097	(12%)	278	(6%)	404.17
			8	537,115	(76%)	4,306	(47%)	2,199	(47%)	253.33
		131,072	1	221,177	(31%)	1,295	(14%)	278	(6%)	413.33
			8	537,827	(76%)	5,885	(65%)	2,199	(47%)	248.00
		524,288	1	221,687	(31%)	1,686	(19%)	278	(6%)	380.00
			8	536,521	(76%)	9,018	(99%)	2,199	(47%)	248.00
1	RK1	2,048	1	362,643	(51%)	2,257	(25%)	1,784	(38%)	295.83
		8,192	1	362,577	(51%)	2,257	(25%)	1,784	(38%)	302.50
		32,768	1	365,740	(52%)	2,257	(25%)	1,784	(38%)	316.67
		131,072	1	363,758	(52%)	2,766	(30%)	1,784	(38%)	297.50
		524,288	1	363,231	(51%)	3,794	(42%)	1,784	(38%)	262.00
	RK2	2,048	1	459,893	(65%)	3,388	(37%)	1,820	(39%)	222.22
		8,192	1	460,654	(65%)	3,388	(37%)	1,820	(39%)	270.83
		32,768	1	458,778	(65%)	3,388	(37%)	1,820	(39%)	183.33
		131,072	1	459,358	(65%)	4,427	(49%)	1,820	(39%)	180.56
Existing FPGA dataflow approach										
0	RK1	2,048	1	95,970	(14%)	2,270	(25%)	455	(10%)	358.33
		8,192	1	105,300	(15%)	5,034	(56%)	455	(10%)	342.50
1	RK1	2,048	1	143,077	(20%)	3,716	(42%)	1,171	(25%)	340.00
		8,192	1	159,529	(23%)	8,604	(96%)	1,171	(25%)	308.33
	RK2	2,048	1	148,954	(21%)	3,843	(43%)	1,200	(25%)	320.00
		*8,192	1	171,980	(25%)	8,155	(91%)	1,200	(25%)	272.50

8,192 elements. CGP achieves this performance while performing only around half of the GFLOP/s (and total Floating-Point Operations (FLOP), not shown in Table 3). This is achieved by optimizations like *SymPy* `simplify`, which can also include shared expressions over two elements within the same stencil, and by differences in the original problem formulation (in particular quadrature-free).

Table 3. Performance of FPGA designs. Times per RK-step correspond to a full time step at $p = 0$. Cycles per update designate cell updates for CGP, element updates for dataflow. FLOP count for GFLOP/s calculation based on report parsing for CGP, manual counts for dataflow. *Arbitration design variant.

p	integrator	elements	replicates	time/RK-step [μs]	time/update [cycles]	Perf [GFLOP/s]	Power [W]
New FPGA CGP							
0	RK1	2,048	1	58.94	24.37	5.19	72.30
			8	7.02	1.80	43.60	82.65
		8,192	1	81.24	8.40	15.07	73.37
			8	21.97	1.26	55.75	84.92
		32,768	1	271.06	6.69	18.07	77.56
			8	61.31	0.95	79.91	90.90
		131,072	1	945.15	5.96	20.73	82.70
			8	216.74	0.82	90.41	93.69
		524,288	1	4,065.92	5.89	19.28	79.43
			8	820.59	0.78	95.52	94.13
1	RK1	2,048	1	68.30	19.73	36.30	81.81
		8,192	1	218.75	16.16	45.33	80.99
		32,768	1	584.51	11.30	67.86	84.05
		131,072	1	2,200.36	9.99	72.11	86.72
		524,288	1	9,567.62	9.56	66.33	86.61
	RK2	2,048	1	296.14	64.27	8.54	78.21
		8,192	1	715.20	47.29	14.15	81.46
		32,768	1	2,946.64	32.97	13.73	77.30
		131,072	1	10,427.00	28.73	15.52	76.99
Existing FPGA dataflow approach							
0	RK1	2,048	1	7.63	1.33	110.66	75.15
		8,192	1	26.37	1.10	128.01	78.32
1	RK1	2,048	1	8.08	1.34	386.67	78.39
		8,192	1	29.35	1.10	425.70	82.21
	RK2	2,048	1	8.57	1.34	364.49	78.21
		*8,192	1	33.17	1.10	376.59	80.83

Next in Table 3, we look at the clock cycles used per basic update (cell update for the CGP design, element update for the dataflow design). For a fully occupied pipeline, this should ideally be 1, or $\frac{1}{s}$ for s temporal replications of the CGP design. We see that the dataflow design is relatively close to this value, with the differences caused by the pipeline latency between two subsequent synchronization points, whereas the CGP designs are farther away, partially due to off-chip bandwidth limitations, partially due to a higher pipeline latency. For larger mesh sizes, this overhead becomes smaller, partially due to reduced impact of the fixed one-time pipeline latency. For the mesh with 131,072 elements, which is beyond the capacity of the dataflow design, the CGP design almost doubles its performance compared to 2,048 elements.

Now looking at $p = 1$ in Table 3, we see that the dataflow designs clearly outperform the CGP designs for corresponding sizes, both in terms of time per RK-step and in GFLOP/s. This is due to the fact that the dataflow designs are not bandwidth limited due to their complete on-chip buffers, whereas the bandwidth limitation of the CGP designs aggravates with more data required per cell, materializing in large deviations from the ideally 1 cycle per cell update also for larger meshes. In contrast to the $p = 0$ case, these can no longer be compensated with temporal data reuse due to resource limitations. Nevertheless, within the CGP designs for RK1, the throughput in terms of GFLOP/s is similar between $p = 0$ and $p = 1$, since more operations are performed per cell update. The dataflow design almost retains its only latency limited ratio of 1.1–1.3 cycles per element update for $p = 1$ and improves its arithmetic throughput to almost 400 GFLOP/s. On the other hand, only the CGP designs scale to 524,288 or 131,072 supported elements (RK1 and RK2 respectively) and also display improved efficiency and throughput with increasing problem sizes.

5.1   Performance of the CPU Reference and Validation

To measure the performance of the CPU reference version, we used the applications generated by *GHODDESS* and *ExaStencils*, which are optimized with cache blocking and vectorization with intrinsics, and compiled them with the GCC 9.4 compiler. The benchmarks were conducted on a *Intel Xeon Skylake Gold 6148 CPU*, where the frequency was fixed to 2.2 GHz. Every setup was executed with 1, 10, 20, and 40 OpenMP (OMP) threads. Every for loop within in *GHODDESS* was thereby parallelized with the OMP pragma *schedule(static)*. Table 4 shows for every setup and number of threads the results for the combination with the lowest execution time. For the smallest grids with 2,048 elements, the execution time actually very similar for all thread counts. The runtime was measured by the application itself and any further metrics were gathered with the *likwid-perfctr* [8] tool.

Table 4 summarizes the measurements of the CPU reference for the presented scenarios and Fig. 4 visualizes them in terms of time/RK-step compared to the FPGA designs. The results show that despite their bandwidth limitations, the FPGA CGP designs are competitive to this highly optimized CPU reference over a large range of experiments, with advantages for $p = 0$ and for smaller grids, but with performance challenges in the RK2 case. For the mesh sizes that are supported by the buffer architecture of the FPGA dataflow design, this takes a clear lead over the other approaches for $p = 1$.

As validation, we show the difference for the free surface elevation $\xi_{fpga} - \xi_{cpu}$ in Fig. 5. With at most 10^{-6}, the differences are within the expected numerical differences for the single precision floating point format used.

Table 4. Performance results for the CPU reference on a *Intel Xeon Skylake Gold 6148 CPU*. Fastest configuration out of 1, 10, 20, and 40 OpenMP threads reported. Cycles relative to base clock of 2.2 GHz.

p	integrator	elements	threads	time/RK-step [us]	cycles/cell update [cycles]	Perf [GFLOP/s]	Power [W]
0	RK1	2,048	20	50.81	109.16	11.91	37.95
		8,192	10	95.89	51.51	25.04	60.10
		32,768	10	159.64	21.44	59.95	60.13
		131,072	20	286.58	9.62	133.32	89.58
		524,288	20	1,163.68	9.77	131.22	138.82
1	RK1	2,048	20	385.63	828.50	9.15	36.07
		8,192	10	344.11	184.82	40.73	59.60
		32,768	40	555.06	74.53	100.67	89.05
		131,072	40	1,628.60	54.67	137.03	96.46
		524,288	40	8,791.08	73.78	101.47	105.25
	RK2	2,048	10	390.35	838.65	9.09	35.95
		8,192	10	364.08	195.55	38.70	59.14
		32,768	40	562.10	75.48	99.94	88.80
		131,072	40	1,788.94	60.05	125.41	96.32
		524,288	40	10,093.75	84.71	88.93	108.19

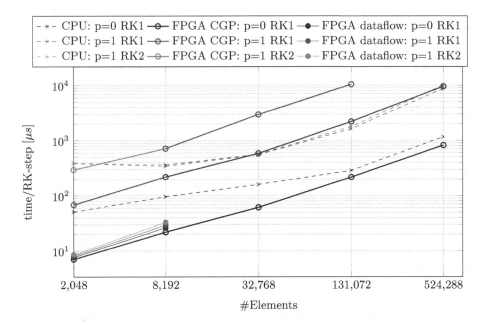

Fig. 4. Double-log line plot of time/RK-step for all designs. The color encodes the setup blue for p = 0, RK1, red for p = 1, RK1, and green for p = 1, RK2. The lighter colors mark the highlighted numbers from the Table 4 and Table 3. (Color figure online)

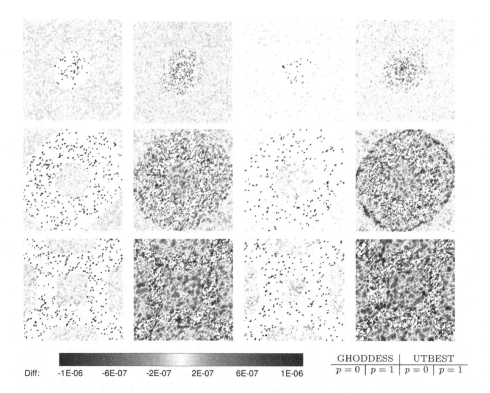

		GHODDESS		UTBEST	
Diff:	-1E-06 -6E-07 -2E-07 2E-07 6E-07 1E-06	$p=0$	$p=1$	$p=0$	$p=1$

Fig. 5. Radial dam break solution: $\xi_{fpga} - \xi_{cpu}$ difference plots at $t = 0.1$ s (top), $t = 1$ s (middle) and $t = 3$ s (bottom).

6   Analysis

The roofline model [22] in its original formulation assumes that the performance of an application is either limited by the peak performance of the execution units (P_{peak}) or the bandwidth between data-path and off-chip memory and gives an intuitive visualization which of them is the bottleneck. The application is characterized by its *Operational Intensity (OI)*, which quantifies the work done per transferred byte, and by its actual performance. In this section, we apply the roofline analysis to the CGP approach, leaving out the dataflow designs, since for those, meaningful bandwidth and *OI* values could only be formulated with regard to on-chip memory.

To calculate P_{peak} for FPGAs, Siracusa et al. [20] have introduced a formulation that takes into account the application-specific configurability of FPGAs. It is based on the hardware operators of an idealized implementation scaled to the available hardware resources and assumes that every operator can produce a useful value within every clock cycle. To model the P_{peak} for *StencilStream* applications, we adapted this procedure. As the base, we use the number of FLOP that are performed within a single call of the kernel function (o_{flop}), obtained from the report generated from the *oneAPI* toolchain.

As described in Sect. 3.3 and shown in Sect. 5, it is possible to increase the performance of kernel functions with low resource usage by replicating the required stages as multiple temporal replications. To take this into account, we introduce the replication factor RF, which predicts how many temporal replications can be synthesized on the device and is similar to the *Scalabilty* as it was proposed by da Silva et al. in [19]. It is obtained by dividing the number of resources that are available for kernels (av_r) by the number of resources that are occupied by the logic for the kernel function (kf_r) of every resource type $r \in R = \{DSP, RAM, ALM\}$ (c.f. Eq 3). As a design can only be replicated completely, this factor is rounded to the next lower integer. These numbers can be obtained from the synthesis report, as it lists the resource usage for each function. Similar to the ideal hardware implementation in [20], we assume that at peak performance the hardware can perform RF-times invocations of the kernel function in a clock cycle. Our formula for P_{peak} is shown in Eq. 4 where f denotes the frequency of the device.

$$RF = \lfloor \min_{r \in R} \frac{av_r}{kf_r} \rfloor \quad (3) \qquad P_{peak} = o_{flop} \times RF \times f \quad (4)$$

To model the maximum bandwidth from the off-chip memory, we used the bitwidths of the memory interface that is used for reading and for writing, and multiplied it by f.

To quantify the amount of work that is done in a kernel function, we use o_{flop} with a single temporal replication and scale this with the number of actual temporal replications. For every invocation of a *StencilStream* kernel function, the transferred data has the size of two grid cells since one is read and the other one is written back. Consequently the OI for CGP designs is:

$$OI = \frac{o_{flop} \times stages}{sizeof(celltype) \times 2} \quad (5)$$

The code generation pipeline maps the whole solve phase from the original CPU formulation to the kernel function, which is then used to generate an FPGA design. Therefore, this kernel function also contains boundary handling and not only the hotspot loops of the application. So the presented model has the same - coarse - granularity.

Figure 6 shows this model applied to the designs generated with the new CGP approach. As a target frequency for the used *Intel Stratix 10 GX 2800* we assumed 432 MHz, which is the target frequency shown in all reports for these designs. We assumed the maximum bandwidth as the maximum throughput for reading and writing as $BW = 64$ Byte $\times$ 432 Mhz $\times$ 2 $= 55.30$ GB/s for the data path from the off-chip memory. P_{peak} and OI are calculated as shown in the previous part of this section and $P_{max} = \min\{P_{peak}, OI \times BW\}$. For the designs for $p = 0$ and RK1, performing a single RK step needs 299 FLOP and, as shown in Table 2, the limiting resource is the ALMs. A single instance of the kernel function uses around 6.5% of the available ALM, which yields $RF = 11$ and $P_{peak} = 299\,FLOP \times 11\times 432\,$MHz $= 1.421$ TFloating-Point Operations per second (FLOP/s). The cell size for this setup is 47 floats, leading to $OI = \frac{299}{47 \times 4 \times 2} = 0.795$ for one temporal replication and 6.36 for eight temporal replications. For the configurations with $p = 1$, the FLOP per RK step are 2421 (RK1) and 2470 (RK2) and for both the $RF = 2$, the cell size is 123 for RK1 and 141 for RK2, consequently the OIs (2.46 and 2.19 FLOP/Byte) and P_{peak} values (2.092 and 2.134 TFLOP/s) are relatively close. Consequently, on the x-axis of Fig. 6, the designs for $p = 1$ fall in between the designs with one replication for $p = 0$ and those with eight replications. Although using more temporal replications leads to increased performance, it shows that the difference between P_{max} and the actual performance is higher with eight temporal replications. This can be explained by lower clock frequency for these designs (c.f. Table 2). It also shows for all setups, that grids with fewer elements are further away from P_{max}. This can be explained by the overhead that it takes to fill the pipeline, which becomes less dominating for larger grids. Furthermore, Fig. 6 shows, that every configuration is below the memory-roofline and left of the ridge point (denoted as RP in the plot). Consequently, further optimizations which either increase the maximum bandwidth or reduce the transferred data would be most beneficial.

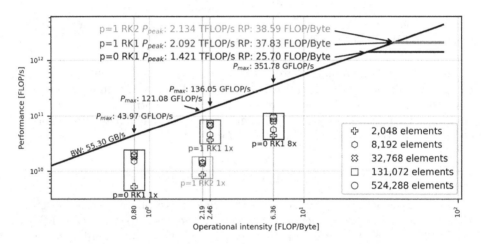

Fig. 6. Roofline plot for all the presented setups. RP is the OI at the point where $P_{peak} = OI \times MAX\_BW$. $N\times$ means the number of temporal replications.

7   Related Work

Other work that shows the use of FPGAs to run shallow water simulations is presented in [15], in [14] and in [18]. All are used for tsunami simulations, using a splitting approach for the SWE and are manually implemented without code generation and do not use a DG discretization. All of them also use temporal pipeline stages, with [18] additionally analyzing spatially parallel pipelines. Architecturally similar FPGA designs [11,25] have also been presented for other stencil applications, whereas an earlier FPGA design [12] with DG discretization on unstructured meshes relied on higher polynomial orders (order 3–6) relied on the high operational intensity of these orders to achieve good overall performance.

Using code generation to increase the productivity of FPGA programming has also been part of other research beyond the *SWE* domain. One example is the SODA framework [3], which generates stencil codes for FPGAs that are optimized for computation reuse, but in contrast to our CGP is not a full stack code generation pipeline. A code generation pipeline for FPGAs was presented in [7], which uses its own high-level stencil description language and implements various FPGA specific code optimizations. Compared to our work, where the FPGA architecture template is provided by *StencilStream*, both [3,7] encode more of the target-specific knowledge in optimization stages.

8   Conclusion and Outlook

In this work, we have presented a new Code Generation Pipeline for shallow water simulations on FPGAs and compared it to an existing, manually optimized FPGA dataflow design approach. Despite many differences, in tooling, mesh representation, quadrature rules, and parallelism, we find that both approaches are able to effectively simulate the presented scenario and achieve performance on par and better than a highly optimized CPU reference. Given the challenging application domain, this result represents a new level of maturity of FPGA design flows that so far were a limiting factor to FPGA adoption in HPC.

Both FPGA approaches have the potential for further optimizations that may enable them to clearly outperform the CPU reference in more scenarios. For the CGP, there is potential to implement further code transformations. In particular, the size of the grid cells can be reduced by storing elements from constant fields in global memory. Also within the library scope, there is optimization potential regarding the global memory interface of *StencilStream*. As *StencilStream* was originally developed to target simple stencils with not more than 512 bits of cell data, it does not fully exploit the four DDR3 memory channels present at the target FPGA board, let alone the bandwidth potential of newer FPGAs with HBM2. When switching to a block-structured grid representation, the manual FPGA dataflow design could also be adapted to a streaming design using DDR or HBM memory to support larger problem sizes – and use temporal parallelism to use more computational resources, particularly for the piecewise constant $p = 0$ designs. In an alternative direction towards support of larger meshes, we have recently made progress with a spatially distributed multi-FPGA design [6] that could be scaled up further after overcoming topology limitations.

Acknowledgments. The authors gratefully acknowledge the funding of this project by computing time provided by the Paderborn Center for Parallel Computing (PC2). The authors gratefully acknowledge the scientific support and HPC resources provided by the Erlangen National High Performance Computing Center (NHR@FAU) of the Friedrich-Alexander-Universität Erlangen-Nürnberg (FAU). The hardware is funded by the German Research Foundation (DFG). The work in this paper was supported in part by the DFG through grant AI 117/6-1 'Performance optimized software strategies for unstructured-mesh applications in ocean modeling'.

References

1. Aizinger, V., Dawson, C.: A discontinuous Galerkin method for two-dimensional flow and transport in shallow water. Adv. Water Resour. **25**(1), 67–84 (2002). https://doi.org/10.1016/S0309-1708(01)00019-7
2. Bauer, M., et al.: Code generation for massively parallel phase-field simulations. In: Proceedings of the International Conference for High Performance Computing, Networking, Storage and Analysis (SC 2019), pp. 1–32. Association for Computing Machinery, New York, NY, USA (2019). https://doi.org/10.1145/3295500.3356186
3. Chi, Y., Cong, J.: Exploiting computation reuse for stencil accelerators. In: 2020 57th ACM/IEEE Design Automation Conference (DAC), pp. 1–6. IEEE, San Francisco, CA, USA (2020). https://doi.org/10.1109/DAC18072.2020.9218680
4. Faghih-Naini, S., Aizinger, V.: p-adaptive discontinuous Galerkin method for the shallow water equations with a parameter-free error indicator. Int. J. Geomath. **13**(1), 18 (2022). https://doi.org/10.1007/s13137-022-00208-3
5. Faghih-Naini, S., Kuckuk, S., Aizinger, V., Zint, D., et al.: Quadrature-free discontinuous Galerkin method with code generation features for shallow water equations on automatically generated block-structured meshes. Adv. Water Resour. **138**, 103552 (2020). https://doi.org/10.1016/j.advwatres.2020.103552
6. Faj, J., Plessl, C., Kenter, T., Faghih-Naini, S., Aizinger, V.: Scalable multi-FPGA design of a discontinuous Galerkin shallow-water model on unstructured meshes. In: Proceedings of the Platform for Advanced Scientific Computing Conference (PASC) (2023, to appear)
7. de Fine Licht, J., Kuster, A., De Matteis, T., Ben-Nun, T., et al.: Stencilflow: mapping large stencil programs to distributed spatial computing systems. In: 2021 IEEE/ACM International Symposium on Code Generation and Optimization (CGO), pp. 315–326. IEEE (2021). https://doi.org/10.1109/CGO51591.2021.9370315
8. Gruber, T., Eitzinger, J., Hager, G., Wellein, G.: LIKWID. Zenodo (2022). https://doi.org/10.5281/ZENODO.7432487
9. Hajduk, H., Kuzmin, D., Aizinger, V.: New directional vector limiters for discontinuous Galerkin methods. J. Comput. Phys. **384**, 308–325 (2019). https://doi.org/10.1016/j.jcp.2019.01.032
10. Kenter, T.: Invited tutorial: OpenCL design flows for Intel and Xilinx FPGAs: using common design patterns and dealing with vendor-specific differences. In: Proc. Int. Workshop on FPGAs for Software Programmers (FSP), collocated with Int. Conf. on Field Programmable Logic and Applications (FPL) (2019)
11. Kenter, T., Förstner, J., Plessl, C.: Flexible FPGA design for FDTD using OpenCL. In: Proc. Int. Conf. on Field Programmable Logic and Applications (FPL), pp. 1–7. IEEE (2017). https://doi.org/10.23919/FPL.2017.8056844
12. Kenter, T., et al.: OpenCL-based FPGA design to accelerate the nodal discontinuous Galerkin method for unstructured meshes. In: Proc. IEEE Symp. on Field-Programmable Custom Computing Machines (FCCM), pp. 189–196. IEEE (2018). https://doi.org/10.1109/FCCM.2018.00037
13. Kenter, T., Shambhu, A., Faghih-Naini, S., Aizinger, V.: Algorithm-hardware co-design of a discontinuous Galerkin shallow-water model for a dataflow architecture

on FPGA. In: Proceedings of the Platform for Advanced Scientific Computing Conference, pp. 1–11. ACM, Geneva, Switzerland (2021). https://doi.org/10.1145/3468267.3470617

14. Kono, F., Nakasato, N., Hayashi, K., Vazhenin, A., Sedukhin, S.: Evaluations of OpenCL-written tsunami simulation on FPGA and comparison with GPU implementation. J. Supercomput. **74**(6), 2747–2775 (2018). https://doi.org/10.1007/s11227-018-2315-8

15. Lavrentiev, M., Lysakov, K., Marchuk, A., Oblaukhov, K., et al.: Algorithmic design of an FPGA-based calculator for fast evaluation of tsunami wave danger. Algorithms **14**(12), 343 (2021). https://doi.org/10.3390/a14120343

16. Lengauer, C., et al.: ExaStencils: advanced multigrid solver generation. In: Bungartz, H.-J., Reiz, S., Uekermann, B., Neumann, P., Nagel, W.E. (eds.) Software for Exascale Computing - SPPEXA 2016-2019. LNCSE, vol. 136, pp. 405–452. Springer, Cham (2020). https://doi.org/10.1007/978-3-030-47956-5_14

17. Meurer, A., Smith, C.P., Paprocki, M., Čertík, O., et al.: SymPy: symbolic computing in python. PeerJ Comput. Sci. **3**, e103 (2017). https://doi.org/10.7717/peerj-cs.103

18. Nagasu, K., Sano, K., Kono, F., Nakasato, N.: FPGA-based tsunami simulation: Performance comparison with GPUs, and roofline model for scalability analysis. J. Parallel Distrib. Comput. **106**, 153–169 (2017). https://doi.org/10.1016/j.jpdc.2016.12.015

19. Silva, B., Braeken, A., Touhafi, A., D'Hollander, E.: Performance modeling for FPGAs: extending the roofline model with high-level synthesis tools. Int. J. Reconfigurable Comput. **2013**, 7 (2013). https://doi.org/10.1155/2013/428078

20. Siracusa, M., Del Sozzo, E., Rabozzi, M., Di Tucci, L., et al.: A comprehensive methodology to optimize FPGA designs via the roofline model. IEEE Trans. Comput. **71**(8), 1903–1915 (2022). https://doi.org/10.1109/TC.2021.3111761

21. Trimberger, S.M.S.: Three ages of FPGAs: a retrospective on the first thirty years of FPGA technology: this paper reflects on how Moore's law has driven the design of FPGAs through three epochs: the age of invention, the age of expansion, and the age of accumulation. IEEE Solid-State Circuits Mag. **10**(2), 16–29 (2018). https://doi.org/10.1109/MSSC.2018.2822862

22. Williams, S., Waterman, A., Patterson, D.: Roofline: an insightful visual performance model for multicore architectures. Commun. ACM **52**(4), 65–76 (2009). https://doi.org/10.1145/1498765.1498785

23. Zint, D., Grosso, R., Aizinger, V., Faghih-Naini, S., et al.: Automatic generation of load-balancing-aware block-structured grids for complex ocean domains. In: 30th International Meshing Roundtable (SIAM IMR 2022). Zenodo (2022). https://doi.org/10.5281/zenodo.6562440

24. Zint, D., Grosso, R., Aizinger, V., Köstler, H.: Generation of block structured grids on complex domains for high performance simulation. Comput. Math. Math. Phys. **59**(12), 2108–2123 (2019). https://doi.org/10.1134/S0965542519120182

25. Zohouri, H.R., Podobas, A., Matsuoka, S.: Combined spatial and temporal blocking for high-performance stencil computation on FPGAs using OpenCL. In: Proc. Int. Symp. on Field-Programmable Gate Arrays (FPGA 2018), pp. 153–162. ACM, New York, NY, USA (2018). https://doi.org/10.1145/3174243.3174248

Massively Parallel Genetic Optimization Through Asynchronous Propagation of Populations

Oskar Taubert[(✉)] ⓘ, Marie Weiel ⓘ, Daniel Coquelin ⓘ, Anis Farshian ⓘ, Charlotte Debus ⓘ, Alexander Schug ⓘ, Achim Streit ⓘ, and Markus Götz ⓘ

Steinbuch Centre for Computing (SCC), Karlsruhe Institute of Technology (KIT), 76344 Eggenstein-Leopoldshafen, Germany
{oskar.taubert,markus.goetz}@kit.edu

Abstract. We present Propulate, an evolutionary optimization algorithm and software package for global optimization and in particular hyperparameter search. For efficient use of HPC resources, Propulate omits the synchronization after each generation as done in conventional genetic algorithms. Instead, it steers the search with the complete population present at time of breeding new individuals. We provide an MPI-based implementation of our algorithm, which features variants of selection, mutation, crossover, and migration and is easy to extend with custom functionality. We compare Propulate to the established optimization tool Optuna. We find that Propulate is up to three orders of magnitude faster without sacrificing solution accuracy, demonstrating the efficiency and efficacy of our lazy synchronization approach. Code and documentation are available at https://github.com/Helmholtz-AI-Energy/propulate/.

Keywords: Genetic Optimization · AI · Parallelization · Evolutionary Algorithm

1 Introduction

Machine learning (ML) algorithms are heavily used in almost every area of human life today, from medical diagnosis and critical infrastructure to transportation and food production. Almost all ML algorithms have non-learnable hyperparameters (HPs) that influence the training and in particular their predictive capacity. As evaluating a set of HPs involves at least a partial training, state-free approaches to HP optimization (HPO), like grid and random search, often go beyond available compute resources [15]. To explore the high-dimensional HP spaces efficiently, information from previous evaluations must be leveraged to guide the search. Such state-dependent strategies minimize the number of evaluations to find a useful model, reducing search times and thus the energy consumption of the computation. Bayesian and bio-inspired optimizers are the most popular of these AutoML approaches. Among the latter, genetic

© The Author(s) 2023
A. Bhatele et al. (Eds.): ISC High Performance 2023, LNCS 13948, pp. 106–124, 2023.
https://doi.org/10.1007/978-3-031-32041-5_6

algorithms (GAs) are versatile metaheuristics inspired by natural evolution. To solve a search-for-solutions problem, a population of candidate solutions (or individuals) is evolved in an iterative interplay of selection and variation [23,30]. Although reaching the global optimum is not guaranteed, GAs often find near-optimal solutions with less computational effort than classical optimizers [8,9]. They have become popular for various optimization problems, including HPO for ML and neural architecture search (NAS) [14].

To take full advantage of the increasingly bigger models and datasets, designing scalable algorithms for high performance computing (HPC) has become a must [40]. While Bayesian optimization is inherently serial, the structure of GAs renders them suitable for parallelization [34]: Since all candidates in each iteration are independent, they can be evaluated in parallel. To breed the next generation, however, the previous one has to be completed. As the computational expenses for evaluating different candidates vary, synchronizing the parallel evolutionary process affects the scalability by introducing a substantial bottleneck. Approaches to reducing the overall communication in parallel GAs like the island model (IM) [34] do not address the underlying synchronization problem.

To solve the issues arising from explicit synchronization, we introduce Propulate, a massively parallel genetic optimizer with asynchronous propagation of populations and migration. Unlike classical GAs, Propulate maintains a continuous population of already evaluated individuals with a softened notion of the typically strictly separated, discrete generations. Our contributions include:

- A novel parallel genetic algorithm based on a fully asynchronous island model with independently processing workers, allowing to parallelize the optimization process and distribute the internal evaluation of the objective function.
- Massive parallelism by asynchronous propagation of continuous populations and migration.
- A prototypical implementation in Python using extremely efficient communication via the message passing interface (MPI).
- Optimal use of parallel hardware by minimizing idle times in HPC systems.

We use Propulate to optimize various benchmark functions and the HPs of a deep neural network on a supercomputer. Comparing our results to those of the popular HPO package Optuna, we find that Propulate is consistently drastically faster without sacrificing solution accuracy. We further show that Propulate scales well to at least 100 processing elements (PEs) without relevant loss of efficiency, demonstrating the efficacy of our asynchronous evolutionary approach.

2   Related Work

Recent progress in ML has triggered heavy use of these techniques with Python as the de facto standard programming language. Tuning HPs requires solving high-dimensional optimization problems with ML algorithms as black boxes and model performance metrics as objective functions (OFs). Most common are Bayesian optimizers (e.g. Optuna [2], Hyperopt [7], SMAC3 [24,27], Spearmint [32], GPyOpt [5], and MOE [38]) and bio-inspired methods such as swarm-based (e.g. FLAPS [39]) and evolutionary (e.g. DEAP [16], MENNDL [40]) algorithms. Below, we provide an overview of popular HP optimizers in Python, with a focus on state-dependent parallel algorithms and implementations. A theoretical overview of parallel GAs can be found in surveys [3, 4, 12] and books [29, 37].

Optuna adopts various algorithms for HP sampling and pruning of unpromising trials, including tree-structured Parzen estimators (TPEs), Gaussian processes, and covariance matrix adaption evolution strategy. It enables parallel runs via a relational database server. In the parallel case, an Optuna candidate obtains information about previous candidates from and stores results to disk.

SMAC3 (Sequential Model-based Algorithm Configuration) combines a random-forest based Bayesian approach with an aggressive racing mechanism [24]. Its parallel variant pSMAC uses multiple collaborating SMAC3 runs which share their evaluations through the file system.

Spearmint, GPyOpt, and MOE are Gaussian-process based Bayesian optimizers. Spearmint enables distributed HPO via Sun Grid Engine and MongoDB. GPyOpt is integrated into the Sherpa package [22], which provides implementations of recent HP optimizers along with the infrastructure to run them in parallel via a grid engine and a database server. MOE (Metric Optimization Engine) uses a one-step Bayes-optimal algorithm to maximize the multi-points expected improvement in a parallel setting [38]. Using a REST-based client-server model, it enables multi-level parallelism by distributing each evaluation and running multiple evaluations at a time.

Nevergrad [31] and Autotune [25] provide gradient-free and evolutionary optimizers, including Bayesian, particle swarm, and one-shot optimization. In Nevergrad, parallel evaluations use several workers via an executor from Python's concurrent module. Autotune enables concurrent global and local searches, cross-method sharing of evaluations, method hybridization, and multi-level parallelism. Open Source Vizier [33] is a Python interface for Google's HPO service Vizier. It implements Gaussian process bandits [19] and enables dynamic optimizer switching. A central database server does the algorithmic proposal work, clients perform evaluations and communicate with the server via remote procedure calls. Katib [18] is a cloud-native AutoML project based on the Kubernetes container orchestration system. It integrates with Optuna and Hyperopt. Tune [26] is built on the Ray distributed computing platform. It interfaces with Optuna, Hyperopt, and Nevergrad and leverages multi-level parallelism.

DEAP (Distributed Evolutionary Algorithms in Python) [16] implements general GAs, evolution strategies, multi-objective optimization, and co-evolution of multi-populations. It enables parallelization via Python's multiprocessing or SCOOP module. EvoTorch [36] is built on PyTorch and implements distribution- and population-based algorithms. Using a Ray cluster, it can scale over multiple CPUs, GPUs, and computers. MENNDL (Multi-node Evolutionary Neural Networks for Deep Learning) [40] is a closed-source MPI-parallelized HP optimizer for automated network selection. A master node handles the genetic operations while evaluations are done on the remaining worker nodes. However, global synchronization hinders optimal resource utilization [40].

Algorithm 1: Basic GA. In each generation, the individuals are evaluated in terms of the optimization problem's OF. Genetic operators propagate them to the next generation: The selection operator chooses a portion of the current generation, where better individuals are usually preferred. To breed new individuals, the genes of two or more parent individuals from the selected pool are manipulated. While the crossover operator recombines the parents' genes, the mutation operator alters them randomly. This is repeated until a stopping condition is met.

Input: Search-space limits, population size P, *termination_condition*, *selection_policy*, *crossover_probability*, *mutation_probability*.

```
1  Initialize population pop of P individuals within search space.
2  while not termination_condition do                        // OPTIMIZE
3      Evaluate individuals in pop.                           // EVALUATE
4      Choose parents from pop following selection_policy.    // SELECT
5      foreach individual in pop do                           // VARY
6          if random ≤ crossover_probability then             // RECOMBINE
7          |   Recombine individuals randomly chosen from parents.
8          if random ≤ mutation_probability then              // MUTATE
9          |   Mutate.
10         Update individual in pop.
```

Result: Best individual found (i.e., with lowest OF value for minimization).

3   Propulate Algorithm and Implementation

To alleviate the bottleneck inherent to synchronized parallel genetic algorithms, our massively parallel genetic optimizer Propulate (***prop**agate* and *pop**ulate***) implements a fully asynchronous island model specifically designed for large-scale HPC systems. Unlike conventional GAs, Propulate maintains a continuous population of evaluated individuals with a softened notion of the typically strictly separated generations. This enables *asynchronous* evaluation, variation, propagation, and migration of individuals. To ensure interoperability with existing data science and ML workflows, we provide a Python implementation. In most applications, evaluating the OF represents the largest contribution to the total resource consumption. Performance-relevant paths inside the OF evaluation are expected to be implemented and optimized in CUDA and C/C++ or Fortran. With the aforementioned workflows, this is typically already the case.

Propulate's basic mechanism is that of Darwinian evolution, i.e., beneficial traits are selected, recombined, and mutated to breed more fit individuals (see Algorithm 1). On a higher level, Propulate employs an IM, which combines independent evolution of self-contained subpopulations with intermittent exchange of selected individuals [34]. To coordinate the search globally, each island occasionally delegates migrants to be included in the target islands' populations. With worse performing islands typically receiving candidates from better performing ones, islands communicate genetic information competitively, thus increasing diversity among the subpopulations compared to panmictic models [11]. Independent from the breeding mechanism used on each single island of a synchronous

IM, this migrant exchange occurs simultaneously after a fixed number of synchronously evaluated generations, with no computation happening in that time. The following hyperparameters characterize an IM:

- **Island number and subpopulation sizes**
- **Migration (pollination) probability**
- **Number of migrants (pollinators):** How many individuals migrate from the source population at a time.
- **Migration (pollination) topology:** Directed graph of migration (pollination) paths between islands.
- **Emigration policy:** How to select emigrants (e.g., random or best) and whether to remove them from the source population (actual migration) or not (pollination).
- **Immigration policy:** How to insert immigrants into the target population, i.e., either add them (migration) or replace existing individuals (pollination, e.g., random or worst).

Propulate's functional principle is outlined in Algorithm 2. We consider multiple PEs (or workers) partitioned into islands. Each worker processes one individual at a time and maintains a population to track evaluated and migrated individuals on its island. To mitigate the computational overhead of synchronized OF evaluations, Propulate leverages asynchronous propagation of continuous populations with interwoven, worker-specific generations (see Fig. 1). In each iteration, each worker breeds and evaluates an individual which is added to its population list. It then sends the individual with its evaluation result to all workers on the same island and, in return, receives evaluated individuals dispatched by them for a mutual update of their population lists. To avoid explicit synchronization points, the independently operating workers use asynchronous point-to-point communication via MPI to share their results. Each one dispatches its result immediately after finishing an evaluation. Directly afterwards, it non-blockingly checks for incoming messages from workers of its own island awaiting to be received. In the next iteration, it breeds a new individual by applying the evolutionary operators to its continuous population list of all evaluated individuals from any generation on the island. The workers thus proceed asynchronously without idle times despite the individuals' varying computational costs.

After the mutual update, asynchronous migration or pollination between islands happens on a per-worker basis with a certain probability. Each worker selects a number of emigrants from its current population. For actual migration[1], an individual can only exist actively on one island. A worker thus may only choose eligible emigrants from an exclusive subset of the island's population to avoid overlapping selections by other workers. It then dispatches the emigrants to the target islands' workers as specified in the migration topology. Finally, it sends them to all workers on its island for island-wide deactivation of emigrated individuals before deactivating them in its own population.

---

[1] See github.com/Helmholtz-AI-Energy/propulate/tree/master/supplementary for pseudocode with migration and explanatory figure.

Algorithm 2: Propulate with pollination.

Input: Search-space limits; hyperparameters $n\_islands$, island sizes P_i
($i = 1, \ldots, n\_islands$), number of iterations $generations$, evolutionary
operators (including $selection\_policy$, $crossover\_probability$,
$mutation\_probability$ etc.), $pollination\_probability$, $pollination\_topology$,
$emigration\_policy$, $immigration\_policy$.

1 Configure $n\_islands$ islands with P_i workers each. Each worker evaluates one
   individual at a time and maintains its own population list pop of evaluated and
   migrated individuals on the island.
2 /* START OPTIMIZATION.   */
3 **for** each worker **do in parallel**
4   **while** $generation \leq generations$ **do** // Loop over generations.
5   Breed and evaluate individual. Append it to pop. Send it to other
   workers on island to synchronize their populations lists:
   `evaluate_individual()`   // BREED AND EVALUATE
6   Check for and possibly receive individuals bred and evaluated by other
   workers on island. Append them to pop:
   `receive_intra_isle_individuals()`   // SYNCHRONIZE
7   **if** $random \leq pollination\_probability$ **then**   // EMIGRATE
8   Choose pollinators from currently active individuals on island
   according to $emigration\_policy$. Send copies of pollinator(s) to
   workers of target islands according to $pollination\_topology$:
   `send_emigrants()`
9   Check for and possibly receive pollinators sent by workers from other
   islands. Add them to pop. Determine individuals to be replaced by
   incoming pollinators according to $immigration\_policy$. Send
   individuals to be replaced to other workers on island for deactivation:
   `receive_immigrants()`   // IMMIGRATE
10   Check for and possibly receive individuals replaced by pollinators on
   other workers on island. Try to deactivate them in pop. If an
   individual to be deactivated is not yet in pop, append it to history list
   $replaced$ and try again in the next generation:
   `deactivate_replaced_individuals()`   // SYNCHRONIZE
11   Go to next generation: `generation += 1`
12   /* OPTIMIZATION DONE: FINAL SYNCHRONIZATION   */
13   Wait for all other workers to finish: `MPI.COMM_WORLD.barrier()`
14   Final check for incoming messages so all workers hold complete population.
15   Probe for individuals evaluated by other workers on island:
   `receive_intra_isle_individuals()`
16   Probe for incoming pollinators immigrating from other islands:
   `receive_immigrants()`
17   Probe for individuals replaced by other workers on island to be
   deactivated: `deactivate_replaced_individuals()`

Result: n individuals with smallest OF values.

In the next step, the worker probes for and, if applicable, receives immigrants
from other islands. It then checks for individuals emigrated by other workers of its
island and tries to deactivate them in its population. Due to the asynchronicity,

Island 1 with *N* workers

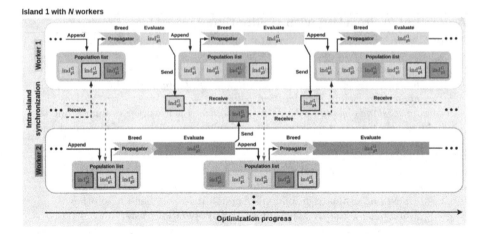

Fig. 1. Asynchronous propagation. Interaction of two workers on one island. Individuals bred by worker 1 and 2 are shown in blue and red, respectively. Their origins are given by a generation sub- and an island superscript. Populations are depicted as round grey boxes, where most recent individuals have black outlines. Varying evaluation times are represented by sharp boxes of different widths. We illustrate the asynchronous propagation and intra-island synchronization of the population using the example of the blue individual ind_{g3}^{i1}. This individual is bred by worker 1 in generation 3 by applying the propagator (yellow) to the worker's current population. After evaluating ind_{g3}^{i1}, worker 1 sends it to all workers on its island and appends it to its population. As no evaluated individuals dispatched by worker 2 await to be received, worker 1 proceeds with breeding. Worker 2 receives the blue ind_{g3}^{i1} only after finishing the evaluation of the red ind_{g2}^{i1}. It then appends both to its population and breeds a new individual for generation 3. (Color figure online)

individuals might be designated to be deactivated before arriving in the population. Propulate continuously corrects these synchronization artefacts during the optimization.

For pollination (see Fig. 2), identical copies of individuals can exist on multiple islands. Workers thus can choose emigrating pollinators from any active individuals in their current populations and do not deactivate them upon emigration. To control the population growth, pollinators replace active individuals in the target population according to the immigration policy. For proper accounting of the population, one random worker of the target island selects the individual to be replaced and informs the other workers accordingly. Individuals to be deactivated that are not yet in the population are cached to be replaced in the next iteration. This process is repeated until each worker has evaluated a set number of generations. Finally, the population is synchronized among workers and the best individuals are returned.

Propulate uses so-called propagators to breed child individuals from an existing collection of parent individuals. It implements various standard genetic operators, including uniform, best, and worst selection, random initialization,

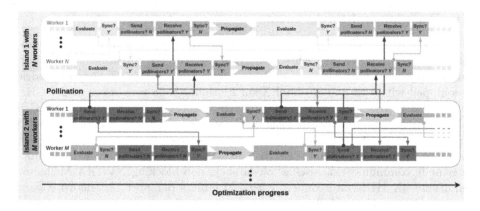

Fig. 2. Asynchronous pollination. Consider two islands with N (blue) and M (red) workers, respectively. We illustrate pollination (dark colors) by tracing worker N on island 1. After evaluation and mutual intra-island updates (light blue, see Fig. 1), this worker performs pollination: It sends copies of the chosen pollinators to all workers of each target island, here island 2. The target island's workers receive the pollinators asynchronously (dark blue arrows). For proper accounting of the populations, worker 1 on island 2 selects the individual to be replaced and informs all workers on its island accordingly (middle red arrow). Afterwards, worker N receives incoming pollinators from island 2 to be included into its population. It then probes for individuals that have been replaced by other workers on its island, here worker 1, in the meantime and need to be deactivated. After these pollination-related intra-island population updates, it breeds the next generation. As pollination does not occur in this generation, it directly receives pollinators from island 2. This time, worker N chooses the individual to be replaced. (Color figure online)

stochastic and conditional propagators, point and interval mutation, and several forms of crossover. In addition, Propulate provides a default propagator: Having selected two random parents from the breeding pool consisting of a set number of the currently most fit individuals, uniform crossover and point mutation are performed each with a specified probability. Afterwards, interval mutation is performed. To prevent premature trapping in a local optimum, a randomly initialized individual is added with a specified probability instead of one bred from the current population.

4   Experimental Evaluation

We evaluate Propulate on various benchmark functions (see Sect. 4.4) and an HPO use case in remote sensing classification (see Sect. 4.5) which provides a real world application. We compare our results against Optuna since it is the most widely used HPO software.

4.1   Experimental Environment

We ran the experiments on the distributed-memory, parallel hybrid supercomputer *Hochleistungsrechner Karlsruhe* (HoreKa[2]) at the Steinbuch Centre for Computing, Karlsruhe Institute of Technology. Each of its 769 compute nodes is equipped with two 38-core Intel Xeon Platinum 8368 processors at 2.4 GHz base and 3.4 GHz maximum turbo frequency, 256 GB (standard) or 512 GB (high-memory and accelerator) local memory, a local 960 GB NVMe SSD disk, and two network adapters. 167 of the nodes are accelerator nodes each equipped with four NVIDIA A100-40 GPUs with 40 GB memory connected via NVLink. Inter-node communication uses a low-latency, non-blocking NVIDIA Mellanox InfiniBand 4X HDR interconnect with 200 Gbit/s per port. A Lenovo Xclarity controller measures full node energy consumption, excluding file systems, networking, and cooling. The operating system is Red Hat Enterprise Linux 8.2.

4.2   Benchmark Functions

Benchmark functions are used to evaluate optimizers in terms of convergence, accuracy, and robustness. The informative value of such studies is limited by how well we understand the characteristics making real-life optimization problems difficult and our ability to embed these features into benchmark functions [28]. We use Propulate to optimize a variety of traditional and recent benchmark functions emulating situations optimizers have to cope with in different kinds of problems (see Table 1).

- **Sphere** is smooth, unimodal, strongly convex, symmetric, and thus simple.
- **Rosenbrock** has a narrow minimum inside a parabola-shaped valley.
- **Step** represents the problem of flat surfaces. Plateaus pose obstacles to optimizers as they lack information about which direction is favorable.
- **Quartic** is a unimodal function padded with Gaussian noise. As it never returns the same value on the same point, algorithms that do not perform well on this test function will do poorly on noisy data.
- **Rastrigin** is non-linear and highly multimodal. Its surface is determined by two external variables, controlling the modulation's amplitude and frequency. The local minima are located at a rectangular grid with size 1. Their functional values increase with the distance to the global minimum.
- **Griewank**'s product creates sub-populations strongly codependent to parallel GAs, while the summation produces a parabola. Its local optima lie above parabola level but decrease with increasing dimensions, i.e., the larger the search range, the flatter the function.
- **Schwefel** has a second-best minimum far away from the global optimum.
- **Lunacek's bi-sphere**'s [28] landscape structure is the minimum of two quadratic functions, each creating a single funnel in the search space. The spheres are placed along the positive search-space diagonal, with the optimal and sub-optimal sphere in the middle of the positive and negative quadrant,

---

[2] https://www.scc.kit.edu/en/services/horeka.php.

Table 1. Benchmark functions.

Name	Function	Limits	Global minimum
Sphere	$f_1 = x_1^2 + x_2^2$	± 5.12	$f(0,0) = 0$
Rosenbrock	$f_2 = 100\left(x_1^2 - x_2\right)^2 + (1 - x_1)^2$	± 2.048	$f(1,1) = 0$
Step	$f_3 = \sum_{i=1}^{5} \text{int}(x_i)$	± 5.12	$f(x_i \leq -5) = -25$
Quartic	$f_4 = \sum_{i=1}^{30} \left(i x_i^4 + \mathcal{N}_i(0,1)\right)$	± 1.28	$f(0,...,0) = \sum_i \mathcal{N}_i$
Rastrigin	$f_5 = 200 + \sum_{i=1}^{20} x_i^2 - 10\cos(2\pi x_i)$	± 5.12	$f(0,...,0) = 0$
Griewank	$f_6 = 1 + \frac{1}{4000}\sum_{i=1}^{10} x_i^2 - \prod_{i=1}^{10} \cos\frac{x_i}{\sqrt{i}}$	± 600	$f(0,...,0) = 0$
Schwefel	$f_7 = 10V - \sum_{i=1}^{10} x_i \sin\sqrt{|x_i|}$	± 500	$f\left(x_1^*,...,x_{10}^*\right) = 0,$
	with $V = 418.982887$		$x_i^* = 420.968746$
Bi-sphere	$f_8 = \min\left(\sum_{i=1}^{30}(x_i - \mu_1)^2,\right.$	± 5.12	$f(\mu_1,...,\mu_1) = 0$
	$\left.30 + s \cdot \sum_{i=1}^{30}(x_i - \mu_2)^2\right)$ with		
	$\mu_1 = 2.5,\ \mu_2 = -\left(s^{-1}\left(\mu_1^2 - 1\right)\right)^{1/2},$		
	$s = 1 - \left(2\sqrt{50} - 8.2\right)^{-1/2}$		
Bi-Rastrigin	$f_9 = f_8 + 10\sum_{i=1}^{30} 1 - \cos 2\pi(x_i - \mu_1)$	± 5.12	$f(\mu_1,...,\mu_1) = 0$

respectively. Their distance and the barrier's height increase with dimensionality, creating a globally non-separable underlying surface.

- **Lunacek's bi-Rastrigin** [28] is a double-funnel version of Rastrigin. This function isolates global structure as the main difference impacting problem difficulty on a well understood test case.

4.3   Meta-optimizing the Optimizer

Propulate itself has HPs influencing its optimization behavior, accuracy, and robustness. To explore their effect systematically and give transparent recommendations for default values, we conducted a grid search across the six most prominent HPs. The search space is shown in Table 2. We ran the grid search five times for the quartic, Rastrigin, and bi-Rastrigin benchmark functions (see Table 1 and Sect. 4.4), each with a different seed consistently used over all points within a search. All three functions have their global minimum at zero. They were chosen for their high-dimensional parameter spaces (30, 20, and 30, respectively) and different levels of difficulty to optimize. For quartic, Propulate found a minimum below 0.01 ± 0.005 for 80.12% of all points across the five grid searches. This increases to 94.94% for minima found within 0.1 ± 0.05 of the global minimum. In comparison, the tolerances have to be relaxed considerably for the more complex Rastrigin and bi-Rastrigin. While only 18.57% of all grid points had a function value less than 1.0 ± 0.5 for Rastrigin, only a single point resulted in an average value of less than 10 for bi-Rastrigin. Although the average value of bi-Rastrigin was only less than 10 once, we found the minimum across each of the five searches to be less than 1.0 for 3.31% of the grid points.

Table 2. Grid search parameters. All experiments use 144 CPUs equally distributed between two nodes. Random-initialization probability refers to the chance that a new individual is generated entirely randomly.

Number of islands	2	4	8	16	32
Island population size	72	36	18	9	4
Migration (pollination) probability	0.1	0.3	0.5	0.7	0.9
Pollination	True		False		
Crossover probability	0.1	0.325	0.55	0.775	
Point-mutation probability	0.1	0.325	0.55	0.775	
Random-initialization probability	0.1	0.325	0.55	0.775	

Considering grid points with at least one result smaller than 1.0, 86.61% used either 16 or 36 islands, while the remainder used eight. As Propulate initializes different islands at different positions in the search space, the chance that one of them is at a very beneficial position increases with the number of islands. This is further confirmed by a migration probability of 0.7 or 0.9 for 61.41% of these points. If one of the islands is well-initialized, it thus will quickly notify others.

With every best grid point using pollination, we clearly find pollination to be favorable over real migration. To determine the other HPs, we compute the averages of the results for the top ten grid points across all three functions. The top ten were determined by grouping over the lowest average and standard deviation of the function values, sorting by the averages, and sorting by the standard deviations. This method reduces the chances of a single run simply benefiting from an advantageous starting seed. Average crossover, point-mutation, and random-initialization probabilities are 0.655 ± 0.056, 0.363 ± 0.133, and 0.423 ± 0.135, respectively. The average number of islands was 28.800 ± 6.009 which equates to an island population of 5.00 ± 1.043. The average migration probability was 0.527 ± 0.150. These values provide a reasonable starting point towards choosing default HPs for Propulate (see Table 3). As the grid searches only considered functions with independent parameters, we assume a relatively high random-initialization probability to be useful due to the benefits of random search [6]. On this account, we chose to reduce the default random-initialization probability to 0.2. As the migration probability might also be lowered artificially by this phenomenon, we set its default to 0.7. The default probabilities for crossover and point-mutation were chosen as 0.7 and 0.4, respectively. The island size was set at four individuals. This is a practical choice as our test system has four accelerators per node and the number of CPUs per node is a multiple of four.

Table 3. Propulate HPs for benchmark function minimization.

Number of islands	38
Island population size	4
Pollination probability	0.7
Crossover probability	0.7
Point-mutation probability	0.4
Sigma factor	0.05
Random-initialization probability	0.2
Generations per worker	256
Selection policy	Best
Pollination topology	Fully connected
Number of migrants	1
Emigration policy	Best
Immigration policy	Worst

4.4 Benchmark Function Optimization

For each function, we ran each ten equivalent Propulate and Optuna optimizations, using the same compute resources, degree of parallelization, and number of evaluations. Figure 3 shows the optimization accuracy over wallclock time comparing Propulate with default parameters determined from our grid search (see Table 3) to Optuna's default optimizer. In terms of accuracy, Propulate and Optuna are comparable in most experiments. For many functions, e.g. Schwefel, bi-Rastrigin, and Rastrigin, Propulate even achieves a better OF value. In terms of wallclock time, Propulate is consistently at least one order of magnitude faster. This is due to Propulate's MPI-based communication over the fast network, whereas Optuna uses relational databases with SQL and is limited by the slow file system. Since the functions are cheap to evaluate, optimization and communication dominate the wallclock time. In particular for problems where evaluations are cheap compared to the search itself, we find that Optuna's computational efficiency suffers massively from the frequent file locking inherent to its parallelization strategy, reducing its usability for large-scale HPC applications.

In addition, we inspected the evolution of the population over wallclock time for both Propulate and Optuna. An example for minimizing the Rastrigin function is shown in Fig. 4. Propulate is roughly three orders of magnitude faster and makes significantly greater progress in terms of both OF values and distance to the global optimum. Due to this drastic difference in runtime, we measured only 46.27 Wh for Propulate compared to Optuna's 2646.29 Wh.

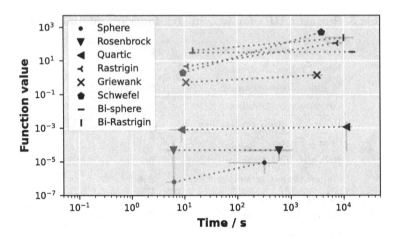

Fig. 3. Benchmark function minimization accuracy over wallclock time. Lowest function values found by Propulate (red) and Optuna (blue) versus wallclock time to reach them, each averaged over ten runs. Step is not shown since both optimizers achieve a perfect value of -25 within 0.6 s and 278.2 s, respectively. (Color figure online)

4.5 HP Optimization for Remote Sensing Classification

BigEarthNet [35] is a Sentinel-2 multispectral image dataset in remote sensing. It comprises 590 326 image patches each of which is assigned one or more of the 19 available CORINE Land Cover map labels [10,35]. Multiple computer vision networks for BigEarthNet classification have been trained [35], with ResNet-50 [20] being the most accurate. While a previous Propulate version was used to optimize a set of HPs and the architecture for this use case [13], a more versatile and efficient parallelization strategy in the current version makes it worthwhile to revisit this application. Analogously to [13], we consider different optimizers, learning rate (LR) schedulers, activation functions, loss functions, number of filters in each convolutional block, and activation orders [21]. The search space is shown in Table 4. Optimizer parameters, LR functions, and LR warmup are included as well. We only consider SGD-based optimizers as they share common parameters and thus exclude Adam-like optimizers from the search. We theorize that including Adam led to the difficulties seen previously [13]. The training is exited if the validation loss has not been increasing for ten epochs. We prepared the data analogously to [13]. The network is implemented in TensorFlow [1].

For both Propulate and Optuna, we ran each three searches over 24 h on 32 GPUs. We use $1 - F_1^{\text{val}}$ with the validation F_1 score as the OF to be minimized. On average, Optuna achieves its best OF value of (0.39 ± 0.01) within (7.05 ± 3.14) h. Propulate beats Optuna's average best after (5.30 ± 2.41) h and achieves its best OF value of (0.36 ± 0.00) within (13.89 ± 5.15) h.

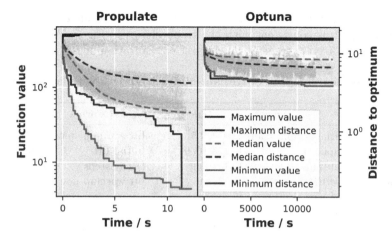

Fig. 4. Evolution of the population over wallclock time for the Rastrigin function. Propulate (left) versus Optuna (right). OF values (blue) use the left-hand scale, distances to the global optimum (purple) use the right-hand scale. Pastel dots show each individual's OF value/distance. Solid (dashed) lines show the minimum (median) value and distance achieved so far. Maximum value and distance are shown in black. Both optimizers perform 38 912 evaluations. Note the difference on the time axis. (Color figure online)

4.6 Scaling

Finally, we explore Propulate's scaling behavior for the use case presented in Sect. 4.5. Figure 5 shows our results for weak and strong linear scaling. Our baseline configuration used two nodes. Since each node has four GPUs, we calculate speedup and efficiency with respect to eight workers. For strong scaling, we fix the total number of evaluations at 512 and increase the number of workers, i.e., GPUs. We average over three runs with different seeds and keep four workers per island while increasing the number of islands. Speedup increases up to 128 workers, where we reach approximately half the optimal value. This is an expected decline since each worker only processes few individuals, so the variance in evaluation times leads to larger idle times of the faster workers before the final population synchronization at the end. Additionally, as the number of workers approaches the total number of evaluations, the randomly initialized evolutionary search in turn approaches a random search. This means that the search performance is likely to be worse than what the pure compute performance might suggest. It is still possible to apply Propulate on these scales, but the other search parameters have to be adjusted accordingly as shown in the weak scaling plot (see Fig. 5 top). The early super-scalar behavior is likely due to the non-sequential baseline. For small node counts, the performance is influenced by effects stemming from cluster utilization beyond the use case studied here, like file system congestion or inter-node distance in the network. With larger node counts relative to total cluster size, these effects average out or approach the worst case, which is consistent with the trend shown in Fig. 5. Weak efficiency only drops to 95% on average at our largest configuration of 128 workers.

Table 4. HP search space of ResNet-50 for BigEarthNet classification.

Optimizers	Optimizer parameters		LR warmup parameters	
Adagrad	Initial accum. value	$[10^{-4}, 0.5]$	LR warmup steps	$[10^0, 10^4]$
SGD	Clipnorm	$[-1, -1000]$	Initial LR	$[10^{-5}, 10^{-1}]$
Adadelta	Clipvalue	$[-1, 1000]$	Decay steps	$[10^2, 10^5]$
RMSprop	Use EMA	Boolean	LR warmup power	$[10^{-1}, 10^1]$
	EMA momentum	$[0.5, 1.0]$		
	EMA overwrite	$[1, 10^3]$		
	Momentum	$[0.0, 1.0]$		
	Nesterov	Boolean		
	Rho	$[0.8, 0.99999]$		
	Epsilon	$[10^{-9}, 10^{-4}]$		

Loss functions			LR parameters	
Binary CE	Categorical CE	Categorical hinge	Decay rate	$[0.8, 0.9999]$
Hinge	KL divergence	Squared hinge	Staircase inverse time decay	Boolean

Activation functions			Decay rate	$[0.1, 0.9]$
ELU	ReLU	Softplus	Staircase poly-	Boolean
Exponential	SELU	Softsign	nomial decay	
Hard sigmoid	Sigmoid	Swish	End LR	$[10^{-4}, 10^{-2}]$
Linear	Softmax	Tanh	Power	$[0.5, 2.5]$

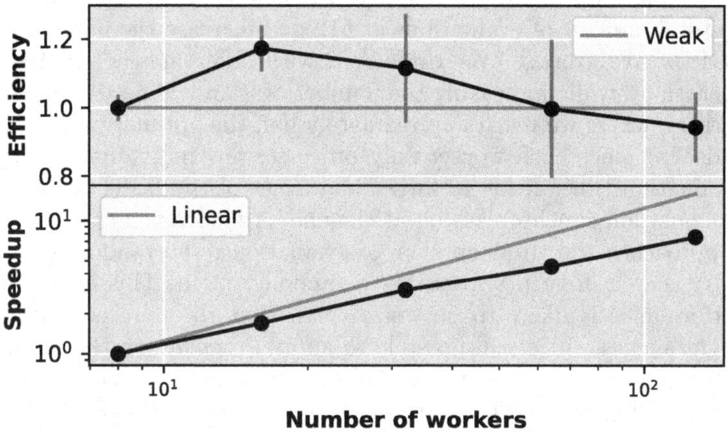

Fig. 5. Scaling with respect to a baseline of eight workers. Weak efficiency (top) and strong linear speedup (bottom). Use case and search space are described in Sect. 4.5. Weak-scaling problem size is varied via the number of OF evaluations. Results are averaged over three runs.

5   Conclusion

We presented Propulate, our HPC-adapted, asynchronous genetic optimization algorithm and software. Our experimental evaluation shows that the fully asynchronous evaluation, propagation, and migration enable a highly efficient and parallelizable genetic optimization. To our knowledge, all existing Python-based genetic optimization tools use synchronization schemes that are not tailored to application in HPC environments. Harder to quantify than performance but very important is ease of use. Especially for HPC applications at scale, some parallelization and distribution models are more suited than others. A purely MPI-based implementation as in Propulate is not only extremely efficient for highly parallel and communication-intensive algorithms but also easy to set up and maintain, since the required infrastructure is commonly available on HPC systems. This is not the case for any of the other tools investigated, except for the not publicly available MENNDL. In addition, Propulate's asynchronicity facilitates a tighter coupling of individuals during the optimization, which enables a more efficient evaluation of candidates and in particular early stopping informed by previously evaluated individuals in the NAS case. Propulate was already successfully applied to HPO for various ML models on different HPC machines [13,17]. Another avenue for future work is including variable-length gene descriptions. Mutually exclusive genes of different lengths, such as the parameter sets for Adam- and SGD-like optimizers in our NAS use case, can thus be explored efficiently. While this is already possible, it requires an inconvenient workaround of including inactive genes and adapting the propagators to manually prevent the evaluation of many individuals differing only in inactive genes.

Acknowledgments. This work is supported by the Helmholtz AI platform grant and the Helmholtz Association Initiative and Networking Fund on the HAICORE@KIT partition.

References

1. Abadi, M., et al.: TensorFlow: a system for large-scale machine learning. In: 12th USENIX Symposium on Operating Systems Design and Implementation (OSDI 16), pp. 265–283 (2016)
2. Akiba, T., Sano, S., Yanase, T., Ohta, T., Koyama, M.: Optuna: a next-generation hyperparameter optimization framework. In: Proceedings of the 25th ACM SIGKDD International Conference on Knowledge Discovery & Data Mining, pp. 2623–2631 (2019). https://doi.org/10.1145/3292500.3330701
3. Alba, E., Tomassini, M.: Parallelism and evolutionary algorithms. IEEE Trans. Evol. Comput. **6**(5), 443–462 (2002). https://doi.org/10.1109/TEVC.2002.800880
4. Alba, E., Troya, J.M.: A survey of parallel distributed genetic algorithms. Complexity **4**(4), 31–52 (1999)
5. The GPyOpt authors: GPyOpt: A Bayesian Optimization Framework in Python (2016). https://github.com/SheffieldML/GPyOpt

6. Bergstra, J., Bengio, Y.: Random search for hyper-parameter optimization. J. Mach. Learn. Res. **13**(10), 281–305 (2012). https://jmlr.org/papers/v13/bergstra12a.html
7. Bergstra, J., Yamins, D., Cox, D.: Making a science of model search: hyperparameter optimization in hundreds of dimensions for vision architectures. In: International Conference on Machine Learning, pp. 115–123. PMLR (2013). https://proceedings.mlr.press/v28/bergstra13.pdf
8. Bianchi, L., Dorigo, M., Gambardella, L.M., Gutjahr, W.J.: A survey on metaheuristics for stochastic combinatorial optimization. Nat. Comput. **8**(2), 239–287 (2009). https://doi.org/10.1007/s11047-008-9098-4
9. Blum, C., Roli, A.: Metaheuristics in combinatorial optimization: overview and conceptual comparison. ACM Comput. Surv. (CSUR) **35**(3), 268–308 (2003). https://doi.org/10.1145/937503.937505
10. Bossard, M., Feranec, J., Otahel, J., et al.: CORINE land cover technical guide - Addendum 2000, vol. 40. European Environment Agency Copenhagen (2000)
11. Cantú-Paz, E.: Efficient and Accurate Parallel Genetic Algorithms, vol. 1. Springer Science & Business Media, Berlin, Heidelberg (2000). https://doi.org/10.1007/978-1-4615-4369-5
12. Cantú-Paz, E., et al.: A survey of parallel genetic algorithms. Calculateurs paralleles, reseaux et systems repartis **10**(2), 141–171 (1998)
13. Coquelin, D., Sedona, R., Riedel, M., Götz, M.: Evolutionary optimization of neural architectures in remote sensing classification problems. In: 2021 IEEE International Geoscience and Remote Sensing Symposium IGARSS, pp. 1587–1590. IEEE (2021). https://doi.org/10.1109/IGARSS47720.2021.9554309
14. Elsken, T., Metzen, J.H., Hutter, F.: Neural architecture search: a survey. J. Mach. Learn. Res. **20**(1), 1997–2017 (2019)
15. Feurer, M., Hutter, F.: Hyperparameter optimization. In: Hutter, F., Kotthoff, L., Vanschoren, J. (eds.) Automated Machine Learning. TSSCML, pp. 3–33. Springer, Cham (2019). https://doi.org/10.1007/978-3-030-05318-5_1
16. Fortin, F.A., De Rainville, F.M., Gardner, M.A.G., Parizeau, M., Gagné, C.: DEAP: evolutionary algorithms made easy. J. Mach. Learn. Res. **13**(1), 2171–2175 (2012)
17. Funk, Y., Götz, M., Anzt, H.: Prediction of optimal solvers for sparse linear systems using deep learning. In: Proceedings of the 2022 SIAM Conference on Parallel Processing for Scientific Computing, pp. 14–24. Society for Industrial and Applied Mathematics (2022). https://doi.org/10.1137/1.9781611977141.2
18. George, J., et al.: A Scalable and Cloud-Native Hyperparameter Tuning System (2020). https://doi.org/10.48550/arXiv.2006.02085
19. Golovin, D., Solnik, B., Moitra, S., Kochanski, G., Karro, J., Sculley, D.: Google Vizier: a service for black-box optimization. In: Proceedings of the 23rd ACM SIGKDD International Conference on Knowledge Discovery and Data Mining, pp. 1487–1495 (2017). https://doi.org/10.1145/3097983.3098043
20. He, K., Zhang, X., Ren, S., Sun, J.: Deep residual learning for image recognition. In: Proceedings of the IEEE Conference on Computer Vision and Pattern Recognition, pp. 770–778 (2016)
21. He, K., Zhang, X., Ren, S., Sun, J.: Identity mappings in deep residual networks. In: Leibe, B., Matas, J., Sebe, N., Welling, M. (eds.) ECCV 2016. LNCS, vol. 9908, pp. 630–645. Springer, Cham (2016). https://doi.org/10.1007/978-3-319-46493-0_38
22. Hertel, L., Collado, J., Sadowski, P., Baldi, P.: Sherpa: hyperparameter optimization for machine learning models. In: 32nd Conference on Neural Information Processing Systems (NIPS 2018) (2018). https://github.com/sherpa-ai/sherpa

23. Holland, J.H.: Adaptation in Natural and Artificial Systems: An Introductory Analysis with Applications to Biology, Control, and Artificial Intelligence. MIT Press, Cambridge (1992). https://doi.org/10.7551/MITPRESS/1090.001.0001

24. Hutter, F., Hoos, H.H., Leyton-Brown, K.: Sequential model-based optimization for general algorithm configuration. In: Coello, C.A.C. (ed.) LION 2011. LNCS, vol. 6683, pp. 507–523. Springer, Heidelberg (2011). https://doi.org/10.1007/978-3-642-25566-3_40

25. Koch, P., Golovidov, O., Gardner, S., Wujek, B., Griffin, J., Xu, Y.: Autotune: a derivative-free optimization framework for hyperparameter tuning. In: Proceedings of the 24th ACM SIGKDD International Conference on Knowledge Discovery & Data Mining, pp. 443–452 (2018). https://doi.org/10.1145/3219819.3219837

26. Liaw, R., Liang, E., Nishihara, R., Moritz, P., Gonzalez, J.E., Stoica, I.: Tune: a research platform for distributed model selection and training (2018). arXiv preprint arXiv:1807.05118

27. Lindauer, M., et al.: SMAC3: a versatile Bayesian optimization package for hyperparameter optimization. J. Mach. Learn. Res. **23**, 54–1 (2022)

28. Lunacek, M., Whitley, D., Sutton, A.: The impact of global structure on search. In: Rudolph, G., Jansen, T., Beume, N., Lucas, S., Poloni, C. (eds.) PPSN 2008. LNCS, vol. 5199, pp. 498–507. Springer, Heidelberg (2008). https://doi.org/10.1007/978-3-540-87700-4_50

29. Luque, G., Alba, E.: Parallel Genetic Algorithms: Theory and Real World Applications, vol. 367. Springer, Berlin, Heidelberg (2011). https://doi.org/10.1007/978-3-642-22084-5

30. Mitchell, M.: An Introduction to Genetic Algorithms. MIT Press, Cambridge (1998)

31. Rapin, J., Teytaud, O.: Nevergrad - A Gradient-free Optimization Platform (2018). https://github.com/FacebookResearch/Nevergrad

32. Snoek, J., Larochelle, H., Adams, R.P.: Practical Bayesian optimization of machine learning algorithms. In: Pereira, F., Burges, C., Bottou, L., Weinberger, K. (eds.) Advances in Neural Information Processing Systems, vol. 25. Curran Associates, Inc. (2012). https://proceedings.neurips.cc/paper/2012/file/05311655a15b75fab86956663e1819cd-Paper.pdf

33. Song, X., Perel, S., Lee, C., Kochanski, G., Golovin, D.: Open source Vizier: distributed infrastructure and API for reliable and flexible blackbox Optimization. In: Automated Machine Learning Conference, Systems Track (AutoML-Conf Systems) (2022). https://github.com/google/vizier

34. Sudholt, D.: Parallel evolutionary algorithms. In: Kacprzyk, J., Pedrycz, W. (eds.) Springer Handbook of Computational Intelligence, pp. 929–959. Springer, Heidelberg (2015). https://doi.org/10.1007/978-3-662-43505-2_46

35. Sumbul, G., et al.: BigEarthNet Dataset with a New Class-Nomenclature for Remote Sensing Image Understanding (2020). arXiv preprint arXiv:2001.06372

36. Toklu, N.E., Atkinson, T., Micka, V., Srivastava, R.K.: EvoTorch: advanced evolutionary computation library built directly on top of PyTorch, created at NNAISENSE (2022). https://github.com/nnaisense/evotorch

37. Tomassini, M.: Spatially Structured Evolutionary Algorithms: Artificial Evolution in Space and Time. Springer, Berlin, Heidelberg (2006). https://doi.org/10.1007/3-540-29938-6

38. Wang, J., Clark, S.C., Liu, E., Frazier, P.I.: Parallel Bayesian global optimization of expensive functions. Oper. Res. **68**(6), 1850–1865 (2020). https://doi.org/10.1287/opre.2019.1966

39. Weiel, M., Götz, M., Klein, A., Coquelin, D., Floca, R., Schug, A.: Dynamic particle swarm optimization of biomolecular simulation parameters with flexible objective functions. Nat. Mach. Intell. **3**(8), 727–734 (2021). https://doi.org/10.1038/s42256-021-00366-3
40. Young, S.R., Rose, D.C., Karnowski, T.P., Lim, S.H., Patton, R.M.: Optimizing deep learning hyper-parameters through an evolutionary algorithm. In: Proceedings of the Workshop on Machine Learning in High-Performance Computing Environments, pp. 1–5 (2015). https://doi.org/10.1145/2834892.2834896

Steering Customized AI Architectures for HPC Scientific Applications

Hatem Ltaief[1(✉)], Yuxi Hong[1], Adel Dabah[1], Rabab Alomairy[1],
Sameh Abdullah[1], Chris Goreczny[3], Pawel Gepner[4], Matteo Ravasi[2],
Damien Gratadour[5], and David Keyes[1]

[1] Division of Computer, Electrical, and Mathematical Sciences and Engineering,
Extreme Computing Research Center, King Abdullah University of Science and
Technology, Thuwal, Jeddah 23955, Saudi Arabia
{Hatem.Ltaief,Yuxi.Hong,Adel.Dabah.1,Rabab.Alomairy,
Sameh.Abdullah,David.Keyes}@kaust.edu.sa
[2] Division of Physical Sciences and Engineering, Extreme Computing Research
Center, King Abdullah University of Science and Technology,
Thuwal, Jeddah 23955, Saudi Arabia
Matteo.Ravasi@kaust.edu.sa
[3] Graphcore, Gdańsk, Poland
chrisgo@graphcore.ai
[4] Warsaw University of Technology, Warsaw, Poland
pawel.gepner@pw.edu.pl
[5] Paris Observatory, Paris, France
damien.gratadour@obspm.fr

Abstract. AI hardware technologies have revolutionized computational
science. While they have been mostly used to accelerate deep learning
training and inference models for machine learning, HPC scientific applications do not seem to directly benefit from these specific hardware
features unless AI-based components are introduced into their simulation workflows, for instance, as a replacement of their numerical solvers.
This paper proposes to take another direction in an attempt to democratize customized AI architectures for HPC scientific computing. The
main idea consists in demonstrating how legacy applications can leverage these AI engines after a necessary algorithmic redesign. It is critical
that the resulting software implementations map onto the underlying
memory-austere hardware architectures to extract the expected performance. To facilitate this process, we promote the matricization technique for restructuring codes (1) by exploiting data sparsity via algebraic
compression and (2) by expressing the critical computational phases in
terms of tile low-rank matrix-vector multiplications (TLR-MVM) and
batch matrix-matrix multiplications (batch GEMM). Algebraic compression enables to reduce memory footprint and to fit into small local
cache/memory, while batch execution ensures high occupancy. We highlight how we can steer the Graphcore AI-focused Wafer-on-Wafer Intelligence Processing Units (IPUs) to deliver high performance for both
operations. We conduct a performance benchmarking campaign of these
two matrix operations that account for most of the elapsed times of four

© The Author(s), under exclusive license to Springer Nature Switzerland AG 2023
A. Bhatele et al. (Eds.): ISC High Performance 2023, LNCS 13948, pp. 125–143, 2023.
https://doi.org/10.1007/978-3-031-32041-5_7

real applications in computational astronomy, seismic imaging, wireless communications, and climate/weather predictions. We report bandwidth and execution rates with speedup factors up to 150X/14X/25X/40X, respectively, on IPUs compared to other systems.

Keywords: BLAS for Graphcore IPU · Low-rank matrix computations · Batch matrix operations · HPC scientific applications

1   Introduction

Heterogeneity is ubiquitous in today's hardware landscape. From large distributed data centers supporting cloud computing to on-premise HPC Supercomputers, the scientific community has witnessed major deployments of mainstream system configurations composed of CPU hosts (e.g., x86/ARM) with accelerator/vector devices. In fact, the adoption of hardware heterogeneity is a clear matter and smartphones equipped with a myriad of specific hardware features (with a neural engine, graphic cores, processing cores, etc.) may represent the ultimate example, which may indicate a pathfinder of where high-end HPC architectures may be heading. While this hardware heterogeneity trend legitimately raises serious concerns on general software development, productivity and sustainability, the advancements of AI-focused hardware technologies have been tremendous during the last decade. These have been supported by a business market continuously expanding in size with applications in natural language processing (with transformers) and computer vision (with convolutional neural network).

This paper demonstrates the capabilities of AI-focused architectures in solving some of the HPC grand-challenge scientific problems in computational astronomy [28], seismic imaging [24,34], wireless communications [10], and climate/weather predictions [5,6,11,13]. In particular, we extend Graphcore AI-focused Wafer-on-Wafer Intelligence Processing Units (IPUs) functionalities [20,21,38] to address the computational challenges raised by the aforementioned applications with regards to real-time constraints and memory-bound mode of execution. The programming efforts required to steer these customized AI accelerators for supporting HPC scientific applications are part of a general call for action. Indeed, while it is true that fast matrix engines may not be inherent to real applications for which sustained bandwidth is the main metric for performance [17], algorithmic innovations are key to make compatible HPC workloads with the underlying AI architectures. This necessitates to express the algorithms in terms of matrix structures to be compliant with the specific features provided by hardware accelerators (e.g., NVIDIA Tensor Cores). Although this may sometimes come at the price of performing more floating-point operations (flops), the computational power of the fast matrix engines may compensate the flops increase. Here, we instead redesign the algorithms that drive the simulations of these four real applications by means of tile low-rank matrix-vector multiplication (TLR-MVM) for the computational astronomy and seismic imaging applications and batch matrix-matrix multiplications (batch GEMM) for the wireless communication and climate/weather applications. The former operation actually reduces memory footprint using algebraic compression to fit in memory-austere environment of IPUs and leverage the high bandwidth of local on-processor memory, while improving time complexity. The latter operation permits to cast original memory-bound operations into batch GEMM operations to improve the hardware occupancy. In particular, MVM accounts for 90% of the real-time controller required on major ground-based deployed telescopes (e.g., the Very Large Telescope [4], the Keck Observatory [2], the Subaru telescope [3], the European Extremely Large Telescope [1], etc.) to compensate for the atmospheric turbulence. For the seismic imaging application, TLR-MVM accounts for 90% of the total elapsed time, as highlighted in Fig. 1 of [24]. As for the batch GEMM kernel, it accounts for 80% of the total elapsed time of the wireless communication [10,15] as well as the climate/weather applications [13,14]. These algorithmic changes turn out to be key in extracting performance across various architectures [11,13,24,28], but most importantly, makes IPUs (and potentially similar wafer-on-wafer chip technologies with limited on-chip memory) and their resource disaggregation compatible with these HPC scientific applications.

We develop TLR-MVM and batch GEMM operations on IPUs and report time-to-solution, sustained bandwidth, and execution rate. The two latter metrics permit to assess how some of the memory-bound workloads on standard x86 or GPUs can translate into compute-bound mode of operation (from an absolute performance perspective) once deployed on IPUs. We compare our implementations against other hardware architectures and highlight the performance superiority of our numerical algorithms. We achieve on IPUs speedup factors up to 150X/14X/25X/40X for computational astronomy, seismic imaging, wireless communication, and climate/weather predictions, respectively, against a myriad of hardware systems. These speedups correspond to the performance improvement of the most time-consuming kernels from these applications that are offloaded to IPUs, while the remaining ones run on the host, similar to the hybrid CPU/GPU trend observed in the HPC community.

The remainder of the paper is as follows. Section 2 presents related work and list our main contributions. Section 3 recalls the batch execution model and the TLR-MVM algorithm, while emphasizing on the importance of the matrization when designing numerical algorithms to remain on par with the AI hardware evolution. We present the Graphcore IPU hardware technology in Sect. 4. Section 5 describes the four HPC scientific applications of interest in this paper. We provide implementations details of our numerical algorithms in Sect. 6. Section 7 reports the performance results in time-to-solution, sustained bandwidth, and execution rate obtained on IPUs and compare our implementation against other hardware architectures. Section 8 discusses current IPU hardware limitations and gives some perspectives moving forward to further steer IPUs as a general-purpose chip. We conclude in Sect. 9.

2 Related Work and Research Contributions

Leveraging AI-focussed hardware architectures for general-purpose HPC workloads is still at its infancy due to the significant efforts it requires to map the existing numerical algorithms on these chips, originally designed for machine learning workloads (i.e., training and inference) as studied in [9,26]. Previous work for accelerating breadth-first graph traversals on IPUs [12] have demonstrated performance improvement for the class of graph algorithms. Stencil computations for solving the 3D wave equation using finite-difference method in seismic imaging applications have been ported into Graphcore IPU [26] and Cerebras Wafer-Scale Engine (WSE-2) [25]. The authors in the latter work rely on a localized communication strategy to mitigate internal data movement overheads, while ensuring data locality for maximum bandwidth extraction from local flat on-chip memory. This matrix-free algorithmic approach that represents the core engine for PDE solvers is friendly to Graphcore and Cerebras hardware technologies thanks to its minimal memory footprint.

In this paper, we revisit the numerical algorithms of real HPC applications, as originally introduced in computational astronomy [28], seismic imaging [24, 34], wireless communications [10], and climate/weather predictions [5,13]. We integrate low-rank matrix compressions and batch executions to reconcile them with IPU hardware design. Based on the numerical kernel primitives used for machine learning on IPUs, we develop these operations by composing higher-level APIs for linear algebra operations, i.e., Level-2 and Level-3 BLAS routines, that were not available natively on the vendor-optimized numerical library. We further tune memory accesses of our algorithms on IPUs and achieve significant performance improvement.

We emphasize the three main contributions of this paper: (1) the matricization approach that enables these HPC applications, otherwise intractable, to exploit IPUs by casting computations on compressed data structures, (2) the batch mode of execution to maintain high hardware utilization, and (3) the reported significant performance speedups that may further democratize AI hardware and accelerate their adoption into the wide HPC application landscape on heterogeneous environments.

3 Batching/Compression or Why Matricization Matters?

We are interested in leveraging IPU computational and throughput capabilities to accelerate HPC scientific applications that rely on matrix formulations. We employ batched kernel executions to map the matrix operation onto IPU local memory and address the resource disaggragation challenge. In addition, if the dataset is large and does not fit on the chip, we exploit Tile Low-Rank (TLR) matrix approximation, an algorithmic technique that consists in splitting the matrix operator into tiles and compressing them using an algebraic method of choice (e.g., rank-revealing QR, randomized SVD, etc.), while enabling matrix algebra on the compressed data structures. Figures 1–6 highlight the compression

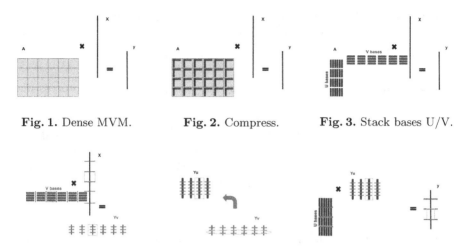

Fig. 1. Dense MVM.   **Fig. 2.** Compress.   **Fig. 3.** Stack bases U/V.

Fig. 4. V-Batch of MVM.   **Fig. 5.** Slicing V->U.   **Fig. 6.** U-Batch of MVM.

procedure for a 4×6 tiled matrix followed by the Matrix-Vector Multiplication (MVM) applied to its compressed form. We refer to [6,7,28] for more technical details. The approximation error introduced is controlled by an accuracy threshold that maintains the application's numerical integrity [5,13,24,34].

Matricization is an approach for enabling numerical algorithms to track AI hardware evolution so that the specific hardware features (e.g., fast matrix engines with support for mixed-precision computations) can be easily integrated and adopted by HPC scientific applications. There is no free lunch and matricization may not be straightforward for all applications. However, when possible, the redesigning efforts may be worth it and these efforts are usually upfront. The main benefits of matricization are twofold: (1) significant performance improvement in bandwidth for memory-bound codes and higher execution rates for compute-bound kernels thanks to dedicated matrix engines (e.g., Intel AMX, NVIDIA Tensor Cores, Graphcore AMP), while being on par with the overall hardware evolution, and (2) high user-productivity when deploying on new hardware architectures across vendors.

4   The Graphcore IPU Hardware Technology

4.1   Architecture Principles and Hardware Details

The Bulk Synchronous Parallel (BSP) model forms the basis for the hardware architecture of Graphcore's Bow Intelligence Processing Unit (IPU) and Poplar graph framework software. The BSP model is fundamental to the operation of IPU processors, which use this parallel computing scheme to schedule data processing and exchange operations. BSP involves a three-step process alternating compute, communication and data synchronisation.

Asynchronous Computation. Each process performs local computations using only local memory. This phase does not involve any communication between processes.

Communication. Data is exchanged by the processes and each process may communicate with its target counterpart. In addition to exchanging intermediate computation results, processes may also engage in remote direct memory access in which they request access to data from remote memories. This remote data is then received in a subsequent communication phase. Each process can therefore access other local memory as a remote memory, effectively enabling it to retrieve any memory from the entire aggregate system memory.

Synchronization. The synchronization phase acts as a check point or barrier. Once a process reaches this phase, it will only continue to the next phase once all processes have reached this check point. This stage does not involve any computation or communication unless the barrier itself specifically requires this.

In terms of its hardware architecture, the IPU is defined as a massively parallel, distributed memory, multiple-instruction, multiple data (MIMD) processor. The IPU has been designed from the ground up to process machine learning algorithms, with explicit programming instructions. The IPU's tile Instruction Set Architecture-ISA [37] comprises of hardware elements such as Accumulating Matrix Product-AMP units (i.e., dot product) and Slim Convolution Units-SLICs, which enable the IPU to complete up to 64 multiply-add instructions per clock cycle. These AMP units are eventually used to compose the necessary kernels and accelerate the HPC applications studied in this paper.

4.2 Programming Model and Poplar Development Kit

Graphcore's Poplar software is designed alongside the IPU to serve as a programming interface. Poplar is a graph programming framework that enables direct programming in Python and C++, building on the capability of C++ to form a new IPU operation model founded on three elements - vertices, computation graphs and control programs. The IPU computation graphs define the input/output relationship between variables and operations. Within the computation graph, there are tensor variables (i.e., the variables in the graph), the compute tasks (vertices) and the edges that connect them. In terms of the tensor variables, data is stored in the graph in fixed-size multi-dimensional tensors. A vertex is a specific task to be performed and the edges determine which variable elements the vertex should process. A vertex can connect to a single element or multiple elements. A codelet is associated with every vertex: this is a piece of code that defines the inputs, outputs and internal state of a vertex. The codelet is implemented in assembly or standard C++11 [26]. Finally, we have the control program, which organizes the selection of processors, loads compiled graphs into the hardware and then executes graph programs. This includes the mapping of data transfers between the IPU and the host, memory structures, and initiating transfers. As soon as the program has been implemented, all the code and data structures required to run the program sit in the IPU's distributed memory [26]. Thanks to the control programs, the appropriate vertices can be executed. On top of low-level Poplar framework, Graphcore provides a PopLibs C++ library that contains higher-level mathematical and machine-learning functions. These underlie the Graphcore implementation of industry-standard ML frameworks, such as TensorFlow and PyTorch, but can also be used for other purposes. The massive parallelism and memory locality of IPU processor is well abstracted by PopLibs. For large data operations like matrix-matrix multiplications, Graphcore software handles the work distribution between IPU tiles to keep even memory and compute utilisation across all cores for load balancing purposes.

5   HPC Scientific Applications

This section describes the background of four major HPC applications in computational astronomy [28], seismic imaging [24,34], wireless communications [10], and climate/weather predictions [5,11,13]. We identify the necessary algorithmic changes before deploying the most time-consuming computational kernels on Graphcore IPUs.

5.1   Adaptive Optics in Computational Astronomy

Using Deformable Mirrors (DM), arranged in closed-loop feedback control with wavefront sensors (WFS) in Adaptive Optics (AO) systems [16], correcting for optical aberrations introduced by atmospheric turbulence, giant optical telescopes are able to acquire sharp high-contrast images of faint and distant targets. As shown in Fig. 7, the real-time controller (RTC) [18] is responsible for interpreting measurements from WFS into commands to the DM actuators, adapting in real-time to the rapidly changing atmospheric turbulence conditions. Thanks to advances in computing, WFS and DM technologies, AO systems are becoming more capable and can be deployed on today's largest ground-based telescopes. However, classical AO correction is only valid in a very small patch of sky. Multi-Conjugate Adaptive Optics (MCAO) solves this by using a series of DMs to compensate the turbulence in volume [35]. This increase in AO complexity inevitably translates into a significant additional load on the RTC sub-system.

A robust control scheme for AO is based on regular dense Matrix-Vector Multiplication (MVM), which has a low arithmetic intensity and is thus limited by sustained memory bandwidth. Assuming a typical atmosphere coherence time of a few ms and in order to compensate for most of the accessible frequency content of the turbulence, the AO RTC latency should be kept below 250 μs [22]. This 250 μs specification leads to a memory bandwidth requirement of about 1600 GB/s for single precision floating-point MVM, i.e., several times larger than what is achievable on current high-end dual-socket CPU servers and typically even higher than on a single high-end GPU. Can the IPUs stand as an alternative hardware solution to outsmart the atmospheric turbulence and meet the real-time computational challenges of ground-based giant optical telescopes? A batched dense MVM is necessary to evenly split the matrix across local memories of the IPUs and match the underlying IPU hardware architecture.

5.2   Seismic Processing and Imaging

Reflection seismology is a remote sensing technique that uses principles of wave propagation to image the Earth's subsurface from reflected seismic waves. Most algorithms for processing and imaging of seismic data, originally developed in the 80's and 90's, operate on individual shot gathers (i.e., ensemble of traces recording the energy produced by a single source at the time); this naturally lends to embarrassingly parallel implementations that loop over the dataset once per processing step. A paradigm shift has however emerged in the early 2000s, with a large portion of modern algorithms relying on wave-equation, inversion-based formulations [42]: such algorithms require repeated access to the entire seismic data in order to evaluate the so-called Multi-Dimensional Convolution (MDC) operator and its adjoint and solve an underlying inverse problem. Examples of such a kind are closed-loop SRME [27], estimation of primaries by sparse inversion [23], multi-dimensional deconvolution [8,33,39], and Marchenko-based processing and imaging [30,31,40,44].

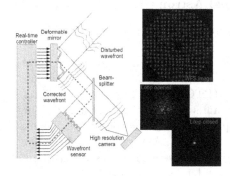
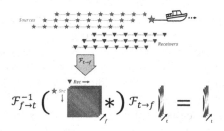

Fig. 7. End-to-end AO simulation [19] relies on MVM in the RTC to outsmart the atmospheric turbulence.

Fig. 8. From seismic acquisition to processing data for the MDC operator that involves TLR-MVM operations.

From a practical standpoint, the MDC operator can be viewed as the chain of the following three linear operations: a Fast Fourier Transform (FFT) to convert the input seismic data from the time to the frequency domain, followed by a batched dense Matrix-Vector Multiplication (MVM) with the frequency representation of the kernel of the MDC operator, and by an Inverse FFT (IFFT) to bring back the output to the time domain (see Fig. 8 and [24,32,34] for more details). Whilst the kernel of the MDC operator varies from application to application, its sheer size renders the batched MVM to be the main computational bottleneck of all of the above mentioned algorithms. As discussed in Sect. 3, TLR-MVM can be used in an attempt to reduce both the memory requirements and computational cost. When performing MDC with dense frequency matrices, the arrangement of sources (along the rows of each matrix) and receivers (along the columns of each matrix) can be arbitrary as long as they remain consistent with that of the input vector. Such reordering becomes much more relevant in the context of TLR algebraic compression as it may lead to better or worse block compression capabilities. Following [34], the Hilbert space-filling curve algorithm has been chosen as the best performing re-arrangement approach. We refer to [24,34] for a detailed study on the impact of accuracy. Compression and reordering are key algorithmic aspects to consider, when deploying big data applications on hardware with limited memory capacities, e.g., IPUs.

5.3   Climate/Weather Prediction Applications

Geostatistical emulations for climate/weather prediction applications rely on computational statistics methods based on the maximum likelihood estimation. The optimization model requires solving a large system of linear equations. This involves a Cholesky factorization of the covariance matrix of dimension the number of geospatial locations, at every iteration of the optimization process. To reduce algorithmic complexity and memory footprint, we exploit the data sparsity structure of the operator and perform TLR matrix approximation based on algebraic compression, as originally introduced in [5,6,13,14]. This necessitates the development of new kernels composed of several successive calls to BLAS/LAPACK functions (e.g., QR/GEMM/SVD), including the most time-consuming, i.e., TLR-GEMM operating on thin-shaped pairs of U/V matrices using the lower part of the symmetric matrix. To increase hardware occupancy, a left-looking variant of the TLR-Cholesky is employed in [11], which then permits to expose opportunities for batched GEMM kernel executions. For instance, Fig. 9 shows the updates on the matrix tile in red that requires batched GEMMs involving the compressed tiles located in the green/yellow/blue (overlapped) regions. These algorithmic steps are critical to make the IPU compatible with such big data applications otherwise intractable.

5.4   Wireless Communications

The increased number of connected devices and data demand under extreme low latency puts today's base station under a huge burden. Massive Multiple-Input Multiple-Output (M-MIMO) technology uses hundreds of antennas at base-station to fulfill the requirement of next-generation networks in terms of data rate and service quality while supporting a huge number of connected devices. However, this technology suffers from high signal detection complexity and accuracy, which is critical for several applications, such as self-driving cars.

Indeed, reducing M-MIMO detection latency to meet the real-time requirement while guaranteeing good detection accuracy represents a challenging problem. Linear detection algorithms maintain low complexity. However, their lack of reliability cannot be accepted [43]. Optimal non-linear detection approaches [41] have high accuracy, but they are not scalable due to the M-MIMO exponential complexity. The multi-level detection approach proposed in [10,15] is a promising scalable and accurate approach for M-MIMO detection problem. It iteratively extends a single path with several symbols within L levels until reaching a complete solution path with the shortest distance among all existing paths. These symbols represent the best combination of aggregating multiple levels. This technique increases the accuracy in terms of error rate performance since it uses coefficients from multiple levels to better distinguish the optimal path. As a result, the more levels used, the more confident we are in getting near-optimal solutions.

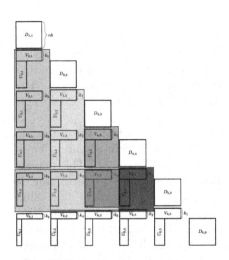

Fig. 9. Tile low-rank Cholesky factorization powered by a batch GEMM for climate applications.

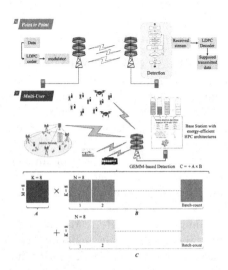

Fig. 10. Massive MIMO workflow powered by a batch GEMM detection for wireless communication.

The computation of these distances can be casted in terms of small matrix-matrix multiplication operations (i.e., GEMM) with dimensions M=K=L and N the number of paths within the window. These well-established GEMM kernels increase the arithmetic intensity of the algorithm and may account up to 80% of the global execution time of the method. However, as highlighted in Fig. 10, the resulting matrix generated by this multi-level algorithm has a short and wide shape, which may prevent it from extracting the full hardware potential, especially in presence of disaggregated memory resources as in IPUs. The single short and wide GEMM must be redesigned into a batched GEMM, while mapping each B_i and C_i blocks along with A onto the local memory.

6   Implementation Details

In the case of the Graphcore Poplar SDK, all linear algebra operations like MVM and GEMM are exposed in form of the PopLibs C++ API that was built from the ground up as a foundation for AI frameworks such as PyTorch and TensorFlow. It is well optimized for this task and allows the user to leverage a high number of independent tiles without needing to manually split the workload among them. It is also based on the concept of computation graphs whereby all compute operations are first compiled into one or more graphs and only then run in this form on the IPU. Those two assumptions make the PopLibs API very different from the standard BLAS interface where parallelism is handled outside of BLAS and compute kernels are run as soon as they are called. It is not straightforward to create a translation layer of BLAS calls which the CPU implementation of TLR-MVM is dependent on to be used on the PopLibs API.

The logical equivalent of MVM and GEMM BLAS calls in FP32 in PopLibs is the matMul function. For the computational astronomy applications, the real datasets fit in IPU local memory so a single call to PopLibs matMul function can be issued, while ensuring proper mapping is done onto the disaggregated memory resources to achieved the required throughput. For the seismic imaging application and its large datasets, the TLR-MVM algorithm comes to the rescue to reconcile the IPU architecture with the application. TLR-MVM algorithm performs multiple MVM kernels on stacked tile columns (Fig. 4) and rows (Fig. 6), with in-between intermediate slicing phase (Fig. 5). PopLibs offers a matMulGrouped call that aggregates multiple independent MVM or GEMM into a single call and schedules all of them to be performed in parallel, distributed amongst IPU tiles. The TLR-MVM implementations on IPUs comes down to a sequence of three functions, as described in Algorithm 1: (1) perform batched MVM on the group of matrix-vector pairs where each pair consists of stacked tile column V_j and corresponding nb portion of the input vector x to get the set of output vectors Yv, (2) project/slice the set of output vectors Yv from V_j bases to U_j bases to get the set of output vectors Yu, and (3) perform batched MVM on group of matrix-vector pairs where each pair consists of stacked tile row U_i and corresponding output vector column of Yu. However, the dimensions in all multiplications must be equal. In TLR-MVM, each stacked tile column/row can have different dimensions after matrix compression, as seen for the seismic imaging application. To leverage the parallelism capabilities of PopLibs, it is then necessary to make all dimensions equal to avoid overheads from stragglers due to the BSP model of IPU, as explained in Sect. 4. Therefore, as shown in Algorithm 2, we need to pad stacked tiles columns/rows with zeros at least up to the size of the biggest element. The actual size of padding is then determined empirically to deliver the best performance with acceptable overheads on memory utilization.

For the climate application, the large dense data-sparse matrix needs to be compressed first using TLR algebraic compression [6,13,14]. The TLR Cholesky factorization can then be redesigned in a left-looking variant [11] to further expose batched GEMM operations that account for most of the elapsed time.

Algorithm 1: Poplar pseudo-code of TLR-MVM.

1: Yv = poplin::matMulGrouped(V,X) (i.e., batch MVM of V bases, see Fig. 4)
2: Yu = popops::multiSlice(Yv) (i.e., project from Yv to Yu via slicing, see Fig. 5)
3: Y = poplin::matMulGrouped(U,Yu) (i.e., batch MVM of U bases, see Fig. 6)

For the wireless communication application, the redesign of the detection algorithm into an efficient GEMM-based approach [10,15] enables to leverage high throughput of customized hardware features for such a massively parallel operation. Both applications can offload their batched GEMM on IPUs by using PopLibs matMulGrouped function to address the computational and curse of dimensionality challenges for the former and to meet the real-time constraints for the latter by achieving high hardware occupancy.

Algorithm 2: Pseudo-code of the offline zero padding step.

Require: Compress A
Ensure: max = 0
1: **for** each tile column **do**
2:     **if** sum of ranks > max **then**
3:         max = sum of ranks
4:     **end if**
5: **end for**
6: **for** each tile row **do**
7:     **if** sum of ranks > max **then**
8:         max = sum of ranks

9:     **end if**
10: **end for**
11: mod = 200 (identified empirically)
12: max = max + mod - max % mod
13: **for** each stacked tile column V_i **do**
14:     append (max - sum of ranks) zeros
15: **end for**
16: **for** each stacked tile row U_i **do**
17:     append (max - sum of ranks) zeros
18: **end for**

---

7   Performance Results

Vendor	Intel	AMD	Fujitsu	NEC	NVIDIA	Graphcore
Family	Cascade Lake	EPYC Milan	Primergy A64FX	SX-Aurora TSUBASA	Ampere GPU	IPU
Model	6248	7713	FX1000	B300-8	A100	Bow
Node(s)/Card(s)	1	1	16	8	1	1
Socket(s)	2	2	4	N/A	N/A	1
Cores	40	128	48	8	6912	1472
GHz	2.5	2.0	2.2	1.6	2.6	1.85
Memory	384GB DDR4	512GB DDR4	32GB HBM	48GB HBM2	40GB HBM2e	3.6GB
Sustained BW	232GB/s	330GB/s	800GB/s	1.5TB/s	1.5TB/s	261TB/s
LLC	27.5MB	512MB	32MB	16MB	40MB	N/A
Sustained BW	1.1TB/s	4TB/s	3.6TB/s	2.1TB/s	4.8TB/s	
Compiler	Intel 19.1.0	GCC 7.5.0	Fujitsu 4.5.0	NEC 3.1.1	NVCC 11.0	POPLAR 2.6
BLAS library	Intel MKL 2020	BLIS 3.0.0	Fujitsu SSL II	NEC NLC 2.1.0	cuBLAS 11.0	N/A
MPI library	OpenMPI 4.0.3	OpenMPI 3.1.2	Fujitsu MPI 4.0.1	NEC MPI 2.13.0	NCCL 2.0	N/A

x86 - ARM - Vector	GPU
MPI + OpenMP	CUDA

Fig. 11. Hardware/software descriptions and programming models.

The experiments are carried on six architectures, i.e., Intel IceLake (codenamed ICX), AMD Epyc Milan (Milan), Fujitsu A64FX (A64FX), NEC SX-Aurora

TSUBASA (Aurora), NVIDIA A100 GPU (A100), and Graphcore Bow IPUs (IPUs). A detailed hardware and software descriptions along with the programming models are illustrated in Fig. 11. We report performance from the median obtained out of 1000 runs on IPUs. All computations are performed using IEEE 754 FP32 arithmetic.

Figure 12 shows the performance of batched dense MVM for the astronomy application. The main numerical kernel, i.e., FP32 Level-2 BLAS MVM, is deployed on single IPU using the real datasets from the MAVIS flagship MCAO instrument for ESO's Very Large Telescope [36], which engenders batched MVM operations on a 5K X 20K matrix size [28] to be performed in real-time. Our batched dense MVM implementation on IPUs achieves 5X speedup factor against Aurora and up to 150X against Milan (DDR4 memory). In terms of absolute performance, our batched dense MVM implementation scores 2 Tflops/s for a Level-2 BLAS operation that is usually limited in performance by the bus bandiwdth. To give a perspective, the obtained performance is equivalent to half of LINPACK benchmark (FP32) on the two-socket 26-core Intel IceLake system.

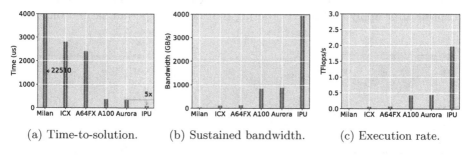

(a) Time-to-solution.   (b) Sustained bandwidth.   (c) Execution rate.

Fig. 12. Performance of Dense MVM for the astronomy application.

For the seismic imaging application, the batched dense MVM is not an option anymore for IPUs since the large matrix size in addition to the single complex precision do not allow the matrix to fit on the on-chip memory. Therefore, we have to use TLR algebraic compression on the matrix and deploy our TLR-MVM kernel. We design our single complex TLR-MVM into two FP32 TLR-MVM for handling the real and imaginary parts. With TLR matrix approximations, the matrices can now fit into the local memory of the IPUs. To further improve performance, we apply two optimizations: reordering and padding, as explained in Sects. 5.2 and 6, respectively. The former reduces memory footprint and time complexity, while the latter ensures load balance on IPUs. Figure 13 shows the impact of padding (represented by the stairs shape since matrices are clustered into bins to mitigate the padding overheads) in terms of MB with limited overhead on all frequency matrices using the default and Hilbert ordering schemes.

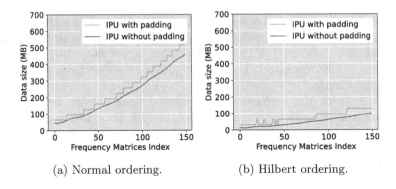

(a) Normal ordering.   (b) Hilbert ordering.

Fig. 13. Overhead (in MB) of padding for the seismic imaging application.

Figure 14 shows the performance of TLR-MVM for the seismic imaging application using Hilbert ordering on two IPUs. We do not show the slower performance obtained for the default ordering due to space limitation. The scalability on two IPUs is a bit limited but this is also expected due to the small memory footprint after applying Hilbert ordering that does not permit saturation.

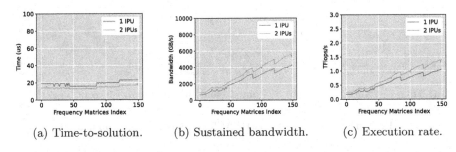

(a) Time-to-solution.   (b) Sustained bandwidth.   (c) Execution rate.

Fig. 14. TLR-MVM performance for the seismic application on two IPUs.

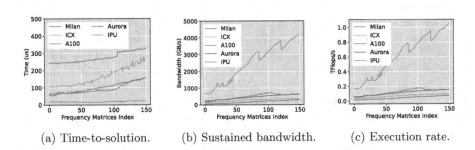

(a) Time-to-solution.   (b) Sustained bandwidth.   (c) Execution rate.

Fig. 15. TLR-MVM performance comparisons for the seismic application.

Figure 15 highlights performance comparisons of TLR-MVM on 150 frequency matrices for the seismic imaging application against other hardware architectures. Our TLR-MVM implementation achieves up to 14X performance speedup against Milan. In terms of absolute performance, our implementation scores more than 1 Tflops/s for a kernel that is intrinsically memory-bound.

Figure 16 shows the performance of batched GEMM for wireless communication and climate prediction applications. We only compare against GPUs since x86/ARM/Vector are not meant for compute-bound kernels. The wireless communication batch size ($M = N = K = 8$) comes from aggregating four tree levels, resulting in a real matrix A with eight rows and columns. The batch count, on the other hand, refers to the total number of possible combinations. For instance, aggregating four levels with 32-QAM modulation generates 8M combinations computed resulting in a batch count close to 1M. The batched GEMM in the climate application needs to be grouped until each single matrix block fits the local memory, while ensuring an even workload distribution. Compared to [10] (but rerun on NVIDIA A100 with 1.1 Tflops/s) and [11] (results obtained on NVIDIA V100 with 1.1 Tflops/s), we achieve 25X and 40X for wireless communication and climate applications, respectively. By launching these kernels in batched mode, we activate all tiles on the IPUs, allowing high absolute performance, while preserving the integrity of the IPU hardware resource disaggregation.

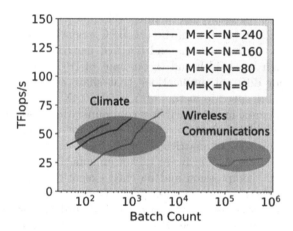

Fig. 16. Batched GEMM performance for MIMO and climate applications.

8   Limitations and Perspectives

While the paper demonstrates the capabilities of IPUs, there are some areas for improvement for Poplar SDK, e.g., enabling support for a standard BLAS/LAPACK interface. Currently, porting HPC applications based on TLR-MVM kernels requires the developer to write a separate implementation for IPU that is fundamentally different from industry-standard solutions. This type of support is a challenging task to accomplish considering how the Poplar SDK is designed. However, Graphcore is already working on delivering this. For instance, this will enable to run the compression phase on IPUs instead of the host and ensure the whole computational pipeline is resident on the chip. While this may not be a problem for seismic imaging application since the compression is needed only once upfront, it may raise performance bottlenecks for the climate/weather applications application that requires matrix factorization and solve at every iteration of the optimization procedure. One element that has not been mentioned yet is the graph compilation time. Poplar builds one compute graph that contains all the operations instead of running small compute kernels. This allows for greater runtime performance as there is very little communication required between the x86 host and the IPU. It also allows Poplar to apply multiple graph-level optimisations that further improves performance, but at the cost of graph compilation time increase. In some cases, this can become problematic and reach minutes of x86 host time to perform a fraction of a second of compute on the IPU. Whereas it can work very well for AI tasks when the same set of operations is run thousands of times, this can become problematic for the one-time compute kernels which are commonplace in HPC.

9   Conclusion and Future Work

This paper presents necessary algorithmic techniques to make the Graphcore Bow IPUs compliant with state-of-the-art HPC scientific applications. Based on low-rank matrix approximations and batched matrix-matrix multiplication, we leverage the high bandwidth and throughput of IPUs and deliver high performance with four different applications that share common matrix algebra operations. We report speedup factors up to 150X/14X/25X/40X for computational astronomy, seismic imaging, wireless communication, and climate/weather predictions, respectively, against a myriad of hardware architectures. This highlights the need to pursue the matricization efforts to ensure HPC applications can keep up with latest AI hardware advancements. In terms of algorithmic innovation, algebraic compression and batched execution appear to be critical ingredients with a significant impact on performance and throughput, not only on IPUs as studied herein, but also on a myriad of hardware architectures from a relative performance perspective. For future work, we would like to explore FP16 for some of these HPC applications and demonstrate the applicability of mixed-precision computations [29].

References

1. The European Extremely Large Telescope (2023). https://elt.eso.org/
2. The Keck Observatory (2023). https://keckobservatory.org/
3. The Subaru Telescope (2023). https://www.subarutelescope.org/en/
4. The Very Large Telescope (2023). https://www.eso.org/public/teles-instr/paranal-observatory/vlt/

5. Abdulah, S., Ltaief, H., Sun, Y., Genton, M.G., Keyes, D.E.: ExaGeoStat: a high performance unified software for geostatistics on manycore systems. IEEE Trans. Parallel Distrib. Syst. **29**(12), 2771–2784 (2018). https://doi.org/10.1109/TPDS. 2018.2850749

6. Akbudak, K., Ltaief, H., Mikhalev, A., Keyes, D.: Tile low rank Cholesky factorization for climate/weather modeling applications on manycore architectures. In: Kunkel, J.M., Yokota, R., Balaji, P., Keyes, D. (eds.) ISC High Performance 2017. LNCS, vol. 10266, pp. 22–40. Springer, Cham (2017). https://doi.org/10.1007/978-3-319-58667-0_2

7. Amestoy, P., Ashcraft, C., Boiteau, O., Buttari, A., L'Excellent, J.Y., Weisbecker, C.: Improving multifrontal methods by means of block low-rank representations. SIAM J. Sci. Comput. **37**(3), A1451–A1474 (2015)

8. Amundsen, L.: Elimination of free-surface related multiples without need of a source wavelet. Geophysics **66**, 327–341 (2001)

9. Arcelin, B.: Comparison of Graphcore IPUs and Nvidia GPUs for cosmology applications (2021). https://doi.org/10.48550/ARXIV.2106.02465

10. Arfaoui, M.A., Ltaief, H., Rezki, Z., Alouini, M.S., Keyes, D.: Efficient sphere detector algorithm for massive MIMO using GPU hardware accelerator. Procedia Comput. Sci. **80**, 2169–2180 (2016). https://doi.org/10.1016/j.procs.2016.05.377

11. Boukaram, W., Zampini, S., Turkiyyah, G., Keyes, D.E.: H2OPUS-TLR: high performance tile low rank symmetric factorizations using adaptive randomized approximation. CoRR abs/2108.11932 (2021)

12. Burchard, L., Moe, J., Schroeder, D.T., Pogorelov, K., Langguth, J.: iPUG: accelerating breadth-first graph traversals using manycore Graphcore IPUs. In: Chamberlain, B.L., Varbanescu, A.-L., Ltaief, H., Luszczek, P. (eds.) ISC High Performance 2021. LNCS, vol. 12728, pp. 291–309. Springer, Cham (2021). https://doi.org/10. 1007/978-3-030-78713-4_16

13. Cao, Q., et al.: Reshaping geostatistical modeling and prediction for extreme-scale environmental applications. In: Proceedings of the International Conference for High Performance Computing, Networking, Storage and Analysis (2022). https:// doi.org/10.5555/3571885.3571888

14. Cao, Q., et al.: Extreme-scale task-based cholesky factorization toward climate and weather prediction applications. In: Proceedings of the Platform for Advanced Scientific Computing Conference, pp. 1–11 (2020)

15. Dabah, A., Ltaief, H., Rezki, Z., Arfaoui, M.A., Alouini, M.S., Keyes, D.: Performance/complexity trade-offs of the sphere decoder algorithm for massive MIMO systems. arXiv preprint arXiv:2002.09561 (2020)

16. Davies, R., Kasper, M.: Adaptive optics for astronomy. Annu. Rev. Astron. Astrophys. **50**(1), 305–351 (2012). https://doi.org/10.1146/annurev-astro-081811-125447

17. Domke, J., et al.: Matrix engines for high performance computing: a paragon of performance or grasping at straws? In: IPDPS, pp. 1056–1065. IEEE (2021). https:// doi.org/10.1109/IPDPS49936.2021.00114

18. Ferreira, F., et al.: Hard real-time core software of the AO RTC COSMIC platform: architecture and performance. In: Schreiber, L., Schmidt, D., Vernet, E. (eds.) Adaptive Optics Systems VII. vol. 11448, p. 1144815. International Society for Optics and Photonics, SPIE (2020). https://doi.org/10.1117/12.2561244

19. Ferreira, F., Gratadour, D., Sevin, A., Doucet, N.: Compass: an efficient GPU-based simulation software for adaptive optics system. In: 2018 International Conference on High Performance Computing and Simulation (HPCS), pp. 180–187 (2018). https://doi.org/10.1109/HPCS.2018.00043

20. Gepner, P.: Machine learning and high-performance computing hybrid systems, a new way of performance acceleration in engineering and scientific applications. In: 2021 16th Conference on Computer Science and Intelligence Systems (FedCSIS), pp. 27–36 (2021). https://doi.org/10.15439/2021F004

21. Graphcore: Tile Vertex ISA (2022). https://docs.graphcore.ai/projects/isa/en/latest/_static/Tile-Vertex-ISA_1.2.3.pdf

22. Gratadour, D,, et al.: MAVIS real-time control system: a high-end implementation of the COSMIC platform. In: Schreiber, L., Schmidt, D., Vernet, E. (eds.) Adaptive Optics Systems VII, vol. 11448, p. 114482M. International Society for Optics and Photonics, SPIE (2020). https://doi.org/10.1117/12.2562082

23. van Groenestijn, G.J., Verschuur, D.J.: Estimating primaries by sparse inversion and application to near-offset data reconstruction. Geophysics **74**, 1MJ–Z54 (2009). https://doi.org/10.1190/1.3111115

24. Hong, Y., Ltaief, H., Ravasi, M., Gatineau, L., Keyes, D.: Accelerating seismic redatuming using tile low-rank approximations on NEC SX-Aurora TSUBASA. Supercomput. Front. Innov. **8** (2021). https://doi.org/10.14529/jsfi210201

25. Jacquelin, M., Araya-Polo, M., Meng, J.: Scalable distributed high-order stencil computations. In: Proceedings of the International Conference for High Performance Computing, Networking, Storage and Analysis (2022). https://doi.org/10.5555/3571885.3571924

26. Jia, Z., Tillman, B., Maggioni, M., Scarpazza, D.P.: Dissecting the Graphcore IPU architecture via microbenchmarking. arXiv preprint arXiv:1912.03413 (2019)

27. Lopez, G.A., Verschuur, D.: Closed-loop surface-related multiple elimination and its application to simultaneous data reconstruction. Geophysics **80**, V189–V199 (2015). https://doi.org/10.1190/geo2015-0287.1

28. Ltaief, H., Cranney, J., Gratadour, D., Hong, Y., Gatineau, L., Keyes, D.: Meeting the real-time challenges of ground-based telescopes using low-rank matrix computations. In: Proceedings of the International Conference for High Performance Computing, Networking, Storage and Analysis (2021). https://doi.org/10.1145/3458817.3476225

29. Ltaief, H., Genton, M.G., Gratadour, D., Keyes, D.E., Ravasi, M.: Responsibly reckless matrix algorithms for HPC scientific applications. Comput. Sci. Eng. **24**(4), 12–22 (2022). https://doi.org/10.1109/MCSE.2022.3215477

30. van der Neut, J., Vasconcelos, I., Wapenaar, K.: On Green's function retrieval by iterative substitution of the coupled Marchenko equations. Geophys. J. Int. **203**, 792–813 (2015). https://doi.org/10.1093/gji/ggv330

31. Ravasi, M.: Rayleigh-Marchenko redatuming for target-oriented, true-amplitude imaging. Geophysics **82**, S439–S452 (2017). https://doi.org/10.1190/geo2017-0262.1

32. Ravasi, M., Vasconcelos, I.: An open-source framework for the implementation of large-scale integral operators with flexible, modern HPC solutions - enabling 3D Marchenko imaging by least-squares inversion. Geophysics **86**, WC177–WC194 (2021). https://doi.org/10.1190/geo2020-0796.1

33. Ravasi, M., Vasconcelos, I., Curtis, A., Kritski, A.: Multi-dimensional free-surface multiple elimination and source deblending of Volve OBC data. In: 77th Conference and Exhibition, EAGE, Extended Abstracts (2015). https://doi.org/10.3997/2214-4609.201413355

34. Ravasi, M., Hong, Y., Ltaief, H., Keyes, D., Vargas, D.: Large-scale Marchenko imaging with distance-aware matrix reordering, tile low-rank compression, pp. 2606–2610 (2022). https://doi.org/10.1190/image2022-3744978.1

35. Rigaut, F., Neichel, B.: Multiconjugate adaptive optics for astronomy. Annu. Rev. Astron. Astrophys. **56**(1), 277–314 (2018)
36. Rigaut, F.E.A.: MAVIS conceptual design. In: Society of Photo-Optical Instrumentation Engineers (SPIE) Conference Series. Society of Photo-Optical Instrumentation Engineers (SPIE) Conference Series, vol. 11447, p. 114471R (2020). https://doi.org/10.1117/12.2561886
37. Rojek, K., Wyrzykowski, R., Gepner, P.: AI-accelerated CFD simulation based on OpenFOAM and CPU/GPU computing. In: Paszynski, M., Kranzlmüller, D., Krzhizhanovskaya, V.V., Dongarra, J.J., Sloot, P.M.A. (eds.) ICCS 2021. LNCS, vol. 12743, pp. 373–385. Springer, Cham (2021). https://doi.org/10.1007/978-3-030-77964-1_29
38. Valiant, L.G.: A bridging model for parallel computation. Commun. ACM **33**(8), 103–111 (1990). https://doi.org/10.1145/79173.79181
39. Vargas, D., Vasconcelos, I., Ravasi, M., Luiken, N.: Time-domain multidimensional deconvolution: a physically reliable and stable preconditioned implementation. Remote Sens. **13**, 3683 (2022). https://doi.org/10.3390/rs13183683
40. Vargas, D., Vasconcelos, I., Ravasi, M., Sripanich, Y.: Scattering-based focusing for imaging in highly-complex media from band-limited, multi-component data. Geophysics (2021). https://doi.org/10.1190/geo2020-0939.1
41. Viterbo, E., Boutros, J.: A universal lattice code decoder for fading channels. IEEE Trans. Inf. Theory **45**(5), 1639–1642 (1999). https://doi.org/10.1109/18.771234
42. Wapenaar, C.P.A., Berkhout, A.J.: Elastic wave field extrapolation: redatuming of single- and multi-component seismic data. Elsevier Science, Philadelphia (2014). https://www.elsevier.com/books/elastic-wave-field-extrapolation/berkhout/978-0-444-88472-5
43. Xie, Z., Short, R.T., Rushforth, C.K.: A family of suboptimum detectors for coherent multiuser communications. IEEE J. Sel. Areas Commun. **8**(4), 683–690 (1990). https://doi.org/10.1109/49.54464
44. Zhang, L., Thorbecke, J., Wapenaar, K., Slob, E.: Transmission compensated primary reflection retrieval in the data domain and consequences for imaging. Geophysics **84**, Q27–Q36 (2019). https://doi.org/10.1190/geo2018-0340.1

GPU-Based Low-Precision Detection Approach for Massive MIMO Systems

Adel Dabah[1]([✉]), Hatem Ltaief[1], Zouheir Rezki[2], Slim Alouini[1], and David Keyes[1]

[1] Division of Computer, Electrical, and Mathematical Sciences and Engineering, King Abdullah University of Science and Technology, Thuwal, Jeddah 23955, Saudi Arabia
{Adel.Dabah.1,Hatem.Ltaief,slim.alouini,David.Keyes}@kaust.edu.sa
[2] University of California Santa Cruz, 1156 High Street, Santa Cruz, CA 95064, USA
zrezki@ucsc.edu

Abstract. Massive Multiple-Input Multiple-Output (M-MIMO) uses hundreds of antennas in mobile communications base stations to increase the amount of transmitted data and the number of connected devices in 5G and beyond. However, M-MIMO systems increase the complexity of recovering the transmitted data (detection phase). To address this challenge, we leverage low-precision arithmetic in recent NVIDIA GPUs to improve the latency/scalability/accuracy of M-MIMO detection. We propose a GPU tree-based detection algorithm that aggregates multiple tree levels and formulates the computation as a matrix multiplication operation followed by a square-norm calculation and sorting (reduction) phase. This process is repeated until reaching the last level of the detection tree. The obtained results show near-optimal data detection with a 10× speedup compared to a two-socket 28-core IceLake CPU implementation. We further deploy low-precision arithmetic operations. We show that moving from single-precision 32-bit floating-point arithmetic (FP32) to half-precision 16-bit representation (FP16) does not affect the accuracy performance while translating into an additional 1.7× speedup. In addition, exploiting 8-bit integer representation results in an acceptable error rate degradation that can be compensated by increasing the number of aggregated levels. In addition, we propose a multi-GPU version that computes the matrix-multiplication operation of subsequent iterations in parallel. This latter operation represents more than 80% of the elapsed time for dense constellations. Results with four A100 GPUs show an additional 2.3× relative speedup compared to our single GPU version. The achieved accuracy/scalability balance may accelerate the deployment of this technology and promote low-precision GPU computations within the wireless communication community.

Keywords: GPU MIMO detection · Low-Precision Arithmetic

A. Bhatele et al. (Eds.): ISC High Performance 2023, LNCS 13948, pp. 144–163, 2023.
https://doi.org/10.1007/978-3-031-32041-5_8

1 Introduction

GPU accelerators enable an increase in computational power by lowering the arithmetic precision. This paper demonstrates the gains achievable by using GPUs with various arithmetic precision to meet the requirements of Next-Generation mobile communication networks in general and Massive Multiple-Input Multiple-Output (M-MIMO) detection in particular. M-MIMO technology is a key enabling technology for 5G and 6G mobile communication networks. It uses hundreds of antennas to send and receive data [7,11]. However, when increasing the number of antennas, the signal detection phase, which estimates the transmitted data, becomes a bottleneck, with an exponential complexity in the number of transmit-antennas for optimal detection. In this context, our goal is to speed up this phase using multiple GPUs with various arithmetic precision. Two main categories of detection methods exist, i.e., linear and nonlinear algorithms. On the one hand, linear detection algorithms operate under real-time constraints but fail to estimate the transmitted data correctly due to noise. On the other hand, nonlinear algorithms, e.g., the Sphere Decoder (SD) [6,8], give an excellent estimation of the transmitted data but require significant execution time. Nonlinear algorithms operate on a search tree that models all possible combinations of the transmitted data. Each path is defined by a set of symbols (data), from which a distance from the received signal can be calculated. The detection goal is to find the path with the shortest distance representing the originally transmitted data.

In this paper, we introduce a low-precision multi-level approach. It iteratively extends one path with several symbols representing the best combination in terms of distance within a window until we reach a complete path (solution). At each iteration, the algorithm combines successive levels within a window and computes all distances via a matrix-matrix multiplication exploiting tensor core capabilities in recent NVIDIA GPUs. The matrix shape is short and wide in dimensions representing the number of levels and all possible paths in a window. We then calculate the square norm and launch a sorting (reduction) phase to select the best extension. By increasing the number of aggregated levels, we improve the accuracy, but this comes at the price of higher complexity, there being a trade-off between complexity and accuracy. To mitigate the complexity and maintain good accuracy, we first exploit low-precision arithmetic (i.e., FP16 and INT8) and engage NVIDIA tensor cores with fast matrix engines. We report results on A100 GPU and achieve a 10× speedup compared to multicore CPU implementation on a two-socket 28-core Intel IceLake CPU. In addition, exploiting low-precision gives an additional 1.7× speedup without impacting the accuracy in terms of error rate. To further reduce the complexity, we propose a multi-GPU version that improves the complexity by reducing the matrix multiplication time, representing more than 80% of the global execution time for dense constellations. The idea is to overlap all matrix multiplication operations performed during the detection process since they are entirely independent and can be processed in an embarrassingly parallel fashion using multiple GPUs. This breaks the inherent sequential behavior of the detection phase, which results in an additional 2.3× improvement. Overall, we achieved up to 40× relative speedup compared to our multi-CPU implementation.

The rest of the paper is structured as follows. Section 2 introduces basic mobile communication concepts. Section 3 reviews the literature on high-performance MIMO processing. Section 4 presents the system model. Section 5 describes the details of our multi-level approach and its implementation. Results and discussions about the complexity and performance are given in Sect. 7. Finally, Sect. 8 concludes this paper and highlights our future plans.

2   Brief Background

M-MIMO incorporates hundreds of antennas in telecommunication base stations to enhance the quality of service for several 5G applications, from video streaming and gaming to self-driving cars and smart cities. The more antennas we integrate, the more data we can send (resp. receive) simultaneously. i.e., One on each antenna.

2.1   Modulation

Modulation is the act of changing a signal to transmit data. It represents a collection of symbols that can be sent directly on one antenna in one transaction. A symbol is represented by a complex number, i.e., real and imaginary parts. The number of symbols in a given modulation is defined as 2^b, where b is the number of bits encapsulated in a symbol. For instance, in Binary Phase-shift keying (BPSK) modulation, one bit is sent per symbol ($b = 1$). Therefore, this modulation includes two symbols (1,0) and (-1,0). In 64 Quadrature Amplitude Modulation (64-QAM), we can send six bits per symbol ($b = 6$). This represents 64 symbols in total. The higher the modulation, the better the data rate. However, it also increases the communication system's error rate and complexity.

2.2   Signal to Noise Ratio (SNR)

The SNR measures the relevant signal strength in decibels (dB) compared to the noise signal that can get in the way. Therefore, the higher the SNR, the better the communication system. A high-SNR value indicates that the user is close to the transmit antenna. A user can be assigned a specific modulation based on the SNR value. For instance, a BPSK modulation in the low-SNR regime versus a 64-QAM modulation if the user has a high SNR.

2.3   Error Rate and Time Complexity

The error rate performance is a ratio between transmitted data and the one recovered correctly at the receiver side. The error rate varies according to the detection algorithm used. The lower the error rate, the better the communication system is. In general, 10^{-2} uncoded symbol error rate (SER) is considered an acceptable error performance for many applications. For systems with powerful error correction codes, the previous SER readily translates into $10^{-5} - 10^{-6}$ SER error performance. The detection latency also depends on the complexity of the detection algorithm and the application area. In general, 10 ms is considered an acceptable latency for mobile communications. A good detection algorithm achieves a good trade-off between complexity and error rate performance.

For more information about communication science and engineering, please refer to e.g., [13].

3   Related Work

Many researchers have exploited multi-core CPUs and GPUs to accelerate non-linear detection algorithms.

Chen and Leib [4] propose a GPU-based Fixed Complexity Sphere Decoder. The authors reported a relative speedup of $7\times$ for large MIMO systems. However, the time of the approach is an order of magnitude higher compared to 10 ms requirements.

Arfaoui *et al.* [3] propose a GPU-based SD algorithm in which a Breadth-First Search (BFS) exploration strategy is used to increase the GPU resource occupancy. However, BFS increases the complexity, especially in low SNR region. The authors reported excellent error rate performance. However, the proposed approach has a scalability limitation, especially for large constellations due to the exponential complexity of the SD.

Husmann *et al.* [9] propose a flexible parallel decoder for MIMO systems using GPU and field-programmable gate array (FPGA) architectures. Their algorithm contains two phases. A first pre-processing phase chooses parts of the SD search tree to explore, and a second phase maps each of the chosen parts of the SD tree to a single processing element (GPU or FPGA). The results are presented for a maximum of a 12×12 MIMO system using 64-QAM modulation.

Nikitopoulos *et al.* [10] propose the design and implementation of a parallel multi-search SD approach using multicore CPU and Very-Large-Scale Integration (VLSI) architectures. After the pre-processing phase, in which they obtain a processing order of the tree branches, the authors split the search tree into several sub-trees. Each sub-tree is then mapped on a processing element and explored using a depth-first strategy. However, the authors do not consider the load-balancing problem, which may arise in modulations with dense constellations. The authors approximate results for a maximum of 16×16 MIMO system using 64-QAM modulation.

Dabah *et al.* [2,5] propose a parallel multi-agent approximate approach that runs simultaneously a single agent with a SD instance while the remaining agents execute concurrent k-best algorithm to accelerate SD search tree.

Despite the decent error rate performance, the above-proposed methods still suffer from scalability limitations. For example, the largest MIMO configuration reported in the above works is for 32 antennas under 10 ms requirements, which is far from massive MIMO potential. In fact, all works mentioned above are based on the SD algorithm, which has an exponential complexity $(2^b)^M$, with M the number of antennas and b the number of bits per symbol. Our GPU multi-level algorithm has a linear complexity $M(2^b)^L$, where L is the number of combined levels $L \in \{1, .., 4\}$. As a result, we report a good error rate performance for up to 100×100 antennas while maintaining an excellent error rate under real-time requirements.

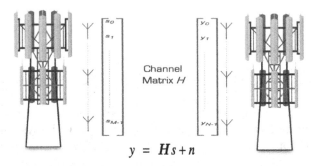

$$y = Hs + n$$

Fig. 1. Example of a MIMO system where the vector s is transmitted by M transmitter antennas via a channel matrix H. The received vector y is a collection of N receiver antennas' observations.

4   System Model

In this paper, we consider a MIMO system consisting of M transmit antennas and N receive antennas, as depicted in Fig. 1. The transmitter sends M data streams simultaneously to a receiver using multiple antennas via a flat-fading channel. i.e., We consider a small-scale fading channel which is a standard model in the literature [3]. The following equation describes the base-band MIMO model: $y = Hs + n$,   where the vector $y = [y_0, ..., y_{N-1}]^T$ represents the received signal. H is an $N \times M$ channel matrix, where each element h_{ij} is a complex Gaussian random variable, with mean 0 and variance 1, that models the fading gain between the j-th transmitter and i-th receiver. The vector $s = [s_0, ..., s_{M-1}]$ represents the transmitted vector, where s_i belongs to a finite alphabet set denoted by Ω. The input s is subject to an average power constraint ρ, i.e., $E[\|s\|^2] \leq \rho$. Finally, $n = [n_0, ..., n_{N-1}]^T$ represents the additive white Gaussian noise with zero mean and covariance I_N, where I_N designates the identity matrix of size N. With regard to the noise and channel normalization, the average power ρ also designates the average SNR per receive antenna. For convenience, let us consider $\mathcal{S}$ as the set of all possible combinations of the transmitted vector s. The possible number of combinations corresponds to the complexity of the MIMO system and it is calculated as follows: $|\mathcal{S}| = |\Omega|^M$.

The two main options for decoding the received signal are linear decoders characterized by low complexity and poor error rate performance and nonlinear (optimal or near-optimal) decoders characterized by good error rate quality but relatively high complexity.

Linear decoders multiply and map the received signal using a matrix denoted by H_{inv} ($M \times N$), obtained from the channel matrix H. The most common linear decoders are Zero Forcing (ZF) and Minimum Mean Square Error (MMSE). As for nonlinear decoders, the Maximum Likelihood [12] is the optimal decoder, exhibiting prohibitive complexity. It calculates a *posteriori* probability for each possible transmitted vector $s \in S$. In other words, the algorithm performs a brute-force exploration of the entire search space, as shown in Eq. 1:

$$\hat{s} = arg \min_{s \in S} ||y - Hs||^2. \tag{1}$$

The SD algorithm [1,14] mimics the ML decoder, but limits the search for the optimal solution inside a sphere of radius r set initially by the user, as shown in the Eq. 2:

$$||y - Hs||^2 < r, \quad \text{where} \quad s \in S. \tag{2}$$

The radius may then be updated subsequently at runtime to further prune the search space and reduce the complexity.

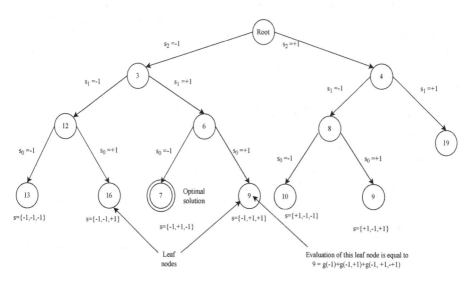

Fig. 2. Detection search tree for a MIMO system with three transmit antennas. One symbol is fixed at each level.

4.1 Tree-Based Representation

The problem in Eq. 2 can be transformed into another equivalent problem by performing the QR decomposition of the channel matrix H as follows:

$$||y - Hs||^2 = ||y - QRs||^2$$
$$= ||\bar{y} - Rs||^2, \text{ where } \bar{y} = Q^H y$$

where $Q \in C^{N \times N}$ is an orthogonal matrix and $R \in C^{N \times M}$ is an upper triangular matrix.

Thus, finding the supposed transmitted vector $(\hat{s})$ in Eq. (1) is equivalent to solving the following minimization problem:

$$\min \sum_{k=1}^{M} g_k(s_{M-1}, ..., s_{M-k}), \quad where \tag{3}$$

$$g_k(s_{M-1}, ..., s_{M-k}) = ||\bar{y}_{M-k} - \sum_{i=M-k}^{M-1} (r_{(M-k),i} s_i)||^2 \tag{4}$$

where (4) represents the partial distance (PD) of a search tree node (path). Indeed, this latter formulation of the problem allows to model all possible combinations of the transmitted vector as a search tree with M layers. To find the path with the minimum distance from the received signal, the SD performs a tree exploration to retrieve the best path.

Algorithm 1: Multi-Level Detection Pseudo-code.

Require: $\bar{y}$, R
  $P = \{\}$ *solution vector L number of aggregated levels M number of antennas*
1: **while** $|P|! = M$ **do**
2:    Generate partial paths P_i $i \in \{1, \Omega^L\}$
3:    Calculate PD_i $i \in \{1, \Omega^L\}$
4:    Locate P_m such that $PD_m = \min\{PD_i, i \in \{1, \Omega^L\}\}$
5:    $P = P \cup P_m$
6: **end while**
7: **return** P

---

5   Multi-level Approach

This section describes a multi-level approach that relies on two factors to keep real-time requirements and a good error rate. The first factor is algorithmic based on our multi-level technique. The second factor is efficiently exploiting the computing power of GPU resources and its large number of processing elements.

As depicted in Algorithm 1, our approach operates on a search tree with M levels (number of transmit antennas) and constructs only one solution named P (complete path). Usually, one symbol is detected at each level, starting from symbol S_{m-1} at level 1 to finally reach symbol S_0 at level M. Our idea is to combine the detection of multiple and successive symbols simultaneously. Despite the increase in the number of successors from $|\Omega|$ to $|\Omega|^L$, combining the detection of L symbols increases the accuracy in terms of error rate performance and reduces the number of iterations of our multi-level approach from M to M/L. Starting from a partial path P (initially empty), our approach creates $|\Omega|^L$ partial paths (P_i / i=1,..., $|\Omega|^L$) that extend P with all possible combinations of L symbols. After that, we calculate the partial distance (PD_i) for each partial path P_i using Eq. (5) Next, we replace P with the best partial path P_i in terms of partial distance (minimum PD_i). We repeat this process until reaching the last level of the tree, where we return P as an approximate solution to the MIMO detection problem.

Increasing the constellation size to 64-QAM (transmitting six bits per symbol) increases the error probability to fall into neighboring symbols instead of the transmitted one due to the noise. Our approach overcomes this issue by using coefficients of the next lower levels to confirm which of these symbols is the right one.

6   GPU-Based Multi-level Approaches

Increasing the aggregated levels increases the accuracy. However, it also increases the complexity. To keep practical time complexity and good error rate even for large constellations, we exploit low precision tensor core capacity in recent GPU hardware. All parts of our Multi-level approach are implemented and executed on GPU to avoid all data-transfer over the slow PCIe bus.

6.1   GPU Multi-level

We formulate our multi-level algorithm as a linear algebra operation that computes the PD (evaluation) of all partial paths simultaneously and then chooses the best one for the next iteration. Indeed, our algorithm is implemented to avoid: (1) thread divergence, especially in generating the partial paths; (2) increasing the compute portion of the algorithm by reformulating this process as matrix algebra operation $A * B + \alpha C$; and finally (3) relying on a reduction process to find the best candidate for following iterations. More detail on efficiently exploiting GPU resources in general, and half-precision in particular, is given in what follows.

Complex to Real Transformation. Wireless communication data are modeled as complex numbers. In order to exploit low-precision arithmetic, we must perform a transformation from complex to real because there is no GPU support for low-precision computation for complex numbers. There are two ways

(a) Replacing each complex number by a 2x2 matrix

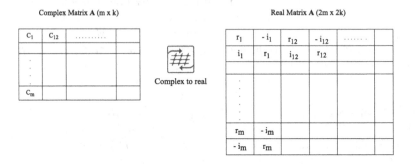

(b) Avoiding redundancy in computation by removing half the columns of matrices **B** and **C**

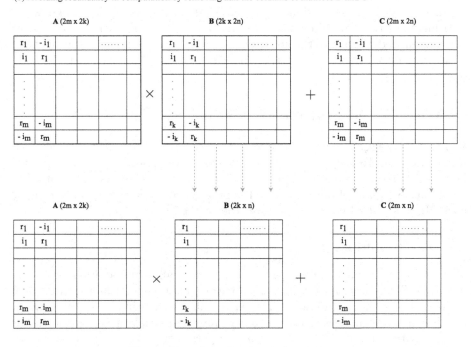

Fig. 3. Complex to real transformation.

to do the transformation. In the first way, we split a complex matrix into two matrices, one matrix representing the real part and the other one representing the imaginary part. This option creates an overhead of managing two matrices instead of one, thus inducing an overhead in computation and memory access. The other interesting option (preferred) is to replace each complex number with a 2×2 matrix. This option is depicted in Fig. 3 (a). Therefore, Matrix **A** with

m rows and k columns will be transformed to a matrix with $2 * m$ rows and $2 * k$ columns. We do the same for matrices B and C.

Matrices B and C can have millions of columns, inducing a huge number of floating-point operations (FLOPS) and memory access. We can notice that matrix C (multiplication result) has duplicated information (r_1,i_1), and $(-i_1,r_1)$ (See Fig. 3 (b)). Here, we exploit this redundancy to cut down by half the number of flops and memory accesses in the multiplication. In this way, we reduce the size of matrix B from $2k * 2n$ to $2k * n$. Similarly, for matrix C. This is important since the number of columns of matrices B and C can reach several million.

Avoiding Thread Divergence. Thread divergence appears when threads within the same warp don't follow the same instruction path (if-else), resulting in negative performance consequences. The thread divergence situation is known when exploring trees on GPU since the branching process has many if-else instructions.

Exploring a search tree and generating partial paths (successor nodes) at each iteration represents a bottleneck on GPU since it involves many if-else conditions. To answer this issue when generating partial paths (all possible combinations of L symbols), we divide a partial path into two parts. A part common with all partial paths (from root to node x) and a distinct part that is unique for each partial path. For instance, the partial paths in Fig. 4 second iteration have two parts: a common part (marked in red) from root to node x, followed by the unique part for each partial path. The distinct part for all partial paths is represented by a matrix B. This latter contains all possible combinations of L symbols such that each column represents a partial path. This matrix is generated once and does not change from one iteration to another. The only thing that changes from one iteration to another is the common part modeled as a vector Vc.

On the one hand, this decomposition allows to avoid thread divergence situations. On the other hand, it also allows reducing the size (memory and flops) of matrix B (resp. C). Without the aforementioned decomposition, the common part will be duplicated for all partial paths $|\Omega|^L$, which can reach millions.

New Incremental Evaluation: The evaluation for each partial path is calculated using Eq. 4. To increase the arithmetic intensity of our algorithm, we grouped the evaluation for all partial paths as a matrix multiplication as follows: $A * B + \alpha C$.

$$E_{Pi} = E_p + \sum_{k=0}^{L-1} \|C_{ki} + V_k\| \tag{5}$$

The evaluation of a partial path P_i is the evaluation of the constructed path P (calculated in the previous iteration) plus the square norm over column $C_i + V$. Following the decomposition we did earlier, the evaluation is divided into two parts, i.e., matrix-matrix multiplication and matrix-vector multiplication. The square matrix A is obtained from matrix R (QR decomposition page 6.), such that it contains the rows of L fixed symbols in the current iteration. The matrix B is defined in the earlier section as all possible combinations of the L symbols, which can reach millions of columns. Finally, the matrix C represents the

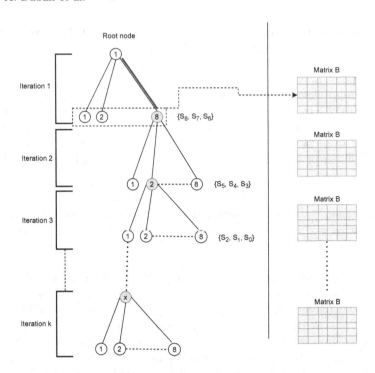

Fig. 4. Branching scheme of the multi-level approach.

elements of $\bar{y}$ corresponding to the L symbols in the current iteration duplicated $|\Omega|^L$ times.

The other part of the evaluation is a matrix-vector multiplication that multiplies Matrix A' obtained from matrix R with the common vector Vc defined earlier. *Sorting (Reduction):* After the evaluation phase, our algorithm chooses the best partial path in terms of evaluation, i.e., distance from the received signal.

6.2 Multi-GPU Version

As earlier stated, the multiplication used to compute the evaluation for each partial path $(A * B + \alpha C)$ requires nearly 80% of execution time (see Fig. 6). In addition to using low-precision mode for computing the above multiplication, we aim to accelerate this phase further using multiple GPUs. Thanks to our path decomposition to avoid thread divergence, matrix B remains the same from one iteration to another. In addition, matrix A for each iteration is known in advance. The idea behind this multi-GPU version is to overlap all the multiplication used during the detection process using multiple GPUs. As depicted in Fig. 5, all multiplications from different iterations are performed on multiple GPUs at the same time. This reduces all the matrix multiplication operations to the complexity of one multiplication. The only phases that need to be done sequentially are the norm calculation and min.

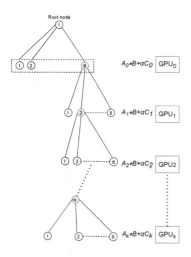

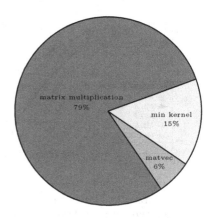

Fig. 5. Multi-GPU version where the matrix multiplication operations during the whole detection process are performed simultaneously on several GPUs.

Fig. 6. Time partition of different kernels (single precision) of our approach for a 100×100 MIMO system with 64-QAM modulation and four levels.

7 Results and Discussions

In the following, we conduct experiments to assess our GPU-based approach's accuracy (error rate) and complexity. For that, we use MMSE linear detection and the optimal GPU-SD in [3]. The exponential complexity of the SD prevents it from dealing with large MIMO systems. For this reason, we include its performance for a small MIMO system. We perform our experiments using a server with four NVIDIA A100 GPUs with 40GB and a two-socket Intel IceLake CPU 2 GHz with 28 CPU-core and 1024 GB of main memory. For all the experiments, we consider the case of perfect channel state information. This means that the channel matrix is known only at the receiver. Each experiment uses randomly generated symbols (data set). As a result, the data sets are different from one execution to another which is close to real wireless data. All level three BLAS operations are performed using the vendor-optimized cuBLAS library.

Figure 7 illustrates the impact of increasing the number of combined levels on the error rate and complexity of our ML approach. We compare our results with the accuracy of the optimal SD algorithm to show how far we are from optimal results. Despite the attractive latency of the MMSE algorithm, this latter has poor error rate performance, which makes it not suitable for M-MIMO. The first observation from sub-figure (a) is the good impact of increasing the number of levels on the error rate performance. Indeed, the accuracy of our multi-level technique is quite close to the performance of the optimal GPU-SD [3] when using four and five levels. However, if we look at the complexity (sub-figure (b)),

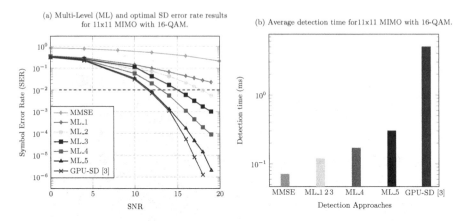

Fig. 7. Accuracy and latency results of our GPU ML approach compared to the linear MMSE and the optimal SD results.

we can see a significant gap in complexity between the two approaches. Indeed, The GPU-SD [3] has high latency since it enumerates all possible combinations of the transmitted signal inside a given radius, which results in a massive number of explored paths. This is not the case with our approach, which combines multiple levels to target the best path in the search tree. This results in a limited number of explored nodes (low latency) while achieving high accuracy. On average, our approach (ML_5) is 40x faster than GPU-SD [3] for this small configuration. By increasing the number of levels of our approach from one to four, we reach the acceptable accuracy (10^{-2}) at 13 dB instead of 22 dB, thus saving 9 dB in power consumption with a slight increase in complexity. This represents a good accuracy/complexity balance for communication users. Thus, increasing the number of levels in our approach is crucial for achieving better accuracy. However, the complexity increases accordingly. To scale the number of antennas while keeping reasonable complexity, we exploit tensor-core capability in recent GPUs.

Figure 6 shows the time partition of our GPU kernels for a 100×100 MIMO system with 64 QAM modulation and four levels. The matrix-matrix multiplication required to evaluate partial paths represents 76% of the total execution time. In this configuration, we have 16777216 partial paths that need to be evaluated as matrix-matrix multiplication with m, k, and n equal to 8, 8, and 16777216, resp. As a result, lowering the time complexity of our approach requires reducing the complexity of the matrix multiplication operation. To achieve this goal and study the impact of low-precision data structure on the wireless communication field in general and MIMO detection in particular, we exploit FP16 and INT8 as follows.

Figure 8 shows the error rate performance of our approach using different arithmetic precisions (FP32, FP16, and INT8) using respectively three and four combined levels (ML_3, ML_4) for a 100×100 MIMO with 64-QAM modulation.

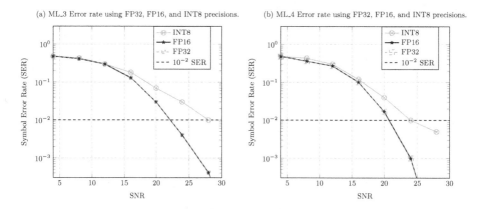

Fig. 8. Error rate performance using different arithmetic precision from float 32 bits precision to the smallest integer 8 bits for a 100×100 MIMO with 64-QAM modulation. Sub-figures (a) and (b) give the results of our algorithm with three levels (ML_3) and four levels (ML_4), respectively.

The interesting observation from both sub-figures (a) and (b) is that our approach performs well and can support precision loss even when using the smallest representation of 8 bits (size of a register). Indeed, we can see from the two sub-figures that passing from FP32 to FP16 representation of matrices A, B, and C has no effect on the accuracy for all SNR regions. This means that the conversion, multiplication, and accumulation in FP16 does not lead to accuracy loss. In turn, this means that the multiplication and accumulation operations performed during the GEMM are all within the range of FP16. Furthermore, when moving to the smallest representation that can fit into a register(INT8), we see a moderate variation in error rate performance. This means we are losing some useful information. Since the accumulation for INT8 is done in integer 32 bits, the precision loss occurs when converting matrix A from Float 32 bits to Integer 8 bits. Indeed, when scaling up matrix A, we may be out of the INT8 range $(-127,127)$, which affects the accuracy in error rate, especially in the high SNR region. Figure 9 shows the effect of increasing the scaling number in the float_to_INT8 conversion of matrix A on the accuracy. We can identify two phases, a first one where increasing the scaling number improves the accuracy, and a second phase where increasing the scaling number negatively affects the accuracy. Indeed, a large scaling number leads to integer values out of the INT8 range $(-127, 127)$. Thus, all values above (resp. under) 127 (resp. -127) are represented by 127 (resp. -127). Therefore, we lose useful information, which explains the decrease in accuracy.

It seems that increasing the number of levels positively impacts the accuracy of the INT8 version. Figure 10 investigates this behavior for 100×100 MIMO with 16-QAM modulation. It shows the impact of increasing the number of levels on the accuracy of the INT8 version in terms of error rate performance. We can see clearly the good impact of increasing the number of levels on the accuracy

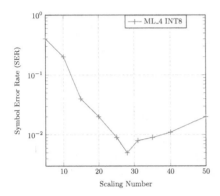

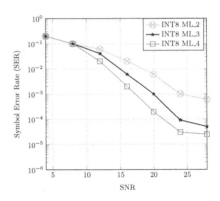

Fig. 9. Impact of scaling number in the float_to_INT8 conversion on the error rate performance for a 100×100 MIMO 64-QAM modulation using ML_4 and SNR = 28 dB.

Fig. 10. Impact of multi-level technique in supporting integer 8-bits accuracy for 100×100 MIMO with 16-QAM modulation.

of the INT8 version by saving up to five dB in power consumption, which is an important aspect in the wireless communication domain.

From Fig. 8, we can identify two SNR regions. Low SNR region between 0 and 16 dB, where INT8 version has a similar error rate compared to FP16 and FP32 versions. After that, a second region begins where we can see the loss in error rate performance of the INT8 version. On the one hand, reducing the precision in the low SNR region affects the chosen path. However, this is not visible since the error rate is very high in this region, even when using the FP32 version. On the other hand, reducing the precision has a visible impact on the accuracy of MIMO detection. However, Fig. 10 shows that combining more levels (ideally four levels) reduces the impact of precision loss. Indeed, increasing the number of levels increases the difference in terms of evaluation between the optimal path and neighboring symbols. This compensates for the precision loss in this SNR region.

Figure 11 gives a general view of INT8 performance for different modulations from BPSK where we send only one bit per antenna, to 64-QAM where six bits are sent together per antenna. We can see from Fig. 11 the limited impact of precision loss on the accuracy of MIMO detection for all modulation and SNR regions. We can see that the more dense the constellation, the more impact of precision loss. Indeed, increasing the constellation size increases the error probability and increases the impact of precision loss since this lost information can influence the chosen path.

Figure 12 shows the impact of using different arithmetic precision on the time complexity of our approach using four levels. We can see that $1.7\times$ improvement in complexity going from FP32 (32 bits) to FP16 (16 bits) without any impact on the accuracy, as we saw earlier. We can also see that INT8 precision does not significantly impact time complexity due to the limited support in CUDA driver 11.6. Indeed, tensor cores are currently not activated for the non-transpose cases when launching this specific CUDA INT8 GEMM kernel. However, even when using half-precision, which has mature support on the GPU hardware, we are not close to the theoretical 18× speedup. Our hypothesis is that the shape of the matrix for our approach deeply affects the performance gain using tensor cores. Figure 13 investigates this and shows the performance gain using driver matrix multiplication with two kinds of matrices. The first is the short and wide matrix shape from our MIMO multi-level detection, i.e., $A(8 \times 8)$, $B(8 \times 16M)$. The second kind is a square matrix $A(4k \times 4k)$ and $B(4k \times 4k)$.

Figure 13 confirms our suggestion that the shape of the matrices significantly impacts the improvement factor using tensor cores. Indeed, with a square shape of A and B matrices, we are getting close to the theoretical peak performance using both FP32 and FP16, with an improvement factor around 15×. On the other hand, the low performance achieved by the wide and short matrices (MIMO shape) is explained by two reasons. The main reason is that this latter shape of matrices engenders a memory-bound regime of execution with an Arithmetic Intensity (AI) in flops per byte of only 4 compared to an AI of 682 square shape matrices. Such matrix shape does not engender enough data reuse for such an operation to be in the compute-bound regime of execution, as usually noticed for traditional square matrix-matrix multiplication. The same conclusion is also valid for INT8 precision.

In addition to using low-precision, we exploit multiple GPUs to overlap the matrix multiplication performed during the detection process. Figure 14 shows

FP32, FP16

Modulation / SNR	0	4	8	12	16	20	24	28	32
64-QAM	4.8E-01	4.8E-01	4.3E-01	2.7E-01	1.0E-01	1.0E-02	1.0E-03	5.0E-05	4.0E-06
16-QAM	3.0E-01	2.1E-01	7.0E-02	1.9E-02	1.6E-03	2.0E-04	3.0E-05	3.0E-05	3.0E-05
4-QAM	2.4E-02	3.0E-03	2.0E-04	2.0E-05	1E-08	1E-08	1E-08	1E-08	1E-08
BPSK	1E-08	1E-08	1E-08	1E-08	1E-08	1E-08	1E-08	1E-08	1E-08

INT8 with FP32 accumulation

Modulation / SNR	0	4	8	12	16	20	24	28	32
64-QAM	4.8E-01	4.8E-01	4.3E-01	2.7E-01	1.0E-01	4.0E-02	1.0E-02	5.0E-03	4.0E-03
16-QAM	3.0E-01	2.0E-01	1.0E-01	2.0E-02	2.0E-03	2.0E-04	3.0E-05	3.0E-05	3.0E-05
4-QAM	2.4E-02	4.0E-03	2.0E-04	2.0E-05	1E-08	1E-08	1E-08	1E-08	1E-08
BPSK	1E-08	1E-08	1E-08	1E-08	1E-08	1E-08	1E-08	1E-08	1E-08

Bad SER — Decent SER — Good SER

Fig. 11. ML_4 error rate heat-map using low-precision arithmetic for different modulations and SNR values for a 100 × 100 with 64-QAM modulation.

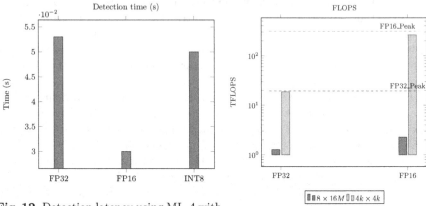

Fig. 12. Detection latency using ML_4 with different arithmetic precision for a 100 × 100 MIMO with 64-QAM modulation.

Fig. 13. FLOPs using ML_4 with different arithmetic precision.

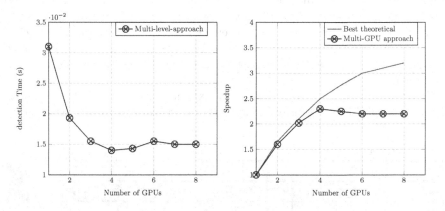

Fig. 14. complexity versus the number of GPUs for our multi-GPU approach for a 100 × 100 MIMO system with 64-QAM using four levels.

the impact of scaling the number of GPUs to further reduce the time-to-solution of the main kernel, i.e., the matrix-matrix multiplication. This latter represents more than 80% of the elapsed time for dense constellations. The idea is to execute matrix-matrix multiplications from subsequent iterations using multiple GPUs simultaneously. However, the remaining 20% of the code must be executed sequentially, which may impede strong scaling performance. Figure 14 shows the complexity (a) and speedup (b) of our multi-GPU approach for a 100 × 100 MIMO system with 64-QAM modulation and four levels. Sub-figure (b) shows the theoretical best speedup (red curve) and achieved speedup (blue curve) by our multi-GPU approach. We can notice two regimes: the first between one and four GPUs, where the complexity decreases, and the second between four and eight GPUs, where increasing GPUs has no effect on the complexity. The first

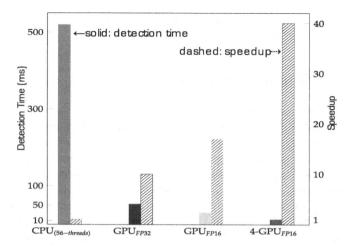

Fig. 15. Complexity and speedup of our proposed approaches for a 100×100 MIMO with 64-QAM modulation.

regime is characterized by a rapid decrease in complexity and a near-optimal speedup. This is due to a high compute-to-communication ratio. After that, increasing the number of GPUs increases the communication-to-computation ratio, which indicates that the increased communication neutralizes the benefit achieved by overlapping addition iterations. Despite the fact that matrix multiplication represents 80% of the execution time, we still need to perform the norm and min kernels. This results in synchronization and data transfer between GPUs. Indeed, the communication when using one to four GPUs is performed using the high-speed NVLink interconnect, whereas increasing the number of GPUs further leads the communication through the slow PCIe bus. This increases significantly the communication, which neutralizes the gain from overlapping more multiplication operations for this particular data set. Adding more levels will allow supporting more than four GPUs; however, the complexity will increase beyond the acceptable threshold for mobile communication.

Figure 15 shows the overall performance against a multi-core CPU implementation on IceLake architecture for a 100×100 MIMO with 64-QAM modulation (ML_4). For a fair comparison, the CPU implementation is also based on real matrix representation as explained in Fig. 3. The best performance for the parallel CPU version is reached around 30 threads and remains the same up to 56 threads. Solid fill indicates the time to solution, while dashed bars report the speedup achieved. Figure 15 shows that going from the multi-CPU version with 30 physical threads FP32 to one GPU A100 with FP32 single precision leads to 10× improvement in complexity. Moreover, exploiting half-precision arithmetic (FP16) pushes the speedup to 17×. Furthermore, our multi-GPU version is 2.3× faster than the single-GPU version with half-precision mode. In total, our multi-GPU version is 40× faster than the parallel CPU implementation. As a result, we achieve a good complexity/accuracy trade-off.

Regarding power consumption, our approach requires an average of 78 W which is below the 90 W cap imposed by wireless vendors.

8   Conclusion and Perspectives

Recent GPUs have fast tensor-core operations that leverage low-precision arithmetic to achieve performance gain. This paper exploits this capability to overcome M-MIMO detection overhead for a large number of antennas. In this paper, we demonstrate the positive impact of low-precision arithmetic operations (32 bits, 16 bits, and 8 bits) on the complexity (1.7×) while maintaining a good accuracy performance of our multi-level detection algorithm. To further reduce the complexity while maintaining the same accuracy performance, we proposed a multi-GPU approach that overlaps the matrix-multiplication operations on subsequent iterations. This resulted in an additional 2.3× speedup. To summarize, we have improved the complexity by a factor of 4× compared to a single-precision single-GPU approach and 40× compared to the multi-core CPU implementation on a two-socket 28-core IceLake.

In future work, we will investigate the potential gain of a Field-Programmable Gate Array (FPGA) on both complexity and power consumption.

References

1. Agrell, E., Eriksson, T., Vardy, A., Zeger, K.: Closest point search in lattices. IEEE Trans. Inf. Theory **48**(8), 2201–2214 (2002)
2. Alouini, M.S., Keyes, D.E., Ltaief, H., Dabah, A., Rezki, Z.: Massive multiple-input multiple-output system and method (14 Dec 2021). US Patent 11,201,645
3. Arfaoui, M.A., Ltaief, H., Rezki, Z., Alouini, M.S., Keyes, D.: Efficient sphere detector algorithm for massive MIMO using GPU hardware accelerator. Procedia Comput. Sci. **80**, 2169–2180 (2016)
4. Chen, T., Leib, H.: GPU acceleration for fixed complexity sphere decoder in large MIMO uplink systems. In: IEEE 28th Canadian Conference on Electrical and Computer Engineering (CCECE 2015), pp. 771–777. IEEE (2015)
5. Dabah, A., Ltaief, H., Rezki, Z., Arfaoui, M.A., Alouini, M.S., Keyes, D.: Performance/complexity trade-offs of the sphere decoder algorithm for massive MIMO systems. arXiv preprint arXiv:2002.09561 (2020). To be submitted
6. Fincke, U., Pohst, M.: Improved methods for calculating vectors of short length in a lattice, including a complexity analysis. Math. Comput. **44**(170), 463–471 (1985)
7. Foschini, G.J.: Layered space-time architecture for wireless communication in a fading environment when using multi-element antennas. Bell Labs Tech. J. **1**(2), 41–59 (1996)
8. Hassibi, B., Vikalo, H.: On the sphere-decoding algorithm I. expected complexity. IEEE Trans. Signal Process. **53**(8), 2806–2818 (2005)
9. Husmann, C., Georgis, G., Nikitopoulos, K., Jamieson, K.: FlexCore: massively parallel and flexible processing for large MIMO access points. In: 14th USENIX Symposium on Networked Systems Design and Implementation (NSDI 2017), pp. 197–211 (2017)

10. Nikitopoulos, K., Georgis, G., Jayawardena, C., Chatzipanagiotis, D., Tafazolli, R.: Massively parallel tree search for high-dimensional sphere decoders. IEEE Trans. Parallel Distrib. Syst. **30**(10), 2309–2325 (2018)

11. Paulraj, A.J., Kailath, T.: Increasing capacity in wireless broadcast systems using distributed transmission/directional reception (DTDR) (6 Sep 1994). US Patent 5,345,599

12. Simon, M.K., Alouini, M.S.: Digital Communication over Fading Channels (Wiley Series in Telecommunications and Signal Processing), 2nd edn. Wiley-IEEE Press, New York (2004)

13. Sklar, B., et al.: Digital Communications, vol. 2. Prentice Hall, Upper Saddle River (2001)

14. Viterbo, E., Boutros, J.: A universal lattice code decoder for fading channels. IEEE Trans. Inf. Theory **45**(5), 1639–1642 (1999)

A Mixed Precision Randomized Preconditioner for the LSQR Solver on GPUs

Vasileios Georgiou[1(✉)] [ID], Christos Boutsikas[2] [ID], Petros Drineas[2] [ID], and Hartwig Anzt[1,3] [ID]

[1] Steinbuch Centre for Computing, Karlsruhe Institute of Technology, Karlsruhe, Germany
{vasileios.georgiou,hartwig.anzt}@kit.edu
[2] Purdue University, West Lafayette, USA
{cboutsik,pdrineas}@purdue.edu
[3] Innovative Computing Lab, University of Tennessee, Knoxville, TN, USA

Abstract. Randomized preconditioners for large-scale regression problems have become extremely popular over the past decade. Such preconditioners are known to accelerate large-scale regression solvers both from a theoretical and a practical perspective. In this paper, we present a mixed precision randomized preconditioner for LSQR solvers, focusing on overdetermined, dense least squares problems. We implement and evaluate our method on GPUs and we demonstrate that it outperforms the standard double precision version of randomized, preconditioned LSQR by up to 20% on the NVIDIA A100. We present extensive numerical experiments utilizing the half-precision and tensorcore units to demonstrate that, in many cases, constructing the preconditioner in *reduced precision* does not affect the convergence of LSQR solvers. This leads to important speedups without loss of accuracy.

Keywords: Mixed Precision · Randomized Preconditioners · Over-determined Least Squares · LSQR · GPUs

1 Introduction

Solving overdetermined least squares problems is a common yet computationally expensive challenge in scientific computing. Standard approaches include a variety of direct and iterative methods. The former rely either on computing the QR factorization of the input matrix or on solving the so-called normal equations. Orthogonalization methods used for factorization utilize variants of the Gram-Schmidt algorithm [5,8,10,33], Householder reflectors [21,32,41], or Givens rotations [7,25]. Additionally, the Cholesky factorization is often used to solve the normal equations [42]. Among the iterative solvers that have been proposed to tackle least squares, LSQR [38] is one of the most popular methods mainly because of its numerical robustness. Alternatives include GMRES [28,37] and CGLS [9,23,35]. The main factor determining the runtime of iterative methods

A. Bhatele et al. (Eds.): ISC High Performance 2023, LNCS 13948, pp. 164–181, 2023.
https://doi.org/10.1007/978-3-031-32041-5_9

is the number of iterations required in order to converge to the specified tolerance. Several techniques for transforming the original problem to one which is easier to solve, i.e., one that requires fewer iterations, have been developed over the years. The most important family of such techniques are the *preconditioning* methods, which are essential in both theory and practice of least-squares solvers.

Preconditioning includes a spectrum of techniques ranging from those tailored to a specific application to general purpose, "black-box" methods, which are broadly applicable but more inefficient in special cases. It is worth noting that constructing the preconditioner could be relatively expensive compared to the overall runtime of the solver, which often argues against using the "tailored" approach, unless the problem input has very specific characteristics. Iterative least squares solvers are often popular for solving *sparse* problems, which has led to a variety of preconditioners based on sparse approximations [16,17] and incomplete factorizations [6,11,18]. On the other hand, there are significantly fewer results for preconditioning *dense* overdetermined least squares problems. Over the past decade, randomized "black-box" preconditioners have emerged as a robust way to solve large-scale regression problems, outperforming dense QR-based approaches [3,4].

Randomization has often been used as a resource in tackling data-intensive linear algebra problems. A popular example is performing principal components analysis (PCA) on massive datasets by sketching or sampling the input matrix. Another example has been randomized preconditioning, which first creates a "sketch" of the input matrix that is used to compute the preconditioner [3]. Theoretical analyses of such methods provide error guarantees that depend on the number of samples or the size of the sketch, which are typically independent of the data size. Such methods effectively reduce the dimensionality of the original data, a process that is somewhat akin to processing a noisy version of the input matrix. This makes randomized linear algebra algorithms perfect candidates for incorporating elements of mixed precision computations, taking advantage of modern hardware to achieve speedups without significant loss of accuracy.

The introduction of native support for 16-bit precision formats on modern GPUs has led to increased interest in mixed-precision versions of numerical methods. Mixed precision algorithms use at least two different precision formats, performing the most computationally intensive steps in lower precision to benefit from faster execution on hardware accelerators. Another way to speedup memory-bound computations is by communicating the data in reduced precision while executing the computations in the original (or higher) precision [2,27]. This is beneficial since for memory-bounded problems the cost of communicating data across devices dominates the overall runtime.

Even though early work on mixed precision numerical algorithms was mostly focused on the solution of linear systems of equations, this has changed over time. Some notable mixed precision methods for solving least squares problems include [15,29], as well as iterative refinement approaches [14] and scaling techniques [30] for recovering (at least partially) the accuracy which is inevitably lost when converting to lower precision. There has also been some work on mixed precision preconditioners in [22, 26]. However, to the best of our knowledge, there has not been much progress in the development and implementation of mixed precision randomized preconditioners for least-squares problems.

In this paper, we address the aforementioned gap. We develop a mixed precision randomized preconditioner to be used with our novel LSQR implementation for solving dense overdetermined least squares problems on GPUs. Despite constructing the preconditioner in lower precision, our results show that this loss in precision does not negatively affect the convergence of LSQR. This leads to significant speedups of up to 140% in terms of the runtime required for constructing the preconditioner, and up to 20% in terms of the overall runtime, without any loss of accuracy. In our analysis we provide some insights, regarding the factors that affect the performance of the preconditioner. Both the randomized preconditioner and the LSQR solver are implemented in C++ using the MAGMA and the CUDA runtime libraries and operate exclusively on the GPU. This is the first implementation and systematic evaluation of mixed-precision, randomized preconditioned LSQR on GPUs.

The rest of the paper is structured as follows: In Sect. 2, we provide some background on randomized preconditioners. In Sect. 3, we explain the details of the implementation of our method, and in Sect. 4 we showcase performance results from our experiments on different datasets. Lastly, in Sect. 5, we summarize our findings and discuss potential extensions.

2   Background

Given a coefficient matrix $A \in \mathbb{R}^{m \times n}$, and a right-hand side vector $b \in \mathbb{R}^m$, the overdetermined $(m \geq n)$ least-squares (LS) solution is the vector $\mathbf{x}^\star$ which minimizes the Euclidean norm residual

$$\mathbf{x}^\star = \arg \min_{\mathbf{x} \in \mathbb{R}^n} \|b - A\mathbf{x}\|_2. \tag{1}$$

For large linear systems, iterative solvers are usually preferred for solving (1). However, such solvers can become impractical and exhibit slow convergence if the condition number of the input matrix A is large (ill-conditioned systems). One potential remedy for this challenge is to transform (1) into a mathematically equivalent problem with more favorable properties. Such a transformation is called *preconditioning*, and in particular, the right preconditioned LS system is given by

$$y^\star = \arg \min_{y \in \mathbb{R}^n} \|b - AM^{-1}y\|_2, \ y^\star = M\mathbf{x}^\star. \tag{2}$$

The matrix $M \in \mathbb{R}^{n \times n}$ is called the *preconditioner*. We can design M having various requirements in mind (e.g., spectral properties, approximating the pseudoinverse, etc.). In practice, we are mostly interested in decreasing the condition number of AM^{-1} (at least compared to the condition number of A) and being able to solve linear systems with M inexpensively. In this paper, we solve (2) using the LSQR (Algorithm 1), which is theoretically equivalent to applying conjugate gradients on $A^T A$, but with better numerical properties [38].

Algorithm 1. Preconditioned LSQR

Input: matrix A, initial solution x_0, right-hand side b, tolerance `tol`, maximum
  number of iterations `maxiter`, preconditioner M
Output: solution x, relative residual `relres`
1: **procedure** $[x, \text{RELRES}] = \text{LSQR}(A, x_0, b, \text{tol}, \text{maxiter}, M)$
2:     $\beta = \|b\|_2, u = b/\beta$
3:     $v = (M^\top)\backslash(A^\top u)$
4:     $\alpha = \|v\|_2, v = v/\alpha$
5:     $w = v$
6:     $\bar{\phi} = \beta, \bar{\rho} = \alpha, \text{iter} = 0$
7:     **while** (1) **do**
8:         $u = A(M\backslash v) - \alpha u$
9:         $\beta = \|u\|_2, u = u/\beta$
10:        $v = M^\top\backslash(A^\top u) - \beta v$
11:        $\alpha = \|v\|_2, v = v/\alpha$
12:        $\rho = \sqrt{\bar{\rho}^2 + \beta^2}$
13:        $c = \bar{\rho}/\rho$
14:        $s = \beta/\rho$
15:        $\theta = s \cdot \alpha$
16:        $\bar{\rho} = -c \cdot \alpha$
17:        $\phi = c \cdot \bar{\phi}$
18:        $\bar{\phi} = s \cdot \bar{\phi}$
19:        $x = x + M\backslash((\phi/\rho)w)$
20:        $w = v - (\theta/\rho)w$
21:        $r = b - Ax$, `relres` $= \|r\|_2/\|b\|_2$, `iter` $+ = 1$
22:        **if** $((\text{iter} == \text{maxiter})\|(\text{relres} < \text{tol}))$ **then**
23:            break
24:        **end if**
25:    **end while**
26: **end procedure**

2.1   Related Work

Over the last two decades, Randomized Linear Algebra has left its mark on constructing preconditioners through sketching-based methods. Rokhlin and Tygert [40] developed a preconditioner for overdetermined systems by applying a Subsampled Randomized Fourier Transform (SRFT) on the input matrix and then pivoted-QR on the preconditioned system. Similar to that setting, Avron *et al.* [3] constructed the randomized solver *Blendenpik* which consists of four steps:

1. Mix the rows of A by premultiplying it by an appropriate random matrix (i.e., the Randomized Hadamard Transform matrix, the Randomized Discrete Cosine Transform matrix, etc.). Let $G \in \mathbb{R}^{m \times m}$ be this random matrix.
2. Sample s rows (uniformly at random) from the "mixed" matrix GA to create the sampled matrix $(GA)_s \in \mathbb{R}^{s \times n}$.
3. QR factorization on $(GA)_s$ to construct the preconditioner M.
4. Call Algorithm 1 to solve (2).

Intuitively, the "mixing" procedure of step (1) distributes the importance of the rows, thus improving the accuracy guarantees of uniform sampling in the following steps. In other words, the mixing procedure uniformizes the so-called *leverage scores* of the rows of the input matrix A; leverage scores play a crucial role in regression problems and random sampling and sketching [20,31]; It is known that the aforementioned transformation *reduces* the maximum leverage score (*coherence*). The *Blendenpik* algorithm is actually a general template for designing randomized preconditioners. For example, [36] proposes the use of a Gaussian matrix instead of the Randomized Hadamard Transform, followed by an alternative approach to the QR decomposition using the Singular Value Decomposition. More recently, Tropp *et al.* [24] described a preconditioner for Conjugate Gradient (CG) via a randomized low-rank Nyström approximation.

The concept of employing mixed-precision arithmetic to improve performance has been recently applied to a range of problems [1]. Furthermore, it has been a well-established approach for linear systems. The recent work of Carson and Daužickaitė, [13] provides an analysis of a Nyström mixed-precision preconditioner for CG. In [12], the authors use a combination of 32-bit and 64-bit floating point arithmetic for iterative refinement of dense linear systems. Also recently, Lindquist *et al.* [34] presented mixed-precision restarted GMRES for sparse linear systems. However, their work differs from ours in various ways: they provide a mix of single and double-precision implementation but do not focus on half precision. Moreover, they construct each preconditioner in double precision and then store it in single precision for the reduced-precision algorithm, unlike our work (see Sect. 3).

3   Design and Implementation of the Mixed Precision Preconditioner

Our mixed precision implementation uses a Gaussian random matrix $G \in \mathbb{R}^{s \times m}$ in order to sketch the input matrix by computing $A_s = G \cdot A$. For the preconditioner we use the triangular factor of the economy qr factorization of the matrix A_s, following the approach proposed in [3]. In MATLAB notation, this is computed as $[\sim, M] = \mathrm{qr}(A_s, 0)$. In Algorithm 2, we present the mixed precision version of this preconditioner. The demote and promote functions convert the matrix entries between the required precisions. All the steps of the algorithm are executed on the GPU, using MAGMA [43] routines for the linear algebraic operations and custom CUDA kernels to perform the conversions to different precisions. The Gaussian matrices are generated using the cuRAND functions[1]. You can access our implementation at https://github.com/vasilisge0/randLS/.

In Algorithm 2, we store matrices in high or low precision, as indicated by the types high_prec and low_prec. The only floating point format for high precision we consider in this paper is double, or fp64. For the low precisions, we experimented with the following types: single or fp32; half or fp16; and TensorFloat-32

---

[1] cuRand v12.0.0 https://docs.nvidia.com/cuda/curand/index.html.

or tf32. The latter is a 19-bit representation for which NVIDIA provides native support on the AMPERE architecture. It uses eight bits for representing the exponent (the same as fp32), but only ten bits for the mantissa (the same as fp16). An additional bit is required to store the sign. Table 1 depicts the precisions used by our implementations of the preconditioner and the solver.

Table 1. Precisions used in implementing our preconditioner and the LSQR solver.

	high precision	low precision
preconditioner	fp64	fp64, fp32, tf32, fp16
solver	fp64	fp64

Algorithm 2. Mixed precision gaussian preconditioner

Input: $m \times n$ matrix A, number of samples s, precision types high_prec, low_prec
Output: $s \times n$ preconditioner M
1: **procedure** $[M] = $ GENERATE_PRECOND(A, s, **high_prec**, **low_prec**)
2:     generate $s \times m$ Gaussian matrix G
3:     $\hat{G} = \text{demote}(G, \textbf{low\_prec})$
4:     $\hat{A} = \text{demote}(A, \textbf{low\_prec})$
5:     $\hat{A}_s = \hat{G}\hat{A}$
6:     $A_s = \text{promote}(\hat{A}_s, \textbf{high\_prec})$
7:     $[\sim, M] = \text{qr}(A_s, 0)$
8: **end procedure**

The central components underlying the construction of the preconditioner and the solver are BLAS operations. The dominant computation for generating the preconditioner is one matrix-matrix multiplication, while the dominant computation for the solver are dense matrix-vector multiplications. For this purpose, we decided to use the MAGMA library [19,43], which ports BLAS operations on various GPU architectures. In this paper, we want to target specifically NVIDIA devices following the AMPERE architecture, in order to test the fp16 and tf32 precision formats. Choosing MAGMA instead of vendor-specific libraries like cuBLAS[2] will allow us to extend our implementation to different architectures in future work. It should be noted that MAGMA provides BLAS functionality either by calling custom CUDA kernels or by directly calling cuBLAS. Mechanisms to make such decision on the fly are also provided.

The following code snippet is our implementation of Algorithm 2. We use `value_type_internal` as the reduced precision type for performing the compute-intensive operations and `value_type` for the original precision of the input data. When `value_type_internal` and `value_type` are different, the entries of the input matrix and the sketch matrix are converted to the precision indicated by `value_type_internal` and the matrix multiplication `dmtx_rp = sketch_mtx` $\times$

---

[2] cuBlas v12.0 https://developer.nvidia.com/cublas.

`mtx` is performed. The output is then converted back into the original precision. If `value_type_internal` is the same as `value_type` then no conversion is required. Afterwards, the economy QR factorization is computed in `value_type` precision and the preconditioner is stored in `dr_factor`.

- **preconditioner::gaussian::generate()**

```
1  // Generates the preconditioner and measures runtime.
2  template <typename value_type_internal, typename value_type,
3          typename index_type>
4  void generate(index_type num_rows_sketch, index_type num_cols_sketch,
5              value_type* dsketch, index_type ld_sketch,
6              index_type num_rows_mtx, index_type num_cols_mtx,
7              value_type* dmtx, index_type ld_mtx, value_type* dr_factor,
8              index_type ld_r_factor,
9              state<value_type_internal, value_type, index_type>&
10                 precond_state,
11              detail::magma_info& info, double* runtime, double* t_mm,
12              double* t_qr)
13  {
14      // Performs matrix-matrix multiplication in value_type_internal
15      // precision and promotes output to value_type precision.
16      if (!std::is_same<value_type_internal, value_type>::value) {
17          cuda::demote(num_rows_mtx, num_cols_mtx, dmtx, num_rows_mtx,
18              precond_state.dmtx_rp, num_rows_mtx);
19          cuda::demote(num_rows_sketch, num_cols_sketch, dsketch,
20              num_rows_sketch, precond_state.dsketch_rp, num_rows_sketch);
21          blas::gemm(MagmaNoTrans, MagmaNoTrans, num_rows_sketch,
22              num_cols_mtx, num_rows_mtx, 1.0, precond_state.dsketch_rp,
23              num_rows_sketch, precond_state.dmtx_rp, num_rows_mtx, 0.0,
24              precond_state.dresult_rp, num_rows_sketch, info);
25          cuda::promote(num_rows_sketch, num_cols_mtx, precond_state.
26              dresult_rp, num_rows_sketch, dr_factor, num_rows_sketch);
27      } else {
28          // value_type_internal == value_type -> no conversions required
29          blas::gemm(MagmaNoTrans, MagmaNoTrans, num_rows_sketch,
30              num_cols_mtx, num_rows_mtx, 1.0, dsketch, num_rows_sketch,
31              dmtx, num_rows_mtx, 0.0, dr_factor, ld_r_factor, info);
32      }
33
34      // Performs qr factorization in value_type precision.
35      magma_int_t info_qr = 0;
36      blas::geqrf2_gpu(num_rows_sketch, num_cols_mtx, dr_factor,
37          ld_r_factor, tau, &info_qr);
38      if (info_qr != 0) {
39          magma_xerbla("geqrf2_gpu", info_qr);
40      }
41  }
```

Listing 1.1. Generate preconditioner.

The object `state<value_type_internal, value_type, index_type>` is a struct containing the input matrix, the sketch matrix and their product computed in `value_type_internal` precision. It also contains the array `tau`, which is allocated on the cpu and used by the QR factorization.

– state<value_type_internal, value_type, index_type>

```
1  template <typename value_type_internal, typename value_type,
2            typename index_type>
3  struct state{
4      value_type_internal* dmtx_rp = nullptr;
5      value_type_internal* dsketch_rp = nullptr;
6      value_type_internal* dresult_rp = nullptr;
7      value_type* tau = nullptr;
8
9      void allocate(index_type ld_mtx, index_type num_cols_mtx,
10             index_type num_rows_sketch, index_type num_cols_sketch,
                   index_type ld_sketch,
11             index_type ld_r_factor) {
12         memory::malloc(&dmtx_rp, ld_mtx * num_cols_mtx);
13         memory::malloc(&dsketch_rp, ld_sketch * num_cols_sketch);
14         memory::malloc(&dresult_rp, ld_r_factor * num_cols_mtx);
15         memory::malloc_cpu(&tau, num_rows_sketch);
16     }
17
18     void free() {
19         memory::free(dmtx_rp);
20         memory::free(dsketch_rp);
21         memory::free(dresult_rp);
22         memory::free_cpu(tau);
23     }
24 };
```

Listing 1.2. State used for storing reduced precision information.

The following code snippet is a our high level implementation of Algorithm 1.

– **solver::lsqr::run()**

```
1  template <typename value_type_internal, typename value_type,
2            typename index_type>
3  void run(index_type num_rows, index_type num_cols, value_type* mtx,
4           value_type* rhs, value_type* init_sol, value_type* sol,
5           index_type max_iter, index_type* iter, value_type tol,
6           double* resnorm, value_type* precond_mtx,
7           index_type ld_precond, magma_queue_t queue)
8  {
9      temp_scalars<value_type, index_type> scalars;
10     temp_vectors<value_type_internal, value_type, index_type> vectors;
11     initialize(num_rows, num_cols, mtx, rhs,
12                precond_mtx, ld_precond, iter, scalars,
13                vectors, queue, t_solve);
14     while (1) {
15         step_1(num_rows, num_cols, mtx, precond_mtx, ld_precond, scalars,
16                vectors, queue);
17         step_2(num_rows, num_cols, mtx, rhs, sol, precond_mtx,
18                ld_precond, scalars, vectors, queue);
19         if (check_stopping_criteria(num_rows, num_cols, mtx, rhs, sol,
20                                     vectors.temp, iter, max_iter, tol,
21                                     resnorm, queue)) {
22             break;
23         }
24     }
25     finalize(vectors);
26 }
```

Listing 1.3. High level implementation of the LSQR solver.

Similar to `preconditioner::gaussian::generate()` the type `value_type_internal` is associated with the precision used in computing the most compute-intensive operations, which, in this case, are the `MV` operations. In this paper, we consider `value_type_internal` and `value_type` to be the same for the solver. The variables `scalars` and `vectors` contain all linear algebraic objects associated with the LSQR algorithm. From an implementation standpoint, Algorithm 1 can be dissected into three consecutive parts: lines 8–11 are implemented in `step_1` and compute the new basis vectors; lines 12–20 are implemented by `step_2` and update the current solution; finally, lines 21–24 are implemented by the `check_stopping_criteria` function, which tests whether convergence has been reached.

4   Numerical Experiments

4.1   Experiment Setup

We evaluate the effectiveness and performance of our preconditioned LSQR implementation as follows: We use a selection of $m \times n$ (with $m \gg n$) matrices $\boldsymbol{A}$ and we set the "true" least squares solution to $\mathbf{x} = \text{randn}(n, 1)$, in MATLAB notation, with $\boldsymbol{b} = \boldsymbol{A}\mathbf{x}$. This allows us to modify the tolerance in the LSQR algorithm, in order to stress-test the effectiveness of the preconditioner. For our numerical experiments, we use the following datasets (Table 2): (a) a human genetics dataset from the Human Genome Diversity Panel and (b) the CIFAR image dataset.

HGDP: HGDP_1 dataset has emerged from a population genetics application; see [39] and references therein for details. The coefficient matrix related to the regression problem is a tall-and-thin matrix whose entries are $-1, 0, 1, 2$. Exact details of the underlying genetic application are not relevant for our work here, since the matrix is only used for numerical evaluations. As regards HGDP_2, we modify HGDP_1 to get an ill-conditioned matrix ($\kappa(\boldsymbol{A}) \approx 10^6$) with different dimensions as follows: Initially, we get the first 6000 rows of HGDP_1 and subsequently, we add a few columns by randomly picking existing ones and change a tiny fraction of their elements ($<1\%$). We carefully act on every change to preserve each entry to be $\{-1,0,1,2\}$. The dimensions of the respective datasets are in Table 2.

CIFAR: The CIFAR dataset consists of $60,000$ 32×32 color images belonging in ten (non-overlapping) classes. In our setting, each row represents an image (we vectorize each $32 \times 32 \times 3 = 3,072$ matrix). Our CIFAR_2 dataset consists of $20,000$ randomly chosen images. We normalize all grayscale values to belong in the $[0, 1]$ interval. For the CIFAR_1 dataset, we created a somewhat "thinner" tall and thin matrix by randomly choosing for each image $1,000$ pixels out of the $3,072$.

Table 2. Matrices used in experimental evaluation.

datasets	rows	columns	cond	aspect ratio
HGDP_1	643,862	425	$O(10^3)$	1.5e3
HGDP_2	60,000	1,000	$O(10^6)$	6.0e1
CIFAR_1	20,000	1,000	$O(10^3)$	2.0e1
CIFAR_2	20,000	3,072	$O(10^4)$	6.5e0

Our experiments were conducted on a system, equipped with AMD EPYC 7742 64-Core Processor cluster CPUs and A100 80GB SXM NVIDIA GPUs. Our tests were run exclusively on a single node and utilized one GPU. The NVIDIA A100, which we ran our tests on, has native support for operations in fp16 and tf32 formats, and features tensor cores for matrix operations in fp64, fp16, and tf32. We used as termination criterion for LSQR, the relative residual norm $\frac{\|b - Ax^{(i)}\|}{\|b\|}$, setting the tolerance to 10^{-10} for our numerical experiments with the HGDP and 10^{-12} for the experiments with the CIFAR dataset. For the reported results, GCC 11.3.0, CUDA 14.4.4 and MAGMA 2.6.2 were used.

The goals of our experiments are three-fold: We seek to demonstrate that *(i)* constructing the preconditioner in reduced precision does not severely affect the convergence of the LSQR solver, and *(ii)* modest speedups can be achieved in constructing the preconditioner, which eventually lead to reductions of the total runtime of the preconditioned solver. In our analysis we also attempt to *(iii)* determine the factors that affect the performance of preconditioned LSQR. Those factors are related to properties of the input matrix, but also on implementation choices and underlying hardware.

For each matrix, we report (for varying values of the *sampling coefficient*) *(a)* the breakdown into preconditioner generation cost and solver iteration cost. This plot forms a *runtime profile* for each test matrix; *(b)* the iteration count of the LSQR solvers using different preconditioners; *(c)* the corresponding runtimes; and *(d)* the speedup with regard to the double precision reference preconditioned LSQR solver. The sampling coefficient controls the number of rows of the sketched matrix (and of the resulting preconditioner) as `rows_sampled = sampling_coeff × rows_mtx`. As the value of the sampling coefficient increases, more random samples are generated leading to preconditioners which are more effective, but also more expensive to generate. The data presented in the plots have been averaged over five executions and collected after five warmup runs.

4.2 Discussion

Every figure presented in this section corresponds to a problem with a unique combination of *runtime profile* and matrix aspect ratio, i.e., the fraction $\frac{\#rows}{\#columns}$. The matrices in descending aspect ratio order are, HGDP_1, HGDP_2, CIFAR_1 and CIFAR_2, (HGDP_1 having the largest and CIFAR_2 the smallest aspect ratio). Their *runtime profiles*, as indicated by the solver to preconditioner-generation runtimes, range from the solver dominating the total runtime (HGDP_1), runtimes being proportional (HGDP_2, CIFAR_1) and preconditioner-generation dominating the total runtime (CIFAR_2). In all of our tests, computing the preconditioner in fp32 is slower than the fp64 implementation. This is related to the lack of specialized hardware units for executing single precision matrix operations (the A100 GPU features tensor cores for fp64, fp16, and tf32 operations but not fp32).

Figure 1 depicts the outcomes of our experimental evaluation for matrix HGDP_1. Firstly, we observe that the convergence of preconditioned LSQR is not affected when the preconditioner is generated in fp32, tf32 or fp16 formats, as depicted in the top-right plot. The corresponding runtimes of the preconditioner generation step are shown in the bottom-left plot. For scaling coefficients greater than 1.5, we notice a significant reduction in the preconditioner generation runtime when tf32 and fp16 are used. The bottom-right plot depicts the speedup for the preconditioner generation and the overall runtime of the fp16

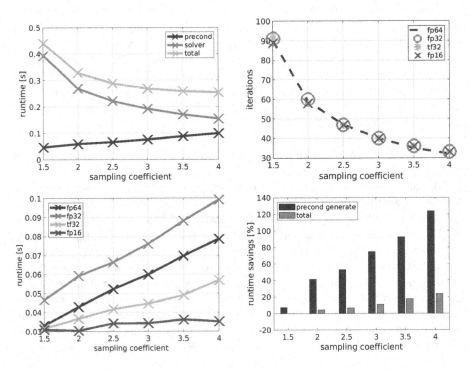

Fig. 1. Evaluation of the mixed precision preconditioner for the HGDP_1 test matrix. Top left: Runtime breakdown of the LSQR algorithm; Top right: Convergence of LSQR using a mixed precision preconditioner; Number of iterations for the 4 precisions overlap. Bottom left: Runtime of the preconditioner generation; Bottom right: Speedup when generating the preconditioner in fp16. Tolerance: 1e−10.

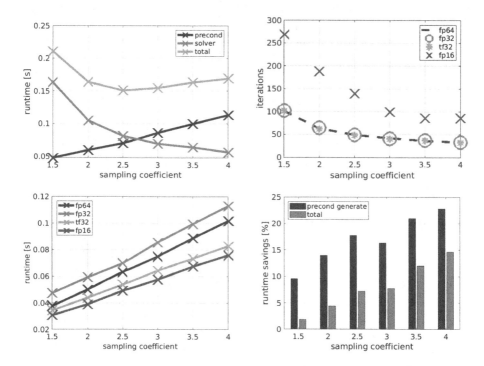

Fig. 2. Evaluation of the mixed precision preconditioner for the HGDP_2 test matrix. Top left: Runtime breakdown of the LSQR algorithm; Top right: Convergence of LSQR using a mixed precision preconditioner; Number of iterations overlap for fp64, fp32 and tf32 precisions; Bottom left: Runtime of the preconditioner generation; Bottom right: Speedup when generating the preconditioner in tf32. Tolerance: 1e−10

implementation. Despite the 2.4× speedup for the preconditioner generation, we only see a moderate 1.20× overall algorithm speedup. This is because of the costly solver iteration phase for the HGDP_1 problem (see top-left plot).

Figure 2 presents the evaluation results for the HGDP_2 matrix. This matrix is generated by manipulating HGDP_1 as described in Sect. 4.1. Computing the preconditioner in fp32 and tf32 formats does not affect the convergence of LSQR but generating the preconditioner in fp16 requires 3× as many LSQR iterations to reach convergence. In the bottom-left plot, we present the runtimes for preconditioner generation and on bottom right the speedup for generating the preconditioner in the tf32 format. The observed speedups of the preconditioner generation step for HGDP_2 are smaller in comparison to HGDP_1. However, the preconditioner overtakes the solver runtime for sampling coefficients greater than 2.5. As a result, the overall speedups are similar to those reported for HGDP_1.

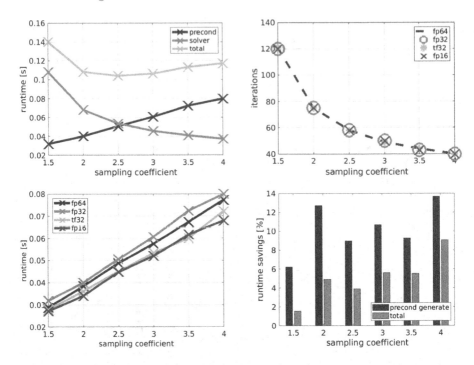

Fig. 3. Evaluation of the mixed precision preconditioner for the CIFAR_1 test matrix. Top left: Runtime breakdown of the LSQR algorithm; Top right: Convergence of LSQR using a mixed precision preconditioner; Iteration plots overlap across different formats; Bottom left: Runtime of the preconditioner generation; Bottom right: Speedup when generating the preconditioner in fp16. Tolerance: $1e-12$

In Figs. 3 and 4, we present experimental results for CIFAR_1 and CIFAR_2 matrices. In both cases, for moderate and large sampling coefficients, the preconditioner generation step becomes more expensive than the solver iteration phase. Convergence is not affected for CIFAR_1 when changing the precision format. Conversely, for CIFAR_2, the convergence suffers when generating the preconditioner in fp16. For CIFAR_2, the preconditioner generation cost is almost independent of the precision format used. This behaviour can be explained by taking into consideration the following; Firstly the aspect ratio of the matrix is too small (approximately 6.5 for CIFAR_2 compared to over 1,500 for HGDP_1), making the theoretical complexity of `qr`, $O(sn^2)$, similar to that of the `matrix multiplication`, $O(smn)$, since m becomes proportional to n. This effect is further amplified by the implementation of the preconditioner on GPU. Even though those components (i.e. `matrix multiply` and `qr`) have similar complexity, implementations of `matrix-matrix multiplication` achieve better performance on GPUs. On the other hand, `qr` is harder to parallelize, because it

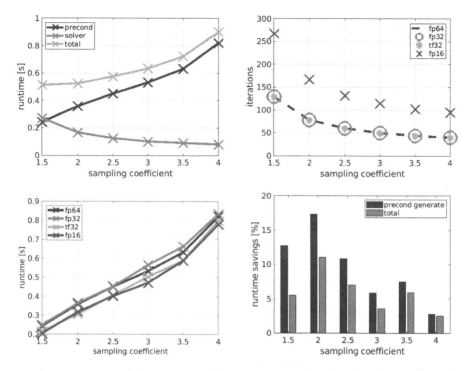

Fig. 4. Evaluation of the mixed precision preconditioner for the CIFAR_2 test matrix. Top left: Runtime breakdown of the LSQR algorithm; Top right: Convergence of LSQR using a mixed precision preconditioner; Iteration plots overlap for fp64, fp32 and tf32 precisions; Bottom left: Runtime of the preconditioner generation; Bottom right: Speedup when generating the preconditioner in tf32. Tolerance: 1e−12

requires operating on the columns of a matrix in a sequential fashion. The above suggest that QR factorization becomes the dominant component of the precon-ditioner generation when the aspect ratio of the matrix is small, and since it is always computed in double precision, the speedup observed is modest at best. This is also evident from Fig. 5, where the runtimes of the major preconditioner components, namely the matrix-matrix multiplication and the qr factorization are presented. We observe that only for the case of HGDP_1 the matrix multi-plication is the dominant operation of the preconditioner generation stage.

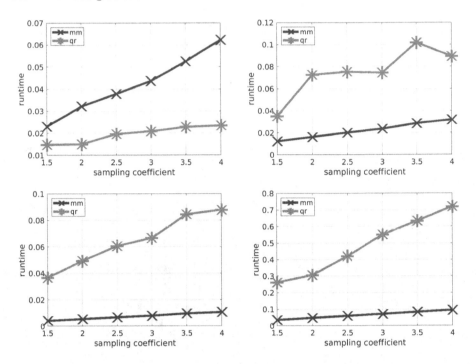

Fig. 5. Runtimes of preconditioner components. Top left: HGDP_1; Top right: HGDP_2; Bottom left: CIFAR_1; Bottom right: CIFAR_2.

5 Conclusion

In this paper, we describe a mixed precision implementation of a randomized preconditioner for solving the dense overdetermined least squares problem and present results on the NVIDIA A100 GPU. In our numerical experiments with matrices from the HGDP and CIFAR datasets, we show that convergence is not affected when using the tf32 format for generating the preconditioner, but we may experience delayed convergence when using fp16 in the preconditioner generation step. Part of our analysis explores how performance is affected by the properties of the input matrix. Attractive runtime savings can be achieved for matrices with high aspect ratio, since mixed precision is applied on the dominant operation of the preconditioner generation stage. Speedups can also be achieved for matrices with balanced row/column ratio, because the preconditioner generation stage requires a significant portion of the total runtime.

In future work, we are interested in combining our preconditioner with a mixed precision implementation of the LSQR solver. This will allow us to further investigate the effect of mixed precision computations on the solution of regression problems. Lastly, we would like to explore the use of mixed precision randomized preconditioning for potentially accelerating sparse least squares solvers and uncovering the factors that impact performance on GPUs.

Acknowledgements. PD and CB were partially supported by NSF grants CCF-2209509, CCF- 1814041, DMS-1760353, and DOE grant DE-SC0022085. This research was also supported by the Exascale Computing Project (17-SC-20-SC), a collaborative effort of the U.S. Department of Energy Office of Science and the National Nuclear Security Administration. The authors would like to thank the Innovative Computing Lab at University of Tennessee, for providing access to their compute cluster, to run the numerical experiments. They are also grateful to the reviewers for their insightful comments that helped improve this paper. CB and VG would like to thank Eugenia Kontopoulou for motivating them to pursue the topic of this paper and Efstratios Gallopoulos for introducing them to the *Blendenpik* algorithm.

References

1. Abdelfattah, A., et al.: A survey of numerical linear algebra methods utilizing mixed-precision arithmetic. Int. J. High Perform. Comput. Appl. **35**(4), 344–369 (2021)

2. Aliaga, J.I., Anzt, H., Grützmacher, T., Quintana-Ortí, E.S., Tomás, A.E.: Compressed basis GMRES on high-performance graphics processing units. Int. J. High Perform. Comput. Appl. https://doi.org/10.1177/10943420221115140

3. Avron, H., Maymounkov, P., Toledo, S.: Blendenpik: supercharging LAPACK's least-squares solver. SIAM J. Sci. Comput. **32**(3), 1217–1236 (2010). https://doi.org/10.1137/090767911

4. Baboulin, M., Becker, D., Bosilca, G., Danalis, A., Dongarra, J.: An efficient distributed randomized algorithm for solving large dense symmetric indefinite linear systems. Parallel Comput. **40**(7), 213–223 (2014). https://doi.org/10.1016/j.parco.2013.12.003. https://www.sciencedirect.com/science/article/pii/S0167819113001488. 7th Workshop on Parallel Matrix Algorithms and Applications

5. Balabanov, O., Grigori, L.: Randomized Gram–Schmidt process with application to GMRES. SIAM J. Sci. Comput. **44**(3), A1450–A1474 (2022). https://doi.org/10.1137/20M138870X

6. Benzi, M., Tuma, M.: A robust preconditioner with low memory requirements for large sparse least squares problems. SIAM J. Sci. Comput. **25**(2), 499–512 (2003). https://doi.org/10.1137/S106482750240649X

7. Bindel, D., Demmel, J., Kahan, W., Marques, O.: On computing givens rotations reliably and efficiently. ACM Trans. Math. Softw. **28**(2), 206–238 (2002). https://doi.org/10.1145/567806.567809

8. Björck, A.: Solving linear least squares problems by Gram-Schmidt orthogonalization. BIT Numer. Math. **7**, 1–21 (1967). https://doi.org/10.1007/BF01934122

9. Björck, R., Elfving, T., Strakos, Z.: Stability of conjugate gradient and Lanczos methods for linear least squares problems. SIAM J. Matrix Anal. Appl. **19**(3), 720–736 (1998). https://doi.org/10.1137/S089547989631202X

10. Björck, A.: Numerics of Gram-Schmidt orthogonalization. Linear Algebra Appl. **197–198**, 297–316 (1994). https://doi.org/10.1016/0024-3795(94)90493-6. https://www.sciencedirect.com/science/article/pii/0024379594904936

11. Björk, A.: SSOR preconditioning methods for sparse least squares problems, pp. 21–25 (1979)

12. Buttari, A., Dongarra, J., Langou, J., Langou, J., Luszczek, P., Kurzak, J.: Mixed precision iterative refinement techniques for the solution of dense linear systems. Int. J. High Perform. Comput. Appl. **21**(4), 457–466 (2007)

13. Carson, E., Daužickaitė, I.: Single-pass Nyström approximation in mixed precision (2022). https://doi.org/10.48550/ARXIV.2205.13355
14. Carson, E., Higham, N.J.: Accelerating the solution of linear systems by iterative refinement in three precisions. SIAM J. Sci. Comput. **40**(2), A817–A847 (2018). https://doi.org/10.1137/17M1140819
15. Carson, E., Higham, N.J., Pranesh, S.: Three-precision GMRES-based iterative refinement for least squares problems. SIAM J. Sci. Comput. **42**(6), A4063–A4083 (2020). https://doi.org/10.1137/20M1316822
16. Cui, X., Hayami, K.: Generalized approximate inverse preconditioners for least squares problems. Jpn. J. Ind. Appl. Math. **26**(1) (2008). https://doi.org/10.1007/BF03167543
17. Cui, X., Hayami, K., Yin, J.F.: Greville's method for preconditioning least squares problems. Adv. Comput. Math. **35** (2011). https://doi.org/10.1007/s10444-011-9171-x
18. Davis, T.A.: Algorithm 915, SuiteSparseQR: multifrontal multithreaded rank-revealing sparse QR factorization. ACM Trans. Math. Softw. **38**(1) (2011). https://doi.org/10.1145/2049662.2049670
19. Dongarra, J., et al.: Accelerating numerical dense linear algebra calculations with GPUs. Numer. Comput. GPUs 1–26 (2014)
20. Drineas, P., Mahoney, M.W., Muthukrishnan, S.: Sampling algorithms for L2 regression and applications. In: Proceedings of the Seventeenth Annual ACM-SIAM Symposium on Discrete Algorithm, pp. 1127–1136 (2006)
21. Dubrulle, A.A.: Householder transformations revisited. SIAM J. Matrix Anal. Appl. **22**(1), 33–40 (2000). https://doi.org/10.1137/S0895479898338561
22. Flegar, G., Anzt, H., Cojean, T., Quintana-Ortí, E.S.: Adaptive precision Block-Jacobi for high performance preconditioning in the Ginkgo linear algebra software. ACM Trans. Math. Softw. **47**(2) (2021). https://doi.org/10.1145/3441850
23. Fletcher, R.: Conjugate gradient methods for indefinite systems. In: Watson, G.A. (ed.) Numerical Analysis, pp. 73–89. Springer, Heidelberg (1976). https://doi.org/10.1007/bfb0080116
24. Frangella, Z., Tropp, J.A., Udell, M.: Randomized Nyström preconditioning. arXiv preprint arXiv:2110.02820 (2021)
25. George, A., Liu, J.W.: Householder reflections versus givens rotations in sparse orthogonal decomposition. Linear Algebra Appl. **88–89**, 223–238 (1987). https://doi.org/10.1016/0024-3795(87)90111-X. https://www.sciencedirect.com/science/article/pii/002437958790111X
26. Göbel, F., Grützmacher, T., Ribizel, T., Anzt, H.: Mixed precision incomplete and factorized sparse approximate inverse preconditioning on GPUs. In: Sousa, L., Roma, N., Tomás, P. (eds.) Euro-Par 2021. LNCS, vol. 12820, pp. 550–564. Springer, Cham (2021). https://doi.org/10.1007/978-3-030-85665-6_34
27. Grützmacher, T., Anzt, H., Quintana-Ortí, E.S.: Using Ginkgo's memory accessor for improving the accuracy of memory-bound low precision BLAS. Softw. Pract. Exp. **53**(1), 81–98 (2023). https://doi.org/10.1002/spe.3041. https://onlinelibrary.wiley.com/doi/abs/10.1002/spe.3041
28. Hayami, K., Yin, J.F., Ito, T.: GMRES methods for least squares problems. SIAM J. Matrix Anal. Appl. **31**(5), 2400–2430 (2010). https://doi.org/10.1137/070696313
29. Higham, N.J., Pranesh, S.: Exploiting lower precision arithmetic in solving symmetric positive definite linear systems and least squares problems. SIAM J. Sci. Comput. **43**(1), A258–A277 (2021). https://doi.org/10.1137/19M1298263

30. Higham, N.J., Pranesh, S., Zounon, M.: Squeezing a matrix into half precision, with an application to solving linear systems. SIAM J. Sci. Comput. **41**(4), A2536–A2551 (2019). https://doi.org/10.1137/18M1229511

31. Ipsen, I.C., Wentworth, T.: The effect of coherence on sampling from matrices with orthonormal columns, and preconditioned least squares problems. SIAM J. Matrix Anal. Appl. **35**(4), 1490–1520 (2014)

32. Kaufman, L.: The generalized householder transformation and sparse matrices. Linear Algebra Appl. **90**, 221–234 (1987). https://doi.org/10.1016/0024-3795(87)90314-4. https://www.sciencedirect.com/science/article/pii/0024379587903144

33. Leon, S.J., Björck, Gander, W.: Gram-Schmidt orthogonalization: 100 years and more. Numer. Linear Algebra Appl. **20**(3), 492–532 (2013). https://doi.org/10.1002/nla.1839. https://onlinelibrary.wiley.com/doi/abs/10.1002/nla.1839

34. Lindquist, N., Luszczek, P., Dongarra, J.: Accelerating restarted GMRES with mixed precision arithmetic. IEEE Trans. Parallel Distrib. Syst. **33**(4), 1027–1037 (2021)

35. Ludwig, R.: Ausgleichung vermittelnder und bedingter Beobachtungen, pp. 58–79. Vieweg+Teubner Verlag, Wiesbaden (1969). https://doi.org/10.1007/978-3-322-98459-3_4

36. Meng, X., Saunders, M.A., Mahoney, M.W.: LSRN: a parallel iterative solver for strongly over- or underdetermined systems. SIAM J. Sci. Comput. **36**(2), C95–C118 (2014). https://doi.org/10.1137/120866580

37. Paige, C.C., Rozloznik, M., Strakos, Z.: Modified Gram-Schmidt (MGS), least squares, and backward stability of MGS-GMRES. SIAM J. Matrix Anal. Appl. **28**(1), 264–284 (2006). https://doi.org/10.1137/050630416

38. Paige, C.C., Saunders, M.A.: LSQR: an algorithm for sparse linear equations and sparse least squares. ACM Trans. Math. Softw. (TOMS) **8**(1), 43–71 (1982)

39. Paschou, P., Lewis, J., Javed, A., Drineas, P.: Ancestry informative markers for fine-scale individual assignment to worldwide populations. J. Med. Genet. **47**(12) (2010). https://doi.org/10.1136/jmg.2010.078212

40. Rokhlin, V., Tygert, M.: A fast randomized algorithm for overdetermined linear least-squares regression. Proc. Natl. Acad. Sci. **105**(36), 13212–13217 (2008). https://doi.org/10.1073/pnas.0804869105. https://www.pnas.org/doi/abs/10.1073/pnas.0804869105

41. Rotella, F., Zambettakis, I.: Block householder transformation for parallel QR factorization. Appl. Math. Lett. **12**(4), 29–34 (1999). https://doi.org/10.1016/S0893-9659(99)00028-2. https://www.sciencedirect.com/science/article/pii/S0893965999000282

42. Terao, T., Ozaki, K., Ogita, T.: LU-Cholesky QR algorithms for thin QR decomposition. Parallel Comput. **92**, 102571 (2020). https://doi.org/10.1016/j.parco.2019.102571. https://www.sciencedirect.com/science/article/pii/S0167819119301620

43. Tomov, S., Dongarra, J., Baboulin, M.: Towards dense linear algebra for hybrid GPU accelerated manycore systems. Parallel Comput. **36**(5–6), 232–240 (2010). https://doi.org/10.1016/j.parco.2009.12.005

Ready for the Frontier: Preparing Applications for the World's First Exascale System

Reuben D. Budiardja$^{(\boxtimes)}$ (iD), Mark Berrill(iD), Markus Eisenbach(iD), Gustav R. Jansen(iD), Wayne Joubert(iD), Stephen Nichols(iD), David M. Rogers(iD), Arnold Tharrington(iD), and O. E. Bronson Messer(iD)

Oak Ridge National Laboratory, Oak Ridge, TN 37831, USA
{reubendb,berrillma,eisenbachm,jansengr,joubert,nicholsss,
rogersdm,arnoldt,bronson}@ornl.gov

Abstract. Frontier, a supercomputer at the Oak Ridge Leadership Computing Facility (OLCF), debuted atop the Top500 list of the world's most powerful supercomputers in June 2022 as the very first computer to produce exascale performance. Making sure scientific applications are optimized on this architecture is the critical link necessary to translate the newly available computational power into scientific insight and solutions. To that goal, the OLCF developed the Center for Accelerated Application Readiness (CAAR) program to ensure that a suite of highly optimized applications is ready for scientific runs at the onset of production operations for Frontier. This paper describes our experience in porting and optimizing such suite of applications in the OLCF's CAAR program.

1 Introduction and Background

Frontier debuted atop the Top500 list of the world's most powerful supercomputers in June 2022 [5] as the very first computer to produce exascale performance. The machine also represents the latest iteration of performance for hybrid CPU-GPU supercomputers that was initiated with the arrival of Titan at the Oak Ridge Leadership Computing Facility (OLCF) in 2012. Since Titan's debut, GPU-enabled scientific computing has moved from a somewhat exotic and perhaps niche methodology for a limited number of algorithms and codes to become the dominant method to achieve maximum performance on today's most computationally demanding applications.

Making sure scientific applications are optimized on this architecture is the critical link necessary to translate the newly available computational power into scientific insight and solutions. Herein we provide the details of code porting and optimization work done to take maximum advantage of Frontier's new exascale architecture.

Notice: This manuscript has been authored in part by UT-Battelle, LLC, under contract DE-AC05-00OR22725 with the US Department of Energy (DOE). The US government retains and the publisher, by accepting the article for publication, acknowledges that the US government retains a nonexclusive, paid-up, irrevocable, worldwide license to publish or reproduce the published form of this manuscript, or allow others to do so, for US government purposes. DOE will provide public access to these results of federally sponsored research in accordance with the DOE Public Access Plan (http://energy.gov/downloads/doe-public-access-plan).

A. Bhatele et al. (Eds.): ISC High Performance 2023, LNCS 13948, pp. 182–201, 2023.
https://doi.org/10.1007/978-3-031-32041-5_10

It was recognized during the project to build Titan at the beginning of the last decade that substantial effort would be needed to bring scientific applications to the point of effective use of hybrid CPU-GPU platforms. The Center for Accelerated Application Readiness (CAAR) was then formed to carry out this program of work. CAAR is a development program designed to ensure that the OLCF's hybrid CPU-GPU platforms deliver on their promise to advance scientific discovery. Following on from an initial small set of applications during the Titan project, CAAR has developed into a larger program with competitive proposals resulting in the formation of integrated teams of code stakeholders and developers, OLCF personnel, and vendor Center of Excellence collaborators brought together to work concertedly on a set of established application codes.

The experience of the OLCF and partners in previous instantiations of CAAR have been provided in [9] and [15]. Like these earlier experiences, the CAAR program for Frontier has a number of related, but distinct, aims. First is to have a suite of highly optimized applications ready for scientific runs at the onset of production operations for Frontier. Via close collaboration with teams dedicated to the development of the Frontier programming environment and tools, CAAR also serves to improve the environment for users and application developers in future, non-CAAR projects. Furthermore, CAAR serves as a laboratory for OLCF staff to develop platform-specific expertise, enabling a smooth transition to and effective support of user programs on Frontier. The experiences of CAAR teams are also translated into a robust training program and used to produce documentation of best practices on the machine.

An important ingredient in the optimization work undertaken by CAAR teams is the formulation of a "challenge problem" to be undertaken on Frontier at the close of development work. Although most modern scientific application codes are under near-constant development and may have a variety of specific simulation aims, the choice of a singular simulation target has proven invaluable to focus the optimization work. Nevertheless, the use of portable and maintainable approaches is a primary design criterion. All of these concerns are, of course, also highly dependent on the specifics of the Frontier platform. Another ingredient of a CAAR project is the formulation of a Figure of Merit (FOM) to allow us to have a quantitative measure of the development work. The FOM represents a performance of a CAAR application. At its simplest, a FOM is a measure of the amount of useful work the code can do per unit of time. A baseline FOM was taken on OLCF Summit at the beginning of the project, with the anticipation that a final FOM will be produced on Frontier at the end of the project. The final FOM captures both software- and hardware- improvements.

This paper is organized as follows. In the next section we briefly describe the pertinent OLCF systems for this work: Summit and Frontier. In Sect. 3 we describe the CAAR applications—their scientific domains, algorithmic motifs, performance characteristics—and the porting and optimization work for these applications for Frontier. We share some initial and early performance results from running these applications on Frontier and Crusher, an early access system with identical hardware to Frontier. In Sect. 4 we share some lessons learned and optimization techniques common to the applications discussed here. We close by providing concluding remarks in Sect. 5.

2 Systems Overview

2.1 Summit

Summit is a production system at the OLCF. Debuted as the number one system in the June 2018 Top500 list, it currently sits as the fifth in the latest Top500 list with the theoretical peak speed at 200 Petaflops.

Summit consists of over 4608 IBM Power System AC922 compute nodes interconnected by a dual-rail EDR InfiniBand network in a non-blocking fat-tree network topology. Each of Summit compute node has two IBM Power9 CPUS and six NVIDIA Volta V100 GPUs. Three GPUs and one CPU are interconnected with NVLink, while the two CPUs are connected by an X-Bus. Each Power9 has 22 cores and is connected to 256 GB DDR4 DRAM, with one core reserved for operating system tasks. Each of the V100 GPUs is connected to a 16 GB High-Bandwidth Memory (HBM). More detailed descriptions on Summit architecture, including the measured speed-and-feeds of the system, can be found in the OLCF User Documentation [19].

Several programming models are supported on Summit: CUDA for GPU programming, OpenMP for multithreading on CPUs, OpenMP offload and OpenACC for directive-based GPU programming. Users have also built portability layers such as Kokkos and Raja on top of these programming models. Common numerical and I/O libraries are also provided as environment modules.

To aid with the development and porting work to Frontier, HIP is also provided on Summit. On systems with NVIDIA GPUs such as Summit, HIP acts as thin portability layers which then called the underlying CUDA compiler (e.g. nvcc). HIP-provided tools for porting are also available on Summit. Prior the deployment of Frontier and its early access systems, Summit was the primary development system for the CAAR program.

2.2 Frontier

Frontier supercomputer consists of 9408 HPE/Cray EX compute nodes and several service nodes. Each compute node has a single 64-core AMD EPYC 7A53 "Optimized 3rd Gen EPYC" processor and four AMD Instinct[TM] MI250X Accelerator. Each of the MI250X Accelerators consists of two Graphics Compute Dies (GCDs) and are being presented to application as two devices (i.e. two GPUs). Therefore from an application perspective, eight GPUs (i.e. GCDs) are available to use. Each GCDs has 64 GB of high-bandwidth memory while the CPU is equipped with 512 GB DDR4 memory. The CPU and GPUs are interconnected with AMD Infinity Fabric, allowing peak bandwidths of 36 GB/s and 200 GB/s between host-and-device and device-to-device, respectively. A unique architectural feature of Frontier is that the four network interfaces are directly connected to the accelerators. The HPE Slingshot interconnect provides inter-node connectivity in a dragonfly topology providing 100 GB/s network bandwidth.

Frontier's programming environment (PE) includes AMD ROCm and ROCm libraries [1] with HIP for GPU programming. HIP, similar to CUDA, is a C++ extension and runtime API to allow developers to write computational kernels for GPUs. HIP's similarity to CUDA, other than pattern-discernible name changes to the API and library routine calls, allows for a straightforward porting of kernels written in CUDA. The HPE Cray provided PE also includes the Cray Compiling Environment (CCE) and AMD compilers capable of OpenMP for multithreading and offload to the GPUs. As with Summit, common numerical and I/O libraries are available via environment modules (see [19]).

The OLCF also provides an early-access system called Crusher. Crusher is virtually identical to Frontier except for its size: Crusher has 192 compute nodes total.

3   Applications

3.1   CoMet

The CoMet (Combinatorial Metrics) application [10] computes similarity metrics between vectors stored in large datasets for the purpose of solving clustering problems in areas such as genomics, climate, bioenergy and pandemics [13]. CoMet searches a very large combinatorial space in order to find clusters manifesting strong similarity relationships that indicate correlation characteristics of scientific interest. Its primary computational expense involves mixed precision GEMM operations comprising up to 90% or more of compute cycles for a typical run.

CoMet was initially ported to AMD GPUs using the HIP interface. Rather than using the HIP interoperability layer, the ported code uses `#ifdefs` in selected locations to allow compilation for either ROCm HIP or CUDA, thus allowing more controlled usage of the relevant libraries such as cuBLAS and rocBLAS. Subsequent development work focused on performance optimizations for the Frontier platform, primarily centered on the highly computationally intensive 3-way vector clustering code path. First, the formation of the matrix taken as input to the GEMMs was moved to the GPU, in keeping with the continuing theme of moving increasingly more computations to the GPU. Second, an algorithm change was made enabling the number of GEMMs required per result to be reduced from three to two with no change in the final answer, resulting in up to 50% performance improvement (see [13]). Finally, the thresholding process for the correlation metrics, which is used to discard all results except for the very small fraction of highly correlated values, was moved to the GPU. This not only made it possible to apply lossless compression (via the AMD rocPRIM library) to the results for much faster GPU-CPU transfer performance but also greatly reduced the CPU memory footprint for storing the metrics, making it possible to solve much larger problems.

Preliminary performance results on Frontier are shown in Fig. 1 for the 3-way CCC method, showing near-perfect linear scaling. CoMet has achieved over **6.71 Exaflops** (FP16/FP32 mixed precision) at scale on Frontier. The FOM or figure of merit for CoMet is measured as the rate of science output in units of vector element comparisons per second of runtime, On Frontier, CoMet achieved 419.9 quadrillion comparisons/second on 9,074 compute nodes, a factor of **5.16X** faster than the Summit baseline of 81.2 quadrillion comparisons per second, this speedup resulting from the combination of algorithmic improvements and increase in mixed precision flop rate of Frontier over Summit.

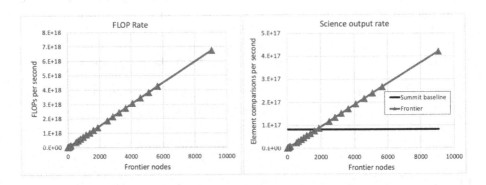

Fig. 1. CoMet Frontier scaling performance

3.2   Cholla: Computational Hydrodynamics on Parallel Architecture

Cholla is as a hydrodynamics code with radiative cooling originally written to run natively on NVIDIA GPUs [25]. It has since evolved and is acquiring additional physics modules relevant for astrophysics and cosmological simulations such as self-gravity solver, particle tracking, and magneto-hydrodynamics. Cholla computational kernels are written in CUDA, with the CPU responsible only to manage inter-process communications via MPI and data movement between CPU and GPU memory. Prior to this project, Cholla has been productively used to perform scientific simulations with published results (see for example, [24] and references therein).

The challenge problem for this CAAR project is to perform simulations of a Milky Way-like galaxy that allow for self-consistent star formation and feedback within interstellar medium. Motivated by recent observational campaigns that have drastically increased the availability of exquisite data about the Milky Way, computational astrophysicists are eager to have simulations results that can reproduce the observational data at the requisite resolutions to be able to make detailed predictions of the galaxy evolution. Considering factors such as the size of the galaxy and star clusters, the target resolutions for such simulations are approximately 10000^3 covering about fifty parsecs of computational domain.

For this project, we define the FOM as $\text{FOM} = \frac{nCells \times nCycles}{Walltime}$, where $nCells$ is the total number of cells, $nCycles$ is the number of cycles, and $Walltime$ is the elapsed wall-clock time in seconds.

Porting Cholla to Frontier is relatively straightforward due to the similarity of CUDA and HIP. Every CUDA library routine used by Cholla map to a corresponding HIP library routine, allowing simple name changes for porting. We started by using the Hipify tool to transition to HIP. The following considerations, however, urged us to come up with an alternative approach. If we had ported everything to HIP as a separate code base, we will be burdened with maintaining two codes: HIP-based and CUDA-based. If we had ported to HIP in-place, Cholla's users on CUDA systems will have the additional burden of installing HIP[1]. Even if performance impact is minimal, we felt that this is a significant burden to users on CUDA system.

Our approach is to instead have a simple conditional compilation file—using C preprocessor—that does the translation from CUDA to HIP calls based on a compilation flag. The small number of CUDA library calls used in Cholla made this a relatively simple process.[2]

When Cholla was originally written, the GPU high-bandwidth memory size was typically only a fraction of the available host memory. It therefore utilized the "sub-grid splitting" technique—where the grid is split into multiple blocks, copied into GPU memory on which computations are performed, and copied back to the CPU consecutively—to fit larger volume than what was possible on GPU memory only. This assumption is no longer true on Frontier, where the size of GPU memory is equal to that of host memory. By removing the subgrid splitting feature, we actually introduced a large speed up by virtue of removing data movement to and from GPU memory while at the same time simplifying the code.

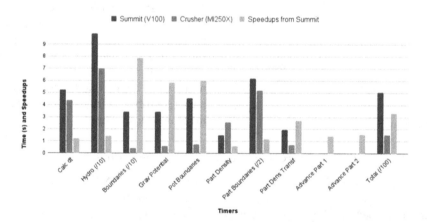

Fig. 2. Timing (green and blue bars) and Speedups (red bars) of computational portions for Cholla on Summit's Nvidia V100 (green) and Crusher's AMD's MI250X GCD (blue). The timing for Hydro, Boundaries, Gravitational potential, Particle boundaries are scaled down by factor of 10, 10, 100, 2, and 100 respectively to fit the scale of the chart. (Color figure online)

Keeping the data persistently on GPU memory is also motivated by another architectural feature of Frontier: hardware- and software-supported GPU-aware MPI. Since

---

[1] On CUDA systems, HIP acts as a thin portability layers that then calls the CUDA compiler nvcc.

[2] How we do this can be observed from the file available from the Cholla public repository: https://github.com/cholla-hydro/cholla/blob/main/src/utils/gpu.hpp.

Frontier's network interfaces are connected directly to the GPU memory, it is more efficient for communications to be done on data residing on GPU memory. We modified Cholla to utilize GPU-aware MPI for the data already residing on GPUs.

Figure 2 shows timings and speedups of computational portions of Cholla for the FOM problem. This test problem was run with 64 GPUs on Summit NVIDIA V100 and 64 GCDs on Crusher's AMD MI250X. This comparison was performed after all the software changes discussed above. As we can see from the plot, most of the computational portions show some speedup on AMD MI250X GCD, with some achieving more than 5X speedup. The total speedup is more than a factor of 3X. We attribute this to mostly two factors. First is the fact that the network interfaces are directly attached to the GPUs. The computational portions that get the most speedups are communication-heavy. The second contributing factor is the higher memory-bandwidth available on Frontier's hardware.

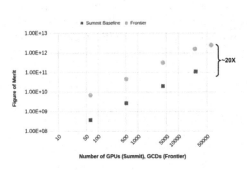

Fig. 3. Cholla FOM as a function of number of GPUs (Summit) or GCDs (Frontier).

Figure 3 shows the total speedup on Frontier over baseline runs on Summit. Note that the baseline runs were performed with the version of the code prior to the developments described above. The FOM speedups on Frontier's 64,000 AMD MI250X GCDS is 20X versus the baseline code on Summit with 26,624 NVIDIA V100 GPUs. From the results shown in Fig. 2, we can infer that software developments contribute a speedup over ~4X, while hardware improvements contribute at least ~4X to make up the total 20X speedups.

3.3 GESTS: GPUs for Extreme-Scale Turbulence Simulations

The GESTS project performs direct numerical simulations (DNS) of turbulent fluid flows across a wide range of scales according to the Navier-Stokes equations. The algorithms developed by GESTS use a Runge-Kutta scheme in time and a Fourier-spectral representation in space to create a pseudo-spectral method that computes the nonlinear terms in physical space and performs all other computations in wave number space. The original GPU-enabled algorithm along with previous results from Summit are presented in [23].

The basic elements of the GESTS algorithm include a domain decomposition among the MPI processes, transposes of the solution domain to allow FFTs to be taken in each direction, local data movements arising from the non-contiguous nature of messages for the required all-to-all communication, as well as data movements between the host and device memory. This 3D FFT problem is in fact well known for being communication intensive, which can limit scalability at large problem sizes. The challenge—which is shared by many other user application codes—is to allow a communication-intensive algorithm to benefit fully from heterogeneous platforms whose principal advantage is fast computation.

The GESTS codes are written in modern Fortran using MPI for communication and OpenMP for CPU multi-threading and GPU offloading. The codes are formed around a custom-built 3D FFT algorithm that computes the FFTs on both CPUs and GPUs via FFTW (for CPUs), CUDA cuFFT (for NVIDIA GPUs), or ROCm rocFFT (for AMD GPUs). OpenMP offloading functionality is used to manage data movement between the host and device, to enable GPU-Direct MPI communications, and to accelerate a variety of array operations on the GPUs.

Two variants of codes have been developed: a "Slabs-" and a "Pencils-" decomposition (see Fig. 4). For a N^3 problem across P MPI processes, the "Slabs" decomposition cuts the domain in only one of the three dimensions at a time to form P partitions. This decomposition allows the code to perform the FFT computations for two of the three dimensions before requiring expensive MPI communications to form contiguous data for the FFT computations in the third dimension. Since each slab must contain a full 2D slice of the domain, the "Slabs" code can have a maximum of $P = N$ MPI processes, which can be a critical limitation for very large problems.

The "Pencils" decomposition divides the domain in two dimensions at a time. This decomposition allows the use of up to N^2 MPI processes, but requires an expensive MPI communication between each FFT computation since only one direction is contiguous at a time. Specifically, for an N^3 problem across P MPI processes, one dimension is divided into P_r pieces and a second dimension is divided into P_c pieces such that $P = P_r \times P_c$. Figure 4 demonstrates both decomposition approaches.

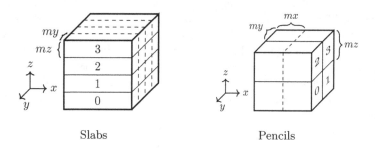

Slabs   Pencils

Fig. 4. Slab vs Pencil Decomposition

As seen in Tables 1 and 2, the MPI communications consume approximately 70% of the runtime for the multi-node jobs while the forward and inverse FFT transforms in the three coordinate directions account for roughly 20% of the runtime. Virtually all of the MPI communications are used to transpose the arrays into contiguous pencils for the FFT computations. As a result, the 3D FFT algorithm consumes upwards of 90% of the runtime for the DNS codes. This demonstrates clearly how efficient DNS computations depend critically on a highly performant 3D FFT algorithm.

The Figure of Merit (FOM) chosen for GESTS is defined as the total number of grid points in the simulation divided by the average time to compute each time step and is presented in Eq. 1

$$FOM = \frac{N^3}{\Delta \tilde{t}} \qquad (1)$$

Table 1. Timings for "Slabs" code on Frontier

N^3	Nodes	Ranks	FFT(s)	Pack+Unpack(s)	MPI(s)	Other(s)	Total(s)
2048^3	1	8	1.364	0.243	1.841	0.635	4.083
4096^3	8	64	1.432	0.246	6.930	0.658	9.266
8192^3	64	512	1.583	0.255	8.110	0.672	10.620
16384^3	512	4096	2.200	0.269	8.427	0.675	11.571
32768^3	4096	32768	3.420	0.276	9.220	0.704	13.62

Table 2. Timings for "Pencils" code on Frontier

N^3	Nodes	P_r	P_c	FFT(s)	Pack+Unpack(s)	MPI(s)	Other(s)	Total(s)
2048^3	1	2	4	1.820	1.092	2.333	0.590	5.835
4096^3	8	2	32	1.643	0.786	8.070	0.791	11.290
8192^3	64	2	256	1.454	0.610	8.760	0.686	11.510
16384^3	512	2	2048	2.340	0.600	9.460	0.730	13.130
32768^3	4096	4	8192	3.385	0.608	10.470	1.337	15.800

The reference FOM was computed on Summit as part of an INCITE 2019 project [23] and is provided in Table 3 along with timings from Frontier (see Tables 1 and 2). As Table 3 shows, GESTS sees a $>5x$ speedup on Frontier on 4096 nodes for both decomposition strategies which exceeds the CAAR project goal of a $4x$ speedup. Tests are ongoing for $N = 32768$ on 8192 Frontier nodes with the "Pencils" code, and full production simulations are expected in the near future. These 32768^3 cases are the largest known DNS computations to date with a point total in excess of 35 trillion grid points. Frontier is the only machine in the world with the memory capacity to complete these simulations.

Table 3. Comparison of FOM on Summit and Frontier

Machine	Decomposition	#GPUs	N^3 (points)	$\Delta \tilde{t}$ (sec)	FOM (points/sec)	Speedup
Summit	Slab	18432	18432^3	14.24	4.398×10^{11}	—
Frontier	Slab	32768	32768^3	13.62	2.583×10^{12}	5.87x
Frontier	Pencil	32768	32768^3	15.8	2.227×10^{12}	5.06x

3.4 LBPM: Lattice Boltzmann Methods for Porous Media

The LBPM software package relies on lattice Boltzmann methods to model transport processes in systems with complex microstructure, including flows through porous media, multiphase flow, and membrane transport processes. Microscope image data— such as 3D data from x-ray micro-computed tomography that reveals the internal structure of complex materials—is commonly used to specify input geometries for LBPM.

Digital rock physics is a core capability of LBPM, particularly direct pore-scale simulations of two-fluid flow through geological materials such as rock or soil. LBPM is freely available through the Open Porous Media project [7, 17]. The LBPM multiphase flow solver uses a color Lattice-Boltzmann model that is defined by a set of three lattice Boltzmann equations (LBEs), corresponding to one momentum transport equation and two mass transport equations. The LBEs are defined based on a quadrature scheme to discretize the velocity space in the continuous Boltzmann transport equation. LBPM includes a thread-based framework to carry out in situ analysis of the flow behavior. The analysis framework is configured to compute integral measures from the flow that capture essential aspects of the behavior. In addition, the analysis framework can identify and track connected and disconnected parts of the fluid performing the integral analysis over these individualized sub-regions [18].

The LBPM code is written in object-oriented C++ using MPI for communication. Analysis routines and I/O are handled in separate CPU threads using the native C++11 thread capabilities. The code used CUDA for the initial GPU capabilities. While the GPU routines represent the computationally expensive portion of the physics, analysis and IO routines are performed on the CPU. The porting effort focused on updating GPU routines to HIP to target the AMD GPUs. The majority of the simulation data remains on the GPU during the calculations over all timesteps with communication from the GPU to the host occurring every n-th timestep for analysis or IO needs. The communication between nodes utilizes pack/unpack routines that are implemented on the GPU to avoid copying the entire domain to the host and the communication can take advantage of the GPU direct MPI communication. The code includes a number of unit tests that were leveraged throughout the porting process to ensure correctness and to test the performance of individual routines such as communication.

To compare performance across multiple architectures and scale the project defined a FOM (Figure of Merit) defined as the number of Millions of Lattice Updates Per Second (MLUPS). Table 4 shows the weak scaling performance data obtained on Summit. Weak scaling demonstrated 80% scaling efficiency on Summit at full machine using the original version of the code. Table 5 shows the weak scaling performance data obtained on Crusher after porting to AMD GPUs.

Table 4. Performance on Summit

Ranks	Nodes	MFLUPS (per rank)	MLUPS (total)
6,144	1024	384	2.36e6
12,288	2048	369	4.54e6
24,576	4096	313	7.71e6

3.5 LSMS

The Locally-Selfconsistent Multiple Scattering (LSMS) code implements a scalable approach for first principles all-electron calculations of alloys and magnetic solid state systems. It is available under an open source license [14]. LSMS solves the Schrödinger

Table 5. Performance on Crusher

Ranks	Nodes	MLUPS (per rank)	MLUPS (total)
1	1	640	640
8	1	610	4880
64	8	594	37,952
512	64	595	304,640

equation for the electrons inside a solid using the Kohn-Sham density functional theory (DFT) formalism [12]. This transforms the interacting many electron problem into a tractable effective one-electron problem. In the transformed problem, the many body effects are captured by the exchange-correlation functional, for which various approximations are available. While most widely used DFT codes diagonalize the Kohn-Sham Hamiltonian, LSMS is inspired by the Korringa-Kohn-Rostoker method [20] and it employs a real space multiple scattering formalism to calculate the electronic Green's function.

LSMS calculates the local spin density approximation to the diagonal part of the electron Green's function. The electron and spin densities and energy are readily determined once the Green's function is known. Linear scaling with system size is achieved in LSMS by using several unique properties of the real space multiple scattering approach to the Green's function, namely: 1) the Green's function is "nearsighted", therefore, each domain, *i.e.* atom, requires only information from nearby atoms in order to calculate the local value of the Green's function. 2) the Green's function is analytic everywhere away from the real axis, therefore, the required integral over electron energy levels can be analytically continued onto a contour in the complex plane where the imaginary part of the energy further restricts its range; and 3) to generate the local electron/spin density an atom needs only a small amount of information(phase shifts) from those atoms within the range of the Green's function. The very compact nature of the information that needs to be passed between processors and the high efficiency of the dense linear algebra algorithms employed to calculate the Green's function are responsible for the scaling capability of the LSMS code. The LSMS code is written in C++ with a few remaining legacy routines written in Fortran and it utilizes MPI for communication as well as OpenMP for multi-threaded CPU execution. GPU acceleration is achieved through CUDA or HIP kernels as well as through the use of dense linear algebra libraries.

For LSMS we defined a figure of merit that captures both strong and weak scaling opportunities as well as increases in the physical accuracy captured during the calculations. Thus FOM_{LSMS} combines the number of atoms in the simulation N_{atom}, the number of energies on the integration contour $N_{energies}$, the number of sites in the local interaction zone N_{LIZ}, the maximum angular momentum l_{max} and time per selfconsistency iteration in seconds $t_{iteration}$ as $FOM_{LSMS} = N_{atom}N_{energies}\left((l_{max}+1)^2 N_{LIZ}\right)^3 / t_{iteration}$. The results for scaling runs on Frontier are shown in Table 6.

The port of LSMS to the AMD GPU architecture of Frontier builds on our GPU implementation for the Titan system at OLCF [9]. The main kernel that accounts for

Table 6. FOM results for LSMS on Frontier and comparison to Summit.

Atoms	Nodes	FOM	FOM/Node	FOM(Frontier)/FOM(Summit)
128	2	2.11E+12	1.05402E+12	6.270912661
1024	16	1.51E+13	9.464E+11	5.63065207
8192	128	1.20E+14	9.37336E+11	5.576724997
65532	1024	9.43E+14	9.21091E+11	5.480073895
65532	2048	1.81E+15	8.85586E+11	5.268835897
65532	4096	3.49E+15	8.52815E+11	5.073863288
131072	2048	1.86E+15	9.09072E+11	5.408568929
131072	4096	3.62E+15	8.84375E+11	5.261631366

more than 95% of the floating point operations in a typical LSMS run calculates the block diagonal parts of the Green's function in the local interaction zone approximation. This requires the calculation of a small block of the inverse of a dense non-Hermitian complex matrix. This task can be readily solved using the dense matrix multiplication, LU factorization and solver routines in the rocBLAS and rocSolver libraries. Additional kernels that construct the matrices that enter the solvers are written in HIP. While these follow the same structure as the equivalent CUDA kernels, the performance was significantly improved by rearranging the matrix index calculations to alleviate the contention between integer and floating point operations on the AMD accelerators.

With the ports to AMD GPUs described above for LSMS we have obtained early scaling and performance measurements on Frontier. In Fig. 5a we show the weak scaling of FePt calculations from 2 nodes to 4096 nodes with 64 atoms per node (8 atoms per GPU). For comparison we show the time on Summit for a single node with the same

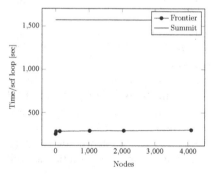

(a) Weak scaling of LSMS for FePt ($lmax = 7$) with 64 atoms per node from 2 to 4096 Frontier nodes.

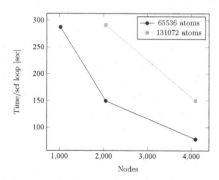

(b) Strong scaling of LSMS for FePt ($lmax = 7$) from 1024 to 4096 Frontier nodes.

Fig. 5. Weak- and strong-scaling of LSMS.

number of atoms per GPU. Additionally we also have early strong scaling results for 65,536 and 131,072 atom systems on Frontier that are shown in Fig. 5b. These results indicate that, together with the CAAR improvements in LSMS, we can, at present, expect an $\approx 5.5 \times$ per node speedup on Frontier when compared to Summit.

3.6   NUCCOR/NTCL

NUCCOR (Nuclear Coupled-Cluster Oak Ridge) is a nuclear physics application designed to compute properties of atomic nuclei from first principles using high-performance computing resources at Oak Ridge National Laboratory (ORNL). From its inception at the start of the millennium [3], it has changed the perception of ab-initio nuclear physics from impractical and too computationally expensive to practical and state-of-the-art. Since NUCCOR uses the coupled-cluster method, a method that scales polynomially with the number of particles present in the atomic nucleus, it has a significant advantage over other competing methods that only scale exponentially. With the exponential growth in the availability of high-performance computing resources at ORNL over the past two decades, NUCCOR has gone from computing properties of oxygen-16, a nucleus with only eight protons and eight neutrons, in 2004 [3], to lead-208, a nucleus with 82 protons and 126 neutrons, in 2022. Frontier will increase the reach of ab-initio nuclear theory to encompass all atomic nuclei and test the theoretical foundations that define low-energy nuclear physics.

NUCCOR solves the time-independent Schrödinger equation for many interacting protons and neutrons, collectively called nucleons, using the coupled-cluster method. The coupled-cluster method rewrites the Schrödinger equation as an eigenvalue problem in a finite basis set. By constructing a similarity transformation for the Hamiltonian matrix using a fixed-point iteration, the eigenvalue problem can be truncated to a smaller basis set and solved at a lower computational cost. However, the basis set is still too large for the eigenvalue problem to be solved exactly, so Krylov sub-space methods, like Arnoldi and non-symmetric Lanczos, are used to extract the lowest eigenpairs to a specified precision.

Due to the inherent symmetries in an atomic nucleus, block-sparse tensor contractions dominate the computational cost of the NUCCOR application. Each iteration consists of multiple tensor contraction terms, where each term is block-sparse. NUCCOR exploits the sparsity patterns to convert them into a series of local, dense tensor contractions of different dimensions. The number of tensor contractions and the dimensions of each contraction depend on the nucleus and the size of the chosen basis set. Typically, the size of the basis set is on the order of thousands, while the dimensions of the tensor contractions vary from less than ten to several million. A balanced distribution scheme among MPI ranks is critical for excellent performance on Summit and Frontier, as well as a highly tuned tensor contraction library.

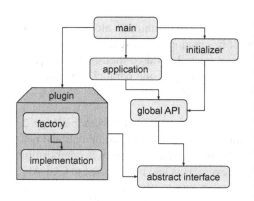

Fig. 6. NTCL implements a plugin structure using the strategy and abstract factory patterns. The application knows only the architecture-independent API, while the main program unit initializes the architecture-dependent API.

NUCCOR uses the Nuclear Tensor Contraction Library (NTCL) [8] to perform distributed block-sparse tensor contractions and dense local tensor contractions. NTCL presents an architecture-independent API to the user and supports multiple hardware backends using a plugin structure. For example, the HIP backend supports Crusher and Frontier, while the CUDA backend supports Summit. For the CAAR project, we ported the CUDA plugin to HIP, which was very straightforward. After a search-and-replace operation, we only had to perform minor adjustments, primarily to accommodate 64 work items in a wave-front, compared to 32 threads in a warp using CUDA.

NTCL and NUCCOR are written in modern Fortran and use features from the Fortran 2018 standard. Internally, NTCL implements the plugin structure using a standard strategy pattern to encapsulate memory, dependencies, and algorithms. In addition, an abstract factory pattern enables the user to write plugin-independent code for maximum efficiency. Figure 6 shows the overall structure.

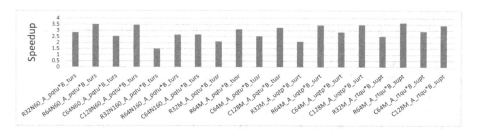

Fig. 7. Tensor contraction speedups in NTCL using a single GCD of the MI250X on Crusher, compared to a single V100 on Summit for different tensor shapes and sizes. The column label denotes the datatype, the tensor dimensions, and the tensor contraction type in Einstein summation notation.

Figure 7 shows preliminary performance results from Crusher. Each column identifies the speedup from an NV100 on Summit to a single GCD on the MI250X on Crusher. We need Frontier to run a representative use case for NUCCOR. If we run a use case appropriate for Crusher, it will result in many small tensor contractions and skew the performance results. Instead, we show a selection of tensor contractions that are important for the figure of merit – the number of tensor contraction operations per second.

3.7 NAMD

NAMD [22] is a C++ molecular dynamics (MD) code that simulates atomistic biological systems on CPU and GPU architectures. It has demonstrated scalable performance on systems consisting of millions of atoms over several hundred thousand cores [21]. NAMD is implemented with Charm++ [11], a message passing parallel programming framework that provides migratable objects, asynchronous methods, and an adaptive runtime system.

As is typical for molecular dynamics codes, the calculation of forces, pairwise 2-body non-bonded, bonded, angle, and dihedral interactions are the computational bottleneck. To reduce the time-to-solution, NAMD uses a spatial-domain decomposition to partition the force calculations over the processor. This had been ported to CUDA.

The methodology of porting NAMD to Frontier was to use HIP. Because HIP and CUDA kernels are syntactically the same, we used a common header file that defines C preprocessor macros to redefine CUDA calls to HIP calls such as the ones shown below:

```
#define cudaGetDevice hipGetDevice
#define cudaStream hipStream
```

HIP does have limitations in adapting to CUDA's API (these limitations are listed in the HIP documentation). Consequently, it is advisable to keep the CUDA code simple to avoid these limitations.

Another difference between HIP and CUDA kernels is that the warp size in CUDA is 32 while that for HIP is 64. Many NAMD kernels had hard-coded the warp size which resulted in deleterious performance effects when run on the AMD GPUs. As part of this project, we improved the code portability on different GPUs by using a variable to represent warp size.

With AMD devices having larger warp sizes that NVIDIA devices, it is important to carefully consider and benchmark performance effects of problem decomposition over the GPUs. In NAMD, the atom's tiles sized was tightly coupled and set equal to the device warp size. This had the side effect of increasing the number of neighboring atoms in which lowered the percentage of effective interacting pairs. This problem was addressed by decoupling the tile sizes from the device's warp size.

For biological MD simulations long-ranged electrostatics effects are significant and are typically calculated with methods that involve Fast Fourier Transforms (FFTs). We initially attempted to use rocFFT to do this but found out that it did not deliver superior performance to the VkFFT library.

NAMD's use of the Charm++ parallel programming framework requires the Open Fabrics Interfaces (OFI) target on Frontier to perform optimally. Unfortunately, the we encountered functionality issue with using OFI on the current Slingshot 11 on Frontier. While we continue to work with the vendor to resolve this issue, we had to resort to using the Charm++ MPI target which is not nearly as performant as the OFI target.

3.8 PIConGPU

PIConGPU is a particle-in-cell code that solves the Maxwell electromagnetic equations simultaneously with the motion a plasma of electrons [2]. Internally, electric and magnetic fields are stored on a staggered, Yee-grid and updated using finite-difference time-domain methods. Electrons are propagated in time by moving 'macroparticles'. Each macroparticle represents a group of electrons within a deformable spatial shape.

This explicit representation of particles and fields is necessary to create high fidelity models of high-energy plasmas because it contains the full relativistic physics of particle-field interactions. Results from these simulations can be used to parameterize continuum, density-based models like the Vlasov-Poisson equation. As a time-domain code, PIConGPU's scaling is governed by a Courant-Friedrichs-Lewy (CFL) condition for the electromagnetic wave velocity.

In the traveling wave electron acceleration experiment (TWEAC) [4], a short, 10-femtosecond burst from two crossed beams of ultraviolet light accelerate electrons to nearly the speed of light. The accelerated electrons leave behind a cavity that can extend 10-s of micrometers. A full simulation of these events requires observing a length scale of 100-s of micrometers over hundreds of femtoseconds, a volume which contains, at minimum, around 10^{14} electrons and 10^{12} grid cells simulated for thousands of time-steps.

For systematically exploring the design of these laser-accelerated plasma setups, it is essential to have a high-performance, parallel application with good weak scaling to large simulation volumes. PIConGPU has shown extremely good weak scaling efficiency, even up to full Frontier scale (Fig. 8). Its strong scaling is essentially limited by needing at least 200^3 cells per GPU in order to saturate the GPU's compute speed. PIConGPU's FOM thus measures number of time-steps completed per second times a weighted average of particles (90%) and grid cells (10%).

PIConGPU faced unique challenges increasing its throughput because of several factors. Primarily, the application had already been heavily optimized for GPU computations: GPU-resident data, use of 32-bit floats in most places, and hand-optimization of kernels ranked slowest on existing hardware. On the other hand, more than 90% of its run-time is already spent in kernels, directly enabling the code able to utilize faster GPUs. Frontier's MI250x GPUs have the same FLOP-rate for 32-bit as 64-bit floats, a factor which doesn't directly benefit existing use cases. Instead, faster double-precision arithmetic enables simulating previously inaccessible laser setups that require high-fidelity.

Figure 8 shows PIConGPU's achieved FOM during a full-Frontier simulation of the TWEAC system. In this particular configuration, the simulation size included $2.7 \cdot 10^{13}$ macroparticles in 10^{12} grid cells. One thousand time-steps completed in a mere 6 and a half minutes. The right panel shows significant variations in the wall-time per simulated time-step. These may potentially be a symptom of network congestion effects. If confirmed, performance will increase with network upgrades.

The average FOM in the run above (65.7 TUpdates/sec) was a factor of 3.9 higher than the Summit benchmark run completed at the start of the project (16.8 TUpdates/sec). Achieving this progress happened in several steps. First, the team added ROCm support to their performance-portability libraries, alpaka and cupla [16]. The team also compiled and tested the I/O backend library, openPMD [6]. The initial test run was 20% slower on a single AMD MI100 GPU[3] as it would have on a NVIDIA

---

[3] MI100 is a previous generation of AMD accelerators.

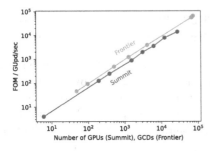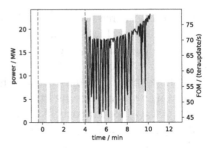

Fig. 8. TWEAC laser simulation weak scaling at 14.6×10^6 cells per GCD (left panel) and (right panel) 9216-node Frontier run showing system power utilization (left scale) and instantaneous figure of merit (units of 10^{12} updates per second, right scale).

V100. There were also program crashes observed during development that originated from within the GPU and MPI library and device driver stacks. Once found, these issues were raised with the compiler and hardware vendors, which lead to help troubleshooting, improved libraries, and issue resolution.

Timing GPU kernels was done without any code changes using nvprof and rocprof. It showed that about 92% of the execution time was spent running GPU kernels on both platforms. Individually, all the kernels were faster on MI100 except for the kernel computing the driving 'background' laser field. This kernel evaluates sin and cos functions, and requires significant GPU register space. After gaining some a few percent speedup by trying some mathematical reformulations, the developers eventually decided to use time-propagation instead of direct calculation for this field. The result was a 25% speedup in the single MI250x GCD vs. V100 comparison. Scaling this up by the number of GPUs available on Frontier, the overall increase in throughput is 4 times higher than Summit.

4   Lessons Learned

We summarize in this section the common insights and lessons learned from porting and optimizing the CAAR applications on Frontier.

We first note that all of the CAAR applications described in this paper had been "production-ready" applications at the beginning of the program. In other words, these applications have been used to perform simulations with published results and have been fairly well optimized on pre-exascale systems such as Summit. Almost by necessity, this means that these applications were already GPU-accelerated at the beginning of the CAAR program.

For porting from CUDA to HIP, the resemblance of the two language extensions tremendously helped the porting efforts. Although the HIP-ify tool was initially helpful, applications chose to instead use a simpler translation layer via C-preprocessor or header include file. This header file provides a name-translation layer between CUDA and HIP routines (for example, see Sect. 3.7 and 3.2). In other cases, developers used OpenMP offloading (GESTS) or reliance on cross-platform libraries (NUCCOR, NAMD, CoMet) to achieve performance portability.

After the initial porting, further optimizations were then obtained by the following techniques common to these applications:

- Abstracting out hardware-dependent limits: GPU thread size, warp size, or work-groups should not be hardwired to the kernel or kernel launch parameters so that they can be changed depending on the system on which the application is being run
- Exploiting larger HBM size: since Frontier has more HBM capacity per GCD, sizing the problem appropriately increases FOM speedups by reducing or eliminating data movement to/from the host DRAM
- Using GPU-aware MPI: with the network interfaces directly connected to the GPUs, MPI communications with data residing on HBM are much more efficient.
- Making data on the GPU as persistent as possible to reduce transfer costs.
- Performing pack/unpack of data on the GPU when appropriate to minimize transfer costs.
- Using OpenMP threads to speed up computations that remain on the CPU.

Beyond this list, specific optimizations due to hardware and algorithmic differences may still be unavoidable (as discussed in Sect. 3.1, Sect. 3.5, and Sect. 3.8).

Some challenges we faced for this work can be attributed to the fact that the programming environments and profiling tools for Frontier were much less mature compared to the ones we had been accustomed to. Through this work and close collaborations with our vendor partners, the programming environments (compilers and software libraries) and profiling tools are now much improved.

5   Conclusions

In this paper, we described the porting and optimization of a suite of applications to be ready for Frontier. Via the CAAR program, this work ensures that these applications are ready to capitalize Frontier's computational power for new scientific insights on the first day of Frontier's production period.

With this suite of applications, we show that Frontier delivers on its performance potential. Most applications described here achieve significant FOM speedups compared to their baseline on Summit. While the initial code porting is generally straightforward, architecture-specific optimizations and tuning are also crucial in achieving those speedups. We have described those optimizations in this paper which would serve as guides for future oncoming applications.

The CAAR program has also served its purpose in improving Frontier's environment by uncovering many initial issues not atypical to a maiden system. The resolutions of these issues benefit applications that will be and are currently being onboarded to Frontier. Meanwhile, we continue to work with our vendor partners to resolve remaining open issues.

Acknowledgments. This research used resources of the Oak Ridge Leadership Computing Facility at the Oak Ridge National Laboratory, which is supported by the Office of Science of the U.S. Department of Energy under Contract No. DE-AC05-00OR22725.

The work described here were collaboratively performed by members of the respective project teams and Frontier's Center of Excellence. We acknowledge their significant contributions to the success of the Frontier's CAAR program. They include P.K. Yeung (Georgia Tech), Rohini Uma-Vaideswaran (Georgia Tech), Kiran Ravikumar (HPE), Steve Abbott (HPE), Matt Turner (HPE), Alessandro Fanfarillo (AMD), Swarnava Ghosh (ORNL), Kariia Karabin (ORNL), Yang Wang (Carnegie Mellon University), Vishnu Raghuraman (Carnegie Mellon University), Franco Moitzi (University of Leoben), Alessandro Fanfarillo (AMD), David Hardy (University of Illinois Urbana-Champaign), Julio Maia (AMD), Josh Vermass (Michigan State University), Tim Mattox (HPE), Morten Hjorth-Jensen (MSU), Gaute Hagen (ORNL), Justin Lietz (ORNL), Rene Widera (Helmholtz-Zentrum Dresden-Rossendorf - HZDR), Klaus Steiniger (HZDR), Sergei Bastrakov (HZDR), Michael Bussmann (HZDR), Fabian Mora (U. Delaware), Richard Pausch (HZDR), Guido Juckeland (HZDR), Jeffrey Kelling (HZDR), Matthew Leinhauser (U. Delaware), Jeffery Young (Georgia Tech.), Franz Pöschl (HZDR), Alexander Debus (HZDR), Sunita Chandrasekaran (U. Delaware), Evan Schneider (U. Pittsburgh), Bruno Villasenor (U. California Santa Cruz, AMD), Brant Robertson ((U. California Santa Cruz), Robert Caddy (U. Pittsburgh), Alwin Mao (U. Pittsburgh), Trey White (HPE), Dan Jacobson (ORNL), Jakub Kurzak (AMD).

References

1. AMD: New AMD ROCM information portal (2022). https://rocmdocs.amd.com/en/latest/. Accessed 01 June 2022
2. Bussmann, M., et al.: Radiative signatures of the relativistic Kelvin-Helmholtz instability, pp. 5:1–5:12 (2013). https://doi.org/10.1145/2503210.2504564
3. Dean, D.J., Hjorth-Jensen, M.: Coupled-cluster approach to nuclear physics. Phys. Rev. C **69**, 054320 (2004). https://doi.org/10.1103/PhysRevC.69.054320
4. Debus, A., et al.: Circumventing the dephasing and depletion limits of Laser-Wakefield acceleration. Phys. Rev. X **9**, 031044 (2019). https://doi.org/10.1103/PhysRevX.9.031044
5. Dongarra, J., Strohmaier, E., Simon, H., Meuer, M.: TOP500 (2022). https://www.top500.org/lists/top500/2022/11/
6. Huebl, A., et al.: openPMD: a meta data standard for particle and mesh based data (2015). https://doi.org/10.5281/zenodo.591699
7. The Open Porous Media Initiative: Open porous media project (2022). https://opm-project.org/. Accessed 30 Dec 2022
8. Jansen, G.R.: NTCL – nuclear tensor contraction library (2022). https://gitlab.com/ntcl/ntcl
9. Joubert, W., et al.: Accelerated application development: the ORNL titan experience. Comput. Electr. Eng. **46**, 123–138 (2015). https://doi.org/10.1016/j.compeleceng.2015.04.008
10. Joubert, W., et al.: Attacking the opioid epidemic: determining the epistatic and pleiotropic genetic architectures for chronic pain and opioid addiction. In: International Conference for High Performance Computing, Networking, Storage and Analysis, SC 2018, pp. 717–730 (2018). https://doi.org/10.1109/SC.2018.00060
11. Kalé, L.V.: Charm++, pp. 256–264. Springer, Boston (2011)
12. Kohn, W., Sham, L.J.: Self-consistent equations including exchange and correlation effects. Phys. Rev. **140**, A1133–A1138 (1965)
13. Lagergren, J., et al.: Climatic clustering and longitudinal analysis with impacts on food, bioenergy, and pandemics. Phytobiomes J. (2022). https://doi.org/10.1094/PBIOMES-02-22-0007-R
14. LSMS: LSMS: scalable first principles calculations of materials using multiple scattering theory (2022). https://github.com/mstsuite/lsms. Accessed 30 Dec 2022
15. Luo, L., et al.: Pre-exascale accelerated application development: the ORNL summit experience. IBM J. Res. Dev. **64**(3/4), 11:1–11:21 (2020). https://doi.org/10.1147/JRD.2020.2965881

16. Matthes, A., Widera, R., Zenker, E., Worpitz, B., Huebl, A., Bussmann, M.: Tuning and optimization for a variety of many-core architectures without changing a single line of implementation code using the alpaka library (2017). https://arxiv.org/abs/1706.10086

17. McClure, J.: LBPM software package (2022). https://github.com/opm/lbpm. Accessed 30 Dec 2022

18. McClure, J.E., Berrill, M.A., Prins, J.F., Miller, C.T.: Asynchronous in situ connected-components analysis for complex fluid flows. In: 2016 Second Workshop on In Situ Infrastructures for Enabling Extreme-Scale Analysis and Visualization (ISAV), pp. 12–17 (2016). https://doi.org/10.1109/ISAV.2016.008

19. Oak Ridge Leadership Computing Facility: OLCF user documentation (2022). https://docs.olcf.ornl.gov/. Accessed 30 Dec 2022

20. Korringa, J.: On the calculation of the energy of a Bloch wave in a metal. Physica **13**, 392–400 (1947)

21. Perilla, J., Schulten, K.: Physical properties of the HIV-1 capsid from all-atom molecular dynamics simulations. Nat. Commun. **8**(15959) (2017)

22. Phillips, J.C., et al.: Scalable molecular dynamics on CPU and GPU architectures with NAMD. J. Chem. Phys. **153**(4), 044130 (2020)

23. Ravikumar, K., Appelhans, D., Yeung, P.: GPU acceleration of extreme scale pseudo-spectral simulations of turbulence using asynchronism. In: Proceedings of the International Conference for High Performance Computing, Networking, Storage and Analysis, SC 2019, pp. 1–22 (2019). https://doi.org/10.1145/3295500.3356209

24. Schneider, E.E., Ostriker, E.C., Robertson, B.E., Thompson, T.A.: The physical nature of starburst-driven galactic outflows. Astrophys. J. **895**(1), 43 (2020). https://doi.org/10.3847/1538-4357/ab8ae8

25. Schneider, E.E., Robertson, B.E.: Cholla: a new massively parallel hydrodynamics code for astrophysical simulation. Astrophys. J. Suppl. Ser. **217**(2), 24 (2015). https://doi.org/10.1088/0067-0049/217/2/24

End-to-End Differentiable Reactive Molecular Dynamics Simulations Using JAX

Mehmet Cagri Kaymak[1]([✉]), Samuel S. Schoenholz[4], Ekin D. Cubuk[3], Kurt A. O'Hearn[1], Kenneth M. Merz Jr.[2], and Hasan Metin Aktulga[1]

[1] Department of Computer Science and Engineering, Michigan State University, East Lansing, MI 48824, USA
{kaymakme,ohearnku,hma}@msu.edu
[2] Department of Chemistry, Michigan State University, East Lansing, MI 48824, USA
merz@chemistry.msu.edu
[3] Google Research, Mountain View, CA, USA
[4] OpenAI, San Francisco, CA, USA

Abstract. The reactive force field (ReaxFF) interatomic potential is a powerful tool for simulating the behavior of molecules in a wide range of chemical and physical systems at the atomic level. Unlike traditional classical force fields, ReaxFF employs dynamic bonding and polarizability to enable the study of reactive systems. Over the past couple decades, highly optimized parallel implementations have been developed for ReaxFF to efficiently utilize modern hardware such as multi-core processors and graphics processing units (GPUs). However, the complexity of the ReaxFF potential poses challenges in terms of portability to new architectures (AMD and Intel GPUs, RISC-V processors, etc.), and limits the ability of computational scientists to tailor its functional form to their target systems. In this regard, the convergence of cyber-infrastructure for high performance computing (HPC) and machine learning (ML) presents new opportunities for customization, programmer productivity and performance portability. In this paper, we explore the benefits and limitations of JAX, a modern ML library in Python representing a prime example of the convergence of HPC and ML software, for implementing ReaxFF. We demonstrate that by leveraging auto-differentiation, just-in-time compilation, and vectorization capabilities of JAX, one can attain a portable, performant, and easy to maintain ReaxFF software. Beyond enabling MD simulations, end-to-end differentiability of trajectories produced by ReaxFF implemented with JAX makes it possible to perform related tasks such as force field parameter optimization and meta-analysis without requiring any significant software developments. We also discuss scalability limitations using the current version of JAX for ReaxFF simulations.

S. S. Schoenholz—Work done while at Google.

A. Bhatele et al. (Eds.): ISC High Performance 2023, LNCS 13948, pp. 202–219, 2023.
https://doi.org/10.1007/978-3-031-32041-5_11

Keywords: reactive molecular dynamics · HPC/ML software · auto-differentiation · hardware portability

1   Introduction

Molecular dynamics (MD) simulations are widely used to study physical and chemical processes at the atomistic level in fields such as biophysics, chemistry and materials science. Compared to quantum mechanical (QM) MD simulations, which involve solving the Schrodinger's equation, classical MD simulations are cost-effective. They enable the study of large systems over significantly long time frames by making certain approximations. In this approach, the atomic nucleus and its electrons are treated as single particle. The atomic interactions are governed by a force field (FF), a set of parameterized mathematical equations that capture known atomic interactions such as bonds, angles, torsions, van der Waals, and Coulomb interactions. To ensure the predictive power of empirical force fields, they must be fitted to reference data obtained through high-fidelity quantum mechanical computations and/or experimental studies.

Classical MD models typically adopt static bonds and fixed partial charges which make them unsuitable for studying reactive systems. To remedy these limitations, different reactive force fields have been developed [10, 27, 30]. In this paper, we focus on the ReaxFF, which is one of the most impactful and widely used reactive force fields [26, 30]. It allows bonds to form and break throughout the simulation and dynamically calculates partial charges using suitable charge models. Due to the dynamic nature of bonds and partial charges, ReaxFF is significantly more complex and computationally expensive than classical force fields.

1.1   Related Work

To enable large-scale and long duration simulations, several ReaxFF implementations with different features and architectural support have been developed over the past couple decades. PuReMD has shared and distributed-memory versions for both CPUs and GPUs (CUDA-based), all of which are maintained separately [2, 3, 14], and several of these versions have been integrated into LAMMPS and AMBER [19]. More recently, to ensure hardware portability and simplify code maintenance and performance optimizations, a Kokkos-based implementation of ReaxFF has been developed in LAMMPS [29]. Kokkos is a performance portable programming model and allows the same codebase implemented using its primitives to be compiled for different backends. The current ReaxFF/Kokkos software also supports distributed-memory parallelism. In addition to the above open-source software, SCM provides a commercial software that includes ReaxFF support [22].

The success of ML techniques in fields such as computer vision and natural language processing has triggered its wide-spread use also in scientific computing. Specifically, in molecular modeling and simulation, a new class of force fields called machine learning potentials (MLP) such as SNAP [28], the Behler/Parrinello potential [7], SchNet [25], OrbNet [18], and NequIP [6] has emerged. More recently, we started witnessing an increase in the number of scientific applications adopting ML libraries such as Tensorflow [1], PyTorch [17], and JAX [9], not only for ML approaches but as a general purpose programming model even when using conventional techniques. This can be attributed to the convenience of advanced tools developed around these programming models and libraries such as auto-differentiation, auto-vectorization, and just-in-time compilation. Such tools have enabled fast prototyping of new ideas as well as hardware portability without sacrificing much computational efficiency.

Intelligent-ReaxFF [12] and JAX-ReaxFF [13] implementations both leverage modern machine learning frameworks. However, they are both primarily designed for force field fitting, and as such they are designed to work with molecular systems typically containing tens of atoms, and they cannot scale beyond systems with more than a couple hundred atoms. More importantly, they both lack molecular dynamics capabilities.

1.2   Our Contribution

The aforementioned features of ML cyber-infrastructure are highly attractive from the perspective of MD software, considering the fact that existing force field implementations are mostly written in low-level languages and tuned to the target hardware for high performance. As such, we introduce a portable, performant, and easy-to-maintain ReaxFF implementation in Python built on top of JAX-MD [24]. This new implementation of ReaxFF is

- **easy-to-maintain** because it only requires expressing the functional form of the potential energy for different atomic interactions in Python. MD simulations require calculation of forces which are calculated by taking the gradient of the potential energy with respect to atom positions at each time step. This can simply be accomplished with a call to the `grad( )` function in JAX,
- **hardware portable** because for its functional transformations, JAX uses XLA (Accelerated Linear Algebra) [23], which is a domain specific compiler for vector and matrix operations. Since XLA has high performance implementations across different CPUs (x86_64 and ARM) as well as GPUs (Nvidia and AMD), porting our ReaxFF implementation does not require any additional coding,
- **performant** because we ensure that our underlying ReaxFF interaction lists are suitable for vectorization, and we leverage just-in-time compilation effectively through a carefully designed update/reallocation scheme,
- **versatile** because we designed our implementation such that the same interaction kernels can be re-used in either a single high performance run (needed for long MD simulations) or multiple small single-step runs (needed for parameter optimization) settings. This allows our implementation to be suitable for force field training as well. Also, it simplifies the study of new functional forms for various interactions in the ReaxFF model.

2   Background

2.1   ReaxFF Overview

ReaxFF uses the bond order concept to determine the interaction strength between pairs of atoms given their element types and distances, and then applies corrections to these initial pairwise bond orders based on the information about all surrounding atoms. The corrected bond order is used as the main input for the energy terms such as bond energy (E_{bond}), valence angle energy (E_{val}), and torsion angle energy (E_{tors}). To account for atoms that may not attain their optimal coordination, additional energy terms such as under-/over-coordination energies, coalition, and conjugation energies are used, which we denote as E_{other} for simplicity. The van der Waals energy (E_{vdWaals}) and electrostatic energy terms (E_{Coulomb}) constitute the non-bonded terms. Since bond orders are dynamically changing, an important pre-requisite for calculation of electrostatic energy is the charge equilibration procedure which dynamically assigns charges to atoms based on the surroundings of each atom. For systems with hydrogen bonds, a special energy term ($E_{\text{H-bond}}$) is applied. Bonded interactions are typically truncated at 5 Å, hydrogen bonds are effective up to 7.5 Å, and the non-bonded interaction cutoff is typically set to 10–12 Å. Equation (1) sums up the various parts that constitute the ReaxFF potential energy, and we summarize the dependency information between them in Fig. 1.

$$
\begin{aligned}
E_{\text{system}} = {} & E_{\text{bond}} + E_{\text{val}} + E_{\text{tors}} + E_{\text{H-bond}} \\
& + E_{\text{vdWaals}} + E_{\text{Coulomb}} + E_{\text{other}}.
\end{aligned}
\tag{1}
$$

2.2   JAX and JAX-MD Overview

Since the new ReaxFF implementation is developed in JAX-MD, important design and implementation decisions were based on how JAX and JAX-MD work. As such, we first briefly describe these frameworks.

JAX [9] is a machine learning framework for transforming numerical functions. It implements the Numpy API using its own primitives and provides high order transformation functions for any Python function written using JAX primitives. The most notable of these transformation functions are automatic differentiation (*grad*), vectorization on a single device to leverage SIMD parallelism (*vmap*), parallelization across multiple devices (*pmap*), and just-in-time compilation (*JIT*). These transformations can be composed together to enable more complex ones. JAX uses XLA, a domain specific compiler for linear algebra, under the hood to achieve hardware portability. This allows any Python code written in terms of JAX primitives to be seamlessly compiled for CPUs, GPUs, or TPUs. Since XLA is also used extensively to accelerate Tensorflow models, XLA is supported for almost all modern processors, including GPUs by Nvidia and AMD. With JIT, XLA could apply performance optimizations targeted specifically for the

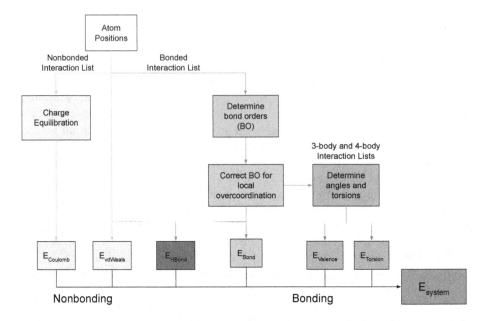

Fig. 1. Task dependency graph for calculations performed in ReaxFF.

selected device. The main limitation of JAX is that it expects the input data to the transformed functions to have fixed sizes. This allows XLA to adopt more aggressive performance optimizations during compilation, but when the size of the input data changes, the code needs to be recompiled.

JAX-MD [24] is an MD package built in Python using JAX. It is designed for performing differentiable physics simulations with a focus on MD. It supports periodic and non-periodic simulation environments. JAX-MD employs a scalable $3D$ grid-cell binning based algorithm to construct the neighbor list for atoms in a given system. It includes integrators for various kinds of ensembles as well as Fast Inertial Relaxation Engine (FIRE) Descent [8] and Gradient Descent based energy minimizers. Various machine learning potentials such as the Behler-Perrinello architecture [7] and graph neural networks including the Neural Equivariant Interatomic Potentials (NequIP) [6], based on the GraphNet library [5], are also readily available. When combined with the capabilities of JAX, this rich ecosystem enables researchers to easily develop and train hybrid approaches for various chemistry and physics applications.

3   Design and Implementation

In this section, we describe the overall design considerations and present the final design for our ReaxFF implementation in JAX-MD. To simplify the design and ensure modularity, generation of the interaction lists have been separated from the computation of partial energy terms. For overall efficiency and scalability, special consideration has been given to memory management.

3.1   Memory Management

To avoid frequent re-compilations, sizes of input to JAX's transforming functions must be known and fixed. As such, we separate the logic for handling the interaction list generation into **allocate** and **update** parts. The allocate function estimates the sizes of all interaction lists (see Fig. 2) and allocates the needed memory with some buffer space (default 20%). Due to its dynamic nature, JAX transformations such as *vmap* and *jit* cannot be applied to the allocate function. The update function works with the already-allocated interaction lists, and fills them based on atom positions while preserving their sizes. Since the update function works on arrays with static sizes, JAX transformations such as *vmap* and *jit* can be and are applied to this function. For effective use of *vmap*, the update function also applies padding when necessary. Finally, while filling in the interaction lists, it also checks whether the utilization of the space allocated for each list falls below a threshold mark (default 50%) where the utilization is the ratio of the true size to the total size. If it does, a call to the allocate function is triggered to shrink the interaction lists as shown in Algorithm 1, which in turn causes JAX to recompile the rest of the code since array dimensions change.

Algorithm 1. General structure of computations in an MD simulation.

1: interLists ← Create the interaction lists using the allocate function
2: **for** *timestep* = 1, 2, . . . **do**
3:     Calculate forces
4:     Update positions using the calculated forces
5:     overflow ← Update the interaction lists
6:     **if** overflow **then**
7:         interLists ← Reallocate based on the most recent utilizations
8:     **end if**
9: **end for**

Another important aspect of our memory management scheme is the *filtering of interaction lists*. In ReaxFF, while bonds are calculated dynamically, not all bonds are strong enough to be chemically meaningful, and therefore they are ignored (a typical bond strength threshold is 0.01). This has ramifications for higher-order interactions such as 3-body, 4-body, and H-bond interactions as well because they are built on top of the dynamically generated bond lists. As

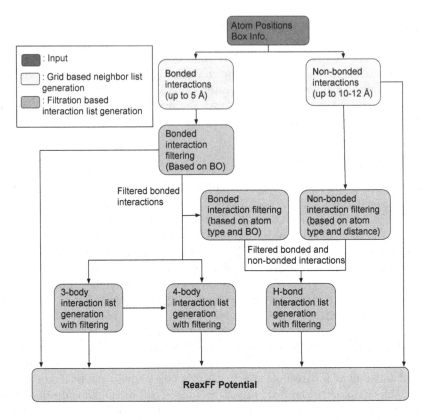

Fig. 2. Flow graph describing the generation of the interaction lists.

we discuss in more detail below, the acceptance criteria for each interaction is different. For 3-body and 4-body interactions, acceptance criteria depends on the strength of bonds among the involved atoms as well as force field parameters specific to that group of atoms; for H-bonds, it is a combination of acceptor-donor atom types and bond strengths. However, the steps for filtering all interaction lists are similar and can be implemented as a generic routine with a candidate interaction list and an interaction-specific acceptance criterion. The interactions that require filtering and their relevant input data are shown as yellow nodes in Fig. 2. First, the candidate interaction list is populated. Then, candidates get masked based on the predefined acceptance criterion. Finally, the candidate list is pruned and passed onto its corresponding potential energy computation function. While actually pruning the candidate list might be seen as an overhead, we note that the number of unaccepted 3-body and 4-body interactions are so high that simply ignoring them during the potential energy computations introduce a significant computational overhead. Also, the memory required to keep the unfiltered 3-body and 4-body interaction lists would limit the scalability of our implementation for GPUs due to their limited memory resources.

The filtering logic discussed above is JAX-friendly because the shapes of the intermediate (candidate) and final (pruned) data structures are fixed. As such, *vmap* and *jit* transformations can be applied to the filtering procedure, too. As with un-pruned lists, filtered interaction list generation also keeps track of utilization of the relevant lists and sets the overflow flag, when necessary.

3.2 Generation of Interaction Lists

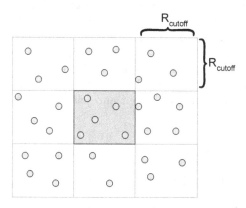

Fig. 3. Illustration of grid-cell neighbor search used to generate neighbor lists.

Pair-Wise Bonded Interactions: In ReaxFF, bond order (BO) between atom pairs are at the heart of all bonded potential energy computations. The BOs are computed in two steps. First, uncorrected BOs are computed according to Eq. (2), where r_{ij} is the distance between the atom pair i-j, and r_o^σ, r_o^π, and $r_o^{\pi\pi}$ are the ideal bond lengths for σ-σ, σ-π and π-π bonds, respectively.

$$
\begin{aligned}
\mathrm{BO}'_{ij} &= \mathrm{BO}^\sigma_{ij} + \mathrm{BO}^\pi_{ij} + \mathrm{BO}^{\pi\pi}_{ij} \\
&= \exp\left[p_{\mathrm{bo}_1} \cdot \left(\frac{r_{ij}}{r_o^\sigma}\right)^{p_{\mathrm{bo}_2}}\right] + \exp\left[p_{\mathrm{bo}_3} \cdot \left(\frac{r_{ij}}{r_o^\pi}\right)^{p_{\mathrm{bo}_4}}\right] \\
&\quad + \exp\left[p_{\mathrm{bo}_5} \cdot \left(\frac{r_{ij}}{r_o^{\pi\pi}}\right)^{p_{\mathrm{bo}_6}}\right].
\end{aligned}
\tag{2}
$$

After uncorrected bond orders are computed, the strength of BO'_{ij} is corrected based on the local neighborhood of atoms i and j. The corrected BO (BO_{ij}) represents the coordination number (i.e., number of bonds) between two atoms. Corrected bonds below a certain threshold get discarded as they do not correspond to chemical bonds. Hence, they do not contribute to the total energy.

To calculate uncorrected BO, for each atom in a given system, their neighbors are found using a grid-cell binning based neighbor search algorithm (Fig. 3). This allows us to generate the bonded neighbor lists in $O(Nk)$ where N is the number of atoms and k is the average number neighbors per atom. The side length of the grid cell is set to 5.5 Å, as a buffer space of 0.5 Å is added to the 5 Å actual bonded interaction cutoff to avoid frequent updates to the neighbors list. Since the cell size is almost the same as the bonded interaction cutoff, neighbor search only requires checking the nearby 3^3 grid cells. Neighbor information is stored in a $2D$ format where the neighbors of atom i are located on ith row with padding and alignment, as necessary. This format which is very similar to the ELLPACK format [32] is highly amenable for vectorization and memory coalescing on modern GPUs. It also simplifies bond order corrections because the neighbor indices for a given atom are stored consecutively. As will be discussed later, it also helps creating 3-body (for valency) and 4-body (for torsion) interactions since they use BOs as the main input. After creating the $2D$ neighbor array, BO terms are calculated and pairs with small BOs are filtered out as described above.

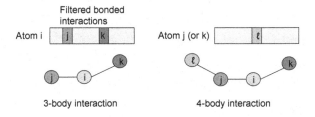

Fig. 4. Atoms and their interactions involved in formation of the 3-body and 4-body interactions.

Higher Order Bonded Interactions: After pruning the bonded interactions, 3-body and 4-body interaction lists are generated (Fig. 4). For each atom, every two neighbor pairs are selected to form the candidate list for 3-body interactions. In a system with N atoms and k neighbors per atom, there will be $O\left(Nk^2\right)$ candidates. Then the candidates are masked and filtered based the involved BO terms to form the final array with shape $M \times 3$ where M is the total number of interactions and columns are atom indices. After that, the finalized 3-body interaction list is used to generate the candidates for the 4-body interactions. For each 3 body interaction i-j-k, neighbors of both j and k are explored to form the 4-body candidate list and then the candidates get filtered based on the 4-body specific mask.

When the molecule involves hydrogen bonds, the hydrogen interaction list is built using the filtered bonded and non-bonded interactions. A hydrogen bond can only be present if there are hydrogen donors and acceptors. While the acceptor and the hydrogen are covalently bonded (short range), the acceptor bonds to the hydrogen through a dipole-dipole interaction, therefore it is long ranged (up to 7.5 Å). Hence, to find all possible hydrogen bonds involving a given hydrogen atom, both its bonded neighbors and non-bonded neighbors are scanned. Using the appropriate masking criterion, the final interaction list is formed to be used for potential energy calculations.

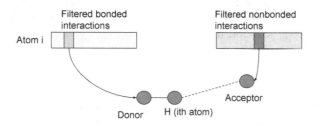

Fig. 5. Atoms and their interactions involved in formation of hydrogen bonds.

Non-bonded Interactions: In ReaxFF, non-bonded interactions are effective up to 10–12 Å, and they are smoothly tapered down to 0 beyond the cutoff. Similar to the pair-wise bonded interactions, the long range neighbor lists are also built using the grid-cell binning approach, this time using a buffer distance of 1 Å to avoid frequent neighbor updates. The neighbors are again stored in a 2D array similar to the ELLPACK format. This simplifies accessing the long range neighbors of a given atom while building the Hydrogen bond interactions list (as shown in Fig. 5). Also, the sparse matrix-vector multiplication kernel (SpMV) required for the dynamic charge calculation becomes simpler and more suitable for GPUs [31].

The non-bonded interaction list is used to compute van der Waals and Coulomb energy terms. While E_{vdWaals} computation is relatively simple as it only involves the summation of the pair-wise interaction energies, E_{Coulomb} requires charges to be dynamically computed based on a suitable charge model such as the charge equilibration (QEq) [21], electronegativity equalization (EE) [16], or atom-condensed Kohn-Sham density functional theory approximated to second order (ACKS2) method [33]. Our current JAX-based implementation relies on the EE method.

The EE method involves assigning partial charges to individual atoms while satisfying constraints for both the net system charge and the equalized atom electronegativities. For a given system with n atoms, let the charges and the positions be $\mathbf{q} = (q_1, q_2, \ldots, q_n)$ and $\mathbf{R} = (r_1, r_2, \ldots, r_n)$, respectively. The electronegativity constraint can be formalized as follows

$$\epsilon_1 = \epsilon_2 = \cdots = \epsilon_i = \underline{\epsilon},$$

where ϵ_i is the electronegativity of atom i and $\underline{\epsilon}$ is the average electronegativity. The net system charge constraint is expressed as

$$\sum_{i=1}^{n} q_i = q_{\text{net}},$$

where q_{net} is the net system charge. The constraints and the parameterized long range interactions can be expressed as a set of linear equations with the partial charges $\mathbf{q}$ being the solution to

$$\begin{bmatrix} \mathbf{H} & 1_n \\ 1_n^T & 0 \end{bmatrix} \begin{bmatrix} \mathbf{q} \\ \underline{\epsilon} \end{bmatrix} = \begin{bmatrix} -\boldsymbol{\chi} \\ q_{\text{net}} \end{bmatrix},$$

where $\boldsymbol{\chi}$ is an $n \times 1$ vector of target electronegativities and $\mathbf{H}$ is a symmetric $n \times n$ matrix describing the interactions between atoms. $H_{i,j}$ is defined as

$$H_{i,j} = \delta_{i,j} \cdot \eta_i + (1 - \delta_{i,j}) \cdot F_{i,j}$$

where $\delta_{i,j}$ is the Kronecker delta operator and η_i is the idempotential. Lastly, $F_{i,j}$ is defined as

$$F_{i,j} = \begin{cases} \dfrac{1}{\sqrt[3]{r_{i,j}^3 + \gamma_{i,j}^{-3}}}, & r_{i,j} \leq R_{\text{cutoff}} \\ 0, & \text{otherwise} \end{cases}$$

where $r_{i,j}$ is the distance between atom i and j, $\gamma_{i,j}$ is the pair-wise shielding term, and R_{cutoff} is the long range cutoff.

Since the size of the above linear system is $(n + 1) \times (n + 1)$, it is prohibitively expensive to solve it with direct methods when n is becomes large (beyond a few hundred). Hence, we employ an iterative sparse linear solver. The iterative solvers available in JAX only expect a linear operator as a function pointer that can perform the matrix-vector multiplication. This allows us to define the SpMV operation directly using the non-bonded neighbor lists provided in an ELLPACK-like format described earlier without applying any transformations. Another optimization to accelerate the charge equilibration is to use initial guesses to warm start the iterative solver. Since the charges fluctuate smoothly as the simulation progresses, we use the cubic spline extrapolation to produce the initial guesses based on past history [2].

3.3   Force Field Training

Predictive capabilities of empirical force fields are arguably more important than their performance. For this, it is crucial for force field parameters to be optimized using high-fidelity quantum mechanical training data. In contrast to MD simulations involving a single system iterated over long durations, this optimization process typically involves executing several (on the order of hundreds to thousands, depending on the model and target systems) small molecular systems

---
Algorithm 2. Gradient-based parameter optimization.

1: $\theta \leftarrow$ Initialize the model parameters
2: training set $\leftarrow$ Align the training set by padding with dummy atoms
3: lossFunction $\leftarrow$ Create a loss function by utilizing vmap(energyFunction)
4: calculateGradients $\leftarrow$ jit(grad(lossFunction))
5: **while** stopping criterion not met **do**
6:     $X_i, Y_i \leftarrow$ Sample a minibatch of data from the training set
7:     Create the interaction lists for X_i
8:     $g \leftarrow$ calculateGradients(θ, interLists, Y_i)
9:     $\theta \leftarrow$ Update the model parameters using g
10: **end while**

---

for a single step using different parameter sets in a high-throughput fashion. While evolutionary algorithms have traditionally been used for Reax force field optimizations, as JAX-ReaxFF [13] and Intelligent-ReaxFF [12] have recently demonstrated, using gradient-based optimization techniques can accelerate the training process by two to three orders of magnitude. However, the gradient information needed for force field optimization is much more complex than that of MD simulation – one needs to calculate the derivative of the fitness function which is typically formulated as a weighted sum of the difference between predicted and reference quantities over all systems in the training dataset with respect to parameters to be optimized (which is usually on the order of tens of parameters for ReaxFF). While this would be a formidable task using analytical or numerical techniques, the auto-differentiation capabilities of JAX enable us to easily repurpose the above described ReaxFF MD implementation for parameter optimization. By composing different transformations, a simple loss function defined for a single sample can extended to work for a batch of training data as shown in Algorithm 2. To fully take advantage of SIMD parallelism, especially on GPUs, we ensure that different molecules in the training dataset are properly divided into small batches. To reduce the number of dummy atoms and the amount of padding within each batch, the training set could be clustered based on how much computation they require. Given the allocate/update mechanism described in Sect. 3.1, the different sizes of interaction lists for different molecular systems in a batch data does not cause additional challenges.

4   Experimental Results

4.1   Software and Hardware Setup

To verify the accuracy of the presented JAX-based ReaxFF implementation, simulations were performed using molecular systems shown in Table 1. The Kokkos-based LAMMPS implementation of ReaxFF was chosen for validation and benchmarking comparisons due to its maturity and maintenance. For this purpose, we used the most recent stable release of LAMMPS (git tag stable_23Jun2022_update3), and experimented on both Nvidia and AMD GPUs.

LAMMPS was built using GCC v10.3.0, OpenMPI v4.1.1, and CUDA v11.4.2 for the Nvidia GPUs, and with ROCm v5.3.0, aomp v16.0, and OpenMPI v4.1.4 for the AMD GPUs (using device-specific compiler optimization flags for both). For the JAX experiments, Python v3.8, JAX v0.4.1, and JAX-MD v0.2.24 were paired with CUDA v11.4.2 for the Nvidia GPUs, and ROCm v5.3.0 for the AMD GPUs. Hardware details are presented in Table 2. The compute nodes at the Michigan State University High-Performance Computing Center (MSU-HPCC) and the AMD Cloud Platform are used for the experiments.

Table 1. Molecular systems used in the performance evaluation section, with the third column (N) indicating the number of atoms, the fourth one denoting the dimensions of the rectangular simulation box, and the last column showing the force field used to simulate the system.

Name	Chem. Rep.	N	Sim. Box (Å)	Force Field
Water	H_2O	2400	$29.0 \times 28.9 \times 29.3$	[11]
Silica	SiO_2SiO_2	6000	$36.9 \times 50.7 \times 52.5$	[11]

Table 2. Hardware details of the platforms used for performance experiments.

GPU	CPU	Cluster
A100	Intel Xeon 8358 (64 cores)	MSU-HPCC
V100	Intel Xeon Platinum 8260 (48 cores)	MSU-HPCC
MI210	AMD EPYC 7742 (64 cores)	AMD Cloud Platform
MI100	AMD EPYC 7742 (64 cores)	AMD Cloud Platform

4.2   Validation of MD Capabilities

Figure 6 shows that the JAX-based ReaxFF energies almost perfectly match those from LAMMPS in actual MD simulations. The deviation only becomes visible after 2000 MD steps which is inevitable due to machine precision limitations. The relative energy difference is around 10^{-7} for both the water and silica systems.

4.3   Performance and Scalability

We compare the performance of JAX-based ReaxFF to Kokkos/ReaxFF package in LAMMPS on both Nvidia and AMD GPUs. While Kokkos/ReaxFF supports MPI parallelism, we use a single GPU for all tests. Kokkos/ReaxFF incurs minimal communication overheads when there is a single MPI process. The performance comparison on AMD GPUs is possible through Kokkos' ROCm backend support, as well as the availability of JAX/XLA on AMD GPUs.

To create systems with varying size, the molecular systems shown in Table 1 have been periodically replicated along the x, y, and z dimensions. The number

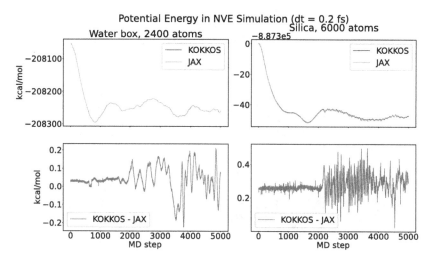

Fig. 6. Comparison of absolute (top plots) and relative difference (bottom plots) in potential energies for NVE simulations with a time step of 0.2 fs and a CG solver with 1e-6 tolerance for the charge calculation.

of atoms vary from 2400 to 19200 for the water systems and from 6000 to 24000 for the silica systems. For each experiment, NVE simulations with a time step of 0.2 fs were run for 5000 steps, and the average time per step in ms was reported. For both the Kokkos and JAX-based implementations, the buffer distance for the non-bonded interactions was set to 1 Å. While reneighboring is done every 25 MD steps for Kokkos, the JAX implementation keeps track of how much atoms move since the last neighborhood update and only reneighbors when atoms move more than the buffer distance. As suggested by the Kokkos documentation, the half-neighbor list option is used.

While written in Python using JAX primitives, the proposed implementation is faster when the system size is small on all GPUs. As the number of atoms increases, while the time increases linearly for the JAX implementation, the Kokkos one increases sublinearly. The sublinear scaling for Kokkos indicates that it cannot fully utilize the resources when the problem size is small unlike JAX. As the problem size increases, Kokkos starts to utilize the GPU better and yield better performance. The Kokkos implementation achieves up to 3.2× speedup for the largest water systems on AMD GPUs (MI100 and MI210). On Nvidia GPUs (V100 and A100), it is around 2.3× faster for the same water system with 19200 atoms. For the silica systems where there are no hydrogen bonds, Kokkos is around 2× faster on the AMD GPUs and 1.5× on the Nvidia GPUs. On the other hand, when the problem size is small, JAX achieves up to 1.8× speedup on an A100 GPU (Fig. 7).

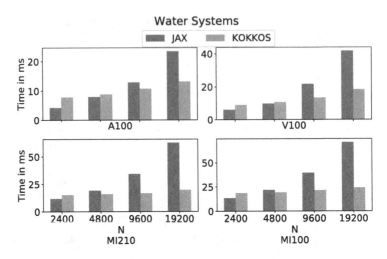

Fig. 7. Average time per MD step (in ms) for the water systems with varying sizes.

4.4 Training

To demonstrate the training performance of the described implementation, we trained the ReaxFF parameters on the public QM9 dataset of about 134k relaxed organic molecules made up of H, C, N, O, and F atoms, with each molecule containing up to nine non-hydrogen atoms [20]. All systems are calculated at the B3LYP/6-31G(2df,p) level of theory. To simplify the dataset, we removed the molecules that contain F atoms which resulted in around 130k molecules. During optimization, 80% of the data is used for training and the remaining 20% for testing. The training is done using the AdamW optimizer [15] from the Optax library [4] with a batch size of 512 and the learning rate is set to 0.001.

The ReaxFF model is typically fit to the training data containing relative energy differences between molecules with the same type of atoms (different conformations and configurations) and the energies of the individual atoms get canceled out. Since the QM9 dataset only contains the absolute energies, we added a new term to the ReaxFF potential to remedy the energy shifts caused by the self-energies of the individual atoms (Fig. 8).

$$E_{\text{system}} = E_{\text{ReaxFF}} + E_{\text{self-energy}}$$
$$E_{\text{self-energy}} = \sum_{i=1}^{N} s_i \tag{3}$$

In Eq. (3), E_{ReaxFF} is the original ReaxFF potential designed to capture the interaction related terms and $E_{\text{self-energy}}$ is the newly added parameterized self-energy term to capture the energy shifts, and s_i is the self energy of atom i solely determined by the atom type. Hence, the new term only contains 4 parameters as there are 4 atom types in the modified QM9 dataset. In total, around 1100 ReaxFF parameters are optimized during the training. The training is performed

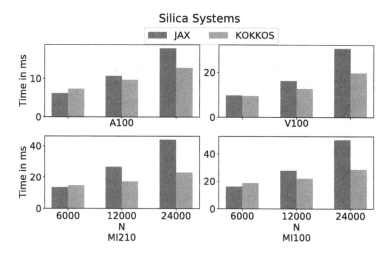

Fig. 8. Average time per MD step (in ms) for the silica systems with varying sizes.

on an A100 GPU with each epoch taking approximately 8 s. Figure 9 shows the mean absolute error (MAE) per epoch. Since the ReaxFF model has a relatively small number of parameters compared to most modern ML methods, the training and test MAE perfectly overlap throughout the training. The final MAE of the model on the test data is 3.6 kcal/mol. While this is higher than the ideal target of 1 kcal/mol error, we note that this is a straight optimization without any fine-tuning to demonstrate the capabilities of the new ReaxFF implementation.

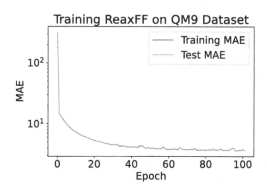

Fig. 9. Training progress of the ReaxFF model on the QM9 dataset, with the final MAE on the test data being 3.6 kcal/mol.

5 Conclusion

With the accelerator landscape changing rapidly and becoming more complex, cross platform compilers gain more importance as they enable the same codebase to be used on different architectures. By leveraging modern machine learning cyber-infrastructure, we developed a new JAX-based ReaxFF implementation that is easy-to-maintain, hardware portable, performant, and versatile. Using auto-differentiation, forces in MD simulations are computed directly from energy functions implemented in Python without requiring any extra coding. It also allows the same code to be used for both MD simulations and parameter optimization which are both essential to study any system of interest with ReaxFF. While Kokkos is an another cross-platform solution, it lacks auto-differentiation and batching optimization capabilities. Although it is more performant for bigger molecules, the JAX implementation is faster for small ones while also providing new functionalities.

References

1. Abadi, M., et al.: TensorFlow: a system for large-scale machine learning. In: 12th USENIX Symposium on Operating Systems Design and Implementation (OSDI 2016), pp. 265–283 (2016)
2. Aktulga, H.M., Fogarty, J.C., Pandit, S.A., Grama, A.Y.: Parallel reactive molecular dynamics: numerical methods and algorithmic techniques. Parallel Comput. **38**(4–5), 245–259 (2012)
3. Aktulga, H.M., Pandit, S.A., van Duin, A.C., Grama, A.Y.: Reactive molecular dynamics: numerical methods and algorithmic techniques. SIAM J. Sci. Comput. **34**(1), C1–C23 (2012)
4. Babuschkin, I., et al.: The DeepMind JAX ecosystem (2020). http://github.com/deepmind/jax
5. Battaglia, P.W., et al.: Relational inductive biases, deep learning, and graph networks. arXiv preprint arXiv:1806.01261 (2018)
6. Batzner, S., et al.: E (3)-equivariant graph neural networks for data-efficient and accurate interatomic potentials. Nat. Commun. **13**(1), 1–11 (2022)
7. Behler, J., Parrinello, M.: Generalized neural-network representation of high-dimensional potential-energy surfaces. Phys. Rev. Lett. **98**(14), 146401 (2007)
8. Bitzek, E., Koskinen, P., Gähler, F., Moseler, M., Gumbsch, P.: Structural relaxation made simple. Phys. Rev. Lett. **97**(17), 170201 (2006)
9. Bradbury, J., Frostig, R., et al.: JAX: composable transformations of Python+ NumPy programs. Version 0.2 5, 14-24 (2018)
10. Brenner, D.W., Shenderova, O.A., Harrison, J.A., Stuart, S.J., Ni, B., Sinnott, S.B.: A second-generation reactive empirical bond order (REBO) potential energy expression for hydrocarbons. J. Phys.: Condens. Matter **14**(4), 783 (2002)
11. Fogarty, J.C., Aktulga, H.M., Grama, A.Y., Van Duin, A.C., Pandit, S.A.: A reactive molecular dynamics simulation of the silica-water interface. J. Chem. Phys. **132**(17), 174704 (2010)
12. Guo, F., et al.: Intelligent-ReaxFF: evaluating the reactive force field parameters with machine learning. Comput. Mater. Sci. **172**, 109393 (2020)

13. Kaymak, M.C., Rahnamoun, A., O'Hearn, K.A., Van Duin, A.C., Merz Jr., K.M., Aktulga, H.M.: JAX-ReaxFF: a gradient-based framework for fast optimization of reactive force fields. J. Chem. Theory Comput. **18**(9), 5181–5194 (2022)
14. Kylasa, S.B., Aktulga, H.M., Grama, A.Y.: PuReMD-GPU: a reactive molecular dynamics simulation package for GPUs. J. Comput. Phys. **272**, 343–359 (2014)
15. Loshchilov, I., Hutter, F.: Decoupled weight decay regularization. arXiv preprint arXiv:1711.05101 (2017)
16. Mortier, W.J., Ghosh, S.K., Shankar, S.: Electronegativity-equalization method for the calculation of atomic charges in molecules. J. Am. Chem. Soc. **108**(15), 4315–4320 (1986)
17. Paszke, A., et al.: PyTorch: an imperative style, high-performance deep learning library. Adv. Neural Inf. Process. Syst. **32** (2019)
18. Qiao, Z., Welborn, M., Anandkumar, A., Manby, F.R., Miller III, T.F.: OrbNet: deep learning for quantum chemistry using symmetry-adapted atomic-orbital features. J. Chem. Phys. **153**(12), 124111 (2020)
19. Rahnamoun, A., et al.: ReaxFF/AMBER-a framework for hybrid reactive/nonreactive force field molecular dynamics simulations. J. Chem. Theory Comput. **16**(12), 7645–7654 (2020)
20. Ramakrishnan, R., Dral, P.O., Rupp, M., Von Lilienfeld, O.A.: Quantum chemistry structures and properties of 134 kilo molecules. Sci. Data **1**(1), 1–7 (2014)
21. Rappe, A.K., Goddard III, W.A.: Charge equilibration for molecular dynamics simulations. J. Phys. Chem. **95**(8), 3358–3363 (1991)
22. ReaxFF, S.: Theoretical chemistry (2020)
23. Sabne, A.: XLA: compiling machine learning for peak performance (2020)
24. Schoenholz, S., Cubuk, E.D.: JAX MD: a framework for differentiable physics. Adv. Neural. Inf. Process. Syst. **33**, 11428–11441 (2020)
25. Schütt, K., Kindermans, P.J., Sauceda Felix, H.E., Chmiela, S., Tkatchenko, A., Müller, K.R.: SchNet: a continuous-filter convolutional neural network for modeling quantum interactions. Adv. Neural. Inf. Process. Syst. **30** (2017)
26. Senftle, T.P., et al.: The ReaxFF reactive force-field: development, applications and future directions. NPJ Comput. Mater. **2**(1), 1–14 (2016)
27. Tersoff, J.: Modeling solid-state chemistry: interatomic potentials for multicomponent systems. Phys. Rev. B **39**(8), 5566 (1989)
28. Thompson, A.P., Swiler, L.P., Trott, C.R., Foiles, S.M., Tucker, G.J.: Spectral neighbor analysis method for automated generation of quantum-accurate interatomic potentials. J. Comput. Phys. **285**, 316–330 (2015)
29. Trott, C.R., et al.: Kokkos 3: programming model extensions for the exascale era. IEEE Trans. Parallel Distrib. Syst. **33**(4), 805–817 (2021)
30. Van Duin, A.C., Dasgupta, S., Lorant, F., Goddard, W.A.: ReaxFF: a reactive force field for hydrocarbons. J. Phys. Chem. A **105**(41), 9396–9409 (2001)
31. Vazquez, F., Garzón, E.M., Martinez, J., Fernandez, J.: The sparse matrix vector product on GPUs. In: Proceedings of the 2009 International Conference on Computational and Mathematical Methods in Science and Engineering, vol. 2, pp. 1081–1092. Computational and Mathematical Methods in Science and Engineering Gijón, Spain (2009)
32. Vázquez, F., Fernández, J.J., Garzón, E.M.: A new approach for sparse matrix vector product on NVIDIA GPUs. Concurr. Comput.: Pract. Exp. **23**(8), 815–826 (2011)
33. Verstraelen, T., Ayers, P., Van Speybroeck, V., Waroquier, M.: ACKS2: atom-condensed Kohn-Sham DFT approximated to second order. J. Chem. Phys. **138**(7), 074108 (2013)

Machine Learning, AI, and Quantum Computing

Allegro-Legato: Scalable, Fast, and Robust Neural-Network Quantum Molecular Dynamics via Sharpness-Aware Minimization

Hikaru Ibayashi[1]([✉]), Taufeq Mohammed Razakh[1], Liqiu Yang[1], Thomas Linker[1], Marco Olguin[2], Shinnosuke Hattori[3], Ye Luo[4], Rajiv K. Kalia[1], Aiichiro Nakano[1], Ken-ichi Nomura[1], and Priya Vashishta[1]

[1] Collaboratory for Advanced Computing and Simulations, University of Southern California, Los Angeles, CA 90089, USA
ibayashi@usc.edu
[2] Center for Advanced Research Computing, University of Southern California, Los Angeles, CA 90089, USA
[3] Advanced Research Laboratory, R&D Center, Sony Group Corporation, Atsugi Tec. 4-14-1 Asahi-cho, Atsugi-shi, Kanagawa 243-0014, Japan
[4] Argonne Leadership Computing Facility, Argonne National Laboratory, Lemont, IL 60439, USA

Abstract. Neural-network quantum molecular dynamics (NNQMD) simulations based on machine learning are revolutionizing atomistic simulations of materials by providing quantum-mechanical accuracy but orders-of-magnitude faster, illustrated by ACM Gordon Bell prize (2020) and finalist (2021). State-of-the-art (SOTA) NNQMD model founded on group theory featuring rotational equivariance and local descriptors has provided much higher accuracy and speed than those models, thus named Allegro (meaning fast). On massively parallel supercomputers, however, it suffers a fidelity-scaling problem, where growing number of unphysical predictions of interatomic forces prohibits simulations involving larger numbers of atoms for longer times. Here, we solve this problem by combining the Allegro model with sharpness aware minimization (SAM) for enhancing the robustness of model through improved smoothness of the loss landscape. The resulting Allegro-Legato (meaning fast and "smooth") model was shown to elongate the time-to-failure t_{failure}, without sacrificing computational speed or accuracy. Specifically, Allegro-Legato exhibits much weaker dependence of time-to-failure on the problem size, $t_{\mathrm{failure}} \propto N^{-0.14}$ (N is the number of atoms) compared to the SOTA Allegro model ($t_{\mathrm{failure}} \propto N^{-0.29}$), *i.e.*, systematically delayed time-to-failure, thus allowing much larger and longer NNQMD simulations without failure. The model also exhibits excellent computational scalability and GPU acceleration on the Polaris supercomputer at Argonne Leadership Computing Facility. Such scalable, accurate, fast and robust NNQMD models will likely find broad applications in NNQMD simulations on emerging exaflop/s computers, with a specific example of accounting for nuclear quantum effects in the dynamics of ammonia to lay a foundation of the green ammonia technology for sustainability.

© The Author(s), under exclusive license to Springer Nature Switzerland AG 2023
A. Bhatele et al. (Eds.): ISC High Performance 2023, LNCS 13948, pp. 223–239, 2023.
https://doi.org/10.1007/978-3-031-32041-5_12

Keywords: Molecular dynamics · Equivariant neural network ·
Sharpness-aware minimization

1   Introduction

Neural-network quantum molecular dynamics (NNQMD) simulations based on machine learning are revolutionizing atomistic modeling of materials by following the trajectories of all atoms with quantum-mechanical accuracy at a drastically reduced computational cost [1]. NNQMD not only predicts accurate interatomic forces but also captures quantum properties such as electronic polarization [2] and electronic excitation [3], thus the 'Q' in NNQMD. NNQMD represents one of the most scalable scientific applications on the current high-end supercomputers, evidenced by ACM Gordon Bell prize winner in 2020 [4] and finalist in 2021 [5]. A more recent breakthrough in NNQMD is drastically improved accuracy of force prediction [6] over those previous models, which was achieved through rotationally equivariant neural networks based on a group theoretical formulation of tensor fields [7]. The state-of-the-art (SOTA) accuracy has now been combined with a record speed based on spatially localized descriptors in the latest NNQMD model named Allegro (meaning fast) [8].

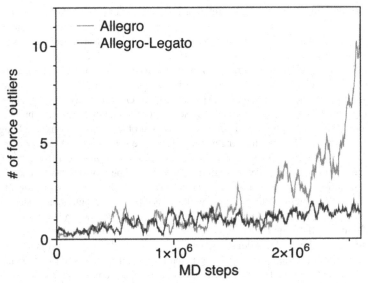

Fig. 1. Number of outliers in atomic force inference during NNQMD simulation: As the simulation progresses, the dynamic of atoms becomes unstable due to an increasing number of unphysically large force values (over 5σ) predicted by the original Allegro model. This resulted in the eventual failure after 2.6×10^6 MD steps (red). On the other hand, the proposed model (Allegro-Legato) maintains a nearly constant number of outliers and the simulation stable (blue). (Color figure online)

Despite its remarkable computational scalability, massively parallel NNQMD simulation faces a major unsolved issue known as *fidelity scaling* [9]. In large-scale NNQMD simulations, small prediction errors can propagate and lead to unphysical atomic forces that degrade the accuracy of atomic trajectory over time. These force outliers can even cause the simulation to terminate unexpectedly (Fig. 1). As simulations become spatially larger and temporally longer, the number of unphysical force predictions is expected to scale proportionally, which could severely limit the fidelity of NNQMD simulations on new exascale supercomputing platforms, especially for the most exciting far-from-equilibrium applications [3, 10].

In this paper, we solve the fidelity-scaling issue taking a cue from a recent development in machine learning. Solving the fidelity-scaling issue requires robustness of the NNQMD model, *i.e.*, reduced number of unphysical force-prediction outliers when simulation trajectories encounter atomic configurations outside the training dataset. It has been observed that the robustness of a neural-network model can be enhanced by sharpness-aware minimization (SAM) [11]—a training algorithm that regularizes the sharpness of the model (*i.e.*, the curvature of the loss surface) along with its training loss. We thus apply SAM to train the fast Allegro model to smoothen its loss landscape, thereby enhancing its robustness. The resulting Allegro-Legato (meaning fast and "smooth") model is shown to increase the time-to-failure $t_{failure}$, *i.e.*, how many MD steps a NNQMD simulation can run under microcanonical ensemble, while maintaining the same inference speed and nearly equal accuracy. Specifically, Allegro-Legato exhibits much weaker dependence of time-to-failure on the problem size, $t_{failure} \propto N^{-0.14}$ (N is the number of atoms) compared to the SOTA Allegro model ($t_{failure} \propto N^{-0.29}$), thus allowing much larger and longer NNQMD simulations without failure. Along with this main contribution, we find that the fidelity-scalability of the NNQMD model correlates with sharpness of the model more than the number of parameters in the model.[1]

The fast and robust Allegro-Legato model has been implemented in our scalable parallel NNQMD code named RXMD-NN. We have achieved a weak-scaling parallel efficiency of 0.91 on 480 computing nodes, each with an AMD EPYC central processing unit (CPU) and four NVIDIA A100 graphics processing units (GPUs), of the Polaris supercomputer at Argonne Leadership Computing Facility (ALCF). The code has also achieved a 7.6-fold single-node performance acceleration using four GPUs over single 32-core CPU of Polaris.

Allegro-Legato allows much larger spatio-temporal scale NNQMD simulations than are otherwise possible. Unlike MD simulation with heat bath often used in "effective" long-time sampling of molecular configurations (*e.g.*, for protein folding), which disrupts dynamic trajectories, Allegro-Legato enables "true" long-time Hamiltonian dynamics that can be directly compared with fine vibrational modes observed in high-resolution spectroscopic experiments. Specifically, we can now satisfy the prohibitive computational demand of accounting for subtle nuclear quantum effects in the dynamics of ammonia based on path-integral molecular dynamics, which is essential for resolving a mystery in a recent high-resolution neutron-scattering experimental observation at Oak Ridge National Laboratory. Synergy between the most advanced neutron experiment and

---

[1] Code is available at github.com/ibayashi-hikaru/allegro-legato.

leadership-scale NNQMD simulation lays a foundation of the green ammonia-based fuel technology for achieving a sustainable society.

2 Method Innovation

This section first summarizes (1) NNQMD simulation method, along with the SOTA Allegro model, and (2) SAM for robust neural-network model training. We then present the key method innovation of SAM-enhanced Allegro model, Allegro-Legato, followed by its scalable parallel implementation.

2.1 Summary of Neural-Network Quantum Molecular Dynamics

Molecular dynamics (MD) simulation follows time evolution of the positions $\{\mathbf{r}_i | i = 1, \ldots, N\}$ (*i.e.*, trajectories) of N atoms,

$$m_i \frac{d^2}{dt^2} \mathbf{r}_i = \mathbf{f}_i = -\frac{\partial}{\partial \mathbf{r}_i} E(\{\mathbf{r}_i\}), \tag{1}$$

where m_i and $\mathbf{f}_i$ are the mass of the i-th atoms and the force acting on it, whereas E is the interatomic potential energy that is dictated by quantum mechanics (QM). In NNQMD, neural networks are trained to reproduce ground-truth QM values, $E(\{\mathbf{r}_i\}_t)$, for a set of atomic configurations $\{\{\mathbf{r}_i\}_t | t = 1, \ldots, N_{\text{training}}\}$ (N_{training} is the number of training configurations) [1–5]. In the SOTA Allegro model, the energy E is composed of pairwise embedding energies, E_{ij}, between atomic pairs (i, j) within a finite cutoff distance to preserve data locality [8]. Key to the high accuracy of Allegro is that all energy terms are group-theoretically equivariant with respect to rotation, inversion and translation, *i.e.*, to the Euclidean group $E(3)$ [6, 7]. This is achieved by representing the energy in terms of tensors up to rank ℓ and tensor products using their irreducible representations. In short, Allegro attains accuracy through group-theoretical equivariance and computational speed through data locality.

2.2 Summary of Sharpness-Aware Minimization

Neural networks are trained by minimizing the loss function $L(\mathbf{w})$ where $\mathbf{w}$ represents the weight parameters of the neural network. Design choice of optimization methods plays a crucial role in machine learning, as it impacts various factors such as convergence speed and generalization performance [12]. In particular, vulnerability to adversarial attacks is a problem unique to neural networks [13], which has actively been studied in various fields such as computer vision [14] and natural language processing [4]. Recent studies suggest that the fidelity-scalability in NNQMD can also be viewed as a robustness against "adversarial attacks" during large-scale simulations [15, 16], where atomic trajectories are "attacked" by the accumulated unphysical predictions, *i.e.*, "adversarial perturbations" throughout the long and large-scale simulation. Therefore, it is natural to expect that optimization methods for adversarial attack would enhance the fidelity-scalability in NNQMD.

Sharpness-aware minimization (SAM) is one of such robustness-enhancing methods proposed in the computer vision area [11]. The key component of SAM is that it minimizes "sharpness" of the model defined as

$$\max_{\|\epsilon\|_2 \leq \rho} \{L(\mathbf{w} + \epsilon) - L(\mathbf{w})\}, \tag{2}$$

where ρ (the size of neighborhood) is a hyperparameter to define sharpness. While computing the sharpness directly is infeasible, it has been shown that minimizing $L(\mathbf{w}) + \max_{\|\epsilon\|_2 \leq \rho}\{L(\mathbf{w} + \epsilon) - L(\mathbf{w})\}$ (training loss + sharpness) can be achieved through the following update rule:

$$\mathbf{w} = \mathbf{w} - \eta \nabla_{\mathbf{w}'} L(\mathbf{w}')\big|_{\mathbf{w}'=\mathbf{w}+\rho \frac{\nabla_{\mathbf{w}} L(\mathbf{w})}{\|\nabla_{\mathbf{w}} L(\mathbf{w})\|}} \quad (\eta : \text{learning rate}), \tag{3}$$

which utilizes first-order derivatives, *i.e.*, $\nabla_{\mathbf{w}} L(\mathbf{w})$. This allows for the optimization of sharpness without the need for computationally expensive second-order derivatives.

2.3 Key Innovation: Allegro-Legato: SAM-Enhanced Allegro

As explained above, our hypothesis is that smoothened loss landscape through SAM enhances fidelity scaling of NNQMD. To quantitatively test this hypothesis, we incorporate SAM into the training of the Allegro NNQMD model [8], which entails SOTA accuracy and computational speed. We call the resulting SAM-enhanced Allegro model as Allegro-Legato (In music, Legato means "smooth without sudden breaking between notes").

To find an appropriate strength of sharpness regularization, SAM's hyper parameter ρ is tuned so as to provide the most robust model, *i.e.*, the longest time-to-failure, t_{failure}, in a small-scale simulation ($N = 432$). Table 1 shows the result of our grid search over $\rho \in \{0.001, 0.0025, 0.005, 0.01, 0.025, 0.05\}$, from which we found that $\rho = 0.005$ gives the longest t_{failure} in our setup. For the small-scale simulation test, we used LAMMPS, which is a widely used open-source MD simulation software (https://www.lammps.org). See Sect. 4.5 for the detailed training settings.

Table 1. SAM strength ρ *vs.* time-to-failure t_{failure}: We tune ρ by conducting a grid search in the range of 0.001 to 0.05. A model with $\rho = 0.005$ gives the largest t_{failure} with a small-scale simulation ($N = 432$).

ρ	0.001	0.0025	**0.005**	0.01	0.025	0.05
t_{failure}	4030	6420	**8480**	4760	4210	3780

2.4 RXMD-NN: Scalable Parallel Implementation of Allegro-Legato NNQMD

For large-scale testing of computational and fidelity scaling, we implement the proposed Allegro-Legato NNQMD model in our RXMD-NN software [3, 9], which is an extension of our scalable parallel reactive MD software, RXMD [17]. RXMD-NN employs a hierarchical divide-and-conquer scheme to realize "globally-scalable and local-fast" (or "globally-sparse and locally-dense") parallelization [18]: (1) globally scalable spatial decomposition that is best suited for massively parallel computing platforms; and (2) locally efficient linked-list decomposition and subsequent neighbor-list construction to achieve the $O(N)$ computational complexity. Interprocess communication is implemented using non-blocking application programming interfaces (APIs) of Message Passing Interface (MPI) library, and the communication pattern is designed to be lock-free with minimal internode-data exchange. While it is one of the most widely adapted strategies in large-scale MD applications, this is particularly suitable for NNQMD algorithm to take advantage of the modern high-performance computing (HPC) architecture, in which a few very powerful GPU cards do the heavy lifting by accelerating computationally demanding kernels while random memory access and out-of-order data processing are concurrently executed by many-core CPUs. In RXMD-NN, CPU is responsible for the adjacency-list construction in parallel. The constructed adjacency list, together with atom position and type information, is converted to PyTorch tensor object for force inference on GPUs. RXMD-NN allows to control the computational granularity, such as the number of atoms per domain and domains per node, to find an ideal balance between horizontal and vertical scalability to utilize available hardware resources.

PyTorch has become a standard Python library in machine learning community due to its APIs for complex model architectures that enables highly efficient training and inference on GPU. However, production platforms such as HPC clusters, mobile devices, and edge nodes often demand a set of requirements that Python is not designed for, *e.g.*, multithreading, low latency computing, and massively parallel distributed architectures. GPU Offloading of Allegro model is realized by TorchScript, which is statically typed intermediate representation to create serialized and optimizable ML models. The serialized model can be loaded from other programming language such as C++ allowing to be deployed in environments that are difficult for python codes to run without sacrificing multithreading and optimization opportunities.

3   Results

We test both fidelity and computational scalability of the proposed Allegro-Legato NNQMD model as implemented in the RXMD-NN code on a leadership-scale computing platform, Polaris, at Argonne Leadership Computing Facility (ALCF).

3.1   Experimental Platform

We conduct numerical experiments on the Polaris supercomputer at ALCF. It is a Hewlett Packard Enterprise (HPE) Apollo 6500 Gen 10+ based system consisting of two computing nodes per chassis, seven chassis per rack, and 40 racks, with a total of 560 nodes. Each Polaris node has one 2.8 GHz AMD EPYC Milan 7543P 32-core CPU with 512 GB of DDR4 RAM, four NVIDIA A100 GPUs with 40GB HBM2 memory per GPU, two 1.6 TB of SSDs in RAID0 and two Slingshot network endpoints. Polaris uses the NVIDIA A100 HGX platform to connect all 4 GPUs *via* NVLink, with a GPU interconnect bandwidth of 600 GB/s. Designed by Cray, the Slingshot interconnect is based on high radix 64-port switches arranged in dragonfly topology, offering adaptive routing, congestion control and bandwidth guarantees by assigning traffic classes to applications. Polaris is rated at a production peak performance of 44 petaflops with node-wise performance at 78 teraflops for double precision.

3.2 Fidelity-Scaling Results

For the fidelity-scaling test, we trained Allegro and Allegro-Legato with $\ell = 1$ and examined their robustness in terms of t_{failure}, *i.e.* the greater t_{failure}, the more robust. The parameters of MD simulation for the test are carefully chosen so that each MD simulation is expected to fail within a reasonable time but not immediately. While the constant-temperature ensemble method based on Nose-Hoover thermostat (*i.e.*, NVT ensemble) is used to study thermal-equilibrium properties, it could suppress and hidden unphysical model predictions by connecting atoms with an external thermostat. Microcanonical ensemble (NVE) method is the most rigorous test on the model robustness by simply integrating the equations of motion without an external control (also it has broader applicability to nonequilibrium processes). In each simulation instance, the liquid ammonia system is first thermalized at a temperature of 200 K using NVT ensemble for 1,000 steps. We subsequently switch the ensemble to NVE and continue the simulation until it fails to determine t_{failure} (see the arrow in Fig. 1). The time step Δt of 2 femto-seconds (fs) is chosen throughout the robustness test. For each system size, over ten independent simulation instances are averaged to measure t_{failure}.

Figure 2 shows t_{failure} as a function of the system size (*i.e.*, the total number of atoms, N) ranging from $N = 432$ to 27,648. Firstly, regardless of the system size, we observe a significant improvement in the averaged sustained MD simulation steps using Allegro-Legato model. We observe the greatest improvement of the simulation robustness in the largest system with $N = 27,648$, where 2.6-times longer MD simulation (14,600 steps) is achieved with SAM in Allegro-Legato than that with the original Allegro model (5,500 steps). In the MD simulation framework, even a single misprediction of atomic force can lead to catastrophe through chain reactions. An error in atomic force is integrated into its velocity, then into atom coordinates. Too large atomic displacement in a single MD step could result in unphysically strong collisions with other atoms, which propagate throughout the system within a few MD steps, known as "the billiard effect." MD simulations with large number of atoms or longer simulation time will inevitably suffer from higher probability of having such model mispredictions, thus fail faster than a smaller system. Our test demonstrates that SAM successfully improves the robustness of model prediction, realizing a stable MD simulation for greater time steps.

To quantify fidelity scaling, we define a fidelity-scaling exponent $N^{-\beta}$ through the scaling relation,

$$t_{\text{failure}} = \alpha N^{-\beta}, \tag{4}$$

where α is a prefactor. A smaller β value (*i.e.*, weaker fidelity scaling) indicates delayed time-to-failure, thus a capability to study larger spatiotemporal-scale processes accurately on massively parallel computers. The Allegro-Legato model has drastically improved fidelity scaling, $\beta_{\text{Allegro-Legato}} = 0.14 < \beta_{\text{Allegro}} = 0.29$ beyond statistical uncertainty (see the error bars in Fig. 2), thus systematically delaying time-to-failure.

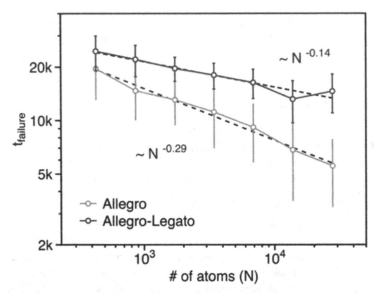

Fig. 2. Fidelity scaling of NNQMD simulation: Here, t_{failure} is measured using NVE ensemble with a timestep of 2 fs. Statistically improved t_{failure} is observed in even the smallest system size, which is further pronounced as the system size increases. The exponent of power law fitting shows nearly a factor of two reduction using Allegro-Legato model.

3.3 Computational-Scaling Results

We measure the wall-clock time per MD step with scaled workload—6,912P-atom ammonia system on P MD domains. In this test, each MD domain consists of 6,912 atoms that are offloaded to single GPU. In addition to the force inference, the execution time includes the adjacency list construction, data transfer between host and GPU memory, and internode communication via network fabric. Figure 3 shows wall-clock time as a function of P. By scaling the problem size linearly with the number of GPUs, the runtime increases only slightly, indicating an excellent scalability.

Here, we quantify the parallel efficiency by defining the speed of NNQMD algorithm as the product of the total number of atoms multiplied by the number of MD steps executed per second. The isogranular speedup is given by the speed on P MD domains relative to the speed of single domain as baseline. The parallel efficiency of weak scalability thus is obtained by the isogranular speedup divided by P. With the granularity of 6,912 atoms per domain, we have obtained an excellent weak-scaling efficiency, 0.91 for up to 13,271,040 atoms on 1,920 A100 GPUs. Despite the relatively large granularity of 6,912 atoms per domain, we obtained a fast time-to-solution of 3.46 s per MD step enabling 25,000 MD steps per day for production runs.

Figure 4 shows GPU acceleration of NNQMD algorithm on single Polaris node. The histogram presents the reduction in wall-clock time per MD step (averaged over 10 MD steps) using the runtime obtained with CPU only (32 cores with 32 threads) as baseline. Here, we examined: (1) three system sizes of $N = 1,728$, 6,912, and 13,824 ammonia

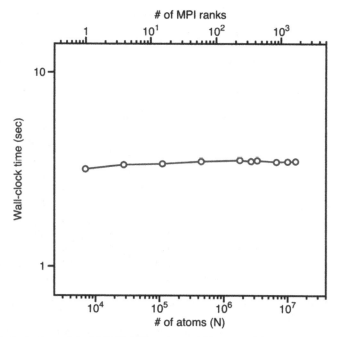

Fig. 3. Wall-clock time of the RXMD-NN code per MD step, with scaled workloads—6,912P atom ammonia liquid using P A100 GPUs ($P = 1,...,$ 1,920).

atoms; and (2) three domain decompositions such as single, double and quadruple sub-domains. Atoms in each domain are assigned to one GPU. With $N = 1,728$ system, we observe a marginal GPU acceleration up to 1.24× speedup, which has been substantially improved with greater system sizes. We have achieved a 7.6x speedup using $N = 13,824$ atom system with four subdomains.

4 Discussions

While SAM-enhanced Allegro model, Allegro-Legato, has achieved improved robust-ness over the SOTA Allegro model as shown in the previous section, we here discuss the imprecation of SAM training to other aspects such as accuracy and computational speed.

4.1 Simulation Time

First of all, MD simulation time is not affected by SAM since SAM only applies to the training stage but not the inference stage in MD simulation. Table 2 compares the simulation time per MD time step for the baseline Allegro model and the proposed Allegro-Legato model. Hereafter, we use the default value, $\ell = 1$, for the maximum tensor rank, thus the same number of parameters for the two models. The simulation time is identical for both models within the measurement uncertainty due to nondedicated access to the experimental platform.

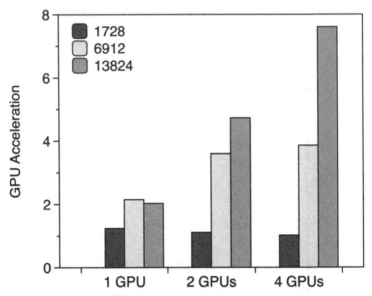

Fig. 4. GPU acceleration of NNQMD algorithm: Three system sizes of $N = 1728$, 6912 and 13,824 atoms are examined. The histogram presents the reduction in wall-clock time per MD step over the runtime with 32 CPU cores without GPU as reference. Detail of the benchmark platform as well as the GPU and CPU architectures are presented in the main text. We have achieved 7.6× speedup using four GPUs with $N = 13,824$ atoms.

As a comparison, Table 2 also shows the baseline Allegro model with two other tensor ranks, $\ell = 0$ and 2. Larger ℓ generates more accurate but larger models (*i.e.*, larger numbers of parameters) and hence incur longer simulation times. Based on the accuracy/computational-cost trade-off, production NNQMD simulations with the Allegro model typically use $\ell = 1$.

Table 2. Simulation-time comparison: As SAM only applies to the training stage and does not modify the size of architecture, the computational cost for simulation is not affected.

Model	# of parameters	Time/step (ms)
Allegro	133,544	916
Allegro-Legato	133,544	898
Reference Models		
Allegro ($\ell = 0$)	95,656	395
Allegro ($\ell = 2$)	183,720	2,580

4.2 Training Time

As mentioned in Sect. 2.2, SAM's shortcoming is that it requires more computation time than the base optimizer, because each epoch has to compute the first-order gradients twice. However, in our setting, SAM converges faster than the default optimizer, and thus the total training time is not significantly affected (Table 3). As references, we also measured the training time of Allegro models with different maximum tensor ranks, $\ell = 0$ and 2 and we observed that the training cost increases drastically for larger ℓ. In summary, Allegro-Legato improves the robustness of Allegro without incurring extra training cost.

Table 3. Training-time comparison: Although SAM takes longer per-epoch training time, it converges faster and thus does not significantly affect total training time. Compared to the reference training times of variations of Allegro models, the extra training cost of Allegro-Legato is negligible.

Model	Total time (hours)	Per-epoch time (seconds)	Epochs
Allegro	11.1	248	161
Allegro-Legato	13.6	433	113
Reference Models			
Allegro ($\ell = 0$)	4.4	127	127
Allegro ($\ell = 2$)	19.6	636	111

4.3 Model Accuracy

While faithful reproduction of system energy is necessary to properly guide model training, the most crucial to MD simulations is accurate force prediction. We obtained the validation error in atomic force as 15.9 (root mean-square error, RMSE) and 11.6 (mean absolute error, MAE) with Allegro-Legato ($\ell = 1$) model, and 14.7 (RMSE) and 10.7 (MAE) with the original Allegro model ($\ell = 1$), respectively. All error values are in a unit of meV/Å. Chmiela *et al.* recently provided a guideline that MAE required for reliable MD simulations is 1 kcal/mol/Å, which corresponds to 43.4 meV/Å [19]. Although Allegro-Legato incurs a slight increase in the force prediction error (about 8% in the liquid ammonia dataset) compared to the original Allegro model, the obtained force error is about a factor four smaller than the guideline for reliably performing MD simulations. Namely, Allegro-Legato improves the robustness without sacrificing accuracy.

4.4 Implicit Sharpness Regularization in Allegro

While we propose to explicitly control the sharpness of models, we found that one control parameter in the baseline Allegro model (*i.e.*, maximum rank of tensors to represent features) implicitly regulate the sharpness of the model. In Table 4, besides our Allegro-Legato model having smaller sharpness, Allegro $\ell = 1, 2$ models have significantly smaller sharpness and higher t_{failure} compared to Allegro $\ell = 0$ model. Namely, Allegro with higher ℓ implicitly regularizes sharpness, resulting in higher robustness (*i.e.*, larger t_{failure}), but with increasing computational cost. Allegro-Legato ($\ell = 1$) model achieves the same level of sharpness as Allegro ($\ell = 2$) model with much less computing time; see Tables 2 and 3.

Table 4. Implicit sharpness regularization by Allegro: While our Allegro-Legato model has smaller sharpness than Allegro, Allegro models with larger ℓ have progressively smaller sharpness. Here, we measure sharpness, $\max\limits_{\|\epsilon\|_2 \leq \rho} \{L(w + \epsilon) - L(w)\}$, by taking maximum of 1,000 independent random samples around the 0.05-neighborhood of each minimum.

Model	Allegro ($\ell = 0$)	Allegro ($\ell = 1$)	Allegro ($\ell = 2$)	Allegro-Legato ($\ell = 1$)
Sharpness	5.0×10^{-4}	3.2×10^{-4}	9.8×10^{-5}	1.2×10^{-4}

Figure 5 visualizes the loss surface of Allegro ($\ell = 0$, 1, and 2) and Allegro-Legato ($\ell = 1$) models. The figure confirms: (1) progressive smoothening (*i.e.*, smaller sharpness) for larger ℓ within the Allegro model due to implicit regularization through accuracy but with increasing computational cost; and (2) explicit smoothening of Allegro-Legato through SAM over Allegro with the same ℓ without extra computational cost.

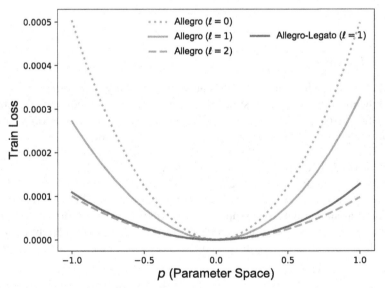

Fig. 5: Loss surface visualization: One dimensional visualization of loss surface of each model. Following the definition of sharpness (Eq. 2), we randomly sample a vector, d, that gives the sharpness direction to compute $L(w + pd)$ for $p \in [-1, 1]$.

4.5 Training Details

Lastly, we provide detailed training configuration for completeness (Table 5). For fair comparison, we used the default hyperparameters that are released as the SOTA model and SAM training uses the default optimizer as its base optimizer.

Table 5. Detailed training setting: All training setups in this paper adopt these parameters unless otherwise noted.

Material type	Liquid NH_3
Number of atoms per a configuration	432
# of training examples ($N_{training}$)	4,500
# of validation examples	500
r_{max} for cutoff	6.0
Maximum tensor rank (ℓ)	1
Batch size	4
Peak learning rate	2e−3
Learning rate decay	ReduceLROnPlateau
Learning rate scheduler patience	50
Learning rate scheduler factor	0.5
(Base) Optimizer	Adam
Adam's (β_1, β_2)	(0.9, 0.999)
Loss function	Per atom MSE
Loss coefficient (force, total energy)	(1.0, 1.0)
Stopping criterion	$\Delta L_{validation} \leq 3e - 3$ for 100 epochs

5 Applications

The improved robustness of the proposed Allegro-Legato model, while preserving the SOTA accuracy and computational speed of Allegro, enables large spatio-temporal scale NNQMD simulations on leadership-scale computers. A compelling example is the study of vibrational properties of ammonia. Development of dynamical models that accurately reproduce the vibrational spectra of molecular crystals and liquids is vital for predictions of their thermodynamic behavior, which is critical for their applications in energy, biological, and pharmaceutical systems [20]. In particular, there has been growing development of green ammonia-based fuel technologies for sustainable society over the past few years. Ammonia (NH_3) has a higher energy density than even liquid hydrogen, but ammonia can be stored at a much less energy-intensive −33 °C versus −253 °C, and thanks to a century of ammonia use in agriculture, a vast ammonia infrastructure already exists [21]. Over 180 million metric tons of ammonia is produced annually, and 120 ports are equipped with ammonia terminals [21]. Development of technologies based on ammonia will be reliant on our ability to understand and model the complex physical and chemical interactions that give rise to its unique properties.

There are multiple complicating factors that require careful considerations such as nuclear quantum effects (NQEs) and its coupling with vibrational anharmonicity when developing computational frameworks that accurately describe vibrational properties [20]. Standard first-principles calculations for vibrational properties only treat electrons quantum mechanically and vibrational properties can be determined by Fourier transform and matrix diagonalization of the unit-cell Hessian, which is at most on the order of a few 100 entries [22]. Evaluating the role of NQEs and its coupling with vibrational anharmonicity is done in the so-called path integral MD (PIMD) approach, which samples the quantum partition function for the entire quantum system [23, 24]. This requires long-time simulations of a large number of replicas of large MD systems that are harmonically coupled to each other as interacting ring-polymers, especially at low temperatures [23, 24]. The background of Fig. 6a shows a typical first principles-based simulation, where the atoms are treated classically and the electron charge density is treated quantum-mechanically to compute atomic forces, which is illustrated as blue iso-surfaces. In the foreground we have highlighted one NH_3 molecule from a PIMD simulation of the same atomic configuration, where each atom has 32 replicas that are harmonically coupled together. The computation of the replica simulations is embarrassingly parallel, with only fixed nearest replica communication, and the major cost is computing the energy and forces for the atoms within each replica simulation, which is typically done from first principles. However, our Allegro-Legato model with enhanced robustness allows for stable long-time MD simulations at near quantum accuracy, and thus can replace expensive first-principles calculations in the PIMD simulations, which would make accurate evaluation of ammonia's low energy inter-molecular vibrational modes intractable.

We have performed massively parallel PIMD simulations with our Allegro-Legato model, computing the energy and forces within each replica simulation to evaluate the phonon spectra for inter-molecular modes of ammonia. The Allegro-Legato model is found to produce the expected softening of high-energy modes at finite temperature with inclusion of nuclear quantum effects in comparison to standard matrix diagonalization within the harmonic approximation, which is illustrated in Fig. 6b. In particular, reduction of the energy of the vibrational modes in the 30–90 meV is consistent with high-end neutron experiments for the vibrational spectrum performed by the authors at Oak Ridge National Laboratory in the last summer (these results will be published elsewhere).

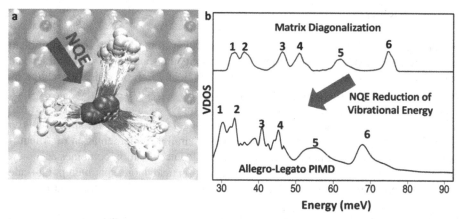

Fig. 6. Computed vibrational spectra of ammonia: (a) While typical first-principles simulation treats atoms classically and electrons quantum-mechanically, PIMD simulation uses multiple replicas of each atom to mimic nuclear quantum effect (NQE). (b) Top curve shows vibrational spectrum computed at zero temperature without NQE, while bottom at finite temperature with Allegro-Legato PIMD simulation. With the inclusion of NQE, Allegro-Legato PIMD correctly shows softening of high-energy inter-molecular modes expected at finite temperature and explains high-end neutron-scattering observations.

6 Related Work

There has been an explosion in the development and application of NNQMD simulations [1–3, 6, 8] and their scalable parallel implementation [4, 5]. On the other hand, it was only recently that the robustness of NNQMD was quantified in terms of time-to-failure $t_{failure}$ [25] and its deteriorating reduction with the problem size (*i.e.*, fidelity-scaling problem) was pointed out [9]. This work is the first to: (1) formally quantify the fidelity scaling by introducing the fidelity-scaling exponent β through $t_{failure} \propto N^{-\beta}$ (N is the number of atoms); and (2) propose the solution to the fidelity-scaling problem using sharpness-aware minimization.

Robustness against adversarial attacks is a central and widely studied issue in machine learning [4, 13, 14]. Compared to typical adversarial attacks, it is nontrivial to generate adversarial perturbations for NNQMD. This is because the attack we consider is not only focused on the accuracy of the model, but also on the time to failure ($t_{failure}$) of the model, which can only be determined through long-time simulations [15, 16]. Generative adversarial network (GAN) is one possible approach for sampling molecular configurations in a learning-on-the-fly setting [26]. However, we remark that the real strength of MD simulation is its ability to compute dynamic correlations that can directly explain high-resolution spectroscopic experiments, which requires a long uninterrupted Hamiltonian trajectory, to which adversarial networks are generally not applicable. In this domain, Allegro-Legato thus provides a unique solution.

7 Conclusion

We have introduced the proposed SAM-based solution to the fidelity-scaling problem into the Allegro NNQMD model,[8] which represents the state-of-the-art accuracy and speed. The resulting Allegro-Legato model has drastically improved fidelity scaling by exhibiting a significantly lower exponent, $\beta_{\text{Allegro−Legato}} = 0.14 < \beta_{\text{Allegro}} = 0.29$, thus systematically delaying time-to-failure. Such improved fidelity scaling is central to ensure that meaningful scientific knowledge is extracted from large-scale simulations on leadership-scale parallel computers. Our scalable parallel implementation of Allegro-Legato with excellent computational scaling and GPU acceleration combines accuracy, speed, robustness and scalability, thus allowing practical large spatiotemporal-scale NNQMD simulations for challenging applications on exascale computing platforms.

Acknowledgement. This work was supported as part of the Computational Materials Sciences Program funded by the U.S. Department of Energy, Office of Science, Basic Energy Sciences, under award number DE-SC0014607. H.I. and K.N. were partially supported by an NSF grant, OAC-2118061. The simulations were performed at the Argonne Leadership Computing Facility under the DOE INCITE program, while scalable code development was supported by the Aurora ESP program. The authors acknowledge the Center for Advanced Research Computing at the University of Southern California for providing computing resources that have contributed to the research results reported within this publication. We are grateful to Dr. Makiko Hirata for valuable discussions regarding Allegro-Legato.

References

1. Behler, J.: Constructing high-dimensional neural network potentials: a tutorial review. Int. J. Quantum Chem. **115**(16), 1032–1050 (2015)
2. Krishnamoorthy, A., et al.: Dielectric constant of liquid water determined with neural network quantum molecular dynamics. Phys. Rev. Lett. **126**(21), 216403 (2021)
3. Linker, T., et al.: Exploring far-from-equilibrium ultrafast polarization control in ferroelectric oxides with excited-state neural network quantum molecular dynamics. Sci. Adv. **8**(12), eabk2625 (2022)
4. Jia, W., et al.: Pushing the limit of molecular dynamics with ab initio accuracy to 100 million atoms with machine learning. Proceedings of Supercomputing, vol. 5. ACM/IEEE (2020)
5. Nguyen-Cong, K., et al.: Billion atom molecular dynamics simulations of carbon at extreme conditions and experimental time and length scales. In: Proceedings of Supercomputing, vol. 4. IEEE/ACM (2021)
6. Batzner, S., et al.: E(3)-equivariant graph neural networks for data-efficient and accurate interatomic potentials. Nat. Commun. **13**, 2453 (2021)
7. Thomas, N., et al.: Tensor field networks: rotation-and translation-equivariant neural networks for 3D point clouds. arXiv:1802.08219 (2018)
8. Musaelian, A., et al.: Learning local equivariant representations for large-scale atomistic dynamics. arXiv:2204.05249 (2022)
9. Rajak, P., et al.: Ex-NNQMD: extreme-scale neural network quantum molecular dynamics. In: Proceedings of IPDPSW21, pp. 943–946. IEEE (2021)
10. Misawa, M., et al.: Application of first-principles-based artificial neural network potentials to multiscale-shock dynamics simulations on solid materials. J. Phys. Chem. Lett. **11**, 4536–4541 (2020)

11. Foret, P., Kleiner, A., Mobahi, H., Neyshabur, B.: Sharpness-aware minimization for efficiently improving generalization. In: Proceedings of International Conference on Learning Representations, ICLR, vol. 1839 (2021)
12. Schmidt, R.M., Schneider, F., Hennig, P.: Descending through a crowded valley - benchmarking deep learning optimizers. In: Proceedings of International Conference on Machine Learning, ICML, vol. 139, pp. 9367–9376 (2021)
13. Goodfellow, I.J., Shlens, J., Szegedy, C.: Explaining and harnessing adversarial examples. In: Proceedings of International Conference on Learning Representations, ICLR (2015)
14. Shafahi, Aet al.: Adversarial training for free! In: Proceedings of NeurIPS, vol. 32 (2019)
15. Schwalbe-Koda, D., Tan, A.R., Gómez-Bombarelli, R.: Differentiable sampling of molecular geometries with uncertainty-based adversarial attacks. Nat. Commun. 12(1), 5104 (2021)
16. Cubuk, E.D., Schoenholz, S.S.: Adversarial forces of physical models. In: Proceedings of NeurIPS-MLPS (2020)
17. Nomura, K., Kalia, R.K., Nakano, A., Rajak, P., Vashishta, P.: RXMD: a scalable reactive molecular dynamics simulator for optimized time-to-solution. SoftwareX 11, 100389 (2020)
18. Nomura, K., et al.: Metascalable quantum molecular dynamics simulations of hydrogen-on-demand. In: Proceedings of SC14, pp. 661–673. IEEE/ACM (2014)
19. Chmiela, S., Sauceda, H.E., Müller, K.-R., Tkatchenko, A.: Towards exact molecular dynamics simulations with machine-learned force fields. Nat. Commun. 9(1), 3887 (2018)
20. Hoja, J., Reilly, A.M., Tkatchenko, A.: First-principles modeling of molecular crystals: structures and stabilities, temperature and pressure. WIREs Comput. Mol. Sci. 7(1), e1294 (2017)
21. Chehade, G., Dincer, I.: Progress in green ammonia production as potential carbon-free fuel. Fuel 299, 120845 (2021)
22. Togo, A., Tanaka, I.: First principles phonon calculations in materials science. Scripta Mater. 108, 1–5 (2015)
23. Feynman, R.P., Hibbs, A.R.: Quantum Mechanics and Path Integrals. McGraw-Hill (1965)
24. Rossi, M., Ceriotti, M., Manolopoulos, D.E.: How to remove the spurious resonances from ring polymer molecular dynamics. J. Chem. Phys. 140(23), 234116 (2014)
25. Fu, X., et al.: Forces are not enough: benchmark and critical evaluation for machine learning force fields with molecular simulations. arXiv:2210.07237 (2022)
26. Jinnouchi, R., Miwa, K., Karsai, F., Kresse, G., Asahi, R.: On-the-fly active learning of interatomic potentials for large-scale atomistic simulations. J. Phys. Chem. Lett. 11(17), 6946–6955 (2020)

Quantum Annealing vs. QAOA: 127 Qubit Higher-Order Ising Problems on NISQ Computers

Elijah Pelofske[(⊠)], Andreas Bärtschi, and Stephan Eidenbenz

Los Alamos National Laboratory, CCS-3 Information Sciences, Los Alamos, USA
epelofske@lanl.gov

Abstract. Quantum annealing (QA) and Quantum Alternating Operator Ansatz (QAOA) are both heuristic quantum algorithms intended for sampling optimal solutions of combinatorial optimization problems. In this article we implement a rigorous direct comparison between QA on D-Wave hardware and QAOA on IBMQ hardware. These two quantum algorithms are also compared against classical simulated annealing. The studied problems are instances of a class of Ising models, with variable assignments of $+1$ or -1, that contain cubic ZZZ interactions (higher order terms) and match both the native connectivity of the Pegasus topology D-Wave chips and the heavy hexagonal lattice of the IBMQ chips. The novel QAOA implementation on the heavy hexagonal lattice has a CNOT depth of 6 per round and allows for usage of an entire heavy hexagonal lattice. Experimentally, QAOA is executed on an ensemble of randomly generated Ising instances with a grid search over 1 and 2 round angles using all 127 programmable superconducting transmon qubits of ibm_washington. The error suppression technique digital dynamical decoupling is also tested on all QAOA circuits. QA is executed on the same Ising instances with the programmable superconducting flux qubit devices D-Wave Advantage_system4.1 and Advantage_system6.1 using modified annealing schedules with pauses. We find that QA outperforms QAOA on all problem instances. We also find that dynamical decoupling enables 2-round QAOA to marginally outperform 1-round QAOA, which is not the case without dynamical decoupling.

Keywords: QAOA · Quantum Alternating Operator Ansatz · Quantum annealing · dynamical decoupling · higher-order Ising · Pegasus graph · heavy-hex lattice

1 Introduction

Quantum annealing (QA) in the transverse field Ising model is an analog computation technology which utilizes quantum fluctuations in order to search for ground state solutions of a problem Hamiltonian [1–5]. D-Wave quantum annealers are programmable hardware implementations of quantum annealing which use superconducting flux qubits [6,7].

© The Author(s), under exclusive license to Springer Nature Switzerland AG 2023
A. Bhatele et al. (Eds.): ISC High Performance 2023, LNCS 13948, pp. 240–258, 2023.
https://doi.org/10.1007/978-3-031-32041-5_13

Quantum Alternating Operator Ansatz (QAOA) is a hybrid quantum classical algorithm for sampling combinatorial optimization problems [8–10], the quantum component of which can be instantiated with a programmable gate-based universal quantum computer. The Quantum Approximate Optimization Algorithm [11] was the first variational algorithm of this type, which was then generalized to the Quantum Alternating Operator Ansatz algorithm [8].

QAOA is effectively a Trotterization of the Quantum Adiabatic Algorithm, and is overall similar to Quantum Annealing. In particular both algorithms address combinatorial optimization problems. The exact characteristics of how both QA and QAOA will scale to large system sizes is currently not fully understood, in particular because quantum hardware is still in the NISQ era [12–14]. For example, there is evidence that QAOA may be more difficult for classical computers to simulate than quantum annealing, which could make it a viable candidate for quantum advantage [15]. Quantum annealing in particular has been experimentally evaluated against classical algorithms in order to determine for what problem types and under what settings quantum annealing could provide a scaling advantage over the next best state-of-the-art classical approaches [13,14,16–18]. Generally these results are encouraging and show that quantum annealing can indeed sample certain problem types better than classical methods such as simulated annealing. There have been a number of studies that directly compare Quantum Annealing and QAOA for a number of different sampling tasks [19–23], however this paper presents, to the best of our knowledge, the largest direct comparison between Quantum Annealing and QAOA to date. There have been experimental QAOA implementations which used up to 40 qubits [24], 27 qubits [25], and 23 qubits [26]. There have also been QAOA experiments which had circuit depth up to 159 [27] and 148 [28].

The contributions of this article are as follows:

1. We provide a direct comparison between QAOA and Quantum Annealing in terms of experiments on D-Wave and IBMQ hardware. This comparison uses a comparable parameter search space for QA and QAOA, uses no minor embedding for quantum annealing, and uses short depth QAOA circuits, thus providing a fair comparison of the two algorithms. A comparison of this problem size has not been performed before to the best of our knowledge. We show that QAOA is better than random sampling, and quantum annealing clearly outperforms QAOA. A comparison against the classical heuristic algorithm simulated annealing is also presented.

2. The QAOA algorithm we present is tailored for short depth circuit construction on the heavy hexagonal lattice (CNOT depth of 6 per round), therefore allowing full usage of any heavy hexagonal topology quantum processor in the future. We use all 127 qubits of the ibm_washington chip in order to execute the largest QAOA circuit, in terms of qubits, to date. Each QAOA circuit uses thousands of gate operations, making these results one of the largest quantum computing experiments performed to date.

3. The Ising models that are used to compare quantum annealing and QAOA are specifically constructed to include higher order terms, specifically three

Table 1. NISQ hardware summary at the time the experiments were executed. The hardware yield (e.g., the number of available qubits or two qubit interactions) for all of these devices can be less than the logical lattice because of hardware defects, and can also change over time if device calibration changes.

Device name	Topology/chip name	Available qubits	Available couplers/ CNOTs	Computation type
Advantage_system4.1	Pegasus P_{16}	5627	40279	QA
Advantage_system6.1	Pegasus P_{16}	5616	40135	QA
ibm_washington	Eagle r1 heavy-hexagonal	127	142	Universal gate-model

variable (cubic) terms. QAOA can directly implement higher order terms, and quantum annealing requires order reduction using auxiliary variables to implement these higher order terms. This is the largest experimental demonstration of QAOA with higher order terms to date.

4. In order to mitigate errors when executing the QAOA circuits, we utilize digital dynamical decoupling. This is the largest usage of dynamical decoupling in terms of qubit system size to date, and the results show that digital dynamical decoupling improves performance for two round QAOA, suggesting that it will be useful for computations with large numbers of qubits in the noisy regime.

In Sect. 2 the QAOA and QA hardware implementations, and the simulated annealing implementation are detailed. Section 3 details the experimental results and how the two quantum algorithms compare, including how simulated annealing compares. Section 4 concludes with what the results indicate and future research directions. The figures in this article are generated using matplotlib [29,30], and Qiskit [31] in Python 3. Code, data, and additional figures are available in a public Github repository[1].

2   Methods

The Ising models are defined in Sect. 2.1. In Sect. 2.2 the QAOA circuit algorithm and hardware parameters are defined. In Sect. 2.3 the quantum annealing implementation is defined. Section 2.4 defines the simulated annealing implementation.

2.1   Ising Model Problem Instances

The NISQ computers which are used in this comparison are detailed in Table 1; the clear difference between the D-Wave quantum annealers and

---

[1] https://github.com/lanl/QAOA_vs_QA.

ibm_washington is the number of qubits that are available. The additional qubits available on the quantum annealers will allow us to embed multiple problem instances onto the chips. The current IBMQ devices have a graph topology referred to as the heavy-hexagonal lattice [32]. Therefore, for a direct QAOA and QA comparison we would want to be able to create QAOA circuits which match the logical heavy-hexagonal lattice and the quantum annealer graph topology of Pegasus. For this direct comparison we target D-Wave quantum annealers with Pegasus graph hardware [33,34] connectivities. The two current D-Wave quantum annealers with Pegasus hardware graphs have chip id names Advantage_system6.1 and Advantage_system4.1. The goal for this direct comparison is that ideally we want problems which can be instantiated on *all* three of the devices in Table 1. In particular, we want these implementations to not be unfairly costly in terms of implementation overhead. For example we do not want to introduce unnecessary qubit swapping in the QAOA circuit because that would introduce larger circuit depths which would introduce more decoherence in the computation. We also do not want to introduce unnecessary minor-embedding in the problems for quantum annealers.

The other property of these problem instances that is of interest is an introduction of *higher order terms*, specifically cubic ZZZ interactions [35] also referred to as multi-body interactions [36], in addition to random linear and quadratic terms. These higher order terms require both QAOA and QA to be handle these higher order variable interactions, which is an additional test on the capability of both algorithms. QAOA can naturally handle higher order terms [37]. Implementing high order terms with QA requires introducing auxiliary variables in order to perform order reduction to get a problem structure that is comprised of only linear and quadratic terms, so that it can be implemented on the hardware, but whose optimal solutions match the optimal solutions of the original high order polynomial (for the non-auxiliary variables) [4,38–41].

Taking each of these characteristics into account, we create a class of random problems which follow the native device connectivities in Table 1. The problem instances we will be considering are Ising models defined on the hardware connectivity graph of the heavy hexagonal lattice of the device, which for these experiments will be ibm_washington. For a variable assignment vector $z = (z_0, \ldots, z_{n-1}) \in \{+1, -1\}^n$, the random Ising model is defined as

$$C(z) = \sum_{v \in V} d_v \cdot z_v + \sum_{(i,j) \in E} d_{i,j} \cdot z_i \cdot z_j + \sum_{l \in W} d_{l,n_1(l),n_2(l)} \cdot z_l \cdot z_{n_1(l)} \cdot z_{n_2(l)} \quad (1)$$

Equation (1) defines the class of random minimization Ising models with cubic terms as follows. Any heavy hexagonal lattice is a bipartite graph with vertices $V = \{0, \ldots, n-1\}$ partitioned as $V = V_2 \cup V_3$, where V_3 consists of vertices with a maximum degree of 3, and V_2 consists of vertices with a maximum degree of 2. $E \subset V_2 \times V_3$ is the edge set representing available two qubit gates (in this case CNOTs where we choose targets $i \in V_2$ and controls $j \in V_3$). W is the set of vertices in V_2 that all have degree exactly equal to 2. n_1 is a

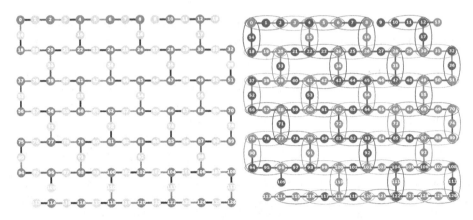

Fig. 1. Left: ibm_washington graph connectivity, where qubits are connected by CNOT (also referred to as cx) gates. The ideal lattice is called the heavy-hexagonal lattice. Note that there are two missing graph edges from the lattice between qubits 8-9 and 109-114. The total number of qubits (nodes) is 127. The edges of the graph are three colored (red, blue, and green) such that no node shares two or more edges with the same color. The node colorings of light and dark gray show that the heavy hexagonal lattice is bipartite (meaning it can be partitioned into two disjoint sets). The three edge coloring is consistent with the QAOA circuit construction in Fig. 2. **Right:** Example of a single random problem instance with cubic terms (see Eq. (1)) on the ibm_washington graph. The linear and quadratic terms are shown using two distinct colors (red and green). The nodes and edges colored red denote a weight of -1 and the nodes and edges colored green denote a weight of $+1$. The cubic terms are represented by ovals around the three qubits which define the cubic variable interactions. Like the linear and quadratic terms, the color of the oval representing the cubic terms represents the sign of the weight on the terms, where green is $+1$ and red is -1. (Color figure online)

function that gives the qubit (variable) index of the first of the two neighbors of a degree-2 node and n_2 provides the qubit (variable) index of the second of the two neighbors of any degree-2 node. Thus d_v, $d_{i,j}$, and $d_{l,n_1(l),n_2(l)}$ are all coefficients representing the random selection of the linear, quadratic, and cubic coefficients, respectively. These coefficients could be drawn from any distribution - in this paper we draw the coefficients from $\{+1, -1\}$ with probability 0.5. Equation (1) therefore defines how to compute the objective function for a given variable assignment vector z.

The heavy hexagonal topology of ibm_washington, along with an overlay showing one of the random problem instances with cubic terms defined on ibm_washington, is shown in Fig. 1. Each term coefficient was chosen to be either $+1$ or -1, which in part helps to mitigate the potential problem of limited precision for the programming control on all of the NISQ devices. 10 random instances of this class of problems are generated and sampled using QAOA and QA, the implementations of each will be discussed next.

2.2   Quantum Alternating Operator Ansatz

Given a combinatorial optimization problem over inputs $z \in \{+1, -1\}^n$, let $C(z): \{+1, -1\}^n \to \mathbb{R}$ be the objective function which evaluates the cost of the solution vector z. For a maximization (or minimization) problem, the goal is to find a variable assignment vector z for which $f(z)$ is maximized (or minimized). The QAOA algorithm consists of the following components:

- an initial state $|\psi\rangle$,
- a **phase separating** Cost Hamiltonian H_C,
  which is derived from $C(z)$ by replacing all spin variables z_i by Pauli-Z operators σ_i^z
- a **mixing** Hamiltonian H_M; in our case, we use the standard transverse field mixer, which is the sum of the Pauli-X operators σ_i^x
- an integer $p \geq 1$, the number of rounds to run the algorithm,
- two real vectors $\boldsymbol{\gamma} = (\gamma_1, ..., \gamma_p)$ and $\boldsymbol{\beta} = (\beta_1, ..., \beta_p)$, each with length p.

The algorithm consists of preparing the initial state $|\psi\rangle$, then applying p rounds of the alternating simulation of the phase separating Hamiltonian and the mixing Hamiltonian:

$$|\boldsymbol{\gamma}, \boldsymbol{\beta}\rangle = \underbrace{e^{-i\beta_p H_M} e^{-i\gamma_p H_P}}_{\text{round } p} \cdots \underbrace{e^{-i\beta_1 H_M} e^{-i\gamma_1 H_P}}_{\text{round } 1} |\psi\rangle \qquad (2)$$

Within reach round, H_P is applied first, which separates the basis states of the state vector by phases $e^{-i\gamma f(x)}$. H_M then provides parameterized interference between solutions of different cost values. After p rounds, the state $|\boldsymbol{\gamma}, \boldsymbol{\beta}\rangle$ is measured in the computational basis and returns a sample solution y of cost value $f(y)$ with probability $|\langle y|\boldsymbol{\gamma}, \boldsymbol{\beta}\rangle|^2$.

The aim of QAOA is to prepare the state $|\boldsymbol{\gamma}, \boldsymbol{\beta}\rangle$ from which we can sample a solution y with high cost value $f(y)$. Therefore, in order to use QAOA the task is to find angles $\boldsymbol{\gamma}$ and $\boldsymbol{\beta}$ such that the expectation value $\langle \boldsymbol{\gamma}, \boldsymbol{\beta}|H_P|\boldsymbol{\gamma}, \boldsymbol{\beta}\rangle$ is large ($-H_P$ for minimization problems). In the limit $p \to \infty$, QAOA is effectively a Trotterization of the Quantum Adiabatic Algorithm, and in general as we increase p we expect to see a corresponding increase in the probability of sampling the optimal solution [42]. The challenge is the classical outer loop component of finding the good angles $\boldsymbol{\gamma}$ and $\boldsymbol{\beta}$ for all rounds p, which has a high computational cost as p increases.

Variational quantum algorithms, such as QAOA, have been a subject of large amount of attention, in large part because of the problem domains that variational algorithms can address (such as combinatorial optimization) [43]. One of the challenges however with variational quantum algorithms is that the classical component of parameter selection, in the case of QAOA this is the angle finding problem, is not solved and is even more difficult when noise is present in the computation [44]. Typically the optimal angles for QAOA are computed exactly for small problem instances [20,45]. However, in this case the angle finding approach we will use is a reasonably high resolution gridsearch over the possible angles. Note however that a fine gridsearch scales exponentially with the number of QAOA rounds p, and therefore is not advisable for practical high round QAOA [9,11]. Exactly computing what the optimal angles are for problems of this size would be quite computationally intensive, especially with the introduction of higher order terms. We leave the problem of exactly computing the optimal QAOA angles to future work.

Figure 2 describes the short depth QAOA circuit construction for sampling the higher order Ising test instance. This algorithm can be applied to any heavy hexagonal lattice topology, which allows for executing the QAOA circuits on the 127 variable instances on the IBMQ `ibm_washington` backend. For the class of Ising models with higher order terms defined in Sect. 2.1, the QAOA angle ranges which are used are $\gamma_1, \ldots, \gamma_p \in [0, \pi)$ and $\beta_1, \ldots, \beta_{p-1} \in [0, \pi), \beta_p \in [0, \frac{\pi}{2})$ where p is the number of QAOA rounds. Note that the halving of the angle search space for β applies when $p = 1$. For optimizing the angles using the naive grid search for $p = 1$, β_0 is varied over 60 linearly spaced angles $\in [0, \frac{\pi}{2}]$ and γ_0 is varied over 120 linearly spaced angles $\in [0, \pi)$. For the high resolution gridsearch for $p = 2$, β_1 is varied over 5 linearly spaced angles $\in [0, \frac{\pi}{2}]$ and γ_0, γ_1, and β_0 are varied over 11 linearly spaced angles $\in [0, \pi]$. Therefore, for $p = 2$ the angle gridsearch uses 6655 separate circuit executions (for each of the 10 problem instances), and for $p = 1$ the angle gridsearch uses 7200 separate circuit executions. Each circuit execution used 10, 000 samples in order to compute a robust distribution for each angle combination.

In order to mitigate decoherence on idle qubits, digital dynamical decoupling (DDD) is also tested for all QAOA circuits. Dynamical Decoupling is an open loop quantum control technique error suppression technique for mitigating decoherence on idle qubits [46–51]. Dynamical decoupling can be implemented with pulse level quantum control, and digital dynamical decoupling can be implemented simply with circuit level instructions of sequences of gates which are identities [50]. Note that digital dynamical decoupling is an approximation of pulse level dynamical decoupling. Dynamical decoupling has been experimentally demonstrated for superconducting qubit quantum processors including IBMQ devices [46,52,53]. Dynamical decoupling in particular is applicable for QAOA circuits because they can be relatively sparse and therefore have idle qubits [46]. DDD does not always effective at consistently reducing errors during computation (for example because of other control errors present on the device [46,49]), and therefore the raw QAOA circuits are compared against the QAOA circuits with DDD in the experiments section. In order to apply the DDD sequences to the OpenQASM [54] QAOA circuits, the `PadDynamicalDecoupling`[2] method from Qiskit [31] is used, with the `pulse_alignment` parameter set based on the `ibm_washington` backend properties. The circuit scheduling algorithm that is used for inserting the digital dynamical decoupling sequences is ALAP, which schedules the stop time of instructions as late as possible[3]. There are other

---

[2] https://qiskit.org/documentation/locale/bn_BN/stubs/qiskit.transpiler.passes. PadDynamicalDecoupling.html.

[3] https://qiskit.org/documentation/apidoc/transpiler_passes.html.

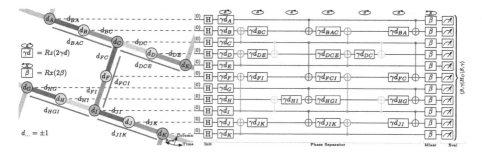

Fig. 2. A 1-round QAOA circuit: **(left)** The problem instance is a hardware-native bipartite graph with an arbitrary 3-edge-coloring given by Kőnig's line coloring theorem. **(right)** Any quadratic term (colored edge) gives rise to a combination of two CNOTs and a Rz-rotation in the phase separator, giving a CNOT depth of 6 due to the degree-3 nodes. When targeting the degree-2 nodes with the CNOT gates, these constructions can be nested, leading to no overhead when implementing the three-qubit terms: these always have a degree-2 node in the middle (see Eq. (1)). (Color figure online)

scheduling algorithms that could be applied which may increase the efficacy of dynamical decoupling. There are different DDD gate sequences that can be applied, including Y-Y or X-X sequences. Because the X Pauli gate is already a native gate of the IBMQ device, the X-X DDD sequence is used for simplicity.

Note that the variable states for the optimization problems are either -1 or $+1$, but the circuit measurement states are either 0 or 1. Therefore once the measurements are made on the QAOA circuits, for each variable in each sample the variable state mapping of $0 \rightarrow 1$, $1 \rightarrow -1$ is performed. For circuit execution on the superconducting transom qubit `ibm_washington`, circuits are batched into *jobs* where each job is composed of a group of at most 250 circuits - the maximum number of circuits for a job on `ibm_washington` is currently 300, but we use 250 in order to reduce job errors related to the size of jobs. Grouping circuits into jobs is helpful for reducing the total amount of compute time required to prepare and measure each circuit. When submitting the circuits to the backend, they are all first locally transpiled via Qiskit [31] with `optimization_level=3`. This transpilation converts the gateset to the `ibm_washington` native gateset, and the transpiler optimization attempts to simplify the circuit where possible. The QAOA circuit execution on `ibm_washington` spanned a large amount of time, and therefore the backend versions were not consistent. The exact backend software versions were `1.3.7`, `1.3.8`, `1.3.13`, `1.3.15`, `1.3.17`.

2.3 Quantum Annealing

Quantum annealing is a proposed type of quantum computation which uses quantum fluctuations, such as quantum tunneling, in order to search for the ground state of a user programmed Hamiltonian. Quantum annealing, in the case of the transverse field Ising model implemented on D-Wave hardware, is explicitly described by the system given in Eq. (3). The state begins at time zero purely in the transverse Hamiltonian state $\sum_i \sigma_i^x$, and then over the course of the anneal (parameterized by the *annealing time*) the user programmed Ising is applied according the function $B(s)$. Together, $A(s)$ and $B(s)$ define the anneal schedules of the annealing process, and s is referred to as the *anneal fraction*. The standard anneal schedule that is used is a linear interpolation between $s = 0$ and $s = 1$.

$$H = -\frac{A(s)}{2}\left(\sum_i^n \sigma_i^x\right) + \frac{B(s)}{2}\left(H_{ising}\right) \tag{3}$$

The adiabatic theorem states that if changes to the Hamiltonian of the system are sufficiently slow, the system will remain in the ground state of problem Hamiltonian, thereby providing a computational mechanism for computing the ground state of optimization problems. The user programmed Ising H_{ising}, acting on n qubits, is defined in Eq. (4). The quadratic terms and the linear terms combined define the optimization problem instance that the annealing procedure will ideally find the ground state of. As with QAOA, the objective of quantum annealing is to find the variable assignment vector z that minimizes the cost function which has the form of Eq. (4).

$$H_{ising} = \sum_i^n h_i \sigma_i^z + \sum_{i<j}^n J_{ij}\sigma_i^z\sigma_j^z \tag{4}$$

The goal is to be able to implement the Ising models defined in Sect. 2.1 on D-Wave quantum annealers. In order to implement the higher order terms, we will need to use order reduction in order to transform the cubic terms into linear and quadratic terms [4,38–41]. This order reduction will result in using additional variables, usually called *auxiliary* or *slack* variables. Figure 3 shows the embeddings of the problem instances onto the logical Pegasus P_{16} graph, including the order reduction procedure which is used. The order reduction procedure outlined in Fig. 3 allows for direct embedding of the order reduced polynomials onto the hardware graph, regardless of whether the cubic term coefficient is +1 or −1. This order reduction ensures that the ground state(s) of the cubic term are also the ground states of the order reduced Ising. Additionally, this order reduction ensures that for every excited state of the cubic term, there are no slack variable assignments which result in the original variables having an energy less than or equal to the ground state of the original cubic term. This order reduction procedure allows any problem in the form of Eq. (1) to be mapped natively to quantum annealing hardware which accepts problems with the form of Eq. (4). Importantly, this procedure does not require minor-embedding, even including the auxiliary variables.

In order to get more samples for the same QPU time, the other strategy that is employed is to embed multiple independent Ising model instances onto the hardware graph and thus be able to execute several instances in the same annealing cycle(s). This technique is referred to as *parallel quantum annealing* [40,55]

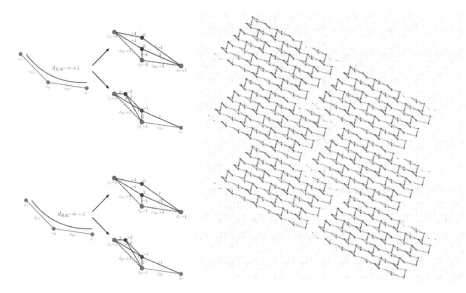

Fig. 3. (left) Two different embeddings for cubic $+1/-1$ terms. Each embedding needs two slack variable qubits. Our overall embedding alternates between these two cubic term embeddings. Any embedding with only one slack variable needs a 4-clique between the slack and the three original variables, which is not possible to embed for consecutive cubic terms. **(right)** Embedding structures of the problem instances with higher order terms embedded in parallel (independently) 6 times onto the logical Pegasus P_{16} graph. The view of this graph has been slightly partitioned so that not all of the outer parts of the Pegasus chip are drawn. The light grey qubits and couplers indicate unused hardware regions. The cyan coloring on nodes and edges denote the vertical qubits and CNOTs on the `ibm_washington` hardware graph (see Fig. 1). The red coloring on nodes and edges denote the horizontal lines of qubits and CNOTs on `ibm_washington`. The green nodes and edges denote the order reduction auxiliary variables. Note that the top right hand and lower left hand qubits are not present on the `ibm_washington` lattice - but for the purposes of generating the embeddings, these extra qubits are filled in to complete the lattice. (Color figure online)

or *tiling*[4]. Figure 3 (right) shows the parallel embeddings on a logical Pegasus graph. Because some of the logical embeddings may use a qubit or coupler which is missing on the actual hardware, less than 6 parallel instances can be tiled onto the chips to be executed at the same time. For `Advantage_system4.1`, 2 independent embeddings of the problem instances could be created without encountering missing hardware. For `Advantage_system6.1`, 3 independent embeddings of the problem instances could be created. The structure of the heavy-hexagonal lattice onto Pegasus can be visually seen in Fig. 3; the horizontal heavy-hex lines (Fig. 1) are mapped to diagonal Pegasus qubit lines that run from top left to bottom

---

[4] https://dwave-systemdocs.readthedocs.io/en/samplers/reference/composites/tiling.html.

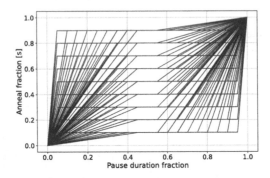

Fig. 4. All modified (forward) quantum annealing schedules which are tested in order to find the best anneal schedule with a pause. The symmetric pause inserted into the normal linearly interpolated schedule defining the $A(s)$ and $B(s)$ functions can provide better ground state sampling probability. The anneal fraction at which this pause occurs is varied between 0.1 and 0.9 in steps of 0.1. The pause duration, as a fraction of the total annealing time, is also varied between 0.1 and 0.9 in steps of 0.1. Although not shown in this figure, the annealing times are also varied between 10, 100, 1000, and 2000 μs.

right of the square Pegasus graph rendering. Then the vertical heavy-hexagonal qubits are mapped to QA qubits in between the diagonal qubit lines.

In order to optimize the quantum annealing parameters, with relatively similar complexity to the angle parameter search done for QAOA, the forward anneal schedule with pausing is optimized over a gridsearch. Pausing the anneal at the appropriate spot can provide higher chances of sampling the ground state [56]. Figure 4 shows this anneal schedule search space - importantly the annealing times used in these schedule are also optimized for. The total number of QA parameters which are varied are 9 anneal fractions, 9 pause durations, and 4 annealing times (10, 100, 1000, 2000 microseconds). Therefore, the total number of parameter combinations which are considered in the grid search is 324. 2000 microseconds is the longest annealing time available on the current D-Wave quantum annealers. The number of anneals sampled for each D-Wave job was 500. The annealing times and the anneal schedules were varied in a simple grid search. Readout and programming thermalization times are both set to 0 microseconds. All other parameters are set to default, with the exception of the modified annealing schedule.

2.4   Simulated Annealing Implementation

In order to provide a reasonable basis of comparison, the 10 Ising model problem instances are also sampled using simulated annealing. Simulated annealing is a standard high accuracy and general purpose classical heuristic algorithm [57], and has been used as a reasonable comparison against quantum algorithms [13]. The simulated annealing implementation that we utilize is an open source implementation[5]. The settings we use are all set to default and 1000 samples are drawn for each Ising model. The simulated annealing implementation does not natively handle higher order terms, and therefore order reduction must be applied to the Ising model's before being sampled by simulated annealing. Order reduction introduces additional variables into the computation. The order reduction is performed using the python package *dimod*[6]. The order reduction penalty `strength` is set to 2, which ensures that the optimal solution of the original higher order Ising matches the order reduced Ising model (excluding the ancillary variables introduced by the order reduction).

3   Results

Figures 5 and 6 combined show the detailed energy distributions for all 10 cubic Ising models sampled using the best parameter choices found for QA and QAOA. These histograms include the four variants of QAOA - 1 and 2 rounds with and without digital dynamical decoupling. The histograms include 10000 random samples (binomial distribution with $p = 0.5$) on the 10 Ising models.

QA Performs Better than QAOA: The most notable observation across these histograms is that clearly quantum annealing results in better variable assignments compared to all tested variations of QAOA; this clear stratification of the algorithms capabilities is consistent across all 10 problem instances. Notice that the minimum energies achieved by QAOA (marked by the solid vertical lines) do not reach the energy distribution sampled by the quantum annealers. The characteristics of each of the 10 problem instances are slightly different, but this trend is very clear.

QAOA Performs Better than Random Sampling: Both QA and QAOA sampled better solutions than the 10000 random samples. Although an obvious observation from the distributions in Figs. 6 and 5, it is not trivial that the QAOA samples had better objective function values compared to random sampling. The reason this is not trivial is because at sufficient circuit depth, which is not difficult to reach, the computation will entirely decohere and the computation will not be meaningful. This result is encouraging because it shows that short depth circuit constructions, combined with increasing scale of near term quantum computers, can begin to yield relevant computations for larger system sizes (in this case, 127 variables).

The Effect of Digital Dynamical Decoupling: The dataset shown in Fig. 6 also allows for a direct quantification of how successful the digital dynamical decoupling passes were at improving the QAOA circuit executions. Table 2 shows a comparison of the four QAOA implementations. For 2-round QAOA, DDD improved the mean sample energy for 10 out of the 10 Ising models. For 1-round QAOA, DDD improved the mean sample energy for 4 out of the 10 problem instances. This shows that digital dynamical decoupling does not uniformly

---

[5] https://github.com/dwavesystems/dwave-neal.

[6] https://github.com/dwavesystems/dimod.

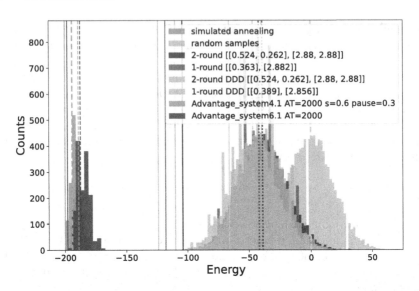

Fig. 5. Direct objective function (e.g. energy) histogram comparison of QA and QAOA results for one of the 10 minimization problem instances. A distribution of simulated annealing energies are also shown to provide a comparison against a reasonable classical heuristic. Here the energies being plotted are the full energy spectrum for the parameters which gave the minimum mean energy across the parameter grid searches performed across the QA and QAOA parameters. The optimal parameter combination for each distribution is given in the figure legend. For QA parameters, the annealing time in microseconds, the forward anneal schedule (symmetric) pause fraction, and anneal fraction, are given in the legend. If the default linearly interpolated quantum annealing schedule performed the best, only the annealing time reported in the legend. For the QAOA angle parameters, the format is $[\beta, \gamma]$, and are rounded to 3 decimal places. The mean for each dataset is marked with vertical dashed lines and the minimum energy found in each dataset is marked with solid vertical lines. The energy histogram plots for the other 9 Ising models are shown in Fig. 6.

improve the performance of the QAOA circuits. This suggests that the qubits in the 2-round QAOA circuits have more available idle time compared to the 1-round QAOA circuits, which would allow for DDD to improve the circuit performance. The 2-round QAOA results had better average energy compared the 1-round results in 6 out of the 10 problem instances.

Optimal Parameter Choices - QAOA: The optimal 2-round QAOA angles for all 10 problems with and without dynamical decoupling is the same. The optimal 1-round QAOA angles are not consistent across all problems, and even vary between the with and without DDD circuit executions. However, even though the exact optimal angle assignments are not consistent across all problems the, they are very close to each other which is notable because it indicates that the optimal angles may be identical or nearly identical but the search space is being obscured by the noise in the computation.

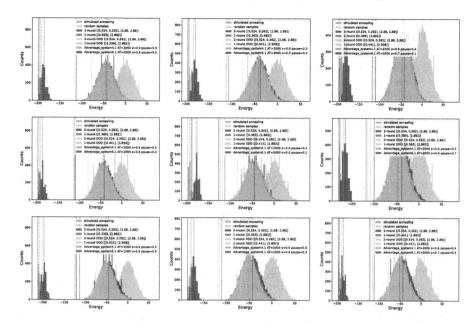

Fig. 6. Direct energy histogram comparison of QA and QAOA results for the other nine problem instances, continuing from Fig. 5. The mean of each energy distribution is marked with vertical dashed lines, and the minimum energy of each dataset is marked with vertical solid lines. Note that for several of the distributions there are overlapping minimum energies.

Optimal Parameter Choices - QA: Figure 6 also allows examination of how stable the different parameters are, both across the 10 Ising models but also within each problem instance. In the case of quantum annealing, but the optimal annealing times are always 2000 and the optimal pause schedule is not incredibly consistent with pause fraction durations ranging from 0.1 to 0.9 and with anneal fractions s ranging from 0.5 to 0.7.

D-Wave Devices Performance Differences: One last observation from Fig. 6 is that there a small but consistent performance difference between the two quantum annealers; the slightly older generation `Advantage_system4.1` yields lower mean energy than `Advantage_system6.1`. Simulated annealing is comparable to the quantum annealing distributions, with simulated annealing performing marginally better than the quantum annealing distributions.

4   Discussion

It is of considerable interest to determine how effective quantum annealing and QAOA are at computing the optimal solutions of combinatorial optimization problems. Combinatorial optimization problems have wide reaching applicability, and being able to solve them faster or to get better heuristic solutions is

Table 2. How the four different QAOA implementations, one and two rounds with and without DDD, compare against each other in terms of in how many of the 10 random instances each method was better than the other three methods in terms of mean objective function value across the 10000 samples (for the best angle combination). There is a clear finding in the order of performance of the four methods; $p = 2$ with no DDD performed the worse, $p = 1$ with no DDD performed the next best, $p = 1$ with DDD performed the next best, and $p = 2$ with digital dynamical decoupling performed the best overall.

	$p = 1$	$p = 2$	$p = 1$ with DDD	$p = 2$ with DDD
$p = 1$ (no DDD) better than –	–	10/10	5/10	4/10
$p = 2$ (no DDD) better than –	0/10	–	2/10	0/10
$p = 1$ (with DDD) better than –	5/10	8/10	-	4/10
$p = 2$ (with DDD) better than –	6/10	10/10	6/10	–

a very relevant topic in computing. In this article, we have presented experimental results for a fair direct comparison of QAOA and quantum annealing, implemented on the state-of-the-art currently accessible quantum hardware via cloud computing. We leave more detailed benchmarking against state of the art classical solvers on these Ising model instances to future work. This research has specifically found the following:

1. Quantum annealing finds higher quality solutions to the random test Ising models with higher order terms compared to the short depth QAOA $p = 1$ and $p = 2$ circuits, with reasonably fine grid searches over the QAOA angles and quantum annealing schedules with pauses.
2. QAOA performs noticeably better than random sampling - this is mostly due to the short depth QAOA circuit constructions which allow reasonably robust computations to be executed without the qubits decohering on current quantum computers.
3. The short depth QAOA circuit construction is notable because it allows for higher order terms in the Ising, and is scalable to a heavy-hexagonal lattice of any size, therefore this circuit construction can be used for future implementations of QAOA on devices with heavy-hexagonal lattices for heavy-hex native Ising models.
4. Dynamical decoupling can improve the computation of QAOA on NISQ computers.

Acknowledgments. This work was supported by the U.S. Department of Energy through the Los Alamos National Laboratory. Los Alamos National Laboratory is operated by Triad National Security, LLC, for the National Nuclear Security Administration of U.S. Department of Energy (Contract No. 89233218CNA000001). The research presented in this article was supported by the Laboratory Directed Research and Development program of Los Alamos National Laboratory under project number 20220656ER and the NNSA's Advanced Simulation and Computing Beyond Moore's Law Program at Los Alamos National Laboratory. This research used resources provided by the

Darwin testbed at Los Alamos National Laboratory (LANL) which is funded by the Computational Systems and Software Environments subprogram of LANL's Advanced Simulation and Computing program (NNSA/DOE). This research used resources provided by the Los Alamos National Laboratory Institutional Computing Program. We acknowledge the use of IBM Quantum services for this work. The views expressed are those of the authors, and do not reflect the official policy or position of IBM or the IBM Quantum team. The authors would like to thank the anonymous reviewers for their helpful comments which helped to improve the manuscript. LA-UR-22-33077.

References

1. Kadowaki, T., Nishimori, H.: Quantum annealing in the transverse ising model. Physical Review E, **58**(5), 5355–5363 (1998). https://doi.org/10.1103/physreve.58.5355

2. Morita, S., Nishimori, H.: Mathematical foundation of quantum annealing. J. Math. Phys. **49**(12), 125210 (2008). https://doi.org/10.1063/1.2995837

3. Das, A., Chakrabarti, B.K.: Colloquium: quantum annealing and analog quantum computation. Rev. Modern Phys. **80**(3), 1061 (2008). https://doi.org/10.1103/revmodphys.80.1061

4. Hauke, P., Katzgraber, H.G., Lechner, W., Nishimori, H., Oliver, W.D.: Perspectives of quantum annealing: methods and implementations. R. Progress Phys. **83**(5), 054401 (2020). https://doi.org/10.1088/1361-6633/ab85b8

5. Yarkoni, S., Raponi, E., Bäck, T., Schmitt, S.: Quantum annealing for industry applications: introduction and review. Rep. Progress Phys. **85**(10), 104001 (2022). https://doi.org/10.1088/1361-6633/ac8c54

6. Lanting, T., et al.: Entanglement in a quantum annealing processor. Phys. Rev. X, 4, 021041 (2014). https://doi.org/10.1103/PhysRevX.4.021041

7. King, A.D., et al.: Coherent quantum annealing in a programmable 2000-qubit ising chain (2022). arXiv preprint arXiv:2202.05847, https://doi.org/10.1038/s41567-022-01741-6

8. Hadfield, S., Wang, Z., O'Gorman, B., Rieffel, E., Venturelli, D., Biswas, R.: From the quantum approximate optimization algorithm to a quantum alternating operator ansatz. Algorithms, **12**(2), 34 (2019). https://doi.org/10.3390/a12020034

9. Cook, J., Eidenbenz, S., Bärtschi, A.: The quantum alternating operator ansatz on maximum k-vertex cover. In: 2020 IEEE International Conference on Quantum Computing and Engineering (QCE), pp. 83–92 (2020). https://doi.org/10.1109/QCE49297.2020.00021

10. Wang, Z., Rubin, N.C., Dominy, J.M., Rieffel, E.G.: Xy mixers: analytical and numerical results for the quantum alternating operator ansatz. Phys. Rev. A **101**(1) (2020). https://doi.org/10.1103/physreva.101.012320

11. Farhi, E., Goldstone, J., Gutmann, S.: A quantum approximate optimization algorithm (2014). https://arxiv.org/abs/1411.4028

12. Phillip, C., et al.: Scaling quantum approximate optimization on near-term hardware. Sci. Rep. **12**(1) (2022). https://doi.org/10.1038/s41598-022-14767-w

13. Albash, T., Lidar, D.A.: Demonstration of a scaling advantage for a quantum annealer over simulated annealing. Phys. Rev. X, **8**, 031016 (2018). https://link.aps.org/doi/10.1103/PhysRevX.8.031016, https://doi.org/10.1103/PhysRevX.8.031016

14. King, A.D., et al.: Scaling advantage over path-integral monte carlo in quantum simulation of geometrically frustrated magnets. Nature Commun. **12**(1), 1–6 (2021). https://doi.org/10.1038/s41467-021-20901-5

15. Farhi, E., Harrow, A.W.: Quantum supremacy through the quantum approximate optimization algorithm (2016). https://arxiv.org/abs/1602.07674

16. Mandrà, S., Zhu, Z., Wang, W., Perdomo-Ortiz, A., Katzgraber, H.G.: Strengths and weaknesses of weak-strong cluster problems: a detailed overview of state-of-the-art classical heuristics versus quantum approaches. Phys. Rev. A **94**(2) (2016). https://doi.org/10.1103/physreva.94.022337

17. Boixo, S., et al.: Evidence for quantum annealing with more than one hundred qubits. Nature Phys. **10**(3), 218–224 (2014). https://doi.org/10.1038/nphys2900

18. Tasseff, B., et al.: On the emerging potential of quantum annealing hardware for combinatorial optimization (2022). https://arxiv.org/abs/2210.04291

19. Lubinski, T., Coffrin, C., McGeoch, C., Sathe, P., Apanavicius, J., Neira, D.E.B.: Optimization applications as quantum performance benchmarks (2023). https://arxiv.org/abs/2302.02278

20. Pelofske, E., Golden, J., Bartschi, A., O'Malley, D., Eidenbenz, S.: Sampling on NISQ devices: "Who's the Fairest One of All?". In: 2021 IEEE International Conference on Quantum Computing and Engineering (QCE). IEEE (2021). https://doi.org/10.1109/qce52317.2021.00038

21. Ushijima-Mwesigwa, H., Shaydulin, R., Negre, C.F.A., Mniszewski, S.M., Alexeev, Y., Safro, I.: Multilevel combinatorial optimization across quantum architectures. ACM Trans. Quant. Comput. **2**(1) (2021). ISSN 2643–6809. https://doi.org/10.1145/3425607

22. Streif, M., Leib, M.: Comparison of QAOA with quantum and simulated annealing (2019). https://arxiv.org/abs/1901.01903

23. Pelofske, E., Bärtschi, A., Eidenbenz, S.: Quantum annealing vs. QAOA: 127 qubit higher-order ising problems on nisq computers (2023). https://arxiv.org/abs/2301.00520

24. Pagano, G., et al.: Quantum approximate optimization of the long-range ising model with a trappedion quantum simulator. In: Proceedings of the National Academy of Sciences, vol. 117, no. 41, pp. 25396–25401 (2020). https://doi.org/10.1073/pnas.2006373117

25. Weidenfeller, J., et al.: Scaling of the quantum approximate optimization algorithm on superconducting qubit based hardware. Quantum **6**, 870 (2022). ISSN 2521–327X. https://doi.org/10.22331/q-2022-12-07-870

26. Matthew, P., et al.: Quantum approximate optimization of non-planar graph problems on a planar superconducting processor. Nature Phys. **17**(3), 332–336 (2021). https://doi.org/10.1038/s41567-020-01105-y

27. Niroula, P., et al.: Constrained quantum optimization for extractive summarization on a trapped-ion quantum computer. Sci. Rep. **12**(1), 1–14 (2022). https://doi.org/10.1038/s41598-022-20853-w

28. Herman, D., et al.: Portfolio optimization via quantum zeno dynamics on a quantum processor (2022). https://arxiv.org/abs/2209.15024

29. Caswell, T.A., et al.: matplotlib/matplotlib

30. Hunter, J.D.: Matplotlib: a 2D graphics environment. Comput. Sci. Eng. **9**(3), 90–95 (2007). https://doi.org/10.1109/MCSE.2007.55

31. Treinish, M., et al.: Qiskit/qiskit: Qiskit 0.34.1 (2022)

32. Chamberland, C., Zhu, G., Yoder, T.J., Hertzberg, J.B., Cross, A.W.: Topological and subsystem codes on low-degree graphs with flag qubits. Phys. Rev. X, **10**, 011022 (2020). https://link.aps.org/doi/10.1103/PhysRevX.10.011022, https://doi.org/10.1103/PhysRevX.10.011022

33. Zbinden, S., Bärtschi, A., Djidjev, H., Eidenbenz, S.: Embedding algorithms for quantum annealers with chimera and pegasus connection topologies. In: Sadayappan, P., Chamberlain, B.L., Juckeland, G., Ltaief, H. (eds.) ISC High Performance 2020. LNCS, vol. 12151, pp. 187–206. Springer, Cham (2020). https://doi.org/10.1007/978-3-030-50743-5_10

34. Dattani, N., Szalay, S., Chancellor, N.: Pegasus: the second connectivity graph for large-scale quantum annealing hardware (2019). https://arxiv.org/abs/1901.07636

35. Tseng, C.H., et al.: Quantum simulation of a three-body-interaction hamiltonian on an NMR quantum computer. Phys. Rev. A, **61**, 012302 (1999). https://link.aps.org/doi/10.1103/PhysRevA.61.012302, https://doi.org/10.1103/PhysRevA.61.012302

36. Chancellor, N., Zohren, S., Warburton, P.A.: Circuit design for multi-body interactions in superconducting quantum annealing systems with applications to a scalable architecture. NPJ Quant. Inf. **3**(1), 1–7 (2017). https://doi.org/10.1038/s41534-017-0022-6

37. Campbell, C., Dahl, E.: QAOA of the highest order. In: 2022 IEEE 19th International Conference on Software Architecture Companion (ICSA-C), pp. 141–146 (2022). https://doi.org/10.1109/ICSAC54293.2022.00035

38. Valiante, E., Hernandez, M., Barzegar, A., Katzgraber, H.G.: Computational overhead of locality reduction in binary optimization problems. Comput. Phys. Commun. **269**, 108102, 2021. ISSN 0010-4655. https://doi.org/10.1016/j.cpc.2021.108102. https://www.sciencedirect.com/science/article/pii/S0010465521002149

39. Ishikawa, H.: Transformation of general binary MRF minimization to the first-order case. IEEE Trans. Pattern Anal. Mach. Intell. **33**(6), 1234–1249 (2011). https://doi.org/10.1109/TPAMI.2010.91

40. Pelofske, E., Hahn, G., O'Malley, D., Djidjev, H.N., Alexandrov, B.S.: Quantum annealing algorithms for boolean tensor networks. Sci. Rep. **12**(1) (2022). https://doi.org/10.1038/s41598-022-12611-9

41. Jiang, S., Britt, K.A., McCaskey, A.J., Humble, T.S., Kais, S.: Quantum annealing for prime factorization. Sci. Rep. **8**(1), 1–9 (2018). https://doi.org/10.1038/s41598-018-36058-z

42. Golden, J., Bärtschi, A., Eidenbenz, S., O'Malley, D.: Evidence for super-polynomial advantage of QAOA over unstructured search (2022). https://arxiv.org/abs/2202.00648

43. Cerezo, M., et al.: Variational quantum algorithms. Nature Rev. Phys. **3**(9), 625–644 (2021). https://doi.org/10.1038/s42254-021-00348-9

44. Wang, S.: Noise-induced barren plateaus in variational quantum algorithms. Nature Commun. **12**(1), 1–11 (2021). https://doi.org/10.1038/s41467-021-27045-6

45. Zhu, Y.: Multi-round QAOA and advanced mixers on a trapped-ion quantum computer. Quantum Sci. Technol. **8**(1), 015007 (2022). https://doi.org/10.1088/2058-9565/ac91ef

46. Niu, S., Todri-Sanial, A.: Effects of dynamical decoupling and pulse-level optimizations on IBM quantum computers. IEEE Trans. Quan. Eng. **3**, 1–10 (2022). https://doi.org/10.1109/tqe.2022.3203153

47. Suter, D., Álvarez, G.A.: Colloquium: protecting quantum information against environmental noise. Rev. Mod. Phys., **88**, 041001 (2016). https://link.aps.org/doi/10.1103/RevModPhys.88.041001

48. Viola, L., Knill, E., Lloyd, S.: Dynamical decoupling of open quantum systems. Phys. Rev. Lett., **82**, 2417–2421 (1999). https://link.aps.org/doi/10.1103/PhysRevLett.82.2417,https://doi.org/10.1103/PhysRevLett.82.2417

49. Ahmed, M.A.A., Álvarez, G.A., Suter, D.: Robustness of dynamical decoupling sequences. Phys. Rev. A **87**(4) (2013). https://doi.org/10.1103/physreva.87.042309

50. LaRose, R.: A software package for error mitigation on noisy quantum computers. Quantum **6**, 774 (2022). https://doi.org/10.22331/q-2022-08-11-774

51. Kim, Y.: Scalable error mitigation for noisy quantum circuits produces competitive expectation values. Nature Phys. (2023). https://doi.org/10.1038/s41567-022-01914-3

52. Ezzell, N., Pokharel, B., Tewala, L., Quiroz, G., Lidar, D.A.: Dynamical decoupling for superconducting qubits: a performance survey (2022). https://arxiv.org/abs/2207.03670

53. Pokharel, B., Anand, N., Fortman, B., Lidar, D.A.: Demonstration of fidelity improvement using dynamical decoupling with superconducting qubits. Phys. Rev. Lett., **121**, 220502 (2018). https://link.aps.org/doi/10.1103/PhysRevLett.121.220502

54. Cross, A.W., Bishop, L.S., Smolin, J.A., Gambetta, J.M.: Open quantum assembly language (2017). https://arxiv.org/abs/1707.03429

55. Pelofske, E., Hahn, G., Djidjev, H.N.: Parallel quantum annealing. Sci. Rep. **12**(1) (2022). https://doi.org/10.1038/s41598-022-08394-8

56. Marshall, J., Venturelli, D., Hen, I., Rieffel, E.G.: Power of pausing: advancing understanding of thermalization in experimental quantum annealers. Phys. Rev. Appl. **11**, 044083 (2019).https://doi.org/10.1103/PhysRevApplied.11.044083, https://link.aps.org/doi/10.1103/PhysRevApplied.11.044083

57. Kirkpatrick, S., Gelatt, C.D., Jr., Vecchi, M.P.: Optimization by simulated annealing. Science **220**(4598), 671–680 (1983). https://doi.org/10.1126/science.220.4598.671

Quantum Circuit Simulation by SGEMM Emulation on Tensor Cores and Automatic Precision Selection

Hiryuki Ootomo[1][(✉)] ⓘ, Hidetaka Manabe[2] ⓘ, Kenji Harada[2] ⓘ, and Rio Yokota[1] ⓘ

[1] Tokyo Institute of Technology, Tokyo, Japan
ootomo.h@rio.gsic.titech.ac.jp, rioyokota@gsic.titech.ac.jp
[2] Kyoto University, Kyoto, Japan
manabe@acs.i.kyoto-u.ac.jp, harada.kenji.8e@kyoto-u.ac.jp

Abstract. Quantum circuit simulation provides the foundation for the development of quantum algorithms and the verification of quantum supremacy. Among the various methods for quantum circuit simulation, tensor network contraction has been increasing in popularity due to its ability to simulate a larger number of qubits. During tensor contraction, the input tensors are reshaped to matrices and computed by a GEMM operation, where these GEMM operations could reach up to 90% of the total calculation time. GEMM throughput can be improved by utilizing mixed-precision hardware such as Tensor Cores, but straightforward implementation results in insufficient fidelity for deep and large quantum circuits. Prior work has demonstrated that compensated summation with special care of the rounding mode can fully recover the FP32 precision of SGEMM even when using TF32 or FP16 Tensor Cores. The exponent range is a critical issue when applying such techniques to quantum circuit simulation. While TF32 supports almost the same exponent range as FP32, FP16 supports a much smaller exponent range. In this work, we use the exponent range statistics of input tensor elements to select which Tensor Cores we use for the GEMM. We evaluate our method on Random Circuit Sampling (RCS), including Sycamore's quantum circuit, and show that the throughput is 1.86 times higher at maximum while maintaining accuracy.

Keywords: Quantum circuit simulation · Tensor Cores · Mixed precision

1 Introduction

Quantum circuit simulators are vital for the development of quantum algorithms and verification of *quantum supremacy*, and are considered as one of the key applications for HPC systems in the Exa-scale era [13,17,30]. In a quantum computer, all operations follow quantum mechanics: preparing qubits (a quantum version of classical bits), applying unitary gates, and measuring qubits to

A. Bhatele et al. (Eds.): ISC High Performance 2023, LNCS 13948, pp. 259–276, 2023.
https://doi.org/10.1007/978-3-031-32041-5_14

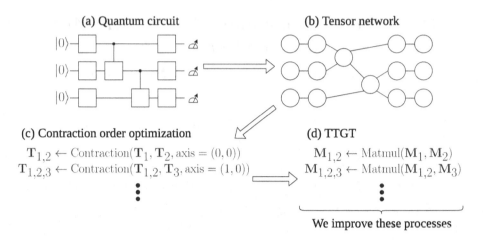

Fig. 1. An image of quantum circuit simulation using tensor network simulation and the part of the computation that we improve.

get classical data. The goal of quantum circuit simulation is to reproduce the classical result obtained by these quantum operations only with a classical computer.

There exist various types of quantum simulators [8,11,28,29]. For general circuits dominated by non-Clifford gates, the two types of simulators: 1) state vector and 2) tensor network methods are widely used. We choose these simulation methods according to the objectives. The state vector simulations require 2^n complex values on memory, where n is the number of qubits. For instance, to simulate Google's Sycamore [1], which has 53 qubits, we would require 128 PB of memory. Since the total memory capacity of the current largest supercomputers is in the order of a few PB, state vector methods are limited by memory capacity. One advantage of state vector methods is that the computational complexity for a circuit of depth d is $\mathcal{O}(2^n \times d)$ and scales linearly with d. Furthermore, there are some studies to reduce the required memory size, such as by splitting the circuit [3]. On the other hand, the tensor contraction method [16] can simulate several thousands of qubits with low-depth layers at a slightly higher computational cost. Therefore, tensor contraction is the method of choice for many recent studies that aim to validate quantum supremacy in both quantum computing and high performance computing [15,22,30]. In tensor contraction methods, the quantum circuit is represented as a tensor network, where each node represents a quantum gate, and the edge represents the quantum wire, as shown in Fig. 1. The appearance probability of an output bitstring is calculated through the contraction of the tensor network. Since the computational complexity of the contraction heavily depends on its order of computation, many studies focus on finding the near-optimal contraction order [7,9,12,22].

The simplest way to compute a tensor contraction is to form nested loops for each tensor index. In practice, the TTGT (Transpose-Transpose-GEMM-

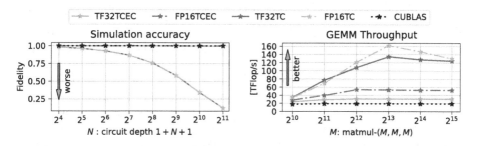

Fig. 2. Left: The comparison of simulation accuracy of a 4×4 rectangular lattice Random Quantum Circuit simulation for each GEMM precision. TF32TCEC, FP16TCEC, and CUBLAS have single-precision mantissa accuracy, and TF32TC and FP16TC have half-precision. The circuit consists of a Hadamard gate layer $(1+)$, N-CZ gate layers, and a Hadamard gate layer $(+1)$. **Right:** The throughput comparison of each CGEMM implementation.

Transpose) algorithm is widely used since it can leverage the existing high performance GEMM implementations on various processors such as Intel MKL and NVIDIA cuBLAS. In this algorithm, the input tensors are first reshaped into matrices, where rows or columns separate the contracted and non-contracted indices. Then, it computes the matrix multiplication of the input matrices and transposes them to fit into the output tensor if necessary. Although this approach requires additional memory to store the transposed tensors, it can leverage the high performance GEMM implementation, which can effectively utilize the hierarchical cache and memory of the target processor.

The chain of GEMM operations in tensor contraction can be accelerated by improving both the algorithm and implementation. In terms of algorithmic improvement, Huang et al. [10] applied Strassen's algorithm to tensor contraction and slightly reduced its computational complexity. With respect to implementation, leveraging the existing high performance GEMM implementations on Tensor Cores would seem like a natural fit, but quantum circuit simulations require at least single precision accuracy, as we will show later. Tensor Cores are mixed-precision matrix multiply-add units on NVIDIA GPUs, and have $7.5 \sim 15\times$ throughput compared to the standard arithmetic units on NVIDIA A100 GPUs. Although the data type of input matrices for multiplication are low-precision (FP16 or TF32), the computation inside Tensor Cores is performed in higher-precision (FP32). However, when we compute an SGEMM on Tensor Cores, we need to convert the input matrices to low precision, which causes accuracy degradation. Markidis et al. propose a method to recover the accuracy through compensated summation, but their method cannot fully recover the FP32 accuracy [14]. Our previous study identified the cause of this problem as the rounding mode inside the Tensor Cores, and developed a method that circumvents this issue with minimal performance degradation [19]. As a result, our method outperforms the theoretical peak performance of FP32 SIMT Cores on NVIDIA A100 GPUs while the FP32 accuracy is fully recovered. This method can be applied to TF32 Tensor Core error correction (TF32TCEC) and FP16 Tensor Core error correction (FP16TCEC). The TF32 version supports almost the same exponent range as FP32, while the FP16 version supports only a limited exponent range but has higher throughput. Therefore, there is a trade-off between the supported exponent range and throughput. In the case of quantum circuit simulation using tensor network contraction, it is difficult to compute the simulation in high precision on Tensor Cores without the error correction when the number of computations is large, as shown in Fig. 2. Therefore, error correction is necessary when using Tensor Cores for the simulation. However, it is difficult to determine which tensor contraction requires TF32TCEC or if FP16TCEC is sufficient. To the extent of the authors' knowledge, there is no framework for automatically selecting between these two operations. Although Liu *et al.* use a dynamic scaling method for FP16 computation in the simulation, they select the parts to be computed with FP16 heuristically [13] by performing an analysis of the tensor network contraction a priori. Furthermore, their method causes overflow in some cases, which causes the entire computation to fail.

In the present work, we drastically improve the throughput of quantum circuit simulation while retaining sufficient accuracy by using the SGEMM emulation on Tensor Cores and automatic precision selection. To select between TF32TCEC and FP16TCEC for each tensor contraction, we use the exponent statistics of elements in the input matrices measured before the GEMM operation.

The summary of our contributions is as follows:

1. We develop a library for SGEMM emulation on Tensor Cores, cuMpSGEMM, that can be used without any change to the source code of the target applications. This library intercepts SGEMM function calls of the cuBLAS dynamic library and executes the SGEMM emulation on Tensor Cores instead, and surpasses the performance of SGEMM while fully retaining the accuracy. This library is not limited to quantum circuit simulation and can be used for any other application that calls cuBLAS SGEMM, CGEMM, and their batched variants and is open-source and available on GitHub[1].
2. We develop a method to select the GEMM precision, TF32TCEC, FP16TCEC, or FP16TCEC with scaling, for improving the throughput by taking the exponent statistics of input matrix elements before the GEMM operation. We have tested our method on a random tensor network contraction and confirmed that it successfully avoids the underflow error with a slight overhead.
3. We evaluate the accuracy and throughput of Random Circuit Sampling (RCS) simulation, including Sycamore's quantum circuit. In RCS, our method improves the throughput by 1.86 times for a quantum circuit of 9×9, depth $= 33$, and 1.44 times for the Sycamore circuit while retaining the accuracy of the baseline implementation.

---

[1] https://github.com/enp1s0/cuMpSGEMM.

2 Background

2.1 NVIDIA Tensor Core and SGEMM Emulation

NVIDIA Tensor Core computes a matrix multiplication and addition,

$$\mathbf{D}_{\mathrm{F32}} \leftarrow \mathbf{A}_{\mathrm{low}} \cdot \mathbf{B}_{\mathrm{low}} + \mathbf{C}_{\mathrm{F32}}, \tag{1}$$

where the subscript denotes the data type of the matrix: the "low" is low-precision, FP16 or TF32, and "F32" is FP32. Although $\mathbf{A}_{\mathrm{low}}$ and $\mathbf{B}_{\mathrm{low}}$ are low-precision, the multiplications and additions are computed in FP32. However, when it comes to computing single-precision matrix multiplication on Tensor Cores, we must convert the input matrices from single-precision to low-precision, which causes a loss of accuracy in the final computation result. To recover the loss of accuracy, Markidis *et al.* propose an error correction method based on compensated summation [14], but their method does not recover the full FP32 accuracy. Our previous study improves upon this method by avoiding the rounding inside Tensor Cores and can recover the full FP32 accuracy with minimum overhead [19]. In this method, a single-precision matrix-multiplication $\mathbf{C}_{\mathrm{F32}} \leftarrow \mathbf{A}_{\mathrm{F32}} \cdot \mathbf{B}_{\mathrm{F32}}$ is computed approximately as follows.

$$
\begin{aligned}
\mathbf{A}_{\mathrm{low}} &\leftarrow \mathrm{toLow}\left(\mathbf{A}_{\mathrm{F32}}\right) \\
\Delta\mathbf{A}_{\mathrm{low}} &\leftarrow \mathrm{toLow}\left(\left(\mathbf{A}_{\mathrm{F32}} - \mathrm{toF32}\left(\mathbf{A}_{\mathrm{low}}\right)\right) \times 2^{11}\right) \\
\mathbf{B}_{\mathrm{low}} &\leftarrow \mathrm{toLow}\left(\mathbf{B}_{\mathrm{F32}}\right) \\
\Delta\mathbf{B}_{\mathrm{low}} &\leftarrow \mathrm{toLow}\left(\left(\mathbf{B}_{\mathrm{F32}} - \mathrm{toF32}\left(\mathbf{B}_{\mathrm{low}}\right)\right) \times 2^{11}\right) \\
\mathbf{C}_{\mathrm{F32}} &\approx \mathbf{A}_{\mathrm{low}} \cdot \mathbf{B}_{\mathrm{low}} + \left(\Delta\mathbf{A}_{\mathrm{low}} \cdot \mathbf{B}_{\mathrm{low}} + \mathbf{A}_{\mathrm{low}} \cdot \Delta\mathbf{B}_{\mathrm{low}}\right)/2^{11},
\end{aligned}
\tag{2}
$$

where "toLow" is the conversion from FP32 to low-precision and "toF32" is from low-precision to FP32. In this scheme, each matrix element in $\mathbf{A}_{\mathrm{F32}}$ and $\mathbf{B}_{\mathrm{F32}}$ is split into two low-precision elements in $\mathbf{A}_{\mathrm{low}}, \mathbf{B}_{\mathrm{low}}$ and $\Delta\mathbf{A}_{\mathrm{low}}, \Delta\mathbf{B}_{\mathrm{low}}$, respectively. Then the single-precision matrix multiplication is computed approximately in Eq. (2) using Tensor Cores, where the multiplication and addition are performed on specialized arithmetic units in a precision that is equivalent to FP32. Furthermore, this method uses FP32 SIMT Cores for addition with RN (Round to Nearest, ties to even) mode for $\mathbf{A}_{\mathrm{low}} \cdot \mathbf{B}_{\mathrm{low}}$ to avoid the RZ (Round toward Zero) rounding inside Tensor Cores. We show the matrix-matrix multiplication implementations and their supporting input accuracy in Table 1. When we use TF32 for the input type of Tensor Cores, we can emulate the single-precision matrix multiplication in both the mantissa and exponent (TF32TCEC). On the other hand, when we use FP16 for the low-precision, the supported exponent range of the input matrices is limited (FP16TCEC). However, the theoretical peak performance of FP16TCEC is higher than TF32TCEC, as shown in the table. Therefore, there is a trade-off between the supported exponent range and the throughput. We can achieve a higher throughput using FP16TCEC without loss of accuracy if the elements of the input matrices are in the supported

Table 1. The comparison of GEMM implementations using Tensor Cores on NVIDIA A100 GPU. Each throughput represents theoretical peak performance and is calculated by an assumption that the Tensor Core instruction is issued every clock.

		Input type of Tensor Core	
		TF32	FP16
Error correction	Yes	**TF32TCEC** Exponent:FP32, Mantissa:FP32 [52 TFlop/s]	**FP16TCEC** Exponent:FP16, Mantissa:FP32 [104 TFlop/s]
	No	**TF32TC** Exponent:FP32, Mantissa:FP16 [156 TFlop/s]	**FP16TC** Exponent:FP16, Mantissa:FP16 [312 TFlop/s]

representation range. Furthermore, we can use these SGEMM emulation methods for a single-precision tensor contraction. In the TTGT algorithm, the input tensors are reshaped to matrices, and the contraction is computed as matrix multiplication. Thus, improving the throughput of GEMM leads to improving the throughput of tensor contraction.

2.2   Quantum Circuit Simulation and Tensor Network Contraction

A quantum circuit consists of quantum gates and wires, as shown in Fig. 1 (a), similar to a classical logic circuit. A quantum state of n qubits is represented as a normalized complex vector of length 2^n. For instance, a typical 1-qubit state called *computational basis states* is represented as $|0\rangle := (1, 0)^\mathsf{T}$ and $|1\rangle := (0, 1)^\mathsf{T}$. The quantum gate for k qubits is represented as a $2^k \times 2^k$ unitary matrix. For instance, the Hadamard gate, which is one of the single-qubit gates, is represented as $\mathbf{H} = \begin{bmatrix} 1 & 1 \\ 1 & -1 \end{bmatrix} / \sqrt{2}$, and T gate is $\mathbf{T} = \begin{bmatrix} 1 & 0 \\ 0 & \exp(i\pi/4) \end{bmatrix}$, where i is the imaginary unit. The change of the quantum states by applying a quantum gate is represented as a multiplication of the quantum gate matrix and the state vector of the quantum states. For instance, applying the Hadamard gate to the quantum state $|0\rangle$, we obtain the new state as follows:

$$|\psi\rangle = \mathbf{H} |0\rangle = \frac{1}{\sqrt{2}} \begin{pmatrix} 1 \\ 1 \end{pmatrix}.$$

The quantum state is a superposition state, from which we can not extract information directly. Instead, we conduct *measurements* to get the information of the quantum state indirectly. In the case of an n-qubits system, a quantum state $|\phi\rangle$ is a superposition of 2^n states, $|00\cdots00\rangle, |00\cdots01\rangle, \cdots, |11\cdots11\rangle$ in the computational basis, and represented as follows:

$$|\phi\rangle = \sum_{j=00\cdots00}^{11\cdots11} \alpha_j |j\rangle,$$

where α_j is called the *amplitude* of the state $|j\rangle$ and $\sum_{j=00\cdots00}^{11\cdots11} |\alpha_j|^2 = 1$. When measuring the state $|\phi\rangle$, we obtain an n-length bitstring j with a probability $|\alpha_j|^2$. We conduct the measurements many times and obtain the distribution of the output bitstrings to extract the information of the quantum state. In contrast, the quantum circuit simulation directly calculates the amplitude of given bitstrings. However, calculating the amplitude of a large qubit system and circuit generally requires large computational costs and memory.

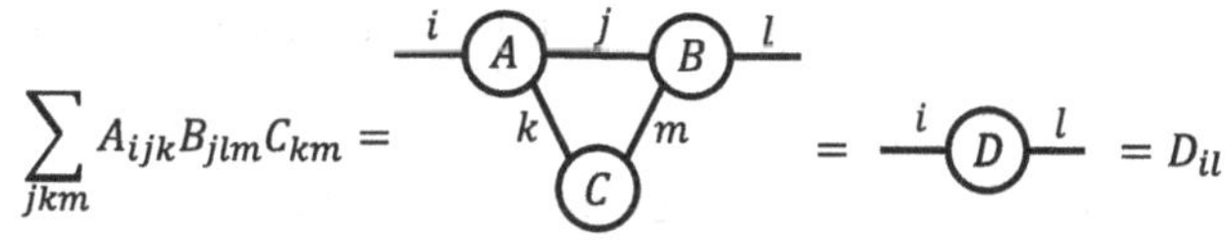

$$\sum_{jkm} A_{ijk}B_{jlm}C_{km} = \quad \text{[diagram]} \quad = \quad \text{[diagram]} \quad = D_{il}$$

Fig. 3. An example of the tensor network diagram.

One of the methods to compute the amplitude is tensor network contraction. A simple example of tensor network formalism is shown in Fig. 3. A rank-r tensor, which is an element of $\mathbb{C}^{d_1 \times \cdots \times d_r}$ with indices of dimension d_i, is represented as a node with r edges. The connection of the edges in a network corresponds to Einstein's summation over the corresponding index. A quantum circuit can be represented as a tensor network. The initial state $|00\cdots00\rangle$ and the measuring state $|x\rangle$ are a set of rank-1 tensors, n-qubits gates are rank-$2n$ tensors, and the wires represent contraction. The amplitude is calculated by the contraction of the whole tensor network. Therefore, the primary workload of the quantum circuit simulation by the tensor network contraction is GEMM.

The time complexity of a tensor network contraction strongly depends on its contraction order or *contraction path*. In the example in Fig. 3, calculating in order

$$\sum_{jkm=1}^{d} A_{ijk}B_{jlm}C_{km} = \sum_{km} C_{km} \left(\sum_{j} A_{ijk}B_{jlm} \right)$$

requires computational complexity $\mathcal{O}(d^5)$. On the other hand,

$$\sum_{jkm=1}^{d} A_{ijk}B_{jlm}C_{km} = \sum_{j} \left(\sum_{km} A_{ijk}B_{jlm}C_{km} \right)$$

requires only $\mathcal{O}(d^4)$. In general, finding the optimal contraction path is NP-complete [4] and even contracting the entire tensor network is #P-complete [27]. Therefore, there is no evidence that quantum circuit simulators by the tensor network contraction method perform well. However, in practice, by using advanced techniques such as hyperparameter optimization and hypergraph partitioning to find a near-optimal contraction order and by massively distributing the computation, the tensor network methods outperform the state vector

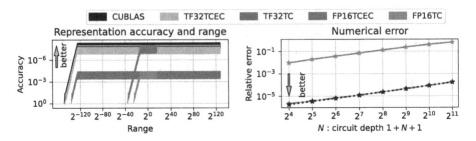

Fig. 4. The evaluation of numerical error of 4×4 Random Quantum Circuit simulation.

method, especially for systems with large qubits and shallow circuits [7,9,13,21]. For instance, [13] performed the Sycamore simulation in only 304 s by carefully selecting the contraction path and parallelizing on tens of millions of CPU cores.

The computation of tensor network contraction for quantum circuit simulation is performed in single precision. For the computation of an n-qubit circuit simulation, it is required to be able to represent $2^{-(n-1)/2}$ by a floating point value at least to represent the resulting amplitude. Therefore, FP16, which only has 5 bits of the exponent, is insufficient. From the perspective of mantissa accuracy, we also need single precision. We show the numerical accuracy of a quantum circuit simulation in Fig. 4, where the qubits are arranged in a 4×4 rectangular lattice, and the quantum circuit is RQC explained later in Sect. 5.3. Since the number of qubits 4×4 is small enough for using FP16 in terms of the exponent range, we can ignore the underflow error and evaluate only the effect of mantissa accuracy. As we can see in the graph, the numerical errors of TF32TC and FP16TC are larger than the others. This results in worse simulation accuracy (fidelity) in Fig. 2, even for relatively shallow circuits. Therefore, using low-mantissa-length arithmetics without error correction is unsuitable for quantum circuit simulation.

3   SGEMM Emulation Library on Tensor Cores

We have implemented an SGEMM emulation library, cuMpSGEMM, that can be used in existing applications that call the NVIDIA cuBLAS SGEMM without modifying the source code of the applications. The implementation is made from scratch using NVIDIA WMMA API (Tensor Core device API), and WMMA API extension library [20]. This library supports single-precision real and complex GEMM (SGEMM/CGEMM) and their batched variants. We extend the SGEMM emulation to CGEMM by decomposing the real part and imaginary part of the input matrices and computing it as 4 SGEMMs as follows:

$$
\begin{aligned}
\mathbf{C}_{\mathrm{F32}}^{\mathrm{complex}} \leftarrow & \mathbf{A}_{\mathrm{F32}}^{\mathrm{complex}} \cdot \mathbf{B}_{\mathrm{F32}}^{\mathrm{complex}} \\
= & \left(\mathbf{A}_{\mathrm{F32}}^{\mathrm{real}} \cdot \mathbf{B}_{\mathrm{F32}}^{\mathrm{real}} - \mathbf{A}_{\mathrm{F32}}^{\mathrm{imag}} \cdot \mathbf{B}_{\mathrm{F32}}^{\mathrm{imag}} \right) + \left(\mathbf{A}_{\mathrm{F32}}^{\mathrm{real}} \cdot \mathbf{B}_{\mathrm{F32}}^{\mathrm{imag}} + \mathbf{A}_{\mathrm{F32}}^{\mathrm{real}} \cdot \mathbf{B}_{\mathrm{F32}}^{\mathrm{imag}} \right) i.
\end{aligned}
$$

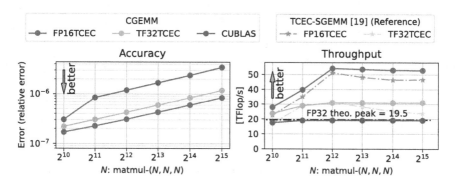

Fig. 5. The accuracy and throughput of the CGEMM implementation on Tensor Cores using the error correction method.

This library intercepts the function calls to cuBLAS SGEMM functions and executes the SGEMM emulation functions instead of the original functions. Therefore, we can use the SGEMM emulation without changing the source code of the target application if the application uses the cuBLAS dynamic library. All we need to do is to build the library, set an environmental variable LD_PRELOAD, and execute the target application as usual. We have confirmed that this library can intercept cuBLAS calls in PyTorch [23], CuPy [18], and our custom applications just by following these steps. The different implementations shown in Table 1 can be selected by defining an environment variable.

We perform a unit test for our CGEMM implementation as shown in Fig. 5. We denote the shape of GEMM as (m, n, k), which is the multiplication of $m \times k$ and $k \times n$ matrices. To measure the accuracy, we calculate a relative error of a single-precision complex matrix-matrix multiplication $\mathbf{C}_{F32} \leftarrow \mathbf{A}_{F32} \cdot \mathbf{B}_{F32}$ as follows:

$$\text{Relative Error} = ||\mathbf{C}_{F32} - \mathbf{C}_{F64}||_F / ||\mathbf{C}_{F64}||_F, \qquad (3)$$

where $\mathbf{C}_{F64}$ is the result in FP64, and each element of $\mathbf{A}_{F32}$ and $\mathbf{B}_{F32}$ is chosen from a uniform distribution $(-1, 1)$. Since the values are in the order of $10^{-7} - -10^{-6}$ for each matrix size, FP32 is sufficient, but FP16 is not. To evaluate the throughput, we measure the computing time and calculate the throughput. The maximum throughput of FP16TCEC and TF32TCEC are 54.2 [TFlop/s] and 31.0 [TFlop/s], respectively. This performance is almost identical to the implementation using NVIDIA CUTLASS [19].

4 Automatic Precision Selection

Although FP16TCEC supports a limited exponent range compared to TF32TCEC, it is faster than TF32TCEC. Therefore, we can improve SGEMM throughput by selecting FP16TCEC when its accuracy loss is permissible. However, it is generally impossible to predetermine whether FP16TCEC is tolerable before the actual computation. To check the tolerance, we take the statistics of

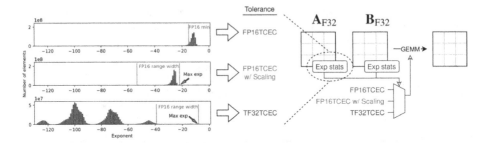

Fig. 6. The overview of the automatic kernel selection by the exponent statistics of the input matrices.

the exponent distribution of the input matrices before the GEMM operation, as shown in Fig. 6, and select the GEMM computing mode dynamically. In addition to FP16TCEC and TF32TCEC, we can select **FP16TCEC w/ scaling** mode. This mode can be used when the required exponent range is sufficient for FP16, even when the values themselves are small enough to underflow in FP16. This requires an additional overhead for scaling all elements in the input and output matrices.

The challenge in implementing the automatic precision selection method is to get the statistics correct while keeping its computational overhead negligibly small relative to the GEMM computing time. To achieve this, we adopt two strategies as follows:

- We check all elements in the matrix to take the statistics. Although we can reduce the overhead by sampling only part of the elements, this can lead to overflow in some cases. We check all elements to prevent overflow and compute the tensor contraction correctly.
- We do not transfer the statistics data from GPU to CPU to minimize the overhead. Although we need the exponent statistics to control which GEMM kernel we use, it results in an additional overhead for synchronizing CUDA kernels and sending the statistics data on the device memory to host memory. To reduce the overhead, we preemptively launch all CUDA kernels and kill some if they are not necessary instead of controlling the kernels to be launched.

We explain the detail of the two components above in the following sections.

4.1   Exponent Statistics and Computing Mode Selection Rule

To determine that a given tensor can tolerate FP16TCEC or FP16TCEC w/ scaling, we take the exponent statistics of each element in two stages.

Stage 1: Obtain the number of elements that are larger than the minimum value of FP16 (N_1) and the max value of the exponent ($e_{\max}$). When N_1 is larger than the underflow admissibility threshold, we mark the matrix that can tolerate FP16TCEC and skip the next stage.

Stage 2: Obtain the number of elements within the shifted FP16 exponent range (N_2), where the range is shifted so that the maximum exponent becomes 14, which is the maximum exponent value of FP16. When N_2 is larger than the threshold, we mark the matrix that can tolerate FP16TCEC w/ scaling; otherwise, we use TF32TCEC.

The threshold is shared in the two stages above and can control the accuracy of the tensor contraction. We check the tolerance for both input matrices. When either input matrix can not tolerate FP16TCEC and FP16TCEC w/ scaling, we use TF32TCEC for the GEMM operation. When either of the input matrices can not tolerate FP16TCEC, we use FP16TCEC w/ scaling. Otherwise, we use FP16TCEC. Note that we only check the underflow since the absolute values of all real and imaginary values of tensor elements in the quantum circuit simulation are smaller or equal to 1.

4.2   Dynamic Kernel Selection

We select the GEMM kernel function depending on the result of the exponent statistics of two input matrices. The simplest way to realize this is to offload the statistics to the host and launch the selected GEMM kernel function. However, this requires GPU-to-host data transfer and may result in throughput degradation. Although NVIDIA provides the Dynamic Parallelism API for such situations that can launch a kernel function from another, we can not use this API since there is a limitation related to the dynamic shared memory size configuration we use. Instead, we use another method: we launch all CUDA kernel functions possibly used and kill some if they are not. For instance, we launch both TF32TCEC and FP16TCEC kernel functions, but one of them exits at the beginning of the execution by checking the computing mode flag on the device memory. The entire flow of execution is shown in Fig. 7. We use two buffers on the device memory to control the kernel execution, **exp stats buffer** and **mode flag buffer**. The kernel function for taking the exponent statistics stores N_1, N_2 and e_{max} on **exp stats buffer** and the tolerance on **mode flag buffer**. Based on the **mode flags** of input matrices, the GEMM mode selection kernel (**select kernel**) selects the computing mode by the selection rule in 4.1. When the mode is FP16TCEC w/ scaling, the scaling kernel (**scale**) scales the matrix elements so that the maximum exponent value becomes 14, and after computing the GEMM operation in FP16TCEC, we scale the resulting matrix to balance out. Note that we do not restore the scaled input matrices since they are not reused in the quantum circuit simulation[2].

---

[2] The library itself has an optional functionality to restore the scaled input matrices for general purpose.

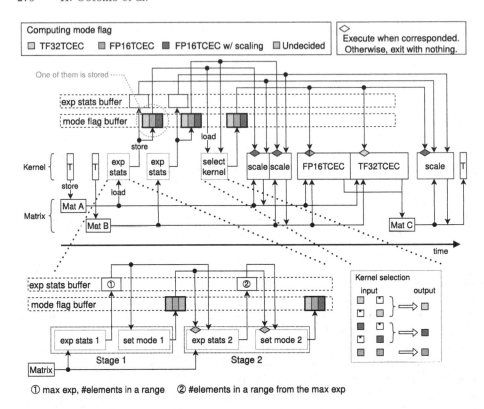

Fig. 7. The dynamic kernel selection mechanism to compute a tensor contraction (TTGT) using the `mode flag buffer` on the device memory.

4.3 The Overhead of the Exponent Statistics

The operations for taking the exponent statistics and scaling elements are memory bandwidth intensive. We have measured their throughput efficiency shown on the left side of Fig. 8. When the matrix size is large, they achieve more than 90 % of the theoretical peak throughput. In the case of $n = 2^{11}$, the throughput of the `Scaling A/B` kernel function outperforms the theoretical bandwidth since the data is on the L2 cache, since it is loaded in the `Exp stats` 2 kernel function executed just prior to it. We have also investigated the time breakdown of the automatic precision selection shown on the right of Fig. 7. When the matrix size is small, the overheads of the automatic precision selection and the scaling operation are not negligible. Therefore, we use the following rule for automatic precision selection when the matrix size is large:

- When $m, n, k \geq 2048$: Use the automatic precision selection.
- Otherwise and when $m, n, k \geq 512$: Use TF32TCEC.
- Otherwise: Use cuBLAS.

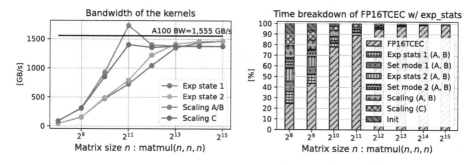

Fig. 8. Left: The bandwidth efficiency of the exponent statistics and scaling kernel function. **Right:** The breakdown of the automatic precision selection in the case where FP16TCEC is selected.

5   Experiment

5.1   Preparation

Quantum Circuit Simulation on GPU. We use the Python library TensorNetwork [25], and quimb [6] for the quantum circuit simulation using the tensor network contraction, cotengra [7], kahypar [26] and opt_einsum [5] for path optimization, and CuPy [18] for the computational backend on GPUs. Although there are several quantum circuit simulators such as NVIDIA cuTensorNet[3], it is not possible to perform a fair comparison against them since their method to avoid explicit transposing on device memory is not open-source. While our method focuses on improving the CGEMM throughput after transposing input tensors, cuTensor, which is used in cuTensorNet for the tensor contraction, focuses on reducing data movement by avoiding explicit transposing on device memory, etc. Therefore, technically, we can apply our method to cuTensorNet if it is open-source. We have confirmed experimentally that cuTensorNet is faster than our methods depending on the problem sizes and contraction paths since the GEMM and transposition time ratio vary.

Fast Implementation for Irregular Shaped GEMM. In quantum circuit simulation, the irregular shape of GEMMs, for instance, $(2, 2^N, 2)$ and $(2^N, 2, 2)$ for $N \geq 10$, are computed many times for the contraction of a single-qubit gate tensor. However, the cuBLAS CGEMM function for these shapes is not optimized. The memory bandwidth bounds the throughput of the GEMMs for these shapes. We have implemented specialized CGEMM kernel functions for these shapes and achieved up to 90% of the theoretical device memory bandwidth on A100 GPU, while that of cuBLAS is 10%. We enable this kernel function in all experiments in all computing modes, including the baseline CUBLAS mode.

---

[3] https://docs.nvidia.com/cuda/cuquantum/cutensornet/index.html.

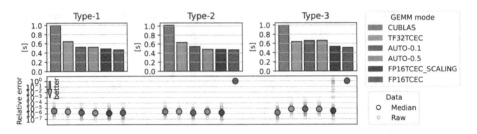

Fig. 9. The computing time (top) and accuracy (bottom) of a random tensor network contraction for different types of element initializations.

5.2 Exploratory Experiment

We check the behavior of the automatic precision selection on a tensor network contraction which is randomly constructed. The tensor network consists of 10 nodes with 2–4°. Each dimension of the tensors is 128, and all elements are initialized as follows.

Type-1: With standard distribution $\mathcal{N}(0, 10^{-4})$. All computing modes can compute with high accuracy.

Type-2: After Type-1 initialization, all elements are scaled 10^{-6}. FP16TCEC can not compute with high accuracy without scaling.

Type-3: After Type-2 initialization, set $10 \sim 20$ elements 1. FP16TCEC can not compute with high accuracy, even with scaling.

The accuracy is the error relative to FP64 computation. We denote our method as AUTO-t, where t is the underflow tolerance threshold. For instance, when $t = 0$, the mode that can avoid all underflows is selected. We show the computing time and accuracy in Fig. 9. Throughout all types, the AUTO modes select the proper computing mode to avoid underflow automatically, and their computing accuracy is close to the same level as the baseline (CUBLAS). In Type-2, the computing time of AUTO-0.5 is shorter than AUTO-0.1 since it selects different computing modes while maintaining accuracy. That implies that the underflow tolerance is being used in some cases. However, it is not feasible to find an appropriate tolerance value t since it is also related to the positional distribution of the input matrix elements, such as sparsity. In Type-2 and 3, the accuracy of FP16TCEC underflows to zero. Although the median error of TF32TCEC, AUTO, and FP16TCEC w/ scaling is larger than the baseline by about 2 bits of mantissa, we consider that the cause is computation order, and the accuracy is considered sufficiently single-precision. However, each result of FP16TCEC w/ scaling sometimes underflows to zero or has low accuracy. In summary, we have confirmed that the AUTO mode automatically selects high throughput computing mode while achieving the same level of accuracy as the baseline.

5.3   Random Quantum Circuit Simulation

We evaluate the automatic precision selection on the Random Circuit Sampling (RCS) problem [2], which is the task to demonstrate the so-called *quantum advantage* [24]. In the RCS problem, we sample the output bitstrings of a random quantum circuit (RQC) U. The bitstring x follows the distribution:

$$p_U(x) := |\langle x|U|0\rangle|^2, \tag{4}$$

where $p_U(x)$ is the appearance probability of x. On a quantum device, the sampling can be accomplished by preparing an initial zero state, applying a unitary circuit U, and measuring each qubit on a computational basis. On the other hand, on a classical computer, we first decide a (random) bitstring and compute its appearance probability through Eq. 4. From the computed probability, we decide whether we accept the bitstring as the output of the quantum circuit or not. Since the computation of one amplitude is independent of other amplitude computations, the throughput scales linearly with computing resources. Generally, the sampling cost on a classical computer can be much higher than on a quantum device since we reject much more bitstrings than we accept. However, in the case of RCS, the *frugal reject sampling* [15] technique can be used to sample them on a classical computer at about the same computational cost as on a quantum device by reducing the number of rejected bitstrings. Therefore, many studies focus on improving the throughput of computing one amplitude.

We evaluate our method on the rectangular lattice RQC defined in [2] and Sycamore circuit [1]. As mentioned above, all quantum circuits and measurements are represented as tensor networks, and one amplitude is obtained by contracting them. Since the computational cost of the Sycamore circuit is high, we typically divide it into slices and merge the result of their contraction. We measure the computing time for one amplitude for the rectangular lattice RQC and one slice for the Sycamore circuit. The computation is conducted 10 times for different output bitstrings, and we show their median.

Rectangular Lattice RQC. The rectangular lattice RQC has $m \times n$ qubits arranged in a lattice, and we apply a specific set of quantum gates. Furthermore, the quantum gates are also arranged in a rectangular lattice, and the number of the rectangular lattice layers is called "depth". We denote the depth $d = 1+X+1$ since we apply the Hadamard gate for all qubits in the first (1+) and last (+1) stages of the circuit. We have evaluated the automatic precision selection on four kinds of rectangular lattice RQCs, as shown in Fig. 10. Throughout all circuits, the AUTO modes avoid the underflow automatically and achieve the same level of accuracy as the baseline (CUBLAS) while achieving higher throughput than TF32TCEC. The AUTO-0.5 mode has achieved up to 1.86 times higher throughput than the baseline in the 9×9 quantum circuit, which has a small computing time ratio for the tensor transposition. The TF32TCEC mode has not been selected in the AUTO modes since it has sufficed to use FP16TCEC w/ scaling in all cases. Therefore, the throughput of the AUTO modes is almost the same

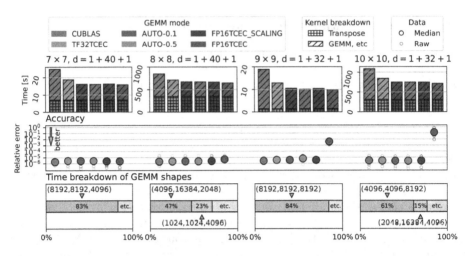

Fig. 10. The computing time (top) and accuracy (center) of obtaining one amplitude for each RQC and the GEMM shape time breakdown in the CUBLAS mode (bottom) of the rectangular lattice RQCs.

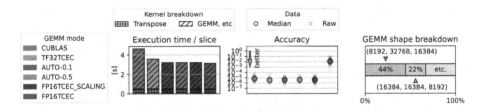

Fig. 11. The computing time (left), accuracy (center), and GEMM shape time breakdown in the CUBLAS mode (right) of Google Sycamore sampling simulation.

as FP16TCEC w/ scaling mode. Although the throughput of FP16TCEC is also higher than TF32TCEC, accuracy loss occurs due to the underflow when the qubit size is large. We have also investigated the computing time breakdown for GEMM shapes in each quantum circuit. In all circuits, a large shape of GEMM dominates the whole GEMM computing time. In this case, we can improve the efficiency of our method since the SGEMM emulation methods achieve higher throughput, and the exponent statistics have a relatively lower overhead.

Sycamore. In the Sycamore circuits, 53 qubits are arranged in 2-D, and we apply $(1 + 20 + 1)$-depth quantum gates layers. The evaluation result of the Sycamore circuit is shown in Fig. 11. The AUTO modes have achieved 1.45 times higher throughput than the baseline (CUBLAS) while achieving the same level of accuracy. In this quantum circuit, the large shape GEMMs dominate the whole GEMM computing time, and we can efficiently improve the throughput of the simulation. Although the underflow ratio of the elements in the large GEMMs has differed from the output strings, FP16TCEC w/ scaling is selected in all computations. As we mentioned above, since the throughput of the RCS is proportional to the throughput of one amplitude computation, we believe our method improves the whole Sycamore circuit simulation to the same extent.

6   Conclusion

We improve the throughput of the quantum circuit simulation using the SGEMM emulation method on Tensor Cores and automatic precision selection. Our method automatically selects the GEMM computing modes in the tensor contractions to improve the throughput while avoiding accuracy loss due to underflow. We have achieved up to 1.86 times throughput in 9×9 RQC and 1.45 times in Google Sycamore circuits compared to the baseline simulation using cuBLAS CGEMM while keeping the accuracy. Furthermore, we have also achieved up to 1.27 times in 9×9 RQC, 1.11 times faster throughput in the Sycamore circuit than SGEMM emulation using TF32 Tensor Core, which clearly can improve the throughput. Through this study, we show an example that Tensor Core, which is developed for machine learning, can be used for another HPC field of research.

Acknowledgements. This work was partially supported by JSPS KAKENHI 22H03598, 21J14694, and 20K03766. This work was partially supported by "Joint Usage/Research Center for Interdisciplinary Large-scale Information Infrastructures" in Japan (Project ID: jh220022-NAHI).

References

1. Arute, F., Arya, K., et al.: Quantum supremacy using a programmable superconducting processor. Nature **574**(7779), 505–510 (2019)
2. Boixo, S., et al.: Characterizing quantum supremacy in near-term devices. Nat. Phys. **14**(6), 595–600 (2018)
3. Chen, Z.Y., Zhou, Q., Xue, C., Yang, X., Guo, G.C., Guo, G.P.: 64-qubit quantum circuit simulation. Sci. Bull. **63**(15), 964–971 (2018)
4. Chi-Chung, L., Sadayappan, P., Wenger, R.: On optimizing a class of multidimensional loops with reduction for parallel execution. Parallel Process. Lett. **07**(02), 157–168 (1997)
5. Daniel, G., Gray, J.: Opt_einsum - a Python package for optimizing contraction order for einsum-like expressions. J. Open Source Softw. **3**(26), 753 (2018)
6. Gray, J.: quimb: a python package for quantum information and many-body calculations. J. Open Source Softw. **3**(29), 819 (2018)
7. Gray, J., Kourtis, S.: Hyper-optimized tensor network contraction. Quantum **5**, 410 (2021)
8. Guerreschi, G.G., Hogaboam, J., Baruffa, F., Sawaya, N.P.D.: Intel quantum simulator: a cloud-ready high-performance simulator of quantum circuits. Quantum Sci. Technol. **5**(3), 034007 (2020)
9. Huang, C., Zhang, F., Newman, M., et al.: Efficient parallelization of tensor network contraction for simulating quantum computation. Nat. Comput. Sci. **1**(9), 578–587 (2021)

10. Huang, J., Yu, C.D., van de Geijn, R.A.: Implementing strassen's algorithm with CUTLASS on NVIDIA Volta GPUs. arXiv:1808.07984 (2018)
11. Jones, T., Brown, A., Bush, I., Benjamin, S.C.: QuEST and high performance simulation of quantum computers. Sci. Rep. **9**(1), 10736 (2019)
12. Liang, L., et al.: Fast search of the optimal contraction sequence in tensor networks. IEEE J. Sel. Top. Sig. Process. **15**(3), 574–586 (2021)
13. Liu, Y.A., et al.: Closing the "quantum supremacy" gap: achieving real-time simulation of a random quantum circuit using a new Sunway supercomputer. In: Proceedings of the International Conference for High Performance Computing, Networking, Storage and Analysis, SC'21, pp. 1–12 (2021)
14. Markidis, S., Der Chien, S.W., Laure, E., Peng, I.B., Vetter, J.S.: NVIDIA tensor core programmability, performance & precision. In: 2018 IEEE International Parallel and Distributed Processing Symposium Workshops (IPDPSW), pp. 522–531 (2018)
15. Markov, I.L., Fatima, A., Isakov, S.V., Boixo, S.: Quantum supremacy is both closer and farther than it appears. arXiv:1807.10749 (2018)
16. Markov, I.L., Shi, Y.: Simulating quantum computation by contracting tensor networks. SIAM J. Comput. **38**(3), 963–981 (2008)
17. Nguyen, T., Lyakh, D., Dumitrescu, E., Clark, D., Larkin, J., McCaskey, A.: Tensor network quantum virtual machine for simulating quantum circuits at exascale. arXiv:2104.10523 (2021)
18. Okuta, R., Unno, Y., Nishino, D., Hido, S., Loomis, C.: CuPy: a numpy-compatible library for NVIDIA GPU calculations (2017)
19. Ootomo, H., Yokota, R.: Recovering single precision accuracy from tensor cores while surpassing the FP32 theoretical peak performance. Int. J. High Perform. Comput. Appl. **36**(4), 475–491 (2022)
20. Ootomo, H., Yokota, R.: Reducing shared memory footprint to leverage high throughput on tensor cores and its flexible API extension library. In: Proceedings of the International Conference on High Performance Computing in Asia-Pacific Region, HPC Asia'23, pp. 1–8 (2023)
21. Pan, F., Chen, K., Zhang, P.: Solving the sampling problem of the sycamore quantum circuits. Phys. Rev. Lett. **129**(9), 090502 (2022)
22. Pan, F., Zhang, P.: Simulation of quantum circuits using the big-batch tensor network method. Phys. Rev. Lett. **128**(3), 030501 (2022)
23. Paszke, A., et al.: PyTorch: an imperative style, high-performance deep learning library. In: Advances in Neural Information Processing Systems, vol. 32 (2019)
24. Preskill, J.: Quantum computing and the entanglement frontier (2012)
25. Roberts, C., et al.: TensorNetwork: a library for physics and machine learning (2019)
26. Schlag, S., Heuer, T., Gottesbüren, L., Akhremtsev, Y., Schulz, C., Sanders, P.: High-quality hypergraph partitioning. ACM J. Exp. Algorithmics **27**, 1–39 (2022)
27. Schuch, N., Wolf, M.M., Verstraete, F., Cirac, J.I.: The computational complexity of PEPS. Phys. Rev. Lett. **98**(14), 140506 (2007)
28. Suzuki, Y., et al.: Qulacs: a fast and versatile quantum circuit simulator for research purpose. Quantum **5**, 559 (2021)
29. Treinish, M., Gambetta, J., et al.: Qiskit/qiskit: Qiskit 0.38.0 (2022)
30. Villalonga, B., et al.: Establishing the quantum supremacy frontier with a 281 Pflop/s simulation. Quantum Sci. Technol. **5**(3), 034003 (2020)

Performance Modeling, Evaluation, and Analysis

A Study on the Performance Implications of AArch64 Atomics

Ricardo Jesus$^{(\boxtimes)}$ and Michèle Weiland

EPCC, The University of Edinburgh, Edinburgh, UK
rjj@ed.ac.uk

Abstract. Atomic operations are indivisible operations guaranteed to execute as a whole. One of the most important and widely used atomic operations is "compare-and-swap" (CAS), which allows threads to perform concurrent read-modify-write operations on the same memory location, free of data races. On recent Arm architectures, CAS operations can be implemented either directly via CAS instructions, or via load-linked/store-conditional (LL-SC) instruction pairs.

In this paper we explore the performance of the CAS and LL-SC approaches to implement CAS operations on recent high-performance Arm-based CPUs, namely the A64FX, ThunderX2, and Graviton3. We observe that CAS and LL-SC instructions can lead to fundamentally different performance profiles. On the A64FX, for example, the newer CAS instructions—often preferred by compilers over the older LL-SC pairs—can lead to a quadratic increase in average time per successful CAS operation as the number of threads increases, whereas the older LL-SC approach shows the expected linear scaling. For high thread counts, this difference translates into a speedup of more than 20x when using LL-SC instructions. We characterise the conditions under which the LL-SC or CAS approaches are superior on each CPU, and the speedup that can be realised by preferring one strategy over the other.

Keywords: A64FX · Graviton3 · ThunderX2 · atomics · benchmarking · compare-and-swap · performance analysis

1 Introduction

In the context of concurrent programming, atomic operations are indivisible operations guaranteed to run to completion without interference from other threads. Atomic operations are essential for the synchronisation and cooperation of threads in a multi-threaded program [1]. One of the most common and general atomic operations is the "compare-and-swap" (CAS), which allows a thread to atomically compare a value stored in memory with another value, and, if the values match, to overwrite the memory with a new value. In practice, CAS operations enable threads to perform generic read-modify-writes on a same memory location concurrently and free of data races. The applicability of CAS operations ranges from low-level synchronisation primitives such as locks and semaphores to

© The Author(s), under exclusive license to Springer Nature Switzerland AG 2023
A. Bhatele et al. (Eds.): ISC High Performance 2023, LNCS 13948, pp. 279–296, 2023.
https://doi.org/10.1007/978-3-031-32041-5_15

higher-level codes such as concurrent data structures [14,17,21] and in-memory databases [19].

Although the performance of CAS and other atomic operations has been considered in the past for x86 targets [11,12,23,28,30], AArch64 CPUs by comparison have received significantly less attention. However, it can be argued that atomic and other synchronisation operations are even more important for Arm-based processors [24] because of Armv8's weakly-ordered memory model, which dictates that the order of memory accesses is not required to follow the program order for load and store operations [2]. This contrasts with the x86 architecture, which offers stronger guarantees such as reads not being reordered with other reads, and writes not being reordered with older reads, for example [16, §8.2].

While evaluating the performance of several Arm-based chips, we identified one kernel from the RAJAPerf suite [15] that scaled particularly poorly on TX2 and A64FX CPUs (Sect. 2.1). The kernel in question stress tests OpenMP atomic floating-point (FP) operations, which, on recent Arm-based CPUs like the two above, are implemented with CAS instructions. In this kernel, those particular instructions caused a *slowdown* of $48x$ on the TX2 and of $70x$ on the A64FX when scaling from 1 to 48 threads (Fig. 1). This led us to question the performance of CAS on Arm-based CPUs and wonder (i) if there was a fundamental issue with these instructions across Arm microarchitectures, and (ii) if the "legacy" method used to implement CAS operations prior to the introduction of Armv8.1, load-linked/store-conditional (LL-SC) pairs of instructions, could offer any benefit over the more recent CAS instructions. We perform our analyses on the Arm-based TX2, A64FX, and Graviton3 processors, and use the x86-based EPYC 7742 and Intel Xeon Gold 6330 CPUs for comparison. Overall, our results show that the newer CAS instructions do not perform well on TX2 and A64FX, and the older LL-SC instructions can bring significant performance improvements on all Arm-based systems tested (Fig. 4). The main contributions of this paper are:

1. We demonstrate the negative impact that the newer CAS instructions (chosen by default by compilers) can have on parallel codes;
2. We perform a detailed performance study of CAS and LL-SC instructions on state-of-the-art AArch64 CPUs;
3. We describe the conditions under which each approach (CAS or LL-SC) delivers better performance when implementing atomic operations, including "latency thresholds" that govern performance on A64FX.

As far as we are aware, this is the most extensive and comprehensive study on the performance of atomic instructions on state-of-the-art Arm-based CPUs.

The remainder of this paper is organised as follows. In Sect. 2 we describe the performance issues we observed with the RAJAPerf kernel that led us to investigate CAS operations on Arm-based CPUs. In Sect. 3 we discuss the ways in which a CAS operation can be implemented for the AArch64 architecture and present the micro-benchmarks we developed to assess their performance. In Sect. 4 we present the main results of the paper, namely the performance of different approaches to implement CAS operations on Arm-based CPUs and their scaling behaviours. In Sect. 5 we discuss related work and, in Sect. 6, we conclude the paper.

2   The Problem

In this section we describe the problem that motivated our study of atomic operations on Arm-based CPUs. Our goal is to (i) contextualise our work and describe how it came into being, (ii) provide concrete examples of codes where the issues we address in this work emerge, and (iii) demonstrate their possible implications for performance.

2.1   RAJAPerf and the `PI_ATOMIC` kernel

The RAJA Performance Suite (RAJAPerf)[1] is a benchmark suite designed to assess the performance of various parallel programming models and runtimes on a wide range of loop-based kernels common to HPC codes [15]. The suite consists of roughly 50 kernels implemented in C++11, and parallel libraries and runtimes such as OpenMP, CUDA and RAJA. The kernels are mainly extracted from HPC applications. Each kernel is implemented in a variety of "variants", such as baseline sequential and OpenMP versions. To allow for a fair comparison between programming models, all variants of a kernel perform roughly the same mathematical operations and their loop bodies are implemented identically.

One of RAJAPerf's kernels is the `PI_ATOMIC` kernel, which calculates an approximation of π via the identity

$$\frac{\pi}{4} = \arctan(1) = \int_0^1 \frac{1}{1+x^2}\,dx. \tag{1}$$

In the kernel's most basic version, the baseline sequential variant, the integration on the right-hand side is carried out in a simple sequential loop. In C-based pseudocode, this corresponds to the code shown in Listing 1. The baseline multi-threaded version of the kernel uses OpenMP atomics to accumulate the value of π in the body of the loop (line 10). Although not a particularly efficient way to parallelise this computation, the code is designed to measure the performance of OpenMP atomics in a context of high contention.

2.2   Performance Results

As we were using RAJAPerf to identify codes where Arm-based processors currently underperform compared to x86 competitors, the `PI_ATOMIC` kernel stood out as the worst-performing kernel on A64FX and TX2 by a large margin. In Fig. 1 we plot the average runtime of the `PI_ATOMIC` kernel (as reported by RAJAPerf) as a function of the number of threads used on the A64FX and TX2 processors, and (as comparison) on the EPYC 7742 (results for the Xeon 6330 are identical). The kernel runs for 50 repetitions of 1,000,000 iterations each (the default parameters of RAJAPerf). Compilers, optimisation flags, and other experiment parameters are those described in Sect. 4.

---

[1] https://github.com/LLNL/RAJAPerf/tree/v0.11.0. Accessed on 29 April 2022.

Listing 1. The `PI_ATOMIC` kernel.

```
1  double PI_ATOMIC() {
2    const int N = ...;    // num
        sub-intervals
3    const double dx = 1.0 / (double)N;
4
5    double pi = 0.0;
6    //#pragma omp parallel for
7    for(int i = 0; i < N; ++i) {
8      double x = ((double)i + 0.5) * dx;
9      //#pragma omp atomic
10     pi += dx / (1.0 + x * x);
11   }
12   pi *= 4.0;
13
14   return pi;
15 }
```

Uncomment for multi-threaded OpenMP version.

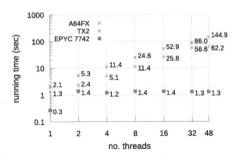

Fig. 1. Performance of the multi-threaded `PI_ATOMIC` kernel on A64FX, TX2, and EPYC 7742 CPUs. (Log-log scale.)

As the figure shows, on EPYC 7742, for runs with at least two threads, the runtime of the kernel stays approximately constant as the number of threads increases. This is the expected behaviour—the atomic operation acts as a serialisation point that prevents much parallelism, and therefore, since the total number of atomic operations is kept constant across different runs, the system as a whole (ideally) takes the same amount of time to perform those operations, regardless of the number of threads that execute them. On the A64FX and TX2 however, this is not the case. On these processors, going from 1 thread to 48 causes a slowdown of about $70x$ on A64FX and of $48x$ on TX2. We observed identical behaviour using non-GNU compilers, namely LLVM (Clang) 11.0.0 and the Arm C/C++ Compiler 21.0. Moreover, we have also measured similar slowdowns with CircusTent [29], a benchmark suite for atomic operations, and with the VTK-m [22] AtomicArray benchmark[2].

2.3 A Closer Look at OpenMP Floating-Point Atomics

Profiling the `PI_ATOMIC` kernel revealed the cause of the slowdown to be the atomic FP addition. To confirm that the scaling issues observed were not due to an implementation inefficiency in the OpenMP runtime, we examined how the atomic addition is implemented in assembly, shown in Listing 2 for the Zen 2 (EPYC 7742) and A64FX microarchitectures. As the code shows, the assembly generated for the two targets is virtually identical. At a high-level, the atomic variable to update is moved from a general-purpose (GP) register to an FP register, the addition is performed (using FP instructions), and the result is moved back into a GP register. Then, an (atomic) CAS instruction is attempted. If it succeeds, execution continues its normal path; otherwise, the whole operation is restarted. A minor inefficiency in the assembly is the

---

[2] https://gitlab.kitware.com/vtk/vtk-m/-/tree/master/benchmarking. Accessed on 04 August 2022.

Listing 2: Snippet of assembly generated by GCC 11.2 for an OpenMP atomic FP addition for Zen 2 and A64FX. Reference C/C++ code on the right. Compiled with -O3 -fopenmp -march=znver2/-mcpu=a64fx.

```
/*         C/C++        */
for(...) {
    #pragma omp atomic
    x += 1.0;
}
```

	/* ASM (x86) */	/* ASM (A64) */	/* Comments */
1			
2	.L2:	.L2:	
3	vmovq %rdx,%xmm2	fmov d1, x2	// move `x' to FP register
4	mov %rdx,%rax	mov x3, x2	// create copy
5	vaddsd %xmm2,%xmm0,%xmm1	fadd d1, d0, d1	// do addition (x+1.0)
6	vmovq %xmm1,%r8	fmov x4, d1	// move result back
7	lock cmpxchg %r8,(%rdi)	casal x3, x4, [x0]	// attempt CAS
8		cmp x2, x3	
9	jne .L4	bne .L4	// retry if unsuccessful
10	...	...	
11	.L4:	.L4:	
12	mov %rax,%rdx	mov x2, x3	
13	jmp .L2	b .L2	

conditional jump to label .L4, which is unnecessary if the registers used for the CAS instructions are changed as done in Listings 4 and 5. Nevertheless, this is a minor issue that does not play any significant part in the slowdowns observed.

3   Benchmarking CAS Operations

In this section we discuss how CAS operations can be implemented and present a set of micro-benchmarks we developed to study the performance of these operations on Arm-based CPUs in more detail.

3.1   Compare-and-Swap Operations

At the machine level, there are two main ways of implementing a CAS operation: either via an explicit CAS instruction, or via a pair of load-linked/store-conditional (LL-SC) instructions. We briefly describe these alternatives below. A third option would be via "transactional memory", which is similar in principle to the LL-SC approach, but allows multiple loads and stores to be effected atomically at once. We do not consider this approach as it is currently not widely available in practice. Nevertheless, the Armv9 architecture considers this option in its (optional) Transactional Memory Extension (TME) [6,7], which might feature in future systems. A more exhaustive discussion on ways to implement CAS and other atomic operations is provided in [18, §6.1.1] and references therein.

CAS Utilising an explicit CAS instruction to perform the CAS operation is, generally speaking, the most straightforward option (assuming there is hardware support for it). In the case of the x86 architecture, this can be accomplished with a `lock cmpxchg` instruction. In AArch64, such an instruction did not exist until the introduction of the Large System Extension (LSE), which first appeared in Armv8.1 [5]. For Armv8.1 and subsequent architectures, a CAS operation can be effected via one of several instructions that vary in the size of the operands on which they operate (from 8 to 128-bits), and in the memory order semantics they utilise for the load and store parts of the operation. For example, for 64-bit operands, the mnemonics for these instructions are `cas`, `casa`, `casl` and `casal`, where in the case of `casa` and `casal` the load is performed with acquire semantics; in `casl` and `casal` the store has release semantics; and `cas` has neither acquire nor release semantics (memory order semantics are discussed in more detail in Sect. 3.2).

LL-SC Prior to the availability of LSE, CAS operations on the Arm architecture (Armv8) were implemented via pairs of load-linked/store-conditional (LL-SC) instructions. In this approach, a store-conditional to a memory address will only succeed, thereby writing to the location, if no other write to the same location has happened since a previous load-linked instruction. This approach closely follows the load/store philosophy of Arm and other RISC architectures. For Armv8 (AArch64) targets, an LL-SC CAS operation can be implemented with `ldxr`, `ldaxr`, `stxr` and `stlxr` instructions. The first two perform a load-exclusive with and without acquire semantics (respectively), whilst the latter two perform a store-exclusive with and without release semantics (also respectively).

The hardware implementations of these approaches vary from microarchitecture to microarchitecture, and are often not public in the case of proprietary designs. Nevertheless, here we briefly describe how these instructions are implemented in Arm's Neoverse cores connected to CHI-based interconnects (like the Graviton3) to illustrate how they can be implemented in general. In Arm's Neoverse cores, LL-SC instructions manage an exclusive monitor in the L1 memory system that keeps track of exclusive access to a cache line. This monitor is set by load-linked instructions and checked (and/or cleared) by store-exclusive instructions. Meanwhile, CAS instructions (on CHI-based interconnects) can be performed either as near (in the CPU), or as far (in the interconnect) atomics, depending on where data resides [3]. Since far atomics cannot be performed speculatively (whereas the read prior to the execution of a near atomic could), by default they are disabled in Neoverse CPUs [4].

3.2   Benchmark Description

To assess the performance of CAS operations on different CPUs we developed a set of micro-benchmarks where a counter is incremented concurrently by a number of threads. The increment is performed atomically using one of the CAS strategies mentioned in the previous section, thereby avoiding data races. Overall, we are interested in measuring the average time required to perform an increment (or iteration) per thread, as well as the average number of times each thread has to attempt the CAS operation, per increment, before it succeeds. Listing 3 presents sample C++ code implementing the benchmark, to facilitate its general understanding. However, it should be noted that most of our benchmark kernels are implemented in assembly so that we have precisely control over the instructions used for the atomic operation, as well as their placement.

Listing 3. Reference C++ implementation of the CAS kernel.

```
 1  #include <cstdint>
 2  typedef uint64_t u64;
 3
 4  template <typename counter_t>
 5  u64 kernel(u64 iters, counter_t* mem,
 6             bool weak, int memorder)
 7  {
 8    u64 attempts = 0;
 9    do {
10      counter_t expected = *mem, desired;
11      do {
12        desired = expected+1; attempts++;
13      } while(!__atomic_compare_exchange(
14              mem, &expected, &desired,
15              weak, memorder, memorder));
16    } while(--iters);
17    return attempts;
18  }
```

Listing 4. Assembly kernels for x86 targets.

```
 1  kernel_dbl_x86:
 2    xor %r8d, %r8d
 3    vmovsd one, %xmm0     Change to
 4  loop_dbl_x86:           lea 0x1(%rax), %rcx
 5    mov (%rsi), %rax      for integer kernel
 6  try_dbl_x86:
 7    inc %r8
 8    vmovq %rax, %xmm1
 9    vaddsd %xmm0, %xmm1, %xmm2
10    vmovq %xmm2, %rcx
11    lock cmpxchg %rcx, (%rsi)
12    jne try_dbl_x86
13    dec %rdi
14    jne loop_dbl_x86
15    mov %r8, %rax
16    ret
17  one:
18    .double 1.0
```

Besides the number of iterations and threads, each benchmark takes three main parameters: (i) the data type utilised for the counter, (ii) the "strategy" used to implement the CAS operation, and (iii) the memory order semantics for the atomic operation. Table 1 summarises the values we consider for these parameters, which we describe below in more detail.

Counter Type. We consider two data types for the counter in the benchmark: uint64_t and double. The former is a conventional 64-bit unsigned integer, whilst the latter is an IEEE 754 double-precision FP type. The main reason for considering these two types is that they indirectly allow us to evaluate how the latency of the CAS loop (i.e. time between loading the value of the counter and computing the value to store) affects the performance of the CAS operation. The version using a double type spends more time setting up the operation, which (as we will see in later sections) can affect performance significantly. Furthermore, the implementation that uses a double counter resembles the PI_ATOMIC kernel described in Sect. 2.1 more closely, and therefore is a more faithful representation of the problem. We also ran experiments with other types, namely uint32_t and float, but, since they exhibited the same performance as their 64-bit counterparts, they are not considered further here.

Strategy. "Strategy" refers to the way in which the CAS operation is implemented, as described in Sect. 3.1. For x86 targets we only consider implementations with CAS instructions, whereas for Arm targets we consider both CAS and LL-SC. Note that if we were concerned with the increment operation *per se*, and we only used an integer type for the counter, then the increment could be achieved directly via, for example, a lock add in x86 or a ldadd in Armv8.1 (and subsequent) architectures. However, in the context of this benchmark, the increment is a mere vehicle to assess the performance of CAS operations, and therefore we do not consider these approaches.

Listing 5: Assembly kernels for Arm targets. From left to right: uint64_t kernel with CAS strategy, uint64_t with LL-SC strategy, double kernel with CAS strategy, and double with LL-SC strategy. Instructions at the same line correspond roughly to the same "high-level" operation.

1	kernel_u64_cas:	kernel_u64_llsc:	kernel_dbl_cas:	kernel_dbl_llsc:
2	mov x9, 0	mov x9, 0	mov x9, 0	mov x9, 0
3			fmov d0, 1.0	fmov d0, 1.0
4	loop_u64_cas:	loop_u64_llsc:	loop_dbl_cas:	loop_dbl_llsc:
5	ldr x2, [x1]	ldxr x2, [x1]	ldr x2, [x1]	ldxr x2, [x1]
6	try_u64_cas:		try_dbl_cas:	
7	add x9, x9, 1	add x9, x9, 1	add x9, x9, 1	add x9, x9, 1
8			fmov d1, x2	fmov d1, x2
9	add x3, x2, 1	add x3, x2, 1	fadd d1, d0, d1	fadd d1, d0, d1
10			fmov x3, d1	fmov x3, d1
11	mov x4, x2		mov x4, x2	
12	cas x2, x3, [x1]	stxr w4, x3, [x1]	cas x2, x3, [x1]	stxr w4, x3, [x1]
13	cmp x2, x4		cmp x2, x4	
14	bne try_u64_cas	cbnz w4, loop_u64_llsc	bne try_dbl_cas	cbnz w4, loop_dbl_llsc
15	subs x0, x0, 1	subs x0, x0, 1	subs x0, x0, 1	subs x0, x0, 1
16	bne loop_u64_cas	bne loop_u64_llsc	bne loop_dbl_cas	bne loop_dbl_llsc
17	mov x0, x9	mov x0, x9	mov x0, x9	mov x0, x9
18	ret	ret	ret	ret

Memory Order. The memory order semantics of an atomic operation specify how memory accesses, including regular, non-atomic ones, are to be ordered around the atomic operation. The semantics of atomic operations are particularly important in architectures such as the Armv8 that employ a weakly ordered memory model, since on such architectures the order of memory accesses is not necessarily required to follow the program order for load and store operations [2]. In this benchmark, we consider a subset of the memory orders defined in the C/C++ 11 standard: relaxed, acquire, release, and acquire-release. In general terms, acquire operations perform a "one-way barrier" that guarantee that all memory operations after the acquire cannot be reordered to take place before it. Similarly, release operations perform a one-way barrier in the opposite direction: they guarantee that all memory operations before the release operation cannot be reordered after it. Acquire-release imposes both an acquire and a release, whilst relaxed does neither. In Armv8 these memory orders are enforced via appropriate CAS/LL-SC instructions as described in Sect. 3.1.

3.3 Assembly Kernels

As mentioned in Sect. 3.2, the kernels used to measure the performance of CAS operations are implemented in assembly. This has been done to control the instructions used in the kernels and to stop the compilers from introducing differences across machines that may affect the kernels' performance. These kernels, presented in Listing 4 for x86 targets and Listing 5 for Arm-based ones, result from an optimised transliteration of the reference C++ kernel (Listing 3) and were specialised for a relaxed memory order on Arm. Other memory orders

Table 1. CAS benchmark parameters. **Table 2.** CPUs and compiler versions.

Parameter	Options
counter type	`uint64_t, double`
strategy	CAS, LL-SC
memory order	relaxed, acquire, release, acquire-release

System	Processor	Compiler
ARCHER2	EPYC 7742	GCC 11.2.0
ICX	Xeon Gold 6330	GCC 11.2.0
Fulhame	ThunderX2	GCC 10.1.0
Isambard 2	A64FX	GCC 11.1.0
C7g	Graviton3	GCC 10.3.1

are achieved by replacing the `cas`, `ldxr` and `stxr` instructions with the appropriate instructions as mentioned in Sect. 3.1. In the A64 assembly, `x0` and `x1` are the kernel arguments, i.e. number of iterations and address of memory location to update, respectively; `x2` is the value loaded from the memory location in a given iteration; and `x9` is used to accumulate the number of attempts of the CAS loop. Other registers are temporaries to compute the increment and set up the CAS operation, for example.

4 Experiments and Observations

In this section we present the main results of this work, concerning the performance of CAS operations on Arm-based CPUs. We utilise the following systems in our tests:

ARCHER2 HPE Cray EX system with dual AMD EPYC 7742 64-core CPUs (128 cores per node). Zen 2 "Rome" microarchitecture (x86).
ICX System with dual Intel Xeon Gold 6330 28-core CPUs (56 cores per node). Ice Lake Sunny Cove microarchitecture (x86).
Fulhame HPE Apollo 70 cluster with dual 32-core Marvell ThunderX2 CPUs (64 cores per node). Armv8.1 architecture.
Isambard 2 HPE Apollo 80 system with Fujitsu A64FX 48-core processors. Armv8.2 architecture.
C7g AWS c7g.16xlarge instance with 64 vCPUs of a Graviton3 processor. Based on a modified Neoverse V1 core (Armv8.4).

All measurements were taken using the system's compute nodes in exclusive mode to guarantee dedicated access to the resources. Threads were pinned to cores and placed close to each other with the variables `OMP_PLACES=cores` and `OMP_PROC_BIND=close`. As such, the cores of a system were occupied sequentially "by NUMA region", i.e. a NUMA region was fully filled before the cores of another were used. All kernels were compiled with GCC using the versions specified in Table 2. In all cases the optimisation flags used were `-O3 -fopenmp -march=native`/`-mcpu=native` (the former for x86-based systems, the latter for Arm-based). Unless otherwise stated, all results were obtained running 100,000 iterations per thread.

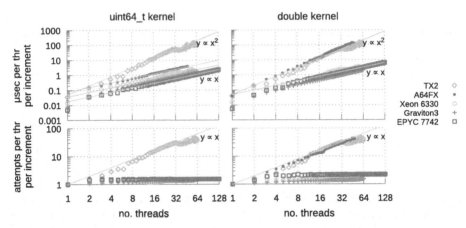

Fig. 2. *Top:* Performance of the new CAS instructions introduced in Armv8.1 LSE on the 64-bit integer and double variants of the benchmark described in Sect. 3. The y axis represents the average time spent by each thread, in microseconds, performing an increment of the kernel. The gray lines are guides to help illustrate the trends of the curves. *Bottom:* Average number of times each thread attempts the CAS loop, per increment, until the loop succeeds. (Log-log scale.)

The results presented in the remainder of this section use relaxed memory ordering since we did not observe significant differences in behaviour when using other, more restrictive memory orders. We confirmed this by computing the Pearson product-moment correlation coefficient between implementations with relaxed memory order and other memory orders. Nearly all coefficients are extremely high (above 0.99), meaning that the trends of the curves are the same. The exception is the LL-SC tests on Graviton3, where the coefficient drops marginally to 0.96–0.98 (still indicating very strong correlation). As we will see in Sect. 4.3, this is due to increased variability in the LL-SC runs on this processor. Finally, note that we also carried out the tests presented throughout this section on Graviton2 using an AWS c6g.metal instance. However, since the results obtained are identical to those obtained on Graviton3, due to space constraints we have omitted them from this paper.

4.1   Evaluating the Performance of CAS

In Fig. 2 (top) we evaluate the performance of the CAS instructions introduced in Armv8.1 LSE. These are the instructions currently used by default by compilers to implement operations such as the atomic FP updates as seen in Sect. 2.3. We carry out this evaluation on A64FX, Graviton3, TX2, EPYC 7742 and Xeon Gold 6330 CPUs. We consider both the integer and double variants of the benchmark, as presented in Sect. 3.2.

We see two main lines of behaviour: in most cases, the average time spent by each thread performing an increment grows roughly linearly with the number of threads attempting the increment concurrently. This is an effect of the serialising nature of the atomic operation mentioned in Sect. 2.2: since the total system throughput to update the counter is fixed, the average time of each operation is bound to increase at least linearly with the number of threads attempting to update the counter concurrently [10]. However, the A64FX (in the double kernel) and the TX2 (in both kernels), exhibit significantly more pronounced slowdowns. Instead of displaying the expected linear scaling, these CPUs exhibit an approximately *quadratic* slowdown: as we increase the number of threads by a factor of two, the time spent by each thread performing an increment grows roughly by a factor of four. In other words, as we double the number of threads, the throughput of the system halves. This behaviour is consistent with the performance issues seen in Sect. 2.2, and it stems from an increase in the number of CAS operations that fail—and therefore have to be reattempted— as more threads run concurrently. This is demonstrated in Fig. 2 (bottom), where we plot the average number of times each thread performs the CAS loop per successful increment as a function of the number of threads utilised. The trends shown in this figure are akin to those seen in Fig. 2 (top): in systems that exhibit linear scaling of average time per increment, the average number of attempts per successful CAS operation remains flat, whereas in systems that exhibit quadratic increase in runtime, the number of attempts grows linearly. This behaviour suggests a lack of built-in backoff mechanisms on the A64FX and TX2, causing threads to interfere more frequently with each other (thus invalidating their work) as more threads run concurrently.

We note that the dip exhibited by the TX2-based system at 32 threads is due to the crossover of NUMA domains (this system has two 32-core processors, each of which corresponds to one NUMA domain). Other systems do not exhibit such clear NUMA effects.

4.2   A Closer Look at A64FX

As seen in the previous section, the A64FX exhibits both linear and quadratic behaviours, the former in the integer and the latter in the double kernel. The body of the CAS loop is the only place where the two kernels differ, implying that it is the source of the difference in performance. The body of the integer kernel consists only of a small number of integer instructions, whereas the body of the double kernel includes instructions to move data between general-purpose and FP registers, in addition to the FP instructions that perform the counter arithmetic itself. Incidentally, these FP instructions have fairly high latencies on A64FX [13]. For example, a scalar integer addition has a latency of 1 cycle, whereas a scalar FP addition has a latency of 9 cycles. The disparate scaling behaviours of the A64FX can be traced back to the latency of the CAS loops of the integer and double kernels. In Fig. 3 (top) we plot the average runtime and number of attempts, per increment, obtained in a modified version of the integer kernel where the kernel's CAS loop was filled with single-cycle instructions to increase the overall latency of the loop body prior to the CAS instruction. The extra instructions were inserted right before the CAS instruction (before

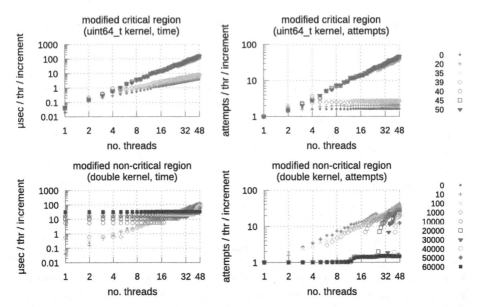

Fig. 3. *Top:* Effect of modifying the CAS loop body size (critical section) on the average running time and average number of attempts of the CAS loop on A64FX (`uint64_t` kernel). *Bottom:* Effect of modifying the size of the region outside the CAS loop (non-critical section) on the average running time and average number of attempts of the CAS loop (double kernel) on A64FX. The legend denotes the number of single-cycle instructions inserted (roughly equivalent to latency in clock cycles).

line 12). The number of instructions added corresponds approximately to the increased latency (in cycles) of the modified kernel. Looking at the average time per increment, the A64FX exhibits the linear scaling behaviour observed in the (original) integer kernel so long as the number of instructions inserted remains below or equal to 39. However, once 40 or more instructions are inserted, the modified kernel shifts to the quadratic scaling observed in the double kernel. Analogous trends are observed in terms of the average number of attempts per increment: whilst the number of additional instructions is kept below or equal to 39, the modified kernel behaves mostly as the integer kernel, whereas for greater values it behaves like the double kernel. These results indicate that the CAS instructions on the A64FX are not optimised for CAS operations with high-latency critical sections (i.e. loop bodies). The high latencies of FP instructions on the A64FX exacerbate the problem, causing atomic FP operations as simple as the addition carried out in the double kernel to exhibit the quadratic scaling we have observed. Indeed, if we consider the double kernel, on A64FX the `fmov` takes around 10–14 cycles depending on the direction of the move, GP to FP register or vice-versa, and the FP addition takes 9, which leads to a total of $10 + 9 + 14 = 33$ cycles. If we consider the latencies of the initial load and of the

CAS instruction itself, which take at least 5 and 8 cycles respectively, we get a grand total of 38–41 cycles, which puts us in the quadratic scaling regime.

Meanwhile, in Fig. 3 (bottom) we plot the average runtime and number of attempts, per increment, obtained using a modified version of the double kernel where the region *outside* the kernel's CAS loop, i.e. the non-critical region, was extended with single-cycle instructions. The figure demonstrates that it is possible to eliminate the adverse linear scaling in average number of attempts on the A64FX by increasing the size of the non-critical region. However, the higher the number of threads attempting the CAS operation concurrently, the bigger the non-critical region needs to be. In our experiments, the smallest non-critical region that exhibits a constant CAS attempt rate for all thread counts is about 60,000 (1-cycle) instructions per CAS operation. The need to increase the non-critical region for higher thread counts means that, unless the increase translates into "useful work", it is not possible to improve the total kernel runtime significantly as the size of the non-critical region will dominate execution time.

4.3   Testing LL-SC Implementations

In Fig. 4 (a–b) we compare the performance of CAS and LL-SC strategies on TX2 and A64FX processors. We consider the Graviton3 independently later since, as we shall see below, it exhibits the peculiar characteristic that, when using the LL-SC strategy, the *average* time per increment *increases* with the number of increments each thread performs (i.e. on Graviton3, the LL-SC strategy is not invariant with respect to the number of operations performed). As the figure shows, on TX2 the LL-SC strategy is consistently faster than the CAS strategy, beating it by a factor of 2–3x in both integer and double kernels. On A64FX however, we observe two distinct trends. On the one hand, the two strategies are similar in the integer kernel, with CAS marginally outperforming LL-SC by a factor of roughly 1.2x. On the other hand, in the double kernel, the LL-SC strategy proves to be far superior to CAS. Indeed, in terms of scaling, LL-SC causes the double kernel to behave like the integer kernel, whereby the average time per iteration scales linearly with the number of threads, instead of quadratically as with CAS. In practice, this causes the *speedup* obtained by LL-SC vs. CAS to *increase* with the number of threads. For large threads counts, this means that the LL-SC strategy outperforms the CAS strategy by factors of over 20x. We presume this difference in behaviour on the A64FX is due to the load-linked instructions on the A64FX reserving the cache line for some time. In case of concurrent access, the CPU owning the cache line is favoured. This does not happen with CAS because the "plain" load before the CAS does not reserve the cache line. Nevertheless, this hypothesis necessitates confirmation from Fujitsu. We confirm that using LL-SC to implement the FP atomic update of the PI_ATOMIC kernel (Listing 1) solves the scaling issues initially observed on the A64FX, leading to a running time of approximately 6.6 s with 48 threads.

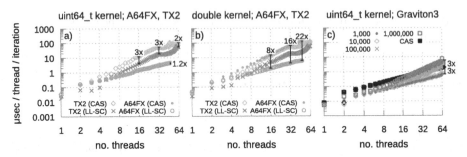

Fig. 4. Performance of LL-SC vs. CAS strategies. (a-b) Results on A64FX and TX2 CPUs for the integer (a) and double (b) kernels. (c) Results on Graviton3 for different iteration counts. In (c) the LL-SC runs are plotted in colour whilst CAS is plotted in black (all CAS lines fall on top of each other); furthermore, only results for the integer kernel are shown since the results for the double kernel are identical. Annotations show speedup ($t_{\text{slowest}}/t_{\text{fastest}}$).

In the case of the Graviton3 processor, a new behaviour emerges. So far, all results we have shown are stable in terms of the number of iterations run, i.e. there are no significant differences between running the kernels for a thousand, ten thousand, a hundred thousand, etc., iterations in terms of the (average) quantities we have shown. On Graviton3, however, this is not true. As shown in Fig. 4(c), when LL-SC is used on Graviton3, the *average* time per iteration *increases* with the number of iterations. In practice, this means that when using 64 threads the average time per iteration at 1,000,000 iterations is almost $10x$ higher than the average time at 1,000 iterations. This behaviour contrasts with that seen using the CAS strategy, where, as expected, the average time per iteration is invariant with respect to the number of iterations. Nevertheless, the LL-SC strategy can still be of interest on Graviton3. Indeed, for low iteration counts (below 100,000) LL-SC can be significantly faster than CAS. For example, at 1,000 iterations, LL-SC is around 2–3x faster than CAS across all thread counts. This means that in scenarios where threads are not expected to contend for the same memory location repeatedly for a long period of time, the LL-SC strategy should be preferred over the CAS strategy as it can provide very substantial speedups. However, given the scope for LL-SC to perform poorly, such an approach should encompass a fallback method that switches to the CAS strategy for instance after a number of failed LL-SC attempts has been reached.

4.4 Summary and Recommendations

Our study demonstrates that CAS instructions do not perform optimally on either the TX2 or the A64FX as the number of threads contending for the operation increases (Fig. 2). On A64FX, however, this behaviour only arises when the time to set up CAS reaches a critical threshold (Fig. 3). Below this threshold we observe *linear* scaling, the expected behaviour given the serialising nature of CAS. The linear behaviour is also observed on the Graviton3 and on the x86 systems used on our experiments. On all Arm-based systems that we tested, the older (pre-Armv8.1) LL-SC instructions can bring significant performance improvements (Fig. 4). On the TX2 and Graviton3, this translates into roughly 2-$3x$ performance improvement over the CAS instructions, though in the case of the Graviton3 this only applies when the number of CAS loops repeated in a quick succession is relatively low. On A64FX, however, the LL-SC instructions improve the runtime to the expected linear scaling; for a large number of threads, this translates into speedups of more than $20x$. Based on our results we make the following recommendations to users of Arm-based systems who would like to verify whether or not atomics are the root cause of poor performance:

1. Test the performance impact of LL-SC by disabling LSE support (and thus CAS instructions) in the compiler, i.e. do not simply rely on the default, CAS, to give the best performance.
2. If possible, verify the impact of reducing work inside the critical section.
3. Verify the impact of *adding* work *outside* the critical section.

The first recommendation can be achieved by using the architecture option `nolse` on GNU and LLVM compilers. Depending on the version of the compilers, the flag `-mno-outline-atomics` might also be necessary to disable wrappers that are otherwise automatically generated. As a caveat, we note that compilers tend to generate inefficient LL-SC code that might limit performance gains. This happens because compilers tend to wrap the LL-SC sequence in a "normal load" prior to the critical section, then do the load-linked (*after* the critical section), and finally check if the value loaded by the load-linked matches the value originally loaded by the normal load; if the values differ, they branch and try from the beginning, otherwise they attempt the store-conditional. A more efficient way of implementing the LL-SC sequence is to do it as we have shown in Listing 5, where the critical region is enclosed with load-linked and store-conditional instructions. Furthermore, it is worth noting that the last two recommendations are largely problem and algorithm dependent. Nevertheless, due to the key roles they play in CPUs such as the TX2 and A64FX, users and implementers ought to be aware of them. As an example, it might be worth moving work to immediately after an atomic operation on A64FX, so as to increase the size of the relevant non-critical region. Compilers and runtimes can help in this task by moving code unrelated to a CAS operation to nearer the CAS non-critical region, where it is safe to do so. The scheduler of a runtime can also fill the CAS non-critical region with pending work (for example, pending OpenMP tasks).

5 Related Work

The performance of CAS and other atomic operations has been extensively considered in the past for x86 targets [11,12,23,28,30]. Here we focus on AArch64 CPUs, which, by comparison, have received much less attention.

In [26] the authors study the performance of CAS and LL-SC instructions on Graviton2 and Kunpeng 920 processors using LockHammer [8] and Splash-3 [27]. They find that CAS instructions tend to perform better on Graviton2, whereas LL-SC usually does better on the Kunpeng 920. Crucially, they do not identify nor characterise the fundamentally different scaling trends we observed on A64FX and TX2, and they do not study how the Graviton2/3 respond to loops of varying duration—and therefore do not realise the speedups that LL-SC instructions can bring in short CAS loops on Graviton2/3 CPUs. Meanwhile, in [25] the authors consider the optimisation of the Hierarchical Mellor-Crummey and Scott (HMCS) lock [9,20] on Kunpeng 920 CPUs. They compare the performance of several variants of the HMCS lock compiled with and without LSE instructions (i.e. with CAS and LL-SC, respectively) and find that, in a single-thread scenario, the targets built without LSE outperform those built with it by 2–4x. However, they do not perform multi-threaded tests to compare the two approaches. Finally, in [10] the authors compare the performance of atomic integer operations implemented with and without LSE instructions on TX2 and A64FX processors. They do not restrict the LSE instructions considered to the cas instructions, and therefore they compare two significantly distinct implementations: one (LL-SC) similar to our integer kernel where a compare-and-swap loop is attempted until successfully performing an increment, and another that utilises ldadd instructions, and therefore needs no such loops. As could be expected, they find that the ldadd approach performs significantly faster than LL-SC.

6   Conclusions

In this paper we have shown that the CAS instructions introduced in Armv8.1 (LSE) do not always bring performance benefits, and can in fact induce a significant quadratic slowdown whereby the average time to successfully preform a CAS operation roughly quadruples as the number of threads attempting the operation concurrently doubles. On the A64FX this behaviour arises in codes where the time to prepare the CAS operation (i.e. the time between the first read from a memory location and the corresponding write attempt) rises above a critical threshold. Graviton3 does not exhibit these issues.

Furthermore, we have shown that the classic LL-SC instruction pairs should not be neglected as they can bring significant performance improvements. Implementing the CAS operation via LL-SC causes the A64FX to exhibit the expected linear behaviour instead of the quadratic slowdown experienced with the CAS instructions. In practice, for high thread counts this means that the LL-SC approach offers speedups of more than 20x over the CAS approach. LL-SC also offers 2–3x speedups on the TX2 and Graviton3, though in the latter case the performance of the LL-SC strategy drops significantly if a high number of CAS operations is performed in a quick succession.

Acknowledgements. This work used the ARCHER2 UK National Supercomputing Service (https://www.archer2.ac.uk); the Isambard UK National Tier-2 HPC Service (http://gw4.ac.uk/isambard/) operated by GW4 and the UK Met Office and funded by EPSRC (EP/P020224/1); and Fulhame, an HPE Apollo 70 system supplied to EPCC, the supercomputing centre at the University of Edinburgh, as part of the Catalyst UK programme, a collaboration with HPE, Arm and SUSE to accelerate the adoption of Arm based supercomputer applications in the UK. We would also like to thank John Linford (Nvidia) and Oliver Perks (Rivos Inc.) for the helpful technical inputs and discussions.

References

1. Alessandrini, V.: Concurrent access to shared data. In: Shared Memory Application Programming, pp. 101–127. Morgan Kaufmann, Boston (2016). https://doi.org/10.1016/B978-0-12-803761-4.00005-8
2. Arm Limited: ARMv8-A Memory Systems. Document ID 100941_0100_en (2017)
3. Arm Limited: Arm Neoverse V1 Core. DDI 101427, 0101-05 (2021)
4. Arm Limited: Do near or far atomics give the best performance on Neoverse systems? (2021). https://developer.arm.com/documentation/ka004706/1-0
5. Arm Limited: Arm Architecture Reference Manual for A-profile architecture. DDI 0487 H.a (2022)
6. Arm Limited: Arm® Architecture Reference Manual Supplement Armv9, for Armv9-A architecture profile. DDI 0608 B.a (2022)
7. Arm Limited: Overview of Arm Transactional Memory Extension. Document ID 102873_0100_en (2022)
8. Arm Limited: Synchronization Benchmarks (2022). https://github.com/ARM-software/synchronization-benchmarks
9. Chabbi, M., Fagan, M., Mellor-Crummey, J.: High performance locks for multi-level NUMA systems. In: Proceedings of the 20th ACM SIGPLAN Symposium on Principles and Practice of Parallel Programming, pp. 215–226. ACM, San Francisco (2015). https://doi.org/10.1145/2688500.2688503
10. Cownie, J.: Atomics in AArch64 (2021). https://cpufun.substack.com/p/atomics-in-aarch64
11. David, T., Guerraoui, R., Trigonakis, V.: Everything you always wanted to know about synchronization but were afraid to ask. In: Proceedings of the Twenty-Fourth ACM Symposium on Operating Systems Principles, pp. 33–48. ACM, Farminton Pennsylvania (2013). https://doi.org/10.1145/2517349.2522714
12. Dice, D., Hendler, D., Mirsky, I.: Lightweight contention management for efficient compare-and-swap operations. In: Wolf, F., Mohr, B., an Mey, D. (eds.) Euro-Par 2013. LNCS, vol. 8097, pp. 595–606. Springer, Heidelberg (2013). https://doi.org/10.1007/978-3-642-40047-6_60
13. Fujitsu Limited: A64FX Microarchitecture Manual. Revision 1.6 (2021). https://github.com/fujitsu/A64FX
14. Herlihy, M., Shavit, N., Luchangco, V., Spear, M.: The Art of Multiprocessor Programming. MA, second edn, Morgan Kaufmann, Cambridge (2021)
15. Hornung, R., Hones, H.: RAJA Performance Suite. Lawrence Livermore National Laboratory (LLNL), Livermore, CA (United States) (2017). https://doi.org/10.11578/DC.20201001.36
16. Intel Corporation: Intel® 64 and IA-32 Architectures Software Developer's Manual, Volume 3A: System Programming Guide, Part 1. Order Number 253668–077US (2022)

17. Klemm, M., Cownie, J.: 6 mutual exclusion and atomicity. In: High Performance Parallel Runtimes: Design and Implementation, pp. 146–193. De Gruyter Oldenbourg, Berlin(2021). https://doi.org/10.1515/9783110632729-006

18. Klemm, M., Cownie, J.: High Performance Parallel Runtimes: Design and Implementation. De Gruyter Textbook, De Gruyter Oldenbourg, Berlin (2021)

19. Makreshanski, D., Levandoski, J., Stutsman, R.: To lock, swap, or elide: on the interplay of hardware transactional memory and lock-free indexing. Proc. VLDB Endowment **8**(11), 1298–1309 (2015). https://doi.org/10.14778/2809974.2809990

20. Mellor-Crummey, J.M., Scott, M.L.: Algorithms for scalable synchronization on shared-memory multiprocessors. ACM Trans. Comput. Syst. **9**(1), 21–65 (1991). https://doi.org/10.1145/103727.103729

21. Michael, M.M., Scott, M.L.: Simple, fast, and practical non-blocking and blocking concurrent queue algorithms. In: Proceedings of the Fifteenth Annual ACM Symposium on Principles of Distributed Computing - PODC 1996, pp. 267–275. ACM Press, Philadelphia, Pennsylvania (1996). https://doi.org/10.1145/248052.248106

22. Moreland, K., et al.: VTK-m: accelerating the visualization toolkit for massively threaded architectures. IEEE Comput. Graph. Appl. **36**(3), 48–58 (2016). https://doi.org/10.1109/MCG.2016.48

23. Morrison, A., Afek, Y.: Fast concurrent queues for x86 processors. In: Proceedings of the 18th ACM SIGPLAN Symposium on Principles and Practice of Parallel Programming - PPoPP 2013, p. 103. ACM Press, Shenzhen (2013). https://doi.org/10.1145/2442516.2442527

24. Oberhauser, J., et al.: VSync: push-button verification and optimization for synchronization primitives on weak memory models. In: Proceedings of the 26th ACM International Conference on Architectural Support for Programming Languages and Operating Systems, pp. 530–545. ACM, Virtual USA (2021). https://doi.org/10.1145/3445814.3446748

25. Oberhauser, J., Oberhauser, L., Paolillo, A., Behrens, D., Fu, M., Vafeiadis, V.: Verifying and optimizing the HMCS lock for Arm servers. In: Echihabi, K., Meyer, R. (eds.) NETYS 2021. LNCS, vol. 12754, pp. 240–260. Springer, Cham (2021). https://doi.org/10.1007/978-3-030-91014-3_17

26. Pardos, V.S.: Characterization and Modeling of Atomic Memory Operations in Arm Based Architectures. Master's thesis, Universitat Politècnica de Catalunya, BarcelonaTech (2022). https://upcommons.upc.edu/handle/2117/363728

27. Sakalis, C., Leonardsson, C., Kaxiras, S., Ros, A.: Splash-3: a properly synchronized benchmark suite for contemporary research. In: 2016 IEEE International Symposium on Performance Analysis of Systems and Software (ISPASS), pp. 101–111. IEEE, Uppsala (2016). https://doi.org/10.1109/ISPASS.2016.7482078

28. Schweizer, H., Besta, M., Hoefler, T.: Evaluating the cost of atomic operations on modern architectures. In: 2015 International Conference on Parallel Architecture and Compilation (PACT), pp. 445–456. IEEE, San Francisco (2015). https://doi.org/10.1109/PACT.2015.24

29. Williams, B., Leidel, J., Wang, X., Donofrio, D., Chen, Y.: CircusTent: a benchmark suite for atomic memory operations. In: The International Symposium on Memory Systems, pp. 144–157. ACM, Washington (2020). https://doi.org/10.1145/3422575.3422789

30. Wu, H., Becchi, M.: Evaluating thread coarsening and low-cost synchronization on intel xeon phi. In: 2020 IEEE International Parallel and Distributed Processing Symposium (IPDPS), pp. 1018–1029. IEEE, New Orleans (2020). https://doi.org/10.1109/IPDPS47924.2020.00108

Analyzing Resource Utilization in an HPC System: A Case Study of NERSC's Perlmutter

Jie Li[1]([envelope]) [ID], George Michelogiannakis[2] [ID], Brandon Cook[2] [ID],
Dulanya Cooray[3] [ID], and Yong Chen[1] [ID]

[1] Texas Tech University, Lubbock, TX 79409, USA
{jie.li,yong.chen}@ttu.edu
[2] Berkeley Lab, Berkeley, CA 94720, USA
{mihelog,bgcook}@lbl.gov
[3] University of California, Berkeley, CA 94720, USA
dulanya@berkeley.edu

Abstract. Resource demands of HPC applications vary significantly. However, it is common for HPC systems to primarily assign resources on a per-node basis to prevent interference from co-located workloads. This gap between the coarse-grained resource allocation and the varying resource demands can lead to HPC resources being not fully utilized. In this study, we analyze the resource usage and application behavior of NERSC's Perlmutter, a state-of-the-art open-science HPC system with both CPU-only and GPU-accelerated nodes. Our one-month usage analysis reveals that CPUs are commonly not fully utilized, especially for GPU-enabled jobs. Also, around 64% of both CPU and GPU-enabled jobs used 50% or less of the available host memory capacity. Additionally, about 50% of GPU-enabled jobs used up to 25% of the GPU memory, and the memory capacity was not fully utilized in some ways for all jobs. While our study comes early in Perlmutter's lifetime thus policies and application workload may change, it provides valuable insights on performance characterization, application behavior, and motivates systems with more fine-grain resource allocation.

Keywords: HPC · Large-scale Characterization · Resource Utilization · GPU Utilization · Memory System · Disaggregated Memory

1 Introduction

In the past decade, High-Performance Computing (HPC) systems shifted from traditional clusters of CPU-only nodes to clusters of more heterogeneous nodes, where accelerators such as GPUs, FPGAs, and 3D-stacked memories have been introduced to increase compute capability [7]. Meanwhile, the collection of open-science HPC workloads is particularly diverse and recently increased its focus

© The Author(s) 2023
A. Bhatele et al. (Eds.): ISC High Performance 2023, LNCS 13948, pp. 297–316, 2023.
https://doi.org/10.1007/978-3-031-32041-5_16

on machine learning and deep learning [4]. Heterogeneous hardware combined with diverse workloads that have a wide range of resource requirements makes it difficult to achieve efficient resource management. Inefficient resource management threatens to not fully utilize expensive resources that can rapidly increase capital and operating costs. Previous studies have shown that the resources of HPC systems are often not fully utilized, especially memory [10,17,20].

NERSC's Perlmutter also adopts a heterogeneous design to bolster performance, where CPU-only nodes and GPU-accelerated nodes together provide a three to four times performance improvement over Cori [12,13], making Perlmutter rank 8th in the Top500 list as of December 2022. However, Perlmutter serves a diverse set of workloads from fusion energy, material science, climate research, physics, computer science, and many other science domains [11]. In addition, it is useful to gain insight into how well users are adapting to Perlmutter's heterogeneous architecture.

Consequently, it is desirable to understand how system resources in Perlmutter are used today. The results of such an analysis can help us evaluate current system configurations and policies, provide feedback to users and programmers, offer recommendations for future systems, and motivate research in new architectures and systems. In this work, we focus on understanding CPU utilization, GPU utilization, and memory capacity utilization (including CPU host memory and GPU memory) on Perlmutter. These resources are expensive, consume significant power, and largely dictate application performance.

In summary, our contributions are as follows:

- We conduct a thorough utilization study of CPUs, GPUs, and memory capacity in Perlmutter, a top 8 state-of-the-art HPC system that contains both CPU-only and GPU-accelerated nodes. We discover that both CPU-only and GPU-enabled jobs usually do not fully utilize key resources.
- We find that host memory capacity is largely not fully utilized for memory-balanced jobs, while memory-imbalanced jobs have significant temporal and/or spatial memory requirements.
- We show a positive correlation between job node hours, maximum memory usage, as well as temporal and spatial factors.
- Our findings motivate future research such as resource disaggregation, job scheduling that allows job co-allocation, and research that mitigates potential drawbacks from co-locating jobs.

2   Related Work

Many previous works have utilized job logs and correlated them with system logs to analyze job behavior in HPC systems [3,5,9,16,26]. For example, Zheng et al. correlated the Reliability, Availability, and Serviceability (RAS) logs with job logs to identify job failure and interruption characteristics [26]. Other works utilize performance monitoring infrastructure to characterize application and system performance in HPC [6,8,10,18,19,23,24]. In particular, the paper presented by Ji et al. analyzed various application memory usage in terms of object access patterns [6]. Patel et al. collected storage system data and performed a correlative analysis of the I/O behavior of large-scale applications [18]. The resource utilization analysis of the Titan system [24] summarized the CPU and GPU time, memory, and I/O utilization across a five-year period. Peng et al. focused on the memory subsystem and studied the temporal and spatial memory usage in two production HPC systems at LLNL [19]. Michelogiannakis et al. [10] performed a detailed analysis of key metrics sampled in NERSC's Cori to quantify the potential of resource disaggregation in HPC.

System analysis provides insights into resource utilization and therefore drives research on predicting and improving system performance [2,17,20,25]. Xie et.al developed a predictive model for file system performance on the Titan supercomputer [25]. Desh [2], proposed by Das et al., is a framework that builds a deep learning model based on system logs to predict node failures. Panwar et al. performed a large-scale study of system-level memory utilization in HPC and proposed exploiting unused memory via novel architecture support for OS [17]. Peng et al. performed a memory utilization analysis of HPC clusters and explored using disaggregated memory to support memory-intensive applications [20].

3   Background

3.1   System Overview

NERSC's latest system, Perlmutter [13], contains both CPU-only nodes and GPU-accelerated nodes with CPUs. Perlmutter has 1,536 GPU-accelerated nodes (12 racks, 128 GPU nodes per rack) and 3,072 CPU-only nodes (12 racks, 256 CPU nodes per rack). These nodes are connected through HPE/Cray's Slingshot Ethernet-based high performance network. Each GPU-accelerated node features four NVIDIA A100 Tensor Core GPUs and one AMD "Milan" CPU. The memory subsystem in each GPU node includes 40 GB of HBM2 per GPU and 256 GB of host DRAM. Each CPU-only node features two AMD "Milan" CPUs with 512 GB of memory. Perlmutter currently uses SLURM version 21.08.8 for resource management and job scheduling. Most users submit jobs to the regular queue that has no maximum number of nodes and a maximum allowable duration of 12 h.

The workload served by the NERSC systems includes applications from a diverse range of science domains, such as fusion energy, material science, climate research, physics, computer science, and more [11]. From the over 45-year history of the NERSC HPC facility and 12 generations of systems with diverse architectures, the traditional HPC workloads evolved very slowly despite the substantial underlying system architecture evolution [10]. However, the number of deep learning and machine learning workloads across different science disciplines has grown significantly in the past few years [22]. Furthermore, in our sampling time, Perlmutter was operating in parallel with Cori. Thus, the NERSC workload was divided among the two machines and Perlmutter's workload may change once Cori retires. Therefore, while our study is useful to (i) find the gap between resource provider and resource user and (ii) extract insights early in

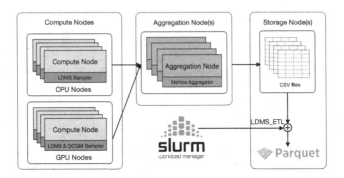

Fig. 1. Data are collected from CPU-only and GPU nodes, aggregated by aggregation nodes, stored in CSV files, and then processed using python's parquet library after being joined by job-level data provided by SLURM.

Perlmutter's lifetime to guide future policies and procurement, as in any HPC system the workload may change in the future. Still, our methodology can be reused in the future and on different systems.

3.2   Data Collection

NERSC collects system-wide monitoring data through the Lightweight Distributed Metric Service (LDMS) [1] and Nvidia's Data Center GPU Manager (DCGM) [14]. LDMS is deployed on both CPU-only and GPU nodes; it samples node-level metrics either from a subset of hardware performance counters or operating system data, such as memory usage, I/O operations, etc. DCGM is dedicated to collecting GPU-specific metrics, including GPU utilization, GPU memory utilization, NVlink traffic, etc. The sampling interval of both LDMS and DCGM is set by the system at 10 s. The monitoring data are aggregated into CSV files from which we build a processing pipeline for our analysis, shown in Fig. 1. As a last step, we merge the job metadata from SLURM (job ID, job step, allocated nodes, start time, end time, etc.) with the node-level monitoring metrics. The output from our flow is a set of parquet files.

Due to the large volume of data, we only sample Perlmutter from *November 1* to *December 1* of 2022. The system's monitoring infrastructure is still under deployment and some important traces such as memory bandwidth are not available at this time. A duration of one month is typically representative in an open-science HPC system [10], which we separately confirmed by sampling other periods. However, Perlmutter's workload may shift after the retirement of Cori as well as the introduction of policies such as allowing jobs to share nodes in a limited fashion. Still, a similar extensive study in Cori [10] that allows node sharing extracted similar resource usage conclusions as our study. Therefore, we anticipate that the key insights from our study in Perlmutter will remain unchanged, and we consider that studies conducted in the early stages of a system's lifetime hold significant value.

We measure CPU utilization from *cpu_id* (CPU idle time among all cores in a node, expressed as a percentage) reported from *vmstat* through LDMS [1]; we then calculate CPU utilization (as a percentage) as: $100 - cpu\_id$. GPU utilization (as a percentage) is directly read from DCGM reports [15]. Memory capacity utilization encompasses both the utilization of memory by user-space applications and the operating system. We use *fb_free* (framebuffer memory free) from DCGM to calculate GPU HBM2 utilization and *mem_free* (the amount of idle memory) from LDMS to calculate host DRAM capacity utilization. Memory capacity utilization (as a percentage) is calculated as $MemUtil = \frac{MemTotal - MemFree}{MemTotal} \times 100$, where $MemTotal$, as described above, is 512 GB for CPU nodes, 256 GB for the host memory of GPU nodes, and 40 GB for each GPU HBM2. $MemFree$ is the unused memory of a node, which essentially shows how much more memory the job could have used.

In order to understand the temporal and spatial imbalance of resource usage among jobs, we use the equations proposed in [19] to calculate the temporal imbalance factor ($RI_{temporal}$) and spatial imbalance factor ($RI_{spatial}$). These factors allow us to quantify the imbalance in resource usage over time and across nodes, respectively. For a job that requests N nodes and runs for time T, and its utilization of resource r on node n at time t is $U_{n,t}$, the temporal imbalance factor is defined as:

$$RI_{temporal}(r) = \max_{1 \leq n \leq N} \left(1 - \frac{\sum_{t=0}^{T} U_{n,t}}{\sum_{t=0}^{T} \max_{0 \leq t \leq T}(U_{n,t})}\right) \tag{1}$$

Similarly, the spatial imbalance factor is defined as:

$$RI_{spatial}(r) = 1 - \frac{\sum_{n=1}^{N} \max_{0 \leq t \leq T}(U_{n,t})}{\sum_{n=1}^{N} \max_{0 \leq t \leq T, 1 \leq n \leq N}(U_{n,t})} \tag{2}$$

Both $RI_{temporal}$ and $RI_{spatial}$ are bound within the range of $[0, 1]$. Ideally, a job uses fully all resources on all allocated nodes across the job's lifetime, corresponding to a spatial and temporal factor of 0. A larger factor value indicates a variation in resource utilization temporally/spatially and the job experiences more temporal/spatial imbalance.

We exclude jobs with a runtime of less than 1 h in our subsequent analysis, as such jobs are likely for testing or debugging purposes. Furthermore, since our sampling frequency is 10 s, it is difficult to capture peaks that last less than 10 s accurately. As a result, we concentrate on analyzing the behavior of sustained workloads. Table 1 summarizes job-level statistics in which each job's resource usage is represented by its maximum resource usage among all allocated nodes throughout its runtime.

3.3   Analysis Methods

To distill meaningful insights from our dataset we use *Cumulative Distribution Functions (CDFs)*, *Probability Density Functions (PDFs)*, and *Pearson correlation coefficients*. The CDF shows the probability that the variable takes a value

Table 1. Perlmutter measured data summary. Each job's resource utilization is represented by its peak usage.

Metric	Statistics of all jobs				Statistics of jobs $\geq 1h$			
	Median	Mean	Max	Std Dev	Median	Mean	Max	Std Dev
CPU Jobs					**21.75% of CPU jobs $\geq 1h$**			
Allocated nodes	1	6.51	1713	37.83	1	4.84	1477	25.43
Job duration (hours)	0.16	1.40	90.09	3.21	4.19	5.825	90.09	4.73
CPU util (%)	35.0	39.98	100.0	34.60	51.0	56.68	100.0	35.89
DRAM util (%)	13.29	22.79	98.62	23.65	18.61	33.69	98.62	30.88
GPU Jobs					**23.42% GPU jobs $\geq 1h$**			
Allocated nodes	1	4.66	1024	27.71	1	5.88	512	23.33
Job duration (hours)	0.30	1.14	13.76	2.42	2.2	4.12	13.76	3.67
Host CPU util (%)	4.0	19.60	100.0	23.53	4.0	18.00	100.0	24.81
Host DRAM util (%)	17.57	29.76	98.29	12.51	18.04	28.24	98.29	20.94
GPU util (%)	96.0	71.08	100.0	40.07	100.0	83.73	100.0	30.45
GPU HBM2 util (%)	16.28	34.07	100.0	37.49	18.88	40.23	100.0	36.33

less than or equal to x, for all values of x; the PDF shows the probability that the variable has a value equal to x. To evaluate the resource utilization of jobs, we analyze the maximum resource usage that occurred during each job's entire runtime, and we factor in the job's impact on the system by weighting the job's data points based on the number of nodes allocated and the duration of the job. We then calculate the CDF and PDF of job-level metrics using these weighted data points. The Pearson correlation coefficient, which is a statistical tool to identify potential relationships between two variables, is used to investigate the correlation between two characteristics. The correlation factor, or Pearson's r, ranges from -1.0 to 1.0; a positive value indicates a positive correlation, zero indicates no correlation, and a negative value indicates a negative correlation.

4   Results

In this section, we start with an overview of the job characteristics, including their size, duration, and the applications they represent. Then we use CDF and PDF plots to investigate the resource usage pattern across jobs, followed by the characterization of the temporal and spatial variability of jobs. Lastly, we assess the correlation between the different resource types assigned to each job.

4.1   Workloads Overview

We divide jobs into six groups by the number of allocated nodes and calculate the percentage of each group compared to the total number of jobs. The details are shown in Table 2. As shown, 68.10% of CPU jobs and 65.89% of GPU jobs only request one node, while large jobs that allocate more than 128 nodes are only

Table 2. Job size and duration. Jobs shorter than one hour are excluded.

Job Size (Nodes)		1	(1, 4]	(4, 16]	(16, 64]	(64, 128]	(128, 128+)
CPU Jobs	Total Number: 21706	14783	2486	3738	550	62	87
	Percentage (%)	**68.10**	11.45	17.22	2.54	0.29	0.40
GPU Jobs	Total Number: 24217	15924	5358	1837	706	318	74
	Percentage (%)	**65.89**	22.04	7.56	2.90	1.31	0.30
Job Duration (Hours)		[1, 3]	(3, 6]	(6, 12]	(12, 24]	(24, 48]	(48, 48+)
CPU Jobs	Total Number: 21706	8879	4109	6300	2393	15	10
	Percentage (%)	**40.90**	18.94	29.02	11.02	0.07	0.05
GPU Jobs	Total Number: 24217	14495	3888	4916	918	0	0
	Percentage (%)	**59.86**	16.05	20.30	3.79	0	0

0.40% and 0.30% on CPU and GPU nodes, respectively. Also, 40.90% of CPU jobs and 59.86% of GPU jobs execute for less than three hours (as aforementioned, jobs with less than one hour of runtime are discarded from the dataset). We also observe that about 88.86% of CPU jobs and 96.21% of GPU jobs execute less than 12 h, and only a few CPU jobs and no GPU jobs exceed 48 h. This is largely a result of policy since Perlmutter's regular queue allows a maximum of 12 h. However, jobs using a special reservation can exceed this limit [13].

Next, we analyze the job names obtained from Slurm's *sacct* and estimate the corresponding applications through empirical analysis. Although this approach has limitations, such as the inability to identify jobs with undescriptive names such as "python" or "exec", it still offers useful information. Figure 2 shows that most node hours on both CPU-only and GPU-accelerated nodes are consumed by a few recurring applications. The top four CPU-only applications account for 50% of node hours, with ATLAS alone accounting for over a quarter. Over 600 CPU applications make up only 22% of the node hours, using less than 2% each (not labeled on the pie chart). On GPU-accelerated nodes, the top 11 applications consume 75% of node hours, while the other 400+ applications make up the remaining 25%. The top six GPU applications account for 58% of node hours, with usage roughly evenly divided.

We further classify system workloads into three groups according to their maximum *host* memory capacity utilization. In particular, jobs using less than 25% of the total host memory capacity are categorized as low intensity, jobs that use 25–50% are considered moderate intensity, and those exceeding 50% are classified as high intensity [19]. Node-hours and the number of jobs can also be decomposed in these three categories, where node-hours is calculated by multiplying the total number of allocated nodes by the runtime (duration) of each job.

As shown in Fig. 3a, CPU-only nodes have about 63% of low memory capacity intensity jobs. Although moderate and high memory intensity jobs are 37% of the

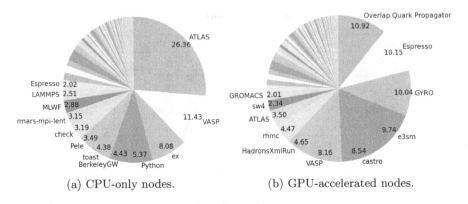

(a) CPU-only nodes.   (b) GPU-accelerated nodes.

Fig. 2. Decomposition of node-hours by applications. Infrequent applications are not labeled.

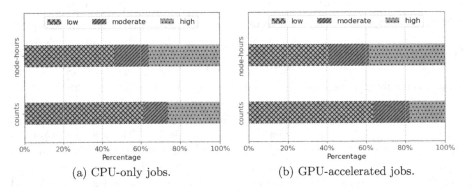

(a) CPU-only jobs.   (b) GPU-accelerated jobs.

Fig. 3. Node-hours and job counts by host memory capacity intensity (utilization).

total CPU jobs, they consume about 54% of the total node-hours. This indicates that moderate and high memory intensity jobs are likely to use more nodes and/or run for a longer time. This observation holds true for GPU nodes in which 37% of memory-intensive jobs compose 58% of the total node-hours. In addition, we observe that even though the percentage of high memory intensity jobs on GPU nodes (17%) is less than that on CPU nodes (26%), the corresponding percentages of the node-hours are close, indicating that high memory intensity GPU jobs consume more nodes and/or run for a longer time than high memory intensity CPU jobs.

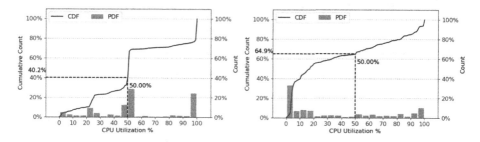

Fig. 4. Maximum CPU utilization of CPU node-hours (left) and GPU node-hours (right).

Observation: The analysis shows that both CPU and GPU nodes have around two-thirds of jobs that only occupy one node. GPU jobs have a higher proportion of short-lived jobs that run for less than three hours compared to CPU jobs. Additionally, jobs rarely allocate more than 128 nodes, which suggests that the majority of jobs can be accommodated within a single rack in the Perlmutter system. Furthermore, the analysis indicates that jobs that are intensive in host memory tend to consume more node-hours, despite representing a relatively small proportion of total jobs.

4.2 Resource Utilization

This subsection analyzes resource usage among jobs and compares the characteristics of CPU-only jobs and GPU-enabled jobs. We consider the maximum resource usage of a job across all allocated nodes and throughout its entire runtime to represent its resource utilization because maximum utilization must be accounted for when scheduling a job in a system. As jobs with larger sizes and longer durations have a greater impact on system resource utilization, and the system architecture is optimized for node-hours, we calculate the resource utilization for each job and multiply the number of data points we add to our dataset that measure that utilization by the job's node-hours.

CPU Utilization. Figure 4 shows the distribution of the maximum CPU utilization of CPU jobs and GPU jobs weighted by node-hours. As shown, 40.2% of CPU node-hours have at most 50% CPU utilization, and about 28.7% of CPU node-hours has a maximum CPU utilization of 50–55%. In addition, 24.4% of jobs reach over 95% CPU utilization, creating a spike at the end of the CDF line. Over one-third of CPU jobs only utilize up to 50% of the CPU resources available, which could potentially be attributed to Simultaneous Multi-threading (SMT) in the Milan architecture. While SMT can provide benefits for specific types of workloads, such as communication-bound or I/O-bound parallel applications, it may not necessarily improve performance for all applications and may even reduce it in some cases [21]. Consequently, users may choose to disable SMT,

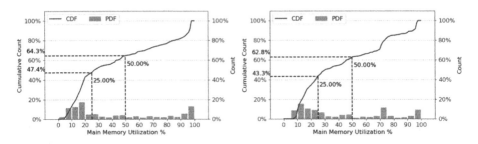

Fig. 5. Maximum host memory capacity utilization of CPU node-hours (left) and GPU node-hours (right).

leading to half of the logical cores being unused during runtime. Additionally, certain applications are not designed to use SMT at all, resulting in a reported utilization of only 50% in our analysis even with 100% compute core utilization.

In contrast to CPU jobs, GPU-enabled jobs exhibit a distinct distribution of CPU usage, with the majority of jobs concentrated in the 0–5% bin and only a small fraction of jobs utilizing the CPUs in full. We also obverse that node-hours with high utilization of both CPU and GPU resources are rare, with only 2.47% of node-hours utilizing over 90% of these resources (not depicted). This is because the CPUs in GPU nodes are primarily tasked with data preprocessing, data retrieval, and loading computed data, while the bulk of the computational load is offloaded to the GPUs. Therefore, the utilization of the CPUs in GPU-enabled jobs is comparatively low, as their primary function is to support and facilitate the GPU's heavy computational tasks.

Host DRAM Utilization. We plot the CDF and PDF of the maximum host memory utilization of job node-hours in Fig. 5. To help visualize the distribution of memory usage, the red vertical lines at the X axis indicate the 25% and 50% thresholds that we previously used to classify jobs into three memory intensity groups. A considerable fraction of the jobs on both CPU and GPU nodes use between 5% and 25% of host memory capacity, respectively. Specifically, 47.4% of all CPU jobs and 43.3% of all GPU jobs fall within these ranges. The distribution of memory utilization, like that of CPU utilization, displays spikes at the end of the CDF lines due to a small percentage of jobs (12.8% for CPU and 9.5% for GPU, respectively) that fully exhaust host memory capacity.

Our results indicate that a significant proportion of both CPU and GPU jobs, 64.3% and 62.8% respectively, use less than 50% of the available memory capacity. As a reminder, the available host memory capacity is 512 GB in CPU nodes and 256 GB in GPU nodes. While memory capacity is also not fully utilized in Cori [10], the higher memory capacity per node in Perlmutter exacerbates the challenge of fully utilizing the available memory capacity.

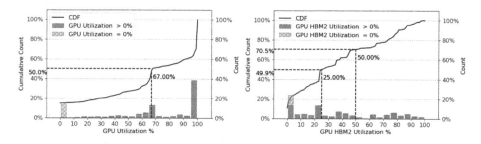

Fig. 6. Maximum GPU (left) and HBM2 capacity (right) utilization of GPU-hours.

GPU Resources. The utilization of GPUs in DCGM indicates the percentage of time that GPU kernels are active during the sampling period, and it is reported per GPU instead of per node. Therefore, we analyze GPU utilization in terms of GPU-hours instead of node-hours. The left subfigure of Fig. 6 displays the CDF plot of maximum GPU utilization, indicating that 50% of GPU jobs achieve a maximum GPU utilization of up to 67%, while 38.45% of GPU jobs reach a maximum GPU utilization of over 95%. To assess the idle time of GPUs allocated to jobs, we separate the GPU utilization of zero from other ranges in the PDF histogram plot. As shown in the green bar, approximately 15% of GPU hours are fully idle.

Similarly, we measure the maximum GPU HBM2 capacity utilization for each allocated GPU during the runtime of each job. As shown in the right subfigure of Fig. 6, the HBM2 utilization is close to evenly distributed from 0% to 100%, resulting in a nearly linear CDF line. The green bar in the PDF plot suggests that 10.6% of jobs use no HBM2 capacity, which is lower than the percentage of GPU idleness (15%). This finding is intriguing as it indicates that even though some allocated GPUs are idle, their corresponding GPU memory is still utilized, possibly by other GPUs or for other purposes.

The GPU resources' idleness can be attributed to the current configuration of GPU-accelerated nodes, which are not allowed to be shared by jobs at the same time. As a result, each user has exclusive access to four GPUs per node, even if they require fewer resources. Sharing nodes may be enabled in the future, potentially leading to more efficient use of GPU resources.

Observation: After analyzing CPU and host DRAM utilization, we find that GPU node-hours consume fewer CPU and host memory resources in comparison to CPU node-hours, likely because the computation is offloaded to GPUs. Although most GPU-hours reach high GPU utilization rates, we find that 15% of them have fully idle GPUs, and 10.6% of GPU-hours do not utilize HBM2 capacity, due to current configurations that do not allow for job sharing of GPU nodes. Allowing GPU sharing could alleviate the idleness of GPU resources and increase their average utilization.

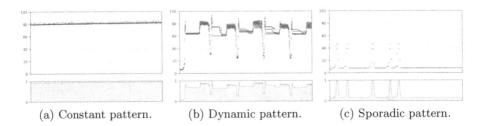

| (a) Constant pattern. | (b) Dynamic pattern. | (c) Sporadic pattern. |

Fig. 7. Temporal patterns illustrated with the memory capacity utilization metrics of randomly selected jobs in Perlmutter, one representative job for each of the three categories. Each color represents the memory capacity utilization (%) of each node assigned to the job over the job's runtime. The area plots at the bottom show the normalized metrics for the node that has the maximum temporal factor among nodes allocated to the job; the percentage of the blank area corresponds to the value of $RI_{temporal}$ of a job. A larger blank area indicates more temporal imbalance.

4.3 Temporal Characteristics

Memory capacity utilization can become temporally imbalanced when a job does not utilize memory capacity evenly over time. Temporal imbalance is particularly common in applications that consist of phases that require different memory capacities. In such cases, a job may require significant amounts of memory capacity during some phases, while utilizing much less during others, resulting in a temporal imbalance of memory utilization.

We classify jobs into three patterns by the $RI_{temporal}$ value of host DRAM utilization: *constant*, *dynamic*, and *sporadic* [19]. Jobs with $RI_{temporal}$ lower than 0.2 are classified in the *constant* pattern, where memory utilization does not show significant change over time. Jobs with $RI_{temporal}$ between 0.2 and 0.6 are in the *dynamic* pattern, where jobs have frequent and considerable memory utilization changes. The *sporadic* pattern is defined by $RI_{temporal}$ larger than 0.6. In this pattern, jobs have infrequent and sporadic higher memory capacity usage than the rest of the time.

Figure 7 illustrates three memory utilization patterns that were constructed from our monitoring data. Each color in the scatter plot represents a different node allocated to the job. The constant pattern job shows a nearly constant memory capacity utilization of about 80% across all allocated nodes for its entire runtime, resulting in the bottom area plot being almost fully covered. The dynamic pattern job also exhibits similar behavior across its allocated nodes, but due to variations over time, the shaded area has several bumps and dips, resulting in an increase in the blank area. For the sporadic pattern job, the memory utilization readings of all nodes have the same temporal pattern, with sporadic spikes and low memory capacity usage between spikes, resulting in the blank area occupying most of the area and indicating poor temporal balance.

The CDFs and PDFs of the host memory temporal imbalance factor of CPU jobs and GPU jobs are illustrated in Fig. 8, in which two vertical red lines separate the jobs into three temporal patterns. Overall, both CPU jobs and GPU

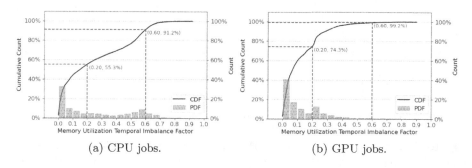

(a) CPU jobs.   (b) GPU jobs.

Fig. 8. CDFs and PDFs of the *temporal* factor of host memory capacity utilization across nodes. The larger the value of the temporal factor, the more temporal imbalance.

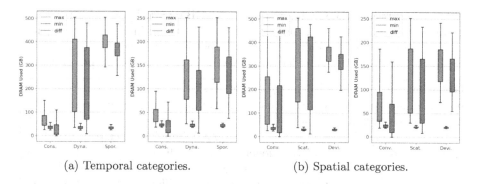

(a) Temporal categories.   (b) Spatial categories.

Fig. 9. Host DRAM distribution by temporal and spatial categories. The left portion of each subfigure represents CPU jobs and the right portion GPU jobs.

jobs have good temporal balance: 55.3% of CPU jobs and 74.3% of GPU jobs belong to the constant pattern, i.e., their $RI_{temporal}$ values are below 0.2. Jobs on CPU nodes have a higher percentage of dynamic patterns: 35.9% of CPU jobs have $RI_{temporal}$ value between 0.2 and 0.4, while GPU jobs have 24.9% in the dynamic pattern. On GPU nodes, we only observe very few jobs (0.8%) in the sporadic pattern, which means the cases of host DRAM having severe temporal imbalance are few.

We further analyze the memory capacity utilization distribution of jobs in each temporal pattern; the results are shown in Fig. 9a. We extract the maximum, minimum, and difference between maximum and minimum memory capacity used from jobs in each category and present the distribution in box plots. The minimum memory used for all categories on the same nodes is similar: about 25 GB and 19 GB on CPU and GPU nodes, respectively. 75% of jobs in the constant category on CPU nodes use less than 86 GB while 75% jobs on GPU nodes use less than 56 GB. As 55.3% CPU jobs and 74.3% GPU jobs are in the constant category, 41.5% CPU jobs and 55.7% GPU jobs do not use 426 GB and 200 GB of the available capacity, respectively. The maximum memory used in the con-

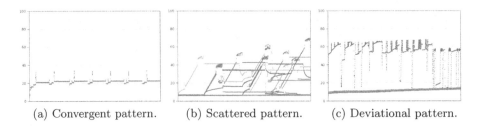

(a) Convergent pattern.   (b) Scattered pattern.   (c) Deviational pattern.

Fig. 10. Spatial patterns illustrated with the memory capacity utilization metrics of randomly selected jobs in Perlmutter, one representative job for each of the three categories. Each color represents memory utilization (%) of a different node allocated to each job.

stant pattern is 150 GB on CPU nodes and 94 GB on GPU nodes, both of which do not exceed half of the memory capacity. Jobs using high memory capacity are only observed in dynamic and sporadic patterns, where 75% sporadic jobs use up to 429 GB on CPU nodes and 189 GB on GPU nodes, respectively.

> **Observation:** Our analysis suggests that GPU nodes exhibit a greater proportion of jobs with temporal balance in host DRAM usage compared to CPU nodes. While over half of both CPU and GPU jobs fall under the category of temporal constant jobs, jobs with temporal imbalance, characterized by dynamic and sporadic patterns, generally require higher maximum memory capacity compared to constant pattern jobs. Furthermore, the distribution of host memory capacity usage among jobs with different temporal patterns reveals that memory capacity is not fully utilized for constant pattern jobs, whereas dynamic and sporadic pattern jobs may achieve high memory capacity utilization at some point during their runtime.

4.4 Spatial Characteristics

The job scheduler and resource manager of current HPC systems do not consider the varying resource requirements of individual tasks within a job, leading to spatial imbalances in resource utilization across nodes. One common type of spatial imbalance is when a job requires a significant amount of memory in a small number of nodes, while other nodes use relatively less memory. Spatial imbalance of memory capacity quantifies the uneven usage of memory capacity across nodes allocated to a job.

To characterize the spatial imbalance of jobs, we use Eq. 2 presented in Sect. 3.2 to calculate the spatial factor $RI\_spatial$ of memory capacity usage for each job. Similar to the temporal factor, $RI\_spatial$ falls in the range $[0, 1]$ and larger values represent higher spatial imbalance. Jobs are classified into one of three spatial patterns: (i) *convergent* pattern that has $RI\_spatial$ less than 0.2, (ii) *scattered* pattern that has $RI\_spatial$ between 0.2 and 0.6, and (iii) *deviational* pattern with its $RI\_spatial$ larger than 0.6.

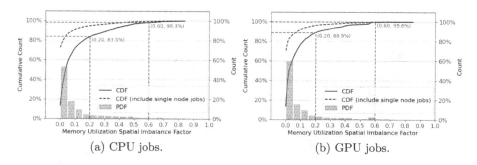

(a) CPU jobs.   (b) GPU jobs.

Fig. 11. CDFs and PDFs of the *spatial* factor of host memory capacity utilization of jobs. The larger the value of the spatial factor, the more spatial imbalance.

As shown in the examples in Fig. 10, a job that exhibits a convergent pattern has similar or identical memory capacity usage among all of its assigned nodes. A job with a scattered pattern shows diverse memory usage and different peak memory usage among its nodes. A spatial deviational pattern job has a similar memory usage pattern in most of its nodes but has one or several nodes deviate from the bunch. It is worth noting that low spatial imbalance does not indicate low temporal imbalance. The spatial convergent pattern job shown in the example has several spikes in memory usage and therefore is a temporal sporadic pattern.

We present the CDFs and PDFs of the job-wise host memory capacity spatial factor in Fig. 11. Overall, 83.5% of CPU jobs and 88.9% of GPU nodes are in the convergent pattern and very few jobs are in the deviational pattern. Because jobs that allocate a single node always have a spatial imbalance factor of zero, if we include single-node jobs, the overall memory spatial balance is even better: 94.7% for CPU jobs and 96.2% for GPU jobs.

We combine the host memory spatial pattern with the host memory capacity usage behavior in each job and plot the distribution of memory capacity utilization by spatial patterns; the results are shown in Fig. 9b. Similar to the distribution of the temporal patterns, we use the maximum, minimum, and difference of job memory to evaluate the memory utilization imbalance. Spatial convergent jobs have relatively low memory usage. As shown in the green box plots, 75% of spatial convergent jobs (upper quartile) use less than 254 GB on CPU nodes and 95 GB on GPU nodes. Given that spatial convergent jobs account for over 94% of total jobs, over 70% of jobs have 258 GB and 161 GB of memory capacity unused for CPU and GPU nodes, respectively. Memory imbalance, i.e., the difference between the maximum and minimum memory capacity usage of a job (red box plots), is also the lowest in convergent pattern jobs. For spatial-scattered jobs on CPU nodes, even though they are a small portion of the total jobs, the memory difference spans a large range: from 115 GB at 25% percentile to 426 GB at 75% percentile. Spatial deviational CPU jobs have a shorter span in memory imbalance compared to GPU jobs; it only ranges from 286 GB to 350 GB at the lower and upper quartiles, respectively.

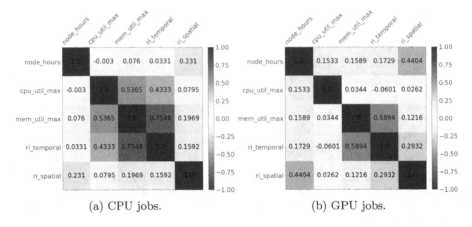

(a) CPU jobs.   (b) GPU jobs.

Fig. 12. Correlation of job node-hours, maximum memory capacity used, temporal, and spatial factors.

Observation: Our analysis shows that a significant number of CPU and GPU jobs on Perlmutter have a convergent pattern of spatial balance for host memory capacity usage across allocated nodes. Even after eliminating single-node jobs, the proportion of jobs with a convergent spatial pattern remains high, suggesting that Perlmutter's jobs generally have good spatial balance. However, jobs with scattered and deviational spatial patterns, albeit fewer in number, tend to consume more memory capacity in some allocated nodes, leading to uneven memory capacity utilization across nodes and some nodes exhibiting low memory capacity utilization.

4.5 Correlations

We conduct an analysis of the relationships between various job characteristics on Perlmutter, including job size and duration (measured as $node\_hours$), maximum CPU and host memory capacity utilization, and temporal and spatial factors. The results of the analysis are presented in a correlation matrix in Fig. 12. Our findings show that for both CPU and GPU nodes, job node-hours are positively correlated with the spatial imbalance factor ($ri\_spatial$). This suggests that larger jobs with longer runtimes are more likely to experience spatial imbalance. Maximum CPU utilization is strongly positively correlated with host memory capacity utilization and temporal factors in CPU jobs, while the correlation is weak in GPU jobs. Moreover, the temporal imbalance factor ($ri\_temporal$) is positively correlated with maximum memory capacity utilization (mem_max), with correlation coefficients (r-value) of 0.75 for CPU jobs and 0.59 for GPU jobs. These strong positive correlations suggest that jobs requiring a significant amount of memory are more likely to experience temporal memory imbalance, which is consistent with our previous observations. Finally, we find a slight positive correlation (r-value of 0.16 for CPU jobs and 0.29 for GPU jobs) between spatial and temporal imbalance factors, indicating that spatially imbalanced jobs are also more likely to experience temporal imbalance.

5   Discussion and Conclusion

In light of the increasing demands of HPC and the varied resource requirements of open-science workloads, there is a risk of not fully utilizing expensive resources. To better understand this issue, we conducted a comprehensive analysis of memory, CPU, and GPU utilization in NERSC's Perlmutter. Our analysis spanned *one month* and yielded important insights. Specifically, we found that only a quarter of CPU node-hours achieved high CPU utilization, and CPUs on GPU-accelerated nodes were typically utilized for only 0–5% of the node-hours. Moreover, while a significant proportion of GPU-hours demonstrated high GPU utilization (over 95%), more than 15% of GPU-hours had idle GPUs. Moreover, both CPU host memory and GPU HBM2 were not fully utilized for the majority of node-hours. Interestingly, jobs with temporal balance consistently did not fully utilize memory capacity, while those with temporal imbalance had varying idle memory capacity over time. Finally, we observed that jobs with spatial imbalance did not have high memory capacity utilization for all allocated nodes.

Insufficient resource utilization can be attributed to various application characteristics, as similar issues have been observed in other HPC systems. Although simultaneous multi-threading can potentially improve CPU utilization and mitigate stalls resulting from cache misses, it may not be suitable for all applications. Furthermore, GPUs, being a new compute resource to NERSC users, may be currently not fully utilized because users and applications are still adapting to the new system, and the current configurations are not optimized yet to support GPU node sharing. Furthermore, it is important to note that in most systems, various parameters such as memory bandwidth and capacity are interdependent. For instance, the number and type of memory modules significantly impact memory bandwidth and capacity. Therefore, when designing a system, it may be challenging to fully utilize every parameter while optimizing others. This may result in some resources being not fully utilized to improve the overall performance of the system. Thus, not fully utilizing system resources can be an intentional trade-off in the design of HPC systems.

Our study provides valuable insights for system operators to understand and monitor resource utilization patterns in HPC workloads. However, the scope of our analysis was limited by the availability of monitoring data, which did not include information on network and memory bandwidth as well as file system statistics. Despite this limitation, our findings can help system operators identify areas where resources are not fully utilized and optimize system configuration.

Our analysis also reveals several opportunities for future research. For instance, given that 64% of jobs use only half or less of the on-node host DRAM capacity, it is worth exploring the possibility of disaggregating the host memory and using a remote memory pool. This remote pool can be local to a rack, group of racks, or the entire system. Our job size analysis indicates that most jobs can be accommodated within the compute resources provided by a single rack, suggesting that rack-level disaggregation can fulfill the requirements of most Perlmutter jobs if they are placed in a single rack. Furthermore, a disaggregated system could consider temporal and spatial characteristics when scheduling jobs since high memory utilization is often observed in memory-unbalanced jobs. Such jobs can be given priority for using disaggregated memory.

Another promising area for improving resource utilization is to reevaluate node sharing for specific applications with compatible temporal and spatial characteristics. One of the main challenges in job co-allocation is the potential for shared resources, such as memory, to become saturated at high core counts and significantly degrade job performance. However, our analysis reveals that both CPU and memory resources are not fully utilized, indicating that there may be room for co-allocation without negatively impacting performance. The observation that memory-balanced jobs typically consume relatively low memory capacity suggests that it may be possible to co-locate jobs with memory-balanced jobs to reduce the probability of contention for memory capacity. By optimizing resource allocation and reducing the likelihood of resource contention, these approaches can help maximize system efficiency and performance.

Acknowledgment. We would like to express our gratitude to the anonymous reviewers for their insightful comments and suggestions. We also thank Brian Austin, Nick Wright, Richard Gerber, Katie Antypas, and the rest of the NERSC team for their feedback. This research used resources of the National Energy Research Scientific Computing Center (NERSC), a U.S. Department of Energy Office of Science User Facility located at Lawrence Berkeley National Laboratory, operated under Contract No. DE-AC02-05CH11231. This work was supported by the Director, Office of Science, of the U.S. Department of Energy under Contract No. DE-AC02-05CH11231. This research was supported in part by the National Science Foundation under grants OAC-1835892 and CNS-1817094.

References

1. Agelastos, A., et al.: The lightweight distributed metric service: a scalable infrastructure for continuous monitoring of large scale computing systems and applications. In: SC 2014: Proceedings of the International Conference for High Performance Computing, Networking, Storage and Analysis, pp. 154–165. IEEE (2014)
2. Das, A., Mueller, F., Siegel, C., Vishnu, A.: Desh: deep learning for system health prediction of lead times to failure in HPC. In: Proceedings of the 27th International Symposium on High-Performance Parallel and Distributed Computing, pp. 40–51 (2018)
3. Di, S., Gupta, R., Snir, M., Pershey, E., Cappello, F.: LogAider: a tool for mining potential correlations of HPC log events. In: 2017 17th IEEE/ACM International Symposium on Cluster, Cloud and Grid Computing (CCGRID), pp. 442–451. IEEE (2017)
4. Gil, Y., Greaves, M., Hendler, J., Hirsh, H.: Amplify scientific discovery with artificial intelligence. Science **346**(6206), 171–172 (2014)

5. Gupta, S., Patel, T., Engelmann, C., Tiwari, D.: Failures in large scale systems: long-term measurement, analysis, and implications. In: Proceedings of the International Conference for High Performance Computing, Networking, Storage and Analysis, pp. 1–12 (2017)
6. Ji, X., et al.: Understanding object-level memory access patterns across the spectrum. In: Proceedings of the International Conference for High Performance Computing, Networking, Storage and Analysis, pp. 1–12 (2017)
7. Kindratenko, V., Trancoso, P.: Trends in high-performance computing. Comput. Sci. Eng. **13**(3), 92–95 (2011)
8. Li, J., et al.: MonSTer: an out-of-the-box monitoring tool for high performance computing systems. In: 2020 IEEE International Conference on Cluster Computing (CLUSTER), pp. 119–129. IEEE (2020)
9. Madireddy, S., et al.: Analysis and correlation of application I/O performance and system-wide I/O activity. In: 2017 International Conference on Networking, Architecture, and Storage (NAS), pp. 1–10. IEEE (2017)
10. Michelogiannakis, G., et al.: A case for intra-rack resource disaggregation in HPC. ACM Trans. Archit. Code Optim. (TACO) **19**(2), 1–26 (2022)
11. NERSC: NERSC-10 Workload Analysis (Data from 2018) (2018). https://portal. nersc.gov/project/m888/nersc10/workload/N10_Workload_Analysis.latest.pdf
12. NERSC: Cori (2022). https://www.nersc.gov/systems/cori/
13. NERSC: Perlmutter (2022). https://www.nersc.gov/systems/perlmutter/
14. NVIDA: NVIDIA DCGM (2022). https://developer.nvidia.com/dcgm
15. NVIDA: NVIDIA DCGM Exporter (2022). https://github.com/NVIDIA/dcgm-exporter/blob/main/etc/dcp-metrics-included.csv
16. Oliner, A., Stearley, J.: What supercomputers say: a study of five system logs. In: 37th annual IEEE/IFIP International Conference on Dependable Systems and Networks (DSN 2007), pp. 575–584. IEEE (2007)
17. Panwar, G., et al.: Quantifying memory underutilization in HPC systems and using it to improve performance via architecture support. In: Proceedings of the 52nd Annual IEEE/ACM International Symposium on Microarchitecture, pp. 821–835 (2019)
18. Patel, T., Byna, S., Lockwood, G.K., Tiwari, D.: Revisiting I/O behavior in large-scale storage systems: the expected and the unexpected. In: Proceedings of the International Conference for High Performance Computing, Networking, Storage and Analysis, pp. 1–13 (2019)
19. Peng, I., Karlin, I., Gokhale, M., Shoga, K., Legendre, M., Gamblin, T.: A holistic view of memory utilization on HPC systems: current and future trends. In: The International Symposium on Memory Systems, pp. 1–11 (2021)
20. Peng, I., Pearce, R., Gokhale, M.: On the memory underutilization: exploring disaggregated memory on HPC systems. In: 2020 IEEE 32nd International Symposium on Computer Architecture and High Performance Computing (SBAC-PAD), pp. 183–190. IEEE (2020)
21. Tau Leng, R.A., Hsieh, J., Mashayekhi, V., Rooholamini, R.: An empirical study of hyper-threading in high performance computing clusters. Linux HPC Revolution 45 (2002)
22. Thomas, R., Stephey, L., Greiner, A., Cook, B.: Monitoring scientific python usage on a supercomputer (2021)
23. Turner, A., McIntosh-Smith, S.: A survey of application memory usage on a national supercomputer: an analysis of memory requirements on ARCHER. In: Jarvis, S., Wright, S., Hammond, S. (eds.) PMBS 2017. LNCS, vol. 10724, pp. 250–260. Springer, Cham (2018). https://doi.org/10.1007/978-3-319-72971-8_13

24. Wang, F., Oral, S., Sen, S., Imam, N.: Learning from five-year resource-utilization data of titan system. In: 2019 IEEE International Conference on Cluster Computing (CLUSTER), pp. 1–6. IEEE (2019)

25. Xie, B., et al.: Predicting output performance of a petascale supercomputer. In: Proceedings of the 26th International Symposium on High-Performance Parallel and Distributed Computing, pp. 181–192 (2017)

26. Zheng, Z., et al.: Co-analysis of RAS log and job log on blue Gene/P. In: 2011 IEEE International Parallel & Distributed Processing Symposium, pp. 840–851. IEEE (2011)

Overcoming Weak Scaling Challenges in Tree-Based Nearest Neighbor Time Series Mining

Amir Raoofy[1,4(✉)], Roman Karlstetter[2,4], Martin Schreiber[3,4], Carsten Trinitis[4], and Martin Schulz[4]

[1] Leibniz Supercomputing Centre, Munich, Germany
amir.raoofy@lrz.de
[2] IfTA GmbH, Puchheim, Germany
roman.karlstetter@ifta.com
[3] Université Grenoble Alpes (UGA), Grenoble, France
martin.schreiber@univ-grenoble-alpes.fr
[4] Technical University of Munich, Munich, Germany
{carsten.trinitis,martin.w.j.schulz}@tum.de

Abstract. The mining of time series data plays an important role in modern information retrieval and monitoring infrastructures. In particular, the identification of similarities within and across large time series is of great importance in analytics and knowledge discovery. For this task, the matrix profile similarity indexing approach, which encodes the correlations among snapshots of a time series, is well-established. However, it is computationally expensive, especially for long time series, as existing exact approaches mostly rely on exhaustive, exact query (search) operations and are inefficient. Similarly, existing approximate approaches are limited with respect to parallelism, scalability, or their extent of practicality. We, therefore, focus on an approximate parallel tree-based nearest-neighbors approach and address the weak scaling challenges raised when applied to large time series in HPC settings.

We build on the existing concept of parallel iterative tree-based nearest neighbor solvers and introduce a novel approach for the approximate calculation of the matrix profile. To improve the performance and overcome weak scalability challenges, we exploit a mix of creating a forest of parallel trees on exclusive ensembles of resources combined with pipelining of iterations. We provide an implementation targeting large-scale CPU-based HPC systems and illustrate the performance of this new approach with experimental data. Finally, we demonstrate the mining of time series at billion-records-scale datasets on the SuperMUC-NG system.

1 Introduction

Time series and their analysis are mainstream in many areas, from infrastructure monitoring [12] (power grid, renewable energy generation, ...) to mobility

© The Author(s), under exclusive license to Springer Nature Switzerland AG 2023
A. Bhatele et al. (Eds.): ISC High Performance 2023, LNCS 13948, pp. 317–338, 2023.
https://doi.org/10.1007/978-3-031-32041-5_17

data [27] (self-driving cars, plane safety systems, ...), from environmental sensors [21] (weather monitoring, data-driven architecture, ...) to factory automation [9] (predictive maintenance, intelligent material flow, ...). As the size of such datasets grows (in many such use cases, billions of data samples are already not uncommon), we need scalable, high-performance approaches to process them, e.g., to extract similarities and patterns with a reasonable time-to-solution (e.g., in order of minutes). This highlights the importance of using suitable parallel scalable algorithms and tools on large-scale HPC systems to meet the processing speed, efficiency, and memory requirements for processing *large* datasets, as they appear in real-world use cases.

Matrix profile [33] is a well-established indexing approach for the explorative analysis of time series data. This approach was introduced in 2016 by Yeh et al. in a series of papers [33,34,39] and has been successfully applied to mine similarities and patterns in datasets from various fields, such as seismology [28] and medical science [5], and used for various data mining and machine learning tasks, such as semantic segmentation, clustering, and anomaly detection [40]. Since its introduction, due to its various performance, scalability, accuracy, and practicality advantages, it has gained significant momentum in research communities as a fundamental approach for time series mining.

The matrix profile itself is a meta index that encodes similarity in time series data and its computation corresponds to a *nearest-neighbors* problem with the well-known classical exact approaches to compute it based on exhaustive search operations for nearest neighbors [8,33]. These *exact* solutions are generally inefficient for *large* datasets as the computational costs scale quadratically with the size of the datasets (i.e., the number of records). These approaches typically rely on mitigating the computational costs for the search operations by extensive arithmetic optimizations of compute kernels [37], or using accelerators for computation [11,39], and deploying on cloud-based [41] or HPC systems [20,24]. On the other hand, *approximate* approaches [26,37] are drawing increasing attention as they can provide solutions that are much more efficient to compute while also being accurate enough in practice. However, existing approaches still suffer either from excessive computational costs [37] (e.g., it takes days to compute matrix profile for 1 billion records on GPUs [41]), are restricted to specific settings [26] and application scenarios [15], or lack parallelization.

To our best knowledge, no research in the literature focuses on classical nearest-neighbor approaches for the computation of matrix profiles to prune the search space and reduce computational costs. In this paper, we focus on these approaches, specifically on the family of the iterative approximate nearest-neighbor exploiting *KD-tree-based* data structures and randomized approximate nearest neighbor approach [1] in distributed memory setting [32] as state of the art. To address computation for *large datasets*, we target large-scale CPU-based HPC systems and use weak scaling as the relevant scenario to scale to larger datasets. We demonstrate that, when applied to matrix profile computation in weak scaling, the state-of-the-art nearest neighbor approach method suffers from excessive communication overheads. We address these scaling challenges.

We specifically introduce two optimizations to address scaling challenges: 1) we *pipeline* the stages of the nearest neighbor algorithm in consecutive iterations to overlap the construction of the parallel tree data structure and the follow-on search operations; and 2) we enable control over the granularity of parallelism by constructing a forest of parallel trees on smaller *ensembles* of resources.

Overall, the tree-based solution enables us to exploit and explore approximate tree-based nearest-neighbor schemes for the first time in matrix profile computation. Consequently, we achieve a competitive solution to the alternatives for matrix profile computation. Additionally, once combined with the weak-scaling optimizations, the tree-based solution outperforms the state-of-the-art nearest neighbor algorithms when applied to matrix profile computation on HPC systems. We make the following contributions:

- We develop and, for the first time, apply an iterative tree-based nearest neighbor algorithm for the approximate computation of the matrix profile.
- We perform a detailed analysis of the performance, accuracy, and scaling behavior of the iterative tree-based approach and demonstrate its benefits.
- We extend the state-of-the-art iterative nearest neighbor with a combination of a pipelining mechanism and creating a forest of trees to scale the matrix profile computation on the HPC systems.
- We demonstrate the region of benefit where the tree-based approach is superior to alternatives when applied to real-world datasets and scenarios.

We further demonstrate that once compared to the prior art, our optimizations improve the scalability of the tree-based matrix profile computation on HPC systems by *doubling* the parallel efficiency when increasing the resources by three orders of magnitude on the SuperMUC-NG system. We also showcase the performance of our approach for large-scale problems by computing the approximate matrix profile for time series with 1 billion records on 48K cores of the system with 99% accuracy in under 20 min, which is 3–100 folds faster than other alternative approaches.

2   Matrix Profile Background and Performance-Accuracy Trade-offs

Matrix profile is an indexing approach to represent the similarities of local chunks of two input time series. These input time series are the *query* time series $T_Q \in \mathbb{R}^q$ with q records, and the *reference* time series $T_R \in \mathbb{R}^r$ with r records. The chunks (also known as segments or subsequences) are small overlapping windows of m consecutive samples of either of the input time series generated by moving a window of size m over the input time series. m is called the subsequence length or window size. The reference time series is often a well-known historical time series dataset and is used to characterize motifs, patterns, and anomalies in the unknown query time series. The two input series can also be identical.

Matrix profile computation is based on comparing all the local chunks of the two input series, and for this, a distance (or correlation) matrix is calculated.

For chunks in the query time series, the best matching fellow chunks in the reference time series, i.e., the chunks with maximum correlations, are determined. This way, the best matching chunks with the most similarities are retrieved. The *matrix profile P* itself is a real-valued vector of the distances of best matching segments of T_Q to their nearest neighbor segments in T_R. The *matrix profile index I* is an indexing vector indicating the location of the aforementioned nearest neighbor segments in T_R. With these definitions, *computing the matrix profile*, i.e., computing P and I, can be done using any nearest neighbor algorithm applied to set of segments, R and Q, as input data. The dimensionality of members of these sets corresponds to the subsequence length m.

Computing the matrix profile for two input time series, each including n records ($r = q = n$) require $O(m \cdot n^2)$ computation corresponding to the cost to compute the distance matrix. However, state-of-the-art methods (e.g., SCRIMP++ [37]) achieve this in $O(n^2)$ by using a so-called *streaming dot product* formulation for distance computation. Tree-based methods cannot employ this formulation; however, they can prune parts of the computation of elements in the distance matrix that are less likely to be needed, rendering sub-quadratic costs in n while keeping the linear cost in m. Therefore the tree-based approach has a performance trade-off compared to the state-of-the-art for different subsequence lengths: In state-of-the-art methods, the runtime does not scale with the subsequence lengths, which is a beneficial feature for the analysis of arbitrarily large sequences and patterns. The tree-based approach trades this property in favor of enabling fast analysis of larger time series. With such a trade-off, this method becomes beneficial for the cases where the number of records n is large (e.g., $n > 1,000,000$), and the window size is relatively small (also see the problem settings in the work of Lu et al. [15]). Additionally, problems with large window sizes are not the ideal setting for tree-based approaches, and the efficiency of the tree data structure might be suboptimal due to the curse of dimensionality [10,32]: Still, often these approximate methods [32] remain effective even in high dimensional settings (depending on the properties of datasets), where this dimensionality can grow and reach 100 s to 1,000 s as they appear in many real-world use cases. On the other hand, we still argue that cases with extremely large window sizes, e.g., $m > 10,000$ (e.g., scenarios reported in this work of Zhu et al. [37]), are typically over-sampled scenarios and can be down-sampled and mapped to problems with much smaller window sizes, where the tree-based approach is still advantageous. We shed light on this trade-off in practice in Sect. 7.1.

Moreover, in the approximate case, only parts of retrieved neighbors match the exact reference segments; an approximate method sacrifices the accuracy of retrieved results in favor of computational efficiency. Consequently, there is a trade-off between the accuracy and computational efficiency of methods (see Fig. 1 – more details in Sect. 7.1).

2.1 Related Work

We identify four main categories of approaches in the literature that relate to our work: Fig. 1 illustrates various approaches and visualizes these categories on a schematic accuracy-efficiency trade-off graph.

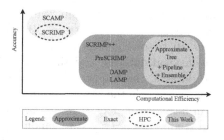

Exact Methods (Blue Region in Fig 1): The state-of-the-art exact method for computing matrix profile, *SCAMP* [41] algorithm, offers $O(n^2)$ complexity. *SCAMP* exploits GPUs for accelerated computation and targets Cloud environ-

Fig. 1. Accuracy vs. comp. efficiency trade-off existing methods. (Color figure online)

ments. Zhu et al. [37] proposed *SCRIMP* which is also an exact approach and has similar computational properties to *SCAMP*. This approach is further extended and deployed on HPC systems [20]. Approximate approaches (e.g., tree-based approach) suggest reasonable alternatives to reduce computational costs.

Approximate Methods(Red Region in Fig 1): Zhu et al. propose the approximate methods, *PreSCRIMP*, and *SCRIMP++* [37]. Although *PreSCRIMP* is introduced as a preprocessing step for the *SCRIMP++* algorithm, it stands as a standalone approximate solution as well. SCRIMP++ itself is both an exact and approximate solution that iteratively refines an initial approximate solution computed using *PreSCRIMP*. However, despite the promising results and properties, none of them accomplish sub-quadratic computational costs. *LAMP* [26] uses a neural network model to approximate matrix profile indices. Although this approach achieves significant speedups in comparison to exact solutions, it targets computation of matrix profile for data streams in *real-time* settings and therefore is not ideal for batch processing of large-scale datasets. Moreover, the authors clarify that the accuracy (e.g., false-positive rates) significantly depends on the quality of a reference dataset used to train the model. Finally, Zimmerman et al. [41] investigate the approximation of a matrix profile using reduced-precision computation and conclude that a single-precision computation suffers from a significant loss of accuracy. Our investigations suggest that this loss mainly stems from the propagation of numerical errors in the streaming dot product formulation used as the core in all existing methods [11]. None of the above-mentioned limitations applies to the tree-based approach.

Tree-Based Nearest Neighbor Methods(Green Region in Fig 1): Tree-based algorithms are traditionally used to accelerate ModSim computations: Barnes-Hut [2] and Fast Multipole Methods [25] are examples of such algorithms that have been used to mainly speedup force computations in N-body problems. These algorithms constantly attract attention in other fields, e.g., in the field of data analytics, where for instance, Van Der Maaten [31] exploits a Barnes-Hut method to accelerate the *t-SNE* method. The family of *nearest-neighbors prob-lems* has also benefited from tree-based algorithms for many years [1]. These problems are proven to gain "substantial speedups" [31] by exploiting tree data structures, such as KD-trees. Xiao et al. [32] use parallel randomized KD-trees [10] to solve nearest-neighbors problems with *approximation* targeting high-dimensional datasets and show that, in case of low intrinsic dimensionality in the dataset, their approach can solve *exact* nearest-neighbors in *linearithmic* time. Although the dual-tree algorithms are the "fastest known way to per-form nearest-neighbor *search*" [4], their distributed memory support is limited, and studies are restricted to smaller dimensionalities [29]. Further, a distributed memory approach based on dual-tree methods would result in similar overheads (e.g., overheads in tree construction and not only search overheads), which we are addressing in our work.

Methods Targeting HPC Systems (Encircled in ¡dashed¦ ellipses in Fig 1): Among all the approaches discussed, only SCRIMP is deployed on large-scale HPC systems. However, it is still implemented as an exact approach with $O(n^2)$ computational costs.

Despite the long history, there are limited tree-based *nearest neighbor* meth-ods targeting HPC systems: main approaches are *FLANN* [17], *PANDA* [19], and *RKDT* [32,35]. Among these, *RKDT* approach [32,35] is well studied on distributed memory systems and works well on large datasets with fairly high dimensionality (which is a requirement in the case of matrix profile computa-tion), and therefore is used as the base in our work. However, as we discuss later, still in the scope of matrix profile computation, it suffers from various effi-ciencies. In this paper, we experimentally demonstrate these inefficiencies and provide algorithmic redesigns and optimizations to enable a more scalable tree-based matrix profile computation on HPC systems.

2.2   Potentials of Tree-based Methods

In real-world cases, we are increasingly dealing with larger datasets, and bil-lions of records in these time series are becoming common. In such scenarios, it is increasingly important to provide the community with algorithms that can facil-itate the analysis of such a large num-ber of records. Tree-based approaches particularly fit these cases and promise sufficiently accurate *approximate* solu-tions with much better computational effi-ciency compared to the state-of-the-art.

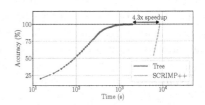

Fig. 2. Tree-based approach compared to the classical SCRIMP++ method, both iteratively progressing (single core runs, $n = 1000K$, $m = 128$).

No method in the literature exploits tree-based nearest-neighbors in the con-text of matrix profile computations and our work demonstrates the benefits (see Fig. 2).

Additionally, the state-of-the-art tree-based method [32] suffers from inefficiency in weak scaling when applied to matrix profile computation (See Fig. 3). Consequently, when exploiting these methods, computing matrix profiles for larger time series becomes inefficient as we increase the size of input datasets along with the number of resources. In our work, we explicitly focus on the scalability issues and provide optimization methods to

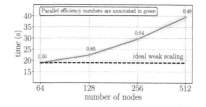

Fig. 3. Weak scaling of the forefront tree-based nearest-neighbor method used for matrix profile computation.

improve the scalability of tree-based approaches. With these optimizations, we are able to compute matrix profiles for large datasets more efficiently.

Nevertheless, as we are targeting large time series, the tree-based method is demanding with respect to compute, memory, and networking resources, and therefore we are targeting HPC systems. However, given accuracy, and computational efficiency, the tree-based approach is highly beneficial and competitive.

3   Current Parallel Tree-Based Approach and Its Shortcomings

Given reference (R) and query (Q) time series $T_R \in \mathbb{R}^r$ and $T_Q \in \mathbb{R}^q$, and subsequence length m, we formulate matrix profile computation by deriving two datasets $R \in \mathbb{R}^{r \times m}$ and $Q \in \mathbb{R}^{q \times m}$ of local chunks by sliding windows if size m on each (Line 2 in Pseudocode 1). Matrix profile computation is formulated as a Nearest Neighbor (NN) solver applied to Q and R to find the best matches with the lowest Euclidean distance: $P, I = \text{NN}(R, Q)$.

Pseudocode 1 Computation of matrix profile based on randomized KD-tree *in parallel*.

Input: The reference and query time series T_R and T_Q.
Output: The matrix profile P and index I.
Sources of overheads and comp. costs are highlighted in red.

```
1:  I ← {-1}, P ← {∞}
2:  R, Q = sliding_window_and_znormalize_distribute (T_R, T_Q)
3:  for i ←0 to T  do
4:      S₀ = random_direction_broadcast ()              ▷ Phase 1 (P1)
5:      R₁ᵒᵗ, Q₁ᵒᵗ = random_transform_parallel (R, Q, S₀)
6:      for l←0 to L  do
7:          med_l = max_var_quick_select (R₁ᵒᵗ, S_l)    ▷ Phase 2 (P2)
8:          S_{l+1},R₁ᵒᵗ_{+1}, Q₁ᵒᵗ_{+1} = split_redist_balance (R₁ᵒᵗ, Q₁ᵒᵗ, med_l)
9:      for leaf in tree leaves  do
10:         I¹ P¹ = NN_parallel (Q₁ᵒᵗ_eaf ,R₁ᵒᵗ_eaf)      ▷ Phase 3 (P3)
11:     I, P = merge_iteration_results_all2all (I, I¹, P, P¹)
```

We propose addressing the computation through an *iterative* and *pruned* method exploiting KD-tree data structures instead of directly solving NN (R, Q) by computing pairwise distances (and streaming dot product formulation). In Pseudocode 1, we provide a method based on the approach of Xiao et al. [32] to compute the matrix profile.

Tree-Based Approach: This approach starts with initializing the resulting matrix profile (P and I) to neutral values (Line 1) and iteratively updates (merges) partial results computed in each iteration (Line 11). This iterative process continues for a predefined number of iterations or until a certain accuracy level estimation is reached. Next, the two datasets R and Q are computed by applying sliding windows on the input series and z-normalizing each sample (Line 2).

Next, in multiple iterations (Line 3), the input datasets (R^{rot} and Q^{rot}) are randomly rotated (Phase 1), specifically, a householder transformation is applied to both the reference and query sets (Lines 4–5). In each iteration, a tree is constructed (Lines 6–8, (Phase 2)) on top of the rotated datasets, where at each level of the tree (Line 6), R^{rot} and Q^{rot} are partitioned (Line 8) into smaller subsets based on the median (Line 7) of the principal direction (i.e., the direction with maximum variance). After building the tree, a pruned nearest neighbor in each leaf of the tree is solved which exploits BLAS (DGEMM) operations (i.e., greedy search on leaves – Line 10). At the end of each iteration, the partial results of iterations are merged (Line 11, (Phase 3)) using element-wise minimum and arg-minimum operations.

Parallelization Approach: When moving to a distributed memory setting, the same scheme with extra parallelization mechanisms, e.g., multi-processing and message passing, is realized [32]. In this approach, a distributed tree data structure is constructed to collocate the reference and query points with the most similarity in the leaf in each node/process. The reference and query sets (Q and R) are statically partitioned among different nodes/processes initially. During the iterations, these sets are partitioned and shuffled around in parallel to construct the tree, i.e., to bring *similar* reference and query data in the same nodes/processes of the tree (Lines 7 and 8 in parallel). Then the matrix profile computation is reduced to a series of BLAS operations (DGEMM) in the leaves of the tree running on different node/processes in parallel (Line 9).

Overall, the parallel approach additionally includes static partitioning of reference and query sets (`distribute` in Line 2), `broadcast`ing the transformation direction (in Line 4), a series of `reductions` and pair-wise data exchanges as part of distributed approximate `quick_select` mechanism used to compute medians (Line 7). The reference and query sets are split according to the median value (`redistribute` and `balance`) using a series of pairwise exchanges during the construction of the tree (Line 8). Also, an additional *all-to-all* operation in Line 11 is used is used to merge iteration results P^i and I^i. This brings the resulting P^i and I^i to the right process/node, where the original reference sets are residing according to the static partitioning in the first step, and finally, it merges the results using element-wise comparisons. All these mechanisms add extra communication overhead. These overheads under the matrix profile setting running on the large number of nodes are extreme, where communication overheads dominate the runtime when compared to the time spent on transformation and DGEMM operations that run fully in parallel. In more detail, in large scenarios, i.e., the *all-to-all* collectives in `merge_iteration_results_all2all` grow drastically and dominate the runtime. Additionally, the pairwise exchanges in `split_redist_balance`, as well as the reductions in `max_var_quick_select`, are another major scaling bottleneck. For instance, our evaluations show that these overheads combined comprise $\approx 50\%$ of the runtime for large jobs (see Sect. 7 for a detailed analysis of overheads).

4   Overcoming the Scalability Challenges

We provide two complementary mechanisms to avoid these extra overheads:

1. Based on the analysis of these overheads (see Sect. 7), we identify three Phases, P1-P3, in Pseudocode 1 (highlighted from top to bottom in green, red and blue) and introduce a scheme to **pipeline the phases** (by adjusting Lines 3 and 6 in Pseudocode 1). This allows for concurrent and partial execution of multiple iterations resulting in the overlap of communication and computation of multiple phases and therefore hiding the communication latencies of the phases. This approach is in particular effective to reduce the latencies of *all-to-all* collectives.
2. Complementary to the pipelining mechanism, we create a **forest of trees on multiple exclusive ensembles** of resources (by adjusting Line 3 in Pseudocode 1). Overall, this allows to coarsen the granularity of parallelism and therefore reduces the communication overheads. This approach is particularly effective in reducing the communication costs in the series of pairwise exchanges in split_redist_balance, and the series of reductions in max_var_quick_select.

4.1   Pipelining Mechanism

We introduce a pipelining mechanism [3] to stagger the communication within the phases in iterations of Pseudocode 1. This pipelining mechanism intends to enable communication/computation overlap for multiple (enough) iterations (the intention is not to introduce more compute parallelism).

Such pipelining mechanisms are well-known techniques for hiding communication latencies of phases in parallel SPMD applications. Specifically, the shallow pipeline with a length of one, i.e., staggering a computation and a communication phase is a straightforward optimization in parallel programs and is typically enabled through non-blocking communication calls. In the case of the tree-based matrix profile computation, lengthier (i.e., deep enough) pipelines are required to enable latency hiding on a larger setup: for the runs on large portions of the HPC systems, the network latency become the bottleneck (e.g., in a fat-tree network topology of the target system). In this case, staggering multiple phases and/or deeper pipelines is beneficial.

Figure 4 provides a simplified schematic representation for this pipelining scheme. We illustrate how the phases of Pseudocode 1 are pipelined, where the benefit of deeper pipelines is visible. While this pipelining mechanism applies to an SPMD program, for simplification, we are only sketching the pipeline for the phases spawned by a single execution process (i.e., a single MPI process). We use a parameter l to represent the pipeline length (depth), as the main configuration setting for the pipelining mechanism, allowing for flexible pipelining of multiple (l) iterations (l is set to three for the sketch in Fig. 4). The value of l can be set according to the experimental setup and tuned based on the overall scale of the problem and the performance on the system. Each phase consists of a

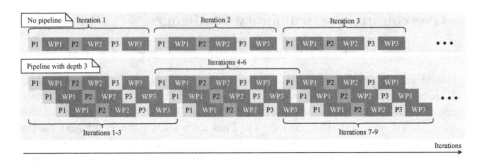

Fig. 4. Pipelining the iteration phases (P1, P2, and P3) in Pseudocode 1. Blocking *wait* operations for phases are annotated with WP1, WP2, and WP3.

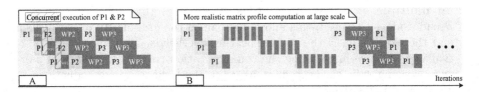

Fig. 5. A : A scenario with potential performance drawbacks due to concurrent execution of P1 and P2 on the same resource. B : More realistic pipeline.

blocking *wait* call (annotated with WP in Fig. 4) to ensure the completion of communications of a phase at the start of the successive phase.

Figure 5 provides more details about this pipelining mechanism: this pipelining mechanism can have a potential drawback in the performance of the phases that are, in the end, scheduled for *concurrent* execution on the same computing resources. An example of such a scenario is illustrated in Fig. 1 left A . We are explicitly preventing this scenario. Moreover, in our evaluations, we observe that the *all-to-all* communications (i.e., *waits* corresponding to MPI_Ialltoall) are the major communication bottleneck at large scale. Therefore at this stage, we end up with a pipeline that is similar to the sketch in Fig. 5 right B , where we stagger the *all-to-all* communications along with other phases, which prevents *all-to-all* communications from dominating the runtime in large jobs (see Sect. 3).

Implementation: Pseudocode 2 describes the pipelining mechanism in more details. However, for conciseness, we are only presenting the pipelining mechanism for Phase 3, i.e., merge_iteration_results_all2all. Specifically, we discuss the non-blocking *all-to-all* communications and their corresponding wait operation (the

Pseudocode 2 Pipeline mechanism to stagger the *all-to-all* communications

```
Input: (l) represents the pipeline depth.
1:  wait_handles_p3 = Initialize_pipeline ()
2:  for i←0 to T+1     with step 1 do in pipes
3:      ...                                    ▷End of P1
4:      wait_all_pipes (syn_handles_p3)        ▷Wait WP3
5:      ...                                    ▷End of P2
6:      ...                          ▷ (Details are removed) P3
7:      for j ← 0 to l do concurrently
8:          merge_iteration_results()
9:          launch_comms_async (wait_handles_p3[j])  ▷Trigger Comm P3
```

same can be applied to other phases as well). In Line 1, we initialize the wait handles as well as separate buffers to enable concurrent execution of l iterations. In Line 2, we start the main iteration loop in which the iterator i is incremented by the pipeLine length l. Another nested loop triggers the concurrent execution of l iterations (Line 7). In particular, in the j loop in Line 7, after calling to `merge_iteration_results`, the asynchronous communications are spawned (l times). We then call the corresponding wait operations `wait_all_pipes` (`wait_handles_p3`) in the next iteration, at the latest point possible.

As we target HPC systems, we realize this pipelining mechanism using non-blocking *all-to-all* communication, i.e., in Phase 3, `MPI_Ialltoall` and `MPI_Waitall` operations are used.

4.2   Forest of Trees on Ensembles of Resources:

While pipelining is promising for improving the performance of Phases 2 and 3, it is not suitable for the optimization of communications in the second phase, namely staggering the communications in the series of `reductions` and pair-wise data exchanges (`redistribute` and `balance`) during the tree construction and embedding phase (2): The main reason is that pipelining the tree construction loop in Line 6 in Pseudocode 1, requires another level of nested pipelining due to the dependency of the iterations of this loop. However, creating another pipeline level would be infeasible in practice due to excessive memory consumption overheads of nested pipes (i.e., another level of the pipeline requires the allocation of extra buffers).

We take a different approach to address the overheads. The key idea here is to utilize the parallelism in the outermost loop at Line 2 of Pseudocode 1. Therefore, instead of using all the resources for constructing a *single* tree (Fig. 6 left), we construct a forest of *multiple* trees of a certain size (four in Fig. 6 right), each of which is built on an *exclusive ensemble of resources (nodes/processes) in parallel*. For example, in Fig. 6 right, the illustrated work corresponds to four iterations, each assigned to one of the ensembles, which then run independently in parallel.

This scheme results in reduced communication overheads, as ensembles of nodes/processes working on different trees do not communicate across. Also, this scheme allows coarsening the parallelism in the inner computations and communications (Lines 4–11 in Pseudocode 1), including the partitioning involved in the KD tree construction (Phase 2 of Pseudocode 1). Specifically, it allows the *reductions* and *pair-wise data exchanges* in `redistribute` and `balance` as well as the *collectives* in other phases to run on coarse-grained parallelism in smaller communication contexts (i.e., communicators). This can

Pseudocode 3 Forest of trees on ensembles of resources

Input: (e) represents the number of ensembles.

```
1: C_ensemble, C-trans = create_ensemble_comm_context (e)
2: Part = partition_iterations (e)
3: for iter^e = Part.start to Part.end do in parallel on ensembles
4:     ...                              ▷Run P1 on C_ensemble
5:     ...                              ▷Run P2 on C_ensemble
6:     I^e, P^e = P3 (C_ensemble)       ▷Run P3 on C_ensemble
7: I, P = merge_partial_results ({I^e ,P^e}, C_trans)
```

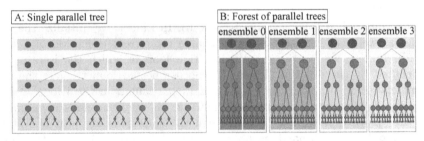

Fig. 6. Single parallel tree vs. forest trees. Pink circles represent the resources, e.g., processes. Rectangular enclosures with unique colors represent the communication contexts (i.e., MPI communicators) at different levels of a parallel tree. Each parallel tree is represented by a hierarchy of boxes with a unique color. (Color figure online)

also be observed in the example in Fig. 6: The largest communication context in Fig. 6 left includes eight processes/nodes, while the forest approach uses only two processes/nodes, at the top level of the tree. The main caveat for this approach is the high memory consumption, which scales with the number of ensembles.

Implementation: Pseudocode 3 provides the details of the forest of trees approach. We split the available resources into smaller sets, i.e., *ensembles* (Line 1 in Pseudocode 3). Ensembles have the same amount of resources (processes/nodes). Assuming fairly uniform iterations, we statically partition the iterations of the loop in Line 2 of Pseudocode 1 and assign them to these ensembles (Lines 2 and 3 in Pseudocode 3). We then run the iteration phases on these ensembles (Line 4–6). We perform a final merging step across the ensembles (Line 7) to aggregate partial matrix profiles in ensembles. This is optionally done during the iterations to estimate the overall accuracy among all ensembles.

We implement this approach in MPI by splitting MPI's default communicator using `MPI_Comm_split`. The resulting communicators represent the communication context and corresponding ensembles. The final merging step is realized using `MPI_Allreduce`.

5   Modeling the Impact of Optimizations on Complexity

To better understand the performance characteristics of the tree-based method, we reuse the complexity analysis of Xiao et al. [32] and adapt it according to the pipelining and forest mechanisms. For this complexity analysis, the following assumptions and simplifications are made: (1) We assume that the size of the reference and query sets are equal (i.e., $q = r = n$). (2) We assume that the tree data structure is fully parallel running on p processes/nodes, and the number of subsequences within each leaf of the tree is represented by n_{leaf}.

We split the time for the execution of a single iteration into smaller chunks (Eq. (1)) based on the phases that we introduced in Sect. 3.

$$T_{Iteration} = T_{P1} + T_{P2} + T_{P3} \tag{1}$$

$$T_{P1} = T_{\underline{transformation}} + T_{\underline{broadcast}} = \mathcal{O}\Big(n \cdot m/(p/e)\Big) + \mathcal{O}\Big(\log(p/e)\Big) \tag{2}$$

$$T_{P2} = T_{max\_var\_\underline{quick\_select}} + T_{split\_\underline{redist\_balance}} =$$
$$\mathcal{O}\Big(\log(p/e)\cdot\log(n) + n/(p/e)\Big) + \mathcal{O}\Big(\log(n)\cdot\log^2(p/e)\Big) +$$
$$\mathcal{O}\Big(n\cdot m/(p/e)\Big) + \mathcal{O}\Big(n\cdot m\cdot\log(p/e)/(p/e)\Big) \tag{3}$$

$$T_{P3} = T_{NN} + T_{merge} = \mathcal{O}\Big(n_{leaf}{}^2\cdot m\Big) + \mathcal{O}\Big(n\cdot m\log(p/e)/(p/e)\Big) + \mathcal{O}\Big(p/e\Big) \tag{4}$$

The first phase (Eq. (2)) only includes the parallel transformations of data as well as a broadcast. The pipelining mechanism staggers and eliminates the overheads of the reduction (the term highlighted in red) in this phase, and the forest mechanism reduces the size of the communication context of the reduction operation.

In the second phase (Eq. (3), only the forest mechanism affects the size of the communicators and slows down the growth of the overheads by a factor e, i.e., the size of the forest.

In the last phase (Eq. (4)), the pipelining mechanism staggers the overheads of *all-to-all* operations (highlighted in red) into other phases. Also, similar to the other phases, the forest mechanism has a similar effect on reducing the communicator size for the *all-to-all* operations (factor e).

From these equations, we observe that the time to run the iterations of the tree-based approach is similar to its parent randomized KD tree method, i.e., regardless of the parameters chosen for the pipelining and forest mechanisms, the time complexity of the iterations of the tree-based method is sub-quadratic. This results in an overall sub-quadratic complexity which is unlike SCRIMP++, that overall scales quadratically with problem size. However, the randomized tree-based approach requires multiple iterations, i.e., multiple rounds of creation and searching in the tree. Therefore, there is an additional multiplier in the overall time complexity and overheads of the tree-based approach. Similar to the assumptions made in [23], we assume that running the tree-based approach with a certain number of iterations can reach a certain accuracy level and eventually converge to the exact solution. Analyzing these conditions falls out of the scope of this paper, but what we want to highlight here is that the overall performance of the tree-based method relies on the content of the time series dataset, as well as the required accuracy level. If the exact solution is needed, the tree-based approach would not be the right scheme.

Note that, unlike SCRIMP++, the tree-based approach cannot benefit from the affinity of neighboring subsequences in the evaluation of distances and does not allow the use of the streaming dot product formulation [41]. Therefore observe the terms in Eq. (3) scale linearly with the parameter m. This suggests that the tree-based approach is more suitable for large time series (large n), and mining of fine-grained patterns (small m). This, however, is a frequent problem setup in analysis use cases where the subsequence length is much smaller than the time series length $m \ll N$. We summarized a list of such use cases in Table 1, which we will discuss later.

6   Experimental Setup

We describe implementation and experimental setup used in this paper below.

Implementation: We implement[1] the tree-based matrix profile approach in C++ using pure MPI for parallelization. Our implementation targets CPU-based HPC systems, and it relies on vectorized sorting and searching kernels as well as optimized DGEMM kernels in the Intel MKL for distance computation.

System Specification: Our targeted system for the experiments of this paper is the SuperMUC-NG system at the LRZ[2] featuring Intel Xeon 8174 CPU with 48 cores per node. In all experiments, we use the Intel OneAPI package v21.2.0, including the Intel C++ compiler v21.2.0, with the highest optimization level (-Ofast) for compilation, and the Intel MPI v21.2.0.

Baseline: We use the C++ implementation of SCRIMP++ (and also Pre-SCRIMP) [37] as the baseline to compare the tree-based method. Due to the limitations of other approximate approaches, discussed in Sect. 2.1, we are limiting our comparisons to SCRIMP++. Besides, in all these implementations, the parallelization support is limited, and often analysis of large datasets is at least an order of magnitude slower in comparison to the parallel tree-based method [15]. We are also excluding downsampling of the input time series as an approximation method in our evaluation as it is out of the scope of matrix profile computation methodologies (see also discussion in Sect. 2). Finally, we are not comparing the performance of the tree-based method to any exact method (except for SCRIMP++), as the performance characteristics of all these methods are similar to SCRIMP++.

Statistical Significance: We report the metrics for the average of 5 repeated runs, and we do not discuss statistical errors where they are insignificant.

Selected Datasets: In our experiments, we use a variety of datasets from different sources listed in Table 1. We selected these datasets carefully to reflect the regions of benefits (see Sect. 7.1) for the tree-based approach. These datasets are mainly derived from real-world applications and scenarios. While various window sizes can be configured for matrix profile computation, we mainly use the configurations listed in Table 1, which reflect analysis scenarios discussed in sources listed in Table 1. Table 1 also illustrates a short snapshot of these datasets together with the recommended window sizes in the mentioned sources.

For stress tests and scaling experiments (Sect. 7.1, and 7.3–7.6), we use random walk dataset [41] (not listed in Table 1). We use problem sizes to enable straightforward comparisons to prior works (e.g., experiments in [32]).

---

[1] The implementation can be provided upon request.
[2] Leibniz Supercomputing Centre.

Table 1. List of datasets used for the experiments. We also include the configurations used in various sources in the literature.

Dataset	Description	Source	n	m	Similar scenario	Sample plot
HPC-ODA	HPC monitoring	[18]	34K	64	[11] Fig. 8	
Earthquake	Earthquake vibrations	[41]	100.00K	200, 100	[41] Sec. 5	
Penguin	Penguin behaviour	[38]	1.000M	28	[38] Fig. 10	
ASTRO	Celestial objects	[14]	1.100M	512	[14] Sec. 6.2	
PSML	Energy grid	[36,15]	1.500M	200	[15] Fig. 9	
GT	Gas Turbine	[12,13]	1.900M	64	[12] Fig. 4	
GAP	Power consumption	[14]	1.950M	512	[14] Sec. 6.2	
EMG	Electromyography signal	[14]	2.860M	512	[14] Sec. 6.2	
InsectEPG	Insect behaviours	[37]	6.400M	50, 256	[7] Sec. E	
ECG	Electrocardiogram signal	[6]	19.2M	421, 256, 94, 128	[6],[22] Tab. 5 & [33] Tab. 7, [15] Fig. 13, [16] Fig. 16	
MGAB	Synthetic anomalies	[30,15]	112.5M	40	[15] Fig. 4	

Metrics of Accuracy: We evaluate the quality of the results by comparing the matrix profile index against the exact computation (i.e., brute force computation). For this comparison, we specifically use Recall[3] ($\mathscr{R}$) on the matrix profile index. Recall is defined [32] as the ratio of the number of the matching (*signum*) matrix profile indices computed by the tree approach (I_i^T) with the exact computation (I_i^E) to the total number of subsequences ($N - m + 1$):

$$\mathscr{R} = \sum_i signum(|I_i^E - I_i^T|)/(n - m + 1) \tag{5}$$

7 Evaluations

In our evaluations, we address the applicability of the tree-based approach, assess its accuracy in real-world datasets, and also discuss its scaling overheads. We start each subsection with a research question (RQ) and address this question subsequently. In the end, we provide a demonstration of computing the matrix profile for a time series with a billion records.

7.1 Region of Benefit

RQ1: Considering the performance advantages and trade-offs discussed in Sect. 2 where is the tree-based approach beneficial in comparison to the existing approximate approaches? We make a comparison of the tree-based method to SCRIMP++ to address this question. Looking back at the discussion in Sect. 2 and 5, the performance advantage of the tree-based method directly depends on the size of the two input time series n, and the windows m. Therefore, we use random walk datasets with different combinations of n and m parameters to compare the two methods. For a fair comparison, we fix the accuracy level and compare the time to get to at least $\mathscr{R} = 99.99\%$ accuracy for both methods.

---

[3] Other metrics are also used in the literature, and some might be subjective to particular practical use cases. An investigation of such alternative metrics is beyond the scope of the present work.

Figure 7 illustrates the results of this experiment by providing a region of benefit (the green area) for the tree-based method. We observe that as the size of the input datasets increase (towards the right in the graph) relative to the window size, the tree-based approach becomes superior. This is also in accordance with the scope and practicality discussions in Sect. 2. Also, again by looking at Table 1, we can observe that many (but certainly not all) real-world scenarios lie in the region of the benefit of the tree-based approach.

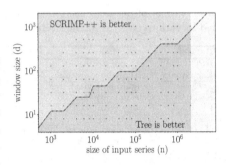

Fig. 7. Color-coded region of benefit, when comparing tree-based approach vs. SCRIMP++ (single core execution). (Color figure online)

Note that to keep this region of benefit relevant for parallel computation, the parallel efficiency of the tree method should be high. One of the main contributions of our work is to address the high parallel efficiency of the tree-based method through the approaches discussed in Sect. 4.

7.2   Performance on Real-World Datasets

RQ2: Considering the performance-accuracy trade-offs discussed in Sect. 2, when applied to real-world datasets, how much is the tree-based approach performant in comparison to the existing approximate approaches? We use the accuracy metric defined by Eq. (5) and run an experiment on various datasets listed in Table 1. We set the input parameters according to columns (n and m) in Table 1. We run all experiments sequentially and compare the time to reach a certain accuracy level

Table 2. Time to 99.9% accuracy among various methods (single-core execution).

Dataset	Time (s) To 99.9% Accuracy		
	PreSCRIMP	SCRIMP++	Tree
HPC-ODA	✗	8.96	16.88
Earthquake	✗	13.47	32.62
Penguin	✗	7070.79	245.15
ASTRO	✗	1156.18	2615.70
PSML	✗	5936.69	303.60
GT	✗	7875.80	3104.13
GAP	✗	3320.65	2482.38
EMG	✗	7648.17	2874.43
InsectEPG	✗	9474.30	1282.58
ECG	✗	6060.12	1240.75
MGAB	✗	10749.50	20.67

(i.e., 99.9% accuracy). Table 2 summarizes the results of this experiment. Our measurements suggest that the tree-based approach is overall faster than SCRIMP++ (8 out of 11 cases in Table 1 highlighted in green for tree approach). Three cases are exceptions: note that these cases do not lie on the region of benefit for the tree-based methods (again see Fig. 7 and parameters in Table 1). Also, we observe that for none of the datasets, PreSCRIMP is able to achieve 99.9% accuracy. Another observation is that the tree-based the approach is superior for the datasets with a larger number of records, i.e., it is superior for the lower rows of Table 2.

Overall, this experiment validates that the tree approach can achieve high accuracy in a reasonable time, and it can be superior to existing approximate methods. While there are real-world cases, similar to the first rows of Table 1 or the experiments in [37], where the tree approach is not superior, many cases similar to the one we report in Table 2 can benefit from it.

7.3   Single-Node Performance

RQ3: Going beyond the single core runs, how does the performance of the tree-based approach scale on a single node, and what are the sources of overheads? Can the proposed mechanism improve the scalability? To answer these questions, we run a set of weak scaling experiments on single nodes of the SuperMUC-NG system. Figure 8 summarizes these experiments. We present four different cases; on the top left graph, we show the runtime and overheads of the tree-based method once scaling on a single node. We observe large overheads ($\approx$100%) even on such a small scale. Digging further into the overheads, we notice that the sources of them are mainly in Phases 2

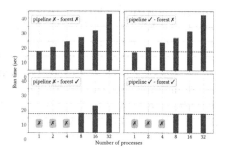

Fig. 8. Single-node performance of the tree approach, with ($\checkmark$) and without ($\times$) pipelining or forest mechanism ($n = 6K$ per core, $m = 512$, random walk dataset). Configurations annotated with $\times$ mark are *algorithmically* not supported.

and 3 of Pseudocode 1. Specifically in all the cases `max_var_quick_select` and `merge_iteration_results_all2all` comprise at least 60% of the run time. However, `merge_iteration_results_all2all` is only responsible for small portion of it, and as we will show, this overhead only appears in larger setups.

We repeat the experiment and enable the pipelining mechanism with a depth of four (top right). We observe almost negligible improvements. However, we observe on the graph at the bottom left, that setting the size of the forest (the number of ensembles) to eight would reduce the overheads significantly. When we combine the two mechanisms (bottom right), we almost completely overcome the overheads and reach $\approx$ 100% parallel efficiency on a single node.

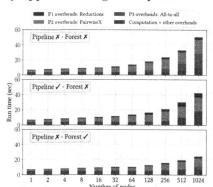

Fig. 9. Breakdown for the time spent in various phases, with ($\checkmark$) and without ($\times$) pipelining or forest mechanisms. ($n = 4K$ per core, $m = 256$, random walk).

7.4   Scaling Overheads

RQ4: Going beyond the single-node runs, how does the performance of the tree-based approach scale, and what are the sources of overheads? We run a set of weak scaling experiments on the

SuperMUC-NG system, with a setup starting from a single node up to 1024 nodes. On the top graph in Fig. 9, we observe the breakdown for the time spent in different phases of Pseudocode 1 for computing matrix profile. As we scale the problem and resources, the overhead in max_var_quick_select, merge_iteration_results_all2all, and split_redist_balance scales drastically; When we use 1,024 nodes, the overheads comprise more than 75% of the runtime, where the largest overhead is traced to the *all-to-all* operations in merge_iteration_results_all2all.

We repeat the same scaling experiments and switch the two mechanisms on, one at a time. Once the pipelining mechanism is switched on (middle graph in Fig. 9), the overhead of *all to all* operations is removed. However, this optimization alone only has around 9% performance improvements. On the other hand, once the forest mechanism is enabled (bottom graph in Fig. 9), the overhead of all the phases is significantly shrunk (by ≈55%).

7.5   Effects of Pipelining and Forest Mechanisms

RQ5: How do the proposed pipelining and forest mechanisms affect the overheads how do they interplay? To better understand the effects of the two optimization mechanisms, we conduct a series of weak scaling experiments on the SuperMUC-NG system with various pipeline depth (l) and forest size (e) configurations. Figure 10 summarizes the results of these experiment: In Fig. 10 top, we revisit the overhead of the *all-to-all* operations in split_redist_balance which only appears in the setups larger than 64 nodes. We observe that in all the cases enabling the pipelining mechanism is highly beneficial, and increasing the depth of the pipeline can help to almost

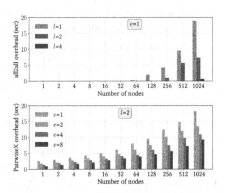

Fig. 10. Effect of pipelining and forest mechanisms on scaling overheads ($n = 65K$ per node and $m = 256$, 32 iterations, random walk).

completely eliminate the *all to all* overheads. In Fig. 10 bottom, we focus on the overhead of split_redist_balance, which was the main target for enabling the forest mechanism. We observe that increasing the size of the forest in all the experiments improves the performance. Also, similar to the results shown in Fig. 9, we also observe positive effects on other overheads (not shown in Fig. 9).

The two mechanisms have a complementary effect on performance improvements. Our further experiments suggest enabling them simultaneously and tuning e and l parameters is beneficial.

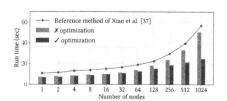

Fig. 11. Weak scaling results with ($\checkmark$) and without ($\times$) optimizations ($n = 65K$ per node, $m = 256$, 32 iterations, random walk).

7.6 Scaling Results

RQ6: How does the tree-based approach scale overall? We conduct a weak scaling experiment on the SuperMUC-NG system to illustrate the overall scaling performance of the tree-based matrix profile approach. In this experiment, we use two cases; in the first case, we disable all the optimization mechanisms, and in the second case, we enable the pipelining mechanism with depth $l = 4$ as well as a forest of size $e = 4$. Figure 11, illustrates the results of this experiment: Again, we observe that the tree-based approach results in scaling bottlenecks if no optimization is used. In this case, starting from one node and increasing the number of MPI processes by 3 orders of magnitude on SuperMUC-NG, i.e., going beyond a single island, results in 14% parallel efficiency, which is also in accordance with the experiments of Xiao et al. [32]. However, applying the two pipelining and forest mechanisms improves efficiency to 31%, which is a large improvement. Note that this efficiency shrinks the region of benefit (i.e., Fig. 7), however overall, the method stays beneficial for larger time series, as discussed in Sect. 7.1. Finally, we trace the remaining scaling overheads to the series of pairwise exchanges in split_redist_balance. Although the forest mechanism improves the overheads of data shuffling and load balancing in Phase 2 of Pseudocode 1, it still does not entirely eliminate the latencies of the blocking calls in this phase.

7.7 Billion Scale Experiment

To showcase the capabilities of the tree-based approach, we run a matrix profile computation on a billion-record random walk dataset ($n = 1$ billion) with a window size $m = 128$, using $48K$ cores of the SuperMUC-NG to 99% in 19 minutes. This run reaches ≈ 338 TFlops maximum kernel performance. There are only 2 previous works that conduct experiments at this scale: 1) Zimmerman et al. [41] computed matrix profile for 1-billion-record time series on AWS spot instances using the SCAMP algorithm, which took between 10.3 h to 2.5 days. Compared to that, the tree-based approach reaches 1–2 orders of magnitude faster speed. 2) Just recently, Lu et al. [15] conducted *anomaly detection* using DAMP algorithm on 1-billion-record in around 1 h on a commodity desktop system in a single run. While the tree-based method is still 3x faster, it is highly inefficient compared to DAMP. However, the matrix profile computed with the tree-based method can be applied to various data mining and machine learning tasks, while DAMP only targets anomaly detection.

8   Conclusions

In this work, we presented an approximate parallel iterative tree-based approach for the computation of matrix profiles, targeting CPU-based HPC systems. We analyzed the scaling bottlenecks state-of-the-art tree-based approach for matrix profile computation in our work. We provided a pipelining and forest mechanisms to improve the scalability of the tree-based approach. Our optimizations improved parallel efficiency on 32K cores by a factor of 2. The optimization mechanisms presented can be generalized and applied to similar problems (e.g., nearest neighbor computations or randomized iterative algorithms).

With the presented work, it is feasible to compute matrix profile for large time series, which previously required days to compute, in just a few minutes. We demonstrated a billion-scale experiment with up to 99% accuracy in 19 min which is 3–100 folds faster than existing approaches. This provides a competitive computation time compared to the alternative approaches.

Acknowledgements. This work is partially funded by Bayerische Forschungsstiftung under the research grants *Optimierung von Gasturbinen mit Hilfe von Big Data* (AZ-1214-16), and *Von der Edge zur Cloud und zurück: Skalierbare und Adaptive Sensordatenverarbeitung* (AZ-1468-20). The authors gratefully acknowledge the Gauss Centre for Supercomputing e.V. (www.gauss-centre.eu) for funding this work by providing computing time on *GCS Supercomputer SuperMUC-NG at at Leibniz Supercomputing Centre* (www.lrz.de).

References

1. Arya, S., et al.: An optimal algorithm for approximate nearest neighbor searching fixed dimensions. J. ACM **45**(6), 891–923 (1998)
2. Barnes, J., Hut, P.: A hierarchical O(N log N) force-calculation algorithm. Nature **324**(6096), 446–449 (1986)
3. Cools, S., et al.: Improving strong scaling of the conjugate gradient method for solving large linear systems using global reduction pipelining. ArXiv abs/1905.06850 (2019)
4. Curtin, R.R.: Faster dual-tree traversal for nearest neighbor search. In: Amato, G., Connor, R., Falchi, F., Gennaro, C. (eds.) SISAP 2015. LNCS, vol. 9371, pp. 77–89. Springer, Cham (2015). https://doi.org/10.1007/978-3-319-25087-8_7
5. Dau, H.A., Keogh, E.: Matrix profile V: a generic technique to incorporate domain knowledge into motif discovery. In: 23rd ACM SIGKDD, pp. 125–134 (2017)
6. Eamonn Keogh: Electrocardiography Dataset. https://www.cs.ucr.edu/~eamonn/ECG_one_day.zip. Accessed 15 Aug 2022
7. Gharghabi, S., et al.: Domain agnostic online semantic segmentation for multi-dimensional time series. In: Data Mining and Knowledge Discovery (2018)
8. Heldens, S., et al.: Rocket: efficient and scalable all-pairs computations on heterogeneous platforms. In: Proceedings of SC 2020. IEEE Press (2020)
9. Jirkovský, V., et al.: Big data analysis for sensor time-series in automation. In: IEEE Emerging Technology and Factory Automation (ETFA), pp. 1–8 (2014)
10. Jones, P.W., et al.: Randomized approximate nearest neighbors algorithm. Proc. Natl. Acad. Sci. **108**(38), 15679–15686 (2011)

11. Ju, Y., et al.: Exploiting reduced precision for GPU-based Time series mining. In: IEEE IPDPS, pp. 124–134 (2022)
12. Karlstetter, R., et al.: Turning dynamic sensor measurements from gas turbines into insights: a big data approach. In: Turbo Expo, vol. 6 (2019)
13. Karlstetter, R., et al.: Living on the edge: efficient handling of large scale sensor data. In: 2021 IEEE/ACM CCGrid 2021, pp. 1–10 (2021)
14. Linardi, M., et al.: Matrix profile X: VALMOD - scalable discovery of variable-length motifs in data series. In: ACM SIGMOD, p. 1053–1066 (2018)
15. Lu, Y., et al.: Matrix profile XXIV: scaling time series anomaly detection to trillions of datapoints and ultra-fast arriving data streams. In: ACM SIGKDD (2022)
16. Mercer, R., et al.: Matrix profile XXIII: contrast profile: a novel time series primitive that allows real world classification. In: IEEE ICDM (2021)
17. Muja, M., Lowe, D.G.: Scalable nearest neighbor algorithms for high dimensional data. IEEE Trans. Pattern Anal. Mach. Intell. **36**(11), 2227–2240 (2014)
18. Netti, A.: HPC-ODA dataset collection (2020). https://doi.org/10.5281/zenodo.3701440
19. Patwary, M.M.A., et al.: PANDA: extreme scale parallel k-nearest neighbor on distributed architectures. CoRR abs/1607.08220 (2016)
20. Pfeilschifter, G.: time series analysis with matrix profile on HPC systems. Master thesis, Technische Universität München (2019)
21. Raksha, S., et al.: Weather forecasting framework for time series data using intelligent learning models. In: 5th ICEECCOT 2021, pp. 783–787 (2021)
22. Rakthanmanon, T., et al.: Searching and mining trillions of time series subsequences under dynamic time warping. In: ACM SIGKDD, pp. 262–270 (2012)
23. Ram, P., Sinha, K.: Revisiting KD-tree for nearest neighbor search. In: KDD 2019, pp. 1378–1388. Association for Computing Machinery, New York (2019)
24. Raoofy, A., Karlstetter, R., Yang, D., Trinitis, C., Schulz, M.: Time series mining at petascale performance. In: Sadayappan, P., Chamberlain, B.L., Juckeland, G., Ltaief, H. (eds.) ISC High Performance 2020. LNCS, vol. 12151, pp. 104–123. Springer, Cham (2020). https://doi.org/10.1007/978-3-030-50743-5_6
25. Rokhlin, V.: Rapid solution of integral equations of classical potential theory. J. Comput. Phys. **60**(2), 187–207 (1985)
26. Schall-Zimmerman, Z., et al.: Matrix profile XVIII: time series mining in the face of fast moving streams using a learned approximate matrix profile. In: IEEE ICDM, pp. 936–945 (2019)
27. Schmidl, S., et al.: Anomaly detection in time series: a comprehensive evaluation. Proc. VLDB Endow. **15**(9), 1779–1797 (2022)
28. Shakibay Senobari, et al.: Using the similarity matrix profile to investigate foreshock behavior of the 2004 parkfield earthquake. In: AGU Fall Meeting Abstracts, vol. 2018, pp. S51B–03 (2018)
29. Steinbusch, B., et al.: A massively parallel barnes-hut tree code with dual tree traversal. In: PARCO (2015)
30. Thill, M., et al.: MarkusThill/MGAB: The Mackey-glass anomaly benchmark (2020). https://doi.org/10.5281/zenodo.3760086
31. Van Der Maaten, L.: Accelerating T-SNE using tree-based algorithms. J. Mach. Learn. Res. **15**(1), 3221–3245 (2014)
32. Xiao, B., Biros, G.: Parallel algorithms for nearest neighbor search problems in high dimensions. SIAM J. Sci. Comput. **38**(5), S667–S699 (2016)
33. Yeh, C.M., et al.: Matrix profile I: all pairs similarity joins for time series: a unifying view that includes motifs, discords and shapelets. In: IEEE ICDM, pp. 1317–1322 (2016)

34. Yeh, C.M., et al.: Matrix profile III: the matrix profile allows visualization of salient subsequences in massive time series. In: IEEE ICDM, pp. 579–588 (2016)

35. Yu, C.D., et al.: Performance optimization for the K-nearest neighbors kernel on X86 architectures. In: ACM SC (2015)

36. Zheng, X., et al.: PSML: a multi-scale time-series dataset for machine learning in decarbonized energy grids (dataset) (2021). https://doi.org/10.5281/zenodo.5130612

37. Zhu, Y., et al.: Matrix profile XI: SCRIMP++: time series motif discovery at interactive speeds. In: IEEE ICDM, pp. 837–846 (2018)

38. Zhu, Y., et al.: Matrix profile VII: time series chains: a new primitive for time series data mining. In: 2017 IEEE ICDM 2017, pp. 695–704 (2017)

39. Zhu, Y., et al.: Matrix profile II: exploiting a novel algorithm and GPUs to break the one hundred million barrier for time series motifs and joins. Knowl. Inf. Syst. **54**(1) (2018)

40. Zhu, Y., et al.: The swiss army knife of time series data mining: ten useful things you can do with the matrix profile and ten lines of code. In: KDD 2020, vol. 34, pp. 949–979 (2020)

41. Zimmerman, Z., et al.: Matrix profile XIV: scaling time series motif discovery with GPUs to break a quintillion pairwise comparisons a day and beyond. In: ACM SoCC, pp. 74–86 (2019)

Porting Numerical Integration Codes from CUDA to oneAPI: A Case Study

Ioannis Sakiotis[1]($\boxtimes$)🆔, Kamesh Arumugam[2]🆔, Marc Paterno[1,3]🆔,
Desh Ranjan[1]🆔, Balša Terzić[1]🆔, and Mohammad Zubair[1]🆔

[1] Old Dominion University, Norfolk, VA 23529, USA
{isaki001,bterzic}@odu.edu, {dranjan,zubair}@cs.odu.edu
[2] NVIDIA, Santa Clara, CA 95051-0952, USA
karumugam@nvidia.com
[3] Fermi National Accelerator Laboratory, Batavia, IL 60510, USA
paterno@fnal.gov

Abstract. We present our experience in porting optimized CUDA implementations to oneAPI. We focus on the use case of numerical integration, particularly the CUDA implementations of PAGANI and m-Cubes. We faced several challenges that caused performance degradation in the oneAPI ports. These include differences in utilized registers per thread, compiler optimizations, and mappings of CUDA library calls to oneAPI equivalents. After addressing those challenges, we tested both the PAGANI and m-Cubes integrators on numerous integrands of various characteristics. To evaluate the quality of the ports, we collected performance metrics of the CUDA and oneAPI implementations on the Nvidia V100 GPU. We found that the oneAPI ports often achieve comparable performance to the CUDA versions, and that they are at most 10% slower.

1 Introduction

Historically, general-purpose GPU programming has been characterized by divergent architectures and programming models. A lack of widely adopted common

The authors would like to thank Intel Corporation and Codeplay for providing technical support in the code migration process. The authors are also grateful for the support of the Intel oneAPI Academic Center of Excellence at Old Dominion University. Work supported by the Fermi National Accelerator Laboratory, managed and operated by Fermi Research Alliance, LLC under Contract No. DE-AC02-07CH11359 with the U.S. Department of Energy. The U.S. Government retains and the publisher, by accepting the article for publication, acknowledges that the U.S. Government retains a non-exclusive, paid-up, irrevocable, world-wide license to publish or reproduce the published form of this manuscript, or allow others to do so, for U.S. Government purposes. FERMILAB-CONF-23-007-LDRD-SCD. We acknowledge the support of Jefferson Lab grant to Old Dominion University 16-347. Authored by Jefferson Science Associates, LLC under U.S. DOE Contract No. DE-AC05-06OR23177 and DE-AC02- 06CH11357. code available at https://github.com/marcpaterno/gpuintegration.

A. Bhatele et al. (Eds.): ISC High Performance 2023, LNCS 13948, pp. 339–358, 2023.
https://doi.org/10.1007/978-3-031-32041-5_18

standards led to the development of different ecosystems comprised of compilers and tools that were practically exclusive to specific GPU architectures. Most importantly, the emergent architectures themselves were not compatible with all ecosystems. Portability could only be achieved through the maintenance of multiple code bases. Traditionally, the proprietary CUDA programming model has been the most popular but is exclusively targeted to Nvidia GPUs.

In the absence of universally adopted standards, a viable solution for achieving general portability is to rely on platform-agnostic programming models that target multiple architectures via a unifying interface. This enables the execution of a single code base across various architectures. These programming models would ideally enable the utilization of platform-specific low-level features on their native hardware. This would allow highly-optimized implementations in such portable programming models to remain competitive with platform-specific alternatives. Without these capabilities, use cases with extreme performance requirements would disqualify the use of such portable models.

The need for performant multi-platform execution is only increasing with the emergence of exascale supercomputers such as Frontier and Aurora that do not carry Nvidia GPUs. Projects requiring computing cores at that scale must develop new software solutions compatible with non-Nvidia GPUs or port existing CUDA implementations without significant loss of performance.

Portable programming models such as RAJA, Kokkos, and oneAPI have been in development and are already available for use. These portable alternatives lack maturity when compared to proprietary alternatives. As such, applications requiring portable solutions must be evaluated to quantify any necessary concessions.

In this paper, we discuss the porting process of two numerical integration implementations, PAGANI and m-Cubes, from CUDA to Data Parallel C++ (DPC++), which is oneAPI's SYCL implementation. The oneAPI ecosystem provides a suite of compilers, libraries, and software tools, including Intel® DPC++ Compatibility Tool (DPCCT), that automates the majority of the porting process. Reliance on the C++ and SYCL standards as well as the capability to quickly port large CUDA implementations, places oneAPI at the forefront of the portability initiative.

We faced challenges during the porting process due to the lack of support for certain libraries utilized by the CUDA implementation. For example, the CUDA implementation of PAGANI uses the Nvidia Thrust library to perform common parallel operations on the host side, such as inner product and min-max. Even though there is a multitude of library options in oneAPI, we encountered difficulties with the DPCCT mapping of Nvidia Thrust library calls, which were not fully supported on all backends.

We also observed performance degradation for the ported oneAPI implementations. We conducted numerous experiments with integrands of various characteristics to identify the issues. Most of these issues pertained to optimization differences between the NVCC and Clang compilers, and time differences when executing mathematical functions. After addressing these challenges, the oneAPI ports were on average 10% slower than the optimized CUDA versions. We observe that the cases with the highest performance penalties for the oneAPI ports, require significantly more registers than the CUDA originals. This decreases the occupancy in the oneAPI implementation and causes performance degradation. When the number of registers is similar to the CUDA version, we observe penalties lower than 5%.

The remainder of this paper is structured as follows. First, we provide background information on oneAPI and other portability solutions in Sect. 2. Then, we discuss the two numerical integration CUDA implementations in Sect. 3. Section 4 details the porting process and challenges we faced using DPCCT and the oneAPI platform. In Sect. 5, we present a performance comparison of the CUDA and oneAPI implementations of PAGANI and m-Cubes. We finish in Sect. 6 with a discussion of our conclusions regarding the oneAPI platform's viability and ease of use. We demonstrate that the oneAPI implementation does not induce significant performance penalties and that it is a viable platform for attaining performance on Nvidia GPUs.

2 Background

There are multiple programming models targeting different architectures. Among the most prominent, are OpenCL [16,24], OpenACC [5], OpenMP [1], RAJA, Alpaka [30], and Kokkos [10]. The Khronos group was the first to address portability by developing the OpenCL standard to target various architectures. The same group later followed with the SYCL standard. SYCL is a higher-level language that retained OpenCL features but significantly improved ease of use with the utilization of C++ and the adoption of a single-source model. There are multiple implementations of SYCL such as DPC++, ComputeCpp, HipSYCL, and triSYCL [28]. DPC++ is conformant to the latest SYCL and C++ standards and is integrated into the oneAPI ecosystem [2].

2.1 oneAPI and SYCL

oneAPI provides a programming platform with portability across multiple architectures at the core of its mission. Intel's implementation of oneAPI includes an oneAPI Base Toolkit that includes various tools along with the DPC++ language which was based on the SYCL and C++ standards [8]. The reliance on these open standards that are intended to evolve over time is one of the most attractive features of DPC++. Such evolution is facilitated by DPC++ extensions with various features that can be later introduced to the standards after periods of experimentation. Such examples include the use of *Unified Memory* and *filtered Device selectors*, which were missing from SYCL 1.2.1 but were later included in the SYCL 2020 standard. DPC++ achieves execution platform portability through its use of SYCL and various backends (implemented as shared libraries) that interface with particular instruction sets such as PTX for Nvidia GPUs and SPIR-V for Intel devices. It is worth noting that there is no reliance on

OpenCL, which is instead one of several available backends. As such, DPC++ implementations can target various CPUs, GPUs, and FPGAs. This is a similar approach to Kokkos, Alpaka, and RAJA.

2.2 CUDA-Backend for SYCL

While CUDA is the native and most performant programming model for Nvidia GPUs, Nvidia provided support to the OpenCL API [25]. As a result, non-CUDA implementations could be executed on Nvidia GPUs. The ComputeCpp implementation of SYCL by CodePlay, provided such functionality through OpenCL, but its performance was not comparable to native CUDA as not all functionality was exposed [3].

As such, CodePlay developed the CUDA-backend for DPC++, which is part of the LLVM compiler project. CUDA support is not enabled by default and is at an experimental stage. To enable the backend, we must build the LLVM compiler project for CUDA. This can be achieved through easy-to-follow instructions that involve CUDA-specific flags, and the use of *clang++* instead *dpcpp* to compile source code. As a result, DPC++ code can generate PTX code by using CUDA directly instead of relying on the OpenCL backend. This approach not only enables the use of Nvidia libraries and profiling tools with DPC++ but also the capability to theoretically achieve the same performance as CUDA.

2.3 Related Work

The oneAPI programming model may not be as mature as CUDA but the literature already includes several examples of utilizing DPC++. The authors of [12] validated the correctness of a DPC++ tsunami simulator ported from CUDA. A Boris Particle Pusher port from an openMP version was discussed in [27], where a DPC++ implementation was 10% slower than the optimized original. In [14], CUDA and DPC++ implementations of a matrix multiplication kernel were compared on different matrix sizes; the execution time on an NVIDIA GPU was slower with DPC++ code by 7% on small problem sizes but as much as 37% on larger ones. On the contrary, [15] and [13] included experiments where a DPC++ biological sequence alignment code showed no significant performance penalty compared to CUDA, and even a case of 14% speedup. Spare matrix-vector multiplication kernels and *Krylov* solvers in [26] reached 90% of a CUDA version's bandwidth. There were also cases with non-favorable performance for DPC++ ports. In [17] a bioinformatics-related kernel performed twice as fast in CUDA and HIP than in DPC++. In [11] DPC++ versions generally reported comparable performance to CUDA but there were multiple cases where the penalty ranged from 25–190%.

There seems to be a deviation in the attainable performance. This is reasonable due to the variety of applications and the relatively early stage of development for the oneAPI ecosystem. We also expect that the level of optimization in CUDA implementations is an important factor. In our experience, highly optimized codes typically yield performance penalties in the range (5–10%). There are multiple cases displaying approximately 10% penalty compared to native programming models. This indicates that DPC++ can achieve comparable performance to CUDA, though careful tuning and additional optimizations may be needed.

3   Numerical Integration Use Case

Numerical integration is necessary for many applications across various fields and especially physics. Important examples include the simulation of beam dynamics and parameter estimation in cosmological models [6,9,21]. Even ill-behaving integrands (oscillatory, sharply peaked, etc.) can be efficiently integrated with modest computational resources, as long the integration space is low dimensional (one or two variables). On the contrary, solving medium to high-dimensional integrands is often infeasible on standard computing platforms. In such cases, we must execute on highly parallel architectures to achieve performance at scale. There are a few GPU-compatible numerical integration algorithms [7,19,22,23,29]. Unfortunately, exploration of execution-platform portability has been limited, with CUDA being the most common choice. Since CUDA is a proprietary language, such optimized implementations cannot be executed on non-NVIDIA GPUs. To our knowledge, the only mentions of potential portability in numerical integration libraries are found in [22] where a Kokkos implementation of the PAGANI integrator is briefly mentioned to be in development and in [23] which compares the CUDA implementation of m-Cubes with an experimental Kokkos version.

3.1   PAGANI

PAGANI is a deterministic quadrature-based algorithm designed for massively parallel architectures. The algorithm computes an integral by evaluating the quadrature rules, which are a series of weighted summations of the form $\sum_{i=1}^{f_{eval}} w_i \cdot f(x_i)$. The computation involves an integrand function f which we invoke at d-dimensional points x_i. Each x_i point has a corresponding weight w_i and there are f_{eval} such points in the summation. PAGANI computes an initial integral and error estimate, and it progressively improves its accuracy until reaching a user-specified threshold. The accuracy improvement is achieved by applying the quadrature rules in smaller regions of the integration space and accumulating those values to get a new integral estimate.

The most computationally intense kernel of PAGANI is the EVALUATE method (listed in Algorithm 2 of [22]) which consistently takes more than 90% of total execution time. Its function is to compute an integral/error estimate for each region and select one of the dimensional axes for splitting. As such, it can be viewed as the core of PAGANI, both from an algorithmic and performance standpoint. For the remainder of this paper, we will refer to this method as PAGANI-KERNEL.

In PAGANI-KERNEL, each thread-group processes a different region and uses all threads in the group to parallelize the integrand function evaluations. The function evaluations are accumulated through a reduction operation at the end of the kernel. Since all threads within a group operate on the same region, we can store region-related data in shared memory and broadcast it to all threads. This avoids repeated access to the slower global memory for each function evaluation. The threads must also access several read-only arrays which are stored in global memory due to their larger size. Once all computations are finished, thread zero of each group writes the computed integral and error estimate of the region in corresponding output arrays.

The CUDA implementation was optimized for the NVIDIA *V100* GPU. The kernel is launched in groups of 64 threads and the function evaluations, which are greater in number than the number of threads in a group, are performed in a strided fashion. This allows the threads to coalesce accesses to the read-only arrays in global memory. For those read-only arrays, the kernel utilizes on the "ldg" intrinsic, to suggest to the compiler their placement in the read-only cache.

3.2   *m*-Cubes

m-Cubes is a probabilistic Monte Carlo algorithm based on the VEGAS integrator [20]. It computes integrals by randomizing the sample generation across the integration space and relies on the standard deviation of the Monte Carlo estimate to produce error estimates for the computation. The algorithm partitions the integration space into m sub-cubes and assigns them in batches to all available threads.

The V-SAMPLE kernel, we will refer to as MCUBES-KERNEL, is the most computational intense method in the algorithm [23]. The kernel involves the sample generation, invocation of the d-dimensional integrand f at the random points, and the computation of an integral and error estimate. At the beginning of the kernel, each thread is assigned a number of sub-cubes and processes them serially. During the sampling of those cubes, the threads randomly generate a series of d-dimensional points within certain bin boundaries and evaluate the integrand at those points. The magnitude of each function evaluation must then be stored in d corresponding memory locations that represent the d bins used to generate the point. The kernel uses atomic addition to perform these memory writes since there are possible collisions due to a lack of one-to-one mapping between bins and threads. Once the threads in a group have evaluated all their points across all their assigned sub-cubes, a reduction operation accumulates the function evaluations within a thread-group. Then, the results of all thread-group are accumulated through atomic addition, providing an integral and error estimate.

The CUDA implementation was optimized for the *V100* GPU. The kernel consisted of 128 threads per block and utilized 500 bins per dimensional axis. The reduction operations utilize warp-level primitives, though limited shared memory is used to accumulate the values from the different warps.

```
1  void cuda_wrapper(const Sub_regions& regions) {
2    const size_t nBlocks = regions.size;
3    const size_t nThreads = 64;
4    kernel<<<nBlocks, nThreads>>>(regions.leftcoord);
5    cudaDeviceSynchronize();
6  }
```

Listing 1.1. Passing Arguments to CUDA Kernel

4 Porting Process

The maturity of the CUDA programming model along with the more widespread utilization of highly performant NVIDIA GPUs make CUDA an intuitive choice for high-performance applications. As such, PAGANI and m-Cubes were designed and optimized for CUDA on a V100 NVIDIA GPU [22,23]. This makes DPCCT the most appropriate tool to facilitate the porting process from CUDA to DPC++. DPCCT is intended to automate the majority of CUDA code migration to DPC++, instead of performing a total conversion [4]. In our experience as well as those reported in [14,18] and many others, DPCCT functions exactly as intended. An easy-to-complete conversion process requires few manual code insertions.

4.1 Challenges

Errors in Automated Code Migration. A source of errors for DPCCT generated code was our use of C++ structures to encapsulate input/output data that resided in the device memory space. We used C++ to automate allocation, deallocation, and initialization for much of the data needed by our CUDA kernels. The constructors and destructors of these non-trivial C++ structures included calls to the CUDA API (cudaMalloc, cudaFree), while member functions involved host-side processing and even invoked CUDA kernels to perform parallel operations.

DPCCT translated the API calls from CUDA to SYCL without errors for all of our C++ structures. The problem arises when passing members of those structures as parameters to the lambda expressions that define the parallel code. This is a problem because the SYCL standard requires that all objects copied between host and device are trivially-copyable. Execution of parallel code is enabled due to the copying of lambda expressions to the device. To make the lambda copyable, any objects captured by the lambda must be trivially-copyable as well. Our C++ structures are not trivially-copyable because they have user-defined constructors and destructors to allocate and free their data on the device. Even though we do not use the objects themselves in the parallel code, but only to conveniently pass their members as parameters, they are captured nonetheless and cause a static assert error.

```
 1 void bad_sycl_wrapper(Sub_regions* regions) {
 2   sycl::queue q(sycl::gpu_selector());
 3   const size_t nBlocks = regions->size;
 4   const size_t nThreads = 64;
 5
 6   q.submit([&](sycl::handler& h) {
 7     using range = sycl::range<1>;
 8     using ndrange = sycl::nd_range<1>;
 9     using nditem = sycl::nd_item<1>;
10     auto total_size = range(nBlocks) * range(nThreads);
11     auto group_size = range(nThreads);
12     auto kernel = [=](nditem item_ct1){
13       // accessing captured wrapper function's argument
14       // yields a run-time error
15       double x = regions->leftcoord[0];
16       ...
17     };
18     h.parallel_for(nd_range(total_size, group_size),
19                    kernel);
20   });
21   q.wait_and_throw();
22 }
```

Listing 1.2. Unsuccessful Passing of Arguments to SYCL Kernel

We demonstrate this in Listings 1.1, 1.2 and 1.3, where we use the *Sub_regions* struct to encapsulate the device-allocated list *leftcoord* and use it as parameter to a kernel. We pass the *regions* objects to the CUDA wrapper-function (Listing 1.1) by reference (line 1). The *leftcoord* member is then passed by value (line 4) to the kernel without issue. In SYCL, the same approach would result in a compilation error due to the lambda capturing the non-trivially-copyable *regions* object. Thus, the SYCL wrapper-function (Listing 1.2) receives a pointer to the *regions* object. This approach removes the trivially-copyable related compilation error, but accessing *leftcoord* in the parallel code causes an *illegal access* run-time error (line 15). To solve this issue, we must store any data that we want to be captured by our lambda, into scope-local variables. We demonstrate this in Listing 1.3, where the local variable at line 5 is captured by the lambda instead of the class member, resolving all issues.

Another issue we encountered in the DPCCT converted code was the incorrect conversion of atomic addition in our parallel code. DPCCT converted the *atomicAdd* CUDA function call to *dpct::atomic_fetch_add*. The use of this particular function triggers an *unresolved extern* error for the *__spirv_AtomicFAddEXT* function. This is an improper mapping for atomic addition to the CUDA-backend. The same command works on Intel devices. We resolve this problem by using a function directly from the SYCL namespace (see Listing 1.4).

```
1  void sycl_wrapper(Sub_regions* regions) {
2    sycl::queue q(sycl::gpu_selector());
3    const size_t nBlocks = regions->size;
4    const size_t nThreads = 64;
5    const double* leftcoord = regions->leftcoord;
6
7    q.submit([&](sycl::handler& h) {
8      using range = sycl::range<1>;
9      using ndrange = sycl::nd_range<1>;
10      using nditem = sycl::nd_item<1>;
11      auto total_size = range(nBlocks) * range(nThreads);
12      auto group_size = range(nThreads);
13      auto kernel = [=](nditem item_ct1){
14        // accessing captured local variable is fine.
15        double x = leftcoord[0];
16        ...
17      };
18      h.parallel_for(nd_range(total_size, group_size),
19                     kernel);
20    });
21    q.wait_and_throw();
22  }
```

Listing 1.3. Successful Passing of Arguments to SYCL Kernel

```
1  //ptxas fatal    : Unresolved extern function
2  dpct::atomic_fetch_add<double,
3    sycl::access::address_space::generic_space>(
4    &result_dev[0], fbg);
5
6  //functional replacement
7  auto v = sycl::atomic_ref<double,
8    sycl::memory_order::relaxed,
9    sycl::memory_scope::device,
10    sycl::access::address_space::global_space>(result_dev[0]);
11  v += fbg;
```

Listing 1.4. Atomic Addition

Porting Issues with NVIDIA Thrust Library. PAGANI uses Thrust to perform common parallel operations on device-data from the host side. Such operations include reduction, dot-product, prefix sum, and finding the minimum/maximum value in a list. DPCCT successfully automates the translation of these Thrust library calls to SYCL, mainly through the use of equivalent functions in the *dpct* namespace. This requires including the *dpct/dpct.hpp* header which is present in the DPCCT installation. In our experience, the one exception where DPCCT fails to translate a CUDA Thrust library call is the *minmax_element* function. DPCCT inserts a placeholder that prevents compilation and inserts a warning in the code to indicate the issue. We addressed this limitation by using the *min_max* function from the oneMKL library's *Summary Statistics* domain. This approach worked on Intel GPUs and CPUs but we later found that there was no mapping for that function in the CUDA-backend, which caused an *undefined reference* error. To solve this issue, we used the *iamax* and *iamin* routines from the oneMKL library's BLAS domain.

We faced a similar CUDA-backend mapping issue with the *dpct::inner_product* method, which caused a *no matching function* compilation error. We first found the *row_major::dot* method as an alternative in the oneMKL library but it was not implemented for the CUDA-backend. Instead, we used the equivalent routine in the *column_major* namespace which worked for both Intel and NVIDIA devices. The only limitation of the oneMKL *dpct::inner_product* routine was that it required the two input lists to be of the same type. In contrast, the Thrust routine allows the user to compute the dot-product between floating point and integer lists. In most cases, any performance impact from this feature would be negligible, but the impact on memory can be critical for PAGANI. Computationally intense integrands, can require multiple lists with sizes in the order of millions and PAGANI uses memory-saving routines when the available memory is close to being exhausted. Using a floating-point type instead of integer-types for certain lists, can trigger costly memory-saving routines in the oneAPI implementation that may not occur in the CUDA original and thus lead to inferior performance. This scenario is applicable in extreme cases and is not expected to impede average-case execution.

Performance Degradation. We encountered more difficulties when attempting to achieve comparable performance to the original CUDA implementations. The parallel codes for SYCL and CUDA were near-identical, yet we found differences in terms of register pressure and shared memory allocation size. These factors contributed to degraded performance in the SYCL implementations, with execution times often being more than 50% larger than the CUDA originals. The critical optimization that on average minimized execution times to within 10% of the CUDA implementation, was manual loop-unrolling but only after setting the inline-threshold to 10,000. In our initial SYCL implementations, the default inline-threshold limited code inlining and loop-unrolling (even when using unroll directives).

Another method to limit register usage in SYCL was the use of one-dimensional *nd_item* objects (used for indexing and coordinating threads in a group). DPCCT defaults to using 3D *nd_item* even when converting CUDA code that does not utilize multi-dimensional indexing. This is the case for both PAGANI and *m*-Cubes which organize multi-dimensional data in one-dimensional lists and thus have no need for 2D grids. Using the one-dimensional *nd_item* in *m*-Cubes decreased register usage by 10 and yielded small (1–2%) but consistent performance improvement.

Additionally, we found that in many cases, using a custom function to perform work-group reduction through shared memory was faster than the built-in *reduce_over_group*. Computing a six-dimensional integral where PAGANI used the built-in reduction, increased the register count from 100 to 132 and the execution time from 757 ms to 778 ms. We observed that the slowdown was sensitive to the inline-threshold. When using the default threshold, the built-in method yielded equivalent performance to our custom function.

Another challenge in our attempt to achieve comparable performance to CUDA was deviations in the performance of SYCL and CUDA mathematical functions. There is no guarantee that the mathematical functions in SYCL have the same implementations as the functions in the CUDA Math API. In some cases, we must use different functions (e.g. *sycl::pown* instead *pow*) which could make small deviations unavoidable. Exponential functions displayed comparable performance on benchmark kernels. On the contrary, we observed a slowdown of various degrees in SYCL when using *power* or trigonometric functions. This is most likely attributed to the compilers utilizing different optimizations. It is worth noting that we did not use any *fast-math* flags, since high accuracy is critical in numerical integration use cases.

Finally, the use of atomic addition in *m*-Cubes caused orders of magnitude slowdown on both the MCUBES-KERNEL and benchmark kernels. This was attributed to the lack of an architecture-specific flag that must be set to enable efficient atomics when supported. After setting the Volta architecture flag, atomic addition was as performant as in the native CUDA implementation.

Software Engineering Issues. We faced non-intuitive compilation errors due to our use of the Catch2 testing framework. Test code which included the same headers as benchmark code (except the Catch2 headers) failed to compile. We found that including oneDPL library and Catch2 headers was causing the issue. Listing 1.5 illustrates a minimal example that causes a compilation error. Removing the oneDPL header at line 4 eliminates the error. It is worth noting that the same issue occurs if we use *dpct/dpct.hpp* and *dpct/dpl_utils.hpp* instead of the headers at lines 3–4. These *dpct* headers were included by DPCCT to utilize the parallel policies of standard library functions such as *std::exclusive_scan* and *std::reduce*.

Utilization of CMake for building executables and tests was largely successful but more error-prone when targetting the CUDA-backend. We had to include separate CMake commands and flags when building for NVIDIA GPUs. As illustrated in Listing 1.6, we needed additional flags for the CUDA-backend (lines 9 and 12) to specify the GPU architecture, CUDA-backend, and the inline-threshold. Using the oneMKL library, required the *-lonemkl* flag to CMake's *target_compile_options* and the oneMKL location to the *target_link_directories* command, which had to be manually set through the initial CMake command. Building for the *P630* Intel GPU was simpler. We did not need any flags to compile a target, and the oneMKL CMake package made the utilization of the library less verbose. Our supplement of extra flags for the CUDA-backend does not follow standard CMake practices and is error prone. As support for the CUDA-backend exits its experimental stage, we expect such software engineering issues will be less pronounced.

```
1  #define CATCH_CONFIG_MAIN
2  #include "catch2/catch.hpp"
3  #include <oneapi/dpl/execution>
4  #include <oneapi/dpl/algorithm>
5
6  //error: ranges/nanorange.hpp:3303:46: error: reference to '
      match_results' is ambiguous
7
8  TEST_CASE("TEST HEADER INCLUSION")
9  {
10   sycl::queue q;
11 }
```

Listing 1.5. Header Inclusion Issues with Catch2 Testing Framework

5 Experimental Results

We conducted a series of experiments to evaluate the performance and correctness of the oneAPI ports relative to the optimized CUDA implementations of PAGANI and m-Cubes. We used a single node with a V100 NVIDIA GPU and a 2.4 GHz Intel Xeon R Gold 6130 CPU. We also used the Devcloud environment to verify that the DPC++ implementations were portable and could be executed on a P630 Intel GPU. Due to the V100 GPU having significantly more computing cores than the P630, we do not make any performance comparisons between the two GPUs. Instead, we focus on the attainable performance of DPC++ on NVIDIA hardware.

When executing the CUDA implementations, we used gcc 8.5 and CUDA 11.6. For the CUDA-backend execution, we used the same environment but compiled with clang 15, an inline threshold of 10000, and the following compilation flags: "-fsycl -fsycl-targets=nvptx64-nvidia-cuda -Xsycl-target-backend –cuda-gpu-arch=sm_70". We verified the correctness of our ports, by comparing the results on both the NVIDIA (V100) and Intel (P630) GPUs, to the results generated by the CUDA originals on a V100 GPU.

In terms of evaluating performance, we chose the same benchmark integrands originally used to evaluate PAGANI and m-Cubes in [22] and [23]. These functions belong to separate integrand families with features that make accurate estimation challenging. We list those integrands in equations 1 to 6. All experiments use the same integration bounds $(0, 1)$ on each dimensional axis. Similar to [22] and [23], we perform multiple experiments per integrand.

We deviate from [22] and [23] in that we do not execute the PAGANI and m-Cubes methods in their entirety. Instead, we execute their main kernels PAGANI-KERNEL and MCUBES-KERNEL, which is where more than 90% of execution is spent. With this approach, we can evaluate the effectiveness of each programming model in terms of offloading workloads to the device. It allows us to separate kernel evaluation from memory management operations (allocations, copies, etc.)

```
1  # For Intel P60 GPU
2  find_package(MKL REQUIRED)
3  add_executable(exec_name filename.cpp)
4  target_link_libraries(exec_name PUBLIC MKL::MKL_DPCPP)
5
6  # For CUDA backend
7  #we must store the path to oneMKL library in the CMake
8  # variable ONEMKL_DIR store GPU architeture in CMake variable
      TARGET_ARCH
9  set(CMAKE_CXX_FLAGS "${CMAKE_CXX_FLAGS} -fsycl -fsycl-targets
      =nvptx64-nvidia-cuda -Xsycl-target-backend --cuda-gpu-
      arch=${TARGET_ARCH}")
10 add_executable(exec_name filename.cpp)
11 target_link_directories(exec_name PUBLIC "${ONEMKL_DIR}")
12 target_compile_options(exec_name PRIVATE "-lonemkl" "-mllvm"
      "-inline-threshold=10000")
```

Listing 1.6. Using CMake

and library usage. This comparison of custom kernel implementations is a better indicator of performance implications when porting CUDA codes to DPC++.

$$f_{1,d}(x) = \cos\left(\sum_{i=1}^{d} i\, x_i\right) \tag{1}$$

$$f_{2,d}(x) = \prod_{i=1}^{d}\left(\frac{1}{50^2} + (x_i - 1/2)^2\right)^{-1} \tag{2}$$

$$f_{3,d}(x) = \left(1 + \sum_{i=1}^{d} i\, x_i\right)^{-d-1} \tag{3}$$

$$f_{4,d}(x) = \exp\left(-625\sum_{i=1}^{d}(x_i - 1/2)^2\right) \tag{4}$$

$$f_{5,d}(x) = \exp\left(-10\sum_{i=1}^{d}|x_i - 1/2|\right) \tag{5}$$

$$f_{6,d}(x) = \begin{cases} \exp\left(\sum_{i=1}^{d}(i+4)\,x_i\right) & \text{if } x_i < (3+i)/10 \\ 0 & \text{otherwise} \end{cases} \tag{6}$$

5.1   Offloading Mathematical Computations to Kernels

A critical stage in PAGANI-KERNEL and M-CUBES-KERNEL is the invocation of the integrand at various d-dimensional points. Integrands with trigonometric or exponential functions and table look-ups will have larger execution times compared to other simple integrands that only contain basic mathematical operations. To attain satisfactory performance, both the invocation of the integrand functions and the remaining operations within the kernels must achieve comparable performance to the CUDA implementation.

We tested the efficiency of the integrand oneAPI implementations with a simple kernel that performs a series of invocations on many d-dimensional points. The points are randomly generated on the host and then copied to device memory. Each thread invokes the integrand serially 1 million times and writes its accumulated results to global memory. Writing the results prevents the NVCC and Clang compilers from disregarding the integrand computations due to optimization.

We first tested simple integrands that contained only a particular function such as *sin, pow, powf, sycl::exp, sycl::pow, sycl::pown*. We invoked these mathematical functions with d arguments that comprise each d-dimensional point. We did not use fast-math flags as accuracy is critical in numerical integration. We observed small but consistent penalties of at most 2% when invoking the *power* and *exponential* functions. On the contrary, trigonometric functions are approximately 40% slower on the CUDA-backend.

We performed the same experiment on the six benchmark integrands for dimensions 5 to 8. We summarize the results in Table 1. The timings in CUDA and oneAPI columns are the means of 10 kernel executions per integrand. The ratio of those timings shows that the oneAPI version is at most 4% slower. The largest penalty is observed in the $f1$ integrand which makes use of the *cos* function. The remaining integrands only make use of *exponential* and *power* functions and yield small penalties.

These experiments on the execution time of the integrand invocations demonstrate that the user-defined computations do not display significant performance penalties. The one exception is the extended use of trigonometric functions. None of the benchmark integrands make extended use of trigonometric functions ($f1$ has one call to *cos* per invocation). As such, we do not expect any slowdown larger than 5% in either PAGANI or m-Cubes to be attributed to the integrand implementations.

Table 1. Mean (μ) and standard deviation (σ) of execution times for invoking $5-8D$ benchmark integrands

id	μ CUDA (ms)	μ oneAPI (ms)	σ CUDA	σ oneAPI	$\frac{\mu\ oneAPI}{\mu\ CUDA}$
f1	1866.4	1952.4	13.3	21.4	1.04
f2	8413.9	8487.3	5012.5	5042.9	1.009
f3	1812.4	1828.3	18.5	27.1	1.009
f4	11416.1	11410.1	2184.9	2148.1	0.99
f5	634.3	654.4	73.5	67.3	1.03
f6	300.4	300.8	32.05	32.6	1.001

5.2 Benchmark Integrands Performance Comparison

Another set of experiments involved the invocation of the PAGANI-KERNEL and MCUBES-KERNEL on the benchmark integrands. To address different degrees of computational intensity, we vary the number of thread-blocks used to launch the kernels. For the MCUBES-KERNEL, we achieve this effect by varying the required number of samples per iteration in the range ($1e8, 3e9$). This leads to different block sizes per kernel. For PAGANI-KERNEL, the number of thread blocks corresponds to the number of regions being processed. We perform high-resolution uniform splits to generate region lists of different sizes and supply them to the PAGANI-KERNEL for evaluation.

We report the penalty of using oneAPI for the benchmark integrands, in the ratio columns of Tables 2 and 3. We used four thread-block sizes for each integrand for the kernel executions. Each kernel configuration (number of thread groups) was repeated 100 times to provide a statistical mean and standard deviation for the execution times.

Across our experiments, the average execution time ratio ($\frac{oneAPI}{CUDA}$) is in the range (0–10%). The $f2$ and $f4$ integrands which make repeated use of the *power* function display the largest performance penalties for both PAGANI and m-Cubes. It is worth noting that both $f2$ and $f4$ display the largest execution times among the benchmark integrands for both integrators.

5.3 Simple Integrands Performance Comparison

In addition to the benchmark integrands, we also evaluate integrands that only perform a summation of the arguments ($\sum_{i=1}^{d} x_i$) where d is the number of dimensions. This avoids any bias in the comparison by avoiding mathematical functions that could either call different implementations, cause differences in register usage or lead to different optimizations. The ratios in Tables 4 and 5, display timings on addition integrands for dimensions five to eight. Once more, we observe penalties smaller than 10% and for both integrators these penalties decrease on higher dimensionalities.

Table 2. m-Cubes: mean (μ) and standard deviation (σ) of execution times for 8D benchmark integrands in CUDA and oneAPI

id	μ CUDA (ms)	μ oneAPI (ms)	σ CUDA	σ oneAPI	$\frac{\mu\,oneAPI}{\mu\,CUDA}$
f1	286.7	286.7	2.1	0.9	1.0
f2	402.1	443.1	2.6	0.9	1.1
f3	284.5	285.8	1.6	1.4	1.0
f4	385.7	423.5	2.4	0.5	1.1
f5	284.3	285.9	2.1	1.7	1.0
f6	283.8	285.4	1.9	1.6	1.0

Table 3. PAGANI: mean (μ) and standard deviation (σ) of execution times for 8D benchmark integrands in CUDA and oneAPI

id	μ CUDA (ms)	μ oneAPI (ms)	σ CUDA	σ oneAPI	$\frac{\mu\,oneAPI}{\mu\,CUDA}$
f1	172.3	177.5	0.9	1.2	1.02
f2	1500.4	1651.0	0.3	2.1	1.1
f3	286.4	290.7	0.8	0.4	1.01
f4	1434.7	1524.9	0.4	1.9	1.06
f5	166.5	170.7	0.6	0.4	1.03
f6	136.8	139.4	0.4	0.2	1.02

5.4 Factors Limiting Performance

Particularly for compute-bound kernels such as PAGANI-KERNEL and MCUBES-KERNEL, which perform thousands of computations for each byte of accessed memory, occupancy is a critical performance factor. The amount of allocated shared memory and registers per thread limits warp occupancy, and thus any large deviation in those values for the SYCL implementation can degrade performance.

In most cases, the SYCL implementations assigned more registers to each thread compared to their CUDA equivalents. We illustrate the magnitude of this difference in registers per thread in Figs. 1 and 2. We observe the largest difference in integrands $f2$ and $f4$, which make extended use of the *power function*. It is the same functions that display the two largest execution time penalties for the benchmark integrands in Tables 2 and 3.

We observe a similar pattern on the simple addition integrands (Table 4 and 5). In those cases, there are no mathematical functions (*pow*, *exp*, etc.) and the integrands only perform a summation. The difference in registers decreases on higher dimensions, leading to degraded performance on low dimensions. This is evident in Tables 4 and 5 where higher-dimensional integrands have smaller values in the $\frac{oneAPI}{CUDA}$ column. The same pattern is observed for the benchmark integrands, where the high dimensional versions perform better than the low

Table 4. m-Cubes: mean (μ) and standard deviation (σ) of execution times for addition integrands ($\sum_{i=1}^{d} x_i$) in CUDA and oneAPI

id	μ CUDA (ms)	μ oneAPI (ms)	σ CUDA	σ oneAPI	$\frac{\mu\, oneAPI}{\mu\, CUDA}$
5D	206.1	214.5	2.1	1.7	1.04
6D	214.1	217.2	2.2	1.0	1.01
7D	234.1	235.2	1.8	0.9	1.005
8D	284.7	285.7	1.9	1.9	1.005

Table 5. PAGANI: mean (μ) and standard deviation (σ) of execution times for addition integrands ($\sum_{i=1}^{d} x_i$) in CUDA and oneAPI

id	CUDA (ms)	oneAPI (ms)	Std. CUDA	Std. oneAPI	$\frac{oneAPI}{CUDA}$
5D	1.5	1.7	0.05	0.06	1.1
6D	24.8	26.7	0.3	1.4	1.1
7D	129.8	131.6	0.7	0.2	1.01
8D	137.4	137.6	1.3	1.0	1.001

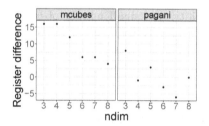

Fig. 1. Register difference on simple addition integrands ($\sum_{i=1}^{d} x_i$). The y-axis displays the number of additional registers per thread in the DPC++ implementation.

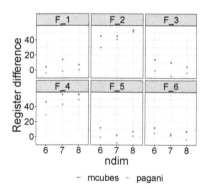

Fig. 2. Register difference on the benchmark integrands. The y-axis displays the number of additional registers per thread in the DPC++ implementation.

dimension equivalents. It can be seen in Fig. 1, that this effect is more prominent in m-Cubes, since it displays a larger deviation across all dimensions. These observations lead us to believe that register difference and its effect on occupancy is the main reason behind the performance degradation.

6   Conclusion

We presented our experience of porting two numerical integration implementations, PAGANI and m-Cubes, from CUDA to DPC++. We utilized Intel's DPCCT to automate the conversion process from CUDA to SYCL and successfully attained the capability to execute the same implementation on both Intel and NVIDIA GPUs. We experimented with various workloads consisting of different mathematical functions. We found that the assigned registers per thread can deviate in oneAPI and CUDA codes. This affects occupancy which in turn can negatively impact performance, particularly in compute-bound kernels. We faced additional challenges with mapping library calls to oneAPI equivalents, matching compiler optimizations of NVCC with Clang, and using build and testing libraries like CMake and Catch2. We addressed those challenges and demonstrated that the performance penalty of using oneAPI ports instead of optimized CUDA implementations can be limited to 10% on NVIDIA GPUs. Additionally, numerous cases exhibited comparable performance to the original CUDA implementations, with execution time differences in the 1–2% range. We compared oneAPI and CUDA implementations on the same NVIDIA V100 GPU. We were able to execute on an Intel P630 GPU but we did not compare these timings with those on the V100 GPU due their significant difference in computing power. In the future, we plan to execute on the high end Intel Ponte Vecchio GPU and compare performance metrics with NVIDIA high end GPUs such as A100.

The vast array of libraries, ease of portability, and small margin of performance degradation, make oneAPI an appropriate software solution for the use case of numerical integration.

References

1. https://www.openmp.org/wp-content/uploads/OpenMP-API-Specification-5.0. pdf
2. Argonne leadership computing facility. https://www.alcf.anl.gov/support-center/ aurora/sycl-and-dpc-aurora#:~:text=DPC%2B%2B%20Data%20Parallel%20C, versions%20of%20the%20SYCL%20language
3. Computecpp^{TM} community edition. https://developer.codeplay.com/products/ computecpp/ce/2.11.0/guides/#computecpp
4. Migrate cuda* to dpc++ code: Intel®dpc++ compatibility tool. https://www. intel.com/content/www/us/en/developer/tools/oneapi/dpc-compatibility-tool. html#gs.lx007q
5. What is OpenACC?. https://www.openacc.org/
6. Giannini, G., et al.: Dark energy survey year 3 results: redshift calibration of the MagLim lens sample from the combination of SOMPZ and clustering and its impact on cosmology (2022)
7. Arumugam, K., Godunov, A., Ranjan, D., Terzic, B., Zubair, M.: A memory efficient algorithm for adaptive multidimensional integration with multiple GPUs. In: 20th Annual International Conference on High Performance Computing, pp. 169–175. IEEE (2013)

8. Ashbaugh, B., et al.: Data parallel c++: enhancing sycl through extensions for productivity and performance. In: Proceedings of the International Workshop on OpenCL, IWOCL 2020. Association for Computing Machinery, New York (2020). https://doi.org/10.1145/3388333.3388653

9. Bridle, S., et al.: CosmoSIS: a system for mc parameter estimation. In: Journal of Physics: Conference Series, vol. 664, no. 7, p. 072036 (2015). https://doi.org/10.1088/1742-6596/664/7/072036

10. Carter Edwards, H., Trott, C.R., Sunderland, D.: Kokkos: enabling manycore performance portability through polymorphic memory access patterns. J. Parallel Distrib. Comput. **74**(12), 3202–3216 (2014)

11. Castaño, G., Faqir-Rhazoui, Y., García, C., Prieto-Matías, M.: Evaluation of Intel's DPC++ compatibility tool in heterogeneous computing. J. Parallel Distrib. Comput. **165**, 120–129 (2022). https://doi.org/10.1016/j.jpdc.2022.03.017. https://www.sciencedirect.com/science/article/pii/S0743731522000727

12. Christgau, S., Steinke, T.: Porting a legacy CUDA stencil code to oneAPI. In: 2020 IEEE International Parallel and Distributed Processing Symposium Workshops (IPDPSW), pp. 359–367 (2020). https://doi.org/10.1109/IPDPSW50202.2020.00070

13. Costanzo, M., Rucci, E., García-Sánchez, C., Naiouf, M., Prieto-Matías, M.: Migrating CUDA to oneAPI: a smith-waterman case study. In: Rojas, I., Valenzuela, O., Rojas, F., Herrera, L.J., Ortuño, F. (eds.) IWBBIO 2022. LNCS, pp. 103–116. Springer, Cham (2022). https://doi.org/10.1007/978-3-031-07802-6_9

14. Costanzo, M., Rucci, E., Sanchez, C.G., Naiouf, M.: Early experiences migrating CUDA codes to oneAPI (2021)

15. Costanzo, M., Rucci, E., Sánchez, C.G., Naiouf, M., Prieto-Matías, M.: Assessing opportunities of sycl and intel oneAPI for biological sequence alignment (2022)

16. Doerfert, J., et al.: Breaking the vendor lock-performance portable programming through OpenMP as target independent runtime layer. Technical report, Lawrence Livermore National Lab. (LLNL), Livermore, CA (United States) (2022)

17. Haseeb, M., Ding, N., Deslippe, J., Awan, M.: Evaluating performance and portability of a core bioinformatics kernel on multiple vendor GPUs. In: 2021 International Workshop on Performance, Portability and Productivity in HPC (P3HPC), pp. 68–78 (2021). https://doi.org/10.1109/P3HPC54578.2021.00010

18. Jin, Z., Vetter, J.: Evaluating CUDA portability with HIPCL and DPCT. In: 2021 IEEE International Parallel and Distributed Processing Symposium Workshops (IPDPSW), pp. 371–376 (2021). https://doi.org/10.1109/IPDPSW52791.2021.00065

19. Kanzaki, J.: Monte Carlo integration on GPU. Eur. Phys. J. C Particles Fields **71**(2), 1–7 (2011)

20. Peter Lepage, G.: A new algorithm for adaptive multidimensional integration. J. Comput. Phys. **27**(2), 192–203 (1978). https://doi.org/10.1016/0021-9991(78)90004-9. https://www.sciencedirect.com/science/article/pii/0021999178900049

21. Ranjan, N., Terzić, B., Krafft, G., Petrillo, V., Drebot, I., Serafini, L.: Simulation of inverse Compton scattering and its implications on the scattered linewidth. Phys. Rev. Accelerators Beams **21**(3), 030701 (2018)

22. Sakiotis, I., Arumugam, K., Paterno, M., Ranjan, D., Terzić, B., Zubair, M.: PAGANI: a parallel adaptive GPU algorithm for numerical integration. Association for Computing Machinery, New York (2021). https://doi.org/10.1145/3458817.3476198

23. Sakiotis, I., Arumugam, K., Paterno, M., Ranjan, D., Terzić, B., Zubair, M.: m-cubes: an efficient and portable implementation of multi-dimensional integration for GPUs. In: Varbanescu, A.L., Bhatele, A., Luszczek, P., Marc, B. (eds.) ISC High Performance 2022. LNCS, pp. 192–209. Springer, Cham (2022). https://doi.org/10.1007/978-3-031-07312-0_10

24. Stone, J.E., Gohara, D., Shi, G.: OpenCL: a parallel programming standard for heterogeneous computing systems. Comput. Sci. Eng. **12**(3), 66–73 (2010)

25. Su, C.L., Chen, P.Y., Lan, C.C., Huang, L.S., Wu, K.H.: Overview and comparison of OpenCL and CUDA technology for GPGPU. In: 2012 IEEE Asia Pacific Conference on Circuits and Systems, pp. 448–451 (2012). https://doi.org/10.1109/APCCAS.2012.6419068

26. Tsai, Y.M., Cojean, T., Anzt, H.: Porting sparse linear algebra to Intel GPUs. In: Chaves, R., et al. (eds.) Euro-Par 2021. LNCS, pp. 57–68. Springer, Cham (2022). https://doi.org/10.1007/978-3-031-06156-1_5

27. Volokitin, V., Bashinov, A., Efimenko, E., Gonoskov, A., Meyerov, I.: High performance implementation of Boris particle pusher on DPC++. A first look at oneAPI. In: Malyshkin, V. (ed.) PaCT 2021. LNCS, vol. 12942, pp. 288–300. Springer, Cham (2021). https://doi.org/10.1007/978-3-030-86359-3_22

28. Wong, M., et al.: Sycl - C++ single-source heterogeneous programming for acceleration offload (2014). https://www.khronos.org/sycl/

29. Wu, H.Z., Zhang, J.J., Pang, L.G., Wang, Q.: ZMCintegral: a package for multi-dimensional Monte Carlo integration on multi-GPUs. Comput. Phys. Commun. **248**, 106962 (2020). https://doi.org/10.1016/j.cpc.2019.106962. https://www.sciencedirect.com/science/article/pii/S0010465519303121

30. Zenker, E., et al.: Alpaka - an abstraction library for parallel kernel acceleration. Cornell University Library, Ithaca (2016)

Performance Evaluation of a Next-Generation SX-Aurora TSUBASA Vector Supercomputer

Keichi Takahashi[1]([⊠]) [ID], Soya Fujimoto[2], Satoru Nagase[2], Yoko Isobe[2],
Yoichi Shimomura[1], Ryusuke Egawa[3] [ID], and Hiroyuki Takizawa[1] [ID]

[1] Tohoku University, Sendai, Japan
{keichi,shimomura32,takizawa}@tohoku.ac.jp
[2] NEC Corporation, Tokyo, Japan
{s-fujimoto,s.nagase,y-isobe-pi}@nec.com
[3] Tokyo Denki University, Tokyo, Japan
egawa@mail.dendai.ac.jp

Abstract. Data movement is a key bottleneck in terms of both performance and energy efficiency in modern HPC systems. The NEC SX-series supercomputers have a long history of accelerating memory-intensive HPC applications by providing sufficient memory bandwidth to applications. In this paper, we analyze the performance of a prototype SX-Aurora TSUBASA supercomputer equipped with the brand-new Vector Engine (VE30) processor. VE30 is the first major update to the Vector Engine processor series, and offers significantly improved memory access performance due to its renewed memory subsystem. Moreover, it introduces new instructions and incorporates architectural advancements tailored for accelerating memory-intensive applications. Using standard benchmarks, we demonstrate that VE30 considerably outperforms other processors in both performance and efficiency of memory-intensive applications. We also evaluate VE30 using applications including SPEChpc, and show that VE30 can run real-world applications with high performance. Finally, we discuss performance tuning techniques to obtain maximum performance from VE30.

Keywords: performance evaluation · SX-Aurora TSUBASA · memory-intensive applications · vector processor · vector supercomputer

1 Introduction

The *memory wall* is a longstanding challenge in HPC that refers to the continuously widening gap between arithmetic computing performance and memory performance in a computing system. Due to the memory wall problem, memory-intensive applications are bottlenecked by data movement and unable to fully utilize the arithmetic computing performance of a system. Not only does this hurt the performance of applications, but it also degrades energy efficiency. The HPC community has therefore been actively exploring novel architectures to tackle the memory wall, such as adopting high-bandwidth memory devices for off-chip memory [4,24], implementing large amounts of on-chip memory [16,21], and reducing memory accesses by directly exchanging data between processing elements [9,11].

ⓒ The Author(s), under exclusive license to Springer Nature Switzerland AG 2023
A. Bhatele et al. (Eds.): ISC High Performance 2023, LNCS 13948, pp. 359–378, 2023.
https://doi.org/10.1007/978-3-031-32041-5_19

However, these exotic architectures completely differ from general-purpose CPUs, and often require the programmer to become familiar with unconventional programming models. For example, the device could require multiple magnitudes larger degree of parallelism than a CPU, or data movement across the memory subsystem might require explicit management by the programmer. As a consequence, developing software for such emerging hardware is generally time-consuming and expensive. If a large body of users exists, the cost for developing optimized software for a specialized system could be amortized (*e.g.*, deep learning). However, it is often the case in HPC that a scientifically important software package is maintained by a handful of programmers and used by a small group of users. In such a case, the development cost becomes prohibitive.

NEC's SX-Aurora TSUBASA (SX-AT) supercomputer aims to achieve both world-class memory performance and high productivity by a unique combination of latest memory technology with the vector architecture. The vector architecture has a long history and recently regained interests from the community. This trend can be seen in the ARM Scalable Vector Extension [28] and upcoming RISC-V Vector Extension [20], both of which are heavily inspired by the vector architecture. Since most HPC applications exhibit high data-level parallelism that can be automatically exploited by a vectorizing compiler, conventional software targeted for general-purpose CPUs can run with minor modifications. To keep feeding data to the high-performance vector cores, High Bandwidth Memory (HBM) is tightly coupled with the processor. As a result, SX-AT offers massive memory performance to applications while ensuring programmer productivity.

NEC has recently been prototyping a brand-new vector processor named Vector Engine 3.0 (VE30) for SX-AT. VE30 takes a big leap from the previous Vector Engine series, and brings a number of architectural advancements beyond peak compute and memory performance increase. Specifically, VE30 introduces bypassable per-core private L3 caches as a new level in the memory hierarchy to accelerate cache-intensive applications. In addition, a new instruction that performs indirectly addressed vector accumulation within a compute-capable LLC is added.

Since these combined improvements are expected to accelerate applications beyond the improvement of peak performance, application performance cannot be trivially estimated. We therefore carry out the first performance analysis of a next-generation vector supercomputer based on the VE30 processor. The main contributions of this paper are summarized as follows.

- This is the first work to evaluate the performance of a next-generation vector super-computer equipped with VE30 processors. Using industry-standard benchmarks and several applications, we assess the basic and application performance of VE30.
- This is the first evaluation of a vector processor using the SPEChpc 2021 benchmark suite. Since the benchmarks included in SPEChpc are carefully selected from a wide spectrum of scientific domains, we believe that our evaluation shows the real-world performance of VE30.
- This paper elucidates the performance gain obtained by each architectural improvement newly introduced in VE30 using microbenchmarks. Understanding the performance benefit of these features is vital for tuning applications for VE30, and establishes a foundation for developing novel tuning techniques.

– This paper discusses several performance tuning techniques to take advantages of the new architectural capabilities of VE30 to accelerate application performance.

The rest of this paper is organized as follows. Section 2 introduces the NEC SX-AT supercomputer and describes the basic architecture of the VE30 processor. Section 3 extensively evaluates the performance of VE30 using standard benchmarks, microbenchmarks and real-world workloads. Section 4 discusses performance tuning techniques to fully exploit the potential of the VE30 processor. Section 5 concludes this paper.

2   Overview of SX-Aurora TSUBASA VE30

In this section, we first outline the architecture of the SX-AT supercomputer, and introduce the newly developed VE30 processor. We then describe the architectural enhancements of VE30 from its predecessor.

2.1   The SX-Aurora TSUBASA Product Family

The *SX-Aurora TSUBASA (SX-AT)* is the latest product family in the NEC SX vector supercomputers series. While SX-AT inherits the well-established and successful design philosophy of its predecessors, it also embraces the current *de facto* standard HPC software ecosystem. The first-generation SX-AT based on the Vector Engine 1.0 (VE10) processor was released in 2018 [13], which was followed by the second-generation SX-AT based on the Vector Engine 2.0 (VE20) processor released in 2020 [7]. The third-generation SX-AT based on the Vector Engine 3.0 (VE30) processor, which is evaluated in this paper, was released in October 2022.

SX-AT employs a heterogeneous architecture consisting of a *Vector Host (VH)* and a *Vector Engine (VE)*. The VH is an x86 server responsible for running the OS and performing tasks such as process and memory management and I/O. The VE is a vector processor implemented on a PCI Express (PCIe) card, and executes the application. The VH communicates with the VE over the PCIe link and controls the VE.

Although on the surface a VE resembles an accelerator such as a GPU, its execution model differs substantially from that of a conventional accelerator. Applications are fully executed on the VE, and system calls are forwarded to the VH and handled by proxy processes running on the VH. This design eliminates kernel launch overhead and reduces data transfer found in conventional accelerators. Furthermore, this design allows users to develop their applications using standard MPI and OpenMP-based programming models, and does not require any knowledge of a vendor-specific programming language or framework.

2.2   Basic Architecture of the VE30 Processor

Figure 1 illustrates an overview of a prototype VE30 processor, and Fig. 2 depicts the memory hierarchy of a VE30 processor. The VE30 processor integrates 16 vector cores, a shared LLC and six HBM2E modules. Each vector core can perform up to 307.2 GFLOP/s (DP) or 614.4 GFLOP/s (SP), and thus a single socket performs

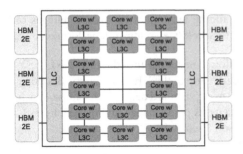

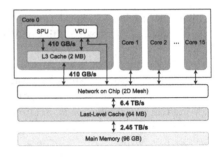

Fig. 1. Block diagram of the VE30 processor.

Fig. 2. Memory hierarchy of the VE30 processor.

4.91 TFLOP/s (DP) or 9.83 TFLOP/s (SP) in total. The six HBM2E modules have 96 GB of capacity and provide an aggregate memory bandwidth of 2.45 TB/s to the cores. The shared LLC is 64 MB in size. The cores and LLC are interconnected through a 2-dimensional Network on Chip (NoC). Similar to the Sub-NUMA Clustering (SNC) [10] in the recent Intel processors, VE30 provides a *partitioning mode*, which splits the cores, LLC and HBM in the processor into two NUMA nodes. This increases the aggregate effective LLC bandwidth by alleviating congestion in the NoC, and benefits LLC-intensive applications.

A vector core in VE30 comprises a Scalar Processing Unit (SPU) and a Vector Processing Unit (VPU). The SPU fetches and decodes instructions, executes scalar instructions and dispatches vector instructions to the VPU. An SPU contains a 64 KB L1 instruction cache, a 64 KB L1 data cache, and a 512 KB unified L2 cache. A VPU contains 64 architectural vector registers that are renamed to 188 physical vector registers. A single vector register holds up to 256 double-precision floating point elements (*i.e.,* 2 KB). A VPU contains 32 vector pipelines, each of which has three Fused-Multiply Add (FMA) execution units. Thus, in total, a vector core can perform 96 FMA operations in a single cycle. The SPU and VPU share a 2 MB unified write-through L3 cache.

2.3 Architectural Improvements from the VE20 Processor

VE30 features a significantly advanced memory subsystem compared to its predecessor. First, the introduction of a new level in the memory hierarchy, per-core private L3 caches, alleviates LLC contention and enables cache-intensive applications to achieve higher performance. Second, the LLC capacity and bandwidth are increased by 4× and 2.13×, respectively. Third, both the capacity and bandwidth of the HBM are also improved. The peak HBM bandwidth is increased by 1.60× from 1.53 TB/s to 2.45 TB/s, and the HBM capacity is doubled from 48 GB to 96 GB. These drastic improvements to the memory subsystem combined are expected to significantly accelerate both memory-intensive and cache-intensive applications.

In addition to the enhancements made to the memory subsystem, the core count is increased from 10 to 16 cores, which increases the peak single-socket performance from 3.07 TFLOP/s to 4.91 TFLOP/s. It should be noted that, despite the increase in the number of cores, the per-core cache and memory performance is either increased or maintained.

Furthermore, a number of improvements are made to the core. First, VE30 relaxes the alignment requirement for single-precision floating point vectors, and improves the performance single-precision applications. Second, VE30 introduces a dedicated hardware mechanism for accelerating vector accumulation with indirect addressing. These improvements do not directly contribute to the peak FLOP/s rate, but are expected to benefit the performance of real-world applications.

3 Performance Evaluation

In this section, we first reveal the basic performance of VE30 using industry-standard benchmarks. We then use microbenchmarks to examine the performance gains delivered by architectural improvements introduced in VE30. Finally, we use workloads that represent practical applications to assess the real-world performance of VE30. Note that the performance measurements on VE30 are conducted using prototype software and hardware. Thus, the results may be subject to change on the final product.

3.1 Evaluation Environment

Table 1. Specifications of the evaluated processors.

	VE Type 20B	VE Type 30A	A64FX	Xeon Platinum 8368	A100 80 GB PCIe
Frequency [GHz]	1.6	1.6	2.2	2.4	1.412
Performance per Core [GFLOP/s]	307 (DP) 614 (SP)	307 (DP) 614 (SP)	70 (DP) 140 (SP)	83.2 (DP)[a] 166 (SP)	181 (DP) w/ Tensor Core 90 (DP) w/o Tensor Core 181 (SP)
Number of Cores	8	16	48	38	108
Performance per Socket [TFLOP/s]	2.4 (DP) 4.9 (SP)	4.9 (DP) 9.8 (SP)	3.3 (DP) 6.7 (SP)	3.1 (DP)[a] 6.3 (SP)	19.5 (DP) w/ Tensor Core 9.7 (DP) w/o Tensor Core 19.5 (SP)
LLC Bandwidth [TB/s]	3.0	6.4	3.6	3.2[b]	4.9[b]
LLC Capacity [MB]	16	64	32	54	40
Memory Bandwidth [TB/s]	1.53	2.45	1.024	0.204	1.935
Memory Capacity [GB]	48	96	32	256	80
Process Rule [nm]	16	7	7	10	7

[a] The peak performance is calculated based on the AVX-512 Turbo Frequency when all cores are active.

[b] The LLC bandwidth (L2 bandwidth on IceLake-SP) is measured using the Empirical Roofline Toolkit (https://bitbucket.org/berkeleylab/cs-roofline-toolkit) since the peak bandwidth is not disclosed by the manufacturers.

Table 1 summarizes the specifications of the processors used in this evaluation. We compare VE30 to a variety of latest processors used in HPC spanning from a vector processor, GPU, many-core processor and general-purpose CPU: NEC Vector Engine Type

20B (an 8-core SKU of VE20) [7], NVIDIA A100 40 GB and 80 GB PCIe models [4], Fujitsu A64FX [24], and Intel Xeon Platinum 8368 (IceLake-SP) [19]. As shown in Table 1, the peak performance of A100 doubles when the Tensor Cores are included. We use the peak performance including the Tensor Cores when calculating the efficiency of HPL, and the peak performance excluding the Tensor Cores for the other benchmarks. This is because all benchmarks except HPL do not use the Tensor Cores.

Multi-node measurements for VE30 are carried out on a cluster composed of 16 VHs interconnected with a dual-rail InfiniBand HDR 200 Gbps network. Each VH is equipped with eight Vector Engine Type 30A cards, an AMD EPYC 7713P processor and 512 GB of DDR4-3200 SDRAM. As for the multi-node measurements for the other processors, the *AOBA-C* system at Tohoku University is used for VE20, the *Flow* Type I Subsystem at Nagoya University is used for A64FX, and the *SQUID* CPU and GPU nodes are used for IceLake-SP and A100.

3.2 Basic Benchmarks

We use four widely recognized benchmarks in HPC to evaluate the basic performance of VE30: the High Performance Linpack (HPL) [6] benchmark, STREAM benchmark, High Performance Conjugate Gradients (HPCG) [5] and Himeno benchmark [8].

HPL is a compute-intensive benchmark that solves a dense system of linear equations using LU decomposition with partial pivoting. The STREAM benchmark measures the effective memory bandwidth. HPCG is a memory-intensive benchmark that solves a sparse linear system using the conjugate gradient method and a geometric multigrid preconditioner. The Himeno benchmark is also memory-intensive, and solves the Poisson equation using the Jacobi method. Only the Himeno benchmark uses single-precision floating point numbers for computation and the rest use double-precision floating point numbers. Since HPL and HPCG executables optimized for the A64FX processor are unavailable to us, the HPL and HPCG performance of A64FX is calculated based on the Top500 result of an A64FX-based system (*Fugaku* [24]).

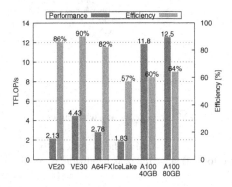

Fig. 3. HPL benchmark performance.

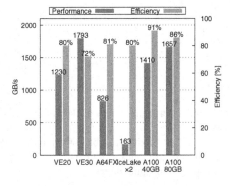

Fig. 4. Effective memory bandwidth.

Figure 3 compares the HPL performance of different processors. The NVIDIA A100 clearly stands out from the other processors. The A100 40 GB model achieves over

11.8 TFLOP/s in HPL performance, and the 80 GB model achieves a slightly higher performance of 12.5 TFLOP/s due to the increased problem size and higher TDP. The VE30 processor delivers 4.43 TFLOP/s and surpasses both A64FX and IceLake-SP. With respect to efficiency, VE30 is the highest with an efficiency of 90%, followed by A64FX and VE20. A100 shows relatively low efficiency as it cannot maintain the GPU boost clock due to power throttling.

Figure 4 compares the effective memory bandwidth of the different processors measured using STREAM. The effective memory bandwidth of VE30 exceeds 1.79 TB/s and is clearly the highest among the evaluated processors. Compared to its predecessor, VE20, the effective memory bandwidth of VE30 is 1.45× higher.

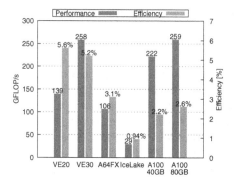

Fig. 5. HPCG benchmark performance.

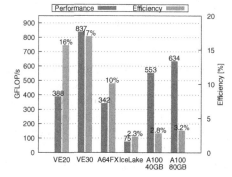

Fig. 6. Himeno benchmark performance (XL size).

Figure 5 shows the HPCG performance of the evaluated processors. VE30 attains 258 GFLOP/s and outperforms VE20, A64FX, IceLake-SP and the A100 40 GB model. It achieves almost identical performance as the A100 80 GB model. In terms of efficiency, VE30 achieves 5.2% of the peak performance, which is considerably higher than that of the other processors: 1.97× higher than the A100 80 GB model and 5.72× higher than IceLake-SP. Furthermore, VE30 achieves the highest energy efficiency among all processors. The energy efficiency of VE30 when executing HPCG reaches 1.034 GFLOP/s/W, while A100 40 GB and 80 GB models achieve 0.909 GFLOP/s/W and 0.999 GFLOP/s/W, respectively. These results highlight that VE30 successfully strikes the balance between memory performance and floating-point performance, whereas other processors heavily prioritize floating-point performance over memory performance.

Figure 6 shows the performance of the Himeno benchmark. VE30 is the best-performing one among all processors. It marks 837 GFLOP/s and surpasses the A100 40 GB and 80 GB models by a factor of 1.51× and 1.32×, respectively. Interestingly, the speedup exceeds the difference in memory bandwidth. For example, VE30 has 1.27× higher memory bandwidth than the A100 80 GB model, but its performance is 1.32× higher. The speedup over VE20 that achieves 388 GFLOP/s is 2.15×, which is again much larger than the 1.60× peak memory bandwidth improvement. This is likely because the alignment restriction for single-precision vectors is relaxed in VE30, and single-precision applications can be executed more efficiently.

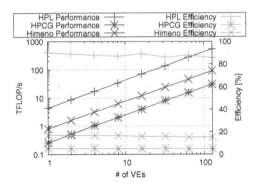

Fig. 7. Multi-node scaling performance of HPL, HPCG and Himeno benchmarks.

Table 2. Summary of the Tohoku University kernel collection.

Kernel	Domain	Bottleneck
Earthquake [1]	Seismology	Mem. B/W
Turbulent Flow [30]	Fluid dynamics	LLC B/W
Antenna [22]	Electronics	Mem. B/W
Land Mine [23]	Electronics	Mem. B/W
Turbine [30]	Fluid dynamics	Mem. latency
Plasma [12]	Geophysics	Mem. latency

Finally, we assess the multi-node scalability of HPL, HPCG and Himeno benchmarks. Figure 7 shows the multi-node performance of the two benchmarks as a function of the number of VEs. The results indicate that all three benchmarks scale almost linearly from 1 VE to 128 VEs with minor drop in efficiency. On 128 VEs, or 16 VHs, the HPL performance reaches 537 TFLOP/s with an efficiency of 85.5%. The HPCG benchmark achieves 30.6 TFLOP/s on 128 VEs with an efficiency of 4.9%. The Himeno benchmark achieves 919 TFLOP/s on 128 VEs with 15.2% efficiency.

3.3   Evaluation of Architectural Improvements

Bypassable L3 Cache. VE30 incorporates per-core private L3 caches into the memory hierarchy. This design choice was made based on the observation that cache-intensive applications suffered from degraded LLC performance on previous generations of the VE. This is largely due to the congestion in the NoC and cache contention in the LLC. The introduction of private L3 caches is expected to improve the effective cache bandwidth by alleviating NoC congestion and LLC contention.

Furthermore, the L3 cache can be bypassed by software. Similar to non-temporal loads and stores in CPUs and GPUs [17], each load or store instruction can specify whether to bypass the L3 cache or not. Selectively caching data that exhibit high temporal locality is expected to reduce cache pollution and allow applications to efficiently utilize the limited cache capacity. From the programmer's perspective, selective caching is enabled by inserting a compiler directive #pragma _NEC on_adb(var) in the source code, where var indicates the array to be L3-cached.

Note that the L3 cache bypassing is different from the LLC retention control [18] that was available in the previous VE generations. The LLC retention control allows applications to mark data as either temporal or non-temporal when issuing loads and stores. The LLC then prioritizes temporal data over non-temporal data when evicting cache lines. However, even if an access is marked as non-temporal, it is still cached in LLC. Thus, non-temporal data can still occupy a certain amount of the cache. The L3 cache bypassing, on the other hand, completely bypasses the L3 cache.

To assess the contribution of the L3 cache to application performance, we utilize the L3 cache bypassing feature and compare the performance of applications with and without enabling the L3 cache. Here, we use the *Tohoku University kernel collection* [13, 26], a set of computational kernels extracted from production applications developed by the users of the Cyberscience Center, Tohoku University. As summarized in Table 2, the kernel collection comprises six kernels spanning a wide variety of scientific domains and performance characteristics.

Figure 8 presents the performance of each kernel with and without enabling the L3 cache. The results reveal that Turbulent Flow, Antenna, Turbine and Plasma clearly benefit from the L3 cache. Since the L3 cache saves LLC and memory bandwidths by serving portion of the memory requests, LLC-intensive and memory-intensive applications such as Turbulent Flow and Antenna are accelerated. Contrastingly, Earthquake and Land Mine do not benefit from the L3. These two kernels are memory-intensive and may either have poor data locality or a large working set size that does not fit in the L3 cache. The memory latency sensitive kernels, Turbine and Plasma, are also accelerated as the L3 cache reduces memory latency. Accessing the LLC incurs higher latency than the L3 cache since the LLC is physically farther away than the L3 cache, and requires communication over the potentially congested NoC.

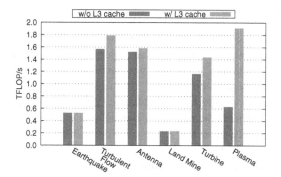

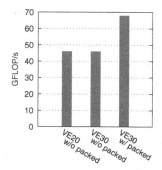

Fig. 8. Impact of L3 Cache on Tohoku University kernel collection performance.

Fig. 9. Single-core performance of a single-precision 27-point stencil kernel.

Relaxed Alignment Restriction for Packed Instructions. The *packed* instructions in SX-AT operate on vectors of 32-bit values, where each 64-bit element of a vector register holds a pair of 32-bit values. For example, a vector register can store 512 single-precision floating point numbers using the packed format. However, previous generations of the VE imposed an alignment restriction, requiring that the starting address of a packed vector is 8-byte aligned. Otherwise, the packed format cannot be used, and each element of a vector register holds only one 32-bit value instead of two. VE30 lifts this restriction and only requires 4-byte alignment for single-precision vectors.

To evaluate the speedup offered by the packed format, we measure the performance of a single-precision 27-point stencil kernel. Figure 9 presents the single-core performance of the 27-point stencil kernel on VE20 and on VE30 with and without using the packed format. Using the packed format on VE30 improves the performance by 1.48× compared to VE20 and VE30 without using the packed format. There is no improvement from VE20 without packed vectors because the per-core memory bandwidth remains the same.

Hardware Support for Indexed Vector Accumulation. The VE30 processor introduces hardware support for vector accumulation with indirect addressing (*i.e.,* axpyi in Sparse BLAS). Such computation is fundamental in applications including finite element and particle methods. An example of an indexed vector accumulation is shown in Listing 1.1. In this example, array y is indirectly accessed using array l[i] as indices. This loop cannot be automatically vectorized by the compiler because loop-carried dependencies exist if some of the indices in l overlap.

Listing 1.1. Indexed vector accumulation.

```
for (int i = 0; i < n; i++)
    y[l[i]] = y[l[i]] + x[i];
```

Prior to VE30, programmers needed to manually examine whether l[i] may overlap, and either insert the ivdep or list_vector compiler directive to the loop. The ivdep directive is specified when there are no overlaps of indices, and simply vectorizes the loop. In the case where the indices do overlap, the list_vector directive must be specified. The list_vector directive instructs the compiler to generate a code that (1) computes the results using vector instructions ignoring loop-carried dependencies, (2) checks the overlaps of indices, and (3) corrects the results for overlapping indices using scalar instructions. However, the overhead incurred by the corrections increases as the number of overlapping indices in vector l increases.

VE30 adds specialized hardware for atomic accumulation in the LLC along with a new instruction, vlfa. The vlfa instruction sends the vector of indices (l in Listing 1.1) and the added vector (x) to the LLC, and then performs the accumulation in the LLC. The vlfa instruction should perform better than list_vector because scalar-based corrections are unneeded, and the latency of vector gather is eliminated. Programmer productivity is also improved since programmers no longer have to spend effort in identifying whether the indices might overlap or not. Note, however, that vlfa still slows down when the number of overlapping indices increases because contention may occur in the LLC.

To investigate the performance of the vlfa instruction, we use the indexed vector accumulation kernel shown in Listing 1.1. Here, we compare the following five variants: scalar-only on VE20 and VE30, list_vector on VE20 and VE30, and vlfa on VE30. We vary the number of overlapping indices to quantify the performance degradation caused by the overlap of indices. This is achieved by initializing the index vector l as the following:

$$l[i] = \begin{cases} 0 & \text{if } i \mod 32 < k \\ i & \text{otherwise,} \end{cases} \tag{1}$$

where k is varied from 1 to 32.

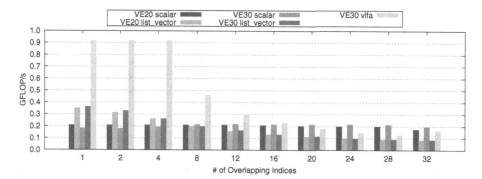

Fig. 10. Single-core performance of indexed vector accumulation.

Figure 10 shows the performance of indexed vector accumulation for each variant. Evidently, `vlfa` outperforms all other variants when the number of overlapping indices is small; it is 3.48× faster than `list_vector` and 4.72× faster than scalar-only when 4 out of 32 indices overlap. The performance of `vlfa` starts to decline with more than 8 overlapping indices, and falls below scalar-only with more than 20 identical indices. However, such large degree of address overlap is unlikely in real-world applications. This indicates that programmers generally do not need to specify the `ivdep` or `list_vector` directives on VE30, hence the productivity is improved.

Listing 1.2. A kernel loop involving indexed vector accumulation.

```
DO N = nstart,nend
  IF(flag3(N)==1) THEN
    COF(7,WI(N),WJ(N),WK(N))=COF(7,WI(N),WJ(N),WK(N))+W_TAUWC(N) * W_AREA_1(N)
    SOC(WI(N),WJ(N),WK(N))=SOC(WI(N),WJ(N),WK(N))+W_TAUWS(N) * W_AREA_1(N)
  ENDIF
ENDDO
```

Listing 1.2 shows a kernel loop extracted from a real-world fluid dynamics application. Here, two 3-dimensional arrays COF and SOC are accumulated in a single loop. In this example, arrays are initialized such that 4 out of 256 indices overlap (there are two pairs of identical indices). Prior to VE30, the VE compiler was unable to vectorize this kind of code. On VE30, the compiler can vectorize this code with the help of the `vlfa` instruction. As a result, this kernel takes 175.6s to run on VE30 without the `vlfa` instruction, but only takes 12.0s to run with the `vlfa` instruction, resulting in a 14.6× speedup.

3.4 Real-World Workloads

SPEChpc 2021 Benchmark Suite. *SPEChpc* [15,27] is a benchmark suite developed by the Standard Performance Evaluation Corporation (SPEC), and comprises a set of carefully selected applications that represent a wide range of real-world HPC applications. The latest version of the SPEChpc benchmark suite, SPEChpc 2021, was released in October 2021. It supports multiple programming models and can run on both CPUs and GPUs. In this evaluation, we use MPI+OpenMP on VE20, VE30, A64FX and IceLake-SP, and MPI+OpenACC on A100.

We first use the *tiny* workload from the SPEChpc 2021 benchmark suite to compare the single-socket performance of the processors. The smallest tiny workload consists of nine benchmarks and requires approximately 60 GB of memory. We plot the speedups to a reference system (a 2-socket 12-core Intel Haswell system) reported by the SPEChpc benchmark script for each processor. If a processor needs more than one socket due to the memory footprint requirement, the speedup is divided by the number of sockets to make a fair comparison. Since the compilers for VE30 are still under development as of writing this paper, we could not obtain the performance results for SOMA and Minisweep on VE30.

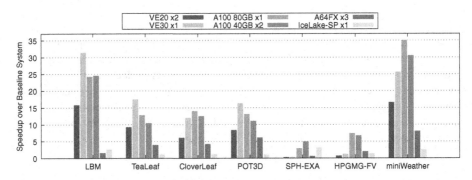

Fig. 11. SPEChpc 2021 tiny workload performance.

Figure 11 summarizes the SPEChpc tiny workload performance on the different processors. VE30 outperforms all other processors in LBM, TeaLeaf and POT3D. The speedups of these three benchmarks over the A100 80 GB model are 1.29×, 1.36× and 1.24×, respectively. The speedups of LBM and TeaLeaf exceed the difference in memory bandwidth, suggesting that the architectural enhancements such as the newly introduced L3 cache and increased LLC capacity and bandwidth, are contributing to the performance gain.

VE30 also clearly outperforms A64FX and IceLake-SP in CloverLeaf and mini-Weather, but slightly underperforms the A100 40 GB and 80 GB models. This is because the time-consuming kernels in CloverLeaf require a large number of vector gather operations, and it appears that VE30 struggles at hiding the latency of vector gather operations compared to A100. The miniWeather benchmark contains a mix of memory-intensive and compute-intensive kernels. Although memory-intensive kernels are faster on VE30 than on A100, compute-intensive kernels are slower on VE30 and dominate the runtime.

SPH-EXA and HPGMG-FV perform poorly on VE30. SPH-EXA [3] is mainly bottlenecked by the construction of an octree-based spatial index and nearest neighbor queries over the index. Both of these functions inherently require recursive function calls and cannot be vectorized. To achieve better performance on vector processors, the nearest neighbor search needs to be changed to a vector-friendly algorithm.

HPGMG-FV suffers from short loop length. The HPGMG-FV tiny workload decomposes a 512^3 cubic domain into 32^3 cubic boxes and distributes the boxes to MPI ranks. The most time-consuming Gauss-Seidel Red-Black smoother kernel sweeps over a box with a triple-nested loop each corresponding to a spatial dimension. As a result, each loop runs for 32 times, but this is too short compared to the vector length of a VE, which is 256 double-precision elements. A potential optimization is collapse the nested loops and increase the loop length. Another possible optimization is to offload the coarse grid levels to the VH and process fine grid levels on the VE.

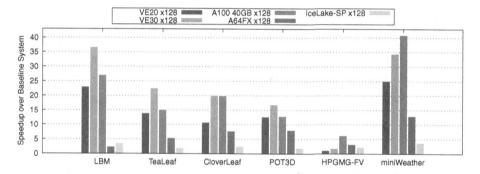

Fig. 12. SPEChpc 2021 medium workload performance.

To evaluate the multi-node scalability, we also compare the performance of the SPEChpc *medium* workload. The medium workload consists of six benchmarks and requires approximately 4 TB of memory. Here, we execute the workload using 128 sockets on all processors. Results for the A100 80 GB model are unavailable since we do not have access to a large-scale deployment of the A100 80 GB model. Figure 12 summarizes the medium workload performance. Here, VE30 is the fastest in four out of the six benchmarks, which are LBM, TeaLeaf, CloverLeaf and POT3D. The speedup of VE30 over A100 40 GB generally shows a similar trend as the tiny workload. For example, the speedup of VE30 over A100 is 1.27× in the LBM tiny workload, while the speedup is 1.35× in the medium workload. Similarly, the performance of miniWeather on VE30 compared to A100 is 0.83× and 0.84× in the tiny and medium workloads, respectively. This would be because both the problem size and the number of sockets are increased, and thus the problem size per socket remains roughly identical to that of the tiny workload.

We analyze the impact of MPI communication time to the total performance on VE30 and A100. Figure 13 shows the breakdown of runtime obtained using MPI profilers.

MPI functions that consume more than 0.5% of the total runtime are shown in the plot. Concordant to previous work [2], `MPI_Allreduce` and `MPI_Waitall` (*i.e.*, non-blocking point-to-point communication) consume majority of the communication time. The difference in communication time between VE30 and A100 is not significant (<1.5×) in LBM, TeaLeaf and miniWeather. However, in CloverLeaf, POT3D and HPGMG-FV, the communication time on VE30 is 2.45×, 1.60× and 2.39× slower, respectively. This may be resulting from the immaturity of the software stack for VE30, or difference in the interconnects of the two systems used for evaluation. These points will be further investigated in our future work.

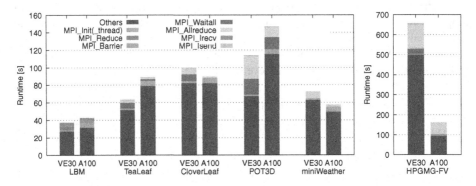

Fig. 13. Runtime breakdown of SPEChpc 2021 medium workload.

Tohoku University Kernel Collection. As described in Sect. 3.3, the Tohoku University kernel collection represents real-world applications developed by the users of the Cyberscience Center at Tohoku University. Figure 14 shows the performance of the Tohoku University kernels on VE20 and VE30. Evidently, VE30 consistently outperforms VE20 with all kernels. The speedup is especially significant for Turbulent Flow, Turbine and Plasma, all of which perform more than 2.3× faster on VE30 than on VE20. Given that Turbulent Flow is bound by LLC bandwidth on VE20, we believe the performance gain is obtained from the 2.13× LLC bandwidth increase and the newly added L3 cache. Turbine and Plasma benefit from the reduction in memory latency thanks to the L3 cache as discussed in Sect. 3.3.

Rainfall-Runoff-Inundation Model. The Rainfall-Runoff-Inundation (RRI) Model [25,29] is a 2-dimensional numerical model that is widely adopted in Japan to conduct flood forecasts. The RRI model discretizes the domain into slope (land) cells and river channel cells. Surface and subsurface flows on slope cells are calculated using a 2-dimensional diffusive wave model, and flows on river cells are simulated using a 1-dimensional diffusive wave model. The interaction between slope and river cells is modeled considering the slope and river water levels. Vertical infiltration is also modeled using the Green-Ampt infiltration model. The governing equations are solved using the fifth-order Runge-Kutta method with adaptive time step control. From the computational point of view, the major kernels in the RRI model are memory-intensive, thereby suited for execution on VEs.

In this evaluation, we use an implementation of the RRI model optimized for SX-AT with OpenMP parallelization [25], and measure the runtime required for conducting a 2-hour flood prediction in the entire *Tohoku* region of Japan. Figure 15 shows the runtime of the RRI model on VE20 and VE30. VE30 achieves 1.32× higher performance than VE20. The speedup of the parallel regions is 1.60×. Considering that the peak memory bandwidth is increased by 1.60× from VE20 to VE30 and the RRI model is memory-intensive, the observed speedup matches the expectation.

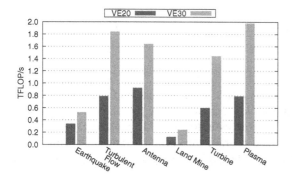

Fig. 14. Tohoku University kernel collection performance.

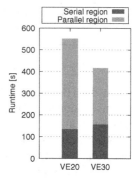

Fig. 15. Runtime of a 2-h flood prediction using the RRI model.

4   Performance Tuning for VE30

Basic optimization techniques for VE include facilitating vectorization by factoring out unvectorizable code from loops, increasing the vector length using various loop transformations, and offloading unvectorizable computation to the VH. In addition to these optimization techniques, further performance can be exploited by utilizing the architectural features introduced in VE30. In this section, we present such tuning techniques and quantify their performance impact.

4.1   Selective L3 Caching

On VE30, programmers can take advantage of the bypassable L3 cache to selectively cache frequently reused data. To demonstrate the effect of selective L3 caching, we use the Himeno benchmark as an example. Listing 1.3 shows the time-consuming Jacobi

Listing 1.3. Jacobi method kernel in the Himeno benchmark.

```
for(i=1 ; i<imax-1 ; ++i)
  for(j=1 ; j<jmax-1 ; ++j)
    for(k=1 ; k<kmax-1 ; ++k){
      s0 = a[0][i][j][k] * p[i+1][j ][k ] + a[1][i][j][k] * p[i ][j+1][k ]
         + a[2][i][j][k] * p[i ][j ][k+1]
         + b[0][i][j][k] * ( p[i+1][j+1][k ] - p[i+1][j-1][k ]
                           - p[i-1][j+1][k ] + p[i-1][j-1][k ] )
         + b[1][i][j][k] * ( p[i ][j+1][k+1] - p[i ][j-1][k+1]
                           - p[i ][j+1][k-1] + p[i ][j-1][k-1] )
         + b[2][i][j][k] * ( p[i+1][j ][k+1] - p[i-1][j ][k+1]
                           - p[i+1][j ][k-1] + p[i-1][j ][k-1] )
         + c[0][i][j][k] * p[i-1][j ][k ] + c[1][i][j][k] * p[i ][j-1][k ]
         + c[2][i][j][k] * p[i ][j ][k-1] + wrk1[i][j][k];
      ss = ( s0 * a[3][i][j][k] - p[i][j][k] ) * bnd[i][j][k];
      wgosa += ss*ss;
      wrk2[i][j][k] = p[i][j][k] + omega * ss;
      // Copy wrk2 to wrk and sum wgosa across all ranks
    }
```

kernel in the Himeno benchmark. Arrays a, b, c, wrk1 and bnd are accessed in a consecutive manner and not reused. On the other hand, array p is accessed in a stencil-like manner. Although ideally 18 out of 19 accesses to p should hit in cache, the accesses to the other arrays pollute the cache and degrade the cache hit ratio of p. This cache pollution can be mitigated by caching p only and bypassing the cache when accessing a, b, c, wrk1 and bnd.

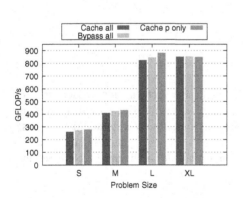

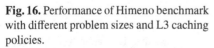

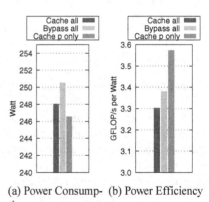

(a) Power Consump- (b) Power Efficiency
tion

Fig. 16. Performance of Himeno benchmark with different problem sizes and L3 caching policies.

Fig. 17. Power efficiency of Himeno benchmark (L size). Note the y-axis is truncated.

Figure 16 compares the performance of the Himeno benchmark under three different caching policies: (1) cache all arrays in the L3 cache, (2) always bypass the L3 cache, and (3) only cache p in the L3 cache. We also compare four different problem sizes: S

$(2^6 \times 2^6 \times 2^7)$, M $(2^7 \times 2^7 \times 2^8)$, L $(2^8 \times 2^8 \times 2^9)$, and XL $(2^9 \times 2^9 \times 2^{10})$. The results indicate that caching all arrays does not show any notable improvement over bypassing all arrays. This suggests that the L3 cache is polluted by non-temporal data and thus the cache hit ratio of p is low. Selectively caching p improves 6.5%, 5.7% and 6.9% over caching all arrays for problem sizes S, M and L, respectively. This indicates that selective caching alleviates cache pollution. Contrastingly, no performance improvement is observed for the XL problem size. This is because p does not fit in the L3 cache in the XL size.

To investigate if selective caching has an impact on power consumption and power efficiency, we use the NEC Monitoring & Maintenance Manager (MMM)[1] tool and measure the power consumption of the VE30 PCIe card while running the Himeno benchmark. Figure 17 compares the power consumption and efficiency of the VE30 card under different caching policies. The plot shows the average of three measurements. The results indicate that selectively caching p reduces the power consumption by 0.6% compared to caching all arrays because the number of memory accesses is reduced. Combined with the performance improvement, selective caching improves the power efficiency by 8.2%, resulting in a power efficiency of 3.57 GFLOP/s/W. Compared to VE20 that achieves 2.21 GFLOP/s/W and the A100 40 GB model that achieves 2.14 GFLOP/s/W [14], VE30 achieves 1.61× and 1.66× higher power efficiency, respectively.

Furthermore, we apply selective L3 caching to the Land Mine kernel to study if selective caching is beneficial for real-world applications. Figure 18 shows the performance, power consumption and power efficiency of the Land Mine kernel under different L3 caching policies. Bypassing the L3 cache yields the lowest performance of 299 GFLOP/s. Enabling the cache slightly improves the performance to 312 GFLOP/s, and selective caching further improves the performance to 339 GFLOP/s. In terms of power consumption, caching all arrays and selective caching both consume slightly more power than bypassing the cache. This is because the increase in cache power outweighs the reduction in memory power. However, the performance gain of selective caching is large enough that its power efficiency is the highest.

4.2 Partitioning Mode

As mentioned in Sect. 2.2, the partitioning mode increases the effective LLC bandwidth by relieving the congestion in the NoC that interconnects the cores and the LLC. Therefore, enabling the partitioning mode may accelerate cache-intensive applications. Although the partitioning mode has been available in the previous generations of VEs, its benefits are expected to be larger on VE30 since NoC congestion becomes heavier due to the increased number of cores.

To assess the effect of the partitioning mode on VE30, we measure the performance of the Himeno benchmark with and without the partitioning mode. The results are shown in Fig. 19. As expected, the partitioning mode does not have a significant impact on VE20 since the NoC is not congested. Contrastingly, the performance is increased by 7.1% by enabling the partitioning mode on VE30. This suggests that the NoC congestion

---

[1] https://sxauroratsubasa.sakura.ne.jp/documents/guide/pdfs/InstallationGuide_E.pdf.

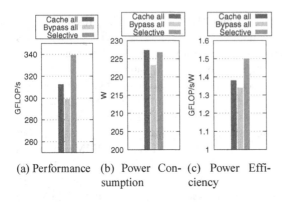

(a) Performance   (b) Power Con-   (c) Power Effi-
                  sumption   ciency

Fig. 18. Performance and power efficiency of the Land Mine kernel under different L3 caching policies. Note the y-axis is truncated.

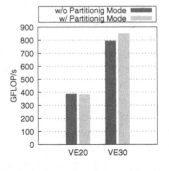

Fig. 19. Impact of the partitioning mode to Himeno benchmark performance (XL size).

is alleviated by the partitioning mode. Thus, the use of partitioning mode should be considered when running cache-intensive applications on VE30.

5   Conclusions

In this paper, we carried out an extensive performance evaluation of a next-generation SX-AT supercomputer equipped with the brand-new VE30 processor. VE30 attains massive performance in memory-intensive standard benchmarks such as the Himeno benchmark and outperforms other processors. The speedup of VE30 over the other processors exceeds the difference in the peak compute and memory performance, indicating the benefits of the novel architectural enhancements introduced in VE30. VE30 also outperforms other processors in many real-world applications such as SPEChpc. Finally, we presented performance tuning techniques to fully exploit the potential of VE30.

These evaluation results clearly demonstrate that VE30 can achieve high sustained performance comparable to latest GPUs and CPUs, while allowing programmers to use conventional programming models, *i.e.*, MPI+OpenMP. This proves the next-generation SX-AT to be an attractive choice for users seeking real-world application performance.

Acknowledgments. This work was partially supported by MEXT Next Generation High Performance Computing Infrastructures and Applications R&D Program "R&D of A Quantum-Annealing-Assisted Next Generation HPC Infrastructure and its Applications," and JSPS KAK-ENHI Grant Numbers JP20H00593, JP20K19808, JP21H03449 and JP22K19764. Part of the experiments were carried out using AOBA-A and AOBA-C at the Cyberscience Center, Tohoku University, SQUID at the Cybermedia Center, Osaka University, and Flow at the Information Technology Center, Nagoya University.

References

1. Ariyoshi, K., Matsuzawa, T., Hasegawa, A.: The key frictional parameters controlling spatial variations in the speed of postseismic-slip propagation on a subduction plate boundary. Earth Planet. Sci. Lett. **256**(1–2), 136–146 (2007)
2. Brunst, H., et al.: First experiences in performance benchmarking with the new SPEChpc 2021 suites. In: 22nd IEEE International Symposium on Cluster, Cloud and Internet Computing (CCGrid), pp. 675–684 (2022)
3. Cavelan, A., Cabezón, R.M., Grabarczyk, M., Ciorba, F.M.: A smoothed particle hydrodynamics mini-app for exascale. In: Platform for Advanced Scientific Computing Conference (PASC 2020), pp. 1–11 (2020)
4. Choquette, J., Gandhi, W., Giroux, O., Stam, N., Krashinsky, R.: NVIDIA A100 tensor core GPU: performance and innovation. IEEE Micro **41**(2), 29–35 (2021)
5. Dongarra, J., Heroux, M.A., Luszczek, P.: High-performance conjugate-gradient benchmark: a new metric for ranking high-performance computing systems. Int. J. High Perform. Comput. Appl. **30**(1), 3–10 (2016)
6. Dongarra, J.J., Luszczek, P., Petite, A.: The LINPACK benchmark: past, present and future. Concurr. Comput. Pract. Exp. **15**(9), 803–820 (2003)
7. Egawa, R., et al.: Exploiting the potentials of the second generation SX-Aurora TSUBASA. In: Performance Modeling, Benchmarking and Simulation of High Performance Computer Systems (PMBS 2020), vol. 2, pp. 39–49 (2020)
8. Himeno, R.: Himeno benchmark. https://i.riken.jp/en/supercom/documents/himenobmt/
9. Hsu, K.C., Tseng, H.W.: Accelerating applications using edge tensor processing units. In: International Conference for High Performance Computing, Networking, Storage and Analysis (SC 2021), pp. 1–14 (2021)
10. Iyer, R., et al.: Advances in microprocessor cache architectures over the last 25 years. IEEE Micro **41**(6), 78–88 (2021)
11. Jouppi, N.P., et al.: Ten lessons from three generations shaped Google's TPUv4i. In: 48th Annual International Symposium on Computer Architecture (ISCA), pp. 1–14 (2021)
12. Katoh, Y., Ono, T., Iizima, M.: Numerical simulation of resonant scattering of energetic electrons in the outer radiation belt. Earth Planets Space **57**(2), 117–124 (2005). https://doi.org/10.1186/BF03352555
13. Komatsu, K., et al.: Performance evaluation of a vector supercomputer SX-Aurora TSUBASA. In: International Conference for High Performance Computing, Networking, Storage and Analysis (SC 2018), pp. 685–696 (2018)
14. Komatsu, K., et al.: Performance and power analysis of a vector computing system. Supercomput. Front. Innov. **8**(2), 75–94 (2021)
15. Li, J., et al.: SPEChpc 2021 benchmark suites for modern HPC systems. In: Companion of the 2022 ACM/SPEC International Conference on Performance Engineering, pp. 15–16 (2022)
16. Louw, T., Mcintosh-Smith, S.: Using the graphcore IPU for traditional HPC applications. In: 3rd Workshop on Accelerated Machine Learning (AccML) (2021)
17. Mittal, S.: A survey of cache bypassing techniques. J. Low Power Electron. Appl. **6**(2) (2016)
18. Onodera, A., Komatsu, K., Fujimoto, S., Isobe, Y., Sato, M., Kobayashi, H.: Optimization of the himeno benchmark for SX-Aurora TSUBASA. In: Wolf, F., Gao, W. (eds.) Bench 2020. LNCS, vol. 12614, pp. 127–143. Springer, Cham (2021). https://doi.org/10.1007/978-3-030-71058-3_8
19. Papazian, I.E.: New 3rd Gen Intel® Xeon® scalable processor. In: Hot Chips Symposium (2020)
20. RISC-V Foundation: RISC-V "V" Vector Extension. Technical report (2021). https://github.com/riscv/riscv-v-spec/releases/tag/v1.0

21. Rocki, K., et al.: Fast stencil-code computation on a wafer-scale processor. In: International Conference for High Performance Computing, Networking, Storage and Analysis (SC20) (2020)
22. Sato, H., Takagi, Y., Sawaya, K.: High gain antipodal fermi antenna with low cross polarization. IEICE Trans. Commun. **E94-B**(8), 2292–2297 (2011)
23. Sato, M., Kobayashi, T., Zeng, Z., Fang, G., Feng, X.: High resolution GPR system for landmine detection. In: Proceedings of International Conference Requirements and Technologies for the Detection, Removal and Neutralization of Landmine and UXO, pp. 548–553 (2003)
24. Sato, M., et al.: Co-design for A64FX manycore processor and "Fugaku". In: International Conference for High Performance Computing, Networking, Storage and Analysis (SC 2020), pp. 1–15 (2020)
25. Shimomura, Y., et al.: A real-time flood inundation prediction on SX-Aurora TSUBASA. In: 29th International Conference on High Performance Computing, Data, and Analytics (HiPC) (2022)
26. Soga, T., et al.: Performance evaluation of NEC SX-9 using real science and engineering applications. In: International Conference on High Performance Computing Networking, Storage and Analysis (SC 2009), pp. 1–12 (2009)
27. Standard Performance Evaluation Corporation: SPEChpc 2021 (2021). https://www.spec.org/hpc2021/
28. Stephens, N., et al.: The ARM scalable vector extension. IEEE Micro **37**(2), 26–39 (2017)
29. The International Centre for Water Hazard and Risk Management: Rainfall-Runoff-Inundation (RRI) model. https://www.pwri.go.jp/icharm/research/rri/index.html
30. Tsukahara, T., Iwamoto, K., Kawamura, H.: Evolution of material line in turbulent channel flow. In: The 5th International Symposium on Turbulence and Shear Flow Phenomena, pp. 549–554 (2007)

Programming Environments
and Systems Software

Expression Isolation of Compiler-Induced Numerical Inconsistencies in Heterogeneous Code

Dolores Miao[1]([⊠]), Ignacio Laguna[2], and Cindy Rubio-González[1]

[1] University of California, Davis, Davis, CA 95616, USA
{wjmiao,crubio}@ucdavis.edu
[2] Lawrence Livermore National Laboratory, Livermore, CA 94550, USA
ilaguna@llnl.gov

Abstract. As the demand for developing and porting numerical applications to heterogeneous computing platforms increases, such programs may exhibit *numerical inconsistencies* caused by architectural differences and aggressive compiler optimizations. These numerical inconsistencies can negatively impact reproducibility and debugging. This paper presents CIEL, designed to identify the root cause of compiler-induced numerical inconsistencies in heterogeneous programs. CIEL uses a floating-point precision enhancement strategy, guided by a recursive bisection search algorithm with increasing search granularity, to identify the *program expressions* that induce numerical inconsistencies due to compiler optimizations. CIEL achieves 99.4% precision in isolating numerical inconsistencies in both CPU and GPU programs, including 330 synthetic GPU programs, benchmark applications like NAS Parallel Benchmarks and Rodinia, and real-world scientific applications such as CLOUDSC, a cloud microphysics parameterization mini-app for the ECMWF IFS. Furthermore, when compared with the state of the art, which only isolates *lines* of code in CPU programs, CIEL runs 24.5% fewer searches for statement isolation, and produces more precise results for 84.9% of the programs. Finally, manual inspection of hundreds of compiler-induced numerical inconsistencies in heterogeneous programs reveals common characteristics.

1 Introduction

Heterogeneous computing uses different processing cores, such as CPUs and graphics processing units (GPUs), to run programs with maximized performance [8]. Software engineers from various fields use GPUs to form heterogeneous architectures and accelerate large-scale parallel computations. General-purpose computing on GPUs (GPGPUs) has become the go-to choice for physics simulations, digital signal processing, machine learning, and climate research.

Compiler optimizations are often the first method software engineers consider when optimizing programs. Aggressive optimization options are also often invoked to push program performance as much as possible. Additionally, switching or upgrading compilers in the middle of a project is also a frequent industrial practice. Unfortunately, such modifications on a project global scale can have a negative impact on software reliability, particularly on floating-point arithmetic which could result in local errors that may propagate to the final program's output. In cases found in the literature [5,18,21], it has required significant effort and domain knowledge to isolate and fix these issues.

Numerical Reproducibility Challenges. Given the large number of hardware architectures, compilers and host environments involved in executing heterogeneous programs, maintaining numerical consistency and reproducibility is equally important to their pure CPU counterparts. Most hardware devices and compilers follow the IEEE 754–2008 standard [1], but offer optimization options, such as `-ffast-math` in Clang, that further push computational performance at the cost of strict IEEE 754–2008 compliance. Such non-compliant optimizations can yield different computation results—*numerical inconsistencies*—between CPU- and GPU-computed results, or for CPU- or GPU-only computations optimized at different levels. These inconsistencies often result in numerical correctness bugs, some of which are reported in widely adopted numerical libraries [15]. Many applications, when ported to GPU platforms, struggle to find a balance between performance speedup and avoiding *compiler-induced numerical variability* impacting the precision of the results [21]. Such impact has already been acknowledged by the floating-point research community concerned with ensuring numerical accuracy on heterogeneous computing systems [17].

Simply disabling compiler optimizations, or increasing precision uniformly across an application, may solve compiler-induced variability, but they are not practical solutions. Instead, developers strive to find the root cause of these compiler-induced inconsistencies and manually fix them to reduce their impact without disabling compiler optimizations. Currently, identifying the root cause of such issues in heterogeneous programs is a manual effort, requires domain knowledge, and is a time-consuming task.

Main Contributions. We present CIEL (which stands for Compiler-induced Inconsistency Expression Locator), the first tool that automatically isolates numerical inconsistencies in heterogeneous programs at the expression level. Prior work [18,28] has proposed automated approaches to isolate such inconsistencies in pure CPU programs. FLiT [28] works at the function level, while pLiner [18] isolates lines of code that cause inconsistencies, but neither targets GPU code nor isolates at expression level, which further reduces developer workload.

In numerical program error analysis, replacing floating-point operations with higher precision variants is widely employed [7,16,30] to more accurately approximate the results of operations in infinite precision. Higher precision operations have a smaller ulp (unit in last place) error, and exceptions such as subnormal numbers and infinity are much less likely to be triggered. It is shown in [18] that compiler-induced inconsistencies can be minimized by enhancing precision. CIEL operates on the same assumption that compilers will produce enhanced precision binary instructions when specific source code regions are in enhanced precision.

Compared to the state-of-the-art [18] for CPUs where each code block at each level is treated individually, our approach traverses the abstract syntax tree (AST) of each function and performs a bisection search for all *adjacent* sibling code blocks, maintaining the adjacency relationship between them; during precision enhancement, adjacent code blocks are either combined into a single code region or have variable checkpoints where redundant type conversions are removed. Furthermore, CIEL isolates code down to the expression level rather than the statement level (line level in [18]). Since the program statements causing the compiler-induced inconsistencies may include many floating-point operations involving different operators, variables, constants, or function calls, isolating at the expression level provides a more precise insight into the inconsistencies, pointing users directly to their root cause and potential fix.

In particular, to adapt to features and limitations on GPU platforms, such as the lack of floating-point arithmetic beyond double precision or the built-in vector arithmetic, CIEL supports extended precision libraries, and can transform built-in vector arithmetic to enhanced precision. CIEL detects code written for different target platforms (CPU or GPU code) and automatically transforms them according to platform specifications, e.g., platform-specific language constructs and data types. CIEL provides a solid foundation for extending support to other platforms, such as OpenMP or OpenCL [3], as long as they are supported by Clang. *To the best of our knowledge,* CIEL *is the only tool capable of isolating code regions in heterogeneous computing programs that, combined with compiler optimizations, produce inconsistent numerical results.*

We evaluate CIEL on a set of heterogeneous programs, including 330 synthetic GPU programs, and on GPU programs from the NAS [6] and Rodinia [10] benchmarks. CIEL achieves a precision of 99.4% in isolating compiler-induced inconsistencies in these programs. Moreover, CIEL finds the root cause of a real-world compiler-induced inconsistency in the C version of ECMWF Cloud Physics mini-app CLOUDSC [14] in only 7 min. The root cause of the inconsistency has been confirmed by ECMWF domain experts. Finally, compared to pLiner [18], the state of the art in isolating *lines* of code in CPU programs, CIEL performs 24.5% fewer searches for statement isolation, and produces more precise isolation results for 84.9% of the pLiner's CPU benchmarks.

In summary, the contributions of this paper are as follows:

- An approach for isolating minimal code regions that cause compiler-induced numerical inconsistencies in heterogeneous programs. Our approach uses a more efficient bisection search compared to the state of the art for CPU programs that operates on simplified ASTs and provides a finer search granularity at the expression level (Sects. 3.1 and 3.2).
- A precision enhancement strategy that more accurately reflects the resolvability of inconsistencies under precision enhancement, and addresses challenges specific to transforming heterogeneous code to higher precision (Sect. 3.3).
- An implementation of our approach in the tool CIEL, and an evaluation that shows (1) efficacy at isolating inconsistencies in a large and diverse set of heterogeneous programs: 330 synthetic GPU programs, NAS and Rodinia GPU benchmarks, and the real-world mini-app CLOUDSC (Sect. 4.1), and (2)

higher precision and efficiency in comparison with the state of the art in isolating numerical inconsistencies in CPU programs (Sect. 4.2).

- A manual inspection of the isolated code that causes compiler-induced inconsistencies, which reveals common characteristics (Sect. 4.1).

2   Examples of Compiler-Induced Inconsistencies

Compilers for CPU and GPU code, such as Clang [4] and nvcc [2], offer various levels of optimization flags from -O0 to -O3. With higher optimization levels, program performance

Table 1. Inconsistencies in BT.S.

Compiler Options	Runtime	Error
nvcc -O0	0.104 s	6.98176E-13
nvcc -O3 -use_fast_math	0.052 s	9.73738E-13
clang -O0	0.349 s	8.32928E-13
clang -O3 -ffast-math	0.059 s	3.50905E-12

is improved, sometimes significantly, but at the cost of potentially generating non-compliant IEEE 754–2008 floating-point code. There are optimization flags that explicitly violate the IEEE 754–2008 standard, but in cases where precision is of less concern, they offer good speedups. For example, consider the CUDA version of the BT NAS program with input class S. Table 1 shows the program runtime and the maximum relative error for each compiler and optimization flag combination. Using -O3 -use_fast_math with nvcc yields 100% speedup compared to -O0, but at the cost of the error being 39% larger. Performance and error with Clang is generally worse, with the largest error in clang -O3 -ffast-math being 403% larger than nvcc -O0.

In real-world applications, such compiler-induced numerical inconsistencies occur frequently. They can happen when migrating software to other hardware/software platforms, switching applications to a new compiler, or just using more aggressive optimization flags for compilation. These inconsistencies may cause major software failures that take tremendous amount of effort to identify and resolve. A documented case [18,21] in the Laghos (LAGrangian High-Order Solver) application [9] is observed when ported to the Lawrence Livermore National Laboratory's Sierra system using the IBM xlc compiler. This triggered an inconsistency in the energy computed by the application under xlc -O3 but not with xlc -O2. In another documented case in [5], the Community Earth System Model (CESM) failed its verification using the CESM-ECT quality assurance framework when it was ported to the Mira machine at Argonne National Laboratory. Both took from weeks to months for scientists and engineers to identify the source code that caused such failures.

Issues like the above are bound to occur when real-world scientific applications are written or ported to new platforms. *Automatically resolving such issues without extensive domain knowledge would save a massive amount of time and increase programming productivity.*

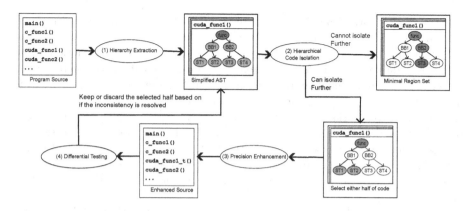

Fig. 1. The workflow of CIEL.

3 Technical Approach

Problem Statement. Given *heterogeneous programs* with known compiler-induced numerical inconsistencies, a practical problem for software developers is how to isolate the *expressions* that cause such inconsistencies in a precise and efficient manner. CIEL is designed with the goal of tackling this problem. Specifically, CIEL takes as input a program P and its associated input, which under compilers $C_1, C_2, ..., C_n$ and optimization flags $O_{i1}, O_{i2}, ..., O_{ik}$ for each compiler C_i, produces inconsistent results. CIEL outputs the *minimal region* R_m in m searches, which means that by generating program variants $P'_1, P'_2, ..., P'_m$ it isolates the root cause of the inconsistency to a code region as narrow as possible. Below we present definitions that will be used throughout the rest of the paper.

Definition 1. *The output of program P given a specific error threshold ϵ under compiler C_i and optimization flags O_{ij} is written as $f(P, \epsilon, C_i, O_{ij})$.*

Definition 2. *Compiler-induced inconsistencies occur if there are two sets of compiler/optimization flag combinations C_i, O_{ij} and C_k, O_{kl}, where $f(P, \epsilon, C_i, O_{ij}) \neq f(P, \epsilon, C_k, O_{kl})$. When any two sets of combinations have the same output, the inconsistencies are considered to be resolved.*

Definition 3. *A region set R of a program P is defined as a set of regions in P, each of which is a straight-line code fragment with an entry point and one or more exit points.*

Definition 4. *A region set R_m is minimal if (a) the inconsistency is resolved when code in R_m is executed in higher precision, and (b) either R_m consists of only one expression, or leaving any expression in R_m in lower precision would result in unresolved inconsistencies.*

CIEL's Workflow. The overall workflow of CIEL is illustrated in Fig. 1. To find the minimal region that causes the numerical inconsistency, CIEL performs *hierarchical bisection search* on the source code—first between functions, then between code regions in the suspected functions. Each iteration increases the search granularity. The search algorithm identifies regions suspected of causing compiler-induced inconsistencies. For each region $R_1, R_2, ..., R_m$, CIEL then creates a mutated variant of the program $P'_1, P'_2, ..., P'_m$ for which code in the corresponding region is in enhanced precision. Whether the variant resolves these inconsistencies is then used to guide the further, narrower isolation of source code that triggers inconsistencies. The isolation process ends when region R_m satisfies the conditions of a minimal region. The modules in CIEL are described below:

(1) *Hierarchy Extraction* traverses the AST of the functions under analysis, extracting information relevant to floating-point operations, and generating a simplified AST for these functions. This is the entry point of the analysis.

(2) *Hierarchical Code Isolation* performs a hierarchical bisection search on the simplified AST to generate regions for subsequent precision enhancement.

(3) *Precision Enhancement* increases the precision of the code regions identified by hierarchical code isolation. The output is the transformed source code with the floating-point operations in specific code regions written in higher precision.

(4) *Differential Testing* compiles and runs the transformed program with specified compilers and optimization flags in parallel. The output of these combinations of compilers and flags is compared to determine if the compiler-induced inconsistencies are resolved.

The rest of the section describes modules 1–3 in more detail.

3.1   Hierarchy Extraction

The hierarchy extraction module traverses the program AST and extracts source code hierarchy information for each function in the form of a *simplified AST*. The simplified AST acts as a data exchange format between modules, and contains additional data specific to CIEL that includes whether a node should be enhanced in precision (enabled/disabled), and the list of all floating-point operations such as reads, writes, declarations, function calls, and constants in every statement under a node. The simplified AST classifies statement structure of a function into five node categories:

1. Each statement that ends with a semicolon (declaration, expression, and *return/break*) is a **statement node** on the simplified AST. Each statement node also contains its expression AST hierarchy.
2. A set of statements with only one entry point and one exit point is grouped as a **basic block (BB) node**.
3. For a selection statement such as *if-else* or *switch-case* statement, one BB node is assigned to each branch; and then a **conditional block node** is assigned for the whole selection statement as a code block.

```
1 void compute(/*var args*/){
2   for(int i=0; i<n; ++i) { //ST1-3
3     comp = x-1.6f; //ST4
4     float t = +1.4697E36f; //ST5
5     comp += t+1.4E-41f; //ST6
6     if (comp < sinhf(y)) { //ST7
7       comp = tanf(z); //ST8
8     }
9   }
10  printf("%.17g",comp); //ST9
11 }
```

(a) Sample function compute. Variables comp, x, y and z are function arguments of type float.

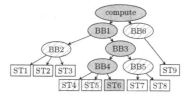

(b) Simplified AST of compute. The inconsistency is in ST6. Dark filled nodes are hierarchically isolated. Stripe filled nodes are considered in the bisection search at each level of hierarchy, but not isolated. White nodes are not considered during bisection search.

Fig. 2. Sample function and its simplified AST.

4. For a loop statement such as a *for* or *do-while* statement, one BB node is assigned to the condition, another to the loop body, and then a **loop block node** is assigned for the whole loop statement as a code block.
5. A **function node** is assigned to the whole function.

The relationship between a sample program and its simplified AST representation is shown in Fig. 2. Each expression statement (for-loop header in Line 2; if condition in Line 6; statements in Lines 3, 4, 5, 7, 10) in Subfigure 2a has its own statement node, which is organized into block nodes. The corresponding simplified AST is shown in Subfigure 2b.[1]

3.2 Hierarchical Code Isolation

When hierarchy extraction is complete, the simplified ASTs for all functions are output to the hierarchical code isolation module. As code isolation progresses, it marks nodes on the simplified ASTs as enabled or disabled depending on whether the node is still in consideration as a potential cause of inconsistencies.

Bisection search is the basis for the approach, followed by a 1-minimal check [31]. Bisection has shown to be an effective search strategy in the context of code isolation in CPU programs [18,28]. CIEL bases its search algorithm on the same idea of partitioning the program into functions, code blocks, and statements, but improves on how the hierarchical search is performed to reduce search time and improve precision. In particular, CIEL proposes a refined hierarchical region isolation with the explicit goal of improving isolation accuracy by reducing unnecessary type conversions when enhancing precision. Furthermore, unlike previous work, CIEL explores expression-level granularity during the search.

CIEL isolates a minimal region of code amongst a set of code regions by recursively bisecting suspicious code regions into two halves and verifying if enhancing

---

[1] Statements and blocks with no floating-point operations are recorded but excluded from precision enhancement.

Algorithm 1: Hierarchical Code Isolation.

```
 1  Function BisectionSearch(regions) :
 2      if regions.size() > 1 then
 3          regions₁, regions₂ = ArraySplit(regions, 2);
 4          if HasResolvedInHighPrecision(regions₁) then
 5          │  BisectionSearch(regions₁);
 6          else if HasResolvedInHighPrecision(regions₂) then
 7          │  BisectionSearch(regions₂);
 8          else
 9          │  BisectionSearch(regions₁);
10          │  BisectionSearch(regions₂);

11  Function RegionIsolation(regions) :
12      BisectionSearch(regions);
13      foreach region in regions do
14      │  if region.hasSubBlocks() && region.inHighPrecision() then
15      │  │  RegionIsolation(region.getSubBlocks());

16  Function FuncIsolation(Funcs):
17      Funcs.setHighPrecision();
18      BisectionSearch(Funcs);
19      minFuncs = Funcs.getHighPrecisionFuncs();
20      foreach func in minFuncs do
21      │  RegionIsolation(func.getBlocks());
```

---

either half resolves the inconsistency (Line 1 in Algorithm 1). Hierarchical search first sets the whole program in enhanced precision (Line 17 in Algorithm 1), then finds the minimal region in increasing granularity, following two stages:

1. **Function Isolation.** During the function isolation stage (Line 16 in Algorithm 1), bisection search is performed at the function level, and the result is a minimal set of functions that cause the inconsistencies.
2. **Hierarchical Region Isolation.** For each function isolated in the first stage, during the hierarchical region isolation (Line 11 in Algorithm 1), bisection search is performed at increasingly granular levels, from code block level to statement level, and ultimately to expression level.

CIEL traverses the simplified AST of each function isolated in the function isolation stage, and isolates child nodes of the current node(s) that cause the compiler-induced inconsistency: from the child nodes of the function node, to child nodes of BB nodes, to all isolated statement nodes, until within the smallest subexpression in a statement node, e.g., a variable, constant, or function call. A difference of this code isolation method, compared to prior work, is that these child nodes are *continuous* blocks or statements, which are split into two continuous sets of code blocks or statements. For example, n continuous code blocks are split into the first $\lfloor n/2 \rfloor$ blocks and the remaining $n - \lfloor n/2 \rfloor$ blocks. Combined with the *region merge pass* (Sect. 3.3), all blocks are merged into as few continuous code regions as possible, reducing redundant type conversions. Section 4.2 shows that by removing redundant type conversions, the transformed program can more accurately and efficiently reflect the resolvability of compiler-induced numerical inconsistencies under precision enhancement.

Furthermore, given how statements in loops could accumulate errors that could exacerbate compiler-induced inconsistencies, our bisection search prioritizes loop structures. Thus, loop BBs at the current level of the AST hierarchy are isolated first. If inconsistencies are resolved then the search is narrowed down to the identified loop BBs; otherwise the search proceeds normally.

We use the sample function from Subfigure 2a to illustrate hierarchical region isolation within a function. The statement that causes the compiler-induced inconsistency is in Line 5 (ST6 in Subfigure 2b). The algorithm first searches in the loop BBs at the top level, between BB1 and BB6. The inconsistency is resolved with BB1 in enhanced precision, thus BB1 is isolated and further split into BB2 and BB3. BB3 is isolated next, which is then split into BB4 and BB5, with BB4 then isolated and split into statements ST4, ST5 and ST6, from which the constant expression $1.4E - 41f$ in ST6 is found to be the root cause of the inconsistency.

3.3   Source-to-Source Precision Enhancement

The precision enhancement module takes as input the marked simplified AST from the hierarchical code isolation module, and produces a transformed program where all floating-point operations in an enabled code region, whether it is a whole function or a continuous code segment, are in enhanced precision. Source-to-source program transformation allows the resulting programs to be successfully compiled by the same compilers that trigger the original inconsistencies. Furthermore, a source-level transformation, in contrast to IR or assembly level, is not affected by aggressive optimization passes such as instruction reordering which would obscure and obfuscate the boundaries between source code statements during binary generation.

CIEL detects and classifies CUDA host and device functions according to language-specific modifiers in the AST, such as the __global__ and __device__ modifiers in the function signature, and transforms code accordingly.

In terms of enhancing precision for CUDA kernels, while CPU programming platforms generally natively support floating-point types beyond double precision, GPU platforms do not. Thus we design CIEL to support precision enhancement with custom extended precision floating-point types that support operator overloading and math functions. Some examples of extended precision libraries include CAMPARY [19] and CUMP [25], but only GPUprec [24] fits the above criteria for integration. GPUprec only requires modest effort to be integrated with CIEL. We use its quadruple precision type to perform precision enhancement because it offers the most support for math functions.

Ideally, all code executed is available to CIEL when isolating code within a code region. However, external functions whose code is not available may be called within a code region. Even though it would not be possible to isolate individual expressions within such external functions, isolating the function call site itself may still be helpful in isolating numerical inconsistencies. In cases where inconsistencies exist in external functions, and an enhanced precision version of the same function is available, replacing the original function calls with calls to their corresponding enhanced-precision functions is expected to resolve the inconsistencies. Thus, for functions called within enhanced code regions, CIEL automatically replaces those given in a customizable *replacement function list*, most of which are math library functions, with an enhanced precision version. In the example in Subfigure 2a, sinhf and tanf would be replaced with sinh and tan, respectively. On the other hand, precision enhancement of variables and constants consists of two stages: region and expression transformation, with targeted strategies for different categories of variables.

Stage 1: Region Transformation. This stage enhances the precision of floating-point operations in a specific code region including scalar variables, built-in vectors and constants. Region transformation consists of three passes: region merge, variable categorization, and code transformation.

Pass 1: Region Merge. This pass merges all basic blocks and statements to be enhanced into as few continuous code regions as possible. Compared to prior work, this pass is added specifically as an improvement in removing unnecessary type conversions in precision enhanced code. If two adjacent code blocks on the same level of the AST hierarchy are to be enhanced, then these blocks are merged into one single block. For example, ST5 and ST6 in Subfigure 2b are adjacent and on the same level in the AST, thus they are merged into one block. If two adjacent code blocks that are on different levels of the AST hierarchy are to be enhanced, we insert a *variable checkpoint* between them so that redundant type conversions can be detected and removed during the Code Transformation pass. For example, ST6 and BB5 in Subfigure 2b are adjacent but on different levels in the AST, a variable checkpoint is inserted here so that there would be no redundant type conversions in between for variables such as comp.

Pass 2: Variable Categorization. This pass iterates through all variable uses in a code region, and categorizes scalar and built-in vector floating-point variables[2] into four groups. Our variable categorization algorithm is based on [18] which, in essence, separates *read-after-write* variables in a code region that require allocating temporary storage from variables that just require casting when referenced. We then categorize the *read-after-write* variables into two groups based on whether the variable declaration is inside (*reviseVars*) or outside (*replaceVars*) the code region since they require different transformation strategies. Finally we group the variables that only require casting when referenced by checking if they are only read (*rdVars*) or only written (*wrVars*). The last category (*wrVars*) was added in CIEL to implement precision enhancement in GPU programs with custom extended precision floating-point types described later in this subsection.

Pass 3: Code Transformation. This pass transforms variables according to their categorization:

---

[2] Pointers and array references are not categorized; their dereferences are directly cast.

T1 For *reviseVars*, the declarations of these variables (originally inside the region) are replaced with a temporary variable in higher precision; any reference to this variable inside the code region is replaced with its corresponding temporary variable; the declaration of the original variable is moved prior to the region's exit points, and initialized with the temporary variable.

T2 For *replaceVars*, a temporary variable declaration is inserted at the entry of the region, initialized with the value of the original variable (declared outside the region); any reference to this variable inside the code region is replaced with the temporary variable; the value of the temporary variable is assigned back to the original variable at region exit points.

T3 For *rdVars*, any reference to the variable inside the code region is explicitly upcast to higher precision.

T4 For *wrVars*, any assignment to the variable inside the code region is explicitly downcast to lower precision (reads may occur only outside the region).

Lastly, type conversion statements from/back to original precision are inserted at the entry/exit point(s) of a code region. Note that calls to functions that are not included in the replacement function list are treated as special exit points of the code region, and their arguments are cast to original precision prior to the function call. Additionally, if the exit/entry of a code region is a *variable checkpoint*, CIEL finds all the variables shared between the two code regions, and simply assigns the enhanced-precision replacement variable in the first region to the one in the second region. By doing so, CIEL prevents redundant type conversions between these two code regions.

Custom extended-precision floating-point types present unique challenges compared to built-in floating-point types. C++ allows implicit conversions among floating-point types, even when such conversions incur precision loss, such as from `double` to `float`. However, such implicit conversions are not possible for custom floating-point types. For example (assuming the type name is `dd_real`):

```
dd_real a = 1.0; dd_real b = a + 2.0;
```

There is ambiguity in `a + 2.0`, which can either be interpreted as an addition of two `dd_real` values or two `double` values before assigning the result to `b`. For such code to pass compilation, CIEL inserts explicit casts back to original precision in value assignments, function arguments, and other possible situations. These explicit casts require CIEL to categorize variables that are only written in a code region, hence a new category, *wrVars*, was added.

Another challenge when enhancing the precision of CUDA kernels is built-in floating-point vector classes. These classes provide vertex and matrix calculation in 2 to 4 dimensions and are widely used. CIEL supports transforming built-in vector type operations to enhanced precision, including type conversions for function arguments passed by reference or by dereferencing. This requires creating temporary variables that are live only during the function call. For this purpose, we implemented converter template class instances as anonymous variables in function arguments. Upon construction, they accept a reference or a pointer of the source variable, convert it to the target type, and provide a reference or a pointer in the target type to the function calls. When the function call is finished, destructors for these converter classes are invoked, and we assign the return value of these references/pointers back to the original variable.

Stage 2: Expression Transformation. This transformation is only applied when the code has been successfully isolated at the statement level. Specified subexpressions in each isolated statement are converted to enhanced precision. CIEL traverses the AST starting from the subexpression node, cast all variable reads and constants from subexpressions to enhanced precision, and the whole subexpression is explicitly converted back to original precision. For example, the subexpression `b*2.0f` in expression `a = b*2.0f+c` would be transformed to `(float)((double)b*2.0)` in enhanced precision.

4   Experimental Evaluation

This experimental evaluation answers the following research questions:

RQ1 How effective is CIEL at isolating compiler-induced numerical inconsistencies in heterogeneous programs?

RQ2 How does CIEL compare with the state of the art in isolating compiler-induced numerical inconsistencies in CPU programs?

4.1   RQ1: Numerical Inconsistencies in Heterogeneous Programs

Benchmarks. We collected a total of 339 compiler-induced inconsistencies: 330 inconsistencies observed in floating-point synthetic GPU programs, 5 inconsistencies triggered in NAS Parallel Benchmarks for GPU (NPB-GPU) [6], 3 inconsistencies triggered in the CUDA version of the Rodinia Benchmark suite for heterogeneous computing [10], and a real-world inconsistency found in the C version of the ECMWF Cloud Physics mini-app CLOUDSC [14].

The synthetic GPU programs were generated with Varity [21], a framework that randomly generates small programs written in CUDA C along with an input for which a numerical inconsistency is observed when using `nvcc -O3 -fastmath` in comparison to `nvcc -O0`. These programs use single-precision floating-point arithmetic, various C syntax mechanisms such as `for-loop` and `if` statements, and calls to external math functions.

The CUDA NAS Parallel Benchmarks demonstrate the ability of CIEL to isolate compiler-induced floating-point inconsistencies in programs originally written for CPU architectures and ported to GPUs. These programs use double precision, which means the extended precision capabilities of CIEL are used. On the other hand, the Rodinia programs are originally written as heterogeneous applications for which single and double precision implementations are available. Therefore, we use the version in single precision.

Finally, CLOUDSC is a standalone mini-app of the ECMWF cloud microphysics parameterization, which tests the CLOUDSC cloud microphysics scheme of the ECMWF Integrated Forecasting System (IFS). We choose CLOUDSC as

Table 2. Numerical inconsistencies in NAS, Rodinia and CLOUDSC programs.

Benchmark	Program	LOC	Input	Epsilon	Compilation Command
NPB-GPU	BT	5062	S	3.0e-12	`clang -O3 -ffast-math`
NPB-GPU	CG	1868	S	1.1e-15	`clang -O3 -ffast-math`
NPB-GPU	CG	1868	W	4.0e-16	`clang -O3 -ffast-math`
NPB-GPU	LU	4437	S	1.9e-12	`nvcc -O3 -use_fast_math`
NPB-GPU	MG	2349	W	2.9e-14	`clang -O3 -ffast-math`
Rodinia	LUD	717	256	1.2e-5	`nvcc -O0`
Rodinia	CFD	647	097K	7.2e-2	`nvcc -O0`
Rodinia	CFD	647	193K	1.9e-1	`nvcc -O0 & -O3 -ffast-math`
N/A	CLOUDSC	2593	N/A	1.0e-11	`gcc -O3 -ffast-math`

a candidate to demonstrate the efficacy of CIEL in finding compiler-induced inconsistencies in real-world applications, and show its capability of adapting to other software platforms and languages supported by Clang.

Experimental Environment. We use a PC with octa-core Intel(R) i7-11800H processors, and NVIDIA RTX 3070 GPU with 5120 CUDA cores, running Ubuntu 20.04 LTS. We use Clang version 14.0.6 to perform source-to-source transformation, which supports CUDA SDK versions up to 11.1 with Compute Capability up to 8.6. Clang 14.0.6 and nvcc 11.1 are also the compiler versions we use to compile transformed GPU programs. For CPU programs, we use gcc 9.4.0. Our methodology is independent of GPU models as long as they have the same Compute Capability. For all compilers, we considered two sets of compiler flags: -O0, and -O3 with fastmath.

Methodology for Triggering Numerical Inconsistencies. The compiler-induced numerical inconsistencies in NAS, Rodinia and CLOUDSC were previously unknown, and were discovered through testing. Specifically, we rely on verification routines that compare the relative errors in output values to an epsilon value ϵ to determine whether the results meet accuracy constraints. A compiler-induced inconsistency exists if a program passes its verification routines for some compiler settings but not for others.

For six of the NAS programs (BT, CG, FT, LU, MP and SP) and Rodinia LUD, we utilize existing verification routines where results are either compared to precalculated ground truth embedded in the program source code, or in the case of Rodinia LUD, the resulting two matrices are multiplied and then compared against the original matrix. For the Rodinia CFD Solver, we calculate the total density energy (TDE) as specified in [22] and compare it to the reference TDE value precalculated by running the double-precision version of CFD Solver compiled with `nvcc -O0`. For CLOUDSC, we compare relative errors for the main variables at the end of program execution against ground truth precalculated by running the original cloud scheme from IFS in FORTRAN.

We follow an existing methodology to *trigger* numerical inconsistencies, first introduced in [18]. Specifically, we set the epsilon value ϵ between the minimum and maximum errors observed amongst all compiler/optimization flag combi-

Table 3. Categorization of inconsistencies found in synthetic GPU programs.

Categories	# Programs	Percentage	Sample Code
Subnormal Arithmetic	125	37.9%	`+1.8922E-42f + var_3`
Inf or NaN Arithmetic	53	16.0%	`+1.3797E-35f / -0.0f`
Math Functions	41	12.4%	`sinf(+1.0195E25f)`
Rounding Errors	18	5.5%	`-16458 / 1.67329e-16`
Program Inputs	164	49.7%	N/A
Print Statements	11	3.3%	N/A

nations for a given program, and maximize the ϵ value such that the program passes its verification routines only for some compiler settings but not for others. Table 2 lists the inputs, epsilon values, and compiler commands used to trigger each of the 9 numerical inconsistencies reported for these programs.

Evaluation Results. We find that CIEL is effective at isolating code responsible for the numerical inconsistencies in 337 out of 339 instances (99.4%). In terms of isolation granularity, CIEL isolates at expression level in 318 out of 339 instances (93.8%), while the rest of the inconsistencies are isolated at line, block, or function level. Below we describe the results per benchmark.

Synthetic GPU Programs. CIEL isolates all inconsistencies: individual expressions in 310 cases, a code block in 18, and a function in the remaining 2. We manually examined the source code, inputs, outputs, and in some cases the assembly code of each of program. Our inspection revealed that CIEL correctly isolated 328 out of 330 (99.4%) inconsistencies while only 2 (0.6%) were false positives.

We identified six categories of *true* compiler-induced numerical inconsistencies isolated by CIEL. Table 3 lists these categories, the number of occurrences, and sample code. Note that an inconsistency may belong to multiple categories.

The first four categories are purely related to floating-point operations. *Subnormal arithmetic* indicates that subnormal numbers are involved in the floating-point operations. *Math functions* are often involved in which extreme values may be computed differently depending on the implementations. For example, nvcc compiles `sinf()` as a single fast approximation instruction instead of a full function. Also in some cases, `Inf` or `NaN` values are involved, which are not strictly IEEE 754–2008 compliant under fast math. We also found that the results of some operations differ under different optimization flags due to *rounding errors*.

The last two categories are related to the setup of the benchmark programs themselves. We observed cases where resolving compiler-induced inconsistencies also required enhancing the precision of their *program inputs*. And lastly, we found a few instances for which the final line of code where the computation result is *printed* byte by byte is the cause of the inconsistency. This is because the result of the computation is subnormal when converted from enhanced precision.

As for false positives, we found two cases where CIEL isolates statements that have no effect on the computation. Specifically, a variable is assigned a value

Table 4. NPB-GPU and Rodinia Experiment Results. Time is given in mm:ss.

		Statement Level			Expression Level		
Program	Isolated Function	Line(s)	# Cfgs	Time	Exp.	# Cfgs	Time
BT.S	exact_solution	1874-1886	10	1:23	zeta	20	2:10
CG.S	sparse	1710,1722	18	1:23	size,shift	24	1:52
CG.W	sparse	1710,1713,1765	19	1:34	size,scale	28	2:24
LU.S	ssor_gpu_kernel_2	4023	8	1:03	tmp	11	1:15
MG.W	rprj3_gpu_kernel	2045-2050	14	1:16	x2,y2	34	3:02
CFD 097K	cuda_compute_step_factor	283	14	6:01	sqrtf, speed_sqd	26	10:10
CFD 193K	compute_speed_sqd	252 257	10	7:29	velocity, speed_sqd	40	22:11
LUD 256	lud_internal	—	17	1:16	—	—	—

that is immediately overwritten by another value. These assignment statements are located inside a loop. When the precision of the entire loop is enhanced, the inconsistency is resolved; but if only the precision of the statements after the initial assignment is enhanced, the inconsistency persists because of type conversions inserted by CIEL at the end of the region inside the loop.

Overall, CIEL took a total of 3 h and 2 min to analyze all 330 programs, and 33 s per program on average.

NAS and Rodinia. CIEL isolated all 8 numerical inconsistencies in NAS and Rodinia programs. Table 4 shows the results for each program for both statement and expression level isolation. For BT.S, LU.S, MG.W, CIEL isolates variable expression(s) in one statement that causes the compiler-induced inconsistency. In CFD 097K, CIEL isolates a function call with a variable parameter. For CG and CFD 193K, CIEL isolates 2 variables across 2 to 3 statements as the cause of the inconsistencies. In all cases above, the isolated expressions are inside deeply nested loops, so even a slight offset can be accumulated into a larger inconsistency that exceeds the error threshold. The only exception is the LUD program where only a function, **lud_internal** is isolated. Upon inspection, the reason seems to be that a variable sum is read and written throughout the function, affecting the whole matrix, and any type conversion would cause the inconsistency to persist.

CIEL isolated each inconsistency within 22 min, used less than 20 searches (configurations) for statement isolation, and used no more than 40 searches for expression isolation. About 1%–5% of run time is used on code transformation.

CLOUDSC. CIEL isolated a constant expression (**float**)0.4 as the cause of the inconsistency. After looking further into the code repository [13] and reporting the issue to ECMWF scientists, we confirmed CIEL's result. It turns out ECMWF scientists had meant to temporarily introduce a bug during testing with the type casting but had forgotten to remove it; CIEL correctly suggests increasing the precision of that same argument to resolve the inconsistency. CIEL took 7 min to isolate the inconsistency, from which 8% is spent on program transformation.

Table 5. NPB CPU Experiment Results. Time is in minutes:seconds.

	CIEL Statement Level				pLiner Statement Level				CIEL Expression		
Prog.	Function	Line(s)	#Cfgs	T_{line}	Function	Line(s)	#Cfgs	T_{line}	Exp.	#Cfgs	T_{exp}
CG.B	sparse	814,819,876	19	16:23	sparse	—	7	3:53	—	—	—
SP.A	tzetar	65,69	16	6:56	y_solve	68	25	7:50	r4,t2	23	9:36
SP.B	exact_solution	44-47	9	17:28	exact_solution	44-47	17	24:51	zeta	19	34:57

Answer to RQ1: CIEL isolated 337 out of 339 inconsistencies in minutes with a precision of 99.4%, which included 328 synthetic GPU programs, NAS and Rodinia programs, and the mini-app CLOUDSC. In 318 cases (93.8%), CIEL isolated expressions. Manual inspection revealed inconsistency characteristics, such as the involvement of Inf, NaN, or subnormal numbers in arithmetic.

4.2 RQ2: Comparison with the State of the Art

Baseline. We compare CIEL to pLiner [18], to the best of our knowledge, the only tool available to isolate inconsistencies at the statement level in CPU programs.

Benchmarks. Due to pLiner capabilities, this evaluation is limited to CPU programs. We adopt benchmarks from the publicly available pLiner repository (SHA ef94b40)[3] originally used to evaluate pLiner, which include 50 floating-point synthetic CPU programs on Intel CPU platforms, and 3 programs from the C version of the NAS Parallel Benchmark: CG.B, SP.A, and SP.B. We use the same compiler, optimization flags, and error thresholds as pLiner in our evaluation.

Evaluation Results. CIEL achieves more precise isolation results than pLiner for 84.9% of the programs. When isolating at the same statement level as pLiner, CIEL is 24.5% more efficient in terms of number of searches. The rest of this section describes the results per benchmark.

Synthetic CPU Programs. In 42 out of 50 programs, CIEL successfully isolates code at the statement level, and subsequently at the expression level. In 36 of these programs, CIEL isolates the same statement (line) as pLiner. In the remaining 6 cases, CIEL isolates at the statement level while pLiner can only isolate at code block or function level. CIEL explores 29.7% fewer configurations to achieve this result. On average, CIEL explores 5.2 configurations for statement isolation compared to 7.4 configurations explored by pLiner. Expression level isolation incurs in exploring additional configurations: 16.5 on average.

For the remaining 8 programs, there are two cases in which CIEL isolates a smaller code block than pLiner. There are four programs for which neither CIEL nor pLiner can resolve the inconsistencies by using precision enhancement. Lastly, there are two programs for which we were not able to reproduce the

---

[3] https://github.com/LLNL/pLiner/commit/ef94b40.

numerical inconsistencies. Note that in these cases, pLiner still proceeded with the search while CIEL immediately detected the absence of an inconsistency.

NAS CPU Benchmarks. Results for the NAS CPU benchmark are shown in Table 5. In CG.B, CIEL isolates three statements in function **sparse**, which has 227 lines of code, while pLiner can only isolate the whole function. pLiner stopped after it failed to resolve the inconsistency even when all basic blocks in **sparse** are in enhanced precision; CIEL prevents this by avoiding unnecessary type conversions between basic blocks. In SP.B, CIEL first isolates the same statement as pLiner in function **exact_solution**, and then further isolates a variable. Finally in SP.A, CIEL and pLiner isolate different functions (**tzetar** vs. **y_solve**) due to exploring different areas of the search tree. We confirmed that precision enhancement of either function resolves the inconsistency. If we were to limit the search in CIEL to only explore function **y_solve**, then CIEL would isolate the same statement as pLiner. Ultimately, CIEL isolates two variables.

In terms of efficiency, CIEL uses fewer configurations than pLiner to isolate inconsistencies in SP.A (16 vs. 25) and SP.B (9 vs. 17) at the statement level. CIEL uses more configurations for CG.B (19 vs. 7), but it isolates the same function with only 4 configurations, and isolates at a finer granularity. Expression isolation requires an additional 7 and 10 configurations for SP.A and SP.B, respectively.

> **Answer to RQ2:** CIEL shows comparable or superior results in isolating the inconsistencies in 44 out of 48 (92%) of synthetic CPU programs and the NAS programs. Overall, CIEL isolates inconsistencies at the same level of granularity than pLiner but with higher efficiency, or at a finer level of granularity with an additional cost, in particular in the case of expression isolation.

4.3   Threats to Validity

While our evaluation set of programs is large and diverse, our results may not generalize to all applications. Also, compiler-induced numerical inconsistencies are input dependent, thus it is possible that other inputs could trigger additional inconsistencies in the same code regions, or elsewhere. Complementary use of dynamic analysis or code coverage information may be useful. CIEL does not handle non-deterministic applications, but some of such programs could still be analyzed by removing certain sources of non-determinism for testing purposes [27].

CIEL's implementation only handles a subset of C/C++ and CUDA platform constructs. Features such as anonymous functions or the **auto** keyword, introduced in C++11, are not currently supported. Handling some of these features may require a new approach in simplified AST generation and code isolation. Nevertheless, given how CIEL can differentiate between host and device code, it could be adapted to any platform supported by the Clang compiler frontend, such as OpenMP and OpenCL [3].

Code isolation may be further impacted by special floating-point values such as ±0.0, Inf, and NaN. The processing of these values, if consistent across precisions but inconsistent between different optimization flags, may become a blind spot for precision enhancement. The choice of extended precision library may also impact search results and efficacy. GPUprec, for example, has known issues with math functions when it should return NaN but returns zero instead, which could affect isolation results. Finally, CIEL requires source code when enhancing precision. However, if the source code for a function is not available, CIEL may still isolate the call site if an enhanced precision variant of the function exists.

5   Related Work

Detecting and Isolating Numerical Errors. pLiner [18] isolates known compiler-induced numerical inconsistencies in C/C++ CPU programs at the line level. pLiner's approach also includes hierarchical code isolation and precision enhancement as a method to isolate inconsistencies. Unlike pLiner, CIEL works on heterogeneous programs, which pose unique challenges when isolating numerical inconsistencies, as described in Sect. 3.3. Furthermore, CIEL isolates inconsistencies to the expression level rather than lines. FLiT [28] generates and runs custom-made tests under different optimization levels to *trigger* compiler-induced numerical inconsistencies, which are then isolated at the function level only. Compared to CIEL, FLiT does not employ precision enhancement for inconsistency isolation, and focuses on CPU programs.

There are also tools that automatically detect or isolate specific categories of numerical errors but not compiler-induced inconsistencies. FPChecker [20] is a tool that automatically detects floating-point exceptions in GPU applications, which also uses Clang to transform CUDA code, but it does so at the IR level. While FPChecker operates on GPU programs, it does not isolate compiler-induced numerical inconsistencies. FPChecker also inspired other tools, such as Predoo [33] in the field of precision testing for Deep Learning (DL) operators. On the other hand, PFPSanitizer [12] detects numerical errors by performing shadow execution with higher precision in parallel. Shadow execution with precision enhancement is also employed by Herbgrind [26] and FPDebug [7] with the goal of finding floating-point precision errors.

Testing Compilers and Numerical Code. CIEL transforms source code in small increments and tests whether numerical inconsistencies are resolved. CIEL is inspired by prior work on compiler mutation testing. Le et al. [23] introduce equivalent modulo inputs (EMI) which mutates programs on unexecuted paths to expose compiler bugs that incorrectly execute these paths. ClassFuzz [11] uses EMI by mutating Java classfiles on predefined mutation operators, and send them to various JVM implementations for differential testing. Zhu and Zaidman [34] propose new mutator operations alongside conventional ones to expose bugs in GPU programs, but their work does not involve floating-point arithmetic. HeteroFuzz [32] introduces a multi-pronged fuzzing approach to detect platform-dependent divergence in heterogeneous programs running on FPGAs, using techniques including dynamic probabilistic mutations to reduce the long latency between invocations to hardware simulators. Overall, none of the above tools focus on exposing or isolating compiler-induced numerical inconsistencies.

CIEL performs differential testing to check whether compiler-induced inconsistencies exist by providing the same input to a series of programs compiled from the same source code but with various compilers and optimization flags. Differential testing has been applied before to numerical programs. FPDiff [29] performs differential testing between automatically identified *synonymous functions* across various numerical libraries to identify inconsistencies between the results from these functions under certain inputs. Unlike CIEL, FPDiff tests *different* implementations of a given function, and it does not consider different compilers or optimization flags.

6   Conclusion

With scientific code ported or developed on GPUs, compiler-induced numerical inconsistencies can arise at various stages of development. Unfortunately, automatic tools to isolate such problems are nonexistent, which harms productivity in GPU computing. In this paper, we demonstrate a practical method to identify the root cause of such inconsistencies in heterogeneous code. We implemented our approach in the tool CIEL based on the effective bisection search algorithm, and improved over the state of the art for CPU programs in both efficiency and accuracy. Most importantly, CIEL addresses a number of challenges to handle heterogeneous code. Our evaluation on synthetic GPU programs, GPU benchmarks, and real world mini-app shows the effectiveness of CIEL at isolating inconsistencies in heterogeneous code with a precision of 99.4%. Our code and experimental data are publicly available at https://github.com/LLNL/Ciel/.

Acknowledgments. This work was performed under the auspices of the U.S. Department of Energy by Lawrence Livermore National Laboratory under Contract DE-AC52-07NA27344 (LLNL-CONF-846081), the U.S. Department of Energy, Office of Science, Advanced Scientific Computing Research, under awards DE-SC0022182 and DE-SC0020286, and the National Science Foundation under award CCF-1750983.

References

1. IEEE standard for floating-point arithmetic: IEEE Std **754–2008**, 1–70 (2008). https://doi.org/10.1109/IEEESTD.2008.4610935
2. CUDA Llvm compiler (2018). https://developer.nvidia.com/cuda-llvm-compiler
3. Clang 14.0.0 documentation (2022). https://releases.llvm.org/14.0.0/tools/clang/docs/ReleaseNotes.html
4. Compiling CUDA with Clang (2022). https://releases.llvm.org/14.0.0/docs/CompileCudaWithLLVM.html
5. Ahn, D.H., et al.: Keeping science on keel when software moves. Commun. ACM **64**(2), 66–74 (2021)

6. de Araujo, G.A., Griebler, D., Danelutto, M., Fernandes, L.G.: Efficient NAS parallel benchmark kernels with CUDA. In: PDP, pp. 9–16. IEEE (2020)

7. Benz, F., Hildebrandt, A., Hack, S.: A dynamic program analysis to find floating-point accuracy problems. In: PLDI, pp. 453–462. ACM (2012)

8. Brodtkorb, A.R., Dyken, C., Hagen, T.R., Hjelmervik, J.M., Storaasli, O.O.: State-of-the-art in heterogeneous computing. Sci. Program. **18**(1), 1–33 (2010)

9. CEED: CEED/Laghos: high-order lagrangian hydrodynamics miniapp (2017). https://github.com/CEED/Laghos

10. Che, S., et al.: Rodinia: a benchmark suite for heterogeneous computing. In: IISWC, pp. 44–54. IEEE Computer Society (2009)

11. Chen, Y., Su, T., Sun, C., Su, Z., Zhao, J.: Coverage-directed differential testing of JVM implementations. In: PLDI, pp. 85–99. ACM (2016)

12. Chowdhary, S., Nagarakatte, S.: Parallel shadow execution to accelerate the debugging of numerical errors. In: ESEC/SIGSOFT FSE, pp. 615–626. ACM (2021)

13. ECMWF: CLOUDSC-V3: re-create the single-exponent bug in the c variant (2019). https://github.com/ecmwf-ifs/dwarf-p-cloudsc/commit/d88c0c8f8d1effd5bd395cb71657629fb242f661

14. ECMWF: Standalone mini-app of the ECMWF cloud microphysics parameterization (2022). https://github.com/ecmwf-ifs/dwarf-p-cloudsc

15. Franco, A.D., Guo, H., Rubio-González, C.: A comprehensive study of real-world numerical bug characteristics. In: ASE, pp. 509–519. IEEE Computer Society (2017)

16. Fu, Z., Bai, Z., Su, Z.: Automated backward error analysis for numerical code. In: OOPSLA, pp. 639–654. ACM (2015)

17. Gopalakrishnan, G., Laguna, I., Li, A., Panchekha, P., Rubio-González, C., Tatlock, Z.: Guarding numerics amidst rising heterogeneity. In: Correctness@SC, pp. 9–15. IEEE (2021)

18. Guo, H., Laguna, I., Rubio-González, C.: pLiner: isolating lines of floating-point code for compiler-induced variability. In: SC, p. 49. IEEE/ACM (2020)

19. Joldes, M., Muller, J.-M., Popescu, V., Tucker, W.: CAMPARY: cuda multiple precision arithmetic library and applications. In: Greuel, G.-M., Koch, T., Paule, P., Sommese, A. (eds.) ICMS 2016. LNCS, vol. 9725, pp. 232–240. Springer, Cham (2016). https://doi.org/10.1007/978-3-319-42432-3_29

20. Laguna, I.: FPChecker: detecting floating-point exceptions in GPU applications. In: ASE, pp. 1126–1129. IEEE (2019)

21. Laguna, I.: Varity: quantifying floating-point variations in HPC systems through randomized testing. In: IPDPS, pp. 622–633. IEEE (2020)

22. Laguna, I., Wood, P.C., Singh, R., Bagchi, S.: GPUMixer: performance-driven floating-point tuning for GPU scientific applications. In: Weiland, M., Juckeland, G., Trinitis, C., Sadayappan, P. (eds.) ISC High Performance 2019. LNCS, vol. 11501, pp. 227–246. Springer, Cham (2019). https://doi.org/10.1007/978-3-030-20656-7_12

23. Le, V., Afshari, M., Su, Z.: Compiler validation via equivalence modulo inputs. In: PLDI, pp. 216–226. ACM (2014)

24. Lu, M., He, B., Luo, Q.: Supporting extended precision on graphics processors. In: DaMoN, pp. 19–26. ACM (2010)

25. Nakayama, T., Takahashi, D.: Implementation of multiple-precision floating-point arithmetic library for GPU computing. In: PDCS, pp. 343–349 (2011)

26. Sanchez-Stern, A., Panchekha, P., Lerner, S., Tatlock, Z.: Finding root causes of floating point error. In: PLDI, pp. 256–269. ACM (2018)

27. Sato, K., Ahn, D.H., Laguna, I., Lee, G.L., Schulz, M.: Clock delta compression for scalable order-replay of non-deterministic parallel applications. In: SC, pp. 62:1–62:12. ACM (2015)
28. Sawaya, G., Bentley, M., Briggs, I., Gopalakrishnan, G., Ahn, D.H.: FLiT: cross-platform floating-point result-consistency tester and workload. In: IISWC, pp. 229–238. IEEE Computer Society (2017)
29. Vanover, J., Deng, X., Rubio-González, C.: Discovering discrepancies in numerical libraries. In: ISSTA, pp. 488–501. ACM (2020)
30. Yi, X., Chen, L., Mao, X., Ji, T.: Efficient automated repair of high floating-point errors in numerical libraries. In: POPL, pp. 56:1–56:29. ACM (2019)
31. Zeller, A.: Yesterday, my program worked. today, it does not. why? ACM SIGSOFT software engineering notes **24**(6), 253–267 (1999)
32. Zhang, Q., Wang, J., Kim, M.: HeteroFuzz: fuzz testing to detect platform dependent divergence for heterogeneous applications. In: ESEC/SIGSOFT FSE, pp. 242–254. ACM (2021)
33. Zhang, X., et al.: Predoo: precision testing of deep learning operators. In: ISSTA, pp. 400–412. ACM (2021)
34. Zhu, Q., Zaidman, A.: Massively parallel, highly efficient, but what about the test suite quality? Applying mutation testing to GPU programs. In: ICST, pp. 209–219. IEEE (2020)

SAI: AI-Enabled Speech Assistant Interface for Science Gateways in HPC

Pouya Kousha$^{(\boxtimes)}$, Arpan Jain, Ayyappa Kolli, Matthew Lieber, Mingzhe Han, Nicholas Contini, Hari Subramoni, and Dhableswar K. Panda

The Ohio State University, Columbus, OH 43210, USA
{kousha.2,jain.575,kolli.38,lieber.31,han.1453,contini.26}@osu.edu,
{subramon,panda}@cse.ohio-state.edu

Abstract. High-Performance Computing (HPC) is increasingly being used in traditional scientific domains as well as emerging areas like Deep Learning (DL). This has led to a diverse set of professionals who interact with state-of-the-art HPC systems. The deployment of Science Gateways for HPC systems like Open On-Demand has a significant positive impact on these users in migrating their workflows to HPC systems. Although computing capabilities are ubiquitously available (as on-premises or in the cloud HPC infrastructure), significant effort and expertise are required to use them effectively. This is particularly challenging for domain scientists and other users whose primary expertise lies outside of computer science. In this paper, we seek to minimize the steep learning curve and associated complexities of using state-of-the-art high-performance systems by creating SAI: an AI-Enabled Speech Assistant Interface for Science Gateways in High Performance Computing. We use state-of-the-art AI models for speech and text and fine-tune them for the HPC arena by retraining them on a new HPC dataset we create. We use ontologies and knowledge graphs to capture the complex relationships between various components of the HPC ecosystem. We finally show how one can integrate and deploy SAI in Open OnDemand and evaluate its functionality and performance on real HPC systems. To the best of our knowledge, this is the first effort aimed at designing and developing an AI-powered speech-assisted interface for science gateways in HPC.

Keywords: HPC · Open OnDemand · Conversational AI · Speech recognition · Natural Language Processing · Knowledge Graphs

1 Introduction and Motivation

High-Performance Computing (HPC) is an integral part of various traditional scientific domains like medical research, weather forecasting, and earthquake prediction, as well as emerging areas powered by Deep Learning (DL) and Machine

This research is supported in part by NSF grants #1818253, #1854828, #1931537, #2007991, #2018627, #2112606, and XRAC grant #NCR-130002.

Learning (ML). The ability to process and analyze large sets of data on current HPC systems has led to remarkable advances in science and engineering and has become an indispensable tool for students, researchers, and industry professionals. Examples include social scientists reviewing massive datasets from sources such as Twitter or Facebook, archaeologists experimenting with LiDAR [18] in mapping subsurface artifacts, and painters harnessing computer-aided design to use archives of ancient works as a style guide.

Unfortunately, HPC use and adoption by many is hindered by the complex way in which these resources need to be used. Utilizing HPC services requires familiarity with command-line interfaces and custom client software of HPC middleware, DL/ML frameworks, and performance analysis tools which creates an accessibility gap that impedes further adoption. For instance, HPC middleware like high-performance MPI libraries and DL frameworks have various advanced features and complex user interfaces. While these interfaces are comprehensive and extensive, they require a *steep* learning curve, even for expert users, making them nearly impossible to use for novice users like medical doctors, domain scientists, and other users whose primary expertise lies outside of computer science.

Recent surveys conducted by supercomputing centers [24] indicate that users are more likely to adopt a GUI-based interface provided by science gateways such as Open OnDemand [5]. Open OnDemand is one of only a few open-source general web interfaces to support remote visualization. It is currently the most well-known and adopted general web interface within the HPC community. Although, Open OnDemand reduces the initial accessibility hurdle to the HPC ecosystem by providing job templates for a small subset of popular HPC applications, there is still much to be desired in extending this support to the other components of the HPC ecosystem such as middleware, frameworks, and tools. While most users are intuitively able to express what they are looking for in words or text (e.g., "train my model with 32 GPUs on TACC Frontera with TensorFlow"), they find it hard to quickly adapt to, navigate, and use HPC interfaces to obtain desired results. Furthermore, surveys of end users conducted by prestigious firms like Deloitte [4] and PriceWaterhouseCooper [6] clearly indicate that users are more likely to use a conversational AI interface as opposed to using older keyboard/mouse-style inputs. **To the best of our knowledge, no interface exists that allows end-users to interact conversationally with state-of-the-art science gateways.**

1.1 Motivation

This challenge leads us to the primary motivation of the proposed work: *can we design an easy-to-use and productive conversational interface, utilizing AI, that enables end-to-end abstraction and automation of the steps involved in execution, monitoring, and evaluation of HPC workloads?* Fig. 1 depicts our vision of how SAI enhances the productivity of end-users. The left side depicts the multiple steps that the end users must traditionally perform to execute their HPC applications. These steps typically include selecting an HPC application; figuring out dependencies and installing them and the actual HPC application (either manually or through package managers); consulting the documentation for appropriate arguments and parameters; and finally creating the job

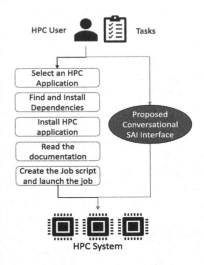

Fig. 1. Motivation behind creating SAI to improve user productivity

launch scripts. All of these steps are complex and require expertise in interacting with HPC middleware and tools using their traditional interfaces. The right side depicts how these same users can extract better productivity by using SAI. The manager of HPC at the U.S Department of Energy Idaho National Laboratory had the following strong and enthusiastic statement for SAI work - *"We have seen early demonstrations of the conversational AI Engine on multiple occasions. We see the proposed work as a paradigm shift that will directly benefit the over 1,200 users on our systems and lower the threshold for HPC usage. The incorporation of the AI Engine in a science gateway will serve to lower the time to science for the vast majority of our HPC users."*

1.2 Challenges in Enabling Conversational Interface for HPC

Challenge #1: Creating Custom Datasets and Models for HPC: While the latest Automatic Speech Recognition (ASR) [9,27] and Natural Language Understanding (NLU) [10,23] models have achieved impressive accuracy rates, such as 2% Word Error Rate (WER) [9] on Librispeech [21], these models often struggle to accurately interpret and understand technical terms (e.g. Allreduce and MNIST) and abbreviations (e.g. CPU and HCA) specific to the HPC domain. Furthermore, current language datasets do not include these technical terms and abbreviations, making it difficult to create ASR and NLU models that can accurately interpret and understand words and sentences commonly used in HPC. Thus, the availability of datasets specifically tailored to HPC domain is crucial and is key to creating new NLU/ASR models capable of accurately interpreting HPC-specific words and sentences. *To the best of our knowledge, HPC-specific datasets and models do not exist for use today.*

Challenge #2: Scalable Representations for Complex Relationships between Components of the HPC Ecosystem: The relationship between HPC applications, parallel hardware, deep learning (DL) models and problems, and datasets/inputs is complex with respect to each other. Researchers currently spend significant time and energy manually understanding and mapping these relationships through the use of documentation, tutorials, and other online resources. However, the representation of these complex relationships can be automated and made more accessible to end-users by leveraging Knowledge Graphs (KGs). An essential aspect of creating such KGs is the use of a portable, simple, yet thorough ontology. Recently, the HPC Ontology [17] has been proposed as a way to formally define and represent HPC-related knowledge, including vocabularies, semantics, and formal representations. *However, it only captures limited aspects of the complex relationships we want to cover for HPC workload execution. Thus, a significant expansion and enhancement is required for the proposed workflow to be truly useful.*

Challenge #3: Automating and Abstracting Installation of Packages: Leveraging High-Performance Computing (HPC) systems requires the use of various libraries, middleware, and applications. MPI implementations such as MPICH, OpenMPI, and MVAPICH2 enable parallel computation at scale. System software like compilers and supporting libraries are vital for accelerating applications. Frameworks like PyTorch and TensorFlow provide high-level APIs for designing and training deep neural networks. However, installing these software packages and their dependencies is a significant challenge, even for those familiar with HPC systems. While package managers such as Spack simplify the process, they can still pose a challenge for novice HPC users whose primary expertise lies outside of computer science.

Challenge #4: Integration of Conversational AI to HPC as Gateway: Developing a conversational interface framework is only the first step, the next challenge is to integrate it into a state-of-the-art science gateway to provide end-users access to it. To achieve this, we need to determine the interface between the conversational AI interface and the science gateways. The conversational interface component must also be modular to adapt to future advancements in DL models and HPC applications without a major revamp. A challenge here is to ascertain and minimize the changes needed to enable the end-to-end pipeline.

1.3 Contributions

In this paper, we take on the challenge of reducing the complexity of executing traditional scientific and ML/DL-based HPC workloads through modern science gateways by proposing, designing, and developing SAI. SAI is a novel conversational AI-based framework that automates and abstracts the cumbersome steps involved in accelerating traditional scientific and ML/DL-based applications on modern HPC systems. SAI simplifies the HPC process for non-experts, such as domain scientists and AI researchers. It eliminates the need to learn about different job queues on a cluster, allowing them to focus on their research without bogged down by technical issues, such as having to learn about the various job queues on a cluster. With SAI, these researchers can easily submit their jobs and get the results they need, without needing to become experts in the intricacies of HPC systems.

To gain a deeper understanding, users can familiarize themselves with the transition flow of SAI (Fig. 7). This will enable them to reproduce results on the terminal using the SAI-generated command as discussed in Sect. 5. To summarize, this paper makes the following contributions:

1. Proposes and develops a conversational AI interface (SAI) for running HPC applications and installing required libraries, packages, and frameworks
2. Describes datasets for text and speech with HPC-specific and fine-tuned state-of-the-art ASR models to recognize HPC terminologies and retrain an Entity-detection NLU model to understand text command
3. Proposes a general ontology to scalably represent the complex relationships between various components of the HPC ecosystem
4. Describes KGs to represent the relationship between different scientific/DL benchmarks/applications, datasets/inputs, package managers, and tools.
5. Integrate and deploy SAI in Open OnDemand and evaluate its functionality and performance on real HPC systems.
6. Provides a comprehensive explainable flow for SAI, including a detailed explanation of the transition from user input to job output along with generated job scripts and installed environments. This helps users to understand how to generate commands and reuse them directly in a terminal in future.

2   Background

2.1   Conversational User Interface

Conversational User Interfaces (CUI) represent a new way for users to interact with applications, moving beyond the traditional Graphical User Interfaces (GUI). Popularized by voice assistants like Siri, Alexa, and Google Assistant, CUIs have the ability to understand and respond to multiple variations of natural language, enabling more intuitive and efficient communication. Studies [12,13] have shown a strong preference for speech interfaces over traditional GUIs due to the ease of use and minimal learning curve. The use of CUIs is becoming increasingly popular in businesses [25] and Data shows that more than half of US adult mobile phone users use virtual assistants such as Siri or Alexa. [3].

2.2   Open OnDemand

Open OnDemand is an open-source, widely-used, customizable web interface for interacting with HPC systems. It allows integration with various HPC resources and job schedulers to make HPC resources more accessible to users who may not be familiar with command-line interfaces. It has features such as job submission, file management, and remote visualization, providing a streamlined and user-friendly experience for researchers, engineers, and scientists.

2.3   Ontology and Knowledge Graphs

Ontology formalizes knowledge of entities in a domain with limited relationships and classes for constructing KGs by adding individuals and instantiating the data and object properties. The data property applies to an individual to capture features or data about the individual while the object property (relationship) links individuals of the same or different classes to each other.

2.4   Spack

Spack is a package manager primarily designed for HPC systems, providing flexibility in build configuration and high compatibility with different systems. It builds packages and dependencies from source, allowing customization without interacting with build systems or resolving dependencies. Users interact with Spack through "specs" specifying package version, compiler, features, and dependencies, which Spack verifies before proceeding with installation.

3   Terminologies

The various terminologies, terms and legends used in this paper are explained below. A parameter is a value that is given by the user for an argument and arguments can have multiple parameters.

- **Entity**: a single or a collection of words that refers to a same class always. For examples, allreduce and ResNet are algorithms/model.
- **HPC-ASR Dataset**: an in-house ASR dataset created by us for HPC and DL terminologies.
- **HPC-NLU Dataset**: an entity detection and classification dataset created by us for training NLU models for HPC and DL terminologies.
- **Speech and Text Query**: Speech query is spoken audio passed to ASR and NLU models, text query is typed text passed to NLU model.
- **WER**: WER is a performance metric for ASR models that works by comparing words in the predicted and the reference text.

4   Proposed SAI Framework

In this section, we elaborate our design and implementation to enable the Speech Assistant Interface (SAI) for the HPC domain. Figure 2 depicts the overall flow of execution and the steps involved in the operation of SAI. We will describe each step in the following subsections.

4.1 Generating HPC Datasets for Speech and Text

To address Challenge-#1 (Sect. 1.2), we create an HPC-datasets for text (**HPC-NLU**) and speech (**HPC-ASR**) containing HPC and DL terminologies (for example NCCL, IntelMPI, ResNet, etc.). ❶ We generate basic text queries and label each entity into five broad categories of model/algorithm, data, system, software, and arguments.

We create a list of arguments that can be given to the application to generate different types of queries on the HPC text dataset. ❷ We generate all the combinations of entities with different arguments for each basic sentence structure. For example, the number of combinations of the commands for running MPI benchmarks amounts to 315K queries. ❸ To handle different ways of saying the same phrase, we develop synonyms for HPC terminologies (like CPU, processor, central-

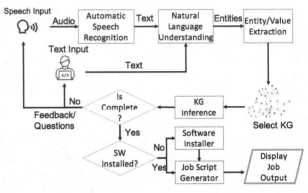

Fig. 2. High-level design of SAI showing the flowchart and SAI components - The blue rectangles are components of SAI while the green boxes show the decision criteria for the direction to proceed based on the processing of user input to continue interacting with the user or moving toward submitting the associated user job. (Color figure online)

processor, and host-processor for CPU) and use them to generate additional queries. The mentioned MPI benchmarks query set extends to 19 million queries by using the synonyms. These queries will cover most of the HPC lexicon and for HPC-ASR we crowd-sourced to 20 different volunteer users—with 6 dialects and speech patterns— recording portions of it to create the HPC-ASR dataset. ❹ We include permutations of phrases to restrict DNN from learning any ordering of arguments in the dataset. The resulting MPI benchmark dataset contains 7 million rows just by including the permutations. Through each step, the labels and queries of both HPC-ASR and HPC-NLU are human supervised. For HPC-ASR, the accents are covered by the TIMIT dataset for training. The recordings are denoised and verified through human supervision. Using the five broad categories mentioned, the entities are classified to these 5 types and are passed to the NLU component for processing and value extraction. Section 6 mentions train-test data split details.

4.2 Fine-Tuning Speech Recognition Model for HPC Terminologies

As the first step of processing speech input shown in Fig. 2 and to address challenge-#1 (Sect. 1.2), we need an ASR model capable of understanding domain specific terminologies (e.g. PyTorch, Allreduce, and IntelMPI) in HPC/DL applications. State-of-the-art ASR models are trained on large speech datasets like LibriSpeech and TIMIT to recognize English's large vocabulary and support different accents. We selected Speech2Text [27] as the base model, pre-trained on the LibriSpeech 1,000 h ASR corpus. To achieve our goal, we combined the HPC-ASR dataset with TIMIT [1] and fine-tuned the model and hyperparameters. TIMIT dataset helps supporting different English dialects and accents. We convert the generated text from the ASR model to lowercase and used SentencePiece [16] to tokenize the words to be passed to the NLU module.

4.3   Designing an Entity Detection and Classification Model for SAI

The next step depicted in Fig. 2 is to apply natural language understanding on user text input or transcribed text from ASR to overcome the rest of challenge- #1 (Sect. 1.2). Therefore, we designed a BERT-based entity detection and classification model [11] to extract entities and classify them into five broad categories: model/algorithm, data, system name, software, and arguments to understand and execute the given command. Figure 3 shows the architecture of the proposed DL model used to detect and classify entities in a sentence. To support multi-word terms, we label the first word as B-Category-Name and consecutive words as I-

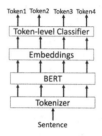

Fig. 3. Proposed BERT-based entity recognition model for SAI

Category-Name. Since arguments can have a numerical value, we create key-value pairs for the argument category by post-processing the NLU output. Arguments could have floating point values; therefore, we support numbers in numerical format only (for example we support "4.56" not "four point five six"). The output of this module is a dictionary of entities with their assigned values like ('Model':'Inception3'). This list is used to query KGs in the next step.

4.4   Creating the HPC Ontology and Knowledge Graphs

The existing ontologies in Sect. 8 do not capture the relationships between HPC components for executing workloads. Hence, to address challenge #2 in Sect. 1.2, we need to create an ontology capable of capturing complex dependencies and the workload relationships between HPC components like systems, software, models/algorithms, data, and their related arguments to construct a complete and useful Knowledge Graph(KG) for different HPC applications. We create a new ontology–called **SAI-O**– with 5 major classes of system, software, model, data, and argument to represent HPC components. Argument has 3 subclasses of software_arg, model_arg, and system_arg. Software has 3 subclass of framework, compiler, and library. A subset of relationships are listed in Table 1.

Table 1. Major object properties in SAI-O ontology

Relation Property	Domain	Range	Description
canBe	any	any	Defines possible values (OR)
runs	any	Software or Model	Captures run capability
depends	Software	System	Captures software dependency
needs	any	any	Defines requirements (no default)
hasArgs	any	Argument	Defines optional values (defaults)
hasSoftware	any	Software	Captures software availability

SAI-O contains data properties like *"version, hasDefault, default, name, description"* that are common between all the individuals in SAI-O. For example, the data property "description" gives a description of the individual to provide further information upon user requests. There are some data properties specific to a class of objects. For example, for a queue class that represents system job queue, we have"size, timeLimit, maximumJobSize, and maxUsable-Memory" data properties to describe a job partition information. Note that not all the properties need to have a value. *Due to the lack of space, only a subset of relationships and data properties are shown in the paper.* Through defining standard and generic"classes/relationships/data" properties in SAI-O, we can capture different asserted and inferred relationships among HPC system, software, model/algorithm, data, and their arguments and query later. SAI-O ontology could be used to add additional HPC applications in the future (Sect. 7.4.)

Using SAI-O, we created the KGs for 3 different HPC applications as a proof of concept in RDF/XML format: OMB Benchmarks [19], Distributed DL training, and NAS parallel benchmarks. In our KGs, synonyms are connected using the "Same individual as" relation to each other. An example of the constructed KG for the Inception3 DL model is shown in Fig. 4 to show the requirements and dependencies to run Inception3 model where green arrows show possible arguments and grey shows "needs".

4.5   Knowledge Graph Selection and Inference

SAI has one KG per application and can support multiple applications. To select the appropriate query for the given query, We define SPARQL [2] queries to query all the available KGs and see which one gives the *max hits* – which KG has the maximum number of entities detected in the given query. We query and process the selected KG to assemble a list of required arguments with their possible values and optional arguments with their default values (Defaults are stored in the KG). The assembled list is compared to the processed user input list if the required parameters are not complete, SAI generates corresponding questions/feedback and interacts with the user back and forth to get the parameters. If a necessary argument has a list of parameters (for example dataset values for Inception3), SAI displays the list to the user to select from it. Otherwise, SAI

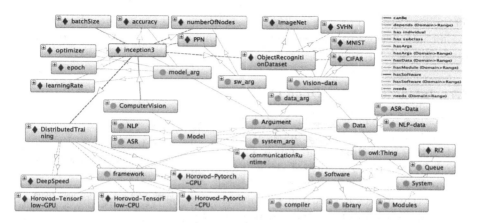

Fig. 4. Screenshot of visualizing Inception3 DL model relations in SAI in constructed DL knowledge graph based on SAI-O ontology - This is only one of the models supported in SAI DL KG. The type of relations are shown at the top left. The yellow rectangles represent classes and purple ones represents individuals in KG (Color figure online)

asks the user to enter the value for a required argument. At the end, we query the KG to get the software dependencies and libraries, which is used in Software Installed module (Sect. 4.6).

4.6 Software Installer Check and Interfacing with Spack

After evaluating the completeness of the user's input, SAI needs to check if the necessary software and packages are in place through the Software Installer component (shown in Fig. 2) to execute the query. For this objective (challenge # 3 described in Sect. 1.2), SAI takes advantage of Spack to resolve installation dependencies, install the requirements, and provide the path of the executables to the Job Script Generator. To enable efficient interaction with Spack, we developed the *Spack Interfacing Layer (SIL)* using Spack's python APIs. To avoid the conflicts with system/user-level Spack environments, SIL utilizes a user-specified directory for software installations and its own configuration file that contains all Spack environments, files, and software installations.

To maintain proper dependencies and correctly bundle software and packages for installing, SIL creates a single Spack file by gathering dependency information about each package and combining them into one spec. The installed Spack environments through SAI can later be activated using Spack when the user wishes to do testing outside of SAI. SAI also reuses these environments if they are compatible with new user requests, in order to avoid redundant environments. SAI uses separate, logical environments that can share installations, ensuring that software is only installed if it does not already exist within SAI.

To increase efficiency and prevent system blockage during installations, SIL implements a multi-threaded installation queue and asynchronous installation.

This allows users to request multiple jobs without SAI being blocked while waiting for installations to complete, even for complex packages like Horovod which may take an hour to install.

4.7   Integration with Open OnDemand

To address challenge #4 in Sect. 1.2, In this section we describe the integration of SAI with Open OnDemand Open OnDemand supports two modes of deployment for applications — "Passenger Apps" and "Interactive Apps" as shown in Fig. 5. Passenger applications run on login nodes and resources are shared among multiple users with a separate directory for each user. Interactive applications, on the other hand, run on top of a node allocation to ensure exclusive resources. For the integration, the authors create YAML files to capture system-level information such as job scheduler, number of available nodes, and partition/queue list. For both deployments, we developed SAI setup scripts and job scripts. For Interactive deployment, we modified the Open OnDemand interface for node allocation to include SAI as an application, configured the cluster to enable running interactive SAI on compute nodes, passed user configuration to the job script, and developed scripts for pre- and post-processing.

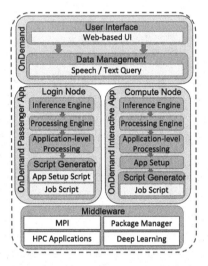

Fig. 5. Integrating SAI with OnDemand

The Passenger SAI application generates scripts for installing dependencies and executing tasks on the login node, while the Interactive SAI application handles dependencies installation on the compute node and submits the task for execution. We also utilize Open OnDemand's job template method to enable the creation of user-defined templates generated by SAI's job script generator. In the future, we plan to generate RPMs, Singularity images, and Kubernetes containers for distributing SAI through Open OnDemand.

5   Insights into SAI Usage and Explainable Flow

Following the flow in Fig. 2, we describe SAI's usage after the integration to OnDemand (Sect. 4.7) to run applications and install dependencies on an HPC system. We describe how SAI addresses the challenges in Sect. 1.2.

❶ Users can access SAI through OnDemand gateway that handles user authentication and remote CLI/GUI connection to SAI. The user selects passenger or interactive deployment of SAI to run. (Challenge #4 in Sect. 1.2)

❷ The user can give tasks using the chat box shown in Fig. 6. SAI converses with the user in natural language to understand their requirements. SAI's chat interface provides a "Mic" button to record the speech command. *SAI does not force a user to use the speech interface every time, it also has a text-based chat interface for users concerned about sending voice.* SAI converts speech to text using ASR model and interpreting the ASR output text or user's text commands with NLU model to prepare commands for HPC application execution, including compilation, running and monitoring. (Challenge #1 in Sect. 1.2)

❸ SAI uses HPC specific ontologies and Knowledge Graphs (KGs) derived from them to assess the user's commands for completeness and correctness. Through the use of these KGs, if SAI realizes that the information provided by the user is not complete, SAI can either use default values for missing information or interacts with the end-user again to get the needed information. (Challenge #2 in Sect. 1.2)

❹ Once the user's input has been obtained and validated, SAI executes the end-user's HPC application on the available hardware resources. Under the hood, SAI installs the application and necessary dependencies, executes the workload, monitors the progress, and reports the results of the application's execution. Users can give the path to the pre-installed software too. (Challenge #3 in Sect. 1.2)

Figure 6 show an example interaction of a user with implementation of SAI where the user tells SAI all the essential parameters in the initial input and changes a parameter. SAI selects and incorporates OMB's Knowledge Graph–based on max hits among all KGs – to validate input accuracy, checking for errors, inconsistencies, or missing information resulting in reducing the risk of errors in the job execution. With all required parameters provided by the user, SAI engages with the user for confirmation and prompts for potential modifications before submitting the job.

SAI Features: SAI's main features include job script generation, job execution, the ability to run jobs on multiple nodes with different architectures including GPUs, and OnDemand integration. SAI automatically finds package dependencies based on HPC system and architecture and supports package instal-

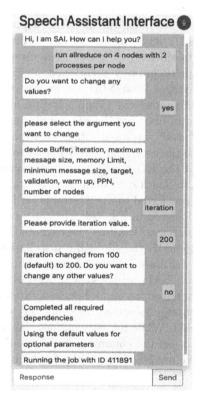

Fig. 6. Screenshot of an user interaction with SAI- the user is running Allreduce benchmark from OMB and changing default values before submitting the job.

lation as well as verification. For applications and job variables, SAI provides the default values, their descriptions, completeness check, and argument validity to reduce the likelihood of errors. The frequency of using SAI chat/speech interface depend on the user's HPC needs. It can be used whenever they want to build or run applications on an HPC system, as well as for tasks such as scaling and job submission. The natural language interface is both user-friendly and accessible, which may encourage more frequent interactions with HPC systems, ultimately resulting in increased overall HPC usage.

Insights into SAI's Flow: Transparency in the internal workflow and output of each component in SAI, from input to output, is of utmost importance. This transparency fosters user understanding and trust, ensuring that SAI is executing tasks as intended. Moreover, it can familiarize new HPC users with the process by showing them the steps taken to understand the flow and reproduce results. To achieve this, we have developed an interface within SAI that offers insights into the transition and output of each component, accessible with a simple click. Additionally, the interface displays the total and component-specific latency for SAI, providing further insight into its performance and enabling users to evaluate its efficiency. Figure 7 illustrates the complete transformation of the user text query initially mentioned in Fig. 6 to job output. In Fig. 7-①, the generated entities from NLU are presented, which are then processed and forwarded to the knowledge graph selection module. Figure 7-② displays the output obtained after querying the KG, revealing a dictionary with required arguments labeled as "need", optional values identified as "defaults", and the selected KG presented to the user. Figure 7-③ showcases the listed –parameters following the processing of the KG query–including required and optional values, along with details of the Spack environment path and working directory path. These parameters are transferred to the job composer by SAI for the creation of the job script. Then, as depicted in Fig. 7-④, the software installer ensures the installation of necessary packages, exhibits the executed commands, and provides users with an option to verify the successful installation of all binaries.

Figure 7-⑤, demonstrates the generated job script by SAI to execute the users job. SAI simplifies the process of submitting jobs to an HPC cluster by creating a batch script and a Spack environment. Once familiar with the process, users can submit jobs directly using the job script and Spack environment generated by SAI. While SAI streamlines the process using SAI is optional, and users are free to use the command line instead with SAI's generated commands and scripts. Figure 7-⑥ displays the final job output of the user's request.

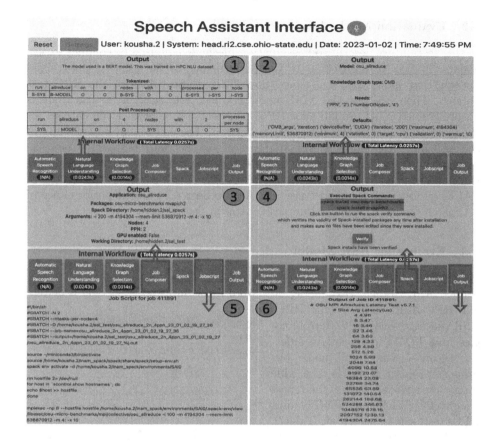

Fig. 7. Visual representation of SAI's implemented pipeline for the user input from Fig. 6: showing series of transformations of through various SAI components, with each step generating an output. The screenshot provides a clear illustration of the flow of data and the transition of input to output at each stage.

6   Experimental Evaluation

6.1   Evaluation Platform

We conduct our evaluation experiments on a 58-node Infiniband EDR cluster. It has two sets of nodes: 1) Intel 28 cores Broadwell(BDW) CPU running at 2.40 GHz nodes with a single NVIDIA Volta V100-32 GB GPU, and 2) Intel 28 cores SkyLake(SKX) CPU running at 2.6 GHz node with two NVIDIA K80 GPUs.

DL Framework: PyTorch [22] defines and trains DNNs for ASR and NLU
DNNs: Speech2Text [27], BERT-based entity detection and classification [11]
Datasets: LibriSpeech [21], TIMIT [1], HPC-ASR, and HPC-NLU

6.2   Evaluation Methodology

In this section, we describe our evaluation methodology used to conduct experiments. In Sect. 6.3, we compare the performance of the existing pre-trained Speech2Text model and fine-tuned Speech2Text (Sect. 4.2) on the HPC test dataset. Then, we test the NLU model trained from scratch – since there is no pre-trained NLU available for HPC – in Sect. 6.4 to predict the entities for the given text query or speech query transcript. The end-to-end performance of the ASR and NLU model is evaluated in Sect. 6.5. Section 6.6 provides the overhead of running the SAI pipeline from deep learning inferencing to determining whether the requested software is installed or not. We evaluate the scaling of SAI as an Open OnDemand Passenger App in Sect. 6.7 and the performance of SAI as an Open OnDemand Interactive App in Sect. 6.8.

6.3   Evaluating ASR Model

We evaluate the performance of pre-trained ASR Speech2Text model on our HPC-ASR dataset. Our HPC-ASR dataset has HPC terminologies and TIMIT dataset has different accents, which will make our proposed design available to a wide range of speakers. The final test results for WER on TIMIT and HPC test set is shown in Table 2. We observed that the existing off-the-shelf ASR model is not suitable for SAI conversational needs as it does not recognize HPC-related terminologies in the test set resulting in high WER. This motivated us to fine-tune our ASR model. Using our fine-tuned ASR model, we were able to improve the performance on the HPC-ASR test set and achieved a better WER, closer to that of state-of-the-art models. Figure 8 shows the fine-tuning of Speech2Text on HPC-ASR + TIMIT datasets. Eval WER is the WER for the ASR model on the validation dataset and Eval Latency is the runtime of one step in ASR model validation.

Table 2. Evaluation of ASR model using Word Error Rate (WER) - Lower is better

Train Dataset	Test Dataset	WER
Base (LibriSpeech)	HPC-ASR	86.2
Base+TIMIT+HPC-ASR	HPC-ASR	**3.7**

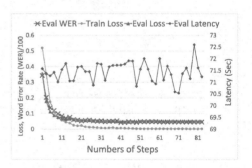

Fig. 8. SAI's ASR Model evaluation for Loss, WER and Latency

6.4 Evaluating NLU Model

Since no pre-trained NLU model is available for HPC terminologies, we trained BERT-based entity detection and classification model (Sect. 4.3) from scratch using HPC-NLU dataset. We evaluate the performance of predicting entities and extracting them for our trained NLU model against human-supervised and labeled HPC-NLU dataset.

The training set consists of 60,000 randomly selected queries for DL, OMB, and NAS phrases from the HPC-NLU dataset including the combinations, permutations, and synonyms. Then, we used 5 million randomly selected queries from the rest of the dataset for testing. We calculated the performance metrics by comparing the NLU output versus the human-supervised labeled HPC-NLU dataset.

Table 3 shows the final test F1-score, precision, and recall on the HPC-NLU test set and achieving 99% accuracy for entity detection and classification. Figure 9 shows the validation loss of the NLU model on the HPC-NLU dataset.

Table 3. Evaluation of NLU model for entity recognition - Higher is better

Test Dataset	F1-score	Precision	Recall
HPC-NLU (5M)	0.999	0.999	0.999

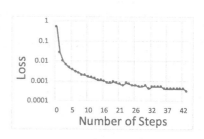

Fig. 9. Validation loss for NLU model of SAI

6.5 Performance Evaluation of Combined ASR and NLU Models

In this experiment, ASR and NLU modules are evaluated together as a pipeline to assess the success rate of SAI for converting speech query to the classified entities. We use our trained NLU and ASR models to calculate inference accuracy. A speech test dataset of 100 queries from 4 individuals' were chosen for end-to-end inference with the following demographic: User 1 with Mandarin accents, User 2 with Middle East accents, and User 3 and 4 with American accents. The testing queries did not exist in the training queries.

As the predicted sentences of the ASR model can have different generated lengths based on the accent from the original sentences, the NLU model cannot compare entities pairwise. Thus, we designate two metrics for end-to-end testing: Metric 1 (M1):

Table 4. Word Error Rate and inference accuracy for ASR+NLU pipeline of SAI on 4 users where the models were not trained on 2 users - Lower is better

Metric	User 1	User 2	User 3	User 4	Average
WER	10.3	8.6	8.3	4.9	8.03
Accuracy M2	0.97	0.90	0.80	0.95	0.907
Accuracy M1	0.84	0.81	0.83	0.92	0.849

if a predicted sentence has more words than the original sentence, we drop the last few words in prediction to make sure they have the same lengths and vice versa. Metric 2 (M2): we first drop less important words like articles, prepositions, and grammatically wrong words inside the ASR-generated query and then repeat the process in metric 1. Table 4 shows the results of end-to-end inference. This end-to-end result shows the practicability of our design because ASR and NLU models have never trained with recordings from User 1 and 4 but still yield 96.8% and 90.7% test accuracy. This implies flexibility of the end-to-end model for recognizing new users' voices.

6.6   Overhead Analysis of SAI

In this experiment, we evaluate the overhead of our full pipeline deployed as a passenger app: from user speech/text input to submitting a job based on the user input. The interactive application performance would be the same or better. Since different packages available through Spack have varying installation times, we skip the overhead of package installation and job execution. In subsequent requests involving the same sets of software, this overhead won't be observed since the software is already installed.

Figure 10 showcases the average end-to-end duration to process speech and text queries of varying lengths in SAI end-to-end pipeline. In general, it can be seen that the time taken to process speech increases with an increase in the number of words in the query. This is expected as the ASR model takes an input of the varying size and hence bigger inputs take more time. The time taken to process a text query is more or less constant as the input size of the NLU model is fixed.

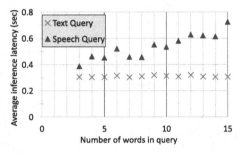

Fig. 10. End-to-end latency evaluation of SAI for 13 different queries on passenger app on speech and text queries consisting of different numbers of words - each data point is an average of 200 iterations

6.7   Overhead Analysis of Scaling Passenger App Users

As mentioned in Sect. 4.7, resources are shared among users of SAI when deployed as a passenger app. This experiment evaluates the end-to-end overhead of SAI when multiple users interact with it at the same time. To do this we use selenium with the chrome web driver to simulate different amounts of users using the SAI passenger app at once for text and speech queries. We use a barrier to ensure the concurrency of users' requests for each iteration. The test uses a text/speech query of 8 words

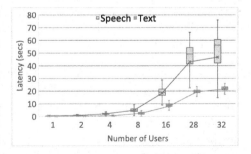

Fig. 11. Boxplot comparison of end-to-end latency of SAI passenger deployment as a varying number of concurrent users utilizing SAI for both speech and text - the host node is equipped with BDW 28 cores CPU

for 200/100 iterations per user. Figure 11 shows the box plot of scaling the users from 1 to 32 concurrent users utilizing SAI as a passenger app. We observe that as the number of users scales up both the average latency and the variance in latency scale up for both speech and text with speech increasing at a greater rate. Moreover, the performance of the login node hosting the passenger app degrades significantly. The increased latency and significant jitters of multi-user passenger apps motivate us to develop SAI as an interactive app to ensure a smooth user experience with lower latency.

6.8   Analysis of SAI Interactive App on Different Architectures

The performance degradation of SAI during scaling up the number of concurrent users motivated us to develop and evaluate SAI as an interactive application to ensure exclusive resources. The user selects the partition/architecture to run SAI. In this experiment, we evaluate the breakdown and the total latency of SAI's both deployment on different architectures for the same 8-word text and speech query running 100 and 400 iterations for speech and text respectively. The passenger test was conducted during the winter break and as many users were not using the system hence, shows the best scenario of the passenger case. The K80 GPU node did not support ASR inference. Table 5 summarizes the median end-to-end latency of total time and breakdown of latency across SAI's sub-components. We observe the latency of ASR and NLU modules decreases when inference happened on the V100 GPU node and overall the total latency is lower than the passenger deployment.

Table 5. Total latency and its breakdown for the deployment of SAI on different 1-node architectures as Interactive and Passenger app inside OnDemand - Numbers show the median of running 8-word speech/text query for 100/400 iterations respectively.

Architecture /Model	Deployment type	Total latency	ASR module	NLU module	KG module
BDW speech	Interactive	0.4919	0.23865	0.02275	0.22655
	Passenger	0.50245	0.2366	0.0217	0.2274
BDW text	Interactive	0.2665	N/A	0.0227	0.24335
	Passenger	0.27125	N/A	0.0218	0.24795
SKX speech		0.44085	0.24105	0.0174	0.1754
SKX text		0.22095	N/A	0.0242	0.19585
V100 speech	Interactive	0.40735	0.16585	0.0172	0.224
V100 text		0.2664	N/A	0.0225	0.2433
K80 text		0.2676	N/A	0.0225	0.2448

7 Discussion

7.1 Security and Authentication

SAI leverages Open OnDemand's user authentication and access privileges validation features and uses "spack verify" command, as shown in Fig. 7, to confirm the integrity of all installed binaries at any time after installation, ensuring that no files have been tampered with or modified. This added layer of security enhances user trust and the reliability of the installed packages.

7.2 Handling Ambiguous Queries in SAI

We discuss the limitations of SAI and the level of ambiguity SAI handles. We seek to see at what point SAI will not understand the user and how we handle those cases. Our developed dataset is limited to popular HPC/DL phrases hence, SAI does not understand all existing HPC synonyms or all available DL models. The HPC-ASR and HPC-NLU dataset contains synonyms and different combinations of the phrases but is limited. We have trained ASR model with 20 volunteer individuals targeting diverse dialect, but our HPC-ASR dataset is still limited. This limitation may result in SAI predicting wrong text output. To address this, SAI displays the transcript in the input text field and allows the user to correct mistakes in speech recognition if there are any. The users can switch between text and speech to resolve any discrepancies on speech recognition during conversation.

SAI shows the internal workflow (Sect. 5) enabling the user to see the parameters and packages and shows the default values. SAI always checks user argument versus the allowed range in the corresponding KG and confirms it with the user. In case anything is missing, SAI provides feedback by asking questions. For example, user can say "train resnet" and as SAI checks the related KG, it inquiries the user for an image dataset and number of nodes/processes as requirements. Currently, SAI does not support directly querying the KG. For example, users cannot ask "what are the datasets for DL image processing?" Also, SAI does not give the option to users to update the KGs.

7.3 Trade-offs for Converting Speech to Entities

There are two ways to convert speech to entities: 1) ASR followed by entity detection and classification, and 2) direct speech to entity detection and classification. Our design uses the first approach, which first converts audio to text then uses NLU to detect and classify entities. We chose this approach for several reasons: first, a speech to entity model requires a large corpus of labeled HPC speech datasets for optimal accuracy; second, since SAI supports both speech and text input, creating separate datasets would be necessary (one for NLU and one for ASR); Third, pre-trained DL models for similar tasks are not available. Fourth, this approach allows for easy integration of new software, only requiring a few minutes of audio recordings containing its terminologies.

7.4   Portability for New Software and Systems

To extend SAI support to a new HPC software, SAI-O ontology can be used to capture the relationships of a new application to be added to SAI. We represent these relationships by using KGs, which capture the connections between software, data, models/algorithms, systems, and arguments.

Adding a new application to SAI requires two steps: (1) creating a KG for the application using the SAI-O ontology and the supported relationships (Table 1), and (2) adding application-specific terms to the HPC-ASR dataset. SAI will provide easy-to-use scripts for fine-tuning the ASR model on new audio samples, enabling support for new terminologies in ASR model. The KG Inference module selects the appropriate KG using "spack verify", allowing us to reuse the general query manager and simplify the addition of new applications. We have trained the NLU module on a large dataset and therefore, it can detect entities and classify them into broad categories based on the sentence structure. In rare cases, the performance of the NLU module may degrade due to new terminologies, but SAI provides an easy-to-use dataset generator script to generate new text commands based on models/algorithms, datasets, software, arguments, and systems to fine-tune the DL model and improve performance for the new application. Figure 7 shows a setting interface where users can upload their customized trained DL models to be used for SAI.

The modularity of our design allows the KG to be ported to multiple systems by updating a template (Sect. 9) with the new platform's system information. Integrating SAI with Open OnDemand makes it even easier to port to new system architectures, as many XSEDE/ACCESS systems use OnDemand. The KG's system portion is the same for all applications on a system, simplifying the deployment of SAI on a new HPC system.

8   Related Work

Our previous work [14] introduced a new conversational AI interface for HPC profiling tools like OSU INAM [15], with a focus on extracting performance-related terminologies, intents, and slots for HPC tools and scope of profiling tools. In this paper, we expand upon our previous work by capturing a broader range of HPC runtime terminologies, and by incorporating an NLU entity recognition model to process user inputs. Additionally, we introduce new features to enhance the interface's usability and effectiveness, such as integration with OnDemand, a software installer component, and job submission capabilities. Several studies [20,26] exist in literature that uses an end-to-end based approach to convert the voice to intent and slots, combining ASR and NLU into one model. The trade-off is discussed in Sect. 7.3 and maintaining and updating a list intent and slots causes the KG query module not to be portable. Another approach is to combine ASR and NLU models to understand the context of speech samples. The state-of-the-art ASR models [9,27] have been proposed in the literature that provides good performance for publicly available datasets and common words found in day-to-day conversation. However, we need to fine-tune these ASR models to recognize technical terms found in computer science and HPC. Similarly, NLU models [7,8,10,23] are trained for publicly available datasets. Hence, to develop a system for HPC software installation and usage tool, we need to generate our own dataset and retrain models from scratch to get better accuracy. To the best of our knowledge, this is the first work that develops a conversational AI-based interface for HPC software installation and execution.

9   Future Work

As part of future work, we plan to simplify the process of creating KGs for HPC software by providing easy-to-use templates to create a KG for a given application and collaborating with multiple HPC centers to identify common applications and make corresponding templates available to users. We will provide examples of existing applications to assist in filling the template. To create a new application's KG, users need to provide the model/application, data, arguments, and dependencies to the KG template. As the repository of model commons for the templates grows, users can update the templates with new features and system information and contribute to the repository, ultimately saving time and effort of generating KGs's template for common applications. Furthermore, we plan to expand the SAI-O ontology to capture a broader range of HPC applications and runtimes, including those with complex inter-dependencies and unique configurations. Finally, we plan to release SAI and our solutions.

10   Conclusion

In this paper, we proposed - SAI, a Conversational AI-Enabled Interface for science gateways in HPC. We created an HPC speech and text dataset to train Automatic Speech Recognition and Entity detection and classification model to understand the input. By defining a new ontology, called SAI-O, we provided a general approach for any HPC application by using knowledge graphs to check and validate the task given by the user. This allowed us to get default values for optional arguments and design a conversational interface to get the required arguments for running the application. We demonstrated the capability of the proposed design by supporting three different HPC applications: 1) OSU Microbenchmarks, 2) Distributed DNN training, and 3) NAS parallel benchmarks. Finally, we integrated SAI in Open OnDemand and deployed it on real HPC systems. We also evaluated its performance and functionality. To the best of our knowledge, this is the first attempt in the HPC field to enhance the user experience by designing a AI-powered speech-assisted interface. Early users have shown interest and found SAI features very useful to onboard domain scientists to HPC.

References

1. TIMIT acoustic-phonetic continuous speech corpus. https://hdl.handle.net/11272. 1/AB2/SWVENO
2. SPARQL query language (2020). https://www.w3.org/TR/sparql11-query/. Accessed 17 April 2023
3. Voicebot research (2020). https://tinyurl.com/4kw4bmz7
4. The future of conversational AI (2021). https://tinyurl.com/2dzxe2w8
5. Open onDemand (2022). https://osc.github.io/ood-documentation/latest/#
6. The impact of voice assistants (2022). https://tinyurl.com/mrx36afk
7. Hosseini-Asl, E., McCann, B., Wu, C.S., Yavuz, S., Socher, R.: A simple language model for task-oriented dialogue (2020). CoRR abs/2005.00796. https://arxiv.org/abs/2005.00796
8. Wen, T.H., Gasic, G., Mrksic, N.S., Vandyke, D., Young, S.J.: A network-based end-to-end trainable task-oriented dialogue system (2016). CoRR abs/1604.04562, http://arxiv.org/abs/1604.04562
9. Baevski, A., Zhou, H., Mohamed, A., Auli, M.: Wav2vec 2.0: a framework for self-supervised learning of speech representations (2020). https://arxiv.org/abs/2006. 11477
10. Castellucci, G., Bellomaria, V., Favalli, A., Romagnoli, R.: Multi-lingual intent detection and slot filling in a joint bert-based model (2019). https://arxiv.org/abs/1907.02884
11. Devlin, J., Chang, M., Lee, K., Toutanova, K.: BERT: pre-training of deep bidirectional transformers for language understanding (2018). CoRR abs/1810.04805, http://arxiv.org/abs/1810.04805
12. Goasduff, L.: Chatbots will appeal to modern workers (2019). https://www.gartner.com/smarterwithgartner/chatbots-will-appeal-to-modern-workers
13. Hauptmann, A., Rudnicky, A.: A comparison of speech and typed input (1990). https://doi.org/10.3115/116580.116652
14. Kousha, P., et al.: "Hey CAI" - conversational AI enabled user interface for HPC tools. In: Varbanescu, A.L., Bhatele, A., Luszczek, P., Marc, B. (eds.) High Perform. Comput., pp. 87–108. Springer International Publishing, Cham (2022). https://doi.org/10.1007/978-3-031-07312-0_5
15. Kousha, P., et al.: INAM: cross-stack profiling and analysis of communication in MPI-based applications. In: Association for Computing Machinery, New York, NY, USA (2021). https://doi.org/10.1145/3437359.3465582
16. Kudo, T., Richardson, J.: Sentencepiece: a simple and language independent subword tokenizer and detokenizer for neural text processing (2018). arXiv preprint arXiv:1808.06226
17. Liao, C., Lin, P.H., Verma G., Vanderbruggen, T., Emani, M.: Hpc ontology: towards a unified ontology for managing training datasets and AI models for high-performance computing. In: 2021 IEEE/ACM Workshop on MLHPC, pp. 69–80 (2021). https://doi.org/10.1109/MLHPC54614.2021.00012
18. National Geographic: LiDAR and Archaeology. https://education.nationalgeographic.org/resource/lidar-and-archaeology
19. OSU Micro-benchmarks. http://mvapich.cse.ohio-state.edu/benchmarks/
20. Palogiannidi, E., Gkinis, I., Mastrapas, G., Mizera, P., Stafylakis, T.: End-to-end architectures for ASR-free spoken language understanding. In: (ICASSP), pp. 7974–7978 (2020). https://doi.org/10.1109/ICASSP40776.2020.9054314

21. Panayotov, V., Chen, G., Povey, D., Khudanpur, S.: Librispeech: an ASR corpus based on public domain audio books. In: 2015 IEEE International Conference on Acoustics, Speech and Signal Processing (ICASSP), pp. 5206–5210. IEEE (2015)

22. Paszke, A., et al.: PyTorch: an imperative style, high-performance deep learning library (2019)

23. Qin, L., Che, W., Li, Y., Wen, H., Liu, T.: A stack-propagation framework with token-level intent detection for spoken language understanding (2019). arXiv preprint arXiv:1909.02188

24. Rothwell, B., Sgambati, M., Evans, G. Biggs, B., Anderson, M.: Quantifying the impact of advanced web platforms on high performance computing usage, PEARC'22. ACM (2022). https://doi.org/10.1145/3491418.3530758

25. Schmidt, A.: The rise of conversational interfaces and their impact on business (2019). https://tinyurl.com/45ppfz9t

26. Serdyuk, D., Wang, Y., Fuegen, C., Kumar, A., Liu, B., Bengio, Y.: Towards end-to-end spoken language understanding (2018). CoRR abs/1802.08395, http://arxiv.org/abs/1802.08395

27. Wang, C., Tang, Y., Ma, X., Wu, A., Okhonko, D., Pino, J.: Fairseq s2t: fast speech-to-text modeling with fairseq (2020). https://arxiv.org/abs/2010.05171

Author Index

A. Bhatele et al. (Eds.): ISC High Performance 2023, LNCS 13948, pp. 425–426, 2023.
https://doi.org/10.1007/978-3-031-32041-5

Printed in the United States
by Baker & Taylor Publisher Services